WAR PLAN ORANGE • • • •

The U.S. Strategy to Defeat Japan, 1897–1945

War Plan
ORANGE
EDWARD S. MILLER

NAVAL INSTITUTE PRESS • ANNAPOLIS, MARYLAND

Naval Institute Press
291 Wood Road
Annapolis, MD 21402

First printing in paperback, 2007
ISBN-10: 1-59114-500-7
ISBN-13: 978-1-59114-500-4

The Library of Congress has cataloged the hardcover edition as follows:
Miller, Edward S.
    War Plan Orange: the U.S. strategy to defeat Japan, 1897–1945 /
    Edward S. Miller.
        p. cm.
    Includes bibliographical references (p.   ) and index.
    ISBN 0-87021-759-3
    1. United States. Navy—History—20th century. 2. Military
    planning—United States—History—20th century. 3. World War,
    1939–1945—Campaigns—Pacific. 4. World War, 1939–1945—
    Naval operations, American. 5. World War, 1939–1945—Naval
    operations, Japanese. I. Title.
    VA50.M53   1991
    359′.03′0973—dc20

                        91-14361 CIP

14 13 12 11 10 09 08 07   9 8 7 6 5 4 3 2
First printing

To Joyce: We planned well together

Contents

List of Maps and Figures

List of Tables

Foreword

Almost twenty years ago, Edward Miller took a break from his hectic schedule as a senior business executive to visit the Naval Historical Center's Operational Archives, where he proceeded to read a number of documents relating to naval strategy in the Pacific. At that time I directed the Operational Archives, which normally served as a source of information for naval officers, other naval professionals, academic historians, and naval veterans. I remember how impressed my staff and I were that Mr. Miller's interest brought him to our specialized office located in one of the former industrial buildings of the Washington Navy Yard, an area far off the beaten path for the usual visitor to Washington. Over the ensuing years Mr. Miller returned many times to the Naval Historical Center, and we became even more impressed as a project begun as an avocation evolved into a highly professional investigation of the origins and evolution of the navy's war plan for a conflict with Japan. The result of those many years of effort is a book that is of central importance to students of American military affairs in the twentieth century.

Despite the fact that Mr. Miller's career was spent in the corporate world, rather than in the classroom, his book is an outstanding example of historical research. His investigation of War Plan Orange led him to numerous records in the Naval Historical Center and the National Archives, as well as in other repositories, that generally see little use by historians. Because he began with no preconceived historical theories, the author posed his own imaginative questions in assessing the meaning of the large body of source materials that he examined. Throughout the process, Mr. Miller took an admirably skeptical point of view in assessing the validity of his evidence.

Although there have been suggestions that little new remains to be said about the background to World War II, this study shows that fruitful research is still being done on that subject. One of Ed Miller's major contributions is to detail the sustained and generally effective planning process that lay behind the preparation of the various versions of War Plan Orange. He rejects the widespread cliché that the navy's leadership in the prewar years was obsessed by battleships and generally out of touch with the realities of modern warfare. Instead, the author finds that many of the navy's strategists were farsighted leaders who devised the flexible strategic concept that led inexorably to Imperial Japan's surrender in 1945. Mr. Miller demonstrates how the long-established principles of this plan were used by Admirals King and Nimitz and the other American naval leaders of World War II as they commanded the American forces that fought across the Pacific to the enemy's doorstep.

Some historians argue that Plan Orange was a failure since it did not prevent the Japanese seizure of the Philippines. Mr. Miller demonstrates, however, that this contention fails to comprehend the major objectives in the minds of naval strategists. For those officers, the plan was not a defensive measure designed to hold territory. Instead, it represented an offensive means of defeating an aggressive Japan, the source of America's security problem in the Far East.

In preparing this book, Mr. Miller benefited from the insights of modern naval strategists based in the Pentagon, at the Naval War College, and at other naval educational institutions. These contacts indicated that the strategy-making of today echoes the planning processes and many of the concepts used in formulating War Plan Orange between 1897 and 1941. This study of how success was achieved in the past becomes all the more relevant under these circumstances—not only to historians, but also to future makers of national security policy.

Throughout its existence, the navy has attracted the interest of many gifted historians. These individuals include uniformed naval personnel as well as civilians with diverse interests and backgrounds. *War Plan Orange* demonstrates how valuable this attention can be. The navy's historians look forward to future contributions from the pen of Edward Miller that will enlighten us on the meaning and current relevance of our institution's rich past.

DEAN C. ALLARD
Director of Naval History
Department of the Navy

Acknowledgments

This book has been a labor of love for eighteen years. I owe a debt of gratitude to many who encouraged and aided it. Prominent among them are the dedicated archivists who guided me through their arcane warrens, especially Dean Allard, Director of Naval History, who believed in my work and gave it his unstinting support. His ever-helpful assistants Cal Cavalcante, Kathleen Lloyd, Mike Palmer, and especially Martha Crawley were tireless. The staff at the Modern Military Branch of the National Archives was ever-accommodating, notably John Taylor, Richard Von Doenhoff, George Chalou, Richard F. Cox, and Gibson B. Smith. So were Evelyn M. Cherpak at the Naval Historical Collection in Newport and the knowledgeable Chuck Haberlein at the Naval Photographic Center.

I was astonished at the warm reception extended by military historians when I first entered their close-knit world. I owe thanks to many: to Roger Pineau, scholar emeritus, for nudging me onward; to the superstar authors of the current strategic scene, Paul M. Kennedy of Yale University, Ronald Spector, recently Director of Naval History, and scholars of strategy including Norman Friedman, Clark Reynolds,

William R. Braisted, Jr., and Forrest C. Pogue, all of whom enrolled me in the club. I wish to express gratitude to my boyhood friend David Kahn, the doyen of the history of military intelligence, for his enthusiastic prodding since junior high school.

I was also heartened by the scholarly naval establishment and those in its orbit who welcomed a serious study of a historical U.S. war plan. They include the incredibly knowledgeable Frank Uhlig of the Naval War College and his colleagues at that birthplace of planning: Robert Wood, David Rosenberg, and John B. Hattendorf, to name a few; their former colleagues J. Kenneth McDonald, chief historian of the CIA, and Michael Vlahos at the Department of State; and Admiral Thomas Moorer, USN (Ret.). Mark Peattie and Thomas Hone wisely advised me on structuring the story. Among those who "put me on the map" by tendering speaking invitations were professors of the U.S. Naval Academy, Naval Post Graduate School, Naval War College, and the National Defense University, along with Takeshi Sakurauchi and the NHK television network of Japan, who enabled me to tell my story to the other side.

I am delighted that the venerable Naval Institute Press is publishing this book. My thanks go to Captain Jim Barber, who heads the Institute, and especially to Deborah Estes, who took a chance when the book was still in my head. I hope she will be pleased with the result. And I hope my readers will be as pleased as I am with the work of editor Trudie Calvert and cartographer Bill Clipson.

A special thank you is tendered to Captain Peter M. Swartz, USN, revealed at last as a principal author of the navy's maritime strategy of the 1980s. He saw in my work something that would fill a gap in the education of the modern planning establishment. His opening of many doors for a rookie historian is deeply appreciated. I hope the book achieves what he wanted.

Bless Susie and Tom, who said, "Go for it, Dad." And finally, I am grateful to Joyce, whose forbearance and love saw me through.

Introduction

War Plan Orange, the secret program of the United States to defeat Japan, was in my opinion history's most successful war plan. In plans developed before the war, Japan was code-named Orange, the United States, Blue, hence the name of the plan developed over nearly four decades by the best strategic minds of the military services. As it was implemented in World War II, it was remarkably successful, especially considering the difficulties of Pacific geography and the many political and technological changes that had occurred over the years. The prewar plans of other great powers proved, by and large, to be costly failures. The vaunted German General Staff, for example, won campaigns but lost wars.

The lack of any other book on Plan Orange has left a gap in the background to World War II that has encouraged misconceptions. Historians have relied on briefs written thirty years ago by U.S. Army scholars who branded Plan Orange a defensive failure because they overlooked the comprehensive offensive strategy developed by the navy to defeat Japan (see Chapter 28). Only fragments of the planning story have appeared in naval journals. Many authors have explored the war plans of 1941, which were published during the Pearl Harbor investigations, but they, too, paid little heed to the offensive strategy. Curiously, many older documents remained classified until the 1960s and 1970s, which inhibited study during the first postwar decades.

War planners were sworn to secrecy, and their attitudes and even identities have not been described heretofore. Memoirs from the years before declassification said little about the duty, and contemporary public reports are almost useless. In the eighteen years during which I researched this book, I tapped the available secondary sources but found most of the information in the formerly classified files of the Modern Military Branch at the National Archives, the Naval Operational Archives, and the Naval War College.

In addition to grand strategy, the book explores plans of campaign, those broad midlevel programs sometimes called theater plans, most of which have never been published. I have not attempted to deal with other events that preceded war with Japan such as diplomatic, economic, or cultural frictions or with American preparations through weapons development, military reorganization, intelligence, maneuvers, or war games except as these were considered by the planners. Detailed comparisons of forces are omitted; they are available in books about fighting ships and similar works.

Neither have I investigated Japan's war plans. Aside from problems of language and access—the Japanese burned many documents before the occupation in 1945—it is my understanding that Japan did not plan as long or as thoroughly as did the United States and that it expected to fight defensively after the first few months. Defensive plans are rarely as specific and certainly not as interesting as offensive ones. American planners, however, assessed enemy intentions rather accurately so the reader will gain valid insights into Japan's strategy through their eyes. Perhaps a future historian will write a comparison of the plans of the two antagonists. I have also omitted Pacific plans of Great Britain or other powers, which appear to have been rudimentary.

Strangely, U.S. war plans rarely included maps except charts of distance. I have prepared twenty-six maps that illustrate the plans. Though these maps are accurate in broad strokes, I had to interpolate missing details. Any errors of interpretation are mine.

Distances are stated in nautical miles of 6,076.1 feet. One nautical mile equals 1.15 statute miles or 1.85 kilometers. Knots are nautical miles per hour; one knot equals 1.15 statute miles per hour. A fathom of sea depth is 6 feet. Tonnages are in American short tons of 2,000 pounds. Place names and spellings are those used at the time of World

War II and not in earlier or postwar periods, for example, Kwajalein, not Kwajalong, and Formosa, not Taiwan.

The book pursues three objectives. First, it presents a detailed account of U.S. Pacific strategy from inception up until Pearl Harbor. Many versions of War Plan Orange, both official and informal, existed at various times. Some were mutually contradictory. I have focused on those that were still valid for the conditions of World War II rather than variants that did not survive the prewar winnowing process. Second, I have described the planning process and the planners in several chapters entitled "The American Way of Planning." Finally, I review the Pacific war of 1941–45 through the filter of the Orange Plan, comparing it to actual wartime events and to alternative strategies conceived during the fighting. The comparisons are necessarily selective, but I have aimed for a balanced interpretation. My analysis concludes that War Plan Orange was a valid, relevant, and successful guide to victory.

The success of the American way of planning in the only case in which a long-term effort was put to the test suggests that Americans may have confidence in modern strategic planners, though they face a world as different from Nimitz's as his was from Mahan's.

WAR PLAN ORANGE ● ● ● ●

Plan Orange and the Global War

O n 6 December 1941, a Saturday, the war plans officer of the
United States Pacific Fleet in Pearl Harbor took note of the location of the fleet's big warships. He then updated a document that was to
govern their response if war erupted in the next twenty-four hours. The
document, the current U.S. war plan, was the latest of a long series
crafted in utmost secrecy over several decades. It rested on the foundations laid down by its earliest progenitors.

In August 1945 the United States dropped two atomic bombs on
Japan. The planners of the prewar era never dreamed of such a weapon,
yet it fulfilled a strategy set forth during the administration of Theodore
Roosevelt of reducing Japan to helplessness by a ruthless siege.

In the years between these two events the United States prosecuted
the Pacific war largely in conformance with the prewar strategic formulation known as War Plan Orange, the most prominent of the color
plans initiated early in the twentieth century. The Joint Army and Navy
Board, a consultative committee, had assigned color code names to
countries; Japan was called Orange and the United States, Blue.[1] The
codes were written both as nouns and as adjectives; hence, Orange
meant Japan or Japanese and Blue the United States or American.

Plan Orange (or simply the plan) is used herein as a synonym for U.S. Pacific strategy before the war. The two dozen or so formal plans that in some cases made up hundreds of pages bore titles such as Navy WPL-13 or Fleet Plan O-1. The Orange designation was dropped at the end of 1940, but the Pacific strategies of the successor Rainbow Plans (so named for multicolored friends and foes of a world war) are included under the same rubric. No Orange Plan was ever enacted by Congress or signed by a president; even in mid-1941 Franklin Roosevelt gave only oral approval to Plan Rainbow Five,[2] the fundamental policy guideline of World War II. The secretaries of war and the navy had signed formal Orange Plans from 1924 onward; previously they were endorsed only by the senior military officers responsible for planning.

American war policy was determined in a varied and often informal manner. The plan was elaborated in such studies as "Estimates of the Situation Blue-Orange" and in correspondence of officials that preceded or interpreted the official versions. The plan was a matter of common understanding more than a set of documents. Before World War II the upper echelons of the armed forces were small societies. About a hundred officers received copies of the written plans.[3] The Pacific campaigns were studied and gamed by a few dozen officers who attended the war colleges each year. They must have been topics of lively discussion in wardrooms and field headquarters. Plan Orange was one of those historical credos that are said to be "noted and filed in the Navy's corporate memory" and "genetically encoded in naval officers."[4] It had been absorbed by the high commanders of World War II as the descriptor of the mission that had shaped their lives and institutions. Many of them had worked on the plan under the tutelage of elder strategists so there was much continuity of attitude. Consciously or unconsciously, they dug into their collective memories during the war. They did not usually pull the old documents from the safe to reread as manuals.[5] The famous remark by Admiral Chester Nimitz (who in 1923 had studied under War College President Clarence Williams, one of the finest strategists of the century) that the war unfolded just as predicted in naval war games applied to the plans as well.[6]

Pacific strategy went through many variations over the decades. Those that were officially revoked, such as schemes for immediate naval offensives to save the Philippines, are deemed "failed strategies" and described only in brief here because they were largely irrelevant to World War II. Those that were not superseded, explicitly or implicitly, underlay wartime strategy and receive greater attention. In cases of contradiction more weight is given to mainstream ideas of long standing than to short-term anomalies. If a recent plan was silent on an issue, earlier models are taken to represent U.S. strategy. This is especially necessary with regard to the war's late stages. Orange Plans before 1934 usually spelled out programs for the entire war, but thereafter operational planning was restricted to early campaigns because of the adoption of a gradualist strategy that would allow ample time for study after the shooting began. The truncation did not nullify the end-game stratagems of older plans, which were still commonly accepted when the war began.

This book deals with the larger aspects of planning: geopolitics, grand strategy, mobilization and logistics, and theaterwide campaigns.[7] Little attention is devoted to tactical plans for defense of small areas like Oahu or Corregidor by local forces, or to landing studies of specific islands that were produced in bulk by army and marine staffs. Naval tactical plans were almost nonexistent; doctrines of ship movement and battle deployment evolved from training maneuvers and war gaming, not from strategic plans.

With these caveats, the story begins with a synopsis of Plan Orange as it was commonly understood until about a year before the war.

The geopolitical premises of the plan held that, in spite of historically friendly relations, a war would erupt someday between the United States and Japan, a war in which neither could rely on the help of allies. The root cause would be Japan's quest for national greatness by attempting to dominate the land, people, and resources of the Far East. America regarded itself as the guardian of Western influence in the Orient. Its popular dogma favored self-determination of peoples and open international trade. To achieve its goal, Japan would feel it necessary to expunge American power from its sea flank by depriving it of bases in the Philippine Islands and Guam.

Japan would mobilize every sinew for a war of vital national interest. When ready, it would strike suddenly. It would easily seize its objectives in the western Pacific but could not carry the war to American shores. It would settle down to a grueling struggle in the belief that the American people would tire of fighting for a faraway region of no vital interest and demand a peace conceding most of Japan's gains.

But Japan's gamble would prove misguided. The United States was pacifistic, but its people would rise in wrath when attacked, especially if the blow fell on Hawaii. They would persevere for a cause they viewed as righteous. U.S. industrial might would be harnessed to a vigorous counteroffensive to recover lost territories, control the western Pacific, destroy Japan's military capacity and economic life, and compel it to complete submission.

It is said that "geography is the bones of strategy," and so it was in the grand strategy of the Orange Plan. The war theater would extend across five thousand miles of the north Pacific from Hawaii to the Asian coast, a region of much water and little land. The United States need not confront the fearsome Orange army en masse, either on the mainland of Asia or in Japan itself. It would win by waging a maritime war.

Distance and geography dictated a three-phase contest. In Phase I Japan would seize the lightly defended American outposts and assure itself of access to the oil and raw materials of territories to the south and west. The U.S. Navy, concentrated at home ports, would be unable to prevent these takeovers but could mobilize in the eastern Pacific, which was considered a sanctuary despite the possibility of hit-and-run raids.

In Phase II, Blue expeditions spearheaded by superior naval and air power would steam westward. Intense but small-scale battles would procure Japanese islands of the central Pacific. Advanced naval and air bases would be established and supply lines secured. Japan would resist with expendable forces, trading distance for time and erosion of the attacking fleet, but the United States would gradually win the attrition battles. After two or three years it would regain a base in the Philippines. A progressively tightening blockade would sever Japanese ocean trade. At a time and place of Japan's choosing, the two battle fleets would meet in a cataclysmic gunnery engagement which American dreadnoughts would win.

In the war's third phase Japan's insularity would prove fatal. American forces would advance northward through islands paralleling the coast of Asia to establish new bases for economic warfare. They would choke off all of Japan's imports and ravage its industries and cities by air bombardment until it sued for peace, even though its proud army stood intact in the home islands and in China.

The particular campaign plans would also be determined by geography. In Phase I American soldiers marooned in the Philippines would fight a sacrificial delaying action on fortress positions at the mouth of Manila Bay. The fleet, mobilized at Pearl Harbor where it would be secure from major attack, initially would limit its action to the relatively favorable waters of the central Pacific, jabbing at fringe outposts and seeking opportunities for battle. Orange shipping would be chased from the world's other oceans. A campaign of trade interdiction would be mounted in the western Pacific despite the great distance. After about six months the United States would commence the Phase II offensive. Amphibious shock troops supported by sea and air power would crunch through Japanese-held islands of Micronesia. Advanced fleet bases would be constructed in the Marshall and Caroline islands and the southern Philippines. The Marianas might also be seized as air bases. After winning the decisive sea engagement at an unknown time and place, a hugely augmented Blue expeditionary force would launch Phase III. When Okinawa was captured, the isolation of Japan would be complete. Blockade and bombardment would compel it to surrender in due course.

The plan was, on the whole, remarkably predictive. Yet there were significant discrepancies between its premises and the events of the war. Chapters 27 through 30 will demonstrate, however, that the divergences did not negate the validity of the plan, which was implemented almost in its entirety in the course of the war. The balance of this chapter will reconcile the most obvious divergence—the global scope of World War II as opposed to the one-theater, two-nation war of Plan Orange (at least until the 1939–41 versions).

Before Hitler's triumphs, it seemed inconceivable that Japan would choose to fight the British fleet or the Russian army simultaneously during a Blue-Orange war. But the European crisis stimulated Japan to grasp for booty, first in China, when the colonial powers and the Soviet Union were distracted by the rise of Germany, and then in the Asian possessions of France, Holland, and Britain, when those powers were defeated or besieged. Plan Orange anticipated Japanese encroachment on China, but it predicted the Europeans remaining neutral and Japan content to purchase raw materials from their colonies after clearing the Blue roadblock in the Philippines. (By 1939 some U.S. planners thought that America would fight to preserve European interests, but mainstream opinion was that war would result from overt attacks on U.S. islands; see Chapter 22.) In 1942, although Japan attained the needed resources by conquest rather than trade, the circumstances approximated the Orange Plan conception of war arising from Japanese expansionism, accompanied by an attack on Blue territory to forestall interference.

World War II was a conflict of coalitions. Yet Japan stood alone, neither receiving from nor giving direct assistance to Hitler and Mussolini, so the plan's concept of a single antagonist held true. The effect of the Allied coalition was more complex. U.S. Allies fought in the Pacific, but their principal achievement was to tie down Orange ground forces. China fought sporadically, diverting about 20 percent of the Imperial Army. The Russians preoccupied other divisions before and during their one-week intervention. Dutch, Australian, British, and other Commonwealth regiments struggled in the southwest Pacific and Burma. Despite their valorous efforts, the sapping of Orange soldiery was irrelevant to the war's outcome. Unlike the Wehrmacht, the Japanese army remained undefeated as a whole. Japan's ruin came when sea and air forces demolished its maritime power and its economic life. Those forces were American (except for limited help from the Royal Navy in the opening and closing weeks). The ground battles that won the truly decisive bases were nearly all fought by United States troops. In the bookkeeping of national efforts and achievements it was a Blue-Orange war, for which the plan was eminently suited.

Japan's population was half and its industrial weight about one-tenth that of the United States. Its financing power was feeble. The plan correctly assumed it would mobilize totally for the struggle, whereas U.S. mobilization generally followed prewar projections despite the simultaneous war in the Atlantic. The planners had long believed that a Pacific maritime war would absorb only a fraction of the nation's vast resources. Their most elaborate calculation, a two-year full-war scenario of 1929, anticipated that Blue would produce an "overwhelming" eighteen thousand airplanes per year, double its submarine and destroyer flotillas within a year, and deploy a thousand cargo ships. These figures turned out to be fairly correct in order of magnitude. In a three-year war Blue would be able to build an entire new fleet of a dozen battleships (an accurate prognosis) although the wartime quadrupling of large aircraft carriers was grossly underestimated (not surprising considering the advances in aviation in the 1930s and 1940s). Ground force requirements, however, had been estimated at a modest three hundred thousand in action plus a reserve of a million for "contingencies." The actual musterings in the Pacific outpaced the forecasts, but the makeup of matériel and men roughly paralleled the prognosis (Chapters 13 and 14). The United States committed to the Pacific nearly all its fast carriers, modern battleships and cruisers, submarines, and marine assault divisions, plus a large share of the merchant fleet. Light warships, airplanes (including every combat B-29), and landing craft were sent out in abundance. But of the wartime army and air force of 8 million, less than a quarter went to the Pacific and Asia.[8]

The embroilment of the Allies extended the fighting to the South

Pacific and eastern Asia. Most Orange Plans had defined the principal theater as the waters from the equator to 35° north between Hawaii and Asia, with other ocean sectors reserved for minor actions and lines of transit. The doubled geographical scope of the Pacific war did not, however, invalidate the plan because the decisive theater was in the predicted area. The reasons, fully discussed in the final chapters, will be summarized briefly here.

The supposed value of mainland allies tempted the United States to adopt alternative strategies during the war. Many American leaders, especially Roosevelt, fancied that China was a great power. Until mid-1944 the United States expected to land there, equip a huge army, and erect bases from which to conduct strategic bombing. China's weakness and the success of the sea offensive, however, vitiated that prospect. China remained isolated and ineffective, and efforts to bomb Japan from Chinese bases proved futile. The British were unable to open a back door into China from India; the struggle to recover Burma was a sideshow. Nor were U.S. pleas for bomber fields in Siberia honored. The Soviet attack on Manchuria in 1945 merely hastened the surrender a little. Despite the searches for continental alternatives, the Orange Plan's ocean path to victory endured.

The South Pacific was largely ignored by prewar planners until 1939–41, when they briefly considered naval expeditions to Singapore, Java, or Rabaul. They did not predict the three major campaigns that raged among the southern territories of the Allies. Nevertheless, each campaign correlated with a principle of Plan Orange, and none grossly distorted its relevance to the actual war situation.

In the first campaign Japan seized the oil and raw materials of Malaya and the Netherlands Indies. The American response followed the dictate of Plan Orange: interception of Japan's shipping at sea by long-range raiders and eventual severance of its trade with the region by a U.S. offensive to the Philippines.

The second campaign, the bitter twenty-month struggle of 1942–43 in the Solomon Islands and New Guinea, was equivalent to the battles of attrition anticipated by the plan during amphibious operations north of the equator. The locale of the fighting was different, but the outcome was as predicted: Japan punished and slowed the U.S. offensive but could not halt it.

The third South Pacific campaign, General Douglas MacArthur's breakout from the "Bismarcks Barrier" and march to the Philippines in 1944, is frequently cited as a crucial departure from prewar plans. Wartime joint staffs and most historians, however, have held that the drive through the central Pacific featured in the Orange Plan was the primary U.S. offensive. It maximized naval dominance, yielded islands that were strategically more valuable, led directly toward Japan, and incited a political upheaval in Tokyo.

The coalition of Allies in a global war opened possibilities that prewar planners had rejected as infeasible. Above all, they had feared a loss of American public will if the fight against Japan dragged on for more than two or three years. In fact, the world holocaust energized U.S. determination to impose unconditional surrender on all its enemies. The decision to beat Germany first braced the country for a lengthy war in the Pacific, one that lasted forty-four months and thus permitted the commissioning of undreamed-of armadas and logistical support. The overpowering muscle accrued during the long war could have been applied to any strategy the United States wished, especially after forces were redeployed from Europe. It was applied to fulfill the Orange Plan.

This synopsis has correlated a few aspects of World War II with War Plan Orange. More detailed comparisons will be made throughout the book. It is remarkable that strategic principles that were relevant—and successful—in the war of global coalition were laid down between 1906 and 1914. The history of the plan begins with a look at the men and the system that spawned it.

The American Way of Planning: The Independent Staffs

F orty years after World War II a chief of naval operations summed up the American way of planning as it applied to modern maritime strategy. A robust plan, he observed, flows best from "plurality of perspective and the resulting competition of ideas. . . . The process may be somewhat untidy, but it is distinctly American. It works."[1]

The American way of planning was complex and sometimes unruly. The power to plan was disseminated among military agencies with differing agendas that did not always coordinate with one another. Some planned actively over long periods. For others planning was an ephemeral assignment. A laissez-faire attitude prevailed; competing ideas were encouraged and dissent was tolerated. Decisions were hammered out in clashes between army and navy, between rival naval staffs, and between individuals of aggressive or cautious bent. Informal practices were as important as bureaucratic structure. Orange Plans more often reflected the personal convictions of talented midlevel officers who were recruited for the elite duty than the dicta of higher authorities.

Almost until the outbreak of World War II the civil government paid scant attention to war planning. Strategy was the domain of uniformed officers who neither got nor expected guidance from their civilian masters. Such lack of coordination between the military and the civil persisted even during the war. Other great powers had integrated their foreign and domestic policies with military strategy, sensible behavior because a major war in Europe could threaten the very survival of nations. For the United States the security of ocean moats, distrust of militarism, and a foreign policy based on assuring the sanctity of the Western Hemisphere and the shunning of alliances all fostered civilian disinterest. Although planning was formalized as a U.S. military function at the start of the twentieth century, politicians usually either knew nothing about the war plans or maintained a discreet pretense that offensive plans did not exist. Euphemistic labels such as the "Peace Plans" of the 1920s or "defense" studies of the 1930s disguised the nature of the exercise.

Congress influenced strategy by fixing the size, composition, and command hierarchy of the services and acting on trade, arms treaties, international organizations, colonies, and overseas bases, but the legislature and its committees were rarely if ever informed about War Plan Orange. Admirals and generals might admire the tightly knit British National Defense Committee,[2] but a civilian strategic agency would never have been acceptable to the home-oriented Congress.

The seven presidents who governed during the years of Plan Orange hardly ever associated themselves with it. Theodore Roosevelt initiated the project, but his interest waned whenever he felt assured of the armed forces' defensive readiness. His administration provided an infrastructure for the plan: a world-class fleet with bases on the Pacific Coast and in Hawaii, and the Panama Canal. William Howard Taft, a former secretary of war and governor of the Philippines, was attuned to Far Eastern policy but was content to stand aloof from the active shaping of Plan Orange that occurred during his term. Woodrow Wilson was overtly hostile to war planners. He curtailed their work in 1913, and soon their attention was diverted to the war in Europe. Nevertheless, he unintentionally aided the creation of offensive campaigns by sponsoring a great dreadnought fleet and by diplomacy that neutralized Japan's Pacific island trophies of World War I. The three Republican presidents of the 1920s were disinterested in war plans and preparations. Governing during a time of Japanese passivity, they put their trust in treaties that restricted navies and bases. (An exception was a murky incident in which Warren Harding's intervention may have suppressed realistic offensive planning; see Chapter 11.) Franklin

Roosevelt despised Japanese adventurism and took a keen interest in rebuilding the armed forces but ignored the war plans until World War II erupted in Europe. He then placed the only existing interservice planning committee under his direct control. In 1940 and 1941 he reacted to his military chieftains' ideas on strategy rather than proposing his own. He was the only president to approve a Pacific warfighting document, Plan Rainbow Five. Nevertheless, the absence of earlier presidential endorsements of war plans did not detract from their value as guides that military leaders understood as defining their missions.

The State Department kept a wary distance from the idea of war planning. In 1912 the members of the Naval War College staff, adherents of Karl von Clausewitz's dictum, "War is only a continuation of state policy by other means," who had struggled to write an Orange Plan, pleaded for political and economic guidance to identify U.S. and enemy motivations. Commander Frank Schofield, later the navy's chief strategist, proposed elaborate flows of information among government agencies and processes of joint action by the State, War, and Navy departments. The senior admirals spurned his idea as academic and complex.[3] Other attempts to bring diplomats into planning councils foundered because offensive strategies conflicted with professed foreign policies of amity, arms control, and a purely defensive military establishment and would tarnish their image among "vociferous pacifist groups."[4] In 1921 Secretary of State Charles Evans Hughes thought it "inadvisable" to sit with army and navy planners except in a national crisis, when, he said, "I shall cordially avail myself of the opportunity to do so."[5] Even suggestions that State (and perhaps the Treasury and Commerce departments) should offer geopolitical advice from a safe distance came to naught.[6] In the threatening atmosphere of 1938 Roosevelt approved a Standing Liaison Committee that Secretary of State Cordell Hull proposed, but it never addressed the Pacific situation and was soon circumvented when the services began reporting directly to the president. Only after mid-1940 did the secretaries of state, war, and the navy assemble informally as members of a "war cabinet."[7]

Absence of civilian direction did not mean that military planners were unaware of global affairs or unaffected by politics. They incorporated current developments into their work, sometimes promptly or even before the event, sometimes after a lapse of time. But the pace of war planning did not necessarily correlate with moods of international tension or tranquility. Crises such as the "war scares" of 1907 and 1913 and Japan's aggressions in Asia of 1937 and 1940–41 did stimulate planning. Perversely, Japan's provocative annexation of Manchuria in 1931 was greeted with lethargy in the planning community, whereas the years of good feelings after the disarmament treaty of 1922 witnessed intensive work on the Orange Plan. The rate of activity often reflected changing military doctrines or the tastes of fresh appointees more than the stresses of the day.

The navy felt no regret about the aloofness of the civilian government. In 1909 it embraced the credo of Commander Clarence Williams, one of its most talented planning aides, who piously conceded the logic of a broad-based agency but believed that policy was so predictable and the strategic situation in the Pacific so clear that the navy could independently and confidently decide its best lines of action. The secretary of the navy concurred.[8] The service was left alone to determine such fundamental issues as whether and why the United States would fight Japan, the sort of war it would fight, and for what goals. It never relinquished its planning autonomy before World War II and even retained it in considerable measure during the war.

The secretaries of war and the navy and their assistant secretaries rarely injected themselves into the planning work of their uniformed subordinates. Their correspondence on the subject was sparse (although they may have communicated verbally). Between the world wars the service secretaries signed about half a dozen Orange Plans or major amendments. They regarded war plans as national policy instruments available for the president's orders in a crisis. Occasionally they reorganized the procedures or nudged the planners to make revisions because of treaties or changes in the balance of power. Usually, however, the planners presented innovations for their endorsement. The secretaries as well as the admirals and generals were often lax in informing their opposite numbers about departmental plans. In public they hardly acknowledged that plans existed, certainly not offensive ones. The secretary of the navy's voluminous annual reports devoted only a few platitudes to the War Plans Division and understandably provided no details.[9] Only on two occasions did the subject of war planning break into newspaper headlines. In 1920, vitriolic testimony by Rear Admiral William S. Sims informed Congress how unprepared the navy had been for war, especially in lacking useful plans against Germany.[10] And in 1939 the navy's proposals for bases on Guam and other islands aroused isolationists to query whether it was planning an offensive war. Assistant Secretary Charles Edison stated "as an absolute truth" that "I have never heard discussed, officially or unofficially, any plan . . . that was based on a desire for offensive action. . . . Never, within the Department, in the field or at social gatherings, or in personal conversations do I get any other impression. The idea that the Navy seeks defense on the surface and offense in the backroom is simply imaginary and untenable."[11] Edison was either misinformed or lying through his teeth.

For the army the planning of a Pacific war was an alien task. The service was a weak constabulary that lacked an overseas orientation. Its strength of 145,000 troops in the 1930s ranked it seventeenth in the world, according to Douglas MacArthur.[12] In a major war it expected to expand behind safe ocean frontiers. Many months would pass before it could dispatch an important expedition so the generals would have plenty of time to mull operations. Army Orange Plans consisted primarily of timetables for mobilization and embarkation in support of navy-designed offensives. The army also prepared narrow tactical plans for defending the Philippines, Hawaii, and the Panama Canal that were complete and workmanlike, but as to wide-angle strategy it was reactive, not innovative. It was also inconsistent. Sometimes its viewpoint harmonized with the navy's, sometimes it prodded the navy to adopt more aggressive programs, and sometimes it prescribed caution. Its schizophrenia arose from the incompatible objectives of supporting the garrison of the Philippines and conserving power for more vital interests in the Atlantic and eastern Pacific.

The army's formal planning organization remained constant over forty years. Inefficiencies revealed during the Spanish-American War led it to adopt a general staff system in which a chief of staff commanded the entire service. An Army War Plans Division (AWPD) functioned directly under his charge. It proved rather sterile of imagination in the designing of plans to win a war in the Pacific. The Army War College also played a muted role in Plan Orange in contrast to its naval counterpart.

In 1903 the Joint Army and Navy Board was created to coordinate interservice matters at a level below the cabinet. The board was a consultative body, not a staff agency, and was empowered to advise the cabinet or president only when asked. It thus had "great responsibility with little corresponding authority." Four officers were selected from the General Staff and four from the navy's General Board. They met at irregular intervals depending on the work load, often after long gaps and never in the summer. Admiral of the Navy George Dewey, the nation's most senior warrior, presided over virtually every meeting until his death in 1917. The Joint Board had no staff; minutes were kept by a junior officer.[13] It did not adopt a rudimentary Orange strategy until 1919 or a formal plan until 1924.

The Joint Board tended to alienate presidents by giving erratic advice. During a 1907 war scare it offered Theodore Roosevelt a sorry agenda for fortifying West Coast ports and outlying territories,[14] then angered him by squabbling over a Philippine naval base. During another war scare in 1913 the board insubordinately convened to mobilize forces against an improbable Japanese attack. Woodrow Wilson ordered a stand-down and railed at it to desist from unwanted activity. Humbled to impotence, it lay moribund during World War I.[15]

The situation of the navy was altogether different. Whereas army planners brooded over the defense of cramped fortress zones, the navy painted Orange Plans on canvases of heroic size. It felt itself ready to fight at any time and believed that sea power was best employed when applying strength over a distance. The Orange Plan, not surprisingly, was primarily a creature of the navy.

The process of naval war planning and of joint planning by the services together was far from consistent. The remainder of this chapter focuses on the methods that brought forth in just a few years the wise assumptions on which Plan Orange always rested.

Before the twentieth century the navy had no tradition of continuous strategic planning. It relied on an ad hoc war council during the Civil War. In anticipation of the 1898 conflict with Spain, individual officers and special committees prepared some elementary plans. The war itself was guided by a temporary strategy board advising Secretary John D. Long. Meanwhile, the Naval War College (NWC), founded in 1884 in Newport, Rhode Island, to instruct favored officers in strategy and scientific war making, had begun to conduct war games and study campaign plans, usually involving combat with Britain in the Atlantic or crisis deployments to the Caribbean.[16] By 1898 the small college had achieved an exalted stature through the fame of its second president, Captain Alfred T. Mahan.

In the Spanish-American War the United States acquired a Pacific empire that stretched from Hawaii to Guam and the Philippines. The obligation to protect it in an age of rampant imperial competition suggested the need of a permanent naval planning agency. But the navy had performed effectively during the war without an omnipotent general staff, and the bureaus that managed its affairs directly under the civilian secretary guarded their turf jealously with the aid of congressional friends. President William McKinley opted to establish a committee with purely advisory powers. On 30 March 1900 a General Board of eleven officers was created at department headquarters in Washington, D.C. Among its principal charges were "to devise plans which will employ our naval force to the best advantage. . . [and]. . . plans of campaign for such theaters of war at home, in our dependencies, or abroad as may . . . become the scene of hostilities; to fix upon naval bases indicated by strategy in such theaters . . . and to recommend to the Secretary such action as may be needed."[17] McKinley appointed Dewey, the lionized hero of the Battle of Manila Bay, as president of the board, thereby shrewdly scotching a minor Dewey-for-president boom that might have challenged his reelection.[18] The admiral occupied this post as well as acting as senior member of the Joint Board until he died.

The NWC and the General Board operated in complementary fashion. The work of the college was seasonal, its process inclusive. It attracted selected officers to summer conferences to mull over strategies which the staff reduced to written findings. Because of its many duties, the board established a Second Committee specifically to prepare war plans. From 1906 to 1910 the committee and college usually worked harmoniously together on Pacific strategy.[19]

Both the Naval War College and the General Board were animated by the prestige of renowned admirals. The NWC was the residence in spirit of Mahan, who had risen from a mediocre naval career to glory in the 1890s following publication of his two-volume *Influence of Sea Power upon History*. As president of the college, prolific writer, honored guest of statesmen, and mentor of Theodore Roosevelt, his own influence grew to global dimensions.[20] He and the other college fathers imbued the officer corps with a set of values extolling the vitality of sea power and especially of strong navies to protect overseas commerce and colonies, which they deemed the main determinants of national greatness and international power. By the time planning for a Blue-Orange war began in earnest Mahan had retired from the navy, but he maintained a liaison with Newport, attended conferences, and offered strategic advice.

Dewey, by contrast, was no intellectual heavyweight. Before his celebrated victory over the Spaniards, the elderly admiral had been a rather ordinary officer, "neither a remarkable thinker nor a brilliant innovator." Some called his General Board a "dignified retreat" for aging flag officers. Although Dewey settled disputes with "exceeding skill" and enhanced board recommendations with the aura of his prestige, he knew his limitations. For planning he recruited and encouraged talented aides.[21]

The easy consensus on policy reflected the shared values of the eminences of Newport and Washington. They believed in America's destiny as a great power and the rightness of its imperial span. They lauded maritime trade as the foundation of national wealth and the need for a strong fleet and bases overseas. They welcomed opportunities to wield power to preserve the new colonies and guard the quasi-wards of Latin America and China. They regarded the Royal Navy as a role model, especially admiring its offensive temperament. They agreed that the proper goal of a great power at war should be total victory.

The college attracted officers of an intellectual bent to study and teach. It was a place where "ideas, facts, and logic were of greater importance than rank and name."[22] Many of them found war planning a congenial exercise of comparative analysis and scholarly deduction. About 1910 the college's president Raymond P. Rodgers adopted the "applicatory system," better known as the "Estimate of the Situation." It was a thinking process recommended by his kinsman Captain William Ledyard Rodgers, who learned it at the Army War College. "A great white light broke on the service" when through this system plans were presented as four reasoned elements: statement of mission, assessment of enemy forces and intentions, assessment of own forces, and evaluation of possible courses of action.[23] The system was used by other naval entities long after the college left the planning scene in 1912.

In search of talented planners, the General Board summoned promising captains and junior admirals. Secretary Long arranged for the part-time assistance of two dozen lieutenants from the fleet, young seagoing officers of proven ability, among them the rising stars William S. Sims and Clarence S. Williams. A tradition arose of rotating a few outstanding individuals through two years of war planning along an almost certain trajectory to flag rank. In 1900 the board identified five attributes it would seek in planning aides: good judgment, aptitude, intelligence, success in handling men and ships, and practical sea experience.[24] For four decades the navy tried more or less conscientiously to select such men, but the recruits it chose seemed to match the list in inverse order.

Planning was quintessentially a staff job lacking command authority, yet the navy always assigned line officers to the top billets. Candidates arrived after ten to thirty years of duty at sea and in the shore establishment. Battleship experience was always overrepresented because ambitious officers pursued that exalted branch, but, myth to the contrary, the planners adapted early to such modern specialties as mine and amphibious warfare, logistics, advanced base designs, and soon submarines and aircraft.

Intellect as a qualification rose in esteem as war became more intricate, to judge from the academic standings of the leaders of the later-established War Plans Division (Table 19.1). Raw brainpower, however, did not assure good plans. Minds able to grasp complexities sometimes cataloged so many contingencies in such turgid prose that their work could be "quite a mystery."[25] Schooling at Newport was a virtual prerequisite in determining aptitude. Since friendship with top commanders was often a factor in selecting aides, however, performance was predictably erratic. Although the heads of planning agencies signed nearly all papers, obscuring the identity of high achievers, energy and enthusiasm seemed to correlate better with bulky output than with excellence.

Good judgment was the most critical trait and the hardest to identify in advance. According to one expert, "constant and unremitting study" was the key to success. Another said it was "imagination; even dreams." A talent for clear and convincing analysis was helpful. The most effective planners neatly balanced an aggressive spirit with realism. One veteran planner defined the hallmark of excellence as "vivid imagination" balanced by pragmatic traits such as an ability to think like the enemy.[26]

War planning brought an elite few to sit at the elbows of supreme admirals but did not usually reward them with promotion to exalted commands. Only one top planner rose to the post of chief of naval operations before World War II (William S. Standley), and only one to commander in chief of the fleet (Frank Schofield). Both had directed the War Plans Division in the 1920s. There was a tendency in the navy to typecast planners as intellectuals, educators, and staff men. Several served as presidents of the War College or returned to planning jobs during World War II. Major wartime commands were rarely offered to former planners except in the new art of amphibious landings.

The most dynamic staff officers of the college and board shared their elders' expansive worldview, which they codified into a geopolitical and grand strategic framework of Plan Orange. Two of them wielded special influence in the formative years. Commander James H. Oliver, an ordnance expert, three-tour veteran of the college, and "student of higher strategy and international relations," was Newport's spokesman.[27] He conceptualized the notions of a maritime strategy to fulfill a continental objective and of a three-phase war. Convinced that the country's intellectual resources were as latent as its material war-making capacity, he urged that war planning be assigned to the best professional minds.[28] Commander Clarence S. Williams, the most articulate voice on the General Board's Second Committee, was a seagoing officer with a flair for strategy.[29] He cared little for the foreign policy analyses that intrigued Oliver but had a better understanding that politicians would never underwrite a chain of Pacific bases that Oliver regarded as vital. He believed pragmatically that any plan was better than none because imperfect models could be amended later and alternatives would offer choices in wartime.[30] Williams's conviction that the navy ought to chart its own course was more in tune with institutional pride than were Oliver's pleas for external guidance. Nevertheless, common goals muted their differences until they turned to the planning of campaigns.

Neither of the two fledgling planning agencies was beholden to a "Prussian" general staff. Both were small, elite bodies with advisory or educational functions, shielded from most outside pressures. Their members were blessed with the freedom to think, debate, and plan. Imagination did coexist with realism. The embryonic American system rendered exceptionally good service in defining the big issues of a Blue-Orange war. The 1906–14 era was one of only three periods when the conditions favorable to real progress in maritime strategy existed, namely skilled naval planning staffs, a warmly supportive senior hierarchy, and the acquiescence of the army. But collegiality and intellectual freedom proved inadequate to the more exacting task of campaign planning. The graybeards of the navy who had applauded their aides' codification of great principles rejected their predictions of an expensive, brutal struggle to defeat Japan. After World War I tight bureaucratic control descended on naval war planning, and the independent staffs faded from the arena of strategy making.

The Geopolitics of the Pacific War

The geopolitical characteristics of a Pacific war included its causes (both long-term and immediate), the nature of the struggle, the goals of both belligerents, and the time and cost of achieving them. In the absence of political direction, military planners had to establish their own suppositions.

Establishing a rationale for war with Japan was not simple. There was no overt reason for anticipating a fight. The nations had enjoyed cordial relations and increased commerce since Commodore Matthew Perry's squadron opened the isolated shogunate to world intercourse in 1853. Americans admired the progressive, westernizing Japanese, and they reciprocated the esteem. Theodore Roosevelt, who like most of his countrymen was "thoroughly well pleased" by Japan's trouncing of Russia,[1] won the appreciation of moderate Japanese leaders and the Nobel Peace Prize by mediating an end to the brutal war in 1905. In the Taft-Katsura Agreement that same year the two nations pledged respect for each others' interests in the Far East.

Before 1906 the only frictions hot enough to kindle a bit of war planning had arisen from suspicions that Tokyo coveted American

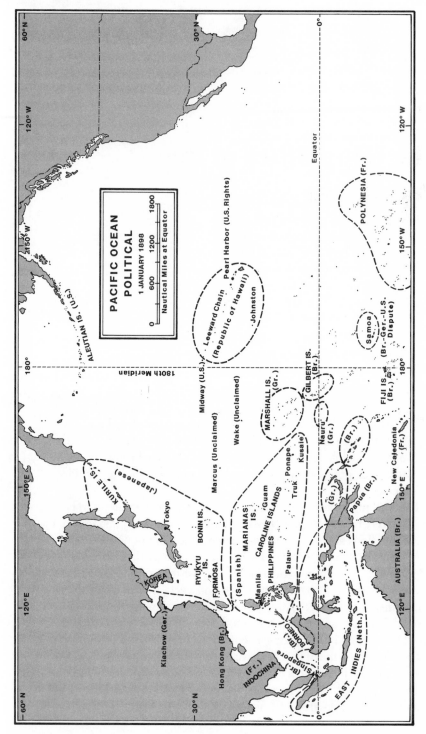

PACIFIC OCEAN POLITICAL
1 JANUARY 1898

Nautical Miles at Equator
0   600   1200   1800

MAP 3.1

islands. In the 1890s many Japanese laborers had emigrated to the Hawaiian republic, which was virtually a U.S. protectorate.[2] When Japanese warships came snooping around, Roosevelt, then assistant secretary of the navy, solicited from his officers a plan of defense in case a need should arise to intervene against a claim by Japan (see Map 3.1).[3] The U.S. annexation of Hawaii in 1898 put such anxieties to rest. In the Social Darwinian atmosphere of the time it seemed plausible that Japan also hungered after the Philippine Islands as a place to resettle its burgeoning population.[4] There was shadowy evidence that Japanese secret societies aided a native insurrection against U.S. rule in the Philippines.[5] Japan's covetousness of Blue possessions was customarily mentioned in Orange Plans as a cause of tension,[6] but the strategists never seriously believed it would foment a war to commandeer such resource-poor archipelagos when far richer prizes in East Asia could be plucked with far less peril.

War Plan Orange was inaugurated by a trivial incident. Between 1891 and 1906 thousands of Japanese emigrated to California. Local white racists agitating to block their entry unfairly stigmatized them as "immoral, intemperate and quarrelsome men bound to labor for a pittance." They victimized Orientals by looting and violence in the tense aftermath of the earthquake and fire that devastated San Francisco in April 1906. Politicians passed laws restricting property rights and segregating schoolchildren—laws that violated treaties. The proud people of Japan were outraged. The American press, the "leprous vampires . . . eager to involve their country in war to sell a few more newspapers," in the words of Secretary of State Elihu Root, brandished lurid tales of menace by the warlike Nipponese who had whipped the czar's legions. Roosevelt's administration calmed matters by coercing bigoted city officials to repeal the measures and negotiated a "Gentlemen's Agreement" whereby Tokyo curtailed the flow of immigrants. But anti-Oriental riots broke out in the spring of 1907, and another "war scare" hit the headlines.[7] So taut was the atmosphere that the Naval War College staff began to ponder a Blue-Orange war scenario. The Second Committee cobbled together a rough plan featuring "preliminary steps to be taken . . . when war is imminent."[8] Even the president became unnerved. A few months earlier he had asked if the navy was studying how to fight Japan. Dewey had told him that the General Board had prepared an "effective" Orange Plan.[9] The Joint Board briefed him on it.[10]

Roosevelt never believed that bigotry and journalistic jingoism could incite a war.[11] Neither did the naval planners, who saw that Japan was absorbed in digesting its conquests in Manchuria and recovering from financial exhaustion.[12] The scare blew itself out by the time the American fleet paid a goodwill visit to Tokyo in 1908. U.S. planners regarded the vigilante flare-ups on the West Coast as "pin pricks" that Japan would exploit for public agitation and world sympathy, not realistic inducements to war.[13]

In 1913 the "yellow press" of both countries again stirred up wrath after the California legislature barred Orientals from owning land. Again the administration urged moderation, but this time President Woodrow Wilson discouraged warlike planning. Angered at plotting of steps for mobilization behind his back, he suspended the Joint Board from all war-planning activity.[14] The scare evaporated. Racist incidents soon faded as a motivation for planners. When the United States passed an immigration act in the early 1920s that excluded most Orientals and provoked bitter feelings in Japan, the strategists took little notice. Nevertheless, the legacy of the bigotry of 1906 was profound because it set the United States to planning war against Japan.

A viable war rationale was identified when the planners scrutinized their country's most prominent Far Eastern policy. The prospect of a lush Chinese market had long captivated American government and business leaders. It had also motivated McKinley to keep the Philippine Islands as a colony after the war with Spain for a commercial entrée to the Orient. But European powers were carving the moribund corpus of Manchu China into exclusive spheres of commercial dominance and preempting Chinese ports as naval bases. The most avaricious imperialists were Germany, France, and Russia. In 1899 Secretary of State John Hay appealed to all nations to preserve free trade throughout China. The following year, after several powers (including the United States) squelched the Boxer uprising of Chinese nationalists against foreigners, the feeding frenzy intensified. Russia virtually annexed the rich province of Manchuria. Hay expanded his plea, asking all states to honor the political integrity of China. The commercial and political appeals, together named the Open Door policy, were popular with Americans for idealistic and practical reasons. With unwarranted confidence, Hay (who joined Roosevelt's cabinet after McKinley was assassinated) assumed that the great powers had assented to America's self-appointed stewardship of the status quo in Asia. Along with the Monroe Doctrine, the Open Door was, Mahan declared, one of the "principal and permanent policies" on which naval planning would stand.[15]

Before the Russo-Japanese War of 1904–5, U.S. planners had searched for ways to maintain the Open Door against predators. It was clear that an isolationist America with a minuscule army could not enforce its high-minded dicta against continental powers like Russia. It needed strong friends in the region. Great Britain and Japan appeared friendly for they were sated for the moment, the former with its vast Eastern empire and the latter with Formosa and Korea, the spoils of its 1894–95 war with China. The British-Japanese alliance of 1902 was applauded in the United States as a stabilizing alignment that would support the Open Door.[16] The General Board therefore set about concocting scenarios of coalition struggles in the Far East that it assembled into War Portfolio No. 2, a collection of vague plans and harbor charts. Rear Admiral Henry C. Taylor, Dewey's right-hand man, mesmerized his colleagues with melodramas that usually pitted the United States and the Anglo-Japanese alliance against a sinister cabal of Russia, Germany, and France. (His naval wars somehow never spread beyond the Orient.) Rear Admiral Frederick Rodgers of the Asiatic Station responded unenthusiastically. When pressed, he grudgingly produced a plan to send his thirteen warships from their rudimentary base at Manila to wreck the weakest opponent, the French squadron, and occupy its Indochinese ports to secure his communications via the Indian and Atlantic oceans. He would then join the larger allied fleets in bottling up the German and Russian squadrons in North China and Siberia.[17] When Rodgers's successor refused to dabble further, the Second Committee and the War College pecked away desultorily at other sketches.[18]

The planning of colonial wars skidded to a halt in 1904, when the army members of the new Joint Board learned of it.[19] Chief of Staff Adna R. Chaffee dismissed the naval scripts as nonsensical. Brigadier General Tasker Bliss of the Army War College called for plans to safeguard the Western Hemisphere and especially the proposed canal at Panama.[20] The navy yielded gracefully. Japan's humbling of Russia and political realignments that set Germany and France on opposing sides in Europe had antiquated Taylor's farcical scenarios.[21] They were never reviewed seriously after his death that year. The final essay, an outline for attacking German Kiaochow in North China, was filed and forgotten in October 1906, when Roosevelt inquired about a plan to fight Japan.[22]

Taylor's studies, though detached from political reality, bequeathed certain legacies to Plan Orange. They envisioned primarily naval contests with little need of Blue ground forces. They emphasized the importance of distant naval bases. A battle-worthy squadron, Taylor declared, would need an industrialized dockyard in the Philippines. Since it would not be able to range as far as the Yellow Sea, it would also need mobile or "flying" bases for replenishment and light repair. The General Board speculated on obtaining a coaling base in China but soon acknowledged that acquiring one in peacetime would be provocative to opinion abroad and that the U.S. government would not sanction it. (Rodgers slyly suggested a permanent anchorage in Korea, which Japan was hardly likely to grant.) During a war, Blue would have to improvise mobile forward outposts, for which the navy began accumulating matériel in the Philippines. Such bases, the board decided, ought to lie conveniently near the fighting zone yet rearward enough to require only portable defenses against light raids.[23] These criteria for advanced bases permeated Blue strategic thinking in the ensuing decades.

Before 1906 nobody of authority, least of all Dewey, had imagined Japan as a threat. The admiral had been charmed by the mikado and empress before steaming off to Manila Bay and liked to contrast the modern constitutional monarchs with the medieval shoguns who had tried to ward off Perry forty years earlier.[24] Even the hyperimaginative Taylor saw no real prospect of fighting Japan, notwithstanding another of his weird scenarios, which pitted Blue against an entente of China, Japan, and Russia.[25] But the Russo-Japanese War (February 1904 to September 1905) radically altered U.S. perceptions of threats to the Open Door. Japan eradicated Russian strength from the Far East. In the following years other European fleets went home to concentrate for a prospective war. Japan had demonstrated astonishing military prowess. Its modern battle line had maneuvered skillfully, its army had fought fanatically, and its economy had withstood the strain of war. It had become the dominant regional power. To project the use of American arms against such a formidable enemy was a more serious business than speculations of colonial squadrons flailing at each other.

The Treaty of Portsmouth that ended the war limited Japanese control of Manchuria, but American planners continued to regard the province as ripe for plucking. Japan was the only conceivable transgressor. When Raymond Rodgers and the War College staff considered the situation in 1911, they predicted that eventually Japan would shift its tactics from gradual economic encroachment to open aggression that would require a "call for action" in support of the Open Door. In the best of circumstances, one or more allies would rally to the cause and check Japan in a continental war in which threats to U.S. possessions would be mere diversions, the role of the Blue navy minor and of the Blue army nil. A more likely situation, they conceded, would involve attempts by Japan to end the American policy of containment and simultaneously cover the sea flank of current and future aggressions while safeguarding its trade lanes. Doing so would entail driving the United States from the western Pacific by seizing the Philippines, Guam, and perhaps Hawaii. In this more difficult situation Blue would fight alone to compel Japan to withdraw from Manchuria, not by continental intervention but by maritime operations that would gain command of the sea, reclaim lost possessions, and throttle Orange commerce.

The NWC planners thus established in 1911 a credible rationale for a Blue-Orange war for which planning had already been under way for five years: Japan would attack American islands to expedite its grandiose ambitions on the mainland. But the college staff committed a political gaffe by recommending alliances with European powers to assure a more conventional war on the mainland that would "drive Japan within the limits of expansion allowed on land and hold it there."[26] The challenge to the traditional loathing of entangling alliances was inflammatory. The secretary of the navy brusquely ordered the college to desist from meddling in political matters.[27] Dewey, who found "extended discussion" of foreign policy by naval officers distasteful, began to loosen the tightly reasoned linkage between Plan Orange and defense of the Open Door. In 1914 the General Board adopted the broad thesis of war arising from Orange intent to expel Blue from the western Pacific, an event of rising probability because the Japanese national character was greedy, combative, overweening, and scornful of American power.[28]

In less than a decade, U.S. strategists had retreated from seeing their nation as the firm guarantor of China to a nebulous restraining force that Japan would assail someday to unblock its ambitions. Though never handed down by higher political authority, this perception by naval officers of the roots of a Pacific war never varied after 1914. It was, in the end, correct. The United States did not fight for Manchuria in 1931 or China in 1937 or 1941. It fought when Japan attacked it to remove the main impediment to conquest of East Asia.

The assumption that Blue would defend its rightful position in the Philippines was far better attuned to national attitudes than was battling for free trade or China. But the assumption was bedeviled over the next thirty years by the uncertain status of the islands. Many Americans wished to be rid of the colony, which was a fiscal burden with disappointing commercial yields. One admiral on the Manila station in later years who advocated withdrawal from the Philippines could not imagine the United States fighting for a "farfetched" possibility of lucrative trade when it could not even shelter its home market from cheap Oriental goods.[29] The Jones Act, passed by Congress in 1916, promised the islanders eventual independence. Nevertheless, ardent Filipinists, notably Generals Leonard Wood and Douglas MacArthur, argued over the years for permanent military support. Wood, as governor-general of the islands in the 1920s, viewed America's interests in terms of morality, prestige, and eventual profits. He persuaded the Harding administration to redirect Plan Orange to the prime objective of foiling a Japanese conquest (Chapter 11). By then the vitality of the armed forces had become so enmeshed in their potential Pacific war missions that they abhorred a voluntary exit from the Philippines.

Joint Board reviews of 1924, 1931, and 1934 complained it would be "unfair" to lay down the "White Nations' burden." Withdrawal from the Orient would forfeit American influence and trade. The Open Door would slam shut. The Filipinos would borrow from wolfish bankers, then default and cede territory. Radicals of other "lesser developed races" would be spurred to expel their European masters. Japan would inherit most of the region. Soon it would grasp for the Philippines. The board, presuming a semiprotectorate obligation as with Cuba, felt the United States would have to return to help its former ward, by combat if necessary. Philippine independence, it warned, would thus increase the probability of war with Japan.

Some naval leaders lobbied for a continued American presence, specifically a fortified base and perpetual rights to use eight harbors. A Joint Planning Committee urged partition of the archipelago with the United States to keep the Sulu Archipelago and western Mindanao (where lay the best sites for an advanced fleet base) while the army retained a few posts and trained native troops. In 1933 Congress approved an independence bill with retention of military stations, but the Philippine legislature refused it. The following year the Tydings-McDuffie Act promised independence in 1946 without sovereign reservations. The war planners railed again about lost markets and influence and Japanese voracity that would compel U.S. protection "if for no other than sentimental reasons."[30]

A military presence was maintained in the Philippines throughout the commonwealth years so Orange planners never had to amend the supposition of 1911 as to what might spark a war. It was possible that the United States might have fought solely to defend European colonies (as some plans of 1939–40 suggested), but the strategists never doubted that Japan, in its compulsion to evict it from Asia, would attack the Philippines. When the commander in chief of the Asiatic Fleet suggested in 1940 that Japan might bypass the archipelago while seizing British and Dutch colonies to the south, he was informed that U.S. war planners deemed an attack on the Philippines, and thus war, inevitable if Japan moved south.[31]

If the causes of war appeared ambiguous at times, the probable situation at the outbreak seemed clear. Japan could mobilize swiftly and secretly. It would choose to attack at an advantageous moment when it considered the United States unready and the U.S. Navy relatively weak. Mahan predicted it would strike unscrupulously without bothering to declare war, as it had done to the Russians at Port Arthur.[32] The planners usually assumed that U.S. politicians would not permit warlike deployments during a period of strained relations, especially not a provocative fleet movement toward the Far East.[33] They sometimes supposed a warning period ranging from two to forty days,[34] but for the most part they expected a sudden thunderbolt as the opening blow.

The American strategists' war objective, simply stated, was to win. They rarely reflected on the chance of a U.S. defeat. Only one circumstance, they reasoned, could bring about that dreadful result: destruction of the battle line early in the war. The fleet's home ports were in the Atlantic, and it would be safe enough at the outbreak. But if it were "expended" soon in the western Pacific, "that would end the war," according to 1907 critics of the Orange Plan,[35] because Japan would achieve strategic supremacy by occupying Hawaii and threatening to seize parts of the West Coast, then "demand peace on her own terms."[36] By 1914 gloomy speculations of defeat disappeared, although the planners remained aware that a naval disaster might forfeit the decision. By 1941, however, when Japan had acquired the means of destroying at a blow the half of the Blue navy that was in the Pacific, U.S. air defenses and Japan's logistical inability to dominate the eastern Pacific had negated any chance of "peace on her own terms" if the United States chose to fight on. Japan's hope of winning lay in enlisting an ally: time.

As the underdog in martial capacity, Orange would fare best in a short war concluded before Blue's power could be fully mobilized, yet its leaders had to anticipate a long war of attrition. Japan's basic military objective, U.S. planners surmised, would be to control the western Pacific as long as possible[37] while maintaining its economy through stockpiling raw materials and importing from North Asia and conserving its fleet for an opportune moment. Planning studies of the 1920s anticipated that Orange would seek to wage a war of endurance until America relented, a war justified by its grandiose political objectives and borne by its obedient people.[38] To win was to outlast America until a bargained peace treaty validated Japan's conquests.

With neither civilian guidance nor dangers to vital U.S. interests, the planners enjoyed considerable latitude in defining a response to the expected enemy strategy. Blue might choose to wage a low-intensity war by sweeping Orange cargoes from all oceans but the western Pacific, raiding outposts, and applying diplomatic and financial pressure to deny foreign loans and trade until Japan came to its senses. Clarence Williams, for one, felt scornful of such a weak riposte that would see American power stagnate while Japan fattened on goods from occupied parts of Asia.[39] Or the United States might conduct a limited offensive to liberate the Philippines and perhaps sink the Orange fleet, then negotiate. It might try to recruit Russia or China to drive back Japan on the mainland. In the most extreme case, it might commit itself to an unlimited war to destroy Japan as a political entity.

The strategy the planners adopted as early as 1906 was one of unlimited *economic* war. Confidence in economic warfare was understandable in the gentlemanly age before World War I, when conflicts were financed through foreign borrowing and belligerents negotiated rationally when facing bankruptcy. Besides, Dewey and his contemporaries had served as young officers in executing the Anaconda Plan of 1861–65 when a world-class U.S. Navy of seven hundred vessels had bottled up the Confederacy. They believed that a relentless blockade, destruction of ports and shipping, and the "final and complete commercial isolation" of Japan[40] were certain to bring about its "eventual impoverishment and exhaustion."[41] It would be the kind of war the United States could wage and win.

The goal of the unlimited war was defined as unlimited victory. War plans rang with triumphant declarations. America's purpose, Oliver proposed in 1907, should be to fight "with the fixed resolve never to end the war until victorious."[42] Or, as Williams later expressed it, "to enforce Japanese submission to our particular aims."[43] Or, simpler still, "to impose our will."[44] Dewey, an uncomplicated sailor, held that the object of war was "to defeat the enemy" and that this was "best attained when defeat is complete." He mistrusted "ulterior" political motives and recommended that Blue should "make war with all its power . . . with the single purpose of accomplishing the objects of the war in the most complete and business-like manner and in the shortest time."[45] These were accurate foretastes of the mind-set of 1941–45, when most U.S. leaders eschewed political ends in favor of strictly military results.

The origins of the navy's gritty determination are not known. Wars to the bitter end had not been the usual rule of history. Instances of success by naval means alone were almost nonexistent. In American experience only the Civil War had been an unlimited struggle, but it had been waged for the most imperative ends. The Blue navy had never fought a modern fleet or conducted an overseas expedition against a first-class enemy. Perhaps its dedication to total victory stemmed from admiration of the Royal Navy's Nelsonian ethic. It did not rest on calculations of America's larger population and output, which ranked high in determining the actual outcome of World War II. Naval planners considered manpower unimportant in a contest that would see no massed army battles, and industrial capacity was not understood as decisive in wars before 1914. Recent examples had suggested that modern conflicts would be brief, measured in months rather than years.

There was no question that U.S. wealth could support a war indefinitely[46] or that the obedient Japanese would fight as long as their leaders demanded. The prime uncertainty was whether the American public would tolerate a lengthy war, say of a year or two years' duration, for goals not vital to national survival. Mahan was certain it would *not*. The perception of a fickle society with a short attention span and no stomach for hardships led him and others to recommend strategies of rapid offensive movement.[47] Oliver took the opposite stance, believing that the nation would willingly suffer "a long and exhausting war" for a just cause.[48] Williams agreed, although he felt that "the patience and temper of the American people would be severely tried."[49]

One provocation would unquestionably energize support for a long conflict: an attack on the United States itself. In 1911 Mahan doubted that Japan would be foolish enough to try to invade the Blue homeland for fear of inflaming popular outrage,[50] a moot point because California lay beyond its reach. The General Board carried the perception further in 1914. Hawaii, it observed, was "truly American territory." A landing, or even a raid, would "arouse a greater spirit of resentment in Blue . . . and result in a more determined prosecution of the war."[51] These were prophetic words, although the admirals wrongly concluded that Japan would never let fly so counterproductive a blow. The specter of U.S. outrage, so clear to Dewey's board, did not deter Admiral

Isoroku Yamamoto from a sneak attack in 1941, to the eventual sorrow of a ravaged Japan.

Conjectures about public tolerance of a long war bore heavily on the formulation of Pacific strategy. The pre-1914 concept that a war might last six to twelve months gave way to a consensus of two years in the 1920s[52] as the delaying power of modern attrition weapons became evident. In two years the United States could churn out awesome quantities of light warships, merchantmen, and airplanes and construct and deliver mammoth dry docks for servicing capital ships at advanced bases in the western Pacific (Chapter 13). But shipyards took three years to build battleships, the unquestioned arbiters of sea power, or large aircraft carriers. In 1923, when naval planners mused of a longer conflict that would allow the building of a second battle fleet, the chief of naval operations thought it such a "large order" that he refused to believe the country would shoulder the cost.[53]

The perception of limited public endurance goes far to explain the lure of a vigorous counterattack to gain rapid advantages. Planners torn between hope and realism spawned such ambivalent statements as "We must expect a long war but we should operate to gain a victorious conclusion in the minimum possible time."[54] The joint planners in 1924 recommended confusingly that government and industry should prepare for a lengthy struggle but could limit mobilization to the needs of a quick victory.[55] In the 1930s more somber strategies guaranteed an even longer war. Although official time estimates were dropped, guesses of four or five years were bruited about.[56] Some planners flirted with notions of less than total victory, but a dedication to absolute triumph was still deeply rooted in the collective military mind when the United States entered the war (Chapter 26). U.S. adoption in 1943 of unconditional Japanese surrender as its preeminent goal vindicated the judgment of the Orange planners, yet doubts about public resoluteness remained to haunt the wartime strategists. The desire to achieve unconditional surrender in an acceptable time led them in 1945 to the most serious of all challenges to the wisdom of Plan Orange—a proposal to invade Japan.

Grand Strategy

T he translation of geopolitics into grand strategy began smoothly
with resolution of the paradox of continental versus maritime
power. Japan's prime objectives were on the mainland, and its trump
card was a large standing army to which American political realities
would allow only a naval challenge. The Blue military mission, therefore, was to defeat land power by sea power. It became an indelible
strategic axiom of War Plan Orange.

Japan's vulnerability to maritime force may seem evident in retrospect, but the axiom was a leap of faith by novice planners in the years
before World War I. In the 1920s it was expanded beyond the initial
themes of marooning the Imperial Army and blockading the Orange
homeland. Rear Admiral Frank Schofield, director of naval war plans,
noted that "the soundest strategy [for Japan] would be one that compelled our Navy to fight her Army" by contesting U.S. access to vital
naval positions with troops and airplanes.[1] The sea-beats-land concept
was applied successfully in World War II even though U.S. strategists
twice recommended large-scale land warfare, in China and then in
Japan itself. America was spared the bloody toll that prewar planners

abhorred because it pursued their maritime vision and avoided massed ground battles.

To fashion the precept into a strategic plan was an onerous chore because of the geography of the Pacific—its vast width and the sparseness of intermediate objectives. (Climate was benign except in the far north.) Distance would initially be Japan's ally in gaining domination of the western Pacific. Before the First World War coal-fired battleships could operate about 2,000 miles from base, torpedo boats and destroyers about half as far (Chapter 9). The American outposts of Manila and Guam were vulnerable, lying 1,500 miles from Japan and only 570 and 900 miles, respectively, from outlying Orange bases in the Pescadore Islands (near Formosa) and in the Bonins. But Hawaii, 3,500 miles from Tokyo, was too remote for extended Japanese operations.

To project its power to the western Pacific the United States would have to overcome unprecedented difficulties. The Blue navy was habitually stationed in the Chesapeake. To reach the main war zone, it would have to travel 14,000 miles via the Atlantic and Indian oceans or 19,700 miles by way of the Straits of Magellan, the latter distance equivalent to nearly 80 percent of the earth's circumference. After the Panama Canal opened in 1914, the cruise shrank to a still formidable 12,000 miles. Even the naval bases proposed for construction in California and Hawaii would lie 7,000 and 5,000 miles from the Philippines. Simply getting to the battlefront would be a heroic effort logistically. The destruction of a weary Russian fleet in 1905 after an arduous voyage from the Baltic to the Battle of Tsushima was a somber omen.

A fleet's power was estimated to erode by 10 percent for each thousand miles it cruised from its base.[2] Wear and tear, prolonged absences for repairs, and tropical growth that fouled hulls and reduced speed by several knots within a few months of leaving dry dock would sap the fleet's potency when far from home. Worse, attrition attacks would inevitably erode American naval superiority. The fighting strength of the fleet would decline steeply in conformance with the "N-squared rule," which decreed that relative power in battle was proportional to the square of the number of ships (or guns) in action.[3] These equations of distance and power underlay the famous five-to-three battleship tonnage ratio negotiated by the United States and Japan in the Washington Treaty of 1922 to equalize their combat power in the western Pacific. (Extension of ship ranges by conversion to oil and later by refueling at sea eased the penalty of distance, but the problem worsened again in the air age because planes had action radii of hundreds, not thousands, of miles.) Furthermore, the long haul from

America's arsenals and coal mines dictated employment of five to ten times as many merchant vessels as Japan to maintain equal strength in the war zone, and they would be exposed to attack during much of their course whereas Japan could service its outposts free of risk until U.S. warships reached the theater.

But distance was a fickle mistress that could be turned against Japan. Once the larger Blue navy established itself in the western Pacific it would be able to sever Japan's trade lifelines, neutralize its outlying stations, overwhelm its fleet in battle, and bombard its homeland. Defeat would follow inevitably. As Williams observed, "Japan's great oversea distance from the United States is her greatest source of strength. . . . Her greatest weakness lies in her island position combined with her dependence upon sea borne commerce."[4]

Geography dictated a Blue-Orange war of three phases (see Map 4.1). The planners easily visualized the opening and closing phases in which the advantages of geography would accrue first to Japan and then to the United States. The strategic suppositions about those two periods were fixed by 1906 and 1911, respectively, and changed little thereafter.

In Phase I Japan was expected quickly to overrun Blue possessions in the western Pacific. Alternative scenarios were occasionally proposed, but the planners always returned to the original thesis; the outlook on the eve of World War II was not much different than that thirty-five years earlier. The complete story of Phase I planning from 1906 to 1941 is compressed into Chapters 5 and 6, which deal with the eastern and western Pacific, respectively.

Phase III was also reasoned out within a few years. Once the Blue fleet and an expeditionary force had established a western base they would advance northward through the islands paralleling the coast of Asia, drawing ever nearer to Japan, to starve it of food, fuel, and raw materials by blockade and bombard accessible targets until it capitulated. This siege scenario was confirmed in 1911 after the secretary of the navy complained that naval planners had "rarely gotten farther than taking the fleet . . . to the scene of hostilities" and had omitted Phase III operations.[5] A more convincing siege plan had to await the advent in the late 1920s of airplanes capable of bombing Japan (Chapter 14). Although further study of endgame strategy was suspended in the 1930s because the timetable of advance had been slowed, the siege remained the commonly understood American policy (Chapter 26).

Over the years Phase II proved to be the most troubling aspect of the Orange Plan. In the standard scenario developed in principle by 1914,

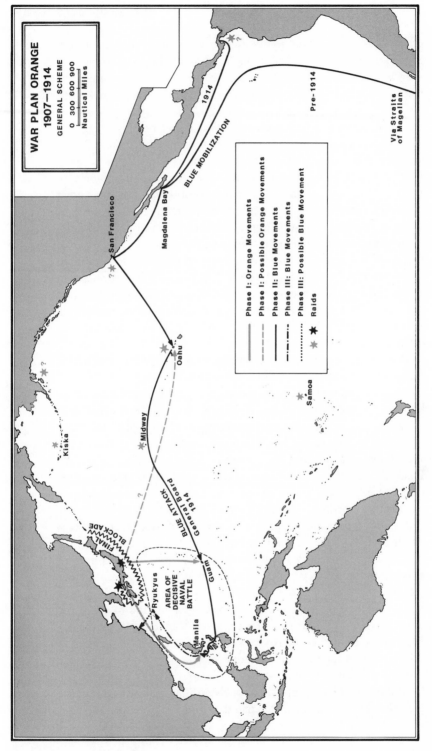

WAR PLAN ORANGE
1907–1914
GENERAL SCHEME
0 300 600 900
Nautical Miles

Phase I: Orange Movements
Phase I: Possible Orange Movements
Phase II: Blue Movements
Phase III: Blue Movements
Phase III: Possible Blue Movement
Raids

San Francisco

Magdalena Bay

BLUE MOBILIZATION

1914

Pre-1914

Via Straits
of Magellan

Oahu

Midway

Kiska

Samoa

BLUE ATTACK
General Board
1914

FINAL
BLOCKADE

Ryukyus

AREA OF
DECISIVE
NAVAL
BATTLE

Guam

Manila

MAP 4.1

the entire Blue navy and an army expeditionary force would advance to the Far East and develop a base, secure their supply lines, and sever Japanese trade with all regions except northeastern Asia, while building strength for Phase III. Many variations were possible within this framework, and from 1906 to 1941 many were proposed. Much of this book is devoted to the unsteady evolution of plans for the war's longest phase, which during World War II lasted from mid-1942 to the end of 1944, or 70 percent of the war's duration.

The problems of designing a Phase II strategy were largely attributable to geography and the long versus short war dilemma. The width of the Pacific would constrain an easy offensive movement. There were neither large land masses nor operative seaports between Hawaii and the archipelagos of Asia. The length of the war would depend on the time required during Phase II to reach and establish a western Pacific base. The location of that base would determine how effectively pressure could be brought against Japan's vital interests.

Over the years three solutions were proposed. The first and simplest demanded construction during peacetime of a naval base in the Far East, an industrial arsenal with impregnable defenses ashore and afloat that could hold out until the fleet arrived. The base, either on Luzon or Guam, would ease the risk and logistical difficulty of projecting power and significantly shorten the war. The concept flourished in the upper echelons of the navy in the first two decades of the century, but the admirals who sponsored it were politically naive. The U.S. government refused to undertake the project and at the Washington Conference of 1922 traded away the possibility in exchange for a deal on mutual arms reductions.

The second solution was to rush the fleet to the Philippines to improvise a base as soon as war began. It was known as the "Through Ticket to Manila,"[6] although after 1925 the destination was shifted to a southern Philippine harbor because the menace of Orange air power over Manila Bay had become unbearable. The movement would entail horrendous logistical difficulties. It would gamble the entire navy on one roll of the dice. Nevertheless, the Through Ticket held out the hope of a short war and so reigned as the generally accepted strategy for most of the years between 1906 and 1934. In the first half of that era it was adopted as a stopgap until a western base could be funded and built. After the idea of a prepared base was vetoed in 1922, the army's clamor for a rescue of its Philippine garrison and the importunings of aggressive naval planners kept the strategy alive until it collapsed in

1934 of its own idiosyncrasies, notably Blue's inferiority in deployable air power.

The prepared western base and the Through Ticket were "failed strategies" that were abandoned long before World War II. Other powers tried to implement comparable policies, with abysmal results. The British fleet base at Singapore turned out to be a disastrous investment; when it fell in 1942, Great Britain was left with no means of fighting Japan at sea. The pitfalls of a Through Ticket attack were vividly demonstrated in 1905 by the Russian death cruise to Tsushima. Nevertheless, an understanding of the failed strategies is important for tracing the evolution of an offensive plan that proved viable.

The correct solution of the Phase II problem, proposed in some of the earliest Orange Plans by a few talented officers, was to advance step-by-step across the Pacific by way of mobile bases set up on intermediate islands. Its advantages were obvious, and it was explored repeatedly. But before 1914 another fact of geography, neutral powers' sovereignty over the most useful islands, discouraged its adoption. Japan had no deep-sea islands suitable for capture and use as naval bases. Among U.S. possessions west of Hawaii, only Guam had limited potential as a base. Samoa and the Aleutians were physically unsuited and poorly located for a war against Japan's economy, and Blue central Pacific atolls were regarded as relatively useless before the air age.

In 1914 Japan gained control of German Micronesia, a hundred islands that sprawled along Blue's best line of approach. Many had excellent natural features. Perceptive strategists understood that a crucial geographic factor had shifted in favor of the gradual offensive. They inserted the step-by-step march across the ocean into Plan Orange, at least briefly in 1911 and 1922, but it was repeatedly suppressed by high commanders obsessed with the short war formulas. Finally, in 1934, it was adopted as the basic U.S. strategy and remained so even after allies and their useful islands were incorporated into the war plans. It was implemented with stunning success in World War II. The long struggle of realists versus adventurists, referred to herein as cautionaries and thrusters, is another theme of this book.

Superimposed on the three-phase concept was the expectation of a single great naval encounter that would determine control of the sea. It would occur at a time and place of Japan's choosing, in either Phase II or III depending on when Japan thought it had whittled down the Blue fleet sufficiently, and probably close to Orange bases along the Japan-Philippines line. (In 1941, after the United States sent half its navy to the Atlantic, the battle was anticipated to occur during Phase I in the central Pacific—Chapter 25.) The fluctuating dates and sites of the battle did not appreciably affect other features of the Orange Plan because the superior Blue fleet was always expected to win it.

The three-phase design co-opted geography into the grand strategy of beating land power with sea power. The planners realized that Japan would gain no advantage from its massive army. Only small garrisons could be sustained on small islands, where control of the sea would assure Blue of an overwhelming concentration of force.[7] The phased war also meshed with the geopolitical objective of full victory at an acceptable cost and, it was hoped, in an acceptable time. The U.S. military embraced these elements of grand strategy between 1906 and 1914. Despite some lapses of enthusiasm and drastic changes in the equations of military power thereafter, the navy's grand strategy persevered as national policy through the end of World War II.

Plan Orange and the Pacific war have sometimes been acclaimed as validations of the credo of Alfred Thayer Mahan. Some Mahanian principles did influence the planners. A navy's primary functions, he felt, were to block enemy commerce and protect one's own. Achievement of these goals would assure victory, he claimed, an oversimplification but one that fit the Blue-Orange case. Yet he was oddly derisive of sending large warships to prey on trade directly. He had drawn heavily from axioms of land combat by the Swiss theoretician Antoine-Henri Jomini. For example, since a fleet's primary target was the enemy navy, it must always operate in full concentration ("Never divide the fleet!") to assure victory in a decisive battle. Mahan's advocacy of interior lines of communication encouraged the development of the Panama Canal and Hawaii. Logistics—the planners adopted his term *communications*—were crucial, he said, but overseas bases should be kept to a minimal number to avoid dispersion for their defense.

Ironically, Mahan's devotion to history blinded him to the current scene. Lacking modern examples, he had looked back to warfare in the age of sail. He had no genuine appreciation of certain new weapons or of the logistics of steam navies. His fascination with the climactic battle and scorn of direct attacks on trade led him to discount the havoc of attrition that an outgunned nation could wreak with expendable light craft and submarines. His edicts did not deter U.S. planners from deft campaigns along exterior lines.[8] But he suppressed his abhorrence of navies engaging land targets—"A ship's a fool to fight a fort," Nelson had said[9]—because amphibious operations would be unavoidable in the Pacific.

Mahan was a mediocre strategist of modern naval war. In 1910–11 he squandered his Olympian prestige by urging on the Orange planners preposterously aggressive advice. Great military achievements, he informed them, resulted from "l'audace, de l'audace et encore de l'audace." (When challenged, he grunted that planners always exaggerated their problems and underestimated the enemy's.[10]) Mahan deserves modest credit for a few principles of Plan Orange, but most of the good ideas flowed from less famous minds. Mahan's unique contribution was to breed into American naval officers an unflagging confidence in sea power, which inspired a plan that overcame unprecedented obstacles in a great maritime war.

.5.
• • • •

The Eastern Pacific Bastion

War Plan Orange designated the eastern Pacific as a Blue sanctuary and zone of mobilization for the offensive. The planners defined the region the same way geographers did, as the waters from the coasts of the Americas to the International Dateline at the 180th meridian. The mid-ocean boundary was politically significant. The United States had declared the Western Hemisphere off-limits to foreign colonizers in the Monroe Doctrine of 1823. The policy was extended to Hawaii by the "Tyler Doctrine" of 1842 and implicitly another thousand miles west to the International Dateline when the United States purchased Alaska and claimed Midway Island in 1867 and at the end of the century acquired parts of Samoa and some minor atolls along with the annexation of Hawaii. By 1941 some naval war planners argued that the Western Hemisphere extended yet a further thousand miles west to include Wake Island and its environs.[1] Guam and the Philippines, however, were always conceded to lie in the Eastern Hemisphere.

The sanctity of the eastern Pacific was not certified until the United States built a large fleet and began constructing naval bases there during the administration of Theodore Roosevelt. Before 1901, studies

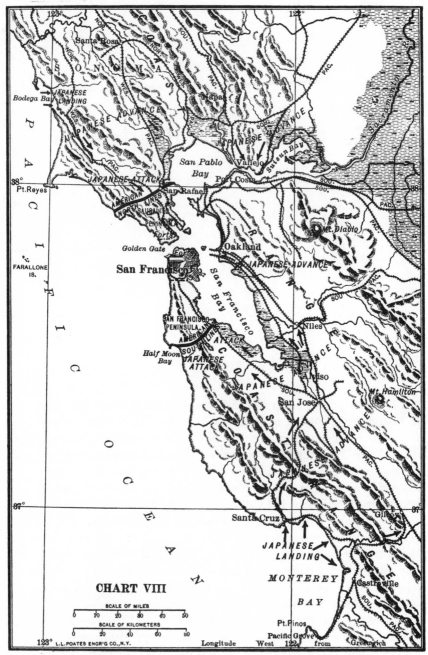

MAP 5.1   *The Invasion of San Francisco, 1909, A Fictional Account*
Source: Homer Lea, *The Valor of Ignorance* (1909; rpt. New York: Harper &
Brothers, 1942), 296a.

by amateur strategists of "a minor Navy still imbued with the operational ethos of a coast defense force"[2] had imagined that the Orange fleet might pounce on Puget Sound from a secret haven in the Aleutians, or sweep into San Francisco Bay,[3] or disgorge a great army at San Diego.[4] After Japan defeated Russia, pulp fiction writers spooked the American public with tales of gory Japanese conquests of the Pacific slope states (Map 5.1). During the war scare of 1907 the Joint Board nervously urged the president to refurbish old forts and lay minefields off West Coast cities.[5]

Such paranoia did not trouble sober analysts at the Naval War College.[6] An Orange expedition to California, they pointed out, would find itself trapped between Blue's army and its fleet steaming around Cape Horn. By 1911 the planners were confident that an invasion was "too fantastic to be seriously contemplated."[7] They were certain Japan would not even gamble big gunships on "eccentric" raids on the American mainland.[8] (Hysterical leaders who uprooted loyal Japanese-Americans from the West Coast in 1942 would have benefited from reading these cool assessments.) After World War I the navy felt no qualms about stationing the fleet on the Pacific Coast or in 1935 ceding to the army responsibility for defending mainland waters out to three hundred miles.[9]

The Panama Canal with its locks and steep-walled cuts appeared vulnerable to an opportunistic enemy attack, but by the time it opened for business in 1914 naval logisticians had demonstrated that Orange warships, even if bearing "aeroplanes," could never threaten it. To mount a raid they would have to wallow along for weeks with dozens of sluggish colliers that would burn most of their own cargo on the 18,000-mile round-trip.[10] Although after 1920 a raid by oil-fired vessels might have been slightly more plausible, the navy never felt it had to assign more than token forces to guard the canal. The army took the chore more seriously. Its Orange Plans of the 1920s proposed a two-hundred-plane air force and rushing forty thousand troops there aboard transports headed from the East Coast toward missions in the Pacific.[11] Sabotage was mentioned in some plans and popularized in a 1925 novel about a Blue-Orange war inaugurated by a suicidal explosion of a Japanese merchant ship in the canal.[12]

Alaska, the westernmost extension of the American mainland, was usually regarded by planners as unimportant and unendangered. Speculations that Japan might seize the territory for its fisheries or as a bargaining chip were scarcely credible.[13] Early Orange Plans allocated a few troops and submarines to police the area.[14] The army mused of a larger garrison to deny bases to enemy sea raiders,[15] but by the mid-1920s Alaska was dropped from the main war theater.[16]

In the late 1930s, strategists began to regard Alaska more seriously. To justify defensive establishments there, the services concocted ludicrous visions of audacious enemy coups. Army planners imagined a Japanese brigade, curiously immune to Blue sea power, strolling ashore on the Alaskan peninsula or other undefended shorelines to rig bases for submarines that would ravage communications between Hawaii and the mainland and hobble a Blue offensive action by diverting units to escort chores. Orange bombers at Alaskan airfields might raid the Pacific Northwest.[17] In 1938 the army allocated 8,100 troops and some planes to hasten to Alaska when a war began. Major Matthew B. Ridgway, G-3 officer of the Fourth Army, pressed for Arctic training and equipment.[18] In 1940 mainland Alaska and nearby islands were designated an army responsibility as a separate command under Colonel Simon Bolivar Buckner, Jr.

The Army Air Corps clamored to develop an aviation center at Anchorage to deal with "surprise aggression." The AWPD called for tanks to defend airfields—against Soviet paratroopers! After the Nazi attack on Russia in mid-1941 the alarmists switched to fretting of a German-Japanese plot against Alaska. But Army G-2 (Intelligence) sensibly observed that Japan would not divert much power to the remote territory, at worst seizing some unoccupied points for light-force bases. Chief of Staff George Marshall considered any threat "highly improbable" but endorsed air-ground defenses against petty incursions. New plans allotted twenty-three thousand men for guard duty. They were sent to Alaska by October 1941 along with fifty aircraft. Nevertheless, as Marshall recalled, "defense of the extreme north Pacific was not a major anxiety of the War Department."[19] In both Plan Orange and World War II mainland Alaska was strategically insignificant.

The Aleutian Islands, although jutting a thousand miles westward from Alaska along the shortest sea track to Japan, were also considered a strategic backwater. Before World War I the navy had studied an offensive via that route but had unequivocally dismissed it because of physical and strategic drawbacks (Chapter 9). The idea was ritualistically exhumed from time to time, even as late as 1945, but always rejected.

Though unsuitable as fleet bases, the Aleutians were marginally useful to both sides as sites for basing raiders. Early Orange Plans assumed that the enemy might establish cruiser nests in the chain but that Blue would promptly root them out.[20] From 1922 to 1936 the Washington Treaty banned military installations in the Aleutians and in the Kurile Islands, Japan's nearest territory. When the treaty lapsed, defending the Aleutians was confirmed as a naval obligation and upgraded by shifting control from the Thirteenth Naval District to the fleet and the Marine Corps.[21] Captain Ernest King, chief of the Bureau of Aeronautics, in 1935 recommended establishing seaplane bases in the group.[22] Surveyors identified favorable locations at Dutch Harbor, off the tip of the Alaska Peninsula, and Adak, at the midpoint of the chain. (Attu and Kiska, the islands nearest Japan, lacked desirable characteristics.)[23] In 1938 a naval commission known as the Hepburn Board advocated establishment of a line of air bases for patrolling the eastern Pacific from the Aleutians to the equator. The board proposed a rear base on Kodiak Island and a minor forward outpost at Dutch Harbor.[24] The following year the daunting problem of operating seaplanes from ice-bound Aleutian harbors was overcome when amphibian flying boats with retractable wheels were successfully demonstrated[25] and the development program was shifted westward to a full base at Dutch Harbor and an outlier on Adak.[26] Only the former was started before the war.

Naval planners who craved Aleutian bases theorized that Japan would covet the islands for self-defense. In 1939, with little fact and much fancy, they supposed that Orange leaders viewed the far north as "the most dangerous of all possible directions" from which a Blue attack might come because northern Japan was not well insulated by distance and defensive outposts. The Japanese would therefore position strong air power in the Kuriles and "at the first opportunity" raid the Aleutians and occupy some of them for submarine and air stations. While granting that such moves would be militarily insignificant, the "northern flank" enthusiasts argued that loss of any sliver of ground that was considered an integral part of the United States would foment "serious political, economic, and psychological repercussions." The navy would be compelled, they warned, to make "material modifications" to Plan Orange to eject the enemy.[27] It was an apt prediction of the diversions to that task in 1943.

The histrionics bore fruit. Congress funded the northern bases; even isolationists agreed that the area was a legitimate defense zone. By 1941 the navy "took Alaskan matters less seriously" because the United States could muster enough power to render an Orange initiative "extremely hazardous."[28] It adopted a low-profile mission of tying down Orange forces that might venture there.

Hawaii was the strategic prize of the eastern Pacific (see Map 5.2). On the island of Oahu lay the port of Honolulu and, at the estuary of the Pearl River, the only sizable harbor within a two-thousand-mile radius. The strategic importance of the islands had been noted as early as 1841 by the navy's global explorer Lieutenant Charles Wilkes.[29] Long before the annexation in 1898, Hawaii had been a virtual protectorate of the United States. Naval leaders hungering for a coaling station to support commerce-protection cruises in Asian waters had been foiled on other Pacific islands twice: in an 1870 attempt to blast a channel through a barrier reef at Midway and by the realization that Samoa, where they had negotiated access to a harbor, was too remote from any place of interest. In 1880, after Lieutenant General John M. Schofield had identified Pearl Harbor as an ideal asset "in the event of war with a powerful maritime nation,"[30] the United States obtained from King Kalakaua the right to develop a base.

Pearl Harbor, though touted as spacious enough to float "the combined navies of the world," was blocked at its mouth by a natural coral bar.[31] The first Orange war studies ignored the problem by dispatching the fleet to the Philippines via Suez, but in 1907 Commander Oliver converted his peers to the wisdom of a transpacific movement (Chapter 9). Oliver's strategy required arsenals and dry docks on the West Coast and a navigable, fortified base at Pearl Harbor.[32] President Roosevelt consented to the establishment of a haven of guaranteed security after the "humiliating" revelation that a Philippine naval base on which he had been lavishing political capital could not be defended (Chapter 7).[33] In 1908 the Joint Board humbly endorsed the Pearl Harbor base.[34] Congress, which then and later distrusted schemes for bases farther west than Hawaii, voted the money. By 1911 a channel for large vessels had been dredged, but construction of dry docks and shore industries proceeded so languidly that Pearl Harbor was unable to accommodate the bulk of the fleet until the eve of World War II.[35]

Confidence in the safety of Pearl Harbor emerged only after several years of study and debate. Before 1898 naval analysts wary of Japanese designs on the Hawaiian republic recommended a preemptive rush of Blue ships and soldiers to the islands if necessary to block a hostile grab.[36] The first Orange war studies of 1906 warned that Japan could descend on Hawaii with "great weight" if the American fleet were sunk in the Philippines after a transatlantic voyage.[37] The decision for a transpacific Blue offensive mandated the "immediate and paramount duty" of retaining Oahu,[38] yet the island appeared so vulnerable to attack that the Joint Board advised Roosevelt during the 1907 war

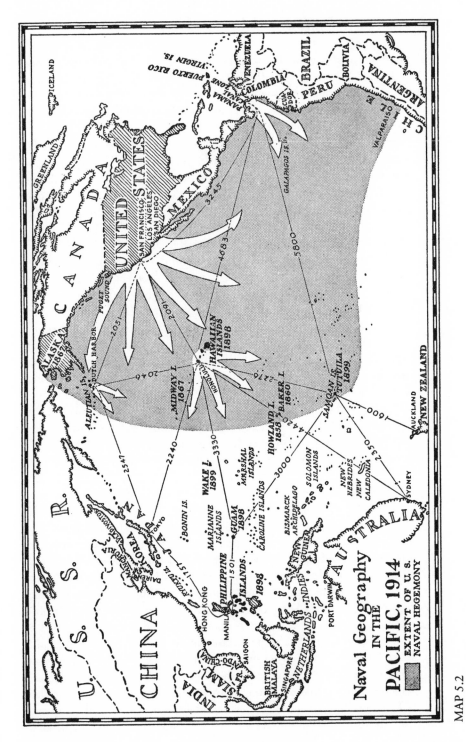

MAP 5.2

Source: Livezey, Mahan, 160.

The map contains the following labels:

ICELAND
GREENLAND
CANADA
U. S. S. R.
KOREA
CHINA
JAPAN
TOKYO
RYUKYUS
BONIN IS.
HONG KONG
SAIGON
FR. INDO-CHINA
SIAM
INDIA
BRITISH MALAYA
SINGAPORE
NETHERLANDS INDIES
MANILA
PHILIPPINE ISLANDS 1898
GUAM 1898
MARIANNE ISLANDS
WAKE I. 1899
MARSHALL ISLANDS
CAROLINE ISLANDS
BISMARCK ARCHIPELAGO
NEW GUINEA
PORT DARWIN
AUSTRALIA
SYDNEY
NEW CALEDONIA
NEW HEBRIDES
SOLOMON ISLANDS
NEW ZEALAND
AUCKLAND
SAMOAN IS. TUTUILA 1899
BAKER I. 1860
HOWLAND I. 1858
HAWAIIAN ISLANDS 1898
HONOLULU
MIDWAY I. 1867
ALEUTIAN IS.
DUTCH HARBOR
PUGET SOUND
ALASKA 1867
UNITED STATES
SAN FRANCISCO
LOS ANGELES
SAN DIEGO
MEXICO
PANAMA CANAL ZONE
COLOMBIA
ECUADOR
GALAPAGOS IS.
PERU
BOLIVIA
BRAZIL
VENEZUELA
PUERTO RICO
VIRGIN IS.
CUBA
ARGENTINA
CHILE
VALPARAISO

Distances shown: 3245, 4683, 1607, 2051, 2046, 2547, 2240, 3330, 1511, 3000, 2350, 1600, 4420, 2216, 5800

Naval Geography
IN THE
PACIFIC, 1914

EXTENT OF U. S.
NAVAL HEGEMONY

scare not to bother with emergency fortifications because it could not be held.[39] Williams and fellow optimists, however, believed that Blue cruisers retreating from the Philippines and troops advancing from the mainland could win a race to Hawaii and fend off the enemy until the battle fleet arrived via Cape Horn.[40]

The worst threat to the American strategic position in the Pacific would be a surprise Japanese seizure of Hawaii at the very outbreak of war. Rodgers and his War College team brooded in 1911 that a twenty-five-thousand-man landing force would swamp the U.S. garrison of five thousand and yet the operation would not be "much more than a diversion" for Orange, hardly requiring exposure of its capital ships. The fall of Oahu would be an "irretrievable disaster" that might well decide the war because a Blue offensive would be "most hazardous and extremely difficult" until it was recaptured.[41] Oliver felt "extremely doubtful" about a counterlanding; at best, the group might be regained in a bloody campaign lasting a year. Mahan disagreed, feeling confident that Oahu could be stormed as soon as the navy set up bases at other Hawaiian harbors. Oliver feared the "insurmountable obstacle" of Japanese heavy mortars that had wrecked the immobile Russian squadron at Port Arthur, but Mahan doubted they could hit moving ships.[42] This debate hastened the fortification of Pearl Harbor, a job conceded to the army because the Marine Corps was too small and the offensive-minded navy abhorred obligations of static defense.[43] Mahan "emphatically" recommended equipping the post for six months of defense, twice the expected time of relief by the fleet.[44] By 1913 the Army Coast Artillery Corps had installed or scheduled twenty 12-inch artillery pieces.[45]

In 1914 an influential naval logistician, Captain William Rawle Shoemaker, proved conclusively that "the great outpost of Blue" lay safely beyond Japan's grasp. The Panama Canal was about to open. American battleships could reach Hawaii in a few weeks. Although a surprise assault by a small force might win Oahu, Japan could not amass the hundred long-range steamers (including colliers to fuel the return trip) needed to deliver in a single voyage the 71,150 men, 4,000 animals, and masses of heavy ordnance believed necessary to repel a U.S. counterassault. A Blue screen of cruisers and torpedo boats would force Japan to guard any convoy with all of its eight capital ships and twenty-one cruisers but without the aid of destroyers and submarines, which could not make the long journey. All vessels would have to flee before the Blue dreadnoughts reached Hawaii. Meanwhile, Japan's operations in the Philippines and its food imports would be curtailed for lack of bottoms. Shoemaker concluded that, regardless of any esoteric benefits to morale and bargaining posture, the enemy could not afford a "misdirected expenditure of effort" and horrendous casualties for a position it would be unable to hold.[46]

Real fear of losing Hawaii rarely surfaced again, but defense of the island group commanded continuous attention. In 1919 the army's primary responsibility was reconfirmed,[47] and during the 1920s it established airfields and pledged strong reinforcement within thirty days of the outbreak of war in the Pacific.[48] In 1928 the Joint Board reexamined the specter of a surprise invasion. Navy planners explained incredulously that slow transports would be sitting ducks for the islands' 139 defending aircraft and that a landing could not succeed before the Blue battleships roared out from California. Still, the army upped its commitment to ninety thousand men sailing on M-Day, the first day of mobilization. The Navy War Plans Division resented preemption of transports from its offensive movement and vowed that no attack troops would offload at Hawaii. In a compromise, the army swore to repel any invasion without hampering the offensive, and the navy sarcastically agreed that before launching a Phase II attack it would reclaim "any necessary portions" of Hawaii.[49]

In 1935 the army once again postulated a Japanese invasion of Oahu, at the beginning of a war when the fleet was in the Atlantic. (It rarely was.) Navy planners assured their colleagues that Hawaiian-based submarines and aircraft could fend off all threats during the month-long rescue voyage of the fleet. Even if the cruise lengthened to seventy days because of sabotage of the Panama Canal, Air Corps bombers flown out from the mainland would help save the base. The army rescheduled its reinforcements to embark before the outbreak,[50] and the navy, cheerfully acknowledging a joint local responsibility to hold Pearl Harbor for seventy days, pledged not to send any of the local submarines and planes to Atlantic maneuvers. The stricture to reclaim "necessary" bits of Hawaii was deleted. "The suggestion of the loss of these islands has no place in [our] Plan," the Joint Board snapped.[51]

The old jitters lay dormant until the eruption of the war. Visceral fears of losing Hawaii loomed in the dark days after 7 December 1941 and again when Japanese forces massed for the move on Midway in 1942. Pragmatic military leaders, however, never lost faith in the long-standing belief that an invasion was far beyond Japan's capabilities.

Hawaii's lines of communication to the mainland did not seem at risk as long as Orange had no raiding base in the eastern Pacific. In the

1930s the planners took another look after Japan had put long-range submarines into commission and especially after the Pacific Fleet took up residence in Pearl Harbor in 1940. The fleet planning officer, Captain C. H. McMorris, estimated in 1941 that Japan could operate submarines served by a secret mother ship, cruisers, "pocket battleships," and even carriers east of Hawaii. His plan diverted some cruisers and convoy guards from offensive tasks, and he reluctantly contemplated detaching a carrier to plug the aerial patrol gap halfway between Hawaii and California.[52] As it turned out, Japan's wartime attempt to sever the lifeline solely by submarines was ineffective.

The most intractable security problem in the eastern Pacific was Pearl Harbor's vulnerability to a raid, especially a surprise initial blow.[53] Although bombardment from the sea was no threat because of its terrain and shoreline defenses, before World War I planners imagined that the Japanese might land a few thousand troops from cruisers, arm disloyal settlers, and demolish the base. (They would also remove Japanese veterans of the war with Russia for renewed service; by the rules of war, Blue would have to consent.[54]) As late as 1935 an army checklist of perils still included demolition landings, uprisings, and blockships sunk in the narrow channel.[55]

The commissioning of large Japanese aircraft carriers in the late 1920s raised the question of the vulnerability of Pearl Harbor more acutely. Army planners in 1928 speculated on a hundred-plane carrier raid, perhaps by obsolescent squadrons that would be recovered at other islands or abandoned. They recommended a defensive air force of 237 planes and plenty of flak. Early detection of the raiders, however, would require a patrol of 310 long-range seaplanes, many more than were available. If the attack were a de facto declaration of war, the base would be caught napping.[56]

It is tempting to ascribe clairvoyance to the prophets of a surprise raid on Pearl Harbor, an operation the U.S. Navy demonstrated in maneuvers and which was discussed in at least seven Orange Plans and studies from 1911 to 1941, except that no planner concerned himself about the safety of the fleet. It was thought to be capable of caring for itself. In pre-1940 Orange Plans it was scheduled to mobilize on the West Coast and to pause at Hawaii only a few days while en route to the western Pacific, primarily at the open anchorage of Lahaina Roads rather than at Pearl Harbor. The raid the planners occasionally postulated for thirty years was supposed to hit the shore facilities, targets Admiral Chuichi Nagumo failed to attack on 7 December 1941.

The threat of Orange carriers and their detection generated interest in outlying bases to screen Pearl Harbor (which would also help the Blue offensive). In the nineteenth century the United States had casually acquired a number of small islands, including the Aleutians, Hawaii's Leeward Chain of atolls, Johnston Island southwest of Hawaii, southern atolls such as Palmyra and Canton, and Samoa. These were unsuitable for fleet bases, but they constituted a forty-five-hundred mile north-south picket line for aircraft and light war vessels that lay parallel to and not far from the 180th meridian. Early planners thought them weak points the Japanese would grab to harass Blue's communications and retard its counteroffensive. Between 1922 and 1936 the islands were demilitarized by treaty. (The Leeward Chain, Johnston, and Palmyra, politically part of Hawaii, were arguably exempt from the ban along with the parent group, but isolationist policy neutralized them anyway.) In 1938 the Hepburn Board's recommendation that a line of air and submarine bases be established in the eastern Pacific won the favor of Congress.[57] The northern and southern ends of the line bore slight relevance to Plan Orange, which assumed that little would happen near the Aleutians or Samoa. The atolls south of Hawaii were regarded as unimportant until 1939, when communication links to Australia, a probable ally, were seen as desirable. The central atolls, especially Midway, were intrinsically the most valuable, as sentinels of Pearl Harbor and support points for a Blue offensive. Midway and the sandspits that backed it up—Johnston and the Leeward atolls—are referred to in this book collectively as the "inner atolls." (Wake Island, a strategically offensive position, is dealt with in later chapters.)

Midway lay near the end of the Leeward Hawaiian Chain of ten atolls, rocks, and reefs that stretched northwestward from the main group toward Japan.[58] Its importance was amply appreciated by 1941. When Admiral Ernest King took the helm of the navy late in December, he overruled his predecessor's panicky assessment that holding it looked "questionable"[59] and awarded the wounded Pacific Fleet the primary task of "covering and holding the line Hawaii-Midway" as a mission coequal with securing communications to Hawaii itself.[60] But that appreciation was of recent origin.

In the early days of Pacific strategy, Midway had enjoyed a temporary vogue among naval planners. They had pointed out that Orange could set up bases among the Leeward atolls for raiding Oahu and its lifeline. These islands would also be of "great military importance"[61] for a Blue offensive toward Guam (Chapter 10). Midway had to be held or, if lost, retaken.[62] But after World War I the transfer of the fleet to California seemed to assure Hawaii's safety, and as offensive plans shifted to a more southerly route, interest in Midway lapsed.

The Washington Treaty of 1922 did not prohibit *mobile* facilities at outlying islands. The commandant of the Fourteenth Naval District, the unit charged with defending Pearl Harbor, was beguiled by Midway's guardian location athwart the direct line of approach from Japan. He had sent a seaplane-bearing vessel to reconnoiter.[63] Undeterred by the negativism of his air-illiterate intelligence officer,[64] he appealed for a skeleton observation post. "Even if forced to abandon or surrender it (destroying base facilities)," he explained, "its use would seem to be fully justified merely for the information thereby gained."[65] In 1924 Lieutenant Commander John Rodgers, a daredevil flyer and scion of a famous naval family, spotted an area of the lagoon that could become an "invaluable" scouting base if a channel were cut through the reef so that ships could enter.[66] But planners in Washington contemptuously dismissed a base on Midway as expensive, an irritant to Japan, and impossible to defend without the fleet. The enemy would seize the base, compelling the United States to destroy or retake it, thereby delaying its offensive—a cardinal sin in an era of aggressive plans. By leaving Midway in its raw and nearly useless state, naval activity there on "any considerable scale" would be rendered unlikely. Forget the base, the planners advised, and expect simply to demolish and abandon the telegraphic cable station erected there in 1903.[67] In 1928 planners again discounted the possibility of air operations in the Leeward Chain such as seaplane raids on Pearl Harbor launched from Orange tenders at French Frigate Shoals, halfway between Midway and Oahu. The army felt that enemy submarines would make the atolls unusable for Blue. Securing Midway, which was too remote for strikes on Pearl Harbor by air, would be "entirely out of proportion" to its value.[68]

In the 1930s senior planners did an about-face. Longer-range seaplanes and the establishment of a commercial Flying Clipper stopover on Midway by Pan American Airways spurred air admirals such as King and Commander in Chief of the Pacific Fleet Joseph Reeves to recommend a base there. Reeves took his ships to the atoll in 1935 for maneuvers, along with forty-six seaplanes, the greatest armada yet to take wing.[69] The chastened war planners decided that the island would prove vital in wartime after all: "We must get there first."[70] Although clumsy attempts to fund a base in the guise of a commercial harbor improvement bogged down in congressional politics,[71] even isolationist politicians agreed to Midway's "very great" defensive value.[72] The Hepburn Board hailed it as second in importance to Pearl Harbor.[73] But when Fleet Commander Claud Bloch tried to enlarge the project as "a vital asset in the event of a fleet movement to the western Pacific," the Navy Department demurred.[74]

The attack-minded navy did not easily adjust to defending fixed points in mid-ocean. It hoped that "ultimately" the army would protect Midway.[75] It thought Orange unlikely to land on or shell the island because of its proximity to Hawaii and because marine experts gave assurance that shore artillery could repel attempts. To Bloch, carrier raids posed a more serious risk, but his recommendation of 1939 to place fighter squadrons at Midway clashed with the naval doctrine that aviation should travel with the fleet. Washington vetoed an airfield. After sifting through odd ideas such as rigging old destroyers as antiaircraft platforms, the navy opted for a marine battalion with AA guns.[76] In 1940 combat reports from Europe eroded the old prejudice. Congressional purse strings loosened, a channel was opened, and an airstrip built. By 7 December 1941 Midway was home to flying boats and landplanes and had been fortified against raids of all types.[77]

Hawaii's smallest sentinel, Johnston Island, lay seven hundred miles southwest of Pearl Harbor. Pre-air-age planners had eyed it as a stepping-stone toward Micronesia,[78] but its trifling sixty-six acres seemed useless.[79] Aerial surveys in the 1920s indicated that a seaplane station was feasible,[80] and by 1933 fleet planners imagined that flying boats could stage through Johnston to help win the Marshall Islands.[81] The Hepburn Board called for a minor scouting base to complete the circuit of Oahu's pickets, with a fly-swatter defense against cruiser floatplanes.[82] Johnston was ready when war came, but, unlike Midway, was never a magnet for the Imperial Fleet.

The reconnaissance stations erected on inner American atolls from 1938 to 1941 covered all feasible approaches to Pearl Harbor except from the north. King and other officers had considered an air shuttle to keep watch on the waters between Midway and the Aleutians,[83] but a sustained effort to cover the two-thousand-mile gap was beyond the capability of prewar aviation. It was through this gap that the Japanese carriers slipped en route to Pearl Harbor.

In May 1940 President Franklin Roosevelt ordered most of the American fleet to Pearl Harbor as a signal to deter Japan from moving against European colonies in Asia. The transfer stimulated defense preparations in the eastern Pacific. Frequent complaints of unreadiness by commanders on the scene did not alter the confidence of planners in

Washington as to the security of the base. Although fleet planner McMorris noted early in 1941 that a strong carrier raid on Pearl Harbor might constitute a surprise opening of the war, he considered the risk so slight that he allotted none of the fleet's seven flying boat squadrons to prewar patrols of Oahu and only one to the mission in the event war began.[84]

The defenses of Pearl Harbor on the eve of the attack have been exhaustively examined in other works. It must be concluded that, despite occasional speculations, the Orange Plan (and its successor, Plan Rainbow Five) did not foretell the Japanese carrier strike. Mc-Morris's final Fleet Plan of July 1941 merely listed it as "possible" and omitted his earlier references to timing and strength.[85] Nevertheless, the plan's strategic perception of the eastern Pacific as a secure American bastion for mounting the offensive was valid on every day of the war except the first. When the Japanese next approached the sanctuary in June 1942, its security was confirmed beyond doubt at Midway.

The Battle of Midway also bore out another premise of Plan Orange with respect to the eastern Pacific: that a naval encounter on the approaches to Hawaii would provide a magnificent opportunity for the United States. As early as 1897 an imaginary mini-battle—each side had only two modern battleships in the Pacific—was seen as settling the fate of the Hawaiian Islands in America's favor.[86] By 1911, however, the planners had come to regard a "supreme test" in Hawaiian waters as idle conjecture because enemy dreadnoughts escorting a surprise landing force would have to depart immediately.[87] In subsequent analyses it was implicit that any Orange action against the Hawaiian islands and atolls would occur only if it bore directly on the defeat of the Blue navy. In 1928 the navy felt confident that it would "utterly defeat" the Orange fleet if it dared appear in those waters.[88] Dreams of a naval battle in the American bastion were then shelved until the middle of 1941, when the Pacific Fleet shaped a plan to induce a battle of annihilation in the waters near Midway (Chapter 25).

The Western
Pacific Capitulation

U.S. planners expected events of Phase I in the western Pacific to be a mirror image of those in the eastern Pacific. A bleak fate awaited the Blue territories in the west. Guam, with a token marine outfit and no defenses afloat, was conceded as lost. In the Philippines, the modest ground and naval units the United States had maintained since 1898 could not long withstand Japan's powerful army and its control of the sea. The Philippine defense forces prepared many tactical plans between 1900 and 1941, but because most of the strategic Orange Plans did not expect them to significantly affect the outcome of the war, they will be sketched here only briefly.

Strategists understood the predicament of defending an archipelago of seven thousand islands with an area comparable to that of Great Britain and a coastline as long as that of the United States. As early as 1906 they assumed that Japan would almost immediately isolate the Philippines by sea and mobilize and transport two hundred thousand troops to the principal island of Luzon to destroy the garrison of twenty thousand, two-thirds of whom were poorly trained Filipino Scouts.[1] A major fleet base that might have justified a sturdier Blue defense program was never built in the Philippines. The navy's endeavors to promote one between 1908 and 1912 foundered (Chapter 7), as did a few later attempts, because of the opposition of politicians and some of its own war planners. Minor stations erected on Luzon for the lilliputian Asiatic Fleet did not merit husky protection because they could not accommodate a relief expedition by the full battle fleet.

The most valued prize of the Philippines was Manila Bay, a splendid thirty-by-thirty-mile harbor on the shores of which sat the capital city and a seaport with excellent commercial infrastructure. In 1916 an army-navy committee proposed that the city and bay should be held as long as possible by local units. Notwithstanding the Joint Board's bluster that it was the only mission worthy of a great power, this was an unrealistic notion. Army War College studies ascertained that at most the garrison could hold a small area for a few months. Critics might huff that merely to "keep the flag flying" over some funk-hole was defeatist, but it was the best that could be done.[2]

Naval optimists hoped to deny Manila to the Japanese navy for a significant period of time, a deprivation that would have been more hurtful in a strictly Blue-Orange war than was the case in 1942, when Japan controlled the South China Sea ports of other powers. They reasoned that without a naval base and port facilities at Manila, Orange opposition to a Blue fleet counterattack would be hobbled because the Japanese could not accumulate enough munitions to resist on Luzon before the U.S. Navy cut their lifeline. An energetic defense of the bay would also distract Japan from occupying harbors of the southern Philippines, where the Blue expedition could pause to improvise a base, and the surviving garrison could assist in recapturing Luzon.[3] The Joint Board was beguiled by this agreeable scenario. It decreed that local forces hold the narrow entrance to the bay.[4] Pessimists thought "defending" a more realistic premise than "holding" because Japan's naval expansion program of World War I would soon triple the mass of its descent.[5] At heart, they always regarded Manila Bay as "without strategic significance" because the American fleet could never arrive in time to save it.[6] The local forces would merely fight a sacrificial delaying action to assuage honor, promote public morale, and inflict some damage before passing into captivity—a correct prognosis of what occurred in 1942. By 1919 the services tentatively adopted the sacrificial mission while hoping that a naval base on Guam might someday allow a more robust strategy (Chapter 7).[7]

Athwart the entrance to Manila Bay lay the island of Corregidor, known as "The Rock," and three smaller islets. In 1904 the army began developing them as citadels. It dug shellproof underground galleries and emplaced heavy artillery that could match that of any battleship. The guns and minefields were expected to keep an enemy fleet at a respectful distance. A foe might take Manila from the landward side, but the corks in the bottle would nullify its value. The concept had a fatal flaw, however. Bataan, a mountainous, jungle-covered peninsula, jutted to within two miles of Corregidor. The Rock could perhaps endure for six months, the time army planners assumed necessary for the fleet to arrive, only if Bataan were also held. If Bataan were lost, bombardment from its reverse slopes would reduce the island fortresses just as Japanese siege mortars had done to the Russian stronghold at Port Arthur. During World War I hopes brightened when entrenched defenders demonstrated great staying power at Gallipoli and in France. Corregidor's tunnel rats might be able to withstand barrages for "a considerable time" and foil landings with machine guns and barbed wire.[8] The Washington Treaty of 1922, however, halted work on the fortifications. The army's Philippine Department was ordered to draft a "Defense Project" recognizing the weakness of the incomplete fortresses.[9]

The navy was well aware of the hopeless outlook, having dabbled with Philippine defense plans since 1900.[10] Its interest in the archipelago waned after its quest for a major base was vetoed (Chapter 7). It shrank the Asiatic Fleet to a handful of light vessels for the purposes of protecting trade and showing the flag in the Orient. In 1907 naval planners heeded Oliver's advice to concede the inevitable fall of Luzon as "no great exercise of generosity."[11] The Orange Plan directed the feeble squadron to escape at the first shot.[12] Williams suggested archly that its war plan need only provide for demolition of its stations.[13]

The War Department did not fully comprehend the navy's indifference until Secretary Josephus Daniels spelled it out in 1915. There was "no justification," he explained, to assume that relief would be timely. Saving small outposts was not the navy's job.[14] The commander in chief of the Asiatic Fleet (CinCAF), Albert Winterhalter, cabled a brutal summary of the situation: "Believe successful defense all Philippines or any part impracticable, prohibitive cost needless sacrifice. Command of sea only proper security. Navy bases undefended useless." He counseled dismantling the naval depots and improvising a minor one on Corregidor for small vessels unable to escape.[15]

The lessons of World War I impressed on a few naval optimists the possibility of a cheap delaying compaign by coastal submarines serviced by floating tenders.[16] The "stop now" dictum of the Washington

Treaty did not prohibit such mobile units, according to an analysis of the language by Williams, then director of war plans. "We are not lawyers," retorted Rear Admiral William Pratt, who had drafted the article. He persuaded the Navy Department to honor its "broad spirit" and refrain from sending more arms to the Philippines.[17] The army agreed and canceled dispatch of a bombing squadron. Williams was satisfied that the archipelago could not effectively resist. He thereupon converted Phase II of the Orange Plan from a much-discussed dash by the fleet to the Philippines into a slow crawl through central Pacific islands (Chapter 10). "The sacrifice of all our forces . . . would be justified by the damage done to the enemy," he opined,[18] a cold-blooded statement that provoked a furious backlash from the army.

The Philippine doomsday assumption that usually pervaded Orange Plans was put aside on two occasions when charismatic generals resurrected fantasies of fighting for great strategic ends. Both were retired chiefs of staff who reigned as proconsuls in Manila. In 1941 Douglas MacArthur assured the U.S. government that he could hold the Philippines if given proper arms. His boast was an echo of a 1923 plea by Leonard Wood, governor-general of the islands. Wood felt betrayed by the navy's callous abandonment. Like MacArthur, he mesmerized both the War Department and the president with his pleas. Unlike MacArthur, he won the support of the navy, in the person of Admiral Robert E. Coontz, the chief of naval operations, who perverted Williams's excellent Phase II strategy into a race to save the Philippines (Chapter 11). Thus in 1923 the services proclaimed that Manila was the best of all possible bases. Defending it would be incomparably cheaper than recapturing it. The entire bay, Wood insisted—not just Bataan and Corregidor—had to be held for six months against a maximum Japanese onslaught.[19]

The keystone of Wood's strategy (and later MacArthur's) was to build a large army of Filipino soldiers backed up by Americans manning the artillery forts and a strong air detachment. All would "resist to the end" and save Luzon if assured of salvation by the navy. "We can do it and will do it," Wood swore.[20] The elated commanders at Manila buried the dreary Defense Project on which they had been laboring and submitted jaunty new plans in 1922–23. They would seal Manila Bay with airplanes, guns, and mines. Regiments of native patriots would harass Orange landings, especially the big one expected at Lingayen Gulf at the head of a valley leading to Manila, then retreat stubbornly to the main line of resistance on Bataan. They would hold the peninsula and Corregidor "to the last" while a detachment went to ground in the mountains of northern Luzon to hector the foe.

Coontz and fellow naval stouthearts devised a pugnacious offshore defense. The Asiatic Fleet would hurl its flea-sized "attack force" at invasion convoys and improvise auxiliary cruisers to badger Orange trade.[21] Admiral Edwin A. Anderson, who had known U-boat war in the Atlantic, was abruptly reassigned to Manila and told to draft a plan.[22] He reported that there was "an excellent chance" of holding *all* of Luzon if a flotilla of submarines with tenders steamed straight across the Pacific to join him immediately after the outbreak of war. Their torpedoes would "almost guarantee" success. The navy would then send destroyers and more converted cruisers to intensify the operations. Anderson would procure help from China and assist the advancing U.S. fleet while preparing a base for it at Subic Bay on Luzon. When the shore station commandant complained that Subic was sure to fall, Anderson retorted that he would shift the submarines to Cape Engano, a Bataan-like peninsula at the northern tip of the island, and there await the fleet.[23]

These heroic boasts were out of touch with reality. Common sense returned in the mid-1920s after the fire-eaters passed from the scene. Prudent naval planners delayed the rescue expedition and routed it to safer islands south of Luzon. The fantasy of a Filipino militia evaporated because of army torpor and naval distrust of the islanders' loyalty. The joint planners in Washington reconfirmed that Luzon would be inundated rapidly. Bataan would fall in 60 days, Corregidor perhaps in 120.[24] Although local generals offered to lay mines seaward of Corregidor to create a precarious anchorage, the navy said it would not send the fleet there and that the treaty forbade mine depots.[25] By the end of the decade the best the naval planners could offer was the possibility of resupplying Corregidor from a base to be established in the southern Philippines (Chapter 13).

Technological advances, especially in air power, caused pessimism to deepen in the 1930s. The chieftains at Manila declared in 1934 that "the tremendous strides made in the art of warfare and the spectacular rise of Orange as a military power" had nullified any value of the bay as an American base. They appealed for a redefinition of their "impossible" mission.[26] Manila G-2 (Army Intelligence) predicted multiple Japanese landings on all sides of Luzon, probably some December or January after the rice harvest.[27] Major General Stanley Embick, soon to head the Army War Plans Division, predicted loss of the city and main airfields by M+15 because Orange troops would debark on beaches close to Bataan and march along a new road to sever the neck of the peninsula. The garrison would have to scramble to get its supplies there before the Manila warehouses were bombed to cinders.[28] Southern Bataan would have to be held for thirty days to assure mining of the bay entrances. The gruesome finale was described by a resident officer in 1936. The men on Bataan could not be evacuated. Vital supplies would be ferried to Corregidor while Filipino demolition squads burned the rest. Guns and animals would be destroyed and the wounded abandoned in field hospitals.[29] In the worst case, even Corregidor might be lost at the outset to a night landing from expendable Orange ships or submarines.[30]

The Japanese onslaught would deprive the Asiatic Fleet of its oil and munitions dumps and reduce it to impotency within a couple of weeks. Pratt, the chief of naval operations, thought it honor-bound to stay and fight anyway but relented when CinCAF Montgomery Taylor petitioned for a stay of martyrdom. Taylor sagely decided to leave on the first day of mobilization.[31] The destination of the refugee ships varied in the Orange Plans. In early versions they were to steam to the aid of Hawaii or perhaps Guam. Later models sent them to a mid-Pacific rendezvous with the onrushing U.S. fleet. In 1936 the surface force—some destroyers and a lone cruiser—was to slip away to the Indian Ocean, meet a liner bearing supplies and thirty prize crews, and hunt down Orange merchantmen and neutrals bearing contraband. Army planners voiced no objection to the navy bugging out; perhaps with a smile, CNO William Standley complimented them on their luck in garnering more of the islands' meager war-making resources.

Only the submarines and mineships of the Asiatic Fleet would stay to aid Corregidor. The obsolescent subs were better suited for scouting and blockade-running than for battle. A proposed service depot on Bataan was reallocated to Corregidor when Embick reported that the peninsula might fall in a month. After two months, he said, The Rock itself would be untenable. The surviving U-boats would slink off to Hawaii, reconnoitering Japanese islands en route and maybe running war patrols from a tender concealed in the South Pacific.[32]

The deteriorating outlook compelled the Joint Board in 1934 to confirm that the only viable mission would be purely sacrificial, denying Orange Manila Bay in the short term.[33] In 1936 the joint planners, ignoring the resurrected boast of a formidable native defense by MacArthur, the recently appointed field marshal of the Philippine

Commonwealth, confirmed the garrison's morbid fate on Bataan and Corregidor.[34]

Local defense studies rarely mentioned the southern Philippine Islands. The War College planners of 1907 noted that a dozen southern harbors were suitable for naval bases, or at least temporary havens, for a fleet cruising to Luzon, and they hoped Japan would be too absorbed in subduing Corregidor to bother with them.[35] But by 1911 the planning staffs predicted that Orange units would swarm southward, occupy or mine all the bays, and post torpedo craft at straits the Blue fleet would have to transit.[36] The army paid little heed to the southern region. A 1925 local plan merely called for levying a regiment to "maintain United States sovereignty" on Mindanao, the largest island of the archipelago.[37]

In the 1930s the planners realized that Orange air power might render even the southern Philippines too dangerous as an initial destination of a fleet offensive. An army plan of 1934 conceded prompt Japanese control of Mindanao.[38] G-2 predicted that the early collapse of Luzon would release two hundred enemy planes in time to render a fleet occupation of a southern base "hazardous and difficult."[39] Naval chart maneuvers showed that even if the United States managed to gain a base on Mindanao, Orange would lure the fleet away to guard its supply line and recapture the island, thus inflicting "a decisive defeat."[40] Captain G. J. Meyers of Navy War Plans predicted that enemy planes would be poised at half a dozen bases to attack the fleet in the southern islands. Engaging Orange landplanes with inferior naval types would be tantamount to fighting the enemy army en masse, a contravention of one of the most sacred principles of Plan Orange. Meyers stood alone in advocating that the Army Air Corps's fifty-six planes in the Philippines be deployed to Mindanao to hold open the door rather than be exterminated over Luzon by a fivefold stronger enemy. He claimed that a further hundred planes placed in the southern area could deny forward airstrips to Japan and fend off its carriers until the fleet reached a safe harbor.[41]

The Army Air Corps resisted being coaxed to the south. In 1935 it decided that at the outbreak it would evacuate Clark and Nichols fields near Manila, disperse to outlying strips on Luzon, and expend its planes against Orange landings.[42] Exercises at Dumanquilas Bay, the best fleet harbor on Mindanao, indicated that it would be next to impossible to construct an airstrip,[43] thereby cooling the navy's ardor for the place just as it contemplated a slow drive through the central

Pacific. Naval planners reviewed other sites such as Leyte Gulf, which was reconnoitered for the first time in 1938, but planning for the southern islands virtually halted.[44]

The wars that began in China in 1937 and Europe in 1939 did not at first alter Philippine defense plans. Japan's occupation of the entire China coast and of Indochina after the fall of France isolated the Philippines from the west in the same way that Orange bases in Formosa and the central Pacific had cut them off from the north and east. In 1939 Admiral Thomas C. Hart pleaded that his Asiatic Fleet be augmented for "neutrality patrols" and for deterrent effect on Japan. Navy planners knew that the army could not protect an expanded flotilla[45] so Hart got only a few flying boats and a suggestion to write "Tension Plans" for demonstrations during times when relations with Japan were strained.[46]

After mid-1939 U.S. leaders anticipated a probable coalition with other democracies to fight Japan and a Japanese occupation of Borneo and New Guinea to complete the encirclement of the Philippines. Planners drafting War Plans Rainbow Two and Rainbow Three flirted with sending a sizable naval force to Singapore or Java or, far less likely, to the Philippines, but canceled all such notions at the end of 1940 (Chapter 22). In 1941 the navy did send Hart some light surface craft, an old cruiser, and PT boats but reconfirmed that it would not fight seriously for the Philippines. Hart was advised to flee Manila with his surface ships "at discretion," abandoning MacArthur in favor of defending Allied territories farther south. His torpedo craft were to scourge "other areas in the Western Pacific" to interdict the lifelines of Orange assaults on British Malaysia and the Dutch East Indies—"very profitable," predicted Chief of Naval Operations Harold Stark as he grandiosely expanded the Asiatic Theater from Tokyo to Australia.[47] Stark ignored many forlorn appeals from Manila. In a typical instance Hart's chief of staff lamented that to expect the obsolescent local units to deny Japan the petroleum of the East Indies was "a wish born of expediency."[48] Stark frostily demanded a plan from him incorporating the no-help decision.[49] When Hart asked for naval dive bombers, he was told to seek air support from MacArthur,[50] not a comforting thought when his staff knew the accuracy of army bombers against ships to be deplorable.[51]

Until the summer of 1941 the army also regarded the Philippines as lost. Its current Plan WPO-3, a derivative of the 1938 Joint Orange Plan, directed the twenty-two-thousand-man garrison to fight on Bataan and Corregidor to the "last extremity" without promise of reinforcement or relief. MacArthur had been laboring to form a self-sufficient army and air force in time for Independence Day 1946 for which the War Department had pledged some equipment only when that date drew near. The general's five-year plan, devised with the aid of the AWPD, called for sealing seven straits with mines, artillery, and PT boats to convert interisland waters into secure lakes. Though defense of the commonwealth without strong naval help was farfetched, his concept was one of deterrence for which he thought a fleet unnecessary.[52]

In April 1941 American, Dutch, and British Far Eastern commanders were instructed to convene their staff planners at a conference known as ADB-1. Their report radiated unwonted confidence in their powers of resistance ashore and afloat. The conferees also proposed an ebullient new mission for theater forces: to attack Japan itself with long-range bombers, a form of violent economic pressure that would bring about its collapse more surely, they argued, than gradual denial of resources. Since Luzon alone of Allied territories lay within extreme bomber range of a few Japanese cities, they urged a commitment to holding it and establishing an offensive air force there.[53] Stark and Chief of Staff George Marshall were unimpressed. Early in July they rejected the planners' theses and chastised them for not focusing on realistic ways to hold the "Malay Barrier," the island chain from Sumatra to Australia.[54]

Suddenly, before the month was out, and for reasons "nowhere explicitly stated" according to its official historian, the War Department decided to mount a stiff fight for the Philippines. Perhaps its leaders were upset by Japan's march along the Asian coast or intrigued belatedly by the drama of air power. MacArthur was recalled to active duty and appointed commander of U.S. Army Forces in the Far East (USAFFE). "An optimist by nature, with implicit faith in the Philippine people," the sixty-one-year-old general refused to belly up to the sacrificial sword. His contagious enthusiasm worked a miracle within a few weeks. His command was awarded top priority for modern weapons. Secretary of War Henry Stimson authorized delivery of 272 B-17 heavy bombers as soon as they rolled out of the factories. A trickle of men and equipment began flowing westward, accelerating into a stream as the year wore on. Marshall promised a doubling of U.S. troops by the end of December and heavy guns for the following year. General Henry H. "Hap" Arnold, chief of the Army Air Forces, scheduled 360 heavy and 260 pursuit planes to arrive before April 1942. (By 7 December 1941, 10 percent and 40 percent, respectively, had been received, along with half the troop increment.) When MacArthur learned that the current war plan, Rainbow Five, still called for martyrdom, he argued stormily for deploying his soldiers to the beaches of Luzon. On 21 November the Joint Board endorsed his program and approved a "strategic defense" of B-17 strikes at invasion forces and bases although not raids on Japan. The Philippines were to become a "self-sustaining fortress," their minimum survival time magically lengthened to 180 days.[55]

The strategy adopted by the army in 1941 was analogous to a naval concept, abandoned thirty-three years earlier, of a fortified Luzon as a great strategic asset. This time the navy refused to help other than to send twelve modern submarines in October to prowl offensively in the surrounding seas.[56] Hart was ordered to stockpile supplies in "the really vital position" of the Malay Barrier and[56] told once again to abandon the Philippines at the outbreak of war.[57]

The army's late bloom of enthusiasm is hard to understand. No sadder self-delusion is to be found in all the prewar planning experiences. In the 1920s Wood's defense fantasy was no more credible than MacArthur's in 1941, but at least it rested on the navy's pledge of rescue. Never after 1934 did the navy intend to move promptly to relieve or even resupply any part of the Philippines (Chapter 17). In the words of the War Department's historian of planning, in 1941, "no one in a position of authority . . . believed that anything like this [relief] would happen. Informed naval opinion estimated that it would require at least two years for the Pacific Fleet to fight its way across the Pacific."[58]

Naval planners spent little time in late 1941 reflecting on operations to save the Philippines. British admirals, who were preparing to send a fleet to Singapore (Chapter 22), spun yarns of their dreadnoughts steaming forward to Manila, where, beneath MacArthur's air umbrella, they would pummel Orange landing forces and save Luzon. "Experience seems to show," the Admiralty opined, "that air threat to Manila from Formosa may not be quite so serious as was formerly thought." Stark and Marshall warned that the port lacked naval facilities and supplies and that its communications were exposed from all directions.[59] The director of naval war plans, Rear Admiral Kelly Turner, doubted that any surface ships could survive there. "It would be dangerous to overestimate the influence of these accretions of Army strength . . . against determined attack," he admonished in November 1941.[60]

When the war began, events in the western Pacific unfolded approximately as predicted by Plan Orange. The Japanese reduced the Philippines with overwhelming sea, air, and land power. Manila fell in three weeks. MacArthur's air force was destroyed on the ground. The raw Filipino army disintegrated during rash attempts to hold the beaches. Within a few days MacArthur bowed to the wisdom of the Orange Plan. His troops scuttled into Bataan just ahead of the Japanese, while most of their food and supplies went up in smoke at Manila. Bataan and Corregidor survived for five and six months, respectively, rather longer than expected, but the sacrifices of their defenders were of minor military import. Manila Bay was, as Embick had said, "without strategic significance." The absence of defenses in the southern Philippines foreclosed all hope of assistance. The Asiatic Fleet escaped to fight in the Indies. The submarines it left behind accomplished almost nothing.

In retrospect the outcome seems preordained. Even in the best of circumstances—hostilities delayed until the spring of 1942, all reinforcements delivered, bombers not wrecked on the ground—MacArthur's position would have been untenable. Japan would still control the sea. The Blue fleet was forbidden to approach within three thousand miles of the Philippines (Chapter 25). British boasts of aid were hollow for the Royal Navy lacked a secure base and a credible air arm. A firm U.S. decision not to send its Pacific Fleet to Singapore, a far better and (it was thought) safer base than Manila (Chapter 22), leaves little room for speculation that if there had been no debacle at Pearl Harbor political pressures might have forced the fleet to relief of the Philippines. MacArthur's defenses, however strong, would therefore have crumbled when supplies ran out.

The Japanese conquest of Southeast Asia and flank extensions to Burma and the Bismarck Archipelago had not been contemplated in Blue-Orange war forecasts (although they had been considered in the Rainbow Plans of 1939–41). Yet the extended Phase I campaign of early 1942 was similar to the Philippines scenario of War Plan Orange. The Japanese mounted overpowering amphibious blitzkriegs. They defeated piecemeal the colonial armies and makeshift sea and air squadrons that opposed them. They encircled and then reduced fortress positions. The campaign secured by conquest rather than by commercial access the resources that American planners knew were essential to Japan. But Japan's long marine lifeline was vulnerable to the interdictory response of the prewar strategy. Plan Orange was a fair template for all Phase I operations in the western Pacific.

The outcome in the Philippines, though predicted, had an unexpected political result: the elevation of Douglas MacArthur to a national hero. His battered command's stubborn resistance raised American morale in a dark hour. His onetime aide Brigadier General Dwight D. Eisenhower was summoned to Washington in late December 1941 to draft an emergency response.[61] The U.S. decision was to extract the general from Corregidor to Australia and there to establish a base for an alternative counterattack that was never projected in Plan Orange.

The Great Western Base

To warriors cast in the heroic mold, eviction from the western Pacific and a long struggle to return was a dispiriting prospect. The agony could be avoided, they believed, if the United States devised a vigorous projection of its naval might. To this end, aggressive strategists pursued two lines of thought over many years: first, the building in peacetime of a grand fortified base in the western Pacific; and, alternatively, rushing the fleet to an improvised base in the region after war commenced. Both proved to be failed strategies that did not resolve the Phase II problem. Both were abandoned long before World War II. Yet they were steps along the path to a formula for victory because planners learned from their frustration to distinguish viable programs from evanescent dreams. They were the awful standards against which better ideas were evaluated and ultimately embraced.

Most high commanders from 1898 to 1922 were fascinated by the idea of the great western base, but civilian authorities refused to sanction it. Their obsession retarded the adoption of a reliable Orange Plan but did not derail it altogether because the admirals and generals never demeaned themselves by embracing plans that violated reality by supposing an imaginary base to be in existence. The other failed strategy, the fleet's dash to an undeveloped Philippine harbor, survived the demise of the western base to dominate Orange Plans for another dozen years until 1934.

At the dawn of the twentieth century overseas naval bases were the symbols and sinews of imperial power. Without them, said Mahan, warships were like "land birds, unable to fly beyond the shore." Battleships devoured thousands of tons of coal, emptied their magazines in a few hours of shooting, and needed frequent docking for repair and cleaning. Great Britain's world-girdling chain of naval stations aroused the envy of every sailor, especially that of Rear Admiral Royal Bird Bradford, chief of the Bureau of Equipment, "a bit of a brute" who irritated his colleagues though convincing them of the importance of distant bases.[1] In 1901 Taylor, Dewey's alter ego on the General Board, presented a petition for a dockyard in the Philippines as the "foundation" for his whimsical colonial war plans.[2]

On the west coast of Luzon sixty miles above Manila lay Subic Bay, which the Spaniards had once dreamed of as a base. Dewey had admired the deep anchorage that was accessible to industrial labor and infrastructure, nestled between hills and behind an island that guarded it from sea attack. "Who holds Subic holds Manila; who holds Manila holds Luzon; and who holds Luzon holds the Philippines," the admiral exclaimed.[3] With "rare energy" he threw himself into promoting its development.[4] By 1901 he had enlisted the General Board and Secretary Long in the cause of a "strong naval base" at the village of Olongapo on Subic Bay.[5] He inveigled French E. Chadwick, president of the War College, whose staff had been considering harbors south of Luzon, to recommend it by instructing him to assume that a European adversary was already ensconced in the southern islands.[6] Olongapo, the college analysts concurred, would prove indispensable in a dispute with Germany over ownership of the Philippines.[7] Theodore Roosevelt was much taken with the notion of developing and fortifying Subic. But unlike the Congresses that funded a gigantic naval base there in the late twentieth century, skeptical lawmakers of the Roosevelt years dragged their feet.[8]

Subic had a fatal flaw: in a confrontation with a naval power it would be vulnerable to amphibious landings from the rear. This prospect troubled the army even before Japan was deemed the enemy, but naval leaders resisted a study of ground defenses[9] until 1904, when the Japanese demolished a Russian naval base at Port Arthur, Manchuria, by mortar fire from surrounding hills. Subic geographically resembled

Port Arthur. Sealing its mouth with a curtain of mines, guns, and torpedoes would be of no avail against siege guns in the mountains. As Major General Leonard Wood warned the president (his former subordinate in the Rough Rider regiment that fought in Cuba), the project would be a "colossal mistake." Subic, said the naval commander on the scene, would become a "rat trap."[10] But Dewey charmed Roosevelt once more.[11] By the time planning against Japan commenced in 1906, a board on coast defenses chaired by Secretary of War William Howard Taft had declared that the base was vital.[12] The navy eked out some money for a small coaling depot and a floating dry dock, aptly named the *Dewey*, for midsized ships.[13]

The war scares of 1906–7 provided an excuse to tout Subic's value in a Blue-Orange war.[14] Dewey reported that "the weight of overwhelming authority" favored a fortified dockyard to which the fleet could steam by way of a chain of bases to be erected in California and Hawaii and on Guam.[15] Strategists recommended that all forces in the Philippines be marshaled to defend Subic "to the last" during the estimated three-month voyage because if the base were lost just before the fleet arrived, the plight of the ships would be "well nigh desperate."[16] Army strategists tentatively accepted that Subic might be held for the requisite time.[17] Roosevelt approved temporary defenses and a start on permanent fortifications.[18] The delighted General Board proposed to send munitions, fuel, and submarines.[19]

But the navy had not reckoned with the iron determination of Leonard Wood, then commanding general of the Philippine Department, and Captain Stanley D. Embick, a coast artillery expert whom Wood sent to look at Olongapo. These two would be nemeses of naval planners for the next three decades. They reported that Subic was utterly indefensible. To hold siege cannon beyond range, 125,000 soldiers would have to man a thirty-five-mile trench line, three times longer than at Port Arthur.[20] (The light guns of the marine guard were uselessly sited to ward off a native uprising.[21]) Wood got the ear of Taft, who was touring Manila. Together they persuaded the president to cancel the project.[22]

Roosevelt felt euchred. For years he had been prodding Congress to approve the base at Subic. Now the admirals and generals had done him "grave harm." He warned them never to proffer advice on a joint matter without first having consulted together. He then turned his energy to promoting a base at Pearl Harbor.[23] On 31 January 1908 the browbeaten Joint Board caved in. Subic, it declared, was too perilous a place for a major base.[24] It could not be defended.

A few naval die-hards continued the fight. After the fleet's world cruise of 1907–9 they boasted that the modern battleships that had performed so swiftly and reliably could reach Subic soon enough while newfangled weaponry held the bay. A General Board planning aide asserted that twenty long-range (150-mile) submarines would sink the enemy's artillery lighters and render the base "well nigh impregnable."[25] Rear Admiral Bradley Fiske proposed that a hundred airplanes could preserve Olongapo. Ridiculous, said Admiral Richard "Fighting Dick" Wainwright—the army had only one fragile machine available.[26]

Wood's motivation, then and later, was geopolitical rather than military. To him the crown jewels of the Orient were Manila and its magnificent bay. There, behind the shield of Corregidor, the United States should erect a base for the avenging fleet.[27] But an army scheme to build a naval base along the city waterfront foundered on pleas to save the commercial port (and the posh Army and Navy Club), and the navy found no other site near the city. Some optimists thought Corregidor could be adapted for a fleet that would need only a coal cache and a few weeks of protected anchorage to turn the tide of war. The army bragged that it could create such an artificial harbor alongside The Rock and hold it for a year "against all comers no matter how strong." On sober reflection, the navy demurred. The expense of a hundred-foot-deep breakwater, poor layouts for service and docking, and a potential rain of explosives from enemy shore guns were too daunting. Even less promising was a proposed base at Caballo, a minuscule island adjacent to Corregidor.[28] These preposterous ideas were exhumed in 1917 by the General Board for an expanding navy that could never have fit inside such cramped and dangerous boxes and were dropped once more.[29]

It was all moonshine. In 1910 NWC strategy conferees decided that no Philippine fleet base could be defended for a useful duration.[30] The navy opted to erect only a minor station for the Asiatic Fleet at Cavite, on a peninsula within Manila Bay that the army could not defend.[31]

Proponents of a Luzon base rallied again a decade later, shortly before the treaty negotiations of 1921–22. While the U.S. government prepared to renounce bases in the western Pacific as a trade-off for Japanese concessions on naval armaments, these enthusiasts argued that a fortified base would guarantee that "Orange would probably not venture to war in this generation." Captain Reginald Belknap of the War College believed that Asiatic Fleet destroyers and submarines could safeguard stockpiles of naval war matériel long enough for the fleet to zip across with only a small train.[32] But the Philippine base was an idea whose time had passed. Further desultory attempts to revive it during the next twenty years came to naught.

After 1908 naval attention turned to America's other outpost of the western Pacific, Guam, southernmost of the Mariana Islands. War planners appreciated the island's position, 1,510 cruising miles east of Manila and 1,360 miles south of Tokyo. Japan would crave it as a bulwark for its empire. For the United States, Guam represented a potential offensive strong point that was more accessible than the Philippines and less prone to quarantine by Orange sea power. But Guam was no Luzon. Its two hundred square miles were nearly all mountainous, its population of ten thousand was a minuscule fraction of Luzon's, and it had no infrastructure. The sole harbor at Apra was cramped, reef-studded, and exposed to violent storms. Williams estimated that only six or seven large ships could coal there simultaneously.[33]

The United States had seized Guam during the Spanish-American War as a transit haven for troopships en route to capture Manila. The Naval War Board selected it because of its convenient location and because it was erroneously thought that coal might be stored there. The island fell after a cruiser lobbed a few shells in its direction. The Spanish governor, unaware of the war, apologized that he had no gunpowder to return what he took to be a salute.[34] After the war Guam's utility as a coaling station became evident. Few steamships could span the five thousand miles between Hawaii and the Philippines without refueling. (American warships usually journeyed via Suez.) Encouraged by Bradford, the navy in 1905–6 installed a five-thousand-ton coal-loading plant but deferred enlarging it because, during the world cruise, the fleet proved adept at replenishing from colliers.[35]

The first Blue-Orange war analyses noted Guam's potentialities but assumed it would be lost unless the Asiatic Fleet raced out from Manila in time to save it. A board appointed to study fortification had reported favorably that Apra and the few other flat beaches could be shielded by minefields and by artillery in the hills. In 1907 the Naval War College undertook a leisurely study of a General Board recommendation to arm the island against minor raids. The languid air of Guam did not hum with the bustle of Corregidor or Pearl Harbor. When some old cruiser guns were dropped off, the marine police unit installed one and returned to drowsing.[36]

The scuttling of the Subic dockyard in 1908 elevated Guam to unexpected prominence. To admirals who yearned for a western base the island was refreshingly free of the snares that had doomed Olongapo. It was small enough to be defended at all points by the navy and marines. Since the island was under naval administration, army nay-sayers would be relegated to junior status. At the NWC conference of 1910 the assembled officers resolved that Guam "could and should" be adapted as a first-class fortified base.[37] The staff's Orange Plan of the following year portrayed a gory campaign of recapture after the unprepared island had fallen, which would seriously retard the rest of the Blue offensive. Mahan (who had sat on the board of 1898 that recommended seizing Guam) insisted on a quicker thrust to the Far East. "Our every interest in the Pacific," he declared, could be secured by converting Guam into "a kind of Gibraltar." From such a stronghold the navy could safeguard Hawaii (or cut off any Orange troops there), drive ahead to save the Philippines, and dominate Japan itself.[38]

The moment was ripe. The aggressive-minded General Board rejected a slow offensive plan proposed by the NWC in 1911. President Raymond P. Rodgers, threatened with termination of the college's planning function, meekly agreed that a base on Guam would be an "absolute necessity" that might "decide the war."[39] The momentum faltered, however, when Captain Bradley Fiske, a prominent voice in naval and joint councils, declared that the battle fleet could neither enter nor defend Apra and that the cost of preparing it would be exorbitant. Fiske derided Mahan's comparison of Guam to Malta, a British base commanding the narrows of the Mediterranean, because hostile ships could give it a wide berth.[40]

In 1912 the Guam movement coalesced. An energetic island governor, Captain Robert Edward Coontz, mounted the old guns and appealed for "defenses of a naval base of the first order."[41] Dewey was won over. He declared Guam the sine qua non of Pacific strategy. As he explained to Navy Secretary George Meyer:

> Guam occupies such a commanding strategic position in the Pacific, and one of such vital importance to our national interests in that ocean, that it is essential to hold it securely against any form of attack. It is axiomatic that a campaign involving the United States in the Far East rests primarily upon the control of the sea. To maintain, or under many circumstances, to attain that control, the fleet's line of communication must be beyond the probability of successful attack. The distance . . . is too long to traverse without an intermediate point of support, and Guam furnishes that point geographically. If, however, it be undefended, or insufficiently defended, it will be taken by our enemy, who, resting

upon Guam, will certainly be able to dispute the control of the sea for a long time, and may be able to prevent us from ever getting it in those waters. The possession of Guam under naval control is a vital necessity to our country in engaging in war in the Far East.[42]

Dewey and Mahan, the naval demigods, had spoken. Around them rallied a "Guam lobby" (a term coined here), a coterie of officers who regarded the base as the foundation of Pacific strategy. The lobby tried to smother dissenters; for a decade it hobbled the search for strategic alternatives. For example, the General Board's Orange Plan of 1914 outdid the professors in describing a murderous campaign to recapture Guam. How different Phase II would look if Blue had a haven armed for a stand "prolonged to the utmost limit." From Guam the fleet could interrupt Orange communications with the Philippines (perhaps forcing evacuation), press against Japan's inner bastion at the Bonins and Ryukyus, and threaten the home islands.[43] In 1917 the board urged the dredging of a capacious anchorage for the hugely expanded fleet just authorized and an arsenal with docks, fuel dumps, and shops to withstand months of devastating blows.[44]

The Guam lobby realized it could not carry the day alone. To avoid another fiasco like Subic it had to co-opt the army. The courtship started off poorly when the generals agreed only to minor works and protection against raids, but soon the Army War College seconded Coontz's proposal,[45] and during the war flap of 1913 it endorsed the full program. The Joint Board urged fortifications that would endure a four-month stand. Woodrow Wilson, no doubt with a sigh, approved a joint survey.[46] The inspectors returned to design a fortress mightier than Oahu or Corregidor where ten thousand troops would man a dozen twelve-inch mortars and clusters of fourteen-inch rifles in turrets and disappearing mounts (Map 7.1). The offshore waters would bristle with minefields and submarines while an "aero squadron" guarded the skies.[47] Then reports from Belgium cast doubt on the survivability of fortresses. The army discovered it had no mortars that could outrange battleships and balked at pouring foundations. Even if mortars were available, they would not be able to hit maneuvering vessels, as Mahan had said.[48]

Mahan and Dewey passed away during the World War. In 1919 the Guam lobby rallied around a new champion, Admiral Robert Coontz, who was appointed to the recently established post of chief of naval operations (CNO). Coontz had helped raise the flag over Guam in

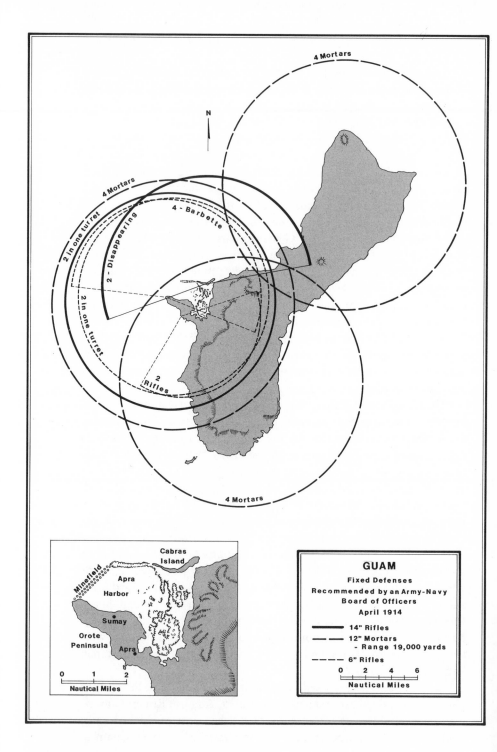

4 Mortars

N

4 Mortars

2 in one turret

2 - Disappearing

4 - Barbette

2 in one turret

2 Rifles

4 Mortars

Cabras Island

Minefield

Apra

Harbor

Sumay

Orote Peninsula

Apra

0   1   2

Nautical Miles

GUAM

Fixed Defenses
Recommended by an Army-Navy
Board of Officers
April 1914

━━━━ 14" Rifles
─ ─ ─ 12" Mortars
        - Range 19,000 yards
- - - - 6" Rifles

0   2   4   6

Nautical Miles

1898, and during his island governorship he had "always had the interests of Guam at heart."[49] He selected as his director of planning (another new billet) the spokesman of Newport's salad days of strategy, Rear Admiral James H. Oliver. After his brilliant theorizing of 1907–11, Oliver had wearied himself trying to manage the creaky Office of Naval Intelligence and had served out the war as governor of the Virgin Islands.[50] The officer who had proposed bypassing Guam altogether now signed aboard the lobby. His detail man, Captain Harry Yarnell, became its mouthpiece.[51] The new planning crew revived the wish list of Pacific bases for a fleet movement and the argument for the one base from whence Blue could dominate the seas and defeat Japan.

Army planners were charmed by the easy solution to the Philippine dilemma. They joined in proposing a massive four-stage transformation of Guam into a Gibraltar that would ultimately shelter and burnish the entire fleet behind powerful defenses (Table 7.1). With the sheath of the Blue sword so near, Japan would not dare attack the Philippines. Indeed, it could not undertake a war "with any reasonable chance of ultimate success." Conversely, an unprepared Guam would invite a war in which Japan would enjoy ample time to foil the Blue offensive by strengthening its conquests behind the screen of Guam and its recently acquired Micronesian islands.[52] At the end of 1919 Secretary of War Newton D. Baker blessed the project.[53] It was the supreme moment of the Guam fantasy.

Then matters began to sour. A naval board chaired by Clarence Williams reported in 1921 that dredging of Apra could neither yield the moorage berths in forty-five-foot depths that capital ships required nor lodge floating dry docks. At best, by excavating to a twenty-foot depth and building simple marine railways for servicing, destroyers and submarines might be accommodated.[54] Army leaders backed away as they began to realize their minor role in a Guam-centered strategy.[55] Coontz turned to the marines for a plan of defense. The corps could offer only 1,900 men with a few guns and seaplanes for a sacrificial delaying fight; even the General Board admitted that their seven-inch cannon would be pulverized by Orange battleships.[56] Coontz, undaunted, pressed for a cordon of 128 torpedo craft that he insisted would keep the enemy at bay. Even so, the battle fleet would find at Guam nothing better than an emergency refuge for "detachments." The base slid down the list of naval priorities.[57]

In late 1921 the CNO and the General Board mounted a last-ditch effort for Guam by haranguing the U.S. delegates to the Washington Conference.[58] Coontz apparently suborned Clarence Williams, his cur-

TABLE 7.1 *Summary of Joint Board Proposal for Development of Guam, December 1919*

Sequence	Army	Navy	Cost ($ million)	Strategic result
First	5,000 troops immediately; increase to 13,500; artillery; aircraft	7 modern submarines with tender; 1,000 contact mines		Limited defense
Second	Construct roads, barracks, magazines, infrastructure	Dredge inner harbor; shore facilities for 20 submarines; shops, fuel, utilities, etc., underground or protected	21.7	Capability to hold out until fleet arrives to base on Guam; operation of 20 submarines offensively
Third	Install two 16″ rifles, four 16″ howitzers	Additional dredging; facilities for 108 destroyers; floating dry dock with capacity for battleship	18.0	Improved capability to hold out until fleet arrives; operation of 20 submarines and 108 destroyers offensively
Fourth	Install additional two 16″ rifles and eight 16″ howitzers	Construct first-class fleet base; berthing of capital ships	59.0	Defense against "any force which could be brought against it"; complete facilities to operate entire fleet offensively; Japan probably dissuaded from engaging in war with United States

Source: JB to SecWar & SecNav, Dev and Def of Guam, 18 Dec 1919, #322, Ser 28, JB Records, RG 225, NA.

rent chief planner, to corrupt Williams's excellent plan of a slow drive through Micronesia (Chapter 10) into a sales pitch for a "very considerable" base on Guam that would assure the usual wonders of war deterrence or rapid victory. Without the base, the delays and sufferings of recapturing Guam might forfeit the war. Williams knew better; his embarrassment was evident in a brusque statement that "in order to save time" he would not explain why Fortress Guam was the only real alternative.[59]

Secretary of the Navy Daniels, a populist ever suspicious of militarism, detested the extravagant base. After withholding his consent for two years, he cynically said in 1921 he would approve it if a disarmament treaty did not materialize.[60] He well knew that President-elect Warren G. Harding had promised "normalcy" and a halt to the fiscally ruinous naval arms race that had bloomed after the war. Harding invited five maritime nations to Washington to discuss limitations of navies and bases. At the conference Theodore Roosevelt, Jr., the former president's son, spoke for the navy. The admirals were reduced to pleading from the sidelines for preservation of their imaginary Pacific Gibraltar.[61]

The Guam lobby lost. Article XIX of the Washington Treaty halted for ten years (later extended to fifteen) military development of Blue possessions west of the 180th meridian, that is, the Philippines, Guam, Wake, and the western Aleutians. It also froze development of Japan's outlying islands of Formosa and the Pescadores, Ryukyus, Bonins, Volcanoes, Kuriles, and Marcus. Britain accepted restrictions that exempted the dominions and Singapore. The younger Roosevelt was smugly satisfied when the conference ended on 6 February 1922, certain he had traded away bases the United States would never build in exchange for those Japan would certainly build, along with a reduction of battleship strengths and a fixing of future U.S.-Japanese capital ship tonnages at a ratio of five to three.[62]

The Guam lobby faded into the shadows. It reappeared briefly in 1938 after the treaty had expired when fleet strategists again sought a base, but their appeals were denied again for political and military reasons (Chapter 22). Guam fell to Japan in the first week of the war. In 1944 U.S. forces retook it and developed it as a naval logistical and repair base, but even that massive effort could not create a harbor ample enough to hold a major part of the fleet.

The doomed quest for western Pacific Gibraltars was oddly relevant to the mobile strategy that was evolved for World War II. The U.S. Navy was compelled to find alternative ways for fighting without a prepared base in faraway seas, which would require range, endurance, and self-sustenance. Each rejection stimulated innovations that met those needs. After the Subic fiasco the navy constructed heavy colliers that could nourish the fleet at raw harbors and clever auxiliary vessels for servicing ships afloat. It researched the management of a large fleet train. In 1922 the navy converted its last coal-burning ships to oil;

other nations did the same, but the United States strove for extreme cruising range. It also designed modular advanced bases and floating dry docks (although acquisition of these lagged because of budget constraints). Finally, after the abortive attempt to revive Guam in 1938, fast oilers for refueling at sea and base construction battalions (Seabees) made their appearance.

Institutions can learn from mistakes. The U.S. Navy put behind it the grand base fantasy twenty years before World War II. So complete was its change of mind that it declined the only true opportunity that ever arose. Early in 1941 Great Britain implored the United States to send its Pacific Fleet to defend Singapore, a base with finer services and fortifications than any the admirals had imagined, with relatively secure communications and access to oil. Yet American strategists spurned the offer (Chapter 22). The Orange Plan's doctrine of mobile bases was by then too deeply ingrained to resurrect the old dream.

The great western base was a terrible strategic idea. Japan's advantages of initiative and proximity probably would have brought any such arsenal to a catastrophic end. Without it, the United States developed the concepts and means of a prudent war strategy, writing off what could not be held and betting on a comeback by way of mobile bases. The doom of Port Arthur and Singapore attests to the fate of nations that built vulnerable dockyards, lost the investments, and failed to find other ways to win in the Pacific.

The American Way of Planning: Thrusters and Cautionaries

Between 1906 and 1914 the independent off-line planning staffs had established the overarching geopolitical and grand strategy frameworks of a Pacific war. They had also defined the Phase I campaigns in both halves of the ocean, settled some elementary assumptions about Phase II, and begun to conceptualize Phase III. The War College and Second Committee worked together smoothly, building on each others' initiatives. In 1906 studies at Newport identified the broad nature of a war for which the committee provided an outline of solutions in the first draft of Plan Orange (which the president requested but which the General Board never ratified). Under Oliver's tutelage the Conference of 1907 cast Phase II as a transpacific attack.[1] When the staffs turned to designing this difficult campaign, however, free-form cooperation broke down. The easy consensus gave way to the truism that modern military establishments are molded by struggles between "heroic leaders, who embody traditionalism and glory, and military 'managers,' who are concerned with the scientific and rational conduct of war."[2] The offensive campaign plan became a football between heroic leaders and managers, whom I label "thrusters" and "caution-

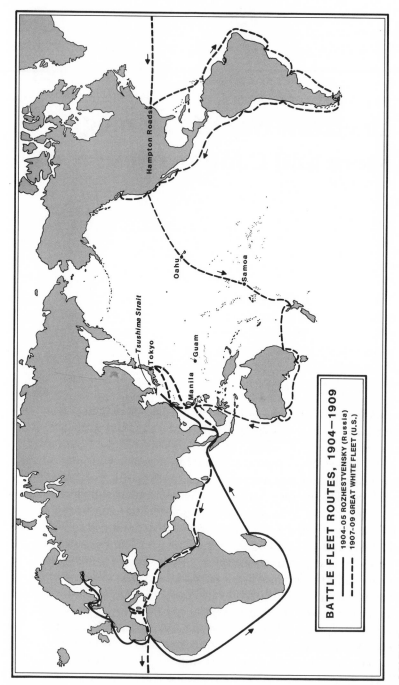

Hampton Roads

Oahu

Samoa

Tsushima Strait

Tokyo

Manila • Guam

BATTLE FLEET ROUTES, 1904–1909

——— 1904–05 ROZHESTVENSKY (Russia)
- - - - 1907–09 GREAT WHITE FLEET (U.S.)

MAP 8.1

aries." They were, respectively, hares and tortoises. Both schools were committed to an all-out attack and absolute victory, but they disagreed about targets, routes, and especially timing.

Thrusters believed that victory had to be won quickly because the American people would not endure a long war. They advocated a rush to the Far East. Power, they said, was a blending of force and time. Blue would "never be stronger" than at the outset of the war. Thereafter, time would favor the defense.[3] A swift riposte would prevent Japan from acting to deny all bases to the fleet and would compel the Orange navy to fight in a region essential to Japanese survival before attrition could erode the U.S. preponderance. Thrusters agitated for an American Gibraltar but understood that unless and until it was built the expedition would have to improvise advanced bases. The Great White Fleet's triumph over distance by ad hoc provisioning on the move was their inspiration (see Map 8.1).

Cautionaries felt that Americans would accept a long war for a righteous cause but would lose heart if the fleet were lost in a premature gamble. A more gradual offensive policy would conserve the battleships while reserve warships and army regiments were made ready, auxiliary vessels converted, and the awesome U.S. industrial machine geared up. They proposed to march across the central Pacific step by step, securing small islands in succession, each step supported by the previous one. The advance would be slow, punctuated by delays to erect naval bases, and flexible when appropriate. The cautionaries also expected a climactic naval battle but imagined it might occur in open waters far from Orange strong points rather than in the narrow China seas. They appreciated that new weapons of attrition—mine and torpedo, submarine and airplane—could exact a heavy toll on Blue during the long campaign yet feared that greater punishment would result from an impetuous lunge. They pointed to the death voyage of Admiral Zinovi Rozhestvensky's "black ships" of 1904–5, an armada that staggered halfway around the world to a theater where it had no accessible base and where the fresh Japanese fleet lay in wait. They dismissed an American Gibraltar as foolhardy because the fleet could not get to it for six months, a year, or even two years. Before 1914, however, the cautionaries faced an insuperable dilemma because the best harbors between Hawaii and the Philippines were owned by neutrals. When Japan seized the Micronesian groups from Germany in World War I, that void was filled and their prayers were answered.

Naval elders bred on traditions of gallantry and audacity were, by and large, thrusters. They controlled the General Board, and after the

World War they took charge of the new centralized entities of Naval Operations and the U.S. Fleet. They usually dominated strategic planning decisions and stifled their adversaries. Cautionaries were prominent among strategists of middle rank who filled the planning slots. Their generation, younger and War College–educated, better grasped the challenges of a modern ocean campaign. They were outranked and outgunned until their vanguard reached high command in the 1930s.

The thruster-cautionary discord lay dormant in 1906 and 1907 because the principles developed by the twin planning staffs were congenial to the views of traditionalist admirals. The outlook for continued synchronization appeared excellent after the officer corps returned from the world cruise in 1909. Secretary of the Navy Meyer bound the staffs even closer when he named as aide for operations Rear Admiral Richard Wainwright, a war hero and intelligence expert, who would supervise the NWC and speak for the Second Committee at General Board meetings.[4] The committee drew up a list of topics that war plans should address: forces and objectives of both sides; theaters, bases, and logistics; means of injuring the enemy and protecting oneself; and, above all, the absolute requirement of offensive movement.[5] Both agencies produced interesting ideas for an offensive campaign in 1910,[6] but the General Board got bogged down in a quest for ideal plans instead of grappling with specific, if awkward, solutions. It lapsed into quarrels over Pacific bases and the lessons of the cruise. Gridlocked, the admirals offered to divest responsibility for Plan Orange to the NWC at the end of 1910. Since Meyer still wanted a cooperative effort, it was agreed that the faculty would study intelligence reports, then draft a strategic plan that addressed the Second Committee's checklist. After the board's preliminary approval, the NWC would recommend tactical doctrines for cruising, patrolling, blockade, and so forth, while the naval bureaus tabulated matériel needs. Upon final approval of the General Board, the plan would be held for use of the secretary and the president.[7]

The family concord did not last. The college's 1911 Plan (submitted in orange-colored binders the board had thoughtfully sent[8]) displeased the thrusters by neglecting to advocate either building or relief of Pacific Gibraltars. In addition, the faculty's reflections on the politics of war did not sit well with Dewey (Chapter 3).[9] The plan was not unequivocally cautionary, projecting a direct advance to the Philippines, for example, but it was damned by Fiske for offering no "reasonable expectation of victory after a long and exhausting war,—if then." Raymond Rodgers, the college president, bristled. It was "a crime" to expect six overburdened officers to plan wars in their spare time. He appealed for a full-time planning staff of seven alumni to try again before others "mutilated" the study. But the admirals were adamant. Meyer repealed his directive and decreed that henceforth Orange Plans were to emanate solely from the General Board.[10] After one harvest, war planning was ruled an unbefitting task for an academy of learning. The college receded into the background; it was to influence future Orange Plans by testing them on the gaming board, training strategists, and submitting occasional studies. Sadly, the college might have produced superior plans had it been given another chance when such bright stars as Captain William S. Sims, Marine Captain Earl H. Ellis, and six future directors of Naval War Plans assembled at Newport in the next few years.[11]

The thrusters of the General Board, having reclaimed authority over the plan, served up two studies before the United States entered World War I. Both were unsatisfactory. In February 1914 the board approved an "Orange Strategic Section" written by its staff, the first Orange Plan to be endorsed by a high military body, albeit an advisory one.[12] (The work may have been guided by Fiske, a frequent adviser to Dewey.[13]) Although it discussed a stepwise central Pacific offensive, its logistical difficulties and the inadequacies of its chosen bases amounted to an oblique testimonial for prepared Gibraltars. At Dewey's death early in 1917 the board passed under another thruster, Rear Admiral Charles J. Badger. Badger's strategic credentials were narrow, but he was respected by Secretary Daniels.[14] By then the senior admirals had begun to understand the significance of submarines and convoys, base defense, and the logistical needs of the vast new fleet authorized the previous year. Yet their response was another stale cry for a chain of impregnable naval bases.[15]

The General Board's warping of Pacific campaign plans into polemics for imperial ambitions was symptomatic of a disorganized Navy Department. The segregation of strategy from operations was no longer tenable. For years reformist officers had been pressing for an army-style general staff because of its supposed efficiency in planning, among other reasons. Opponents countered that a navy had no need of special staffs, that cramped sea quarters were unsuitable for them, and that the army usually did things wrong anyway.[16] Under the loom of war in 1915 Congress brushed aside its traditional fear of surrendering civilian mastery and established the Office of the Chief of Naval Operations (OpNav).[17] The many responsibilities assigned to the uniformed head of the navy included war planning, but though he controlled the

War College and Naval Intelligence directly, on the General Board he was only one among equals who reported to the civilian secretary. The first CNO, Admiral William S. Benson, had little interest in strategizing. His assistant, Captain William V. Pratt, set up a planning staff that got sidetracked into administration during the World War[18] so the older agencies bid to regain the function. President Austin Knight of the War College offered to round up a knowledgeable squad to draw plans for Benson's edification, but the NWC shut down for the duration and nothing came of it. Dewey and Badger brandished the order of 1900 that had designated the General Board as the lawful seat of planning.[19] In the absence of real competition, the board held de facto control of the Orange Plan until 1919 and retained an important say until 1923.

When the United States declared war on Germany in April 1917 the Navy Department was in a chaotic state. It had no useful war plan for the Atlantic, a fact disclosed during Senate interrogations of Admiral William S. Sims after the Armistice. Sims, commander of U.S. naval forces in Europe, charged that the country had suffered tragic losses of vessels and lives because warships were unready for action and the premise of War Plan Black—a naval showdown against Germany in the Caribbean—was ludicrous.[20] During the war Sims took the initiative in assembling a fine planning staff in London, calling on "brilliant graduates" of the War College from many parts of the service. In 1918 Benson reclaimed Captain Harry E. Yarnell to organize a similar group in Washington. By the end of the war "a considerable number of capable youngsters . . . full of vim and vigor," including Captains Frank H. Schofield, Dudley W. Knox, and Thomas C. Hart and Commander William S. Pye, were probing into subjects like peace negotiation tactics and postwar force levels.[21]

The contrasting wartime experiences of Washington and London spurred the formalization in August 1919 of the Planning Division under the CNO, known as OpNav Plans Division or familiarly by its numerical designator, Op-12. Its twenty officers were grouped into eight sections that focused on current issues such as organization, training, and weaponry more than on plans for future wars. It proved so cumbersome that most of its functions were gradually vested in other agencies. In 1921 the remnant of eight or nine officers was renamed the War Plans Division (WPD) and instructed to deal solely with that activity.[22]

The energetic crew ought to have overhauled the obsolete Orange Plan. Had Benson stayed on, he might have encouraged the rise of a cautionary faction for he was an outsider to the thrusting cabal that dominated Pacific strategy and a loyal minion of Daniels, who opposed faraway bases. In late 1919, however, Rear Admiral Coontz took charge of OpNav. The new CNO viewed Japan as the next enemy and soon eased one of the dilemmas facing the planners by transferring the fleet to the Pacific Coast. Yet he had no head for realistic campaign planning.[23] His fanatical devotion to Fortress Guam derailed both thrusting and cautionary versions of the mobile strategy. His planning aides, Oliver and Yarnell, pandered to their chief's conceit, blind to the political trend toward restriction of naval arms and Pacific bases.

After 1920 the founders of the Planning Division drifted away, and its stature waned. Oliver was succeeded in 1921 by the unimpressive Captain Lusius A. Bostwick.[24] Meanwhile, the General Board under William L. Rodgers waged a stubborn rear-guard action for American Gibraltars with the usual ineffective result. Not until the Washington Treaty expunged all hope for Guam in 1922 did the moment for a cautionary program ripen. The navy's most talented strategist, Clarence Williams, moved into the planning vacuum and integrated the innovative ideas brewing among the college, marine, and logistical staffs into a rational island-hopping campaign plan (Chapter 10).

The cautionary ascendancy was brief. The heroic ideals of audacity and quick victory were still too deeply ingrained. A bureaucratic struggle for turf once again yielded a kind of Gresham's Law of strategy: bad thrusting plans drove out good cautionary ones. It was the army, surprisingly, that prodded the naval thrusters to repossess Plan Orange.

After the war the generals wished to redeem the Joint Board from the purgatory to which Wilson had consigned it. With a political nudge from Theodore Roosevelt, Jr., the navy consented. Secretaries Baker and Daniels reconstituted the board with six powerful members, serving ex officio by virtue of their offices: the army's chief of staff and the heads of its Operations and War Plans divisions and the CNO, assistant CNO, and senior naval war planning officer. No clutch of randomly chosen graybeards, they spoke with authority for their services. Since the chiefs and their staffs occupied adjacent buildings on Constitution Avenue in Washington, relationships were close and informal. In a radical reform, the Joint Board was empowered to initiate studies without waiting for requests from the cabinet secretaries. The work of the board was thenceforth considered impressive; it issued about twenty-five formal papers a year. A civilian secretary kept minutes of the monthly meetings until replaced in 1936 by a military officer for security reasons.

The Joint Board appointed a Joint Planning Committee (JPC) of six midlevel officers, three from each War Plans Division, who formed army and navy sections of the committee. The sections worked nearly continuously. The full committee had no office space of its own and met once a week on average. To encourage free exchange it assembled in informal settings and kept no minutes. It operated by consensus. In addition to carrying out planning assignments from the parent board, the JPC was also granted the cherished right to initiate studies. Duty on the JPC was an attractive career opportunity. The chosen few gained insights into joint matters and made contacts that ripened into personal friendships. The committee was also a useful conduit for Op-12 in its formative years because the naval planners could funnel ideas through it without tangling with the jealous General Board. Navy members dominated the work on the Orange Plan. In their haughty view, army plans were simple affairs compared with fleet deployments. Their military colleagues had devoted little study to the Orange strategic problem and fell meekly in line.[25]

In 1919 the Joint Board obligingly approved its staff's paper "Strategy of the Pacific," a Fortress Guam polemic.[26] But the army leadership, which had been preoccupied with a reorganization bill, soon realized that Guam would be a dead issue and began to distance itself from it.[27] After the Washington Treaty of 1922 the rhetoric of Leonard Wood booming from Manila animated the generals to demand a strategy to preserve the Philippines by a thrusting offensive. The proposal beguiled Coontz, but he had dug himself into a bureaucratic hole by endorsing Williams's cautionary solution. The CNO therefore turned to the independent General Board of the Navy to procure backing for the army's gambling proposition. Its advocacy of that rash undertaking proved to be the General Board's swan song in war planning (Chapter 11). After 1923 it faded out of the strategy business to settle into niches of advising on ship characteristics and force levels.

The bureaucratic flux in the navy was not matched in the army planning system. In 1921 the army adopted the General Headquarters (GHQ) concept, which assumed that in wartime a separate field command would be set up overseas and take most of the AWPD staff along. It remained a theoretical arrangement; until World War II the Army's War Plans Division functioned as its sole strategic planning entity.[28]

The simplification of naval war planning into a single headquarters unit was challenged from another quarter in 1925. Coontz, from his final billet as commander in chief of the U.S. Fleet, manipulated himself into control of Pacific campaign planning again. His flagship staff produced an attack plan that was the high-water mark of mindless offensivism. It was so aggressive that it embarrassed the navy. When he retired, OpNav disowned his plan and in 1926 restored the WPD's authority. The fleet did no more planning until the late 1930s; though still the spiritual home of the thrusting faction, it was limited by then to seeking peppery shortcuts compatible with a universally accepted cautionary doctrine.

Two messages are evident in the changing circumstances of the American planning system from 1911 through the mid-1920s. First, the formalisms of the agencies—membership, charter, and place in the chain of command—mattered less in determining campaign strategy than the mind-set of high commanders. The thrusting ideals of the chieftains with heroic visions set the standards for most of the Orange Plans, whether originating from the War College faculties, the general staffs, or the operating units of the services. Only after they passed from the scene did the planning institutions provide more appropriate cautionary solutions. Second, the pluralistic system generated sturdy agencies that were to blossom during World War II. The revitalized and integrated Joint Board of the 1920s was the ancestor of the far more powerful Joint Chiefs of Staff of the 1940s. The JPC evolved into the Joint Staff Planners and Joint War Plans Committee of 1942–45. Op-12 continued under a new name as the wartime strategic planning arm of the Navy Department. The fleet staff, a failure at planning in the 1920s, made a fresh start in time for the conflict and matured as the principal designer of Pacific naval campaigns. The banished Naval War College and the General Board never regained their former glory as planners. Their independent staffs, so admirable at theorizing on geopolitics and grand strategy but so unsuited to offensive campaign planning, had retired from the field of strategy.

The Through Ticket

F or all their yearning for greater means, planners must work with the assets at hand. U.S. strategists refrained from injecting fictitious bases or battleships into their scripts, but they succumbed to fantasies about a Through Ticket counterattack in spite of the missing tools. They proposed a massive, instantaneous Phase II naval advance, uninterrupted except for brief pit stops, to an improvised base in the western Pacific. This thrusting response that dominated most Orange Plans from 1906 to 1934 was a failed strategy, yet it bequeathed useful legacies to the future. It compelled the planners to devise methods of surmounting the penalties of time and distance; some of their solutions, especially of logistical quandaries, were absorbed into better plans in time for World War II. But the main value of the Through Ticket was in providing a negative example. Like the great western base, it served as a dreadful miscalculation against which to study sounder alternatives. Realization of its faults helped U.S. planners find better campaign strategies.

The Through Ticket was invented as a way to implement the grand strategy of Plan Orange. In 1906 the General Board recommended advancing the fleet to the Philippines "at as early a date as possible" for the sensible reasons of curtailing the enemy's time for conquests and its ability to brace for battle.[1] (Grander benefits, like deterring Japan from war or at least from assaulting the Philippines, were mentioned but not taken seriously.) As Dewey informed Theodore Roosevelt in 1906, a bold naval stroke would assure within ninety days "sufficient preponderance of forces to enable us to command the sea in Eastern waters."[2] The army joined in, urging the president to accept a thrusting expedition "as soon as practicable."[3]

One means of facilitating the rapid stroke would be to station the navy closer to its objective. Captains Nathan Sargent and Sidney Staunton of the General Board proposed in 1907–9 the formation of a separate Pacific Fleet more powerful than the entire Imperial Navy. It could sail from the West Coast and fetch up at the Philippines in thirty-eight days (or twenty-two from Hawaii).[4] But the board refused to violate the Mahanian dogma of concentration; the navy had to operate en masse or face defeat in detail.[5] The battle fleet remained united in the Atlantic, poised against conjectural European threats until after World War I.

To sortie promptly, an expedition would have to be held in a high state of readiness. The Naval War College staff assumed conveniently that during a time of strained relations preceding war a compliant government would order full mobilization.[6] The General Board felt less sanguine, expecting timorous politicians to forbid mobilization, at least in overseas possessions, as Wilson had done during the 1913 scare.[7] Nevertheless, in 1914 it adopted Shoemaker's supposition that under duress civilian leaders would permit the working up of fleet and train in home ports.[8] Dewey swallowed his skepticism because the premise fitted his advocacy of diplomatic stalling while making ready (the same policy that was to be urged on the administration by military commanders in 1941). The rosy assumption licensed the planners to project a departure of the battleships only two to seven days after the outbreak of hostilities. Reserve vessels and much of the train could follow two weeks later, they reckoned, overruling bureau chiefs who counted on three months to ready all units and procure ordnance.[9]

The voyage of the Atlantic Fleet was to be an ambitious undertaking. As Roosevelt's expansion program neared fruition, the battleship roster rose from fourteen in 1906 to twenty-two in 1914. But it was an unbalanced fleet. Its complement of cruisers shrank from twenty or thirty (including armed liners) to only a dozen as old units were phased out, leaving destroyers to handle most of the scouting and screening chores. By 1914 thirty-five seaworthy destroyers, mostly oil-fueled, were available for the journey. Moving them in synch with the capital ships was a constant challenge to the planners because their 2,500-mile range fell short of the 3,000- to 3,500-mile segments of an optimized battleship advance. To assure a united fleet at the approaches to the Philippines, the "tin cans" would either travel separately with a mother depot ship to a rendezvous at the edge of the war zone or be taken in tow by large ships, a technique learned during the world cruise that conserved engines and fuel. Submarines, which were added to the expedition after the opening of the Panama Canal in 1914, were also short-legged problems;[10] ironically, when their endurance improved in later decades, they were severed from the fleet voyage and assigned to independent missions.

The fleet's rate of advance would depend on cruising speed and the duration and number of fuel stops, which conservative planners estimated at ten knots and pauses lasting one week apiece. Optimists pointed to the performance of newer battlewagons and improved coaling techniques and predicted a twelve-knot advance and three-day replenishments, thereby taking a month off the passage time.[11] The principal time determinant, however, would be the route of the voyage. The four possibilities were excruciatingly long, as shown in Table 9.1.

A commander in chief would face extraordinary difficulties at every stage of the trip. During the long passage to the fighting zone, his concerns would be fuel, upkeep, and the goodwill of powerful neutrals. During the final surge to a war base, speed, security, combat readiness, and destination would dominate his thoughts.

Naval planners initially advocated a track via the Suez Canal primarily because it was the shortest but also for its good weather and civilized amenities such as commercial ports, telegraph links, and an active coaling trade. Steaming around Africa was also an option; the weather was less certain and the facilities poorer, but secrecy would be easier to maintain. The Asiatic squadron, having fled Manila, would await the expedition in the Indian Ocean. A shuttle service of colliers over the same route would nurture it after arrival.[12]

But the Atlantic–Indian Ocean tracks were fraught with political complexities. Before the traumas of the World War neutral rights were scrupulously honored. According to the Hague Convention, only three warships of a belligerent power could enter a neutral port, and they could stay no more than twenty-four hours. They could not call again at any port of that nation within three months. Great Britain prohibited any men-of-war bound *toward* a combat zone from replenishing at

TABLE 9.1   *Typical Cruising Data, U.S. East Coast to Philippines, ca. 1910*

Route	Nautical miles	Days	Number of stops
Atlantic routes			
Via Suez	13,418	74	4
Via Cape of Good Hope	14,265	79	5
Pacific routes, by way of California and Hawaii			
Via Straits of Magellan	19,725	111	7 to 9
Via Panama Canal (after 1914)	11,772	65	3 to 5
Earth's semicircumference	10,825		

Source: GB 1910 Plan, 15–16; Panama estimated.

empire harbors except for emergencies or breakdowns.[13] The Blue commander would have to find havens without transgressing international rules. Planners compiled catalogs of sheltered bays along the way that had wide mouths and anchorages more than three miles (one marine league) offshore, the accepted limit of sovereignty.

The Atlantic route came under frequent challenge between 1907 and 1914. Sargent deemed it "madness" because Britain, Japan's ally, controlled the Suez Canal and most of the ports. Shoemaker pointed out that heavily laden battleships could not negotiate the shallow canal; they would have to round the Cape and meet the destroyers in the Indian Ocean, risking the attendant dangers and supply difficulties of dividing the fleet.[14] Williams fretted that an eastbound voyage would expose Hawaii to attack.[15] But the principal impetus for switching to a Pacific route came from the experience of the Great White Fleet.

During the 1907 immigration crisis with Japan, Roosevelt had decided to flaunt the new American navy in a display of Big Stick diplomacy. He dispatched sixteen battleships around South America, across the Pacific, and around the world. The immaculate white vessels, gold crests agleam on their bows, received thunderous ovations in every port of call, including Tokyo. They steamed forty-six thousand miles in 434 days, expending more powder in salutes than was ignited in all the battles of the Spanish-American War. The gala parade exhilarated the thrusters. Modern warships had proven sturdy. They were capable of steaming great distances with the ministrations of a small retinue of repair and cargo auxiliaries. But American ports of the

Pacific were found to lack the capacity to service the fleet under wartime conditions, and procurement of fuel had bedeviled the cruise. Forty-nine colliers, mostly British, had had to be chartered. They often turned up late with inferior coal. (Some suspected the English of trying to embarrass Uncle Sam.)[16] A fighting expedition would need reliable control of its fuel sources and deliveries.

After the world cruise, naval opinion tipped in favor of the route around South America and across the Pacific in spite of its distance. Prodded by Oliver, the college and the Second Committee blessed it in 1910 as the one option that would assure retention of Hawaii and minimize political vexations in transit. The armada could fuel in large embayments three miles off the coasts of Venezuela and Brazil. After passing the Straits of Magellan it could rely on the harbors of Chile and Peru because of a legal loophole that permitted depleted warships to load enough coal to reach their nearest national base, in this case Panama. If the rules of neutrality had to be violated, however, diplomacy and money would soothe the Latin republics more easily than they would touchy European powers.[17]

The formidable problems of coaling induced the planners to undertake a serious study of logistics, which became a feature of all Orange Plans. En route to the Orient the fleet would consume 197,000 to 480,000 tons of coal, depending on its size, speed, and path. Coal that produced high energy with low smoke output was mined only in Wales and Appalachia, not in the Pacific Basin. (Coal from the western states and Alaska was awful. The Australian product was so bad that 50 percent more was required per mile.) Delivery of good coal from the Atlantic would be a herculean task. Early twentieth-century colliers could haul 3,000 to 5,000 tons. The navy had only six, decrepit relics purchased in 1898, some rigged with sail. The U.S. mercantile marine had another thirty-seven, which were needed to serve railroads and industries. The NWC calculated that a hundred foreign bottoms would have to be purchased or chartered by agents fanning out ahead of the fleet.[18]

Transfer of coal afloat was a primitive process. Hundreds of sailors grubbed in the colliers' holds filling cloth drawstring bags, which were hoisted aboard warships, emptied on deck, and dropped down scuttle holes to the bunkers where other men leveled the piles with shovels. It was filthy work, "the bane of every crew's existence [that] helped explain the long standing nostalgia for sail among seamen."[19] At a rate of 10 to 30 tons per hour, it was hopeless to try to fill the 2,000-ton bunkers of a battleship except at shore loading towers. A recent invention promising greater efficiency, a marine transfer, mechanically hoisted the sacks and drew them along a horizontal boom to the receiving ships. Although it had been invented in the United States, the Blue navy experimented listlessly while the Royal Navy installed hundreds of the rigs aboard warships to feed from England's plentiful merchant colliers. The Russian fleet used them in 1904, as did German cruisers for looting captured prizes in World War I. But American experts reasoned that in the wide Pacific the navy would need large colliers fast enough to steam with the fleet and equipped with their own transfers. In 1908, after experiences reported by the Great White Fleet, the navy allocated an astonishing 59 percent of ship appropriations to building them.[20]

The rest of the fleet train could be relatively simple. American battleships were designed to carry ample food and stores for long cruises. Nineteen prime merchantmen were to be commandeered from U.S. shiplines for cargo haulage, hospital care, water distilling, and for use as tugs. The navy commissioned a repair ship and figured out how to convert steamers into safe ammunition carriers, a challenging task then and later. For troop movement, the few seagoing U.S. passenger liners could haul a regiment or two of marines (five to ten thousand men) with arms to secure an advanced base. (The corps commandant, remembering the crowded, unsanitary transports of the Spanish-American War, appealed for berths on the battleships.) After a few months, however, dispatch of up to one hundred thousand soldiers to the Philippines would require another armada of foreign ships.[21]

In 1912 Captain William Shoemaker, chief of staff of the Atlantic Fleet, arrived for duty on the General Board.[22] His creed that strategy had to conform to logistics, not vice versa as his contemporaries thought, was summed up in the slogan "communications dominate war."[23] Shoemaker drew up an Administrative Section of the Orange Plan that weaned the navy from relying on the largesse of foreign shipowners. The Panama Canal was about to open. He proposed stockpiling coal for the fleet at U.S. bases in Cuba and the Canal Zone, and in the Pacific Coast states and Hawaii, where naval depots already had enough loading capacity for a Pacific crossing. (A stop at Magdalena Bay, on the west coast of Mexico, was to be an optional convenience.) Shoemaker arranged inspections of civilian colliers and liners and parceled out mobilization chores to the bureaus and shore districts.[24]

By 1914 the problem of concentrating the fleet in the eastern Pacific had largely been solved. The remaining quandary was the route from

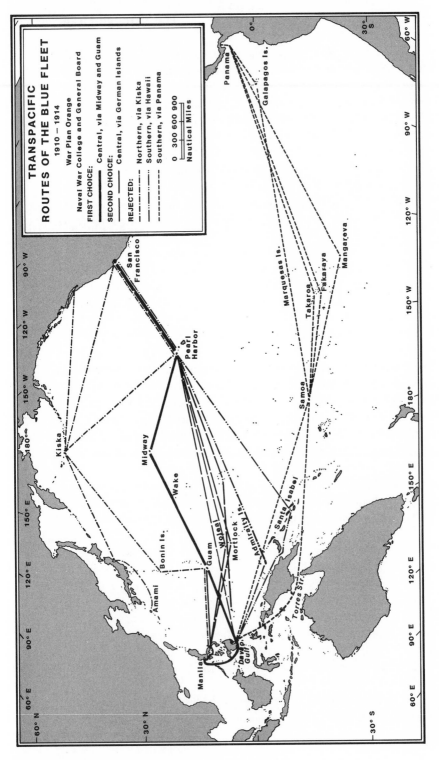

TRANSPACIFIC
ROUTES OF THE BLUE FLEET
1910 – 1914
War Plan Orange
Naval War College and General Board

FIRST CHOICE:
——— Central, via Midway and Guam

SECOND CHOICE:
——— Central, via German Islands

REJECTED:
–·–·– Northern, via Kiska
–··–··– Southern, via Hawaii
– – – Southern, via Panama

0 300 600 900
Nautical Miles

MAP 9.1

there to the Orient (see Map 9.1). The shortest track lay along the great circle by way of Alaska and the Aleutian Islands, but the vile weather and meager harbors of the region were daunting. An expedition from that quarter would find its advance parried by a shift of the enemy fleet to northern Japan.[25] Only Mahan, in his passion for a short war, prescribed the northern route. From a flanking position at Kiska in the western Aleutians, he said, the fleet could compel the withdrawal of any Japanese forces from Hawaii, then descend on Guam or even directly on the Ryukyus. He dismissed the climate, saying that white men thrived in the cold.

Commander Oliver was dismayed. A northern offensive, he protested, would be "playing the enemy's game for him." The cove at Kiska was minuscule and remote from any worthwhile objective. An Aleutian expedition could not menace Japan's territory or trade or entice its navy to battle and would strand itself if it tried. Mahan backed down. He had not appreciated the physical drawbacks, he alibied; he had been thinking of how to outflank Hawaii if it had fallen.[26] He forgot about the Aleutians and began lobbying for a base on Guam. Thereafter, the northern route was analyzed perfunctorily in most Orange Plans but was never again championed by a prominent strategist before the start of World War II. The most serious reconsideration took place in 1922, when Petropavlovsk, a large harbor on the Kamchatka Peninsula of Siberia, was available for seizure because Japan had occupied it during the Russian Revolution. But the idea of a base there was rejected because of vulnerability to air raids,[27] and, in any case, Japan soon withdrew from the place.

The South Pacific as an avenue of advance, either directly from Panama or via Hawaii, generated little enthusiasm. Even though the fleet would be relatively immune from attack in those remote seas, its journey would be excessively long. The United States had only the picayune harbor of Tutuila in Samoa and would have to risk offending an imperial power by coaling in French Polynesia, the British Solomon Islands, or the German Admiralty group. The planners agreed to relegate the South Pacific, like the Atlantic, to a supply lane for a Philippine war base.[28]

By 1914 it was agreed that the Phase II drive would cross the central Pacific, a course of strategic flexibility that used Hawaii's "immeasurably superior" position for concentration while assuring its safety.[29] But in the final stage of its journey the fleet would have to run a gauntlet of Orange attacks (unlike approaches through the narrow seas south of the Philippines, where Orange warships would dread being cut off).[30]

Oliver considered the final three thousand miles to constitute a war theater. Japan would use its "wearing down policy" to ravage the Blue armada by long-range cruisers from the Bonins and Guam and by torpedo boats near the Philippines.[31] Some planning essays envisioned a mid-ocean chain of raider nests across its path. During Japan's three months of free rein in the western Pacific it would occupy the "notoriously weak" islands of Guam, Midway, Wake, Kiska, and possibly Samoa to form, with its own outlying positions in the Kuriles, Bonins, and Marcus, a barrier from which cruisers would sally to blind U.S. scouts and wage "a vigorous offensive-defensive" far out at sea. They might summon the main fleet from Japan for opportunistic forays. If the Blue fleet got by, a continuous *guerre de course* would badger its supply cargoes all over the ocean.[32] When Mahan scoffed that one American army division could recoup the islands, Oliver retorted that Orange would gladly sacrifice a few men to ensnarl its foe in time-wasting actions for minor places.[33] Oliver's rudimentary vision of a Japanese oceanic defense line, adopted by the General Board in its 1914 Orange Plan,[34] was a prescient glimpse of future conditions when Japan fortified the Micronesian groups.

Breaking through the outer gauntlet would be of no avail unless the expedition reached the Philippines with its warships and train intact and with 125,000 to 225,000 tons of coal for a month or two of operations.[35] The Through Ticket plan required a refuge at the edge of the war zone where bunkers could be replenished and efficient means devised to transfer coal. But the new colliers were proving a disappointment. The first six could haul about 12,000 tons apiece but were slow travelers and could hand-load only 120 tons per hour. (They were later converted to supply and repair auxiliaries.)[36] By 1910, however, seven larger colliers, giant vessels as big as battleships, were laid down, beginning with the *Cyclops*. (Colliers were named for gods of the Roman pantheon.) With a "veritable forest of derricks and kingposts" rigged with high-speed winches and grab-buckets for direct dumping, their stability and long booms assured safe ladings at the astounding rate of 1,000 tons per hour. One collier could fill a battleship in a couple of hours, or load two simultaneously in four hours, or feed a torpedo boat in minutes. A few men on the winches replaced the shovel brigades. By 1914 naval colliers fitted with the rig could top up the fleet in any quiet haven. The planners expected to requisition enough fast civilian ships to bring the balance of the fuel quota with the fleet.[37]

There remained the quandary of finding a harbor where replenishment could take place within striking distance of the Philippines. Battleships of four thousand-mile range could not span the five thousand miles from Hawaii. The "unfortunate" torpedo craft would exhaust both their fuel and crews within twenty-five hundred miles; towing would be perilous but unavoidable.[38] Experiments at coaling vessels on the high seas had been in vain. In 1898 American warships had of necessity coaled at sea near Cuba, with terrible results. Their protruding gun sponsons punched holes in the flimsy colliers that pitched and rolled alongside. Other trials of passing coal in floating boxes or by overhead rope had failed. A clever system of running coal sacks along a tensioned aerial wire did enable two vessels to pass forty to sixty tons per hour while proceeding end-to-end under tow. That method was useful for British ships topping up in the North Sea but would have been of little use on a long ocean voyage.[39]

The want of a mid-Pacific haven was the greatest drawback of a Through Ticket movement. The American atolls west of Hawaii had no sheltered anchorages. Guam's harbor was too small. Japan owned no suitable islands that might be seized. But there were sailors' nirvanas in neutral hands. Streaming for two thousand miles along the route lay dozens of fine lagoons in German Micronesia that might afford safe and secret asylum and permit flexible itineraries. Between 1907 and 1914 three studies of the little-known islands were assembled by Williams, Pratt, and Shoemaker. (Williams had to rely on charts from the 1830s. A feeble attempt to promote an on-site inspection ended when the commander of the Pacific Station balked and intelligence officers warned of provoking German displeasure.)[40]

Replenishing the fleet in Micronesia would pose two substantial risks. First, it would violate international law. The problem might be avoided by coaling more than three miles from land, either adrift in the lee of a large island or at anchor on an open shelf extending offshore. A more efficient and safer evasion would be to enter a lagoon (assuming that narrow entries were not sovereign waters) and moor inside one league from dry land. Pratt believed such "legal" anchorages were abundant (see Map 9.2). For example, the lagoon of Kwajalein in the Marshall Islands, the world's largest atoll, was big enough for coaling several miles "off the reef." Eniwetok, also in the Marshalls, was reported to have a lagoon spacious enough to qualify as international waters and (erroneously) a seven-mile-wide entry.[41] The planners hoped that Berlin would not feel "kindly" toward Japan—England's Pacific ally—and would accept American encroachments "with complaisance." But if the kaiser sent gunboats to enforce strict neutrality, the fleet would have "very great" difficulty advancing.[42]

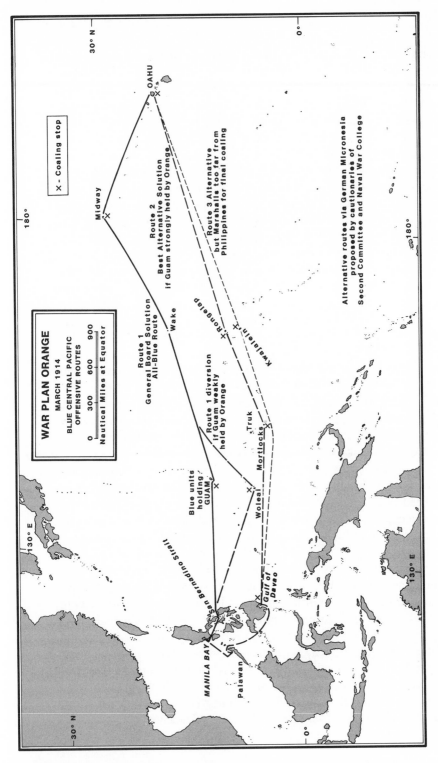

WAR PLAN ORANGE

MARCH 1914

BLUE CENTRAL PACIFIC
OFFENSIVE ROUTES

0 300 600 900
Nautical Miles at Equator

X – Coaling stop

Route 1
General Board Solution
All-Blue Route

Route 1 diversion
if Guam weakly
held by Orange

Blue units
holding
GUAM

Route 2
Best Alternative Solution
if Guam strongly held by Orange

Route 3 Alternative
but Marshalls too far from
Philippines for final coaling

Alternative routes via German Micronesia
proposed by cautionaries of
Second Committee and Naval War College

OAHU

Midway

Wake

Rongelap

Kwajalein

Truk

Mortlocks

Woleai

Gulf of
Davao

Palawan

San Bernadino Strait

MANILA BAY

30° N

180°

0° N

130° E

MAP 9.2

Second, a pause in Micronesia would be militarily perilous. The fleet would be stalked by Orange scout vessels equipped with wireless. Any lagoon might prove a trap, yet there would be no choice but to stop and replenish. Enemy submarines and torpedo boats might penetrate into the anchorage before the passes could be mined. Orange battleships maneuvering outside at high speed could obliterate artillery set up on perimeter islets and wreck the vessels pinned inside.

Only absolute secrecy could reduce the political and military risks to acceptable levels. The fleet could not stop at populated centers with radio stations such as Truk and Jaluit. It would have to seek out the merest reefs, places barely inhabited and rarely visited, like Woleai or the Hall group of the Carolines. Several Marshalls atolls also fit the bill but lay so far from the Philippines that fuel would be depleted again on the resumed journey. The best positions seemed to lie in the central Carolines, especially at the Mortlocks, an atoll cluster with dabs of land so tiny that legal anchorages were sure to be found and with narrow passages for easy defense and escape in two directions. Sheer remoteness would conceal the fleet at this vacant refuge, Shoemaker prayed, and allow it to "pass on before intelligence [could] reach any central authority or the outside world."[43]

Once safely past Micronesia, a Through Ticket fleet would face the dilemma of finding a haven in the Philippines. Thrusters boasted that the majestic battleships that had circled the globe would arrive "in better condition to meet an enemy than when they left home" and with no "imperative necessity" of overhaul. A coal dump on Corregidor would suffice for its needs, they claimed; even repair ships could be dispensed with because wounded ships would be able to limp home to California.[44] But realists appreciated that if the fleet dashed through the western Pacific under enemy persecution, it would arrive damaged and low in fuel. Since all ports of Luzon would be untenable, the convoy would have to make for a bay to the south.[45] (Cautionaries dreaded a politically inspired order to a "wasting effort" of relieving Corregidor.[46]) The General Board in 1911 conceded Williams's premise that Orange would be in control of all Philippine harbors[47] but three years later reverted to the congenial assumptions of still earlier plans that the fleet would somehow bull past all hazards to shelter at a defensible port where it would secure its communications. Since the Philippines were rich in such harbors, the choice could be made with an eye to future strategic maneuvers. A bold commander in chief might steam to Palawan, an island in the South China Sea only 250 miles from Manila, to block Orange forays south of Luzon and probe toward

Formosa, where the Imperial Navy might accept a fight. A more conservative admiral might select a bay on the south coast of Mindanao, far from real danger and easily supplied although ill-sited for aggressive operations. (Polillo, Fiske's favorite island off the east coast of Luzon, lay too close to the Orange stronghold at Manila.)[48] The locale of a southern Philippine base was to be intensively reviewed in the 1920s and once more in 1944, when the strategic pros and cons differed little from those cited in primeval Orange Plans.

To recap the evolution of the Through Ticket before World War I, naval strategists fixed on a direct central Pacific route both because of its advantages and the defects of other paths. (The army was deemed of little account in this operation and provided almost no input.) The government supported the choice by authorizing bases in the eastern Pacific, warships of longer range, and a train that would free the expedition from dependence on foreign help. The planners studied coaling on the move at secret islands. But the strategy was riddled with uncertainties: the fleet's dubious readiness for rapid sortie, reliance on neutral havens and stealth, and luck in finding a base on arrival. The long-term contribution of the Through Ticket to meeting the test of World War II was its emphasis on logistics. As Shoemaker put it, "A war with Orange demonstrates how absolutely all operations depend upon the logistics . . . the exacting, ever present questions of equipment, supply and communications. . . . If the means are lacking to insure the arrival of the full naval strength . . . where the decisive battles of the war must be fought, and to keep it adequately supplied in that area, it [will be an] overpowering national calamity."[49]

The Through Ticket's logistical hardships multiplied after the authorization of a huge battle fleet during World War I and its accelerated construction after the Armistice. Since Japan was undergoing a parallel naval growth, the Orange Plan was updated in 1917 by assigning far greater forces to the Blue advance. The fuel tonnage of the enlarged expedition was set at five to seven times the prewar estimates. The General Board, with Shoemaker back to guide it, multiplied the train tenfold to 646 vessels, including 494 colliers and tankers aggregating 2 million tons capacity and cubage for bountiful cargoes of base matériel and an expeditionary force swollen to half a million men.[50]

The problem of a bloated Through Ticket crossing was somewhat ameliorated by other contemporary trends. The U.S. merchant marine had been greatly expanded during the war. With German naval power gone, the fleet relocated its battleships to California in 1919 and 1922, reducing their wartime journey by four thousand miles. Op-12 worked up a list of ten desirable naval bases, mostly on the West Coast, which the Joint Board and the cabinet secretaries approved.[51] Congress cooperated in spirit, although it was so niggardly with funds that the battlewagons had to settle at San Pedro, a cramped seven-hundred-acre anchorage behind an artificial breakwater. There they remained for twenty years.[52] The fuel problem eased when the navy converted from coal to oil. Torpedo craft were adapted early in the century, and the first oil-fired battleship was designed before 1910. By the mid-1920s the conversion of the fleet was virtually completed. With turbines displacing relatively inefficient reciprocating engines, cruising ranges increased 40 to 50 percent. Rich petroleum fields in the western United States untethered the ships from Atlantic bases near coal mines. Since industrial refining assured uniform quality, oil for operations from a Philippine base might be purchased in wartime from the Dutch East Indies or Persian Gulf. Fuel transfer through flexible hoses from oilers, or from large to small warships, speeded replenishment in harbors (although experiments in open-sea fueling were not conclusive until shortly before World War II).

But the glaring deficiency of the Through Ticket remained the lack of real ocean bases. Oliver ranked Pearl Harbor first in development priority. It could hold at most three battleships and eight cruisers until a long-term dredging program gradually upped its capacity fivefold. Meanwhile, the great offensive convoy would have to assemble at the open roadstead of Lahaina Roads, off Maui.[53] For a base west of Hawaii the planners devoted their energies to promoting the arsenal at Guam. When the project was canceled by the treaty of 1922, the thrusters' formula seemed doomed to oblivion.

Lying ignored on their charts were the islands of Micronesia. During World War I they passed under Japanese control and were subject to a nonfortification agreement after the war. After 1914 a Blue expedition could openly take advantage of their splendid harbors, free of the old risks of offending neutrals or lapses of stealth. But the thrusting faction refused to grasp the opportunity. In 1919 the joint planners brushed off an occupation of Micronesia as a wasteful diversion from their Guam-centered strategy.[54] By 1922, however, with the status of both Blue and Orange Pacific islands altered by the treaty, the gate was opened to a different breed of strategist. It was the cautionaries' moment of opportunity.

10

● ● ● ●

The Cautionary Strategy

T he cautionary version of Phase II was a long time in coming. As enacted in World War II, it involved sequential occupations of islands adaptable as naval and air bases, not merely outposts for momentary servicing or resupply of convoys as in the Through Ticket. Though both attack formulas converged on a Philippine port where the United States would establish its largest outlying base, the cautionary strategy first emplaced such dockyards in the central Pacific.

In the central ocean Blue would be less handicapped by distances than in the Far East. Opening objectives were relatively nearer to U.S. and farther from Japanese naval stations, as shown in Table 10.1.

In 1907 Oliver first advocated "a gradual step by step advance" across the central Pacific. He envisioned it as a Blue salient pushing westward, anchored by flank positions in the South Pacific (Samoa) and the Aleutians (roughly as happened in World War II). He conceded that the strategy might seem "unduly cautious and slow," but it would conserve priceless capital ships, ease the logistical burden, and avoid the Japanese army. It was sure to bring success in "a long and exhausting war."[1]

Oliver's view was flawed, however, because he tied it to the expectation of prewar fortified bases at Hawaii, Guam, and Luzon. In 1909 Clarence Williams proposed the politically more realistic theme of establishing mobile mid-ocean bases as wartime launching pads to the Far East.[2] In actuality, however, no suitable positions were available until 1914. Among Japan's outlying islands, the Bonins had a useful small harbor, but it was heavily armed and mined and much too close to Tokyo for a secure U.S. base.[3] (In a 1925 novel of an imaginary Pacific war, Hector Bywater, a journalist and confidant of American admirals, imagined the bloody repulse of a Blue expedition assaulting the Bonins.[4]) Marcus Island and Iwo Jima had no harbors whatsoever and were rarely mentioned in Orange Plans.

Between Hawaii and Guam the United States owned a few uninhabited atolls that aroused the curiosity of naval officers. (In the early 1900s Japanese poachers visited most of them to slaughter sea birds for their plumage, which was in demand for stylish ladies' millinery, provoking naval-inspired diplomatic protests lest Tokyo seek to annex them.[5]) Midway, which was claimed in 1867 as the United States's first noncontiguous possession, was especially enticing. The navy had sought to develop it in 1869 as a coaling station in cooperation with the Pacific Mail Steamship Company "midway" along the route of its paddlewheel liners between California and the Orient. It told Congress that the island, having "one of the finest harbors in the world . . . [for] . . . an immense fleet of the largest vessels afloat," would be useful should the nation need to use naval force to protect its trade with Asia. In reality, Midway's wide lagoon was too shallow and foul except for a small pocket, Welles Harbor, that was storm-swept and barred to large ships by a submerged coral ledge. The hard rock defied blasting, and the navy abandoned the effort in 1870.[6] In 1903 the island was placed under naval administration and a cable repeater station was built there.[7]

Despite its deficiencies, Welles Harbor was visualized by early Orange planners as the prize in a seesaw struggle for cruiser bases in the leeward Hawaiian atolls. Strategically more important was an undersea shelf in the lee of Midway's reef upon which the entire battle fleet might anchor (at least seasonally when wintry gales didn't howl). In 1914 the General Board designated it as the "final resting place" of the fleet during an advance along an all-Blue route toward Guam.[8] A similar outside shelf at Johnston atoll, southwest of Hawaii, could hold 350 vessels at anchor.[9] After the havoc caused by U-boats during the

TABLE 10.1 *Distances and Ratios, Thrusting versus Cautionary Strategies*

Possible first objectives of Blue offensive	Distance from main base (nautical miles)		Distance ratio, Blue vs. Orange
	Blue[a]	Orange[b]	
Thrusting strategy			
Luzon	5,000	570	8.8 to 1
Mindanao	5,000	1,150	4.3 to 1
Cautionary strategy			
Before 1914			
Guam	3,300	1,500	2.2 to 1
After 1914			
Central Carolines	3,150	1,950	1.6 to 1
Western Marshalls	2,450	2,100	1.2 to 1
Eastern Marshalls	2,050	2,500	0.8 to 1

Note: There were no Orange main naval bases in Micronesia until around 1940.
[a] From Pearl Harbor.
[b] From home islands or Pescadores/Formosa.

World War, however, notions of open-sea anchorages were discarded from the plans.[10]

Wake Island, tantalizingly situated halfway between Midway and Guam, lacked any martial advantage whatsoever. Lieutenant Charles Wilkes, its first naval visitor, mapped it in 1841 during his renowned exploration voyages. He found that the sole passage into the shallow lagoon was barely knee-deep, while the fringing reef fell away so steeply that no bottom could be plumbed for offshore holding ground.[11] (Settlers of the 1930s told gullible newcomers that the island was shaped like a toadstool and might slide off its stem into the sea because it seemed to sway in the pounding surf.[12]) In 1899, at Bradford's insistence, the United States claimed Wake as a cable landing, but surveyors found no amenities, not even fresh water.[13] An army general who examined the atoll doubted if it had "much, if any" value for coaling.[14] Rear Admiral Robley Evans, however, thought that skillful seamen might improvise a way. In 1904, while steering the Asiatic Squadron back to Manila after a demonstration to cover Roosevelt's stage-managed revolution in Panama, he hove to at Wake. Observing calm seas, Evans mused of fueling a fleet while it drifted at the edge of the breakers.[15] This terrifying expedient was never adopted in an Orange Plan. The 1911 version speculated on a Japanese scouting post at Wake but envisioned no use by Blue,[16] and the 1914 Plan merely noted its position along the line of advance.[17] Wake and the other Blue atolls had to await the air age for serious consideration in the plan.

Guam was, by default, the only conceivable base between Hawaii and the Philippines, and it was the place to which cautionaries turned. Despite its deficiencies, they predicted great benefits to the side that controlled it. Japan would undoubtedly seize and prepare the island as a roadblock to compel the Blue navy to fight well short of its real objective and "seriously compromise" its strategy.[18] Orange cruisers from Guam might destroy the train, the 1911 Plan observed, "a calamity that would stagger the Blue fleet . . . if it did not in fact jeopardize the security of the fleet itself." If the expedition slipped safely by, the Orange marauders would "heavily handicap" its supply convoys as far away as Torres Strait, near Australia, and drain the fleet's combat power by forcing its cruisers to escort duty and patrols off Guam. But in American hands, the anchorage at Guam would be a godsend for nursing and mending the expedition to the Philippines. Blue men-of-war would steam forth from the haven to guard supply lines, divert Orange forces by threatening outlying bases or Japan itself, and crimp Japan's communications with the Philippines so badly as perhaps to compel withdrawal.[19]

Unfortunately, the hope of preserving Guam for American use was ill-founded. The War College staff in 1911 drummed up a stopgap defense by Asiatic Fleet monitors and destroyers with three thousand marines arriving, they hoped, before the outbreak. At Corregidor the men would just be excess mouths to feed; on Guam, though they would likely succumb, they would bleed the enemy and delay his other conquests.[20] Williams and the Second Committee, however, considered any defense futile and recommended against reinforcing the island.[21] The General Board concurred. The paltry police garrison was shrugged off with a worthless order to delay Japanese capture and fortification by a stand "obstinate and prolonged to the utmost limit."[22]

In the expectation that Guam would be lost, the essence of the cautionary strategy before World War I was to reclaim it by assault prior to advancing to the Philippines. On Williams's advice, the War College was asked in 1910 to design a campaign of recapture and the preparation of a base where reinforcing echelons would gather.[23] At Newport, Rodgers and Oliver decided the operation would be highly risky. Japan would fortify the island so massively, especially with the much-feared heavy mortars, that the United States would have to commit its entire expeditionary force. The fleet and transports would arrive with bunkers two-thirds depleted and no haven within reach if they failed to secure Apra Harbor. Rodgers and Oliver urged bypassing Guam and proceeding to the Philippines after fueling secretly in the Carolines. Orange, they were sure, would fail to discover the rendezvous or at least decline to risk its battleships so far from home bases. After arrival in the Philippines, Blue patrols could harass and bottle up enemy vessels at Guam, while heavy units guarding the convoy line would drop by to batter them. About six months into the war the superior Blue fleet, securely berthed in the Philippines within round-trip range, would return to occupy Guam.[24]

The bypassing recommendation displeased the thrusters of the General Board (and gave them further impetus to defrock the college war planners). In 1914 the admirals called for a plan of recapture during the fleet passage on about the sixtieth day of war. The Second Committee accepted the premise that Guam would be "obstinately defended" by Japan with large guns and mortars of improved precision and by warships poised in the Bonins. Blue would "pay dearly" in capital ships; or the attack might fail altogether. Nevertheless, the board insisted that it should proceed unless the carnage would be so awful as permanently to dissipate U.S. naval superiority. Yet the options the planners suggested for a defeated assault force were ludicrous. It might ignore losses and plunge forward if Orange were frantically evacuating the Philippines. It might retire to Kiska and commence a dreary campaign against northern Japan. It might about-face and return to the war zone via the Atlantic! Such absurdities branded the board's exercise as another ploy of the Guam lobby to justify a fortified base.[25]

Over the next eight years American strategists reargued the pros and cons of making Guam the first objective. In 1917 the General Board decided that in its pristine state the island would be worthless to the expanding navies of both sides. Japan would not fight hard to keep it, and Blue would gain little by retaking it.[26] In 1919 the Joint Board resuscitated the tale of a gory assault degenerating into a long war unless Guam were prepared in peacetime as an arsenal of "decisive influence."[27] In yet another plea for a Gibraltar, Op-12 warned in 1921 that it would be "absolutely necessary" to recapture Guam despite "many costly losses"; pausing first to develop a base in Micronesia would only worsen matters by granting Orange more time to fortify Guam. The result might be a stalemate that would severely test the resolve of the American people.[28]

The Washington Treaty of February 1922 demolished all hopes of a Fortress Guam. Later in the year, Williams, as director of war plans, wrote finis to the island as a major objective by proposing the stepwise campaign through Micronesia. If a commander in chief established a mobile base at Truk as Williams proposed, he would realize that Apra could shelter only "detachments" of his mighty fleet. It would be "of no value" as a main base. "Years would be required to develop it during war," the director said. A wise CinC would choose to shun an expensive battle merely to eradicate an Orange submarine nest and gain an "auxiliary" post for his raiders. He would isolate Guam and move on.[29]

For eight years before the treaty, the thrusters had conspired to suppress a cautionary drive through Micronesia, which Japan had seized in 1914. Those islands were to become the focal points of Phase II campaign strategy both before and during the Second World War. Without them a viable offensive plan against Japan would not have been possible, at least until 1941, when the United States acquired allies and access to their territories in the Pacific.

The three archipelagos of Micronesia (Greek for "tiny islands") contain a hundred islands aggregating a mere 716 square miles of land sprinkled across an area of the North Pacific equal in extent to the continental United States. (The Gilberts, a British protectorate south of the equator, were ethnographically Micronesian but are excluded from the definition here.) The Mariana Islands had been Spanish fiefdoms since Magellan discovered them in 1521 and the Caroline Islands since the 1600s. The Marshall Islands had been colonized by German planters and traders in the nineteenth century and were declared a protectorate of Berlin in 1885.[30] After World War I the groups were known as the Japanese Mandated Islands or simply the Mandate. Between the wars they supported one hundred thousand residents, half native islanders and the rest mostly Japanese. U.S. plans referred to both the islands and the surrounding seas as the Mandate.

The groups were physically and strategically different (see Table 10.2). The Marianas, named for Queen Maria Anna of Spain, stretched northward from Guam (which was geographically but not politically a member of the group) halfway to Tokyo. They were rugged, relatively large volcanic islands; Saipan and Tinian were forty to fifty square miles in extent. But they had no lagoons. The sole roadstead, at Saipan, was worse than Guam's petty harbor. Thus though they lay within round-trip steaming range of the Philippines, U.S. naval planners usually overlooked the Marianas except as flank guards for the fleet's advance. Their decisive role in World War II was owing to the advent of the long-range strategic bomber in 1944–45.

The Carolines, the most extensive archipelago, were named for Spain's King Charles II. The fifty-five islands spanned two thousand

TABLE 10.2 Islands of Micronesia Important in Plan Orange, Geographical Data

Islands	Type[a]	Number of islands and islets	Areas (square statute miles)			Population, 1935	
			Land total	Largest islet	Lagoon	Native	Other
Marianas							
Saipan	H	1	47.5	47.5	0	3,282	20,290
Tinian	H	1	39.3	39.3	0	25	14,108
Uracas	H	1	.8	.8	0	0	0
Carolines, Eastern							
Kusaie	H	5	42.3	42[b]	c	1,189	31
Ponape	C	26	129.0	125[b]	69	5,601	2,499
Carolines, Central							
Truk	C	98	38.6	13.2	822	10,344	1,992
Mortlocks (Nomoi)	A	83	3.6	0.6	175	2,200	17
Hall Islands	A	62	1.4	0.2	257	445	0
Carolines, Western							
Woleai	A	22	1.7	0.6	11	570	1
Yap	C	15	38.7	35[b]	10	3,713	392
Ulithi	A	49	1.8	0.4	210	433	1
Palaus	C	343	188.3	153.2	479	5,679	6,760

Marshalls, Southern and Eastern

Wotje	A	75	3.2	0.7	241	590	10
Maloelap	A	75	3.8	0.9	376	460	3
Majuro	A	64	3.5	2.0	114	782	3
Mili	A	92	6.2	1.2	295	515	4
Jaluit	A	91	4.4	1.0	266	1,989	433

Marshalls, Northern and Western

Taongi	A	10	1.3	0.6	30	0	0
Bikar	A	7	0.2	0.1	14	0	0
Eniwetok	A	44	2.3	0.4	388	94	0
Bikini	A	36	2.3	0.7	229	159	0
Rongelap	A	61	3.1	0.8	388	98	0
Kwajalein	A	93	6.3	1.1	839	1,079	6

U.S. Islands

Guam	H	1	206	206	0	20,177	2,113[d]
Midway	A	2	1.4	1.0	21	0	28[d]
Johnston	A	2	.05	.04	11	0	0
Wake	A	3	2.9	2.2	3	0	0[d]

Source: E. H. Bryan, Jr., comp., Guide to Place Names in the Trust Territory of the Pacific Islands (Honolulu: Bernice P. Bishop Museum, 1971). U.S. islands calculated from pre–World War II maps.

[a] H = high island; A = atoll; C = complex (high plus reef islets).
[b] Estimated.
[c] Harbors only.
[d] Prior to airline station.

miles of sea in an east-west direction. At the eastern extremity lay Kusaie and Ponape, large, mountainous islands with minor harbors. The gem of the central Carolines was Truk, a "complex" cluster of steep islands (the peaks of sunken mountains) inside a lagoon encircled by a coral seawall a hundred miles in circumference that could accommodate the largest imaginable naval base. At the western end of the Carolines another complex group, the Palaus, were also suitable for a fleet base but strategically less important because many useful harbors lay just beyond in the Philippines. Between and around the major Carolines were speckled many atolls, a few with spacious lagoons.

The Marshalls were named for Captain William Marshall, a less royal personage who happened to sail by. On a map they look like loops of beads carelessly tossed on a floor. (Table 10.1 subdivides them into strategic sectors rather than the two chains customarily described by geographers.) The thirty-one atolls are narrow reefs lined with dozens of islets with a total area of only seventy square miles. A typical atoll contains two to six square miles of sandy land rising barely ten feet above sea level. Even the largest islets, rarely greater than one square mile, were considered inadequate for a major shore base. But Marshalls lagoons are ample and some are vast—two to three hundred square miles of calm waters, large portions of which are deep and unfouled by shoals. The coral reefs enclosing them were boons to navies. The windward sides grow stout, nourished by current-borne nutrients. On the lee sides waves erode the coral in places to form deep natural channels.[31] Such atolls could serve as excellent mid-ocean anchorages for floating logistical trains. In the air age the flat, elongated islets and smooth seaplane fairways became priceless assets. In the Marshalls geography would uniquely favor the U.S. advance because the group lay closer to the Blue main base at Hawaii than to those of Japan and because defenders would have to disperse themselves among many islands while attackers could concentrate their efforts.

Before 1914 American planners had frequently speculated on Micronesia's strategic utility. During the Spanish-American War Dewey had recommended taking one of the Carolines as a coaling station in lieu of Guam.[32] The Navy War Board, prodded by influential missionary societies that had founded churches there, considered diverting troopships bound for Manila to occupy the group. The army balked because of the lack of naval escort and means of communicating.[33] When the war ended, they were still in Spanish hands. At the peace conference Royal Bradford, the navy's logistical conscience, urged that at least one Caroline Island be claimed for strategic needs:[34] "Of what value will be a fleet of fifty magnificent ships of war on the Pacific coast if the enemy is located in the China Sea and there is not a chain of coaling-stations . . . ? Why, without them the fleet will be helpless. . . . In possession of a hostile nation, [the Carolines] are capable of becoming very formidable naval bases from which attacks on the line of communication [to] the Philippines can be made."[35]

Telegraph companies were also eager to get island stations for a government-subsidized cable to the Philippines. Roosevelt and his naval advisers insisted that the cable follow an all-Blue route. But a thirty-five-hundred-mile uninterrupted span from Hawaii to Guam would have reduced profits intolerably because transmission rates fell off as the square of the distance between repeater stations. Of the uninhabited American atolls, only Midway proved suitable.[36] By November 1898, when President William McKinley directed the peace commissioners to purchase one of the Carolines for the cable, Germany had negotiated a deal with a bankrupt Spain to buy them all. The Americans backed away.[37] Berlin then offered to swap a Marshall atoll for one of the Sulu group of the southwestern Philippines. Bradford, who was also an expert on cable systems, contemptuously dismissed the Marshalls as ill-sited and useless for any purpose, while he thought the Sulus were essential for defending the Philippines.[38] Desultory negotiations continued through 1899 until an imbroglio over colonial rights in Samoa soured U.S.-German relations.[39] Bradford had been right to sneer at the first German offer of Taongi, a low reef said to be awash,[40] but he sorely underestimated the strategic virtues of Berlin's second offer, Eniwetok. That strategically located atoll had a vast lagoon with two deep passages and land sufficient for a base. (One may wonder at the subsequent history of the Pacific if the United States had gotten Eniwetok and Germany a port in the Sulus, which Japan might have seized in 1914.)

World War I affected the planning of a Blue-Orange conflict in many ways: expansion of fleets and merchant marines by both antagonists, the proving of submarines and aircraft, and especially the Japanese annexation of Micronesia, where those attrition weapons might offset America's naval dominance and cause its defeat.

Until 1914 Japan had shown no military curiosity about islands more than a thousand miles from its coast. Occasional American anxieties about its supposed designs on Hawaii or the Blue atolls had little basis in fact. Notwithstanding some empire-minded publicists, Japan's pursuits in Micronesia had been peaceably commercial.[41] But the war in Europe offered an irresistible opportunity. At the outbreak, Great

Britain needed protection for troops and cargoes heading to its aid from Australia because a formidable German cruiser squadron commanded by Admiral Graf Maximilian von Spee was at large in the Pacific. Tokyo obliged its ally by declaring war and seizing the Germans' only base, at Kiaochow, in China. Von Spee was foiled from executing his mission of *Kreuzerkrieg* (cruiser warfare). He fled toward Cape Horn and home, feeding from colliers at remote Micronesian islands that had neither facilities nor fortifications. He destroyed a British squadron off Chile only to be annihilated by a superior force at the Falkland Islands in December 1914.

Allied squadrons groping about the Pacific for von Spee turned to imperial aggrandizement. Australian troops occupied the kaiser's South Pacific realms of Bougainville, New Britain, the Admiralty Islands, Nauru, and the German sectors of Samoa and New Guinea. The British Admiralty hoped they would seize Micronesia as well. But Tokyo acted first. In the autumn of 1914, two Japanese naval squadrons, allegedly hunting for von Spee, methodically hoisted the Rising Sun over the German islands of the North Pacific long after he had departed. Britain, alert to Australia's anxieties, asked Japan to halt at the equator and refused its assistance in taking the southern colonies, ostensibly to avoid the protocol of an Australian serving under a senior Japanese admiral but in reality to block further penetration.[42]

After the occupation, pride and strategic advantage nudged the Japanese government toward a claim of permanent ownership. Its wish was assured in February 1917 in a bargain with Britain, which badly wanted destroyers in European waters. Japan agreed to send a flotilla in exchange for retention of its spoils. Foreign Secretary Arthur Balfour concurred and obtained the consent of other Allied nations to allow retentions of all occupied colonies, including, of course, those seized by British Empire forces. He acted quickly because, as the War Cabinet noted, "The possible entry into the war of the United States of America increased the necessity for an early decision in regard to [Micronesia] in order to avoid negotiations on the subject with another power." Britain's haste smacked of a sinister motive: to weaken America's strategic position in the Pacific in case of postwar rivalry. The United States, on the verge of gaining a voice in alliance policies, deserved better consideration. Only later did Secretary of State Robert Lansing learn of the deal assuring Japan of its "souvenirs."[43]

American strategists well understood the "prime importance" to the Orange Plan of Japan's souvenirs.[44] Cautionaries regarded them as manna in the wilderness. The requisites of a stepping-stone offensive, a line of mid-ocean harbors available for seizure in wartime, had suddenly materialized. Shoemaker, backed by Williams and the junior staff officers of the General Board, applauded the situation in August 1914 even before the Japanese marines had landed: "If all the German possessions in the South seas went to Orange, and Blue had the stronger fleet, Blue would be in a better position to carry war across the Pacific. . . . For the islands required for war operations would always be at the disposal of the stronger force on the spot. [To] fortify all islands, in the Marshall and Caroline groups and . . . to make Pacific Gibraltars . . . is far beyond the resources of Orange."[45] The U.S. advantage would be still sweeter if the islands were disarmed and left ripe for plucking.

To the majority of naval leaders (who were also thrusters), however, Japan's action was a calamity. Mahan wrote to Assistant Secretary of the Navy Franklin Roosevelt to plead for a vigorous protest through London, warning of the "very critical" situation America would face if Japan stood permanently astride its communications to Guam and the Philippines. Mahan visited Washington late in 1914 but was unable to see Roosevelt. He died a few weeks later.[46] Perhaps Roosevelt remembered in May 1940, as German armies once again massed before Paris, when he ordered the American fleet to Hawaii to intimidate Japan from grabbing European colonies again.

The aging sea dogs whom Roosevelt called the "old lady dowagers" of the navy closed ranks.[47] To the Guam lobby, Japanese possession of the Marianas posed "a perpetual menace" to their cherished Gibraltar. Through Ticket advocates despaired of a dash to the Philippines when once-vacant lagoons of the Marshalls and Carolines would be spiked with mines and torpedo craft and homes to scouts with high-powered wireless. The Battle of the Atlantic was demonstrating the vulnerability of sea lanes, raising specters of Orange submarine and surface raiders lurking in the mid-Pacific. The admirals demanded relief. Rear Admiral Alfred P. Niblack, guilelessly thinking the British would favor American control, declared Micronesia "absolutely within our strategic frontier, on our Pacific coastline, as it were." The General Board needled the CNO to demand U.S. annexation and arming of the islands.[48] OpNav's young planning staff suggested that Japan might yield them if granted a "free hand" in revolution-torn Siberia.[49] At the State Department sympathetic diplomats and consultants proposed odd schemes such as awarding the islands to a trustworthy third power, or to a minor nation, or returning them to Germany and later buying them by waiving indemnity payments.[50]

The protesters were out of touch with reality. Woodrow Wilson felt "comparatively slight" concern about Micronesia because a claim would violate his pledge that America sought no territory and because he favored withdrawal from the Philippines anyway.[51] Some naval planners warned that a heavy-handed attempt to strip Japan of its winnings would arouse undying enmity—a "gratuitous affront," according to one diplomat.[52] Stanley K. Hornbeck, the State Department's loudest voice on Far Eastern affairs, and other like-minded advisers, recommended internationalizing the islands under the aegis of a proposed League of Nations. The General Board regarded the idea as a desperate last resort, but it fit the president's instincts.[53]

The chief of naval operations cast his lot with the renegade cautionaries. Admiral William S. Benson had been elevated to the job from an obscure career, to the annoyance of more senior admirals, because he would kneel to the will of Secretary Daniels. Not "one of the bright men in the navy,"[54] Benson had previously played no hand in Pacific strategy. After the Armistice he set off for the Peace Conference of Versailles, taking along Captain Frank H. Schofield of his planning staff to prepare the navy's position papers.[55] Schofield, who was to dominate war planning ten years later, earned a medal there for "exceptionally meritorious service in a duty of great responsibility."[56] At Versailles the naval advisers sagely recommended conceding Japan's control of Micronesia subject to a demilitarization clause, which would achieve the strategic advantages that Shoemaker had foreseen in 1914. The undefended islands would lay "hostage" to Blue naval strength. The recommendation was blessed by Colonel Edward M. House, Wilson's confidant. The president suspected that a "grab game" was going on beneath the veil of trusteeships of former German colonies known as League of Nations Mandates, but he acknowledged Japan's claim to get its consent to demilitarization. On 28 June 1919 the Treaty of Versailles awarded the islands as a Class C Mandate to be governed as an integral part of the Japanese Empire. Japan promised not to erect "military or naval bases . . . or fortifications." Its naval leaders were assuaged because the islands could be fortified in wartime, and meanwhile they represented bargaining chips for subsequent negotiations on Pacific security.[57]

A myth has grown over the years that the Mandate award was a dreadful setback for America's strategic position. England's doyen of modern naval history believed that the United States "had virtually surrendered to Japan the dominance of the central and western Pacific." Other "naval authorities" declared that Japan gained "national immunity from naval coercion by sea."[58] They were wrong. Benson and his staff demonstrated "naval statesmanship at its highest level."[59] They had the wisdom to see a demilitarized Mandate as a highway for a cautionary offensive rather than a barrier to an impossible direct thrust across the Pacific.

The die-hard thrusters and the Guam lobby—often the same officers—did not yield gracefully. For three more years they obstructed any attempt to shift to a gradualist offensive. They indulged in an odd belief that Japanese control was illegal and could be undone because U.S. diplomats apparently had thought that the dispositive authority was to be the council of Allies rather than the League of Nations.[60] Admiral Hugh Rodman urged the navy to pursue "redistribution and equal division at least" with Japan.[61] Captain Lusius Bostwick, second director of war plans, tried to bend a treaty clause on "free and open communications" pertaining to a cable station on the island of Yap into a right of naval transit in the Mandate.[62] But the United States had forfeited its leverage by declining to join the League.

By the eve of the Washington Conference on disarmament in late 1921 the General Board's mind-set had degenerated to outrage. The Mandate agreement did not explicitly forbid movable weapons such as mines and submarines or quasi-military structures such as fuel dumps and repair yards. The board was certain that eventually Japan would claim unfettered sovereignty and fully prepare the islands for war. The United States was therefore entitled to access and inspection in peace and war. Japan's refusal, the admirals said, would indicate a plot, permitting America to take over those islands "most suited to our strategic needs."[63]

The shellbacks of the navy knowingly ignored the value of the Mandate settlement to a cautionary plan because to concede a campaign via mobile bases would undermine both the Fortress Guam and Through Ticket orthodoxies. The General Board had amended its prewar Orange Plan only to acknowledge the islands as "possible assets" in trifling ways. The Carolines, for example, might afford bases for American cruisers, while Blue submarine and destroyer stations in the Marshalls would help the battlewagons and their communications as they thundered to the hallucinatory base at Guam. The board slyly deflected talk of a mobile fleet base in the Mandate by declaring the only suitable site to be in the Palaus,[64] a group that could not be reached without a prior stop and that was strategically unimpressive because of its proximity to the Philippines. When Rodman, the CinC of the Pacific Fleet, who had once cruised in Micronesia, proposed a wartime fleet base at Truk,[65] Commander Pye of the Planning Division countered that it would be better to develop Guam into "a first class naval base . . . in the same general vicinity" and avoid international complications.[66] The board did concede that at least five Mandates harbors could accommodate a "great fleet" better than Apra[67] but scarcely admitted the utility of seizing one and then only as a prelude to retaking Guam. Yet if Guam were so unattractive, why bother with it? Squirming to reconcile the paradox, the admirals tendered the hoary case for holding a prepared citadel.[68]

In October 1921, as the conference approached, Op-12 shifted to a politically more realistic cautionary posture. According to Pye, the Mandate was completely legal, but in wartime the United States could occupy it. Secretary of the Navy Edwin Denby acknowledged that Japanese suzerainty was "undoubtedly advantageous."[69] Accepting this mature counsel, Secretary of State Charles Evans Hughes refrained from challenging the Mandate award except tangentially to prod Japan on other issues. After the conference the United States conceded the Mandate's legality and dropped all pretense of shared rights. Japan promised open commercial access and reaffirmed the nonfortification pledge.[70]

The treaties of Versailles and Washington undid fifteen years of U.S. war planning. Article XIX of the latter agreement crushed the dream of Fortress Guam. The Mandate award outmoded a Through Ticket rush via surreptitious havens. The time had come for American strategists to take up the cautionary alternative.

In the summer of 1921 Rear Admiral Clarence Stewart Williams took command of the War Plans Division and installed a competent staff that included such eminent future wartime planners as Wilson Brown and Russell Willson and Major Holland M. Smith, USMC. Unremembered today—no portrait hangs in Newport's hall of college presidents—the stubby admiral was the most astute campaign strategist of the pre–World War II era. He had graduated in the top 10 percent of his Naval Academy class (the highest standing of the first dozen war plans directors). He had gone to sea in every class of warship and risen to command squadrons of dreadnoughts. He had toured the Naval War College as a student in the coveted long course and as chief of staff. As head of a joint committee, he had judiciously recommended in 1916 that the army retain its coast artillery (a naval arm in most countries) to assure that the fleet would remain free of static defense obligations. Before the war he had introduced the General Board to the study of Micronesia and to the strategic criteria of an island-hopping advance. Williams had the right temperament for a war planner: analytical, mature in judgment, unswayed by eloquence, yet a good listener who demanded facts and asked penetrating questions. On the board they had called him "the Oracle" for his grasp of the future. His classmates had dubbed him "Parson" for his sober demeanor, yet his eye held a twinkle when he spun a sailor's yarn.[71]

During Williams's tenure, from July 1921 to September 1922 (which bracketed the Washington Conference), Phase II of the Orange Plan was recast into a cautionary advance through the Mandate. The strategy was laid out in half a dozen papers that he orchestrated rather than in a single official plan, an example of how strategies came forth in the multipolar American planning system. Among the seminal papers were Estimates of the Blue-Orange Situation submitted by students and staff of the Naval War College class of 1921, which included two future Op-12 directors.[72] Williams kept in touch with Sims, the college president, and probably invited the estimates. (Sims had wanted Williams for his Strategy Department, rating him the equal of the next two contenders combined.[73]) A year earlier Sims had told a hostile General Board that Guam was useless and that a major fleet base in the Mandate would be essential for a return to the Philippines.[74] Williams tested the stepwise strategy with the board as it gathered advice for the diplomats until he was sidetracked—no doubt by Coontz—to a distasteful casting of a Mandate occupation simply as a prelude to reclaiming Guam.[75] After the conference, the army prodded Assistant Secretary Theodore Roosevelt, Jr., to urge a full revision of Plan Orange.[76] He probably expected a broad pronunciamento on national policy from the General Board. What he got was a tightly reasoned campaign plan from the WPD. On 1 September 1922 the division submitted a far-reaching Estimate of the Situation Blue-Orange, an unsigned document bearing the unmistakable style and imprint of Williams.[77] (The Director had hoped to process it through the Joint Planning Committee, but army planners seemed paralyzed after the defense freeze in the Philippines.[78]) A few months later, the CNO and Secretary Denby approved the estimate, with modifications, to serve as the foundation of a formal War Plan Orange.[79] Additional logistical data were supplied by Op-12's specialists and the Board for Development of Navy Yard Plans.[80] Rich operating details were presented in a brilliant paper entitled "Advance Base Operations in Micronesia" by Major "Pete" Ellis, USMC, an enigmatic figure and a legend in the

Marine Corps today, whose mentor, Commandant John A. Lejeune, adopted the study as the foundation of a doctrine for assault landings.[81]

The strategy of the cautionaries was conceptually simple. The navy's customary mission of gaining control of the western Pacific required both a superior fleet and advanced bases to serve it. But the Philippines and Guam could not be held, and the latter was physically unsuitable. A Through Ticket sprint to the Philippines would be a desperate gamble entailing hasty preparation, uncertain destination, and vulnerable communications. Blue control of the central Pacific, however, would assure it of "free foot" because there an offensive could proceed in jumps of moderate length and at a flexible pace consistent with logistical means. America's "natural line of advance" led through the Mandate. Without those islands, a Blue offensive would be "practically impossible."[82]

The navy felt it was under no legal or ethical restraint just because the islands were nominal wards of a world organization. Pye had coaxed the State Department to confirm this belief, warning that if the navy were unable to target them in war it would press embarrassingly for annexation.[83] Williams put the morality issue to rest permanently; the League, he predicted, would ignore Japanese complaints and U.S. propaganda would dissuade other powers from criticism.[84]

The naval geography of the Mandate had been analyzed several times since Williams first compiled war routes in 1907. By 1914 the planners had identified harbors of refuge for a Through Ticket fleet and calculated trade-offs among distance, security, and logistics. A nonstop advance to the western Carolines made no sense because of distance and the gauntlet of Orange squadrons en route. Williams had preferred Truk for its central location and security, although other analysts thought it still too forward for cruising range and safety. The Marshalls were a "happy mean," within reach of small ships and far from perils, where many a fine lagoon offered flexible choices, but the run from there to the Philippines would require another stop in a dangerous place.[85] In 1914 Shoemaker pointed out the benefits of multistage movements of sensible length, with a first replenishment in the safe northwestern Marshalls and a full servicing in the central Carolines before moving on to the Philippines.[86] His geographical reasoning presaged the cautionary plans adopted in 1922, the 1930s, and World War II of a gradual crossing of the Pacific in steps of convenient intervals to balance aggressiveness with security.

The campaign was to commence with a steady mobilization of the fleet and train in Hawaii. The armada of 1922 was to be far larger than that of earlier Orange Plans, ultimately nearly eight hundred vessels. The fleet had grown enormously since the war, and the mercantile marine had burgeoned from 557,000 registered tons in 1910 to 17 million tons. The campaign would no longer depend on foreign bottoms, although it would absorb 35 percent of U.S. civilian tonnage and nearly all the country's tankers because the fleet was 80 percent oil-fired by that date.[87]

On the sixty-first day of war (D+60) the expedition would set sail to acquire an advanced fleet base in the Marshall Islands (see Map 10.1), specifically at Eniwetok, westernmost atoll of the group, a splendid potential base that Williams had nominated as "the first choice" as early as 1907.[88] The 2,375-mile voyage would be feasible for the smallest warships and would give a wide berth to other Japanese islands. The naval cautionaries anticipated easy pickings because Japan would refuse to expose capital ships so far from home and the Blue fleet would squelch any lesser craft that dared appear.[89] It had long been an article of faith that an atoll could not withstand naval power because it could be swept everywhere by fire.[90] (The belief was probably heightened by the slapstick adventures of a marine squad that had blown up its gun magazines while encamped on Midway fifteen years earlier.[91]) Ellis warned, however, that Japan would rush troops to the atolls to mount "universal shore resistance," especially "stacked-up" defenses of the three best lagoons of Eniwetok, Jaluit, and Wotje. Blue ships would be forced into "long-drawn-out operations" in support of beachheads, and they would fall prey to attrition by torpedo, mine, and aircraft. Orange would, in effect, pit its army against Blue sea power. To foil that stratagem Ellis urged simultaneous landings on a "broad front" of several islands, tactics assuring speedy victories ashore, and dispatch of Blue capital ships on forward interdiction cruises to assure theater sea control. The marines would have to make do with secondary naval support.

Ellis's description of the method of assaulting an armed atoll like Eniwetok was a military classic. Following an aerial reconnaissance, troopships would arrive in the lee of the island under cover of darkness and offload at dawn. Orange might waft poison gas downwind and submarines might take a toll, but he reckoned the attack would proceed even if a third of the force were lost. Air strikes—from where he did not say—and naval bombardment from ships on the flanks of the transports would keep enemy troops pinned to one or two fortified islets. Because it would be impossible to debark in the surf of a seaward reef,

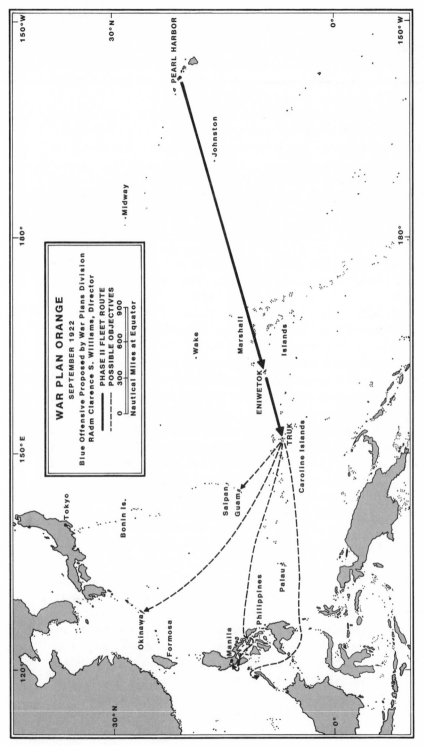

WAR PLAN ORANGE
SEPTEMBER 1922
Blue Offensive Proposed by War Plans Division
RAdm Clarence S. Williams, Director

PHASE II FLEET ROUTE
POSSIBLE OBJECTIVES

0   300   600   900

Nautical Miles at Equator

MAP 10.1

minesweepers would clear a path into the lagoon. Artillery would be lightered to empty islets. Then the defended islets would be assaulted by the main echelons, three waves of combat-loaded marine units in strings of towed ships' boats (a far cry from the tough landing craft of World War II). The battle, Ellis declared, would "entirely succeed or fail practically on the beach." Movement inland and mopping up would conclude it in a few days. After the main bases were won, the rest of the Marshalls, probably defended lightly or not at all, would be occupied and denied to Orange.

Eniwetok would immediately be adapted as Base One (known also as B-1 or X-1) to service the returning fleet. As long as Blue controlled the sea, a Japanese counterinvasion of B-1 would be impossible, but a brigade with five- and eight-inch guns would stand guard to repel raids while nets, mines, and listening devices shielded the passes. Sixty light warships would patrol the island and escort convoy traffic. Forty-eight landplanes would be essential to the defenses because primitive antiaircraft guns could at best keep bombers at a respectful height.[92]

Two weeks after the victory, the fleet would sail eight hundred miles westward to Truk, the island that Japan had used as naval headquarters during the occupation of Micronesia and that was to become its main oceanic base of World War II.[93] U.S. planners had long admired the great lagoon with its high islands that could protect ships from gunfire.[94] Admiral Rodman had listed among its security features mineable entrances and surrounding atolls for small craft and airplane stations.[95] Since the Japanese would also recognize these attributes, the campaign would be a "long and laborious undertaking." Ellis, though omitting a detailed battle outline, observed that rugged peaks would favor a many-layered defense and counterattacks by enemy reserves. At Truk Blue would have to expose first-line battleships, not just obsolescent pre-dreadnoughts, to the ravages of submarines, mines, and uncharted reefs. But in time, working from havens at outlying atolls, it would reduce Truk by sustained pressure. Afterward Blue would need to clear out the high Carolines—Kusaie and Ponape because they might threaten Eniwetok, the Palaus and Yap to assure the neutering of Guam. The contest for the Carolines would be long and brutal.

Truk was to be fashioned into permanent Base Two, a fleet harbor with lavish shoreside facilities and with airfields and other strong defenses to fend off sea attack. (It would lie beyond reach of 1922-vintage bombers.) Its communications, however, might be plundered by Japan's long-range battle cruisers. Blue would have to deploy old battleships and cruisers against them to avoid scattering its modern battle line.[96]

The most disputatious aspect of the cautionary plan was the time it projected for equipping Truk as "a central point for operations to secure and support advanced bases nearer the trade routes."[97] Optimists expected that service and industrial facilities could be ready for a westward movement on D+180.[98] But Williams objected to advancing the fleet beyond the point at which Pearl Harbor's dockyards could maintain it at 25 percent superiority over the Orange navy. From estimates of distances, hull damage, maintenance, and the time and risk of journeys to and fro, he reckoned Truk to be the practical limit. Because the navy owned only one small floating dock, it would have to mark time at Truk while at least one huge mobile dry dock was built and towed out, a project that would take eighteen months or longer.[99] Furthermore, the logistical staff calculated, five of the behemoths would be needed at the next fleet base to the west of Truk.[100]

Additional U.S. goals and timetables would depend on the situation after Truk was taken. Williams presumed that the commander in chief would delay advancing until the floating base and docks were ready to follow.[101] The drive to war-winning positions was bound to be "a long drawn out operation," "a tremendous undertaking" possible only for a rich and determined country.[102] The prospect belied the quick victory that thrusters regarded as essential for public support. Williams dodged the issue by refusing to specify targets and dates after Truk.

At the end of September 1922 Clarence Williams stood down from the War Plans Division for his next billet as president of the Naval War College and finally commander of the Asiatic Fleet in 1925–27.[103] He and his supporters had bequeathed to the nation a sound war plan for advancing at least halfway across the Pacific. They assumed correctly that landings on small islands would encounter furious shore resistance. To avoid attrition losses at sea and ensure the assaults, they projected that the fleet would operate far beyond the beachheads. They foresaw air power as a major force in a future ocean campaign. Their plan allowed for flexible timing and targets after Truk was taken. It was, as a whole, strikingly similar to the Pacific strategy of Plan Rainbow Five, the governing policy of the United States when it went to war in 1941, which specified the precise sequence of Eniwetok and Truk. It also foretold, less accurately, the events of 1944, when the United States bypassed Truk in favor of a great advanced fleet base in the strategically equivalent Admiralty Islands and used Eniwetok as a springboard to the Marianas instead of to Truk (Chapter 28).

The 1922 plan contained some faulty assumptions that were not fixed until a cautionary strategy was reinstated between 1934 and 1941. Its supposition that every Mandated Island had to be cleared was much too pessimistic; the better choice was to bypass most of them. Yet it was too optimistic (as were all prewar U.S. plans) about the rapidity of mobilization and movement. It identified the need for air power over the beachheads but could not explain how to get it there. Finally, it assumed, erroneously, that Orange would not be so foolhardy as to send capital ships to do battle for the Mandate. Japan's ill-fated commitment of its carriers to defense of the region in 1944 was an unforeseen windfall for the strategy.

In spite of its flaws, the cautionary campaign plan of 1922 was a giant step toward a war-winning strategy. Unfortunately, army and navy high commanders turned their backs on it the following year. Its recission in 1923 was a setback that retarded for ten years the study of a true oceanic war and the development of appropriate weaponry and auxiliaries. The military majority recoiled from a slow campaign that would forfeit the last vestige of hope of saving the Philippines and, worse, would prolong the war unbearably. These inadmissible prospects galvanized the thrusters to resistance as furious as any contemplated on central Pacific beaches.

The Thrusters' Resurgence

The thrusters had reluctantly accepted the cautionary solution after the Washington Treaty. But embers of a fiery counteroffensive flickered in their minds, ready to be fanned to life in 1923 when politics intruded into campaign strategy.

Leonard Wood, governor-general of the Philippines, reignited the flame. Wood was a legend in his time: a doctor, Indian fighter, commander of the Rough Riders in Cuba, and army chief of staff, who was a grave father figure popular among the rank and file. Republican progressives had nudged the general toward the presidential nomination of 1920. Harding won the office and offered his stiff-necked rival a consolation prize far from Washington. Wood responded to the "tremendous call for duty" and set sail to enhance America's influence in the Orient.[1]

Navy Secretary Denby was visiting Manila late in 1922 when Wood learned with dismay that naval planners had decided to sacrifice the Philippines should a war occur. He protested to his superiors at the War Department.[2] Though Wood understood that only sea power could guarantee the islands' security, he believed a native army augmented by mobile American units allowed by the treaty could hold Manila until naval relief came and heartily endorsed a boast by the CinCAF that Blue submarines could guarantee the job (Chapter 6).[3] He wrote to Secretary of War John W. Weeks:

> I protest to you most earnestly and beg that you will appeal to the Secretary of the Navy and to the President against the fatal assumption on the part of the Navy that . . . the Philippine Islands could not be defended, must be abandoned, and a long war waged to take them and reestablish ourselves in the Far East. Such a policy of abandonment spells . . . national dishonor and the beginning of a retrogression which God alone can see the end of. Abandonment will be highly injurious to us abroad and far-reaching in its disintegrating and demoralizing effect upon our own people. . . . The Philippine Islands must [be] succored by the Fleet.[4]

The general's outcry struck a responsive nerve. Harding believed in the American empire. He liked to compare himself with McKinley, who had "unsheathed the sword on behalf of suffering humanity" and brought enlightened stewardship to the islands. He opposed Philippine independence and backed his friends who sought trade and investment profits.[5] It is likely (but cannot be proved from known records) that the president was stirred by the aging hero's warranty to keep the flag aloft over "the greatest outpost of Christianity and Western civilization in the Far East" and passed the word to revise the Orange Plan.[6]

By 1923 the confidence levels of the services had reversed. The army had regained its aplomb after a postwar reorganization. Weeks was an influential politician. The stern General John J. "Black Jack" Pershing chaired the Joint Board. Army strategists who had gone along with plans for a prompt naval advance to the Philippines, whether by way of Fortress Guam or the Through Ticket, rallied to decry the fatalism of the cautionary clique. The navy, in contrast, had lost its self-assurance as its magnificent new warships went to the scrap pile. Denby was a nonentity who became ensnarled in the Teapot Dome oil scandal and soon lost his job. Coontz was nearing the end of his stint in Washington and yearned to return to sea. Nicknamed "the Senator" for his bureaucratic wiliness,[7] he sniffed a change in the political air that might rekindle the glow of a naval blitzkrieg. He delayed ratifying Williams's distasteful legacy[8] and maneuvered Op-12 into the hands of the pliable Captain Sinclair Gannon as acting director. Gannon, who had built a career as a popular staff aide, was the youngest chief planner with the most junior staff of the era before World War II.[9]

During the first half of 1923, the CNO deftly orchestrated a fanfare of studies and pronouncements by five military planning agencies that recast the Phase II campaign into a fury of aggressiveness. Like the preceding cautionary montage, many inputs were linked to form a comprehensive Pacific strategy that was refined into a detailed Orange Plan over the next two years.

Coontz arranged for Gannon to doctor Williams's estimate of the situation by inserting "corrections" that negated the detested Mandate campaign.[10] Perhaps to spare himself embarrassment he (or Denby, or TR, Jr.) petitioned the independent General Board for an updated strategic survey of the Pacific. The board, still a hotbed of thrusting zeal, wrote a swaggering Through Ticket scenario. It was, Coontz lied, "in general agreement with existing war plans." Alert to the political quagmire of interservice rivalry, he promised to build a new naval Orange Plan on the foundation of a joint army and navy estimate of similar philosophy.[11] Gannon meanwhile solicited the cooperation of soldiers who needed little coaxing.[12] Williams's cautionary plan was flawed, he explained, because a sluggish Blue offensive would grant Orange time to fortify its inner island ramparts so impregnably that the army would be obliged to mount a "tremendous" ground campaign in China to win the war. To limit the ground fighting to acceptable small-scale island battles compatible with the Orange Plan's grand strategy, a Through Ticket campaign was indicated. The Joint Board agreed enthusiastically, and both secretaries approved the Joint Planning Committee's estimate.[13] Gannon then finished degrading Williams's opus by attaching to its cautionary arguments decisions to pursue the opposite policy.[14]

By midsummer of 1923 Wood was informed that everyone in Washington was in "complete accord" that Manila would not be abandoned.[15] The JPC worked the planning papers into a Joint Basic War Plan Orange, which the Joint Board adopted in August 1924. When it was approved by the cabinet secretaries, the nation had its first official Joint Orange Plan, endorsed at the highest seat of civil authority save the presidency.[16]

The revamping process continued during 1925 as the armed forces wrote their supporting plans. The AWPD's exercise was rather routine. The army was content to flesh out its assignments of securing Luzon and helping the navy get the bases it needed.[17] The navy's approach was anything but doctrinaire. CNO Edward Eberle decided that the immense scope of a modern Blue-Orange war required delegation of "unusual powers" of planning to the United States Fleet (the successor to the postwar Atlantic and Pacific fleets that had been merged on the West Coast in December 1922). Observing that history showed the folly of rigid direction by a distant central authority, Eberle declared the commander in chief of the U.S. Fleet (CinCUS) to be the "principal naval agent" in a war. That officer was to prepare a fleet contributory plan that would be melded with OpNav's essay into an Orange Master Plan.[18] In 1925 the CinCUS was none other than Robert E. Coontz, and his assistant chief of staff was the servile Captain Gannon. (That a CNO would return to a seagoing billet may seem odd to later generations, but between the world wars the CinCUS commanded most of the navy's combat power and rivaled his nominal commander in authority and prestige.) Whether the devolution of authority came from headquarters' disinterest or string-pulling by Coontz, the admiral was ready to embark on a Through Ticket spree.

The thrusting doctrine of the army and navy planning agencies of 1923–24 had combined two principles, one old and one new. The first, conforming to the traditional grand strategy of Plan Orange, stipulated that the war would be offensive and primarily naval. The sea service would operate "with extreme boldness from the earliest stages of the war" and "seek the initiative in all operations." The Blue fleet, supplemented by "overwhelming" air power, would ensconce itself "at the earliest date . . . in strength superior to that of Japan" at a western Pacific base for the conduct of naval and economic warfare.[19] These generalities differed little from the cautionaries' doctrine.

The second principle was derived from Wood's political credo that the Philippine Islands were a commercial eldorado and a political resource whose loss would fatally undermine national prestige, respect of neutrals, and public support for a war in the Pacific. The Joint Board, having hypocritically declared that it had "always been in general accord" with Wood's view,[20] was obligated to present a military strategy harmonizing with the political rationale. The planning staff met the challenge by arguing that Manila Bay was the "strongest [and] best available site" for a western Pacific naval base.[21] Holding it would be immeasurably cheaper than a campaign of recapture that would "seriously retard" the pace of the war.[22] Since the local defenders, even if reinforced within treaty limits, could hold only a short while, the "first and governing" task of American arms was to be an "immediate naval advance" with all available troops.[23] As Leonard Wood put it bluntly, the navy had two distinct missions: "First, the relief of the Philippines and the establishment of its base in Manila. . . . Second, the destruction of the Japanese fleet."[24]

It is astonishing that a generation of naval officers reared on the code of Mahan hailed a strategy that subordinated mobility and sea battle to holding a fixed position. They finessed the paradox by reasoning that although sea power should ordinarily remain unfettered when the enemy fleet was at large, Manila was unique and securing it would constitute the navy's "most effective initial use."[25] Dedication to the fixed objective was correct, agreed Op-12, because "a bold move at the outset" would deny the enemy time to brace and ultimately would prove less costly.[26]

The absurdity of the Through Ticket campaign was never more evident than in the ocean crossing of Coontz's imagination. A mind that never grasped the fatuousness of American Gibraltars hatched a preposterous cavalry charge across the Pacific. The CinCUS had delayed until the departure from Op-12 of the pragmatic William Shoemaker and the accession of Captain Standley, a friend whose career he had assisted, before testing his scheme. Hearing no objection from Washington, he proceeded with gusto.[27] His fleet had no war plans officer, but two WPD veterans were attached to its staff: Commander G. J. Rowcliff probably drafted the force analyses and Gannon the operating scenario.[28] In January 1925 they completed Fleet Orange Plans R-3 for readiness and O-3 for operations.[29] (Naval contributory plans were numbered 1 through 13; the U.S. Fleet's number 3 was later changed to 1.)

To rescue Manila, a vast expedition would have to be assembled and dispatched with lightning speed. Wood had boasted that Americans had always solved impossible logistical problems in wartime.[30] With the fleet already moored on the West Coast, it could concentrate in Hawaii by Z+10 a force 25 percent superior to the Imperial Navy.[31] (Z Day in navy parlance meant the simultaneous start of mobilization and war. The army designated the two events M Day and D Day, which might or might not be one and the same.[32]) In anticipation, mobile service units were to be built and Pearl Harbor's facilities upgraded.[33] Vessels unable to squeeze inside would anchor behind minefields at Lahaina Roads.[34] Op-12 protested that not every ship could be manned and made ready in ten days and that recommissioning of reserve ships would lag while most of the trained sailors steamed westward. The fleet might have to split itself and go over in echelons.[35] Coontz shrugged off the problem with an assumption he had championed as CNO, that a clairvoyant government would assure ample time for docking and stocking by ordering mobilization forty days in advance of the war.[36] Nor was he fazed about sailing without four battleships that were in overhaul; the broadsides of his fourteen active battlewagons, he felt certain, could put down Japan's ten capital ships. He also expected to leave behind obsolete prewar cruisers and all submarines except twenty of the longest range. The United States Asiatic Expeditionary Force (USAEF), as he named it, would aggregate 551 vessels (see Table 11.1). For "overwhelming" air power it would have to rely on the experimental carrier *Langley*, floatplanes aboard the gunships, and 300 seaplanes carried on converted tenders. The fuelships of the train could be fewer than in previous estimates, however, because oil could be purchased in the Orient. Instead, extra bottoms would haul munitions and sustenance to last three months as insurance against communications mishaps.[37] Converted transports would carry an army corps of fifty thousand whose heavy equipment would be foresightedly stockpiled in the Philippines.[38]

The Joint Board had decreed a Phase II counterattack "with the least possible delay."[39] The fleet planners assumed that the Philippines could hold out for sixty days (although Guam would be lost immediately). Therefore, even if the train and troop buildups were incomplete, the commander in chief would order anchors aweigh at 0700 hours on Z+14, "convinced that a bold offensive move would contribute largely to victory."[40]

Ostensibly the CinCUS was free to head for any base of his choice in the western Pacific. To no one's surprise, his planners spurned all harbors save one—Manila Bay. He was also authorized to select a route of advance between the parallels of 30° north and 20° south (which eliminated only the Aleutian track) and to decide whether and where the USAEF would pause.[41] Perhaps to test the fleet's capability, Coontz dispatched fifty-six ships on a cruise to Australia (to the joy of the Prohibition-era bluejackets), a voyage the same length as to the Philippines.[42] Nevertheless, his staff dismissed all courses south of the equator as too slow for a war mission. They also decided to avoid Mandate waters because of raiders and uncharted reefs. To maintain punctuality and secrecy, only a direct nonstop voyage would do. The quicker the crossing, they argued, the fewer days of exposure to attack and the least amount of fuel burned, permitting a smaller train and/or carriage of more matériel. They opted for the fastest track that did not pass too near Japan, along a rhumb line hugging 23° north latitude threading between enemy-held islands as far as 145° east, "thence North about Luzon to Manila Bay" (see Map 11.1).

Regarding replenishment and defense en route, Plan O-3 lapsed into surrealism. It earmarked none of the few islands of the transit zone

TABLE 11.1 *Numbers of Ships in Naval Expeditionary Force to Far East, 1922–1925*

| | Campaign via Marshalls and Carolines to Western Base | | | Direct voyage to Philippines | |
| | WPD,[a] Nov. 1922 | | | WPD Jan. 1924 | U.S. Fleet Jan. 1925 |
	Mandates	Western	Total		
Battleships	3	15	18	18	14
Aircraft carriers		2	2	2	
Aircraft carriers, old		1	1	1	1
Heavy cruisers, old	4	7	11	6	
Light cruisers		14	14	10	10
Subtotal, large combatants	7	39	46	37	25
Mine vessels	22	40	62	23	48
Destroyers	76	233	309	208	190
Submarines	19	47	66	52	20
Tenders and miscellaneous	6	20	26	18	20[b]
Subtotal, small combatants	123	340	463	301	278
Total, all combatants	130	379	509	338	303
Floating dry docks, large and medium		5	5	1	
Troop transports	4	8	12	32	39[c]
Hospital ships	4	5	9	2	6
Dry cargo, ammunition, tug, miscellaneous	48	58	106	22	83
Subtotal, train, nonfuel	56	76	132	57	128
Tankers	88	28	116	116	100
Colliers	19	8	27	32	20
Subtotal, train, fuel	107	36	143	148	120
Total, all train	163	112	275	205	248
GRAND TOTAL	293	491	784	543	551

[a] Estimate of Board for Development of Navy Yard Plans at Request of WPD.
[b] Seaplane tenders, estimate, number unstated.
[c] 12 marine, 27 army.

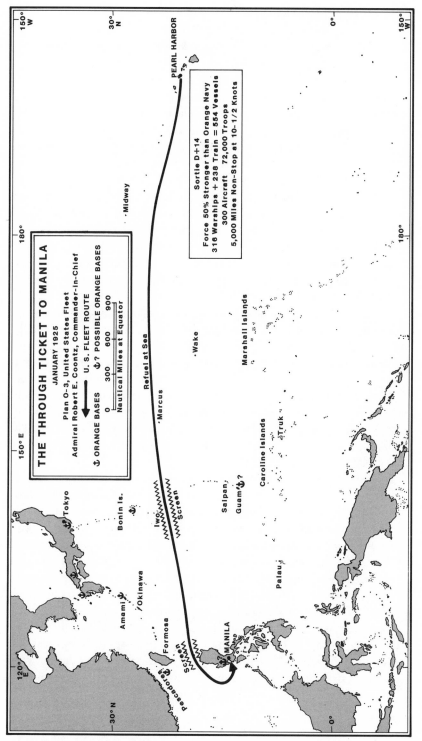

THE THROUGH TICKET TO MANILA

JANUARY 1925

Plan O-3, United States Fleet
Admiral Robert E. Coontz, Commander-in-Chief

⚓ ORANGE BASES   ⚓? POSSIBLE ORANGE BASES

→ U. S. FLEET ROUTE

0   300   600   900
Nautical Miles at Equator

Sortie D+14

Force 50% Stronger than Orange Navy
316 Warships + 238 Train = 554 Vessels
300 Aircraft   72,000 Troops
5,000 Miles Non-Stop at 10-1/2 Knots

PEARL HARBOR

Midway

Wake

Marshall Islands

Marcus

Refuel at Sea

Iwo
Screen

Bonin Is.

Tokyo

Saipan
Guam ⚓?

Caroline Islands

Truk

Palau

Amami ⚓
Okinawa

Formosa

Pescadores
Screen

MANILA
Screen

MAP 11.1

for fueling because none was suitable. Of the American atolls, the Leeward Chain, Midway, and Johnston were written off as too small or perilously exposed, and Wake was not even mentioned. Lagoons of the Mandate would be barbed with Orange mines and submarines.[43] Nevertheless, Op-12 had advised that a means of fueling en route would have to be found.[44] The fleet planners responded that replenishment would be arranged somehow before crossing 160° east (halfway between Wake and Marcus); the small ships were to tank up again farther west or else be taken in tow. How fueling would be done was left unstated. In experiments during the 1920s the navy developed methods of oiling under way by having tankers tow shorter-ranged battleships or other large vessels end-to-end at speeds below even the "laborious and tedious" ten and a half knots of the convoy. Fueling of destroyers riding abeam, for which some naval tankers carried proper gear, had progressed further. Vigorous experimentation in under-way oiling was then shelved until about 1938.[45]

As the USAEF lumbered ahead, its warships spread over twelve hundred square miles of ocean and the soldiers distressed by the rough northern seas, it could expect a lively reception. In the worst nightmare, Japan's four speedy battle cruisers would swoop down upon it. Coontz toyed with detaching his warships from the train to confront them but decided they might slip by and obliterate the auxiliaries. The Blue battleships would have to avoid combat except in a dire emergency or to grasp a chance to destroy the Japanese main body if it appeared. The planners predicted, however, that Japan would suppress a natural impulse for a "spectacular" battle on the high seas and adopt a strategic defensive, holding back its big ships for fear of "disastrous" failure. Instead, it would wage a tactical offensive, making the most of position and mobility. Orange submarines would track the expedition from Hawaii. Light forces from the Mandate would harass it. Other units would foreclose potential harbors of refuge. But the USAEF would thwart its tormentors by means of aerial reconnaissance and outriders of "aggressive power" on its flanks. When it turned west-southwest near Iwo Jima, within a few hundred miles of Orange bases at Guam and the Bonins, hostile submarines and aircraft would be deflected by a close screen of warships and by Blue's "power of air offense"— whether from the *Langley,* catapults, or open-sea takeoffs was not disclosed. Finally, the armada would run another gauntlet between Orange airfields on Formosa and Luzon, turn to port, and make for Manila Bay.[46] At that point, the plan mercifully ended.

Fleet Plan O-3 was the reductio ad absurdum of imposing an impossible political goal onto a military campaign strategy. America's premier fighting asset and its merchant marine were to be risked on a suicide voyage to a distant and weak position. The navy had learned that the army was a power to be reckoned with in Pacific war plans. The ground service's intentions would thenceforth receive due consideration.

After 1925 the burdening of strategy with immediate political objectives eased, at least in the sense of prizing a fixed target above freedom of maneuver. Not until 1940–41 did political decisions again loom in plans for the first campaigns of a Pacific war, and then for mature rationales of deterrence or alliance building. In 1944 an echo of the inversion of priorities of the 1920s reverberated in a policy decision that sent U.S. forces to liberate Luzon after a lodgment in the southern Philippines, a decision made by Franklin Roosevelt at the behest of MacArthur and against the protests of a navy that saw no military advantage in it (Chapter 30).

The Navy Department had erred in appointing its most rabid thruster to write its operational plan. After Coontz hauled down his flag in October 1925, the worst extravagances of his mad voyage were revoked, but by then a Through Ticket rush to the Philippines had congealed into the fundamental campaign strategy of Phase II. The concept, however, held the seed of its own demise. The joint directive of 1923, "To establish at the earliest date American sea power in the Western Pacific in strength superior to that of Japan,"[47] was an oxymoron, a self-contradictory statement. The United States could advance to the war zone either quickly or in superior strength. It could not do both. The conundrum was to absorb the wits of American war planners for another decade until they conceded the unreality of the mission.

The American Way of Planning: The Professionals

I n the late 1920s, high-ranking thrusters passed from the scene, and Pacific war planning settled into a more orderly pattern. Wood and Coontz ceased meddling in strategy. The General Board's trumpet calls for boldness were stilled when William Rodgers left to run the Naval Institute; the board was rarely consulted about war plans thereafter. Harding took ill and died. Presidents Calvin Coolidge and Herbert Hoover, governing during a time of amicable relations with Japan (until the Manchurian crisis of 1931), showed no interest in the subject, nor did their civilian advisers, and the service chieftains scarcely any. The generals dropped their quixotic crusade for Manila and turned to parochial concerns about the army's stature in other war contingencies. Three consecutive chiefs of naval operations—Eberle, Charles F. Hughes, and William V. Pratt—treated war planning with indifference and, in the case of Pratt, with antagonism.

Responsibility for Plan Orange devolved onto the professional strategists of the two war plans divisions and on their common forum, the JPC, as the Joint Board slackened the reins and let its junior staff mature from analyst to architect. Within the navy planning broadened into a servicewide effort adroitly guided by Op-12. The times favored technicians willing to avoid fratricidal strife by shaping cooperative solutions rather than the wrangling visionaries of the previous competitive system. The new breed of professionals designed campaigns that stayed carefully within the boundaries of universally accepted grand strategy. They defused the thruster-cautionary feud by compromises, especially by mitigating the Through Ticket's extreme belligerence while keeping its core principles of speed and deep penetration. In their finest hour, the experts designed a Phase III siege of Japan and calculated the requirements of the long war it would climax, providing for future planners accurate forecasts of the final campaigns of World War II.

The improved planning process of the late 1920s owed much to the relaxation of the army. Its planning staff lapsed once more into the comfortable role of satellite to naval ambitions, for example by acquiescing in precise offensive itineraries and dropping the usual army preference for probing for weak spots before choosing targets.[1] As tokens of goodwill the services conformed their terminology, adopting army M Day as the start of mobilization and war and, in the manner of the navy, the title of CinCUSJAF for the head of the Joint Asiatic Force whose headquarters would be labeled GHQ, army-style.[2] The colonels appreciated the navy's frankness in dealings on the JPC, and the lure of new missions it dangled before them like "maximum effort in air forces" throughout the war. The navy-animated Orange Plans were, they agreed, "excellent."[3]

The General Staff, however, resented the army's second-class status in a maritime war, a rankling issue that was not resolved until World War II and then only by the drastic expedient of carving the Pacific into separate theaters. In a conciliatory gesture the JPC recommended in 1924 that because sea actions would dominate the war, the CinCUS should command all offensive forces and report to the president through the secretary of the navy. The generals balked. Independent commanders with joint staffs, they said, ought to suffice. The professional planners next proposed co-management wherein an admiral would take charge at sea and a general ashore, and they would defer in joint actions to the one having "paramount interest" at the moment. As a badly chosen example it was suggested that if the siege of the home islands failed, the army might oversee a "Conditional Subsequent Phase" and conduct "such further action as will cause Japan to sue for peace,"[4] a meaningless concession because everyone regarded ground fighting in China or Japan as unthinkable (Chapter 14). Army staffers next tried out another two-stage formula of unified subservience to a supreme admiral who would pass the baton to a general when the offensive reached a large fortified island such as Luzon. But their bosses held fast; command, they insisted, had to be decentralized at all times. They accepted only the principle of paramount interest for specific operations and conceded the navy's paramountcy in the western Pacific in exchange for the army's in the eastern ocean. The Joint Board adopted this premise of command and control and never altered it until World War II began. To underscore the army's sphere as a serious defense arena, Blue territory was classified as to potential risk. The U.S. coasts in categories A through C were deemed virtually free of peril, but Category D places (Panama and Hawaii) might be subject to major attacks and category E locales (Alaska and Samoa) to invasion.[5]

The vigor of naval planning provoked an identity crisis in the army. Envious of the sea service's glamorous role, it pined for a mission of great commitment, one that might attract scarce funds from Congress. The General Staff insisted that the Orange Plans include the buildup of a home reserve, which grew in the 1920s plans from 250,000 to 500,000 and finally to 1,200,000 men.[6] Only a few hundred thousand soldiers would be needed in the Pacific; the others were to stand guard against intervention by Great Britain (Red), the one other nation that could harm the United States. A Blue-Red war, the army warned, could erupt over trade rivalry brought to a head by unavoidable atrocities against neutral ships during a blockade of Japan. American preoccupation in the Pacific might tempt England to strike. Army planners drew up a blueprint for combat between the mightiest sea powers that was in no way a maritime plan. It canceled the Pacific offensive, ceded control of the Atlantic to the enemy, relegated the navy to coast defense, and barred marines from seizing British outposts. In the centerpiece of War Plan Red the army, engorged to 4,600,000 men, would throttle Canada by land and air. These Red and Red-Orange Plans, written "in consultation" rather than jointly because of naval skepticism, were approved in 1930 by the Joint Board (which chose to ignore the navy's prediction that Canada would foil the strategy by declaring itself neutral).

Desultory studies of war with Britain continued in army circles until 1939, but the navy showed no further interest.[7] Claims of some historians that the Red-Orange melodramas were useful trial exercises for the two-ocean plans of World War II are not convincing. A march over the border to hold Canada hostage bore no resemblance to projections of land, sea, and air power across the Atlantic to fight Germany in coordination with powerful allies.

In the Navy War Plans Division the Orange Plan remained the major preoccupation. Left alone by the CNOs "to work out its own Salvation,"[8] the division swelled in competence and confidence during the watches of well-qualified directors and their senior aides. In mid-1923 Eberle recruited his former commander of battleships, Rear Admiral William Rawle Shoemaker, a veteran of two General Board tours, who had earned a Navy Cross for imposing the discipline of logistical planning on the service. Shoemaker upgraded the featherweight staff by hiring Captains William S. Pye and William H. Standley.[9] He induced the CNO to install a heirarchical planning system that emphasized material preparation for war. The foundation of planning became the Basic Readiness Plan, WPL-8, an idealized guidebook shrewdly dubbed the "Peace Plan." A Basic War Operating Plan, WPL-9, contained emergency directives for mobilization and logistics and, most important, a Basic Strategic Plan. Every bureau, district, board, and fleet was ordered to write practical contributory plans to complete the package; as in the building of a ship, each was to lend its expertise to the common goal. The paperwork was burdensome but, as Eberle apologized, war plans were a serious and complex business that could not be set down "on a few sheets of paper and in words of one syllable."[10]

Shoemaker, a lifelong cautionary, had the misfortune to represent that faction among a den of thrusters he could not tame through orderly analysis. Standley, another practical member of the fleet staff who followed Shoemaker as director in the summer of 1924, chose to stand aside while Coontz, his former mentor, inflicted the awful Plan O-3 on the navy. Standley contributed little to Plan Orange. His grooming of army contacts and travels throughout the navy, however, gave him a mature perspective on strategy.[11] Eight years later, as CNO, he succeeded in reintegrating planning with command for the shaping of the ocean campaign that was to be executed in World War II.

A serious reform of the Orange Plan began under Pye's guidance in 1926 and got into high gear after the appointment of Rear Admiral Frank H. Schofield as director of Op-12 near the end of the year. For the next two years Schofield was the epitome of the professional strategist. "Cold in personality and intensely logical in planning," he was a gaunt and tight-lipped figure with rimless spectacles. His bonding with other brilliant minds in his early years at the War College had propelled him, despite fragile health, into a career as a sought-after staff man. He had served in Sims's London cadre, as Benson's scribe at Versailles, and as the General Board's mouthpiece for the Through Ticket in the early 1920s.[12] Upon taking charge of the WPD, he doubled its roster to ten or twelve officers and grouped them into eight sections called Op-12-A, Op-12-B, and so on, to deal with such specialties as readiness, logistics, bases, landings, and aviation. An Orange Strategic Section oversaw all operating plans. The sections were not rigid; everyone pitched in as needed. The division also advised the CNO on peacetime forces, ship and aircraft types, and training. Its annual estimate was the foundation of the navy's budget.[13]

Schofield supervised two bursts of Orange planning before and after his attendance at the 1927 Geneva Naval Conference. During the first period his chief assistant was Pye, former war plans officer of the 1918 battle fleet and an adequate strategist although inclined to view a Pacific war simplistically as a racial struggle.[14] In 1927 Captain Frederick J. Horne came aboard. Horne was a rare catch, an alumnus of both war colleges, a writer on the Japanese navy who had served a hitch in Tokyo, and a wearer of aviation wings who brought air-mindedness to planning. Since Schofield earnestly wished to avoid another fracas with the army, he was fortunate that his aide's "down-to-earth, old shoe" personality humored the colonels and mitigated his own tautness. Horne exemplified the long-term continuity of the American planning system throughout a fifty-year career that culminated as vice-CNO and logistics administrator of the navy in World War II.[15]

During 1927 Op-12 and the AWPD churned out Blue-Orange studies that were blended by the JPC into a voluminous Joint Estimate of the Situation in January 1928. After some wrangling, a simplified version of the essay was adopted in June by the Joint Board and cabinet secretaries as the nation's revised Joint Plan Orange. Four volumes of naval supporting plans followed in 1929; the logistics plan alone ran over a hundred pages. Contributory plans, also logistically oriented, were sent in by force and shore commanders.[16] The new constellation of Orange Plans survived as official documents until 1938, albeit with frequent amendments.

The prodigious planning labor of the late 1920s must be accounted both a success and a failure. Most of the features of the Phase III siege of 1945 were devised in this period (Chapter 14). On the other hand, the planners clung to an unworkable Through Ticket solution of Phase II. "Power is the product of force and time," Schofield insisted, so America's relative strength would be greatest at the outset and thereafter

Admiral of the Navy George Dewey presided over the General Board of the Navy and the Joint Army and Navy Board from their inception at the turn of the century until 1917. Dewey presented to Theodore Roosevelt America's first War Plan Orange. (NH 50577, Naval Historical Center)

Alfred Thayer Mahan, a guiding spirit of the Naval War College. The Philosopher of Sea Power inspired faith in a maritime strategy but was inept at planning campaigns for a modern steam navy in the Pacific. (NH 126, Naval Historical Center)

The General Board in 1900 with Dewey at the head of the table. War plans were classified at the highest level of secrecy. Photographs of planners at work are almost nonexistent. (NH 53150, Naval Historical Center)

Vision of the Blue offensive, 1907. The round-the-world cruise of the Great White Fleet emboldened thrusters who advocated a rush of the battle fleet to the Far East in wartime. (NH 92067, Naval Historical Center)

Coaling a battleship. The U.S. Navy built huge colliers to service the battle fleet at primitive bases. Cautionary planners considered the Micronesian islands as coaling bases even before they were occupied by Japan in 1914. (NH 44364, Naval Historical Center)

Conquering Japanese gawk at the big guns of Corregidor in May 1942. The fate of American soldiers in the Philippines was a rankling issue for the army. Naval plans wrote off the islands. (NH 73577, Naval Historical Center)

Apra Harbor, Guam, still undeveloped in 1941. Admirals Dewey, Mahan, and Coontz dreamed of an "American Gibraltar" there, even though the port could accommodate relatively few ships. (80-G-451193, National Archives)

In 1945 the United States recaptured Guam and developed a naval base. If built before the war, however, the base would have suffered the fate of an "American Singapore." (80-G-346147, National Archives)

The navy formed a professional War Plans Division after World War I. The 1920 staff under Rear Admiral James H. Oliver [center] was larger than the typical inter-war staff of ten or twelve officers. (NH 83688, Naval Historical Center)

Rear Admiral Clarence S. Williams [right] devised the island-hopping offensive through the central Pacific when the Washington Treaty ruled out a base on Guam. He is shown here at Newport in 1922 with Assistant Secretary of the Navy Theodore Roosevelt, Jr., and Commander Robert L. Ghormley [center], who became director of war plans in 1938–39. (NH 56936, Naval Historical Center)

[Above, left] General Leonard Wood persuaded the Harding administration to reject the slow offensive across the Pacific and to pledge a rescue of Manila for God and national honor. (111-SC-84786, National Archives) [Above, right] Admiral Robert E. Coontz, chief of naval operations, 1919–23. He fostered the "Through Ticket to Manila," a fanatical ocean blitzkrieg of the thrusting faction. (NH 51699, Naval Historical Center)

Rear Admiral Frank H. Schofield [left], prolific writer of Orange Plans in the late 1920s and advocate of wrecking the Japanese economy by blockade and bombing. Admiral William V. Pratt [right], chief of naval operations in the early 1930s, trusted in disarmament treaties and curbed work on the plan. (NH 75865, Naval Historical Center)

Visions of the great Blue offensive: [left] U.S. battleships, 1919. (NH 59950, Naval Historical Center); [below] the aircraft carrier USS *Hornet,* 1942. (NH 95380, Naval Historical Center)

Rear Admiral Montgomery Taylor, chief
war planner of the early 1930s, with
humorist Will Rogers. The Orange Plan
of the era was a joke, "literally an act of
madness," to army defensivists. (NH
43955, Naval Historical Center)

Sanity returned to Plan Orange when
Rear Admiral Samuel W. Bryant teamed
up with CNO William Standley in 1934
to reinstate the cautionary strategy. The
navy never again deviated from the ocean
campaign it was to execute in World
War II. (NH 64339, Naval Historical
Center)

would sag in favor of Japan. A two-year struggle was admissible if early successes roused the public will. A gradual comeback was intolerable.[17]

After Schofield's departure, naval war planning sank into five years of ineffectiveness. The strong-willed experts who had flourished in the laissez-faire environment gave way in the early 1930s to pedestrian appointees. Captain Merlyn Grail Cook, no magician despite his name, was a journeyman planner who was invalided out of the navy after a few months as head of Op-12 in 1929.[18] Rear Admiral Montgomery Taylor, seven years a flag officer, was no intellectual luminary although his energy, interest in the Pacific, and studies of invasions and blockades augured well for the task.[19] Yet during two years in Op-12 the walrus-mustachioed admiral left no imprint on Plan Orange. He submerged it under his most junior aide, perhaps because of his belief that Japan deserved both American friendship and control of China. Hughes ignored the division and turned to the General Board for policy guidance. Pratt, the next CNO, was a former planner and NWC president. He was also the willing tool of Hoover's pacifism and parsimony. Pratt decided in 1931 that the Orange Plan could not be enacted for lack of ships and downgraded the War Plans Division "to handle routine and dispose of minor matters of operations."[20] His four successive directors were caretakers. After Taylor came the portly Rear Admiral Edward C. Kalbfus—chairs were known to collapse under him—who was a celebrated teacher of strategy and later president at Newport and director of naval history, yet he sat in the (presumably sturdy) chair at Op-12 for only six do-nothing months.[21] Captain George Julian Meyers was an alumnus of both war colleges and sometime author on strategy but had a reputation for "no achievements, a clean sleeve."[22] Worse, he was a flaming thruster when the situation in 1932 called for prudence. Pratt soon demoted Meyers and sensibly appointed Captain Samuel W. Bryant, a cautionary who was keen to reform the plan. But Bryant had to await his chief's retirement in 1932 before altering the status quo (Chapter 16).

During the decade of 1924 to 1933 the chiefs of naval operations abdicated their responsibility to plan war. The Orange Plans of the era ranged from mediocre to terrible. Even the best of the self-guided planners of the late 1920s felt they could not—even had they wished—discard the holy principle of a thrusting rejoinder. Only in relatively noncontentious matters did they install war-winning conceptions, notably in matters of logistics and in Phase III operations.

The U.S. Fleet took no hand in Orange planning after Coontz's

1925 fiasco. Every commander in chief declined the routine invitation to submit an offensive Plan O-1 and to send aides to headquarters for help,[23] even men such as Schofield, who had been strategists, or had drawn to their staffs able planners such as Captains Royal E. Ingersoll and Robert L. Ghormley.[24] The historian is left pondering bureaucratic politics. The Navy Department was leery of another clash with the generals even though the army's loyalty to the Philippines was waning in the late 1920s. If a CinCUS had asserted that a Through Ticket attack was unsound, OpNav might have edged away from it; the army, having no operating officer of equivalent prestige—the top soldier of the USJAF would not be chosen until M Day[25]—would have been hard put to protest. But after Coontz's botchery the seagoing commanders dodged the hot potato. The next Fleet Orange Plan was not drawn up until 1933, and the flagship did not become an influential fount of war planning until the late 1930s, when it was assigned qualified officers who could match the professionals in Washington.

A Marginally Saner Policy

After the frenzy to save Manila of 1923–25 abated, the planners began to recognize the constraints that U.S. leaders were to face in counterattacking during World War II. They realized that it would take longer than had been thought to mobilize and deliver a transpacific expedition and longer still to develop advanced bases and gather strength for the finale. The constraints suggested a war of at least two years' duration. Yet the thrusters, who still dominated planning, intended to grant the foe no breathing time. They worked out a plan that preserved the grand strategy of pressure against Japan's navy and commerce by a rapid surge to the Orient but scrapped the irrational fantasies of saving Manila City or even Bataan. The heart of the revision was a shift of the initial goal to the southern Philippines to establish a fleet base where none had stood before. A five-hundred-mile southward deflection at the end of a voyage of five thousand miles may seem a minor deviation, but it restored the primacy of military over political objectives in Phase II because there would be neither a capital nor a large garrison to rescue. The campaign plan edged further toward realism by incorporating strenuous features such as landings in the teeth of opposition and battles for control of the skies. Compared with the fanatical thrust to Manila, it was a marginally saner policy.

The half-step toward prudence was a far cry from a cautionary march through mid-Pacific islands. Schofield spurned that choice because it would dissipate Blue strength and initiative while granting Japan time to stockpile resources and garner prestige and foreign loans. The result would be a war of "indefinite and exhausting duration." "I don't believe in it," he declared.[1]

An outlying Philippine harbor as the fleet's destination had appeared in Orange Plans as early as 1906.[2] In 1914 the General Board had envisioned a haven south of Luzon where the fleet could lick its wounds and park the train securely between the stormings of Guam and Manila but not the construction of a real base.[3] When the Through Ticket to Manila became the approved strategy in 1923, Schofield and the other board members recommended that the southern Philippines not be occupied until after the garrison on Luzon was relieved.[4]

After 1925 army and navy planners became more aware of the threat of Orange aviation and the difficulty of deploying American air power. They began to see that Manila would be a suicidal destination. The fleet required a base in a more secure locale, preferably one attainable without "serious" fighting. The United States would have to "dismiss for all time" the reverie of quickly liberating Luzon.[5] Still unwilling to revert to the Mandate strategy of the cautionaries, they turned to the southern Philippines as the most appropriate objective. A direct advance to that region, they believed, would guarantee a fleet base at low cost and tip the prestige and morale factors in Blue's favor. But speed would still be vital; after a year into the war all Philippine ports would be so well fortified by Japan that an attempt to carry one would probably end in disaster.[6]

The cautionaries had felt that, in contrast to a seagirt outpost at Truk, a southern Philippine base would be vulnerable to bombing and its communications "forbidden" unless Blue armies were emplaced on the many islands from which Orange aircraft could strike.[7] Shoemaker struggled with little success to resurrect even a limited Mandate campaign to support the advance, proposing that a marine unit be permanently stationed in Hawaii to seize lagoons for fueling the fleet. At a minimum, he argued, the Marshalls and Carolines should be occupied soon after the fleet passed by.[8] Though Schofield saw little need of mid-ocean communications bases, other thrusters acknowledged the peril of raiders and the value of Blue convoy stations after the crossing.[9] The JPC proposed an "early" seizure of the Mandates and earmarked some troops, but the Joint Board, opposed to any taint of gradualism, scaled back the program.[10] The final Plans of 1928–29 grudgingly scheduled occupation of the Mandates after four to six months of war when the entire fleet would have reached the Philippines (Chapter 14, tables).

The exact locale of a base in the southern Philippines was no trivial matter because it would govern Blue operations for at least a year. In 1928 the Asiatic Fleet surveyed three large, strategically placed harbors (see Map 17.2). The most aggressive choice was Malampaya Sound, on Palawan, only 260 miles from Manila and abeam the trade routes, but the army vetoed the idea because Japan could easily establish airfields within the 200-mile range of its bombers. The most conservative option was Tawi Tawi, near the Borneo oil fields and an unassailable 540 miles from Manila. But the small island was topographically ill-suited for air defense and so far to the rear that, in the words of one surveyor, it would hardly be an advanced base at all.

The "measurably superior" choice was Dumanquilas Bay on the southwestern coast of Mindanao. The deeply indented anchorage could accommodate four hundred ships with room for seaplane fairways and deep coves for dry docks. The Blue armada could approach it through deep waters untroubled by submarines or mines. Miles of firm shoreline and hinterland were available for a naval base and the encampments and airstrips of a large army. The fleet would lie snug between minefields at the entrance and guns on the heights above, insulated from overland attack by rough backcountry terrain. Most important, Luzon lay four hundred air miles away across intervening mountain ranges, and the layout for aerial defense was excellent. From such a base the CinCUSJAF could roam freely to intimidate Orange carriers from attacking it.[11]

The Joint Planning Committee opined that an occupation of Dumanquilas would not require "any great effort" if done quickly while the Japanese were busy whipping Luzon's defenders and reinforcing other outposts. The Imperial Fleet would not risk its carriers against the expedition as it steamed across the Philippine Sea under the umbrella of the mighty new flattops *Lexington* and *Saratoga*. Unsure of Blue's destination, it would hang about Japan and Formosa to screen its main bases.[12] (Schofield declared, "I don't belong to that school that fills the air with airplanes thousands of miles at sea."[13]) The joint planners predicted that only a few of the 593 Orange planes it expected in the Philippines would contest a Mindanao landing because the rest would be engaged on Luzon or hoarded on carrier decks as reserves for sea battle. The USJAF would therefore enjoy a three-to-one air ascendancy during its approach and occupation.[14]

The Joint Board was not beguiled by this breezy optimism. More sober reports reckoned that Orange could disgorge two hundred thousand troops in the Philippines every month and fortify every harbor.[15] The Army Air Corps warned that many Orange planes would mass to pounce on the fleet as it neared Dumanquilas;[16] Blue would have to rely on outnumbered carrier planes since its seaplanes would be outclassed and army machines crated below decks. Rear Admiral William A. Moffett of the Bureau of Aeronautics considered the air complement too weak unless augmented by "temporary" carriers. Some army planners wondered if Blue had enough aviation "to go over at all."[17] The Joint Board therefore asked the planners how the expedition might fare if it had to fight its way in.[18]

Schofield convened his staff to study how to overcome strong resistance at Dumanquilas (Map 13.1). They assumed that the Imperial Fleet would advance to the Sulu Sea in the central Philippines whence it could hurl planes and light warships against the expedition but would hold back its big gunships unless it saw a chance to finish off a crippled U.S. fleet. The CinCUSJAF would immobilize them with submarines, sending his modern boats to converge from several directions to wreak confusion while older ones sealed off the straits between the two navies. The Blue fleet could then refuel south of Mindanao, comfortably out of air range. Meanwhile, at Dumanquilas, a division of Japanese would lie in wait with over a hundred artillery pieces, supported by minefields, light warships, and sixty seaplanes. The CinCUSJAF's urgent task would be to get his great convoy into shelter. He would launch a preemptive strike by a carrier and fast gunships, mindful of the theorem of Lieutenant Forrest P. Sherman (then at the Naval War College) that air control could be attained only by smashing hostile planes where they squatted, not aloft. Pressed for time, U.S. troops would have to land in the teeth of fire rather than on a quiet beach and slow-march across bad ground. The Japanese, outnumbered and swept by gun and air power, would succumb after a short but stiff fight.[19] The Americans would have to accept heavy losses stoically. "There could be no turning back on our part," the planners concluded.[20]

The Dumanquilas battle scenario of 1928 foresaw many of the conditions of World War II. As at Guadalcanal, Saipan, and Leyte (and unlike atoll landings), Blue would encounter strong air resistance and division-sized garrisons on large, hilly islands, with an imperial fleet in the offing. Many of the solutions offered in the plan became familiar

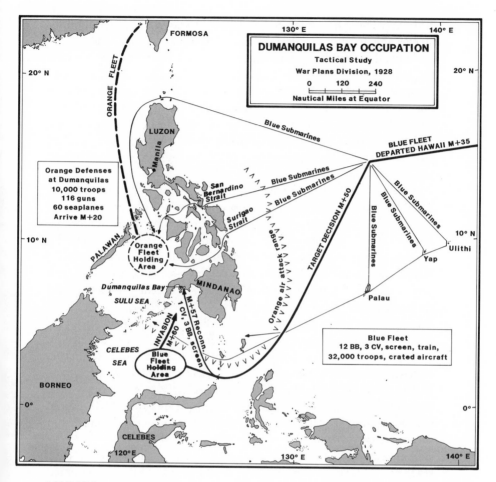

MAP 13.1

during the war: scouting and ambush by submarines, carrier strikes to neutralize shore-based air power and fortifications, a three-to-one margin of invaders over defenders, and a devotion to winning the objective at all costs.

Another important legacy of the scenarios devised in the late 1920s was the logistical preparation for Phase II. The planners painstakingly analyzed mobilization, supply, transport, and base development. Shoemaker tried gamely to wield his logistical expertise against launching a premature advance. He did not believe the government would permit a concentration at Hawaii forty days in advance, an act provocative of war.[21] He thought an offensive might commence four months after the outbreak. Though he managed to delete the war-warning assumption, he was able to impose a delay of only two weeks on the sortie.

Hawaii was still to be the jumping-off point even though most of the armada could not enter Pearl Harbor and would have to gather at the open roadstead of Lahaina. The Bureau of Ordnance designed a thirty-one-mile girdle of fifteen thousand mines and hoped that their long, whisker antennae would bar submarines from slipping through and that torpedoes fired from outside would run dry short of their targets.[22] The risks appeared acceptable because the vessels would tarry at Hawaii only a few days.[23]

Shoemaker challenged the prevailing notion that the United States could instantly assemble a force equivalent to 125 percent of Japan's naval strength, the minimum to assure victory in battle. Readiness, he asserted, was the "controlling consideration."[24] If one assumed the Blue navy had a five-to-three predominance over Japan per the treaty— actually it was below the permitted ceiling—a strength ratio of 167 percent versus 100 percent, a condition of 75 percent readiness would suffice (i.e., 167 percent × 75 percent = 125 percent). The criterion was difficult but not impossible. But when Shoemaker deducted vessels to protect the train he found the fleet would need a strength ratio of 150 percent to assure a 125 percent margin for battle, which equated to 90 percent readiness (167 percent × 90 percent = 150 percent) of the entire navy in Hawaii by Z+14, an impossible standard in peacetime. He therefore proposed that the USJAF should sail in echelons, the less ready units delayed until Z+60. Advancing in successive waves would be feasible if the Imperial Navy cooperated by shunning battle before the Blue concentration in the western Pacific reached the 150 percent mark about Z+90.[25] In 1924 the JPC accepted his premise.[26]

By 1926 the planners understood that the attack schedule needed "considerable improvement." Tactfully forgiving Coontz because he supposedly had not known of the decrepit condition of vessels outside the active fleet,[27] they set about developing an elaborate schedule that was completed in 1929. They delayed the initial sortie from M+14 to M+30, an interval that would allow those battleships, cruisers, and submarines that were habitually manned to be supplemented by 40 percent of the navy's destroyers to create a force of 125 percent superiority. The rest of the warships would follow in monthly waves: on M+60 the remaining battleships and submarines with more destroyers, on M+90 another batch of recommissioned "tin cans," and on M+120 the last of the mothballed vessels. By M+150 virtually all

American naval assets would have reached the Philippines (Table 13.1). (Revised schedules of the early 1930s deducted three battleships undergoing modernization and many destroyers that had been stricken from the lists but added cruisers from recent building programs.)

After about a year of fighting, newly constructed vessels would begin to weigh in. New submarines would be sent out. Fifty liners would join as auxiliary cruisers. Hundreds of special barges would be shipped out for landings under fire, in lieu of flimsy launches and boats. Eventually the cruiser and destroyer complements would be doubled. The expansion was to be manned by reserve crews organized in peacetime, by combing the merchant marine, and, if a Selective Service Act were invoked, by awarding the navy first choice of draftees.[28]

Blue air power would bulk large in the campaign. In 1926 Congress authorized a five-year doubling of naval aviation, and the army anticipated similar growth. By 1928 America's 1,612 combat planes clearly outmatched Japan's 1,100. (Most planners believed them to be qualitatively superior as well, although some warned against complacency.)[29] The army air staff hungered for potent missions of attacking Orange forces and defending bases. The navy recognized the advantages of land-based planes, including the freeing of its own aircraft to operate with the fleet, and allocated liberal shipping space to them.[30] Blue strength in the Philippines was to grow to about 500 aircraft, net of losses, by M+90. After M+180 newly minted army squadrons would arrive in quantity, and naval flying boats might be flown out via Mandates lagoons.[31] (In the early 1930s navy and air corps planners doubled their early deliveries to about a thousand planes each, and the latter pledged a flow of nearly a thousand a month beginning M+120.[32]) Output of naval planes was projected to soar to 9,015 in the first year.[33] These production forecasts were plausible, but another aviation element proved mistaken. The planners hoped to convert fast passenger ships into supplemental fleet carriers (XCVs) at the rate of one per month. But U.S. liners were unimpressive in speed and range, and it was found that elevators and other gear could not be easily installed in them. Besides, they would be needed as troopships. The XCVs soon faded from Orange Plans. The abundant escort carriers (CVEs) of World War II performed supporting missions unlike those hypothesized for the fleet XCVs of the 1920s.[34]

As late as 1927 the planners were lackadaisical about assigning ground forces to the offensive. The first echelon was to sail with no troops at all and the second with a few to seize "localities not occupied by the enemy in force." The army earmarked its only ready units,

TABLE 13.1   *Expeditionary Forces, First Year of War, 1928–1929 Plans*

	Departure date from Hawaii				
	M+30	M+60	M+90	M+120	M+150 to M+360, cumulative
Fleet combatants					
Battleships	12	4	–	–	2
Aircraft carriers	3	–	–	1[b]	12[a, b]
Cruisers	10	–	–	–	–
Old cruisers	–	–	4	6	2
Destroyers	84	41	73	32	27
Submarines	31	16	–	–	51
Minelayers	6	5	5	–	–
Minesweepers	19	18	24[b]	24[b]	–
Train and base patrol					
Fleet auxiliaries	25	24	30	6	5
Fuel ships	101	54	78	33	na
Troop transports	24	26	27	35	39/mo
Other train	40	39	39	48	60/mo
Base patrol boats	34	59	12	–	–
Total ships	389	286	292	161	
Landing craft and barges	117	193	100	100	320
Naval personnel	53,568	21,831	24,311	na	na
Marines	20,000	–	10,000	na	na
Army	16,000	55,000	40,000	50,000	50,000/mo
Aircraft					
Navy: on carriers	168	23	9	36	1,449
on battleships and cruisers	58	13	–	–	–
on train, crated	–	87	106	90	incl above
long-range flying boats	–	–	–	–	60
Army, crated	200	135	93	8	na
Marine, crated	36	–	–	–	na
Total aircraft	462	258	208	134	

Sources: CNO Plan, Mar 1929, 1:4, 6, 11, 76–77. JB Plan, Jun 1928. JPC Plan, April 1928.

Note: Each wave with materials and supplies for voyage, base establishment, ninety days of operations and, from M+60, thirty days of replenishment for preceding waves.

[a] Including 4 converted seaplane tenders.
[b] Converted types.
na = not available (unstated).

twelve to sixteen thousand men, for holding a bloodlessly captured base lying out of bombing range since they had no antiaircraft capability.[35] But the 1928 assumption of "landing operations against opposition" changed the situation. The planners endowed the first wave with a "spearhead" of twenty to twenty-eight thousand marines. Army leaders objected that the Marine Corps had no experience in storming beaches, or indeed in any large-scale operations. If the Corps were to conduct invasions for the entire war, it would have to grow to two hundred thousand—larger than the peacetime army. The navy backed down. Marines would handle the early landings, but their strength in the Pacific would be capped at forty thousand. Soldiers would join the later invasions in increasing strength (another prediction that came true in World War II). With its mission clarified, the army pledged a monthly quota of fifty thousand men.[36] Movements of this scale would require imaginative devices, for example, distilling ships to supply the transports with drinking water.[37] A somber analysis of overall shipping constraints showed that amassing in the western Pacific the five hundred thousand combatants the Army War College judged necessary to win the war would take two years.[38]

Estimates of American casualties, and hence of replacement needs, were matters of some delicacy. Shoemaker anticipated tonnage losses of 1 percent per month for large warships, 2 percent for merchantmen, and 3 percent for destroyers, submarines, and mineships.[39] Hospital ship allowances suggested a diminution of naval personnel of 3 percent per month. Ground force wastage was also set at 3 percent monthly, although Horne's guess of 10 percent per month for marine assault units correlated better with a presumption that half the landing barges would be lost. Flying units of both services were expected to suffer casualties of 25 percent per month; squadrons were allocated 50 percent reserves of men and machines.[40]

Haulage of fuel and cargo to the war zone was recognized as a daunting problem. (The navy insisted on a supply line across the Pacific, rejecting both an Atlantic route and purchases from Asia and Australia.[41]) The United States had in commission or layup 2,517 steamships of 11.5 million gross tons excluding war-built wooden ships that were useless. The navy inspected those suitable for war use;[42] by M+120, 1,128 of them would be pressed into service. The CinCUS-JAF was expected to group them into monthly convoys and guard them with destroyers, old cruisers, and, if necessary, a battleship or two.[43]

The Mobile Base Project (also known confusingly as "the train") was another innovation of the 1920s. Looking far beyond the simple cargo and service auxiliaries of earlier plans, Shoemaker called for a prefabricated naval base able to service the entire fleet at a raw harbor like Dumanquilas. (The idea, as was often the case in Orange Plans, had long roots. In 1911 the War College had imagined a train arriving "in the wake of the fleet" with matériel to transform a Philippine harbor into a military-industrial port and defended encampment.[44]) Prepackaged items embarked on vessels of ten-thousand-mile range were to include barracks, workshops, terminals for fuel, supplies and ordnance, and defense paraphernalia. The Western Base, as it came to be called, was to be erected on a grand scale. First, repair ships would be positioned, air stations put in commission, and three months worth of supplies laid in. Next, fifteen to twenty naval battalions skilled in construction and crafts would build warehouses, oil tanks, magazines, hospitals, and sophisticated maintenance works such as foundries and air engine shops. The tropical shoreline would blossom with the impedimenta of a great seaport—piers, cranes, dredges, tugs—and multiple depots for submarines and planes. In due course, five thousand skilled workers would perform on Mindanao every class of industrial job except gun relining. To save time, the project was supposed to be manufactured during peacetime. Most planners hoped the entire base could be functioning soon after the M+180 echelon arrived; pessimists expected completion about M+360.[45]

The most intractable difficulty of operating from the Western Base would be its lack of dry docks. In 1922 Williams had delayed a cautionary advance beyond Truk for eighteen months to await them.[46] Shoemaker investigated the matter. The fleet could survive topside injuries and do without hull cleaning for a while, he reckoned, but torpedoes and mines would take a heavy toll. His analysis indicated a need for nineteen docks of various sizes to go with the early waves and eight more after Z+180 for bottom cleaning. In full swing, they would be servicing seventeen hundred ships per year.[47] But no one knew how to build and deliver an eight hundred-foot-long battleship dock (or even the use of simple caissons to isolate damaged propellers and hull plates). Construction of just two Class A types for capital ships would take two years and, Shoemaker feared, extend the war beyond popular endurance.[48] Schofield was angered by talk of "throwing up the sponge"[49] but eventually admitted to "grave concern" about dockage. In 1928 Op-12 worked out a program calling for nine mobile docks, with destroyer-sized units to arrive in six months and Class A's in twelve to sixteen months,[50] just in time to help win the war in the two years he thought public patience would accept.

The prepackaged naval base was an excellent concept for World War II, when many were built throughout the Pacific. The delay in building dry docks had also been correctly postulated. Early in the war, heavy American ships had to retire to Pearl Harbor, the West Coast, or Australia. The first cruiser-sized dock appeared at an advanced base after eighteen months and mobile docks for capital ships about thirty months after the outbreak.[51] The lifting capacity installed in the western Pacific by the final year of war bore out the estimates of the 1920s logisticians. The U.S. offensive was not seriously hobbled because of the low effectiveness of Japanese submarines and mines (unlike the widespread topside mutilation by kamikazes), improved damage control and antifouling paints, and the drawn-out war that allowed time to construct 152 floating docks of all sizes.[52]

The Phase II campaign that the planners fashioned between 1926 and 1929 pioneered many valuable concepts for the operations and logistics of World War II, although the Through Ticket strategy they labored to preserve was abandoned five years after they completed it. Their most far-reaching contribution, however, was to design the only prewar campaign plan for the total defeat of Japan in Phase III.

The Siege of Japan

S ince the first Orange Plan the Pacific struggle had been expected to culminate with the reduction of Japan by a siege from offshore. The concept meshed with the plan's basic tenet of defeating land power with sea power. The United States would not have to destroy the Imperial Army on the Asian mainland or in Japan, either alone or with allies. Air power was added to the equation in the General Concept of 1923, which summarized Phase III as a campaign "directed towards the isolation of Japan through control of all waters surrounding Japan, through the equivalent of blockade operations, and through the capture and occupation of all outlying Japanese islands, intensified by an air war over Japanese territory."[1] The endgame of the war would be "a tremendous undertaking," a "long drawn out operation" against fanatical resistance, with rising casualties as the battlefront approached Japan.[2] Nevertheless, the siege had unfailingly been identified as the best means to achieve total victory.

Phase III evolved between 1906 and 1929 into a sequence of offensive operations to achieve specific geographic and economic objectives. It was to commence as soon as the USJAF established itself at a secure

Western Base and to build in intensity as the base expanded and reinforcements arrived. In short order the fleet would sever Japan's trade with regions south of Formosa, drive its navy from the East China Sea, and rupture its communications with its forces in the Philippines. If Corregidor were still holding out, it would be relieved. The expanding USJAF would then commence a drive northward along the ladder of islands paralleling the coast of Asia from the southern Philippines to the shores of Japan. It would either clear Luzon in a major ground campaign or bypass it. Its sea and air power would neutralize Formosa. In the most decisive amphibious campaign of the war a massive Blue expedition would capture the Ryukyu Islands against violent opposition. A fleet base would then be established within a few hundred miles of Japan. At every stage the Japanese would mount tactical attacks of attrition but would hoard their capital ships until, hard-pressed by Blue successes, they sortied for a decisive engagement. The great naval battle might occur at any time during Phase III in waters between Luzon and the coast of Japan. The superior Blue fleet would win. With control of the sea assured, the United States would cinch the blockade noose tightly around Japan. If need be, it would seize additional small islands close to Japan as posts for completing the blockage of imports from northeastern Asia. In the 1920s the plans added massed bombing attacks on Japanese industry and transportation. The siege would continue relentlessly until Japan was utterly exhausted and sued for terms.[3]

In the opening operation of Phase III, as soon as the USJAF arrived in the Philippines it would snuff out Japanese commerce with every region of the world except North China, Korea, and Siberia. (U.S. patrols would meanwhile have swept the Western Hemisphere and Atlantic clear of Japanese merchantmen.) The sea lanes between Japan and the resource areas of Malaysia and the Indian Ocean were important arteries; thrusters had always cited early severance of them as a reason for a quick drive to the Philippines. They could not be interdicted from bases in the central Pacific; the Guam lobby's claim of 1919 that the job could be done from its proposed base was overridden by Williams's insistence that Truk—and by implication Guam—was too remote for the purpose.[4] He was right. The navy was chronically deficient in long-range cruisers, the only blockade tools operable over such long distances (although it hoped to improvise armed liners as auxiliary cruisers). After World War I the planners assigned most of the blockade duty to the hundreds of emergency-built destroyers that could work only from bases close to the trade routes because they lacked range and sea-keeping ability.[5]

A Through Ticket to Manila, the thrusters argued, would simplify the blockade by enabling the fleet to close the narrows between Luzon and China. Removal of the Western Base to Mindanao after 1925 meant that a dispersed effort would be necessary to seal the many straits through the Netherlands East Indies. When the plan was fully refined by the early 1930s, a patrol cordon was projected north of the Indies from Singapore to New Guinea, a line close to Dumanquilas and with relatively few passes that could be covered by small craft and VPs (flying boats) until auxiliary cruisers arrived later in the year. (A patrol line south of the Indies from Singapore to Australia would have been safer from Orange naval interference but less effective because of the distance from Dumanquilas and the need to scatter to guard fifteen straits.) This barrier, along with denial of Western Hemisphere and Atlantic trade, would choke off two-thirds of Japan's normal commerce.[6]

The use of submarines as commerce raiders was a sensitive topic. U.S. policy makers abhorred the unrestricted U-boat attacks that had compelled the nation to fight Germany in 1917, both on moral grounds and for the practical reasons that indiscriminate sinkings would alienate neutral powers by killing foreign passengers and would invite Japanese retaliation. Submarines could not honor the gentlemanly code of the Hague Convention. They could not search vessels, remove passengers and seamen, or accommodate prize crews or prisoners. Submarines were slow when submerged and vulnerable on the surface even to armed merchantmen. The Orange Plans refrained from assigning them to trade warfare, although they could scout for and protect the surface patrols. (Aircraft, by implication, would have to be similarly restricted.) The policy ceded to Japan a sanctuary of trade with northeastern Asia until nearly the end of the war, although it was hoped that shipping in those waters might be disconcerted by undersea prowlings for legitimate military prey. The planners expected Japan to live by the same rules yet wondered if it might turn in desperation to unrestricted sinkings, inducing the United States to follow suit.[7]

The first offensive of the USJAF would commence within a few weeks of arrival at Dumanquilas. The objective might be Luzon—or it might not. Before 1930 about half the Orange planning studies called for reoccupation of the island (usually when the army view prevailed) while the others recommended bypassing it. Some early studies suggested that the Blue fleet would so frighten the Japanese that their army on Luzon would be evacuated, or abandoned to fight in the hills, or eradicated in some unspecified way.[8] The 1914 Plan stipulated that Luzon would be cleared and the fleet established at Manila without saying how. The crowning optimism appeared in the Joint Board's 1924 assumption that a mere fifty thousand Blue troops sprinting on a Z+14 Through Ticket to Manila could easily regain it. But more temperate analysts had calculated as early as 1907 that the task would require a far stronger expedition that would take many months to organize and probably would not embark until the Orange fleet was sunk.[9] All estimates of U.S. capability, however, paled in contrast with Orange's ability to land 100,000 to 200,000 soldiers on Luzon before Blue could intervene. Discerning thrusters of the early 1920s conceded that 250,000 American troops would be needed for large-scale operations in the western Pacific, perhaps including Luzon.[10]

Not surprisingly, naval strategists usually advocated bypassing Luzon and neutralizing it by sea power deployed from advanced bases on smaller islands such as Guam, Palawan, or Truk. Yet they recognized that political pressures might compel the navy to rescue Corregidor.[11] In 1928 the Joint Board inquired about plans for relieving the fortress island. Horne believed the survivors, if any, should be the army's responsibility. Granting that permanent denial of Manila Bay to Orange would enhance the security of Dumanquilas, however, naval planners proposed occupying Malampaya Sound on M+90 and setting up a depot for relief runs by expendable small auxiliaries. The post would also help forces attacking Orange communications with Luzon.[12]

In the late 1920s army planners gauging a campaign to recapture Luzon escalated the need to three hundred thousand motorized troops, triple the presumed Orange garrison, for a battle that would rage from M+270 through M+360. It would preempt all available shipping and compel the fleet to shift to a risky anchorage like Olongapo for close support. Yet a defeat on Luzon was entirely possible. It might cost Blue the war.[13] The General Staff therefore vetoed the campaign, to the satisfaction of the navy (two days after Leonard Wood's death). The joint planners assured their chiefs that it would be "entirely practicable" to skip Luzon except for occupying a minor base at the northern tip. The USJAF would simply eliminate Japanese air power from the island and ignore the trapped enemy garrison.[14]

The decision to bypass Luzon held until Schofield left Washington at the beginning of 1929. In another of those startling discontinuities to which American planning was prone, the army demanded recapture of

Manila Bay "as early as practicable after the outbreak of war." Op-12 was nonplussed. The operation would be brutal and the battered port facilities of little value.[15] The joint planners suggested leaving open the choice of Manila or Dumanquilas as the first destination; the board tightened the wording to "Manila or some other location."[16] The navy, anxious to salvage its Mindanao strategy, proposed using Manila as its *second* base. The fleet would still make for Dumanquilas but would erect there only a transient station, deferring the great civil engineering works "until the campaign has developed to such an extent that the place where the Western Base will finally be located has been determined and the place secured." The USJAF might, for example, clear Manila and Subic bays about M+180 and take up residence there. Naval base specialists refined and stretched out the Philippine two-step over the next few years. Dumanquilas could be operational on M+120 as a simple anchorage with floating services. A permanent base at Manila with grander facilities (although not yet dry docks) might be commissioned on M+360. The naval "commitment" to Manila, however, was tucked away in a supporting plan intended as an exercise for logisticians, not a directive to the CinCUSJAF.[17] In reality, the navy continued actively designing the grand base for Mindanao. The admirals had nodded in mock assent to avert another revolt of thrusting generals. In this they were abetted by army staffers who failed to write a supporting plan for Luzon. The locale and date of the Western Base remained swathed in deliberate ambiguity until 1935, when a revised Orange Plan omitted Philippine operations altogether.

Regardless of the dispute over the base, it was clear in the planning studies that an offensive movement from the southern Philippines did not require taking Luzon. The Orange planners anticipated an issue that strategists of World War II would face. Well-researched findings of the 1920s had indicated that bypassing was the better course militarily, but in 1944 MacArthur renewed the army's call for advancing from the southern Philippines to Luzon. The navy again wished to bypass the big island. The debate, one of the fiercest within the wartime high command, was settled by intervention of President Roosevelt in MacArthur's favor primarily to fulfill a political pledge to return.

A possible alternative to Luzon was Formosa, which Japan had owned since 1895, but the navy had no interest in its modest harbors and the army wanted no part of a major campaign to subjugate the entire large, mountainous island. The joint planners opted to isolate it by a bold series of invasions of small islands, beginning with the Sakishima Group just north of Formosa (Tables 14.1 and 14.2; Map

TABLE 14.1 *Full War Scenario, January 1928: Estimate of Possible Progress of Operations*

Operation	From	To
Prepare first concentration	M day	M+30
M+30 group to Western Base	M+30	M+60
Seizure and occupation of Western Base	M+60	M+90
Reinforcement of Corregidor	M+60	M+90
Organize and equip Western Base	M+60	M+600
Operations against Japanese fleet	M+60	End
Operations against Japanese commerce	M+60	End
Air attacks against Japanese main islands	M+60	End
M+60 group to Western Base	M+60	M+90
Seizure and occupation of Malampaya Sound	M+90	M+120
M+90 group to Western Base	M+90	M+120
Seizure and occupation of Marshall Islands	M+105	M+135
Seizure and occupation of Sakishima Islands	M+120	M+150
Seizure and occupation of Pescadores Islands	M+150	M+180
Operations in Carolines and Marianas	M+180	M+240
Seizure and occupation of Keelung (northern Formosa)	M+240	M+300
Seizure and occupation of Okinawa Islands	M+300	M+360
Air attacks on Amami Oshima	M+390	M+450
Seizure and occupation of Amami Oshima	M+450	M+540
Seizure and occupation of Osumi Islands	M+540	M+570
Intensive air attacks upon Japanese home islands	M+540	End
Seizure and occupation of Goto Islands	M+570	M+600
Operations against Tsushima Island	M+600	M+690
Operations for complete control of sea in immediate vicinity of Japanese home islands	M+690	End

Source: JPC Est, Jan 1928, 80–81.

14.1). The Sakishimas were unsuited for a naval base but would be critical for later air operations. Next, the good port of the Pescadore Islands, between Formosa and China, would be taken despite its heavy fortifications. Only then would a lodgment be secured on the northern tip of Formosa as a link for ferrying aircraft northward, a function so vital that the planners were willing to tie down for perimeter defense the largest U.S. garrison of any base, four times the number guarding

TABLE 14.2 *Full War Scenario, January 1928: Estimate of Possible Number of Troops Required*

Begin operations	Operations	Troops in principal theater	Troops required for operations	New troops required from U.S.	Troops required for defense
M+60	Occupy base in Western Pacific	20,000 M 16,000 A	20,000 M 16,000 A	16,000 A	16,000 A
M+90	Occupy base in Western Pacific	20,000 M 71,000 A		55,000 A	
M+90	Occupy Malampaya	20,000 M 71,000 A	8,000 M 16,000 A		16,000 A
M+105	Occupy Marshalls	30,000 M 71,000 A	10,000 M	10,000 M	10,000 M
M+120	Seize Sakishimas	30,000 M 71,000 A	8,000 M 16,000 A		15,000 A
M+150	Seize Pescadores	30,000 M 81,000 A	16,000 M 24,000 A	10,000 A (to Marshalls)	10,000 A
M+180	Occupy Carolines	30,000 M 101,000 A	10,000 M 20,000 A	20,000 A	10,000 M 20,000 A
M+240	Seize Keelung	30,000 M 147,000 A	30,000 M 60,000 A	46,000 A	60,000 A
M+300	Seize Okinawas	30,000 M 187,000 A	20,000 M 40,000 A	40,000 A	15,000 A
M+450	Seize Amami Oshima	40,000 M 242,000 A	40,000 M 80,000 A	10,000 M 55,000 A	40,000 A
M+540	Seize Osumi Islands	40,000 M 242,000 A	10,000 M 20,000 A		20,000 A
M+570	Seize Goto Islands	40,000 M 242,000 A	20,000 M 40,000 A	20,000 A	20,000 A
M+600	Seize Tsushima	40,000 M 382,000 A	40,000 M 120,000 A	120,000 A	

Source: JPC Est, Jan 1928, 80–81.
A = Army.
M = Marine.

Dumanquilas.[18] (Alternative outposts on Chinese coastal islands or ports were given little consideration. Planners of colonial wars at the dawn of the century had mused of bases there, but analysts of the Blue-Orange war had vetoed them as too provocative of neutral interests and vulnerable to the Orange army.[19])

Strategists agreed unanimously that the decisive positions of the entire conflict would be in the Ryukyus, a chain of midsized islands

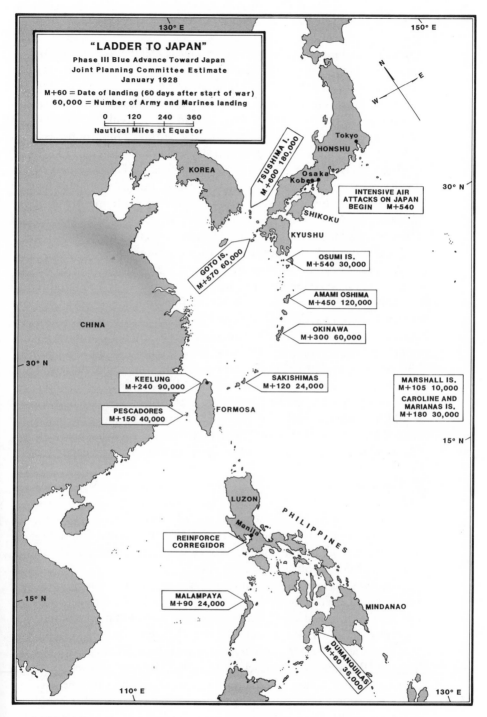

"LADDER TO JAPAN"

Phase III Blue Advance Toward Japan
Joint Planning Committee Estimate
January 1928

M+60 = Date of landing (60 days after start of war)
60,000 = Number of Army and Marines landing

0   120   240   360
Nautical Miles at Equator

TSUSHIMA I.
M+600 180,000

Tokyo
HONSHU

Osaka
Kobe

KOREA

INTENSIVE AIR
ATTACKS ON JAPAN
BEGIN   M+540

30° N

SHIKOKU

KYUSHU

GOTO IS.
M+570 60,000

OSUMI IS.
M+540 30,000

AMAMI OSHIMA
M+450 120,000

OKINAWA
M+300 60,000

CHINA

30° N

KEELUNG
M+240 90,000

SAKISHIMAS
M+120 24,000

MARSHALL IS.
M+105 10,000

CAROLINE AND
MARIANAS IS.
M+180 30,000

PESCADORES
M+150 40,000

FORMOSA

15° N

LUZON

Manila

PHILIPPINES

REINFORCE
CORREGIDOR

MALAMPAYA
M+90 24,000

MINDANAO

15° N

DUMANQUILAS
M+60 36,000

110° E

130° E

MAP 14.1

stretching six hundred miles between Formosa and the southern tip of Japan. In 1911 Mahan had pronounced them "the most effective position for the Blue Fleet."[20] From bases in the group the navy could isolate all Japan's forces to the south, terminate almost all its imports, and compel its fleet to battle.[21] From airfields in the Ryukyus waves of bombers could wreck the Japanese economy. Seizure of the group was a cardinal theme of U.S. strategy from 1906 to the final battle of 1945.[22]

The island of Amami Oshima was perceived as the best siege base of the Ryukyus because of its excellent harbor, but it was staunchly fortified and within close supporting distance of the home island of Kyushu 200 miles away. Good anchorages were also to be found at Okinawa, the largest island. Lying 150 miles farther south, it would be, as Sims noted in 1921, a prudent intermediate target.[23]

A Ryukyus campaign presented formidable problems of logistics and operations. Having neither Manila nor Formosa as an assembly point, Blue would have to mount the assault from a base seventeen hundred miles away in the southern Philippines (a stroke that Commander Oliver had judged "bold but not unwise") or, in the cautionary model of 1922, from Truk. The most brazen scheme of all had been Mahan's proposal of 1911 of a surprise descent from the Aleutians to Amami. The expedition would pause to coal at a deserted cove on the coast of Japan itself! Oliver pointed out that artillery sped by railway would hammer the anchorage while the fully alerted Japanese hardened the defenses of Amami. Even if Mahanian audacity paid off, Oliver added, supply convoys from the Aleutians would be candy for the Orange fleet.[24]

Estimates of strength to win the Ryukyus in pre–World War I plans had ranged from a low of 20,000 troops that might succeed by a "determined dash," to an army corps of three divisions totaling 43,191, to triple that number. But before 1918 the United States had transports enough for only one division; it would have had to resort to chartering foreign bottoms for an assault.[25]

The Ryukyus campaign would be fraught with extreme peril. Fortifications had been halted by the Treaty of 1922, but thrusters still warned that if Blue delayed beyond one year it would find the islands impregnable[26]—a key argument for the Through Ticket to Manila. Whatever the date, enemy artillery and torpedo boat defenses would be fierce and the weight of air attack formidable.[27] American forces would have to attain absolute air superiority to win the Ryukyus. The fleet could not supply enough aerial punch to take Amami, but it could cover the softer Okinawa operation by carriers and seaplanes and expect support from army planes in the Sakishimas and the Formosa enclave. The planners hoped to mount a four-division landing on Okinawa soon after the Western Base was in full commission. (The landings of 1945, covered primarily by fleet aviation, began with four divisions and built up to seven.) Blue air bases on Okinawa would be critical for the attack on Amami, especially since the navy would not expose battleships until the shore guns were knocked out.[28] (One curious suggestion was to invade just before the typhoon season dampened enemy air activity. It did not explain what a typhoon would do to the Americans.[29]) In the 1928 plan the buildup of eight divisions to assault Amami meant delaying the operation to M+450. The entire fleet would be committed to their support, by then hugely enlarged in weaponry of all types including special gunships to help the invasion.[30]

The Ryukyus operations would forge ahead even though a failure at any stage "might prolong the war almost indefinitely, and would certainly increase the cost enormously,"[31] because the islands were essential to the siege strategy. Base Y would be developed there. Its shore facilities and dry docks, guarded by powerful sea and air units, would be designed to service the entire fleet and train for a year. It would make the blockade almost fully effective. Base Y and other advanced bases would include army cantonments for defense and for staging to islands nearer Japan.[32]

The decision during World War II to occupy the Ryukyus was another instance when wartime planners reverted to principles of the Orange Plan. American strategists of 1945 coveted these islands as bases for conventional bombers redeploying from Europe, as naval stations, and as assembly depots for a possible invasion of Japan. Their campaign plan called for seizure of five islands along a 340-mile front, from just off Formosa to one adjacent to Amami,[33] resembling the 1928 outline, although the war ended after only Okinawa and nearby islets had been taken. Japanese suicide bombers, modern analogs of savage torpedo boat and airplane defenses, exacted the dreadful price in capital ships—especially carriers—that peacetime strategists had feared.

War Plan Orange consistently anticipated a great naval battle during Phase III that would defeat or neutralize the Imperial Fleet. To a service spellbound by the Mahanian concept, Williams had preached in 1910 an "unrelenting and undiverted effort to bring the enemy's fleet to action, to crush their naval force and to drive their vessels from the sea."[34] The plans rang with declarations that the navy's "main objective throughout the war" was to "seek and destroy" the Japanese battle line and thereby assure the final victory.[35] Planners occasionally wondered if Japan might adopt a "fleet in being" strategy of shunning contact[36] and inhibiting the Americans by the ever-present threat of its navy until war weariness induced negotiations. But the consensus held that Japan's national character and military necessity would compel it to accept the gauntlet. Japan, however, would dictate the terms of the engagement. Its leaders, confident of their disciplined people, would play a waiting game "knowing that the Blue fleet must come to her and fight." The Orange fleet would emerge only after expendable ground, sea, and air units had reduced Blue's big naval guns to parity or less and only when it was best positioned and prepared.[37]

In 1910 the General Board had reflected that the Japanese could benefit from multiple combats; they might lose each battle but could refit wounded ships at home bases, while Blue, without a dockyard in the western Pacific, would lose the war through cumulative mutilation.[38] But American naval imaginations were obsessed by the dramas of Trafalgar, Tsushima, and Jutland. Besides, a single battle was a congenial planning assumption given the preponderance of U.S. battleships always concentrated for action, with their numerical advantage augmented by the N-squared law that combat effectiveness was proportional to the square of the number of guns in action. A ratio of 5 to 3, for example, translated into a 2.8-to-1 battle superiority and almost certain victory. (Strategists did not concern themselves with battle tactics, which were the provenance of training, maneuvers, and war games. Such exercises sometimes rehearsed the Orange Plan scripts and at other times variant themes, including interception of the USJAF en route to the Philippines.)[39]

Planners' opinions diverged as to the time and place of the clash. Some supposed it would occur early in Phase III near the Western Base, others staged it along the island ladder, and still others at the end of the war off the coast of Japan. They universally agreed that the Orange main body would not challenge the fleet's Pacific crossing during Phase II (excepting the Guam lobby's assertion that a movement to a prepared base might draw out the main body.[40]) Thrusters felt confident that Japanese dreadnoughts would not strike at a secret rendezvous in Micronesia or on the high seas, cavalier assumptions because destruction of the train would admittedly "stagger" the United States into an ignominious retreat and perhaps cost it the war.[41] Cautionaries believed the big Orange ships would not venture so far afield as to oppose a Blue occupation of the Mandates.[42] Not until 1941 did American planners develop a hypothesis of mid-ocean battle (Chapter 25).

The Philippines were a popular combat milieu in plans before World War I. Analysts who projected a quick arrival and immediate forays by the Blue fleet hoped to trap the Orange navy at Luzon and whip it there, perhaps as it scrambled to evacuate.[43] The Second Committee speculated more grimly that the main body might intercept a Blue expedition to the southern Philippines and sink the battleships after cruisers and torpedo craft had scattered them.[44] But the NWC Plan of 1911 fixed the standard presumption that Japanese dreadnoughts would avoid their Blue counterparts in the Philippines unless attrition attacks had taken a nasty bite, an assumption adopted, for example, in Op-12's Battle of Dumanquilas scenario of 1928.[45]

By the late 1920s planners agreed that naval attrition would be a slow process. Japan, seeking to discourage its foe psychologically and militarily, would trade space for time.[46] Its battleships would not fight during the first year. They would not fight for Formosa, which lacked good harbors, or for the Pescadores, which would prove to be a trap if they were cut off there.[47] The main body would emerge only when Japan felt threatened by a Blue advance that imperiled national survival. Most Orange Plans nominated the Ryukyus as the point of contact because Japan could not yield them and still survive. There, close to home bases, waves of torpedo boats could be loosed in near-suicidal night attacks for a final orgy of attrition before a gunnery climax.[48]

An engagement off the coast of Japan itself had rarely been hypothesized. (Mahan had once imagined the possibility if a Blue surprise attack early in the war scattered the Orange battle line.[49]) But in the late 1920s Schofield and his aides adopted that locale. To maximize the attrition period, they reasoned, the main body would hole up until Japan faced absolute suffocation, which would occur after about two years. It was a comforting assumption because it meant the United States could develop the western dockyard and Ryukyus bases within the supposed time limit of public tolerance. The battle would thus constitute the final event of the war.[50]

American strategists felt confident of winning the great clash. Images of defeat were rare. (In one 1907 scenario shattered Blue remnants slunk home via the Indian Ocean or interned in neutral ports and the war ended.[51]) The United States always had more battleships than Japan. In 1906 it had thirty-three versus fourteen.[52] In 1922 the margin was eighteen to ten. But American superiority was less impressive if measured in large-caliber guns, and U.S. dreadnoughts were slower and lacking in such modern protections as antitorpedo blisters and antiaircraft guns.[53] Cruiser strengths were roughly equal at most times. Predominance in light units fluctuated. In 1906 the 116 torpedo boats that Japan had used so effectively against Russia would have been a potent equalizer.[54] The building programs of World War I yielded a Blue supremacy of four- or fivefold in destroyers and submarines,[55] but in the 1920s obsolescence and penury gradually eroded the margin. Nevertheless, Schofield's team remained certain of a victory late in the war because two years' outpourings of airplanes and light warships would go far toward offsetting attrition losses of capital ships.

The single climactic battle projected in the Orange Plans never happened. In World War II there were about a dozen major naval engagements during Phases I and II but not in Phase III (i.e., not north of the Philippines). They were fought thousands of miles from Japan in the central and South Pacific. The principal combatants were aircraft carriers and cruisers and occasionally small detachments of battleships. Each side enjoyed a numerical superiority on various occasions. The United States won most but not all of the battles. A full comparison of Plan Orange to wartime reality must await the closing chapters of this book, but it is instructive to bear in mind the grand strategy of the plan as well as its campaign details. It stipulated destruction of the Imperial Navy as a prerequisite to winning the war. Japan, it predicted, would allow this to happen, neither adopting a "fleet in being" policy nor diverting capital ships to such functions as raids on base facilities or communications. Its battleships and carriers were primed to fight their counterparts. When the test came, they did, and their loss paved the way for U.S. victory. The naval battle hypothesis of Plan Orange was, in essence, correct.

A key element of America's victory strategy was "the final and complete commercial isolation of Japan."[56] The concept of total blockade, originated in 1906 and formalized in the 1911 plan, was to be implemented by interception of Orange shipping and searching of neutral vessels for contraband. The planners expected little difficulty in confining trade to lands within a thousand miles of Japan after the fleet was in the Philippines, but the economic analyses that prefaced their strategic studies showed that the enemy could survive and even prosper as long as it had access to goods from (or transshipped through) Korea, Manchuria, North China, and possibly Siberia. Blue would be unable to stop this traffic by sealing off the harbors of the homeland with inshore patrols as the Federal navy had done to the South in the Civil War, even if the Orange fleet were sunk, because most Japanese ports lay in narrow bays or sounds like the Inland Sea that bristled with modern defenses.[57] Physical layout also discouraged the mining of harbors and straits despite the sophisticated U.S. minelaying achievements of 1918 in Europe. In World War II Japanese waters were not mined effectively until long-range aircraft accomplished the task in 1945.

The "prime consideration" in isolating Japan from northern Asia was the gaining of a base within five hundred miles of the Strait of Tsushima, the shortest crossing to the mainland. Even so, Japan could probably survive by importing across the Sea of Japan into ports on its west coast.[58] To impose total closure, the planners considered and rejected advanced bases in Korea[59]—another idea resurrected in World War II and again declined. In 1928 they chose instead to extend Phase III by mounting the biggest amphibious operation of the war to capture Tsushima Island, within the strait. A base there would lay bare the Sea of Japan and complete the blockade.[60]

The Tsushima operation was to be the capstone of a series of eight major assaults over sixteen months. The joint planners offered this itinerary for its "empirical value" of demonstrating the scope of Phase III;[61] the Joint Board agreed with the strategic sequence but declined to endorse the punctilious timetable.[62] Nevertheless, the planning schedule of 1928 was historically significant as the only full-war campaign agenda drawn before the final year of World War II.

An airtight blockade would have to be maintained for a "considerable time," at least a year, to deplete Japanese stockpiles and longer for effective strangulation.[63] Although the planners of the 1920s adopted a hypothesis wherein Japan would sue for peace after two years of fighting, there were few if any historical precedents of victory by blockade alone. For centuries, reductions of citadels immune to storming had been accomplished by bombardment in combination with isolation. It was optimistic to think that the warrior nation of Nippon would capitulate merely because resources were denied for the brief span most planners believed American public tolerance would accept. Until the air age, however, infliction of physical damage on Japan's onshore economy would have been impossible. At the dawn of U.S. planning there had been speculations of Blue warships forcing the channels of the Inland Sea and shelling the rich cities of Kobe and Osaka and later passing beyond Tsushima to bombard ports on both sides of the Sea of Japan.[64] Mahan, too restless for the slow tourniquet of blockade, urged cruiser strikes on Japanese harbors, actions that would frighten and dislocate coastwise shipping and cause overburdening of the railroads.[65] Even before World War I demonstrated that mines, guns, and torpedo craft could render home ports inviolable, the planners concluded that sea raids on Japan would be "unlikely" and the results "fruitless."[66] Their surmise was correct. As late as 1945, U.S. gunships could only shell minor towns fronting on the open Pacific. They could not navigate the fortified passes to major cities. In the 1920s aircraft carrier strikes on Japan were also pondered, but the planners considered them blows unsuitable for economic warfare and better concentrated against naval bases such as Yokosuka and Kure, preferably as surprise raids early in the war.[67]

The credibility of winning by economic siege was vastly increased by strides in aeronautics during the 1920s. Strategic bombing of Japan was mentioned in studies early in the decade. By 1928 it was adopted in the Joint Orange Plan. Ironically, although air power would accelerate Japan's final collapse, it would slow the campaign of approach in an era of limited flight ranges because, to assure dominance over each island, Blue would have to capture more of them spaced at closer intervals. For the bombing finale, bases very close to Japan would be necessary. Since landplanes and seaplanes of that vintage could not reach Tokyo from the Ryukyus, the JPC proposed to occupy the Osumi and Goto islands, barely forty miles from the Kyushu coast, and build bomber fields with stout defenses against retaliation.[68]

A strategic air effort circa 1928 could have been surprisingly robust. By M+390 U.S. aircraft production would have risen tenfold to eighteen thousand planes annually,[69] a fair approximation of the Pacific deployments of World War II. Nevertheless, army officers felt ambivalent about bombing civilian targets. Some considered warships the only decisive targets of a Pacific war.[70] But General Billy Mitchell, the air service's most outspoken booster and publicist, called Japan's densely populated wood and paper cities "the greatest aerial targets the world has ever seen." He imagined squadrons from Alaska, staging through Siberia by virtue of a deal with the Soviets, laying them waste by incendiary and gas bombs.[71] The planning staff suggested raids on the production and transportation of war goods but not on populations.[72] Army Intelligence recommended hitting aircraft factories, steelworks, and arsenals in Tokyo, Osaka, Yawata, and Nagoya,[73] a list similar to targets actually hit from mid-1944 until the United States switched to city-burning raids in March 1945. Though further air studies were shelved until 1939,[74] the Orange Plans of ten years earlier had shaped Phase III to include procurement of air bases and unleashing of strategic bombers to ruin Japan's economy.

In most previous wars, the victor had won by vanquishing the enemy army, as most recently demonstrated in the Russo-Japanese and First World wars. U.S. planners did examine the possibility of accelerating victory by beating the Japanese army in the field. Their thoughts on the unpopular subject were shrouded in euphemisms like "conditional further action" that would "compel submission."[75] The notion of combat on the Asian mainland was so at odds with maritime thinking that it was not even considered until 1923, and then only to discredit a cautionary ocean advance that, the thrusters argued, would allow Japan to arm the Ryukyus invincibly and forever bar a victory from the sea. The army was advised to study the landing of a huge force in south China and an advance to the Yangtze River to clear depots supporting the island strongholds, a campaign of "tremendous" cost that would alienate the American people.[76] Upon reinstatement of the Through Ticket that year the notion was filed away. Later in the 1920s army planners reported that adequate shipping would never be available to undertake a China expedition.[77] When the Joint Board pressed for hypothetical examples of such a campaign, G-2 sullenly listed three options: a landing at Canton and a long march north, a bolder entry near Shanghai, and a reckless descent directly on Manchuria or Korea.[78] The navy, lacking data and inclination, refused to respond. Planners of both services agreed that grappling with the Japanese army "might well result in disastrous defeat." One gruesome scenario depicted Blue losing control of the sea and unable to extricate its trapped soldiers.[79]

It was an article of faith among all planners that the United States need never invade Japan. To make their studies complete, however, the professional strategists of the 1920s considered the possibility. Williams concluded in 1922 that invasion offered "almost no prospect of success." America could mobilize and arm enough troops over several years, he reckoned, but the entire merchant marine could barely maintain in the Far East a grossly inadequate legion of 1 million.[80] Army planners in 1927 considered the outcome of an invasion "extremely doubtful . . . regardless of our greater potentiality in man power and munitions, because the enemy can always concentrate forces greatly superior to the successive Expeditions into which our land forces must be organized for overseas transportation."[81]

The Army War College reported Japan to be "almost invulnerable." The ferocity of the Imperial Army was legendary. The countryside was mountainous, the valleys filled with rice paddies. Suitable roads were few, and the bridges were designed for farm carts. Heavy equipment, the U.S. trump card, would have to be discarded.[82] Invasion, the staff

166 • WAR PLAN ORANGE

of the AWPD declared, "we honestly believe is a physical impossibility."[83] Nonetheless, the Joint Board inquired about potential landing sites.[84] G-2 responded that all ports were unassailable. If the deed had to be done, the least daunting place was Kagoshima Bay in Kyushu because it lay relatively near prospective Blue bases, had a good anchorage and passes inland, and appeared to be lightly fortified. The second choice was the Tokyo Bay area.[85] These were exactly the landing sites designated in the final U.S. war plans of 1945.

Although they shunned an invasion, the planners observed that massing troops on islands near Japan would suggest such an operation, imposing on the enemy unbearable expense to guard all beaches and thus prodding him toward the peace table.[86] World War II leaders who favored invasion and postwar apologists for the decision later declared similarly that the ability and apparent intention to invade expedited Japan's surrender as surely as the other incentives of August 1945.[87]

The architects of Phase III were sensitive to the question of how long Japan could resist. The answer would determine whether the United States would press on to subjugate it completely or settle for a limited victory. The premise of a two-year war was a compromise. A shorter struggle was unlikely in view of the time needed to mobilize U.S. muscle, Japan's steely determination, and the assumption that it would hoard its battle fleet while maximizing the attrition period. A longer forecast, however, would raise the politically objectionable issue of constructing a second battle fleet during the war. In 1923 the General Board recommended that course, a three-year endeavor, implying a need of plans for a very long war, but OpNav shied away from such a "large order."[88] To propose it would have called into question the national will for unlimited victory and thus the Orange Plan's fundamental thesis (and perhaps even funding of the navy whose mission it defined). Similar questions were to arise in 1944–45. A vast new fleet had already been launched and siege operations were far advanced, but strategists still did not know whether Japan would yield to siege within a time and cost that America would endure.

Quest for a Strategy

T he years of Herbert Hoover's administration were dispiriting for Pacific war planners. The Through Ticket gambit on which rested their design for crushing Japan within two years fell prey to second thoughts after Schofield and Horne departed. International developments boded ill for the gung ho philosophy when the Japanese government fell under the sway of military cliques bent on territorial aggrandizement. In September 1931 they annexed Manchuria and the following year raided Shanghai, undeterred by outcries from the League of Nations and America's "nonrecognition doctrine." In the spring of 1933 Tokyo decided to quit the League but to retain control of the Mandated Islands. Realists in the United States expected Japan to renounce the ban on fortification of the islands and withdraw from the naval treaties that for a decade had limited numbers of warships and strengthening of Pacific bases. Meanwhile, American public sentiment increasingly favored independence for the Philippines, a cession that might call into question the relevance of Plan Orange by removing a major rationale for conflict with Japan.

It was also a time of economic depression and stringent U.S. military budgets. Warships were decommissioned with no evidence that Japan would follow suit. The merchant marine sagged into a state of decay. After 1930 Naval War College analysts figured that American capacity to fight in the western Pacific had slipped to "decided inferiority." The wartime destroyer flotillas had withered away, crippling the fleet for night combat. Japanese aviation loomed larger as a threat to offensive movements. Critics of the Orange Plan sought to tame its excesses by amendments prohibiting the fleet from crossing the Pacific unless explicitly authorized by the president of the United States. (Fragmentary evidence suggests that Clarence Williams sponsored this caveat after his cautionary plan was discarded.[1]) The Joint Board "understood" the president's authority but felt sure he would unsheathe the Blue sword in response to public cries for revenge.[2]

A cautionary backlash gripped Newport. On the gaming floor the Blue train and its escorts were always wrecked by the Orange team. Warships fared no better in the crossing. In the 1923 game fifteen battleships had arrived in the Philippines, but in 1928 only ten made it, and in 1933 only seven got through unscarred by vicious torpedo attacks. The postmortems scorned the Through Ticket as "pure fantasy . . . unfeasible . . . it could not be done."[3] Senior staff members advised that an immediate advance of the fleet "might well result in its complete loss." The Orange Plan, they concluded, was "founded on quicksand."[4]

Army dissidents joined the nay-sayers. The Through Ticket, they warned, was like the Russian suicide cruise and should not be executed "merely because it is the only thing that we see can be done."[5] They coalesced around Brigadier General Stanley D. Embick, commander of the Corregidor fortress and a rising star among strategic thinkers. In 1933 Embick uttered his now-famous denunciation of War Plan Orange as "literally an act of madness." The outmatched U.S. Navy, he predicted, would suffer catastrophic defeat. Since the country could not strengthen itself because of treaties and economic duress, he recommended pulling out of the Orient and retiring into the eastern Pacific behind the perimeter Alaska-Oahu-Panama. The nation might then, if it wished, spend several years and a great fortune building a formidable attack navy, an option Embick derided as a foolish waste to regain worthless possessions.[6]

Early in 1933 the experts at the Naval War College studied the nature of a Pacific war should Embick's defensive strategy be adopted. Captain R. A. Koch, in a paper forwarded to the newly elected President Franklin Roosevelt, foresaw a Phase I lasting three years during which the United States would build capital ships. The navy would cordon off the eastern Pacific at the Midway-Unalaska line and limit offensive actions to submarine stalkings of Orange warships and occasional raids on the nearest of the Mandated Islands. When it had regained a five-to-three ascendancy, equivalent to battle parity after allowances for escort, raiding, and incapacitations, the navy would attack through the Mandate to a western Pacific base. It would advance to blockading positions near Japan and deploy specially designed forty-knot cruisers to strangle Orange trade. Victory would be "practically certain" in four or five years. The head of the college Research Department concurred, urging OpNav to plan for a four-year conflict and a fleet four times the size of Japan's.[7] These academic estimates correctly anticipated the circumstances of World War II, when a great new fleet embarked on a central Pacific advance after two years (or three years after the tremendous Naval Expansion Act of 1940) and Japan succumbed after three years and eight months of fighting.

Thrusters, too, had considered a much-delayed offensive but rejected it as "too remote to warrant the attempt." During a long grace period, Japan would plunder China, stockpile materials, fortify all potential bases, and hone its navy. Petty sea joustings of a long-range Phase I would scarcely trouble it. The American people, they predicted, would either balk at the stupendous expense of a second fleet or, goaded by pride, hurl the navy against a toughened enemy at tragic cost. Quick counterattack, the Joint Board had concluded by the end of the 1920s, was "the only way" to "win the war and impose our will upon Japan."[8]

Under pressure, the thrusters did retreat on details of targets and forces. They could stomach a regression of the Western Base from Manila to Mindanao and after 1933 to Truk. They could accept a stretchout of the attack force into successive waves and ultimately a diminishment of U.S. combat power in the Pacific when it became necessary to stiffen Atlantic defenses. In 1941 they even acceded to naval demonstrations in lieu of landings as the initial offensive actions. But *immediate* naval response, their bedrock principle, remained embedded in American plans until 7 December 1941.

The ultracautionary proposals of the early 1930s to defer attacking for several years made no headway, but the foibles of the Through Ticket could no longer be ignored. Naval planners turned to searching for modifications to overcome its worst drawbacks. In 1932 Op-12, guided by Captain Meyers, worked up a "Battle Problem—Quick Movement" that postulated a Blue expedition setting sail for the Philippines during a period of "more or less acute" tensions before war broke out (see Map 15.1). The navy would dispatch almost instantly from the West Coast twelve battleships and three carriers, a force equal to Japan's capital ships; a cruiser and destroyer screen of somewhat less than parity; and a mini-train of two dozen fast auxiliaries. Smaller vessels would fuel at Lahaina while the big ships bypassed Hawaii to conceal their whereabouts. Japan would be deceived by tales of maneuvers or of excursions to Guam or the Aleutians while the units rendezvoused in utmost secrecy in the South Pacific. A nimble task force would sprint ahead with a handful of picked troops and secure Dumanquilas as a base. When the expedition came to anchor, the United States would mobilize openly and hasten reinforcements along routes south of New Guinea. Meyers expected the "mere presence" of the fleet to deter Japan from invading Luzon. A Quick Movement might ruin the chance for peace, he admitted, but it was a risk worth taking because of the strategic benefit of holding Luzon.[9] A prewar advance, however, was utterly beyond the norms of American politics. It was never translated into an official war plan. Nevertheless, the study introduced the worthwhile notion of a streamlined expeditionary force surging ahead unburdened by hundreds of wallowing merchant tubs.

Naval headquarters in Washington felt no pressure to recast Pacific strategy as long as the anti-planning Pratt was in charge. It sought only to obtain viable proposals from the fleet for establishing itself in the western Pacific in "superior strength" and "at the earliest practicable date."[10] But the calls for a fleet plan were ignored by successive commanders in chief from 1929 through 1932. Early in 1933 CinCUS Richard H. Leigh's staff suggested it might be "quite a simple matter" to adapt the readiness and timing suppositions of the Quick Movement into a "realistic" operating plan. The WPD agreed to the suggestion for want of anything better,[11] but nothing came of it until August 1933, when Admiral David F. Sellers, the next CinCUS, submitted Tentative Contributory Plan O-1. It turned out, to his chagrin, to be the first lurch toward a cautionary policy.

Sellers, a battleship officer who had nearly won the CNO's berth, had been exposed to strategy in staff and command assignments and at the War College, but he lacked the philosophical turn of mind for war planning, preferring the tangible satisfactions of training the fleet under combat conditions.[12] He was a thruster heart and soul. He imagined his carriers laden with army planes galloping to rescue Manila, a fantasy the air corps rebuffed. More plausibly, the CinCUS borrowed the idea of a quick movement in which an elite force would beat Japan

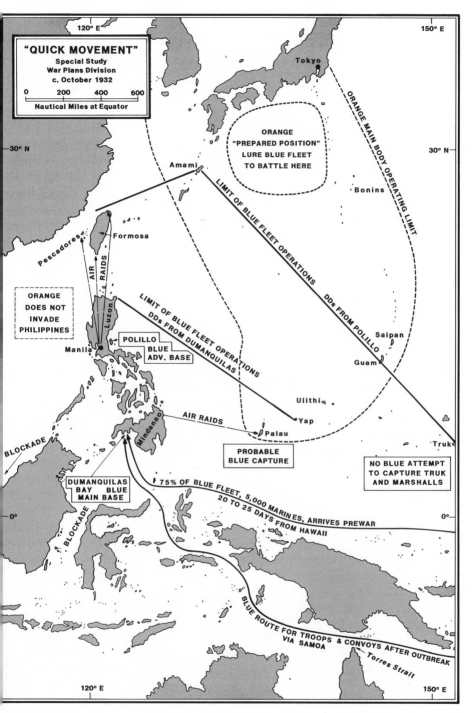

"QUICK MOVEMENT"
Special Study
War Plans Division
c. October 1932

0   200   400   600
Nautical Miles at Equator

120° E

150° E

Tokyo

ORANGE
"PREPARED POSITION"
LURE BLUE FLEET
TO BATTLE HERE

ORANGE MAIN BODY OPERATING LIMIT

30° N

30° N

Amami

Bonins

LIMIT OF BLUE FLEET OPERATIONS

Pescadores

Formosa

DDs FROM POLILLO

AIR RAIDS

Luzon

ORANGE
DOES NOT
INVADE
PHILIPPINES

LIMIT OF BLUE FLEET OPERATIONS

DDs FROM DUMANQUILAS

Saipan

Manila

POLILLO
BLUE
ADV. BASE

Guam

Ulithi

Yap

AIR RAIDS

BLOCKADE

Mindanao

Palau

Truk

PROBABLE
BLUE CAPTURE

NO BLUE ATTEMPT
TO CAPTURE TRUK
AND MARSHALLS

DUMANQUILAS
BAY   BLUE
MAIN BASE

75% OF BLUE FLEET, 5,000 MARINES, ARRIVES PREWAR
20 TO 25 DAYS FROM HAWAII

0°

0°

BLOCKADE

BLUE ROUTE FOR TROOPS & CONVOYS AFTER OUTBREAK
VIA SAMOA

Torres Strait

120° E

150° E

MAP 15.1

to the southern Philippines even though sailing *after* the declaration of war. If conducted with "vigor, determination and aggressiveness . . . in accordance with Blue national spirit," he boasted, the gambit would "break the will to resist of Orange." Success would depend on mobilizing at a moment's notice a streamlined U.S. Asiatic Force (USAF— "Joint" was dropped, perhaps as a bureaucratic ploy).

Rear Admiral Joseph M. Reeves, commander of Sellers's battle force of capital ships, laid out frenetic programs to man, dock, and provision the USAF; procure spare aircraft; and strip Hawaii and the Canal Zone of munitions. To avoid the delay of converting ammunition ships, the men-of-war would lug extra ordnance. Plane-transport and escort vessels would sortie almost immediately along with thirty of the best civilian ships. They would fuel at Lahaina so swiftly that no minefield need be laid. On M+10 three-fourths of the combat navy and liners with five thousand marines aboard would weigh anchor and overtake them at sea. By dint of prompt departures and fast steaming the expedition would reach Dumanquilas three weeks *sooner* than the first wave projected in Plan Orange. On M+20 a supporting detachment would follow, consisting of tardy gunships, submarines from the Atlantic, and a slow train of forty-one vessels, including twenty-six transports bearing a thousand troops apiece. Sixty-three oilers would service both movements, the fastest streaking with the first wave and the rest taking positions along the route. The combined force of 318 ships and 504 aircraft would, said the feisty CinCUS, be "thoroughly prepared to fight and destroy every enemy that we may be fortunate enough to encounter."[13]

For purely logistical reasons Sellers inserted short stops in the Marshall Islands—and unintentionally cracked the door for the cautionaries. He projected the two echelons to refuel in the group on M+27 and M+40, respectively, "strictly practicable" dates because Orange forces could not reach the atolls any sooner, he believed,[14] and because Meyers thought there was no need to protect such temporary havens. But officers of the Fleet Marine Force (FMF, formed in 1933) worried about Orange raids on vessels in unguarded lagoons.[15] Sellers agreed to offload the marine spearhead for a few days of defense but expected to reembark it with the first wave for Dumanquilas (reminiscent of pre-1914 coaling scenarios in German Micronesia). He felt amenable to more solid anchorage defenses for the weak second wave,[16] another idea that was soon co-opted by cautionary minds.

Sellers's version of the Quick Movement was as impracticable as the original, but its deviation from Through Ticket orthodoxy permitted others to twist it into a cautionary campaign plan. By the autumn of 1933 many naval strategists believed that a scenario of a rush to the Philippines could not be salvaged by tinkering with timing, itinerary, or forces. Yet the defensive solution of Embick and the college analysts was antithetical to the tradition embodied in the Orange Plan. Another solution, one that preserved the principle of prompt counter-attack—an island-hopping campaign through the Mandate—had been brushed aside in 1923. Yet before 1933 was out it was resurrected permanently as the American strategy of the Pacific.

Two other conditions motivated adoption of a cautionary Orange Plan: a suspicion that Japan was preparing the Mandates for war and strides in aviation that eliminated the gravest risk of naval operations in the central Pacific.

For two decades Japan had shrouded the Mandated Islands in mystery, barring visits by foreign vessels and rarely admitting travelers and then only to five ports.[17] Scientists observing a solar eclipse, for example, had to travel on Japanese warships.[18] Japan's secrecy is not easily explained because it had honored its other obligations to the League of Nations. It withdrew its military units after World War I. Naval vessels called occasionally, a permissible activity, but no construction of quasi-military value was undertaken before 1934 or any fortification until 1939. A Japanese historian later explained that his country felt embarrassed lest the world see how little it was doing to improve the lot of the inhabitants.[19] Postwar American investigators could only suggest an "apparent" Japanese fetish for secrecy or an obsession with commercial monopoly.[20]

U.S. intelligence officers tended to credit rumors about Japan's activities in the Mandates as "strong indications" of transgression.[21] Gossip about "impregnable island bastions" circulated despite accounts of reliable witnesses, including a museum ornithologist, church missionaries, and an assistant U.S. naval attaché, who saw no forbidden activity. Naval and marine planners believed native seafarers who gossiped about artillery at Truk and ten-inch cannon on the heights of Palau and an AWOL marine who jabbered of "many, many guns" on Saipan.[22] Army G-2 speculated in 1927 that Japan had thirteen submarine and seaplane depots in the islands, and the JPC half believed that guns and mines were already installed.[23]

The United States managed to conduct one useful espionage in 1923, when the cruiser *Milwaukee* toured the islands that Williams had targeted in his 1922 plan. The Office of Naval Intelligence (ONI) proposed an inspection voyage disguised as a routine shakedown cruise of a new vessel. The State Department acquiesced because sister ships were calling at other foreign ports. (Its request for entry went astray in the turmoil of the great Tokyo earthquake, and by the time the Japanese government learned about it the mission had been completed.[24]) At the northernmost Marshall atoll of Taongi the *Milwaukee* found no lagoon passes. At Rongelap and Eniwetok it entered the harbors and lofted its seaplane to take photographs, identifying an excellent anchorage at the latter. The sole Japanese resident raised no objection.[25] At Truk the Americans saw only a small coaling station. The Japanese governor prohibited overflights, but the U.S. intelligence officer noted harbors and aviation sites that confirmed Truk as the best island in the region for a major fleet base.[26]

Emboldened by the results, the ONI and Op-12 plotted the following year to observe eighteen other islands by seeking permission to park naval oilers in the Mandate for replenishing destroyers transiting the Pacific. Eberle demurred, "Not at present time."[27]

A more colorful but inept espionage was conducted simultaneously with the *Milwaukee* cruise by Lieutenant Colonel Earl H. "Pete" Ellis, the brilliant originator of the Marine Corps's landing doctrine (Chapter 10). Ellis, a scholar, war hero, and Japanese linguist, suffered from medical disabilities and a drinking problem. His journey may have been authorized by Commandant Lejeune or it may have been a private adventure. Ellis boarded a Japanese steamer under false identity and toured the Marshalls and Carolines. In the Palaus he died from mysterious causes. Foul play by Japanese officials was rumored but never proved. Ellis's notes were never found.[28]

Proposals for further naval visits were squelched by Tokyo in 1929.[29] After Japan announced in 1933 that it would resign from the League, American strategists grew frantic for hard facts. The FMF began assembling a thousand-page catalog containing every shred of data about Micronesia.[30] Inquisitive officers suggested secret flights to unpopulated islands.[31] Reeves pressed for transpacific or round-the-world tours of naval flying boats as excuses for spy flights. The CNO again refused.[32] No U.S. ship or airplane visited the Mandate again until 1942.

Mysterious ocean redoubts had been tolerable to the war planners as long as they pursued a Through Ticket strategy. But as their minds turned to a campaign in the central Pacific, they visualized the Mandate as a deep barrier that could neither be ignored nor left to a leisurely mopping up. Reduction of the putative web of enemy air and sea nests would require nothing less than the might of the entire U.S. Asiatic Force at the very outset of its drive.

By 1933 the evolution of naval weaponry had encouraged advocates of a cautionary campaign. The oil-burning fleet had a markedly
extended combat range, reflected in planners' visions of sweeps
through the Philippine Sea.[33] Shipborne aircraft could scout and strike
over the horizon. A glaring deficiency of the navy, however, was its
inability to reconnoiter wide areas of sea efficiently—a talent essential
for security in mid-Pacific. A fleet in the Philippines could nest behind
the ramparts of densely packed land masses and narrow straits that
would discourage sea raiders while friendly planes at outlying fields
and coves guarded the skies. But the security of central Pacific anchorages would depend on aircraft that could search a thousand miles
in all directions. No such aircraft were available.

Long-range scouting would also be critical for combat in open seas,
where hostile armadas might close upon each other by five hundred
miles overnight. The aircraft carrier had introduced the "frightening
possibility" of a superior fleet suffering defeat through inferior reconnaissance. It had long been expected that when battle lines clashed, the
greater number of guns would prevail in accordance with the N-
squared law; the underdog could triumph only by tactical excellence of
shooting first, or more steadily, or by "crossing the T" of the enemy
column to bring more guns to bear. A carrier, however, could hurl its
air wing as a single salvo of "pulsed power" and sink an enemy carrier
or battleship. The side that fired its squadrons soonest might even
destroy the enemy carriers before they launched their strikes, an
"unanswered salvo" enabling it to escape harm from the skies altogether. Studies in the 1930s indicated that a lesser fleet, perhaps of
two-thirds the opponent's strength, could win a sea-air battle. Victory
in future engagements would depend on striking first and thus on
intelligence from long-range scouting aircraft.[34]

The United States needed planes that could fly to Hawaii and the
Mandate and concentrate rapidly anywhere in the Pacific. Speed, altitude, ruggedness, and armament were important, but the vital charac-
teristic for ocean reconnaissance was range. Planes capable of flying a
thousand-mile radius could survey ten to twenty times the area that
small shipborne types could. The only aircraft suited to the task before
World War II were flying boats, known in the navy as VPs—V for
heavier than air, P for patrol.[35]

The flying boat had been developed before World War I by the
American genius Glenn H. Curtiss, whose twin-engined biplanes with
notched wooden hulls outperformed pontooned seaplanes. During the
war the United States and Great Britain flew the seven-hundred-mile
endurance craft on anti-U-boat patrols. (Larger NC boats that flew the

first Atlantic crossing in 1919 proved too fragile for naval service.) The Curtiss boats were so serviceable that innovation in the navy was retarded until they wore out in the mid-1920s. The Joint Board in 1923 recommended a force of 84 VPs for the navy (414 in wartime), only 4 percent of all military planes.[36] In 1925 the Scouting Fleet had fourteen.[37]

The craving for aerial scouts escalated when arms treaties of the 1920s limited construction of cruisers. The navy wanted VPs that could accompany the fleet "in all waters of the globe,"[38] especially in the Pacific, where airfield sites were scarce. In the second half of the decade the Naval Aircraft Factory manufactured improved versions with air-cooled radial engines and hulls of duralumin alloy. The "flying forest" of struts between the wings was thinned out. Yet each model disappointed the navy, and few were put into service. Landplanes, in contrast, were booming ahead in performance and range, as highlighted by Charles Lindbergh's famous transatlantic flight of 1927. But landplanes were reserved for the army and forbidden to the navy. The army's coast artillery function had been updated to encompass overwater flights for shore defense including protection of naval bases. In 1931 Pratt signed a pact with Chief of Staff Douglas MacArthur that barred the navy from acquiring large wheeled aircraft. Naval aviation was to be "based on the fleet and move with it,"[39] which confined it to single-engined tactical planes for carriers and the marines and to seaplanes and flying boats. The Pratt-MacArthur deal kept the navy from operating long-range landplanes until 1942.

VPs of the late 1920s were designed for surveillance flights of six hundred to eight hundred miles radius at one hundred knots. But in maneuvers they covered only four hundred miles, scarcely better than the boats of 1918. To fight in mid-Pacific the navy needed a plane with twenty-four-hour endurance that could take off at midnight and begin searching at dawn halfway along a thousand-mile radial line.[40] The engineers of the Bureau of Aeronautics (BuAer) tried again with the P2Y boats of 1932–33, sesquiplanes with stubby underside wings. They were able to exercise at Blue atolls up to seven hundred miles from Oahu, but they still suffered from the "eternal problems" of performance and range that constrained operations with a long-legged fleet.[41]

When trying to participate in rehearsals of offensive naval movements, VPs were prone to a peculiar immobility. They could neither take off from nor land on the ocean (although the navy experimented hopefully until 1934).[42] Notions such as building transports with stern doors to admit folding-winged planes at sea were dismissed as impractical. The VP squadrons (VProns) needed sheltered harbors for lift-off and landing and for the ministration of seaplane tenders, mother ships that were hybrids of fuel, repair, and barracks vessels. After World War I the navy converted one merchantman and several small minesweepers with such lyrical names as *Swan, Thrush,* and *Pelican* as tenders.[43] The shallow-draft "Bird" class vessels were well suited for uncharted lagoons, but their sluggish speed, as Captain Ernest J. King pointed out, retarded aerial mobility. Each tender nurtured a VPron of twelve planes. They worked in pairs, one sailing off to lay moorings at an advanced base while the other stood by until takeoff, then chugged gamely after. The net rate of advance was one-third that of the surface fleet.[44]

During the Depression so many tenders were laid up as virtually to preclude their movement with a war expedition. The shortage was considered "the most serious deficiency in the U.S. Fleet."[45] On 1 April 1933 Pratt detached the VProns from the Battle and Scouting forces, the power centers of the fleet, and banished them to a new command, Aircraft, Base Force, for stodgy defensive patrols of bases. Beyond the search arcs that VPs could reach, carriers and catapulted floatplanes would have to cover the fleet.[46] The disgrace of the lumbering geese was reflected in the Vinson-Trammel Act of 1934, which funded most naval aircraft generously but authorized only thirty VPs a year through 1941.[47]

To some airmen dirigibles seemed a credible alternative for Pacific scouting. In the 1920s the navy experimented with airships that had ten times the range of VPs at triple the speed of cruisers. But during exercises the fragile gasbags proved exceedingly vulnerable to "hostile" airplanes even though they were filled with nonflammable helium rather than hydrogen. Their backers, including Rear Admiral William A. Moffett, the chief of BuAer, argued that they could reconnoiter far out at sea beyond range of Orange planes, observe enemy ships while hovering out of reach of gunfire, and peek at the supposedly unarmed Mandates. At worst, a timely sighting of the enemy fleet would justify loss of a machine costing no more than a destroyer. Two great dirigibles commissioned in the early 1930s were capable of seven thousand-mile round-trips carrying small planes; each airship-plane system could sweep a wider swath than four cruisers. Op-12 wished to base them in Hawaii, but they were unstable in bad weather and were frequently "shot down" in maneuvers. The fleet refused to have them. In 1933 the *Akron* crashed, with Moffett among the dead. In 1935 the *Macon* fell. By then the navy could buy twenty-six VPs for the price of a dirigible. The "flying aircraft carriers" were finished.[48]

Reappraisals of the Orange Plan during the second half of 1933 brought to a head the destiny of the naval flying boat. Reeves, a faithful believer in the type, insisted that the fleet could not enter Philippine waters or even pause in the Marshalls without a security umbrella of five to seven VProns. Op-12 dutifully incorporated them in the first attack wave. Reeves reckoned they could fly to the Marshalls via Johnston Island,[49] but they would have to travel onward to Mindanao as deck cargo. His mobilization tables reserved space aboard all ship classes, yet many of the big planes would have to be lashed precariously on minesweepers under tow.[50] The absurdity of the "eyes of the fleet" struck blind during the dangerous passage further discredited the Through Ticket.

In October 1933 an aeronautical design breakthrough suddenly brightened the credibility of a mid-ocean campaign. An excellent prototype VP had evolved from a successful commercial machine. The navy placed orders for the plane that evolved into the most-produced flying boat of all time, the Consolidated PBY Catalina.[51] The aerodynamically clean, high-winged monoplane soon achieved the long-sought thousand-mile range—fifteen hundred for some wartime models.[52] War planners could look forward to delivery within three years of flocks of far-winging scouts for an ocean offensive. Design work also proceeded on giant VPs that might achieve endurances of five or six thousand miles,[53] but Standley, as chief of naval operations, pressed for masses of the relatively cheap Catalinas for reasons of flexibility and concentration, including the option of deck transport. Numbers and mobility would matter more in the central Pacific than a few superlative planes.[54] The Catalinas formed the backbone of the navy's seaplane surveillance force until larger Coronado and Mariner boats appeared in quantity after World War II was well under way.[55]

The flowering of the cautionary campaign plan after 1933 owed much to enchantment with the Catalinas. They performed superbly as scouts and in massed exercises at U.S. atolls.[56] A few influential officers, notably Ernest King, urged their adaptation as a striking arm of the fleet (a possibility that significantly affected war plans of the late 1930s), although most high-ranking officers advised the CNO against the notion. Standley agreed with Kalbfus, president of the War College, that VPs ought to be information gatherers exclusively. Meyers argued for restricting them to solo flights from protected bases, near the fleet or over sea lanes, to conserve them.[57] Even Reeves conceded their primary mission to be surveillance, though he ached to try them out as attack planes.[58]

The fixation on scouting "to the practical exclusion of all other missions" incited King to a diatribe. King was an air power devotee who had attended flight school in middle age and then commanded the carrier *Lexington*. Moffett's death brought him to the top of the Bureau of Aeronautics in April 1933.[59] He believed that aerial scouts, like cruisers, should also fight. The VP, he asserted, was "distinctly a naval weapon for use over the sea against naval objectives." A modern VPron could haul twenty-four tons of explosives, almost as much as the air wings of both of the large American carriers, to targets five times more distant. King pleaded for unlimited development of the flying boat and its strategic role. If the Navy Department skimped on "the most promising development in the future of Aviation," he warned, the air corps would monopolize the long-range strike mission to the navy's eternal regret.[60]

King stood as a lonely prophet until Rear Admiral William Pye took charge of Op-12 again in 1935. Pye thought massed formations of VPs could probably act as effective bombing forces[61] and encouraged others in the belief. King returned to the fleet to command the VProns. Soon he was operating them as bombers and asking for torpedoes.[62] (The high wing of the Catalina permitted ordnance to be loaded afloat at primitive bases.) King and Pye rounded up supporters among the fleet leadership. Since the VProns could, at last, keep up with the warships, Commander in Chief Arthur Hepburn transferred them in 1937 from the defensive Base Force to a new command, Aircraft, Scouting Force.[63] Claud Bloch, the next CinCUS, continued the attack training.[64] King's vision was apparently vindicated when the navy redesignated the Catalina as the PBY, the first seaplane to sport a "B" for bomber along with "P" for patrol ("Y" was the symbol designating the manufacturer).[65]

King's crusade may seem naive inasmuch as seaplanes were obsolescent as combat craft by the time World War II began. But who could have known, a few years earlier, how modern planes would perform in battle? The vision of a seagoing air armada was alluring. Imaginations the world over were agog at coveys of large bombers such as the B-17 Flying Fortresses, first flown in 1935. By the time the navy jettisoned the notion of the lumbering VPBs as a striking force in 1940, it was irrevocably committed to a central Pacific offensive. The flying boat, the workhorse of naval reconnaissance of World War II, was never an important attack weapon. Nevertheless, in the 1930s its formidable possibilities gave a final impetus to the conversion of Plan Orange to an oceanic strategy.

The American Way of Planning: Cooperation and Campaign Plans

From the end of 1933 to the middle of 1937, approximately the period of Franklin D. Roosevelt's first administration, there occurred a flourish of Pacific campaign planning. Foreign and domestic political events induced among strategists a sense of wariness conducive to the conception of prudent plans but not yet of alarm. The rise of Hitler and the fascist incursions in Spain and Ethiopia were not perceived as threats to U.S. interests. Japan completed its withdrawal from the League of Nations and in September 1934 served notice that it would abrogate the arms treaties at the end of two years. A Blue-Orange war still seemed the most likely military contingency the United States might face. As the nation struggled to climb out of the Depression in 1934, the Vinson-Trammell Act decreed that naval strength be rebuilt to treaty ceilings. Congress confirmed a pledge of Philippine independence but set the fulfillment date ten years in the future. The Through Ticket faded into history not because of that deadline of colonialism but because a gradual offensive was at last recognized as the better military alternative against Japan.

The mid-1930s stand out as an era of harmony among the war-planning agencies. An atmosphere of shared values fostered agreement on large issues and settlement of details by mutual accommodation or at least by orderly debates that yielded results all parties could accept. The army and navy high commands closed ranks with each other and with their planning staffs. The naval triumverate of the CNO, CinCUS, and director of war plans collaborated on most of the new strategic principles, and resolved occasional disputes over operating details by clever bureaucratic footwork or by compromising. Subordinate naval agencies were recruited into the war-planning effort, especially those concerned with island warfare and bases: the marines, the Fleet Base Force, and the Bureau of Yards and Docks (BuDocks). A fleet war plans officer was appointed for the first time, although the post was not influential until 1938.

The prime instigator of change in 1933 was Captain Samuel Woods Bryant, director of the Naval War Plans Division. A man of high intellect who had seen action in two wars, he had served at the War College and in intelligence and observed aviation on the job as chief of staff of the Scouting Fleet.[1] Bryant strongly favored a cautionary policy and demoted Meyers, an unrepentant thruster, to ivory-tower contemplation of the "epitome of the world situation." He buried the Red Plan under a junior aide and vacated the Red-Orange billet. He assigned Plan Orange to a veteran planner, Captain R. F. Dillen, with instructions to focus on ocean routes and bases. He handed amphibious planning to Colonel Thomas Holcomb, USMC. The director ran a taut division and personally screened the staff's output.[2]

Bryant deliberately snubbed the army by ordering his crew to shun the JPC. He had a sound reason: he wished to produce a cautionary plan that conceded loss of the Philippines before having to confront a General Staff that since 1923 had fixed a return to Manila as its highest priority. His ploy involved end-running the collegial joint planning system by attributing the plan to the only officer named to lead Blue forces in war, the commander in chief of the U.S. Fleet. Eberle's 1923 dictum that had assigned a central role in planning to the CinCUS was nominally still in effect; it had applied, for example, to regular updates of the 1929 Orange Plan that had adapted it to his presumed logistical needs.[3] But the fleet had failed to write an operating plan in support. Schofield, the master planner turned CinCUS, had ignored the call,[4] and his successors, Leigh and Sellers, had promoted the unacceptable Quick Movement. Bryant hoped to coax the fleet to produce something better[5] but was stymied as long as Pratt was in charge of OpNav. He had to mark time awaiting a like-minded CNO.

The much-needed turnover occurred on 1 July 1933, when Roosevelt appointed Admiral William H. Standley as chief of naval operations. Standley was the only prewar CNO to have served as a top war planner. Since his lethargic stewardship of Op-12 in 1924–25 he had grown in stature as vice-CNO and in sea commands. By 1933 he was genuinely concerned about Pacific strategy. He wisely retained Bryant as his chief planner. Both officers sought to foster a joint cautionary plan by selling it to the army as the strategic choice of the fleet.

Sellers soon learned that a new Plan O-1 was "a matter of urgent importance" to OpNav.[6] He passed the job to Joseph "Bull" Reeves, the fleet's foremost air enthusiast. Reeves had taken up flying at age fifty-three, then startled the surface admirals by launching mock carrier raids on Panama and Pearl Harbor. The imaginative air admiral was considered a student of Pacific strategy; an ocean campaign featuring naval aviation appealed to him. (Fortunately, the new principles were well established when he moved up to CinCUS in June 1934 because thereafter he alienated Standley by his stubbornness and criticism of the WPD. The CNO made sure that fleet campaign plans were prepared under his eye in Washington.[7])

Late in 1933 Standley, Bryant, and Reeves formed a partnership for change. Standley ordered the fleet to desist from its Through Ticket machinations and recast Tentative Plan O-1 into a drive through the Mandate that was to conform with a checklist Bryant drew up.[8] The CNO's order canceled the Through Ticket, permanently and irrevocably.

Commander in Chief Sellers threw up his hands in disgust. To explore a profusion of campaign schemes, he grumbled, would drown his staff in paperwork. He was happy to punt to the WPD, provided the chairbound planners did not constrain his freedom in wartime. Standley, with indecent haste, reassigned Plan O-1 to Bryant's control.[9] After a decade of ineptitude and neglect the fleet surrendered to Washington its authority to plan Pacific campaigns.

Sellers soon regretted his petulant abdication to a gang of cautionaries whose ideas were "based on mere speculation,"[10] but his moment had passed. During the first half of 1934, Commander Cary W. Magruder of Op-12 wrote a cautionary Plan O-1 on behalf of the fleet. Magruder was an experienced destroyerman and staff aide and, though no intellectual, had learned under Bryant at the War College.[11] He whimsically subtitled his hundred-page opus "The Royal Road," perhaps after Richard Halliburton's popular adventure book *The Royal Road to Romance,* or perhaps as a reminder of Eberle's old apology for bulky plans, "There is no royal road to victory."[12]

Bryant's tour ended just after the Royal Road plan was completed in July 1934. For the next ten months Op-12 was entrusted again to the hawkish Captain Meyers, but, hemmed in by cautionaries Magruder, Holcomb, Reeves, and CNO Standley himself,[13] it became Meyers's sardonic fate to pronounce last rites over the Through Ticket.

The navy kept Plan O-1 to itself for six months before disclosing it to the army. It awaited the appointment to Army War Plans of Brigadier General Embick, who had called the Through Ticket "madness" and would be sure to welcome a change. At the beginning of 1935 Meyers told the AWPD that the fleet had proposed a stepwise drive through the Mandate toward Truk and that marine planners were studying how to make landings. Citing the old authority conferred on the CinCUS to select the attack route, the navy solicited the soldiers' acquiescence. It shrewdly said nothing about the implication of delayed arrival in the Philippines.[14]

Embick loved Plan O-1. He set his staff to laboring with the navy on a tightly scheduled campaign to conquer the eastern Mandate and on allocations of forces for subsequent steps. The joint planners' only mention of the Philippines was to note offhandedly that the Orange Plan ought to contemplate a prompt move after Truk to "Manila Bay or some other location." They then dropped the subject. They fashioned amendments to the 1928 Plan that the Joint Board and service secretaries approved in May 1935. They subverted, de facto, the Through Ticket decision of that earlier document into a national commitment to the Royal Road.[15] Embick told Chief of Staff Douglas MacArthur that the fleet merely wished to perfect its line of communication before setting sail for the western Pacific, that the army should support it, and that the amendments altered only the *initial* goal of the offensive. The Orange Plan had "not been changed materially," he added disingenuously.[16]

MacArthur did not object. No stern voice thundered to save Manila for God and country or even to aid its garrison. The general, as senior member of the Joint Board, reported to the secretaries that "minor" adjustments of early deployments had been made but that the General Concept of the War had not changed.[17] An irony of history (missed by his biographers) was that in 1935 MacArthur signed the death warrant of Bataan and Corregidor.[18] He then retired and set out for Manila with his aides, Majors James B. Ord and Dwight D. Eisenhower, to serve as military adviser to the government of the commonwealth and prepare it for war.

Standley kept up the charade that "no fundamental change in strategy" had taken place, merely the insertion of steps to safeguard communications to the "Western Pacific." Meanwhile, OpNav energetically consolidated the breakthrough by updating its four volumes of 1929 Orange Plans, WPL-13 through 16, and ordering contributory plans that conformed.[19] It discouraged any revival of thruster sentiment by forbidding the planning of movements farther than Truk. The nature of the war beyond that mid-ocean goal drifted into limbo; a few mentions in later naval plans added little to the old scenarios. The army remained passively acquiescent during the mid-1930s about planning for the later stages of the war except for an imaginative study by Colonel Walter Krueger, a rare soldier who kept in mind the grand strategy of a Pacific war by focusing on the Marianas as a pivotal site for military dominance and political pressure that would bring about the surrender of Japan (Chapter 18).

Once the initial offensive had been recast, thruster-cautionary disputes narrowed to campaign details. In mid-1935 Standley summoned a familiar face, Rear Admiral William S. Pye, to a third tour in Op-12. Pye, a middle-of-the-road cautionary and a stickler for detail, was a benign presence in a time of microscopic analysis. The ground services prepared elaborate assault studies of selected islands of the Mandate and agreed to design joint attacks on the toughest targets in meetings umpired by Op-12.[20]

The role of aviation and its bearing on the nature and pace of amphibious war was the most difficult issue for the planners to reconcile. Naval and air corps planners stressed flexible concentrations to destroy Orange air power in massed battles. Op-12 thought that aircraft carriers should range deeply into enemy waters on missions of interdiction. The ground services, however, felt entitled to close air coverage of landings where bitter resistance was likely (a dilemma unresolved as late as 1943). The air problem led the planners away from old notions of occupying nearly all the Mandated Islands to a philosophy of taking as few as needed and bypassing the rest. A bypassing policy would also permit a speedier advance to the Far East, still a motive of all planners. The realization gradually dawned, however, that naval bases could not be developed as rapidly as hoped so the crossing of the Pacific would turn into a drawn-out series of campaigns.

The planners of the mid-1930s shed the illusion of immediate return to the Philippines and adopted a rational central Pacific offensive. Embrace of the cautionary formula ended debates that had clouded the Orange Plan for thirty years, freeing them to design amphibious campaign blueprints that were sound models for World War II.

Implicit in the new strategy was the assumption that the nation would be willing to fight a longer war for the still sacrosanct goal of subjugating Japan completely.

The era of cooperation came to an abrupt end in mid-1937 when Japan turned overtly aggressive by invading China while European dictators embarked on courses that might threaten the interests of the United States, casting doubt on the premise of maximum American effort in the Pacific.

Royal Road: The Ocean Campaign

The energies of war planners from 1934 through mid-1937 were devoted to a cautionary Phase II drive as far as the central Carolines. The armed services produced voluminous studies that constituted the most thorough investigation of any Pacific campaign. Their legacies to World War II strategy included doctrines for amphibious landings, naval interdiction strikes, and air battles; criteria for selecting island targets; policies of bypassing superfluous strong points and keeping the enemy off balance by momentum; and designs for advanced bases.

The concept of using Micronesia as a naval highway had appeared in studies of momentary havens as early as 1907. It had flowered in 1922, when the navy briefly adopted the Williams-Ellis proposals to establish true fleet bases there. But the thrusters who reinstated the Through Ticket in 1923 had demoted Mandates occupations to sideshows; in the 1928 Plan the islands were to be taken by second-line regiments with minor naval help between M+105 and M+180, long after the USJAF would have reached the Philippines, and then only for protection of the supply line.[1] The Quick Movement of 1932 eliminated the operations in Micronesia by presuming that supply vessels could avoid Orange raiders, even battle cruisers, by sailing on dispersed routes through the South Pacific.[2] A hint of the Mandate as a primary theater appeared in Tentative Fleet Plan O-1 of 1933. Admiral Sellers, though still intent on a dash to Mindanao, admitted a "very difficult, if not impracticable" situation would arise if Orange foreclosed all ports in the Philippines. He would have to halt the fleet in the Carolines, or even the Marshalls, seize "the more important bases," and regroup for a stronger advance.[3] Bryant snatched at this contingent thought to promulgate an OpNav directive for a full-blown plan of a Mandate campaign. He demanded a program of attacks across Micronesia, with detailed assumptions about sea and air deployments, landing forces and tactics, and erection and defense of bases.[4]

When Sellers balked, Op-12 drew up the Royal Road Plan on behalf of the fleet in 1934, fibbing to the Army that it was simply an improved way of fulfilling the joint policy of rapid movement to the western Pacific. Commander Magruder, stressing the contradiction of the previous Orange Plan's quest for both speed and power, finessed the call for the fleet's "early arrival" in the Philippines by interpreting it as a date shortly after it solved the threat of being cut off by an Orange naval deployment to central Pacific bases. That would be the earliest moment the fleet could safely meet the plan's other condition of being "ready to act offensively" when it arrived. The Through Ticket had failed to guarantee the vital element of communications security. It was therefore "more glamorous than real" and had to be discarded.[5]

Magruder envisioned the Pacific as barricaded by insular defense lines (Map 17.1) at which Japan would make successive stands to inflict attrition until it was able to defeat the Blue navy in battle and compel American withdrawal from the western Pacific. The Royal Road was a blueprint for cracking the outermost cordon, the eastern and central Mandate, and getting into position to penetrate the remaining barriers. The Blue mission, restated, was "to proceed to the Philippines by a progressive movement through the Mandates,"[6] or, as the Joint Board phrased it, to establish "a secure line of communications to the western Pacific" by clearing the Marshalls and Carolines and emplacing naval bases there.[7]

The geography of the central Pacific would favor the United States in relative distances, force deployments, and sequence of operations. The Royal Road prescribed serial captures of islands on which Japanese defenses (presumably absent before the war) could not be emplaced more than a few weeks or even days before the landings. Blue

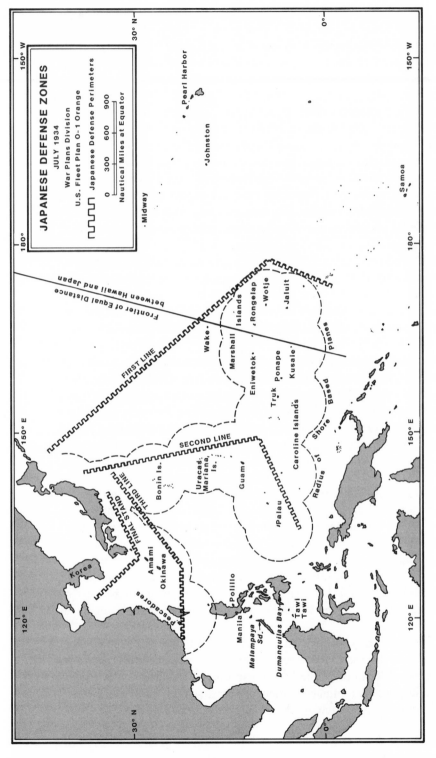

MAP 17.1

would commence at Japan's weakest possessions and proceed stepwise to Truk, establishing mutually supportive fleet and air bases along the way. A drive via small islands could be executed with less land and air strength and a smaller train than would be needed in a Through Ticket drive. It could get off to a lightning-fast start and finish within three months, satisfying the public clamor to "do something." The program was flexible, "logical and sound," even foolproof. Properly managed, it could not be thrown back.[8]

The Royal Road began in the eastern Marshalls, the only enemy islands nearer to a U.S. than to a Japanese main base. There Blue would enjoy superiority, concentration, and surprise. Its attacks would immobilize Orange garrisons on their sandspits and isolate its air squadrons so they could not support each other. The Marshalls contained many lagoons suitable for a Fleet Base One. (Magruder did not consider it feasible to bypass the group and descend directly on Truk because the assault force would have to refuel at sea, make do without shore-based air help, and then put about to clear the Marshalls anyway.) After securing an atoll, the fleet would improvise a service port and concentrate there "with impunity." Expeditions would probe westward to occupy other islands for a chain of forward air stations stretching toward Truk, an island that beckoned as a superb position for controlling the entire Mandate and bordering seas. A larger assault force would be needed to overcome division-strength opposition (but not as large as for big islands later in the war). At Truk the Americans would erect Fleet Base Two, a great arsenal that could be supplied and defended more readily than Mindanao, and then pursue various routes on a flexible timetable to the Orient and the ultimate defeat of Japan.

Magruder recognized the potholes along the Royal Road. Japan could pour aerial reinforcements to the battlefront through its island web (although not as freely as to the Philippines because of flight distances and interdiction by the Blue fleet). The United States would have to expose heavy ships to gain relatively modest objectives. Yet these risks were acceptable to attain a secure fleet base in a U.S.-dominated central region to serve as the foundation for further advance.[9]

The plan envisioned the deployment of overpowering Blue strength to the Mandate. Augmented by the rebuilding program, the Navy could assemble a first wave of 331 fast, long-ranged vessels, including 14 modernized battleships and 15 heavy cruisers (versus 11 and 9 in the earlier Mindanao Through Ticket), and more seaplane tenders and other specialized vessels.[10] The fleet's 4 carriers (the *Lexington*, the

Saratoga, the smaller *Ranger,* and the experimental *Langley*) were still too few, but the keels of 3 more were to be laid during 1934 and 1935. Within a few more years the planners would be able to assign another battleship, raise the cruiser tally to 36, and eliminate nearly all make-shift conversions.[11]

The capital ships would not call at Hawaii, a welcome change because Pearl Harbor could accommodate only five, and no large carrier had yet entered. The Lahaina mine barrage was canceled after it was reappraised at 20 percent effectiveness on M+20 and 50 percent on M+60, the approximate sortie dates of the first waves.[12] Pearl Harbor would service the smaller vessels. The Hawaiian submarine force, released from guarding Lahaina, was assigned to reconnoitering the Mandate, a task of "tremendous value" even though the performance of the small S-boats was limited.[13] But in a couple of years the submarine flotilla would grow from nineteen to thirty-nine, and the modern boats could attack as well as scout.[14]

A crucial supposition of the new plan was that the Japanese main body would not emerge to fight for the Marshalls or Carolines even though outlying fuel stations gave it the capability to cruise anywhere in the Mandate and a thousand miles beyond. Magruder pondered whether enemy leaders might post carriers at Truk to raid the first Blue captures or yield to public outcry at the loss of B-1 and, ignoring Blue's positional advantage of that nearby base, provoke a premature battle on the approaches to Truk.[15] Aggressive U.S. admirals salivated at the thought of ravaging Orange capital ships in the Mandate with "vigor and determination,"[16] but the planners' consensus in the 1930s was that prudence and logistics would constrain Japan to hold them within six hundred miles of home. The planners estimated that Orange would, however, commit to the central Pacific a strong attrition force of sixty to seventy warships, half submarines and the rest destroyers, light cruisers, and some seaplane tenders, which could pop up anywhere in the Mandate from a web of bases.[17]

In the absence of a challenge from the main body, the function of U.S. capital ships became a subject of intense dispute. They could either closely support the landing forces or insulate them by interdicting Orange sea and air units at their forward bases or en route to the beachheads. Subdivision for both tasks was not considered practicable.

A threshold question of Plan O-1 was how many islands Blue should occupy (see Map 17.2). The answer would determine the speed, complexity, and force requirements of the drive and influence the mission of the fleet. The Marshalls alone consisted of thirty-one atolls spaced over half a million square miles. Ten to eighteen were thought to have military value,[18] but hydrographic and air experts later reduced the figure to eight.[19] Although a single atoll would suffice for Base One, naval thrusters at first advocated clearing *every* enemy-held island (Table 17.1). This idea derived from studies of the 1920s about guarding convoys with very short-ranged aircraft (all that were then available), which had called for four or five air bases spread across the group. AWPD planners had disagreed, observing sagely that a navy, unlike an army, did not need to possess every point along its communication line. JPC and marine analysts in 1928–29 decided that the Marshalls could be frugally sterilized by air surveillance and roving landing parties working from only two additional bases.[20] After the navy adopted the Royal Road, it continued to insist on gathering up many island air bases, justified in 1934 for defense of B-1 and assisting the advance on Truk. It assumed that it could eradicate the foe from "any and all" islands it desired.[21] The WPD acknowledged that multiple invasions would expose the fleet to greater attrition but asserted that losses could be minimized by pouncing simultaneously and with "utmost celerity."[22]

The selection of an atoll for Base One was a subject of lively inquiry. Naval desiderata—a large lagoon with a few narrow entries easily corked against U-boats, ten-fathom depths for capital ships, and quiet waters for VPs—were easily met (Table 17.2). But fleet bases also required hundreds of acres of dry land, as did aerodromes for runways oriented to the prevailing winds and especially for parking large numbers of planes. The main physical discriminator was, therefore, the availability of a sizable reef islet, a scarce feature in the Marshalls. Five atolls appeared to meet the criteria.[23] Wotje, the Japanese administrative center, had long been regarded as a prime candidate[24] because of its "striking feature," a 735-acre islet adequate for a naval base and a first-class airport with hangars, shops, and tankage.[25] (Its area was later determined to be exaggerated by 50 percent, but the choice held because other "large" islets in that part of the group were too narrow or too low-lying.[26]) Wotje also fit the navy's preference for a base at the eastern edge of the Marshalls. Standley insisted on this sector, the nearest to Pearl Harbor,[27] because of its unobstructed access and its remoteness from most Orange strong points, especially the thousand-mile moat that would preclude bombing from Truk. In 1935, at Bryant's suggestion, the Joint Board designated Wotje as B-1.[28]

The second best lagoon of the region was believed to be at Jaluit at the southernmost border of the Marshalls. But it was poorly located for

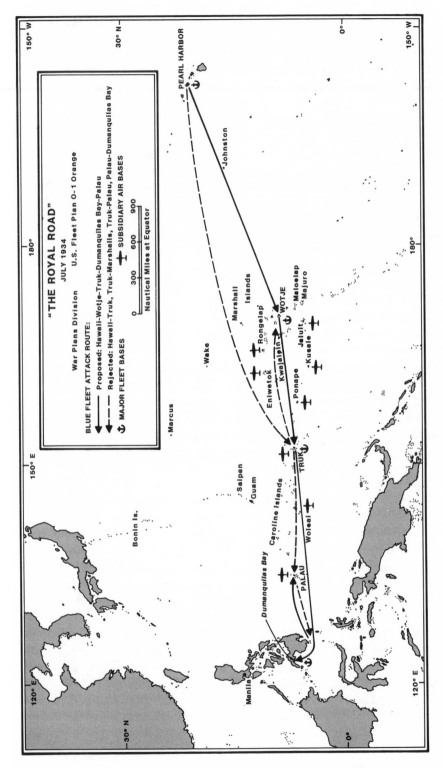

MAP 17.2

TABLE 17.1 *Marshalls Campaign, Mid-1930s: Thruster versus Cautionary Attitudes*

	Thrusters	Cautionaries	Common agreement
Orange defenses	Light ground and air	Heavy ground and air	Naval attrition forces; main fleet to avoid Marshalls
Blue attack units	Modest landing force	Large landing force	Entire fleet deployed
Speed of campaign	Swift reduction of group	Deliberate reduction of group	Fastest possible start of campaign
Locale of main target	Western, most advanced sector (some thrusters)	Eastern (nearest) sector	Island suitable for fleet base
Sequence and completeness	Take few islands except as needed for next advance, bypass and neutralize others	Take all islands of value in uninterrupted sequence	
Blue defenses after capture	Light	Heavy	
Blue Base One on main target	Minimal facility, no delay of advance	Elaborate facility, take time to develop	

movement toward Truk,[29] and when BuDocks assessed its capacity at only twenty landplanes it was demoted to an optional seaplane station. (During the war it was the only Japanese base in the Marshalls without an airfield.) Among other atolls rejected for Base One were Majuro and Kwajelein, the former because it had a single channel through the reef and poor topography for an airfield and the latter, despite its admirable central location for policing the group, because its reef was pierced with twenty-five openings.[30] (In World War II the United States developed both atolls as mutually supporting sea-air bases that offset each other's shortcomings.) Some analysts considered islands in the western Marshalls, but Op-12 spurned them as dangerous places not in accord with the CNO's criteria until changed circumstances in 1939 induced the planners to shift Base One to that sector (Chapter 21).

TABLE 17.2 *Summary of Militarily Useful Marshall Islands, 1927 Study*

	Protected anchorage data				Seaplanes	Landplanes	
	Capacity, number of ships	Number of entry passes	Best entry depth (fathoms)	Submarine protection	Capacity, number of squadrons	Longest airstrip (feet)	Feasibility of airstrip
Eastern							
Wotje	2,000	4	15	Excellent	40+	7,000	Good
Jaluit	1,500	4	9	Good	25	?	Good
Majuro[a]							
Maloelap[a]							
Central							
Kwajelein	Unlimitd	25	20	Poor	Unlimited	5,000	?
Northwest							
Eniwetok	2,000	2	12	Excellent	15+	?	Good
Rongelap	1,000	7	13	Fair	15+	?	Fair
Taongi	None	None	0	–	Unsuited	?	None
Ujelang	Many[b]	1	3	Excellent	12	?	None
Bikini[a]							

Source: WPD, Study of Certain Pac Is, 6 Aug 1927.

[a] Not reported.

[b] Small vessels only.

Opinion was unanimous that Truk was the best potential base in the Carolines because of its ample land and fine anchorages. (The reef had sixteen breaks, but all except two were considered impassable.[31]) The planners also targeted Kusaie and Ponape, the large islands of the eastern Carolines. Although useless as naval bases, they were coveted by the Army Air Corps as perches on the way to Truk because each squadron of eighteen bombers required 160 acres of land.[32] But the mountainous islands were dropped from the itinerary in 1937 after reappraisals indicated that the time and cost to occupy them would be excessive, a decision repeated for identical reasons during World War II. The low atolls of the Carolines were viewed as useful air stations for both sides during the battle for Truk. Blue aviators imagined them also as a bridge to the Philippines for both seaplanes and landplanes, the latter possibly fitted with pontoons.[33]

The intensity of ground battles on Marshalls atolls would depend on how quickly Japanese defenders arrived.[34] Marine planners expected to find important islands held by a regiment of thirty-five hundred infantry entrenched behind mines and beach obstacles and equipped with field guns but not big-caliber cannon.[35] Air resistance troubled them most acutely. The FMF dourly envisioned a web of Orange air stations that could loft two hundred planes over Wotje by M+14.[36] The War Plans Section at Corps headquarters adopted a more sanguine assumption that the Wotje garrison could not arrive until M+22, just two days before the invasion, with only sixty planes that the assault force would overwhelm. Enemy pilots stranded outside combat radius on other atolls because they were denied Wotje's airfield would gnash their teeth in frustration.[37] Army planners felt even more optimistic, clinging to joint assumptions of the 1920s which regarded the Marshalls as pushovers.[38] Colonel Walter Krueger of the AWPD slighted all islands east of Truk as forming a salient or shank intended for sniping by Orange light forces to wound and delay the Blue approach to Truk. Since it was "not in the Orange tradition" to sacrifice big units without compensating gain, he observed, only battalion-sized outfits would guard Marshalls airfields against raids.[39] On Wotje, a measly twelve hundred Japanese with two guns and a dozen planes would be blown away by Blue invaders. Indeed, Orange might not even bother with airstrips; Americans swarming ashore on Wotje could find themselves greeted by smiling natives and a handful of Japanese policemen.[40] OpNav sent the study to the fleet without much comment.[41]

Everyone regarded Truk with deadly seriousness. Japan would understand Blue's need of the island and, believing its loss to be a threat to the security of the empire, would expend great effort on defense.[42] Time would be of the essence for both sides. Within a month Orange could deliver 27,663 troops, although they would not have time to emplace heavy artillery before a Blue invasion force appeared a few weeks later. Japan's trump card, however, was flexible air power. Truk was the place "above all others" to play it. Several American estimates of the hostile concentration converged on four hundred planes, some on Truk, some at fields and coves of twenty surrounding islands, and some standing by in Japan as reserves. The marines credited the widely dispersed air armada with "powers of evasion so great that its attack operations cannot be countered with assurance,"[43] overlooking the superhuman logistical job of servicing at so many bases.

To assault the Mandates against opposition of realistic proportions, Blue would not have to embark a huge army. Estimates for the battles prior to Truk ranged from twenty-three thousand[44] to thirty-three thousand, half marines and half soldiers. Typical estimates were seven thousand five hundred to fifteen thousand to carry a well-defended atoll, three thousand for a minor atoll, and ten to thirteen thousand for one of the eastern Carolines (Map 17.3).[45] Logistics for such units could be kept simple. The train would be of manageable size, with quality emphasized over quantity. Only 41 naval auxiliaries and 99 of the best civilian ships (mostly oilers but including 18 liners) would suffice, in contrast to the 500-plus vessels of Through Ticket plans of the 1920s. The assault outfits would need 15-knot transports that could outrun submarines and about 260 special landing craft; the requirements for both grew throughout the late 1930s. After the capture of B-1, a second convoy of 139 merchantmen escorted by minor warships would deliver the wherewithal to develop and guard it. The train would include such exotic craft as surveying vessels, lighthouse tenders, and seagoing dredges.[46]

The Truk campaign would pose strenuous obligations. With most of the Marine Corps already bloodied in the Marshalls, the army would have to provide the bulk of a fifty thousand-strong landing force armed with 75-mm guns and light tanks.[47] The planners scheduled the units of the first waves to reembark for Truk immediately after their battles in the eastern Mandate despite 10 to 20 percent casualties and another 10 percent "attrition" from sinkings and illness. (In World War II troops needed many months of rehabilitation between landings.) The troop estimates of the 1930s were about one-third lower than the numbers employed in World War II, when, for example, twenty thousand Americans assaulted fortified atolls like Tarawa and each main islet of Kwajelein and sixty-seven thousand landed on the rugged island of Saipan.

Ground battles in the Mandate were subjects of painstaking analysis, most of which was tactical. For atolls, the procedure fixed by Ellis in 1921 (Chapter 10) remained fundamentally unchanged. The Truk operation evolved through several permutations reflecting possible enemy dispositions with mutually supportive artillery on the half-dozen larger islands inside the lagoon. Assuming that Orange troops were massed on the most valuable islands of Dublon and Eten, the Americans would seize the more isolated Tol Island and reef islets, then clear the rest by amphibious movements within the lagoon. (The Pacific Fleet's 1943 draft plan for Truk adopted this program almost verbatim, a clear illustration that some prewar plans were consulted during the war.[48]) Casualties would be heavy in the battle of Truk—25 percent U.S. dead or wounded.[49] Since no island of similar configuration was ever attacked, comparisons with other World War II operations are difficult. But at least one senior planner who studied the Truk operation before the war was so appalled by its difficulties that he undertook a crusade in 1944 to persuade naval leaders to bypass the island,[50] a recommendation sensibly adopted because by then an excellent harbor was available at a strategically comparable location in the Admiralty Islands.

Protection of the ocean bases was another subject of concern. Japanese raids were expected but counterinvasions were not. Defense proposals for B-1 ranged from a few thousand men with a few guns to thirty thousand marines—the entire Corps—if many outlying atolls were also to be held.[51] Some planners contrarily rejected fortification as unnecessary because Orange air power would be suppressed by the fleet and soon by a local air force, or even considered the anchorage expendable after a few weeks because Truk could be supplied by other routes.[52] The Joint Plan of 1935 settled on an army garrison of nine thousand for which BuDocks designed invulnerable channel defenses and onshore stockpiles for prolonged resistance.[53] The shore defenses of Truk, though designed to be more powerful than those of the atolls, were not markedly so considering the importance of the base, presumably because of the fleet's long-term residence there and its capability of falling back from Dumanquilas to protect it.[54]

Japanese flyers would be the most dangerous foes encountered in the Mandate. The main purpose of enemy resistance ashore would be to trap the Blue fleet into protracted support of the landing operations, where attrition could be wrought, especially from the air. The U.S. Navy would not fall into the trap.[55] Preinvasion carrier strikes on Wotje and other atolls (which might destroy 25 percent of Orange air power in the Marshalls) were hinted at but not clearly articulated.[56] During landings the precious carriers, accompanied by the battleships, would cruise forward to reconnoiter, assure naval and air control of the wide theater, and cordon off the beachheads from retaliation (see Map 17.3).[57] In particular, they would block Japanese air replenishment by strikes on their staging bases.[58] During the Marshalls campaign, the fleet would venture five hundred to one thousand miles westward, raiding as far as Truk. By M+45, working from the anchorage at B-1, it would isolate Truk so Orange vessels could no longer use the big lagoon.[59] During the battle for Truk itself, it would operate as far ahead as Woleai in the western Carolines.[60]

Marine Corps planners understandably believed that their comrades were entitled to close support, especially from the carriers "at very near full strength," for as long as needed.[61] Their appeals for more air power in the Marshalls than the navy possessed posed dilemmas. Which of the simultaneous landings would be supported? How soon could the carriers be relieved?[62] General C. H. Lyman of the Fleet

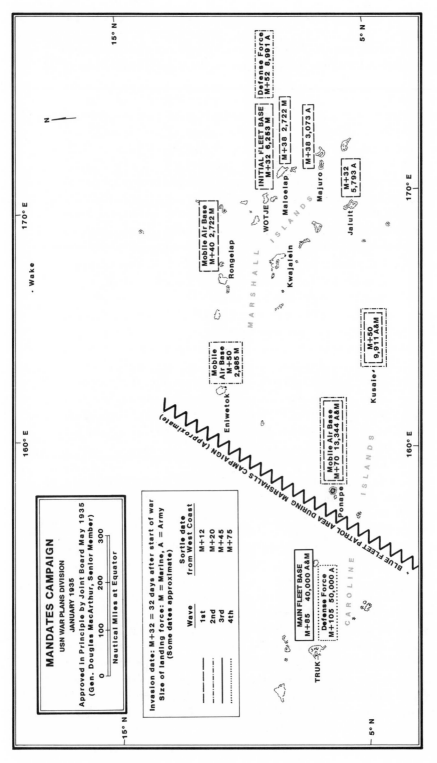

MANDATES CAMPAIGN

USN WAR PLANS DIVISION

JANUARY 1935

Approved in Principle by Joint Board May 1935
(Gen. Douglas MacArthur, Senior Member)

0   100   200   300
Nautical Miles at Equator

Invasion date: M+32 = 32 days after start of war
Size of landing force: M = Marine, A = Army
(Some dates approximate)

Wave	Sortie date from West Coast
1st	M+12
2nd	M+20
3rd	M+45
4th	M+75

N

· Wake

Rongelap

Mobile Air Base
M+40 2,722 M

WOTJE
INITIAL FLEET BASE
M+32 6,253 M
M+38 2,722 M

Maloelap

M+38 3,073 A

Defense Force
M+52 8,991 A

Majuro

Eniwetok
Mobile Air Base
M+50 2,985 M

Kwajalein

MARSHALL ISLANDS

M+32
5,793 A

Jaluit

BLUE FLEET PATROL AREA DURING MARSHALLS CAMPAIGN (approximate)

Kusaie
M+50
9,911 A&M

Ponape
Mobile Air Base
M+70 13,344 A&M

ISLANDS

TRUK

MAIN FLEET BASE
M+85 40,000 A&M

Defense Force
M+105 50,000 A

CAROLINE

15° N

170° E

160° E

5° N

170° E

160° E

15° N

5° N

MAP 17.3

Marine Force appealed to the navy's self-interest. If it were stingy in support, he warned, the land battles and thus the fleet's sallies in dangerous forward waters would be prolonged.[63] His staff demanded two-to-one air dominance at Wotje, an impossibility given his doomsday prediction that two hundred enemy aircraft would orbit the island.[64] The marines also wanted all flattops to stand by after the battle until hundreds of high-performance landplanes were ashore to fend off Orange carriers.[65] USMC headquarters assumed a less worrisome count of Orange planes, but its *Tentative Landing Operations Manual* called for three-to-one air superiority—five-to-one had been discussed—which indicated the need for the fleet's two largest carriers at Wotje.[66] At weak targets such as Majuro the FMF felt it could do without capital ships as long as they were hovering in or near the Marshalls, but added, no doubt facetiously, that they would serve nicely as bait to lure Orange subs away from the tougher beachheads.[67]

Op-12 flintily rejected all pleas for the fleet to provide close air cover of landings. In addition to the risk of immobility, a diversion from striking in the Carolines would grant the enemy time to fortify Truk, which would discourage a rapid assault on it and ultimately prolong the war.[68] The ground forces would have to provide their own air support. But marine aviation was minuscule—138 pilots in 1935[69]—and the navy refused to provide carrier decks for them. Seaplane-carrying ships, with or without catapults, were considered but were not promising.[70] Fortunately, the Army Air Corps offered to fill the breach by accelerating its agreed contribution of 375 planes for the opening drive. The problem was how to get them airborne over Wotje. Major Carl Spaatz apologized that the two-engined Martin bombers of 1935, which had an endurance of fourteen hundred miles, could not fly the two thousand miles from Hawaii because the only possible refueling site, Johnston Island, was too small for an airstrip. The navy declined to ferry landplanes of any size on carriers. Army planes would arrive as cargo, fighters semidismantled, and attack planes crated.[71]

General Lyman came up with a solution: preliminary seizures of lightly held atolls about a hundred miles from the main battles—Maloelap to support Wotje and Majuro if Jaluit were also taken. His concept seemed reasonable in 1936 when expectations were shifting toward softer resistance in the Marshalls. Single-engined seaplanes of all three services could be operative within a day of securing a lagoon.[72] But pontooned aircraft were grossly inferior to wheeled types, so construction outfits would level airstrips and assemble landplanes for the main assaults, a process that might take a week.[73] Meanwhile, Orange planes on and headed for Wotje would be suppressed, presumably by carriers, because the marines advised against occupying advanced interdiction bases in the western Marshalls until a Blue air force was operative at Wotje.[74]

A lesser debate addressed bombardment support. The FMF wanted seven battleships and swarms of cruisers and destroyers to shell Wotje continuously. Op-12 dismissed the operation of battleships at the beaches as "highly improbable." The navy would assign "less valuable" ships.[75]

The Carolines posed an even worse conundrum. Naval planners again told the army and marines to provide their own air power. Although plenty of American planes would be operative at B-1 in time for Truk, it would be difficult to deploy them for a battle a thousand miles away, except for two-thirds of the VP force that would be dispersed with tenders at lagoons nearer to Truk. Wotje could apparently accommodate 226 landplanes, a figure raised in 1936 to 326. (By 1938 it seemed likely that four-engined Air Corps bombers would be sent too.) Naval engineers challenged the consignment of excess planes to shabby strips on outlying atolls because of the unknown topography. BuDocks decided to redesign B-1 to link Wotje's smaller islets into three airfields.[76]

Truk presented a far tougher air target than the atolls. The United States would have to expend scarce VPs on reconnoitering and warm-up raids from the Marshalls during the four-to-six-week buildup of air power at Base One (suggesting a need to double the number of VProns). Unfortunately, Truk would remain "reasonably secure" from air corps bombers poised on Wotje or on scratchy, ill-defended advanced fields. Thus marine planners raised the issue of air support again in 1937. To attain three-to-one superiority over Truk, all 392 planes of Blue's expanding carrier wings would be needed, even assuming a 25 percent kill by preinvasion raids and no diminution for Blue (presumably by spares making up for losses). Carrier cover would be needed for occupations of the atolls around Truk, and, unless these atolls were developed into high-capacity aerodromes by dint of much time and effort, they could not hurt the main target any more than the carriers and certainly not as soon.[77]

The planners of the mid-1930s could not solve the problem of attacking heavily defended islands beyond range of shore-based aircraft. The navy remained adamant that the carriers must roam free. A solution was not arrived at until 1939, when B-1 was relocated to

Eniwetok in the western Marshalls, an island within long-range air support of a proposed American base on Wake Island, and itself within bombing reach of Truk (Chapter 21). During World War II the debate about the carriers' role surfaced again, and the navy and ground forces took the same stances. The dilemma was eventually resolved by production of longer-ranged landplanes and especially of vastly more carriers, large and small, than foreseen in the 1930s. In the one invasion that required the longest support of shore fighting by heavy fleet units, at Okinawa, they paid a dreadful price.

In 1937 the central Pacific campaign plan was amended significantly by adoption of a bypassing policy. Op-12's itinerary of 1935, as ratified by the Joint Board, had called for seizing eight of the Marshalls and eastern Carolines before moving on Truk (Map 17.3). Furthermore, all the invasions had to commence promptly after the outbreak and nearly simultaneously and finish quickly to meet Meyers's dogged insistence that the Mandate was merely a way station on a gallop to the Orient.[78] In his program, the first Blue echelon was to sortie on M+12 to seize Wotje and Jaluit (the expected points of major resistance), the adjacent atolls of Maloelap and Majuro, and Rongelap as a forward air base to protect the flank. Eight days later a second echelon would scoop up Eniwetok and invade in sequence Kusaie and Ponape in the Carolines, all difficult targets subject to air interference from Truk. The campaign would crescendo when a third wave joined the others for an M+75 landing on Truk itself.[79]

Revised analyses in 1936 and 1937 revealed Meyers's agenda to be impossible because of mobilization constraints and air resistance. The notion that regiments could assault many targets in rapid succession was unrealistic. The expedition could take Wotje and an extra atoll or two without strain, but invasion of the eastern Carolines would be time-consuming and devastatingly costly. Captain Damon E. Cummings of the Fleet Base Force, almost surely coached by Reeves, challenged the sanity of the latter operations. Kusaie, which afforded "practically no opportunity" for a base of any kind, posed no threat to Blue[80] and should be skipped. The study of Ponape brought the bypassing concept to full fruition. It was the sort of large island, lying only 375 miles from Truk, that interested the air corps.[81] But when the Marine War Plans Section contemplated a three-dimensional model of the craggy island, it did not like what it saw. An attack would have a "reasonable chance" only with a third wave to reinforce it. But "frittering away" of the force that was earmarked for Truk would defer that climactic assault by at least a month, and it would then be all the more hellish. A rapid conquest of Truk would be impossible if Op-12 and the air corps insisted on a bloody prelude at Ponape.[82]

The marines and the Fleet Base Force devised a scenario to demonstrate the efficacy of bypassing. Orange, they believed, would opt for a forward defense of Truk by placing a whopping 358 planes on Ponape (an insight of Japan's wartime tendency to waste air power in battles for secondary outposts). Blue could attain local air superiority when the third reinforcement echelon boosted its strength to 450 planes and it seized atolls for advanced strips near Ponape.[83] Then, in great air battles, it would destroy Truk's sky shield and obviate the need for the expensive intermediate invasion, "killing two birds with one stone."[84] The eastern Carolines could be kept neutered by bombers from the Marshalls. Fifty thousand troops fresh from home or rested after the atoll battles would therefore be freed for a "bold and expeditious" descent on Truk by M+59, well ahead of schedule. The breathing space would also allow the Base Force to set up services at Wotje before the Truk assault.[85] The marine planners summarized the concept:

> To nibble at the Mandates, after . . . [B-1] . . . has been gained, would be playing into the hand of Orange. Prompt seizure of Truk before it is fully organized . . . seems to offer greater chances of success [to gain] as much as could be expected in many months of the other type of operations. . . .
>
> "Playing safe" by venturing too little may end in greater loss than that resulting from a bold stroke with its chances of strategic surprise and its effect on enemy morale. Such strokes have the greatest possibility of success and offer the largest rewards.[86]

The elaborate central Pacific scenarios of the mid-1930s established a policy of assaulting only as many island strongholds as needed for U.S. bases while neutralizing the rest and leaving them to "wither on the vine." The process would unquestionably speed up the pace of the offensive and limit the fleet's exposure to attrition.[87] It was the U.S. strategy adopted in the central and South Pacific during World War II. Far more Japanese defenders were isolated on bypassed islands than were destroyed in invasion battles. It was one of the most farsighted campaign doctrines handed down from the authors of Plan Orange to the wartime architects of victory.

Royal Road: The Path Divides

C autionaries had advertised the Royal Road as the most secure way of advancing to the Far East to fulfill the Orange Plan's grand strategy of winning by sea battle and economic siege. In December 1934, however, Standley made a momentous decision, on the eve of presenting the plan to the army, that fleet operations would not be projected beyond the capture and development of Truk.[1] The record does not reveal his motives. Perhaps he recalled Eberle's instruction a decade earlier to focus planning on initial gambits that would lead "directly toward the execution of the general concept of the war and meet the probable first moves of the enemy"; thereafter, he had admonished, "the fog of war" would limit the sketches to broad themes.[2] Bryant and Meyers shared the feeling that detailed fleet plans ought to extend "up to the seizure, occupation and defense of the first Advanced Base" with only subsequent generalizations because the situation later in the war seemed "too speculative [to be] profitably discussed."[3] Standley observed that a cautionary movement would allow plenty of time to identify longer-term objectives after the outbreak.[4] Besides, fleet commanders had historically disliked projecting longer than about thirty days ahead.[5]

The truncation of fleet plans was soon extended to all navy and joint plans for a Blue-Orange war. Comprehensive programming beyond the central Pacific ceased from 1935 until the middle of World War II. The cutoff did not mean that American strategists stopped thinking about the next campaigns, but the situations they imagined unfolding west of Truk were hinted at in commentaries and peripheral studies rather than prescribed in formal Orange Plans.

The Royal Road opus, issued half a year before the edict to stop at Truk, was the last naval plan to spell out explicitly the further steps of Phase II. Commander Magruder understood that Blue could not win the war by resting at Truk because the fleet would still be too far from the trade lanes to interrupt Japan's imports, especially of oil. The stretched-out timetable also forfeited Corregidor and gave Japan time to strengthen its inner bastions. The fight to crack the outer barrier was justifiable only as a prelude to knifing into Japan's vital areas.[6]

Bryant's first outline of the Royal Road had visualized continuing operations past Truk to break the next barrier of the Bonins-Marianas-Palaus line and advance to the southern Philippines.[7] The director of war planning viewed the Palaus as a logical target. Magruder disagreed, recommending bypassing the group, suppressing it by air from Mindanao, and, if necessary, taking it at a later date.[8] Other studies had suggested that atolls of the western Carolines, such as Woleai, could be used for air operations and ferrying (although nobody appreciated Ulithi, a major U.S. advanced base during World War II, because planners, although aware of its strategic location, thought its good anchorage area too small and too exposed through a wide gap in the reef).[9]

Magruder's Royal Road of 1934 extended to Dumanquilas, where the fleet would develop a Western Base (B-W). The outpost remained a fixture of strategic commentaries through the late 1930s, although its locale grew hazier. Amendments to the plan in 1935 cryptically defined it as a place "in sufficient nearness to the Orange Main Islands to permit prompt initiation of offensive operations."[10] Sometimes it was to be preceded by a Base Three at "a destination to be assigned later";[11] the sequence of B-3 and B-W would have fit either a Palaus-Mindanao or Mindanao-Manila concept. Mentions of the Philippines grew sparse. In 1936, either to preserve secrecy or to deter speculation, Standley ordered that specific names such as the Palaus, Dumanquilas, and Manila be omitted from new plans.[12] Base designers thereafter obfuscated the sites, identifying the largest prospective depot only as someplace in the Philippines.[13]

The army was at first reluctant to truncate Plan Orange in mid-ocean. Its mobilization program looked ahead six to twelve months. In 1935 the Joint Board, coaxed by Embick, listed army forces for post-Carolines actions to consist of monthly levies of fifty thousand troops and 150 aircraft (the same numbers as the Mindanao buildup of 1928).[14] Although their destination was unstated, such large outfits would be useful only on land masses like the Philippines, but the board merely reaffirmed the goal of capturing bases for "contemplated operations" on the approaches to Japan.[15] Officially, the 1935 reprogramming was an amendment to the 1928 Joint Orange Plan. The United States therefore remained formally committed to Mindanao and the island ladder to Japan.

As planners of the 1930s contemplated operations in the western Pacific, they began to envision long-range sea and air strikes as the dominant features of campaigning in those waters. Op-12 decided in 1932 that the Philippine Sea would appeal to both belligerents for naval operations more than the restricted China Seas. For example, Orange task forces could more readily threaten Dumanquilas from the Pacific side of Mindanao. The division felt confident that modern techniques could counter such threats from the open sea. VPs at outlying coves would track enemy carriers and summon the fleet to rout them. If Orange subs and seaplanes continued to pester the base from the Palaus, their nests would be "wiped out" by Blue carriers and flying boats and perhaps occupied. Similarly, the planners shifted the north-ward movement away from the confined Palawan–Manila Bay axis and chose as the fleet outpost after Mindanao the island of Polillo, off the east coast of Luzon. Unlike Manila, from which Blue ships would have to run a 450-mile gauntlet of enemy-patrolled passages to the open Pacific, from Polillo they could sweep freely to the Bonins and Ryukyus to discourage the Orange fleet from becoming adventurous. The war would devolve into long-range sparring up and down the Philippine Sea (Map 15.1). Orange battleships would demonstrate along the Bonins-Marianas-Palaus line to support raids on American bases and to screen convoy movements, while hoping to lure U.S. battlewagons into well-patrolled waters south of Honshu, "almost a prepared position" for fleet combat. But the Blue dreadnoughts, con-stricted by the radius of their escorting destroyers, would shun the trap and range no farther than the Ryukyus.[16] To accommodate to this vision, the logistical annexes of Plan Orange were amended in 1932 to supply more fuel for high-speed carrier sorties and distant submarine patrols and, to prepare for possible earlier fleet contact, more armor-piercing shells, torpedoes, and air munitions. Depth charges on base patrol boats would free scarce destroyers to run with the big ships. Conversely, ammunition rations for shore bombardment were curtailed because assaults on inner Japanese citadels would occur later in the war.[17]

The Mindanao-Polillo sequence of 1932 was predicated on an unlikely retention of Luzon by a prewar Quick Movement, but the game of hit-and-run in the Philippine Sea could equally well have been played by poising the Blue fleet at Truk. Feinting and jabbing, however, would not win the war. Only a renewed amphibious advance from Truk would prove decisive. A few imaginative planners observed that a fleet established in the central Pacific need not restrict its horizon to the Philippines because it could as readily penetrate to "more vital areas to the West and Northwest."[18] The possibility of an aggressive advance toward the Marianas or Ryukyus had been mooted in Williams's studies of 1922 and in earlier notions of a Midway-to-Guam advance. Even Embick was willing in 1935 to speculate on thoughts, until recently anathema to soldiers, of forgetting the Philippines and heading from Truk along a more direct course toward Japan.[19]

The most innovative proposal for a northwesterly advance did, in fact, come from the army (see Map 18.1). In preparing a Strategical Plan Orange in 1936 Colonel Walter Krueger did not feel bound by the navy's boycott of post-Truk conceptualizing. He accepted the premise of the Royal Road that Truk was the "indispensable" prelude for breaking the second Japanese barrier that extended from the homeland to the Bonins, Marianas, and Palaus. In the parlance of land warfare he called it the Main Line of Resistance (MLR), the rampart at which Japan would make its crucial stand. The key points of the MLR were middle-sized, defensible, high islands. They were also "naturally built aircraft carriers" that could support each other, despite average separations of five hundred miles (too great a gap for most planes), because Orange could shuffle planes through intermediate fields in the northern Marianas and western Carolines.[20]

Krueger reasoned that to reach any position in the Far East Blue would have to punch through the MLR. But at what point? The Bonins were out of the question. Fortified before the Washington Treaty and only five hundred miles from Tokyo, they were the strongest point of the line and impregnable while the Orange fleet was at large. The Palaus, at the opposite end, were vulnerable because logistical difficulties would cause Japan to spread defenses of the western Mandate thinly among several islands. By seizing the Palaus, Blue could turn the

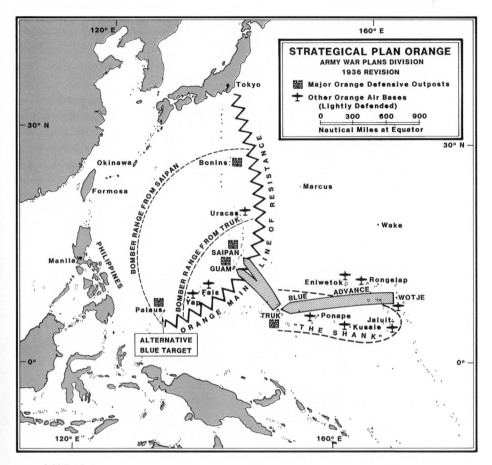

MAP 18.1

flank of the MLR, gain a fleet anchorage and potential springboard to the southern Philippines, and commence a partial blockade of Orange trade, all worthy objectives of the Orange Plan. Krueger decided, however, that the decisive point of penetration would be found "much nearer Orange proper," at Saipan and Guam.[21]

War planners had almost forgotten the Marianas after the Washington Treaty squelched hopes of a base on Guam. The 1928 Orange Plan had slated their incidental capture without saying why.[22] That year Admiral Mark L. Bristol sailed the Asiatic Fleet to Guam for a mock invasion. He found Apra Harbor tiny, naked to seaward fire, and of "no value as a haven for vessels of war." Its "truly deplorable" defenses amounted to old guns that could not track vessels and a few modern fieldpieces easily outranged by warships. The local plan anticipated surrender of the island's 409 U.S. Marines within two days. A few officers had floated odd ideas for reincorporating Guam into the Blue offensive. One island commandant had tried to level some land for an "athletic field" (an illegal airstrip), but the troops balked at the hard work. Montgomery Taylor had fancied that reinforcements could be "infiltrated" onto Guam during a time of strained relations. But marine analysts who calculated a need for a naval squadron and 16,000 troops for a few months of resistance showed they could neither be delivered in time nor stand up against air raids from Saipan. The CNO agreed that diverting energy to Guam would impede the main drive for no good reason because in enemy hands the island would pose no hazards as serious as those already in the Mandate. In 1931 the garrison was halved and all ordnance except a saluting cannon sent home (to the chagrin of the quirky Taylor, who pleaded for the guns at Manila to fight a Red War).[23] In 1935 the remnants of a marine seaplane station on Guam were leased to a civilian airline.[24]

The trifling harbors of the Marianas and their aviation sites far off the main track held no appeal for naval planners of the Royal Road. Nor did they expect Japan to prize the islands except as airway stations to more important places. Naval studies occasionally mentioned interdiction of Orange planes as they transited the Marianas, probably by carrier strikes and later by VPs from Truk.[25] But for Krueger, Saipan was an exciting goal, "the most important or key point" of the MLR. Since the work-sharing compact among the services delegated studies of the Marianas primarily to the army,[26] he proposed a campaign to seize Saipan and Guam.

The Army War Plans Division was abuzz with rumors of Japanese airfields, gun platforms, and bombproof excavations in the Marianas. It expected strong resistance—two Orange divisions with 155-mm guns supported by planes and minefields. Fortunately, air corps bombers of 1936 could span the 550 miles from Base Two at Truk and reduce the artillery and airports to rubble. Blue control of the sea would then assure successful invasions.[27] Krueger did not calculate the Blue assault force; a two-to-one superiority factor would have required two American divisions per island. (Three were landed on Saipan in 1944.) Marine analysts took a more optimistic tack, assuming only twenty-six hundred Orange troops and some civilian reservists holding Saipan, who could be overrun by a ten thousand-man outfit, preceded by a heavy naval and air bombardment of the one beach suitable for a wide-front operation since marine units had nothing more potent than pack howitzers.[28] (Marine Corps studies also contemplated an advance through the northern Marianas in the direction of Iwo Jima. Uracas, a rough island 300 miles north of Saipan reputed to have an underground hangar, would be taken by an infiltration force while other minor operations cleared Tinian, Rota, Maug, and Pagan.[29])

Capture of the Marianas would yield naval benefits such as outposts for trade war and interdicting Orange traffic with the Philippines and would assure the fall of the Palaus. But these were minor payoffs for a major campaign. In Krueger's expansive vision, the winning of the Marianas equated to winning the war because the campaign would draw out the Imperial Fleet. Until then, he believed, Orange naval detachments would "exert the Blue Navy to the utmost" by surprise attacks on task forces and convoys, but Japan would keep its capital ships in home waters. They would be "compelled to fight," however, once Blue "penetrated, captured in its entirety, or turned" the MLR. The loss of Saipan, Krueger declared presciently, "of course, would force the Orange fleet to give battle soon to avoid collapse at home."[30] Punching through the MLR at its fulcrum would provoke Japan militarily and politically to a climactic moment far sooner than would a move to the Philippines.

The Army Strategic Plan of 1936 also assigned the Marianas a role in long-range aerial warfare. Krueger had to limit his vision to neutralizing the end points of the MLR, the only important targets which thousand-mile-radius B-17s (test flown in 1935) could hit from the Marianas. Such raids from the Marianas would not be decisive, however, because the Palaus could also be suppressed from a cheaply won atoll in their neighborhood, and the Bonins's importance would shrivel after the United States severed the Orange flyway at Saipan. Army strategists may conceivably have thought of raiding Japan from the Marianas; Air Corps design work on a plane of five thousand-mile endurance had begun in 1934.[31] As it turned out, serious research on a very long range (VLR) bomber was delayed until November 1939, and the resulting B-29 prototype was not test flown until 1942[32] so any such thoughts in 1936 would have been clairvoyant indeed.

The reawakening of strategic interest in the Marianas was cut short in 1938 by another of those flip-flops that characterized American planning. Soon after Japan invaded China in mid-1937, the army abbreviated its support of the central Pacific offensive and revoked its pledge of forces for targets west of Truk. Naval planners reacted by promoting the ancient chestnut of a fleet base on Guam, only to run into a political stone wall (Chapters 19 and 20). Not until 1944 were the sea and air power rationales for seizing the Marianas reconciled and the islands escalated to decisive targets. The American assault of that year did precipitate a fleet battle and a political upheaval—the fall of the Tojo cabinet and the stirrings of peace cliques in Tokyo—that Krueger had anticipated, and the Marianas soon became launching pads for the aerial coup de grace against Japan.

The course of the war after Truk would depend not only on Blue's geographical objectives but on its timetable. Mobilization data shed little light on the subject. Sailings of reinforcements approved by the Joint Board in 1935 implied that troops might arrive in the Far East, presumably the Philippines, by M+120.[33] A "conservative" marine study, however, contended that the army would need a year to raise five hundred thousand soldiers for full-scale war in the western Pacific.[34] In any event, the fleet was not to renew the attack until Truk was equipped as a first-class base. After 1934, therefore, the sense of an evolving timetable derived mainly from engineering plans. Construction blueprints usually lagged about two years behind operational plans. Thus strategists who dreamed of a swift extension of the ocean blitzkrieg only gradually learned that logistics would decelerate the pace.

The U.S. Navy led the world in mobile base techniques.[35] It designed advanced depots to be assembled from standardized packages by skilled artisans organized in construction battalions and trained to "stand up to the shock of frequent raids."[36] The planners conceived Base One as an exercise of speed and make do, a floating service station with limited shore facilities. But in 1937, when BuDocks completed the full layout for a "typical island group" in the Marshalls, it looked substantial: magazines, shops, fuel dumps, hospitals, infrastructure, and life-support systems for 13,757 resident personnel. And, although the matériel could be delivered by M+70, it would take six months for a work gang of 8,292 laboring night and day to finish the job "disregarding enemy action."[37] It was dismaying news for the planners' M+75 descent on Truk. CNO William D. Leahy scolded the engineers for gold plating the project and demanded completion about M+60.[38] The chastened designers went back to the drawing board to accelerate shipments and construction. By 1939 they hoped to commission B-1 in time for the early Truk operation.[39]

Other logistical constraints were not so easily fixed. OpNav calculated that fleet manpower could not be filled out until M+165.[40] Worse yet, the outlook for readying Base Two lagged with each successive review. Guesstimates in 1935 had Truk up and running within a few months of occupation. As late as 1937 designs showed a skimpy facility capable of patching up ships for limping home but without dry docks;[41] further upgrading to a "Main Outlying Base" relied on adaptation of old Dumanquilas blueprints[42] until March 1939, when Op-Nav issued definitive specifications for a "Large Advanced Base" in the Carolines unquestionably contoured to Truk. It was to be a great arsenal of a scale previously envisioned only for the Philippines: destroyer and submarine depots in lieu of floating tenders, adequate fuel storage for the entire fleet, ample warehouses and barracks, and six large hospitals. A 666-plane contingent for base and fleet was to be dispersed among six land or water stations. Lifted bodily from the Philippine base design of 1928–29 was an industrial plant employing five thousand men per shift and capable of all overhaul work except relining of guns and manufacture of steel castings.

Truk was also to house a battery of floating dry docks.[43] The ability to repair underwater damage near the war zone and obviate return voyages of cripples was of paramount value. But the acquisition of mobile docks had long frustrated the navy. For many years ship architects and war planners had deadlocked over the relative merits of one-piece "shipshape" craft and those built from modular U-shaped sections joined on site. The former promised greater lifting power but could not easily be towed or self-dock if damaged by raids. Procurement was also mired in politics. The navy had easily justified fixed graving docks at home ports, which were relatively cheap and enjoyed local support, for maintenance and home defense. But petitions for movable docks invited conjecture about their purpose. To avoid signaling its offensive intentions, the navy always specified sites in the United States or Hawaii. In the 1930s the planners estimated that for a Pacific war the navy would need four Class B docks for capital ships, three Class C's for cruisers, and eight Class D's for destroyers and submarines. (Class A, an even larger type, had been eliminated.) Yet the navy had procured only one, a Class D, since the venerable *Dewey* was towed to Luzon early in the century. In 1935 it obtained funding for a Class B shipshaped leviathan, but Reeves's insistence on building a sectional type for better survivability and towing ease, as well as cost problems, delayed progress for years.[44] World War II was well along before the fleet received any large mobile docks, and they were sectional ones.

Planners speculating on a renewed offensive had to make assumptions about the pace of Truk's development as a base. Equipment was scheduled to trickle out in six monthly shipments. Logisticians ruefully acknowledged that it could not fully service the fleet until M+360, even if troops labored alongside the construction battalions. When the time to build and deliver large docks was included, the date slipped to M+720. In 1936 OpNav still hoped to stockpile materials for B-2 in peacetime. But by March 1939 a less confident high command advised the bureaus to forget about assembling the goods for Truk before M Day.[45]

The time frame of the Royal Road was becoming inexorably longer as the 1930s drew to a close. As the thrusters had warned, a cautionary war would be a long one. Yet the day of the Through Ticket had passed, never to return, even when Allied bases in the Far East became available for American use in 1941. The United States was committed to the cautionary program even as the terminus and timetable of that strategy receded toward a murky horizon.

The American Way of Planning: The Defensivists' Revolt

P ortents of a global war hung heavily over U.S. planners after the middle of 1937. Japan, having renounced the naval limitation treaties, had joined with the Axis powers, Germany and later Italy, in the Anti-Comintern Pact. On 7 July 1937 Japan launched a full-scale attack on China and soon overran the northern provinces and most seaports. Roosevelt huffed of an international "quarantine" to discipline Japan, but U.S. public reaction was negative. When Japanese planes sank the American gunboat *Panay* in China, the president, perhaps titillated by Rear Admiral Harry Yarnell's coaching on the efficacy of "strangulation," secretly sent the director of naval war plans to discuss with the British naval planners actions to interrupt Japanese trade. Nothing came of the idea.[1] More pragmatically, Congress underwrote a major naval expansion. Meanwhile, another European war loomed with the German *Anschluss* with Austria and dismemberment of Czechoslovakia by the Munich Pact in 1938. Hitler signed a nonaggression pact with the Soviet Union, invaded Poland on 1 September 1939, and the Second World War began.

During the two years before the outbreak of war in Europe, American planning leadership passed to conservative military and naval officers who were either extreme cautionaries doubtful of the country's capacity to execute an early Pacific offensive or outright defensivists alarmed at Axis threats to vital U.S. interests. Both schools were dismayed at the nation's unpreparedness for war and resented the Orange Plan's unbridled aggressiveness. In opposition stood a determined band of naval offensivists, mostly midlevel naval staff officers, who labored to preserve the essence of the plan through compromises and innovations. But Germany's defeat of France in June 1940 and fears that England might follow spelled doom for the policy of all-out effort in the Pacific. Thereafter the naval high command led the way in redirecting America's strategic priorities to the Atlantic. At the end of 1940 Plan Orange was abandoned as a formal war policy, although in 1941 the thrusters were to rally one last time and keep the offensive embers aglow for reignition when battle was joined.

As global war approached, the U.S. planning establishment focused on home security. The core premises of Plan Orange—of a two-nation, one-ocean war featuring a swift counterstroke and a goal of unlimited victory—came under challenge. The retreat from offensivism was led by Brigadier General Embick, the army's senior strategist. As early as December 1935, only six months after prompting MacArthur to endorse the Royal Road, he had signaled a change of heart about the plan in a paper that reached the White House.[2] But his complaint was deflated by Op-12's insistence on a naval offensive and Leahy's notice to FDR that naval plans would still concentrate on Japan as the most likely enemy and maximum exertion in a Pacific war.[3] Embick bided his time. In 1937 he met some ambitious German generals while on a visit to Berlin, where his son-in-law Captain Albert C. Wedemeyer was studying. Perceiving the democratic world to be endangered, he turned harshly against the Orange Plan.[4] By using his leverage as deputy to Chief of Staff Malin Craig, Embick harnessed the General Staff and the AWPD to his assertion that the plan was a potential "national disaster."[5] Its extreme aggressiveness, he informed Roosevelt, was incompatible with national security and violated "the very spirit of America."[6]

Embick's criticisms prompted intensive negotiations between the army and navy from November 1937 to February 1938. The high commanders of both services were hopeful that the planning staffs could hammer out a new Orange Plan. After fifteen years of generally harmonious campaign studies, the stature of the Joint Planning Committee was high. It had added officers specializing in industrial mobilization and affirmed in a "Joint Action of the Army and Navy" that its most important duty was the development of common war plans.[7] But the opinions of the services were virtually irreconcilable. The army insisted that both should assume a defensive posture at the start of a Pacific war. The navy just as adamantly demanded a prompt offensive, conceding only a brief delay if needed to clear Latin America and the western Atlantic of fascist encroachments, a contingency it thought improbable. The army, mindful of its chronic weakness, argued that new war plans should address only defense of the Western Hemisphere, a mission assured of firm public support that might, it hinted, allow a buildup for assertive tasks later.[8] The navy again insisted on planning a Pacific attack. It had its way, in a rather ambiguous Orange Plan of February 1938, but its victory was Pyrrhic because the army reduced its pledge of land and air forces so sharply that a meaningful ocean offensive would be a dubious prospect.

The JPC also pondered how to plan a unilateral American response to worldwide threats until May 1939, when the services agreed to develop five joint blueprints for multinational wars between the Axis coalition and the United States alone or in coalition with allies, called Rainbow Plans for their participants of many hues. Over the next eighteen months Rainbow Plans One and Four were completed to appease the army's craving for strategies to defend the Western Hemisphere and waters out to two thousand miles from U.S. shores. The navy's thirst for offensive plans against Japan was slaked by writing drafts of Joint Rainbow Plans Two and Three, which anticipated wars in coordination with European democracies that had colonial interests in Asia, and by updating the naval Orange Plan. (Rainbow Five, which set defeat of Germany as America's first priority, was not addressed until 1941.)

Because the Rainbow series offered something for everyone, a renewed mood of cooperation blossomed on the JPC. The status of the parent Joint Board was simultaneously enhanced when on 5 July 1939 Roosevelt ordered it to report to him rather than to the civilian secretaries. The board was thus elevated from cooperative council to direct military adviser to the president, a step toward the establishment of the wartime Joint Chiefs of Staff.[9] Nevertheless, the generals and admirals still tended to stand aloof from the detailed work of the staff planners. They rubber-stamped the noncontroversial hemisphere security plans, but offered only loose guidelines regarding the Pacific until early 1941, when discussions with British planners forced them to present a strong common front in bargaining with a future ally.

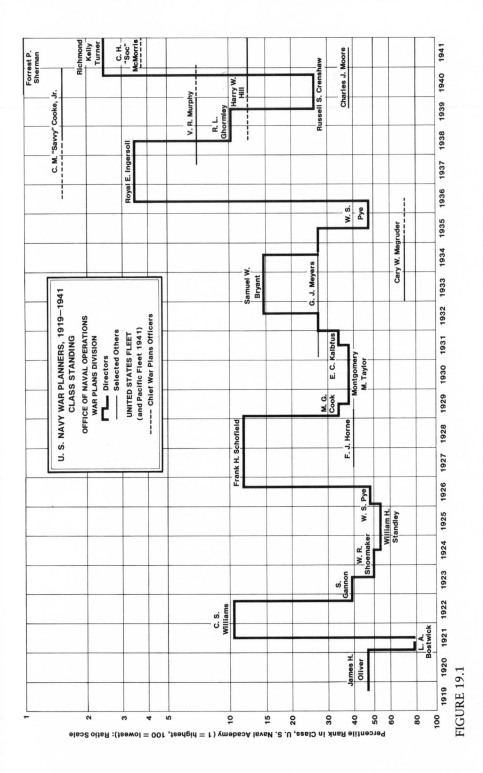

FIGURE 19.1

Neither the priority of the Rainbow studies nor the war in Europe pried the navy away from Plan Orange. In October 1939 the WPD's secret diary noted a navywide order that it still held precedence among naval war plans.[10] It continued in force for another year as the nation's only complete strategy, although its riskier aspects were modified in deference to a world full of threats. Unlike the mid-1930s, however, when reform had been imposed from the top, from mid-1937 to the end of 1940 Plan Orange was restructured by middle-echelon believers who struggled against high commands that had lost faith.

The two chiefs of naval operations of the period shared similar backgrounds. William D. Leahy succeeded Standley in January 1937 and was followed by Harold Raynsford Stark on 1 August 1939. Both admirals were orthodox surface sailors and former "big shots of the Gun Club," as chiefs of the Bureau of Ordnance were known. Both were Anglophiles. Leahy's political acumen was legendary; a personal relationship with FDR dating from the time of the Wilson administration ripened into a wartime appointment as the president's personal chief of staff and chairman of the Joint Chiefs of Staff. Stark, too, was a friend and loyal subordinate of Roosevelt's. Leahy understood grand strategy in a general way. Stark's more impressive credentials included duty with Sims's 1918 London planners and in the remarkable War College class of 1923 with future admirals Nimitz, Hart, and Horne under the tutelage of Clarence Williams. Both CNOs came to office sympathetic to the Orange Plan but grew chary as the world situation deteriorated. In 1937–38 Leahy backed his lieutenants' struggle against the army to preserve the Blue offensive, but near the end of his term he squelched construction of island bases needed to support it. Stark, an honest and modest man of intuitive caution, was shocked by the Nazi blitzkrieg of 1940. He defected from Plan Orange to the Rainbow Five concept that deferred a Pacific counterattack. He prodded political leaders and war planners toward an Atlantic-first policy, but in matters of Pacific strategy he vacillated and allowed strong-willed subordinates to manipulate him.[11]

The directors of naval war plans were oddly ineffective during the gathering crisis. Leahy's choices matched in raw brain power the stars of the past (Figure 19.1). Captain Royal E. Ingersoll, a courtly man trained in intelligence and diplomacy as well as sea command, had been exposed to Plan Orange as early as the 1910 planning conference at Newport and later was involved as a teacher of gaming and tactics and an understudy in Op-12.[12] During Leahy's final year as CNO, Rear Admiral Robert L. Ghormley ran the division. "A rather colorless fellow" but keen-minded and diligent in staff work, he was considered one of navy's best sea planners.[13] But the energies of both chief planners were depleted by their rear-guard struggles to save the navy's strategic inheritance. Ingersoll was a loyal caretaker of the Orange Plan, but he sponsored no improvements. Ghormley wrestled gamely with the army to preserve the plan but was hobbled by Leahy's turn away from a venturesome policy and the diversion of his best aides to the Rainbow projects. He updated WPL-13, a navy Orange Plan that fleshed out the Joint Plan of 1938, and awarded logistical priorities to central Pacific bases and a train of quality and endurance but did not significantly modify the ocean campaign agenda.[14] The inertia of Ingersoll and Ghormley was not attributable to personal shortcomings; both were talented officers who were elevated to assistant CNOs and to wartime theater commands. Rather, their experience illustrated that in the new circumstances of global threat naval headquarters planners could not accomplish much without the backing of a strong chief and a willing army.

In August 1939, Stark, for no discernible reason except seniority, promoted to director of war plans Captain Russell S. Crenshaw, head of the division's Policy and Projects Section. Crenshaw was a weak choice at a crucial time. He had drifted through an unremarkable career in such irrelevant specialties as radio and mines before a brushup at the War College. Under his aegis Op-12 took "a rather lackadaisical approach to the planning problem." It sluffed off a comprehensive review of readiness to the General Board. Studies that Ghormley had initiated of ways to overcome Japanese resistance, WPL-35 to 41 entitled Landing Operations Blue-Orange, languished; for example, the volume on the Mandates did not appear until October 1940 and then added little of value. Crenshaw's lukewarm support of Plan Orange turned chilly when Stark wavered. One searches in vain for any meaningful result of his fifteen-month tenure. Apparently he stayed out of the way of competent aides his boss recruited for the WPD, a clever gang who contrived their own access to the CNO, while Stark discussed strategy with his fleet commanders through chatty personal letters. Crenshaw never made it to flag rank and spent the war in obscure administrative jobs.[15]

The commanders in chief also balked at sponsoring improved fleet operating plans. Admiral Arthur J. Hepburn, a gentlemanly engineer who was considered an incisive strategist, recruited a good planner for his staff but kept him on a short tether and opposed a reorganization intended to free his own time for planning.[16] Admiral Claud C. Bloch, who fleeted up at the beginning of 1938, was a big-gun connoisseur with "an exceptionally keen and clear-thinking mind" that had been trained in War College analytical methods. OpNav wanted him to conform Plan O-1 to the new Joint Orange Plan and pointedly excused him from work on the defensive Rainbows One and Four.[17] Bloch set his aides to work on solving the "devious and frustrating" problem of a practical fleet mission.[18] They drafted an updated O-1 (which cannot be located), but the CinCUS found it full of ambiguities and discrepancies, and Leahy did not bother to approve it for eighteen months.[19] Bloch's most useful legacy to strategic plans was his championing of island bases in the central Pacific.

A long shadow fell over War Plan Orange on 6 January 1940, when the fleet command passed to Admiral James O. "Joe" Richardson. This steel-spectacled expert on steam engineering was a respected administrator in budgeting and personnel. He had also served as deputy to Reeves and Leahy and as commander of the Battle Force. Believing himself a qualified strategist through experience and War College training, he vowed to make planning "my own field for personal day-to-day attention." Richardson paid lip service to Plan Orange's stimulative effects on weaponry and sense of mission, but no naval officer in all its long history so despised the plan as he did. He abhorred the precise targets and timetables and protested against circulating secret details. He objected especially to the mission of instant revenge by a fleet he insisted should stay home until it was enlarged and trained for real war. Richardson exhorted his aides to "assist mightily" in reshaping Plan Orange.

At the beginning of his tour the new CinCUS, worried lest a fleet plan should amplify what he considered the gross errors of judgment of Op-12, submitted only a rough sketch. He preferred to hurl a barrage of criticism that he hoped might sink Plan Orange.[20] His vendetta soon bogged down in wranglings against its supporters and against the even more reckless Plan Rainbow Two (Chapter 22). Then, in May 1940, his attention was diverted when Roosevelt ordered the fleet to a permanent station in Pearl Harbor, a gesture meant to deter Japan from grabbing the colonies of France and Holland, which had been crushed by Germany, and of beleaguered Great Britain. While the admiral was swamped with the problems of settling into the inadequate base, OpNav was in a whirl of emergency planning for the Atlantic. Through the summer of 1940 Plan Orange hung in limbo.

Richardson's moods were a seething brew. He sulked at his impotence to mold high policy. He considered Stark a lightweight and berated other leaders. After the war he wrote a venemous autobiography, *On the Treadmill to Pearl Harbor,* that accused Roosevelt of luring the country into war and tarred him with a "direct, real and personal" onus for the navy's early losses. He let himself be soothed by assurances that the fleet was parked in Hawaii solely to place diplomatic pressure on Japan and that the administration had no thought of provoking war until, at a meeting with the president in October 1940, Richardson sensed that Roosevelt was in a combative temper against Japanese greed. Believing it his "solemn duty" to condemn a suicidal offensive policy, he let fly the most scathing condemnation of the Orange Plan, and of war planning itself, ever written by a naval high commander. It was a sham, he said, its faults disregarded "in order that the Department might have for budget purposes and presentation to Congress the maximum justification for the necessary enlargement of the Navy." He knew of no flag officer who wholeheartedly endorsed it. The so-called fleet supporting plan, concocted by a small, overburdened staff, was a flimsy outline resting on "unsupported assumptions." Ever since raising his flag, the CinCUS had implored Stark to educate the president about the huge costs and minor rewards of a Pacific offensive. He feared that FDR, "blithely inspired by his own impetuosity," might launch an attack regardless of strength or public willingness to see it through. The right solution, he advised, was diplomatic accommodation with Japan.[21]

Roosevelt was displeased and decided to fire the dour admiral. Nevertheless, Richardson's diatribe made its mark at OpNav. Within a month Stark produced the most important American strategic assessment of the era, convincing the nation's leaders that a Pacific conflict should hold lowest priority in the global Armageddon that lay ahead.

In the years between the invasion of China in the summer of 1937 and the Battle of Britain in the summer of 1940 the highest American commanders and planners regarded Plan Orange with attitudes ranging from mild approval to loathing. Who, then, were the loyalists who kept it alive? Primarily, they were the strategy officers of the fleet.

The billet of fleet war plans officer had been created as an experiment in 1935. OpNav assigned to Reeves an aide it had promised for war plans and logistics, Commander Cary W. Magruder, author of the Royal Road. Magruder turned out to be a bad choice; he produced nothing of significance and later spent the war in a training command.[22] The excellent campaign ideas that did emanate from the fleet in the mid-1930s flowed from subordinate staffs of the Base, Battle and

Marine forces, perhaps orchestrated by Samuel Bryant, who had boarded the flagship as chief of staff in 1935.[23] (Bryant contracted tuberculosis and died in 1938, a sad loss of a talented strategist.) When J. O. Richardson replaced him later in 1935, war planning by the CinCUS staff came to a standstill.[24]

In 1936 Hepburn recruited for the fleet planning berth an outspoken thruster, Commander Charles M. Cooke, Jr. (Richardson, then in Washington handling personnel assignments, tried to veto the appointment.) Cooke was a former submariner, a Newport graduate, and a brilliant thinker known throughout the navy as "Savvy." But Hepburn felt dubious about formal war planning and tapped his aide's mind for short-range operating counsel. Thus it was not until Claud Bloch took command in 1938 that Cooke became the foremost champion of the navy's offensive mission. For nearly a decade Cooke was to serve as an influential adviser of supreme commanders, always pushing for aggressive options. His counsel matured over the years, from a futile attempt to revive a naval base on Guam (Chapter 22), through increasingly sophisticated Rainbow Two and Three strategies, and finally to an exalted role as King's principal adviser during the war, when he was commended as "an astute strategist [with] an unsurpassed clarity of vision and power of analysis and . . . a profound grasp of principles governing the art of war."[25]

In 1938 Cooke developed an intimate working relationship with Lieutenant Commander Forrest P. Sherman, the fleet aviation officer. The intellectual "Fuzz" Sherman had served as flag secretary to powerful admirals between stints as a carrier fighter pilot. At age forty-two his brains and aviation know-how conferred on him an influence far beyond his rank.[26] In May 1938 Captain Harry W. Hill, also a protégé of several commanders in chief, followed Cooke as fleet planner and extended the phenomenon of close liaison between CinCUS and handpicked strategist. Similarly, Richardson plucked from Op-12 Commander Vincent R. Murphy, another smart submariner whose "realism" he admired; Murphy, however, lacked the stature to be much more than a scribe to his petulant boss.[27] In 1941 Captain C. H. "Soc" McMorris, another of the navy's brightest, restored the eminence of fleet planning on the eve of war.

The fleet war planners of 1937–40 maximized their influence when they were summoned from the flagship to Op-12. Cooke was called in at Leahy's insistence in mid-1938[28] and Sherman and Hill by Stark in 1940. Although they were conscripted to study rearrangement of the fleet for a two-ocean crisis,[29] their taste for combative policies kept the

Blue offensive high on the naval planning agenda. For the drafting of Rainbows Two and Three Stark eased the torpid Crenshaw off the JPC in favor of Cooke,[30] whose rampaging ideas overwhelmed army confreres and aroused Richardson's consternation. Hill and Sherman also stood up for the Pacific backlash though with somewhat less determination. The transplanted fleet strategists instilled in the Navy Department an admiration for decentralized campaign planning. Fleet planners reached full bloom during World War II, eclipsing the Washington establishment after 1943. Standing high among the wartime campaign architects were the prewar masters: Cooke as King's favorite strategist, Sherman as Nimitz's top thinker, McMorris and Hill as experts in fleet and amphibious planning, respectively, and Murphy in a high logistical policy job.

A few officers outside the fleet helped perpetuate the offensive mind-set against the gloomy tide. Rear Admiral Ben Moreell of BuDocks, the "King Bee of the Seabees," spurred the building of advanced Pacific bases. Rear Admiral J. W. Greenslade, another pro-offensivist, highlighted preparedness in his "Are We Ready?" studies. Ernest King, the tart voice of aviation, used his position on the General Board as a pulpit to urge assaults that capitalized on naval air power, the same theme he later urged at the pinnacle of his wartime power.

From mid-1937 through 1940, the American way of planning evolved erratically. The ranking army and navy leaders and their plans divisions retreated from a vigorous Pacific response, understandably in view of the threat in the Atlantic. A dedicated band of naval staff officers kept alive the ideal of striking boldly for absolute victory over Japan, the essence of Plan Orange. The fleet war planners, insulated from political pressures and quarrels with the army, prodded their superiors by mental prowess and by casting bold ideas into rational operating plans. They emerged as the men best equipped to translate grand strategy into campaigns that could win a Pacific war.

20. ••••

Defensivism versus Plan Orange

In a world changing with "kaleidoscopic rapidity," as the Army War Plans Division observed in November 1937, nobody could fathom the nature of a great conflict that seemed likely to threaten vital national interests.[1] Yet the Orange Plan granted the president a single option: to launch an attack across Japan's front, against fortress islands, aiming toward a toehold on its remote flank. A Pacific struggle of this nature would be long and "very risky." The navy might be sunk, the regular army's cadre squandered, and its scanty air and antiair forces—the shields of America itself—lost. The cost would strain the economy "to the utmost," yet the army would be hard-pressed to equip an expedition to the Orient because building a navy strong enough to beat Japan would consume 75 percent of America's munitions capacity (the reverse of the World War I allocation). To bring a first-class power to its knees primarily by naval action was "contrary to logic and to historical precedent." The Orange Plan had become, in the army's view, "strategically unsound and unwise."[2]

A judicious leadership in an uncertain world, the army advised, should reject a rigid formula "that definitely involves aggressive action, no matter what happens."[3] It should accumulate strength, stay flexible, and "make no war plan . . . beyond the necessity of defense and provision for contingencies."[4] To convert advice to policy Embick drafted a Joint Board directive to rescind Plan Orange and adopt a defensive strategy.[5] Unless this were done, he hinted unsubtly, the War Department would confess to isolationists in Congress that it had been conspiring in offensive war planning.[6]

The challenge to the Orange Plan caught the navy by surprise. It consented at first to a recasting, then rallied to try to save the plan. Under a barrage of memos from both services, the JPC came up with a stew of contradictory ideas that pleased no one. The impasse between the services was rooted in cultural differences, General Craig observed, "since the Navy is practically ready for instant action at all times and accordingly looks far afield," whereas the army was "far from ready for a venture of any magnitude" and had to look to defense of American territory. The Joint Board, exasperated at the deadlock, appointed Embick and Assistant CNO Richardson to resolve what differences they could and especially to try to define the subjects war plans should address. Again, little more was achieved than rehashing the divergent viewpoints.[7]

The army pressed for a plan that would confine the armed forces in the Pacific to a "position of readiness" within the strategic triangle Alaska-Oahu-Panama.[8] It acknowledged a possible secondary mission of preparing for overseas interventions and, as a tertiary and very contingent task, participation in a maritime offensive, as long as the latter two activities did not undermine U.S. safety. As for the goal of a Pacific war, it would accede only to a nebulous objective of applying "pressure" against Japan.

The navy had for three decades regarded a Pacific attack as its primary mission and the template for shaping its forces. It expected to conduct itself in accordance with a plan having "the defeat of Orange as its concept," and its planners therefore insisted on a "complete" plan that guaranteed the navy's freedom of movement and defined at least one specific program leading to victory. Naval strategists thought the army's principal function was to provide troops and planes to help "destroy" enemy forces. They conceded only the possibility of marking time in the strategic triangle before launching the attack.[9]

Craig tried to offer a compromise. The army would accept an offensive movement "coincident" with the position in readiness if the impetuous lunge of the Orange Plan were toned down. He offered to cooperate in writing several *contingent* plans that would be flexible, feasible, and relevant to vital interests and that would suggest loosely what might be done with means at hand without projecting actions beyond initial steps or prescribing them in detail. They would not be binding commitments; they would be options available for use when the realities of war became clear. Specifically, the army would draw a Strategic Concentration Plan for the position in readiness while the navy prepared a Strategic Operations Plan setting forth choices for joint offensives west of the triangle.[10]

The navy agreed to the compromise. The JPC manufactured it into a Joint War Plan Orange that was approved at the end of February 1938 by Secretary of War Harry H. Woodring and Secretary of the Navy Charles Edison. The Orange Plan that had been in effect since 1928 (although radically altered in 1935) was retired.[11] The navy had preserved its offensive mission after a pause it hoped would be brief and the goal of completely defeating Japan. The army imposed a delay on the central Pacific advance and limited penetration by curtailing contributions of troops and planes. It also learned a lesson: the navy would not sacrifice Plan Orange to a vague fear of the unknown. When the army next tried to rein in the fleet it would have to raise the apparition of a two-ocean emergency.

The opportunity arose in November 1938, two months after the Munich Pact had eviscerated Czechoslovakia for the aggrandizement of Nazi Germany. The Joint Board directed the planning staff to explore a xenophobic nightmare in which Germany and Italy violated the Monroe Doctrine in Latin America and Japan exerted a baneful "influence" against the Philippines while the European democracies sat indolently on the sidelines.[12] Alone in a hostile world, America would have to protect the regions critical to its security: the western Atlantic, the eastern Pacific, and the canal that linked them.[13]

The JPC bogged down again in metaphysical arguments about the nature of war plans. The Navy Section wished to write a variety of operating plans, each projecting rapid joint deployments overseas. As Cooke explained, navy plans had to assume a hostile fleet at large that could prevent seizure of vital positions unless the United States moved instantaneously. Furthermore, each operating plan should gaze far into the future, as long as four years ahead. Colonel F. S. Clark of the Army Section insisted that, in addition to mobilization, plans should address only deployments of forces in being, presumably naval, because the army expected to be virtually immobile for at least six months.[14] Op-12 blustered about all-navy expeditions but knew it would have to compromise.[15] By 21 April 1939 the JPC was able to cobble together a rambling study lauded by the Joint Board as "a monument"—an undeserved tribute except in reference to its bulk.

The joint planners slipped their imaginations into overdrive to invent a credible threat from Europe. Although they sensibly ruled out scenarios in which the paltry Axis navies prowled the North Atlantic or the Luftwaffe bombed the Panama Canal from subversively obtained airfields, they ginned up an even more freakish melodrama. Germany and Italy would co-opt Spain and Portugal and their colonies, build a great base in west Africa, and launch vast new fleets. When ready, they would advance an expedition to the African base—via Suez—and hurl half a million storm troopers ashore in Brazil. Fortunately, the United States would have plenty of time to brace itself. The navy would interdict the expedition at sea and raid its bases, a task Ghormley said could be done by one-fourth of the U.S. gunships.[16] Joint expeditionary forces with massive air corps power would then decontaminate South America in short order.[17]

Meanwhile, in the Pacific, where the Orange navy was already "practically foot-loose," Japan would capitalize on American preoccupation to incite a war. It would grab the Philippines and screen its empire by gobbling up the Blue atolls and the Aleutians. The U.S. battle line, reduced temporarily to an inferiority of 0.75 to 1, could not assure against raids on eastern Pacific positions or Oahu's lifeline, but, aided by light warships and planes, it would prevent invasions of Hawaii and Alaska. Then, as soon as the all-clear sounded in the Atlantic, the navy would launch a Phase II offensive virtually unassisted. The fleet would reunite, embark the Marine Corps, and steam out to the central Pacific. It would save any surviving advanced bases and conquer the Marshalls, Carolines, and even the Marianas while the army fattened itself for future campaigns in the Far East. Army planners worried that if the Nazis delayed their adventure the navy might sail prematurely and get "inextricably committed" in the western Pacific instead of hovering near home to fend them off. The navy conceded the need of a common understanding as to how far it should penetrate across the Pacific and the losses it might tolerate in a situation of possible recall.[18] In 1941 that issue was to dominate strategic debate *within* the navy as well.

The navy had demonstrated once more that offensive planning was its birthright. Savvy Cooke had outfoxed the colonels. Every hypothetical situation climaxed with a joint attack against Japan. No matter that the army considered Pacific objectives "in no wise commensurate with the time, effort, and cost involved" or that the campaign might fritter away the heavy bombers of the GHQ Air Force, or suck American troops into immense battles to save European colonies or to overrun Korea to flush out the Orange fleet.[19] Hitler might delay the naval attack of Plan Orange, but he could not stop it.

To resolve the quarrel over whether to shield vital areas or march across the Pacific, the army appealed for a presidential policy directive.[20] Cooke, switching to the role of conciliator, offered to cooperate in drafting plans for various contingencies, from limited conflicts to massive coalition wars. He insisted, however, that an Axis attack on the Western Hemisphere be shelved as "decidedly remote" because of the bulwark of the British Empire. Theatrical studies to counter a farfetched invasion would be "useless work" as the defunct Red Plan had been. The new plans might be called Black, Purple, or Rainbow, Cooke suggested, but they must be "realistic."[21]

The Joint Board concurred. At historic meetings of 11 May and 30 June 1939 it solicited from the JPC plans for five multinational contingencies. Each would assume simultaneous threats of Axis encroachments in the Atlantic and Japanese grabs of Western colonies in Asia. The United States might respond in either ocean or both, acting alone, in concert with friends, or in full alliances. The senior leaders balked at Cooke's insistence that "realistic" plans must always include offensive action. They assigned priority to Rainbow One, a purely defensive script for protecting the Western Hemisphere.

It took the JPC only a few weeks to churn out Rainbow One, with Cooke doing most of the writing.[22] The committee supposed Britain and France to be either cowed or defeated. The United States would defend its ocean moats and the hemisphere as far south as the ocean narrows where Brazil bulged toward Africa. In the Atlantic it would easily achieve its goals of "rendering aggression unprofitable," while the safety of Oahu and Alaska would be underwritten by naval squadrons and army reinforcements. But Japanese conquests in the western Pacific could not be prevented. Cooke inserted a hint of offensiveness by a laconic comment that at some unknown time, when all vital areas were secure, there would ensue a "subsequent extension of United States' control into the Western Pacific as rapidly as possible."[23]

The Joint Board and the cabinet secretaries approved Rainbow One in August 1939, two weeks before the start of World War II in Europe. Roosevelt okayed it orally two months later,[24] the first known instance of a president approving a war plan. The army and navy were supposed to provide supporting plans and annexes from subsidiary and local units,[25] but during the winter "sitzkrieg" on the French-German border further work on Rainbow One languished. OpNav merely alerted the East Coast naval districts to prepare for defensive tasks.[26]

During 1938 and 1939, despite the drift to global scenarios, the navy clung tenaciously to Plan Orange as its premier obligation.[27] In the Joint Orange Plan of February 1938 the army had reduced its pledge of forces to a level barely adequate to carry out the B-1 campaign in the Marshalls, which was scarcely half the strength needed for an advance to Truk. It was "useless," the colonels said, to plan to send additional regiments to the western Pacific at an early date. The air corps's contribution to the opening campaign plummeted from 600 planes to 150.[28] Gone was the promise to provide fifty thousand troops and thousands of aircraft every month.

The army pullback took the starch out of the advocates of a swift drive to the central Mandate. Despite their arguments that capturing Truk would remove "a tremendous threat" to communications with probable allies or that no other objective "would lead more directly to the defeat of Japan," the army had clipped their wings.[29] Ghormley hotheadedly vowed to enlarge the Fleet Marine Force and carry on the attack alone; the WPD conveniently predicted that only two Orange divisions would be holding the ocean outposts, a dispersed body the marines could whip.[30] He cooled down after more sober calculation showed that even if the Corps expanded to maximum size and intermediate objectives were scrubbed, a landing force *might* be ready for Truk about M+180.[31] Worse, Blue shore-based air power would be limited to fewer than a hundred fleet VPs and some marine planes. The latter could not reach Truk, which would be unassailable unless the navy dedicated its carriers to close support or the air corps stationed heavy bombers at Hawaii (justified for training and defense) that could fly directly to Base One and Truk, neither a likely commitment of forces.[32]

The ancient thruster-cautionary confrontation came to life in the navy, distilled down to whether *some* amphibious blow could be launched immediately. If so, the Marshall Islands were the only credible targets. Naval planners tried to insinuate a Marshalls campaign into Rainbow One by geographical finagling that placed the eastern Mandate within the U.S. defensive zone. The Joint Board had defined the "Western Hemisphere" as extending into both oceans. Cooke, snatching at the imprecision, proposed to set the Atlantic boundary at 30° west, the Azores-Greenland line. The Joint Board concurred. Adding 180° of longitude brought the Pacific frontier to 150° east, which encompassed Hawaii, the Aleutians, the Blue atolls, and (Cooke neglected to mention) the Mandate as far as Truk.[33] The board sensibly ruled out Truk but allowed Wake Island to be deemed within the American hemisphere.[34] The concession was a victory for the thrusters because if Wake were part of Blue's "vital area" the Marshalls, which occupied the same longitude, might be too.

An attack on the Marshalls might succeed cheaply, its supporters reasoned, if done while Japan was engrossed in the Orient. The army's grudging promise of twenty thousand men, approximately the number slated for the Marshalls and eastern Carolines in the 1935 plan, should be adequate to take the former alone. Bloch asked that they be delivered to the fleet as two reinforced brigades for assaulting two atolls. Army planners, however, advised that their embarkation would be delayed a few weeks so landings on Base One and outlying atolls could not take place on M+35 even though Corps Commandant Holcomb vowed to deliver twenty thousand marines by then. The B-1 campaign could not start until M+55. Bloch advised the air corps to hold up plane deliveries until M+65, when Wotje's fields would be ready, and to send defensive fighters and machines for sea patrol and attack rather than assault support types. How the landings would receive air cover remained a mystery.[35]

By such tinkering with details the navy preserved a slightly delayed Marshalls attack plan until Richardson's appointment to the fleet in January 1940. The CinCUS resolved to challenge the quick thrust by explaining the fleet's dismal state of readiness. In March he submitted a sketchy outline of a Plan O-1 that has been lost. Apparently it hewed to the standard drill of establishing Base One and advancing on Truk, adding warm-up raids, and providing forces to stiffen Blue ocean bases. The known shards suggest it was a typical Orange Plan lunge, fast and aggressive. It was also a sham because as Captain Hill (who brought it to Washington) lamented, the fleet lacked transports and landing boats (marines debarked from battleships in exercises) and know-how for creating advanced bases.[36]

In April 1940, after the Nazis bested the Royal Navy in Norway, Stark grew uneasy about the Pacific strategy. On 1 May he laid its fate before a rare collective meeting of the General Board and Op-12. Forrest Sherman, newly arrived from the flagship and still fronting for Richardson and perhaps for Stark, proposed to limit the fleet to defensive actions in waters just west of the strategic triangle. Operations would be facilitated by shifting the fleet to Hawaii. (The president obliged the young officer with such an order a few days later.) From Pearl Harbor the fleet could support outposts under construction on

atolls that formed a north-south defense line in front of Hawaii—
Midway, Johnston, Palmyra, and possibly Canton. To stretch the operating zone farther west, say to guard Wake or the Aleutians and their
supply lines, would expose the fleet to erosion of battle strength and
was not advisable.[37]

Most of the conferees liked the proposal of a slightly more permissive naval defense theater. Crenshaw derided the fleet's straw-man
outline of a Mandates attack as a delusion of grandeur. Admiral Walter
Anderson of Naval Intelligence called for an even lower-profile strategy
of defense and disruption of distant trade. As Hill recalled, "One after
another of these officers of outstanding professional reputation took
the floor and in effect declared the Orange Plan was impractical." The
thrusters fought back—Cooke, Hill (assigned to Op-12 and liberated
from Richardson's steely gaze), and Admiral J. W. Greenslade. King
was "really disturbed." He "lit into" his flaccid colleagues: "What an
incisive and fighting defense of the plan he made! One of his mottoes
was, 'Do your best with what you've got. . . .' He was bitterly scornful of those present who would propose keeping the fleet in port at
home for a long period after the declaration of war in order to obtain
the proper tools to take the offensive with. As he plainly told them,
public opinion would force the fleet to sea in spite of such a Fleet
Commander's orders." Not one of the nay-sayers would get a wartime
command under King.[38]

Ernest King had saved the offensive plan, at least temporarily. Stark
held his tongue. He accepted the fleet's O-1 outline with a face-saving
remark that it might be suited to a coalition war. In fact, he was trapped
between the navy's instinctive appetite for attack and the time bomb
ticking in Europe. The CNO was to vacillate many times, a naval
Hamlet sounding the alarm about Hitler, then blessing a Blue offensive,
then again shrinking from it.

In June 1940 the shock of France's collapse catapulted hemisphere
defense plans back to top priority. Op-12 slapped together the overdue
WPL-42, an unimpressive naval supporting plan for Rainbow One. It
called for deploying most of the fleet to the Caribbean and Brazil and
leaving a few depleted squadrons to guard the eastern Pacific. Its only
spark of "dynamic attitude" was the adoption of Sherman's policy of
protecting outposts, stretched to assist Blue units already on Midway
and in the Aleutians and possibly to shield undefended atolls—a lot to
ask of a mini-fleet reduced to three battleships, a carrier, and eighteen
destroyers. But WPL-42 survived only four months. Its principal value

was that it got the lethargic shore districts started on logistical tasks that would be applicable to other war situations.[39] The army did not write a Rainbow One supporting plan but turned to Rainbow Four.[40]

The summer of 1940 was the low-water mark of abject defensivism. The JPC told the president that Britain could not survive through the winter, and the ONI recommended helping evacuate much of its population.[41] The Joint Board demanded Plan Rainbow Four, an improved hemisphere defense plan. The JPC whipped up a ghastly scenario in which the British and French fleets were in German hands and being readied to descend on South America. The U.S. defense perimeter would have to be extended to Cape Horn and probably to the Atlantic island possessions of the beaten democracies and Portugal. The General Board clamored to move all battleships and flying boats to the Caribbean immediately.[42] The commander of the fleet's VPs concocted a scheme for a two thousand-plane continuous patrol of the Western Hemisphere and all U.S. outlying possessions. Richardson called it preposterous because the navy had only two hundred flying boats.[43] Since the dispersion of American strength specified in Rainbow Four would grant Japan even greater freedom, Op-12 restricted the fleet units left in the Pacific to the Midway-Unalaska line and to symbolic occupations of British and French islands of Polynesia. The planning of a Blue offensive was forbidden. The Joint Board received Rainbow Four on 31 May 1940, during the evacuation of the British army from Dunkirk, and promptly endorsed it. In August the president approved it.[44]

Then, like a summer storm, the flap dissolved in the sunshine of reassuring events: the bottling up of the French fleet, the swap of American destroyers for British Atlantic bases, and especially Churchill's bulldog resistance during the air Battle of Britain. Roosevelt steadfastly believed the British would hold. By September 1940 U.S. naval planners were disowning the embarrassing defensive plans. Cooke condescendingly called Navy Rainbow Four a "prewar" plan and discouraged the writing of annexes. Stark dismissed it as an informal study. But the army was laboring on its version so desultory joint discussions continued until October, when Captain Kelly Turner took charge of the WPD. Turner declared all hemisphere defense plans "defective in the extreme" and canceled supplemental work such as designing ports of embarkation for expeditions to South America. The army then decided to quit.[45] Rainbows One and Four, the Fortress America plans, were formally rescinded in mid-1941. They had been out of synch with national tradition and especially with naval gospel that home territory was sacrosanct and that war must be carried across the seas to enemy shores, east and west.

The rebound from defensivism in the autumn of 1940 brought the planning establishment back to contemplating whether and how to mount a Pacific attack. By then the question was sandwiched between two modes of strategic thought. The United States was about to award grand strategic priority to defeating Germany first and to downgrade its commitment to the Pacific. Stubborn thrusters were seeking campaign options compatible with that decision to sustain the aggressive heritage of Plan Orange.

21

Tilting the Offensive Northward

A glaring deficiency of the 1930s Orange Plans was America's inability to deploy large aircraft to the central Pacific. Enemy bases in the Marshalls would be backed by a network of air stations, whereas Blue planes would have to cross the two-thousand-mile waste from Hawaii as cargo. The planners understood that an air-age offensive would require perches for shore-based planes to cover the fleet, support landings, and intercept threats. The Blue atolls in the void—Midway, Johnston, and Wake—could provide such sites. Wake, in fact, lay so far to the west that it could also support a direct assault on the northwestern Marshalls preparatory to a bolder advance to Truk and beyond. The prospect stimulated the downtrodden thrusters in 1939 to shift the attack route away from Wotje to a more aggressive Midway-Wake-Eniwetok line, a gambit better attuned to Orange Plan traditions of speed and audacity. It was a change that helped significantly in preserving the navy's commitment to an offensive strategy during the last two years of peace.

A five-hundred-mile shift of Base One from Wotje to Eniwetok may seem a small deviation, but it changed the course of U.S. strategy just as the switch from Manila to Mindanao had done a decade earlier. A base at Eniwetok would lie closer to Japan and would be more threatening to Truk and even the Marianas. By early 1941 naval thrusters also believed that the Orange main body would emerge to challenge an American attack in that part of the North Pacific. Cautionaries were troubled by the risky initial campaign in the northwestern Marshalls but did not present a counterproposal until May 1941, when they suggested mounting a drive from the South Pacific after it became clear that Allied islands would be available as bases. Their strategy, which somewhat resembled MacArthur's during World War II, had little effect on the decision makers before the outbreak of war.

The American invasion of the Mandate in 1944 did not unfold precisely in accordance with prewar plans, but it did owe much to the efforts of 1939–41. The thrusters, by riveting the navy's attention in those years on a vigorous central Pacific sweep, helped assure that it would not play second fiddle to MacArthur when the test came.

U.S. capture of Eniwetok would isolate all other Orange bases in the Marshalls and establish its air power seven hundred miles from Truk, a much easier radius for modern planes than the thousand-mile flight from Wotje. The fearsome eastern Carolines would be neutralized. Eniwetok could also be a stepping-stone to the Marianas, a thousand miles to the west. The Blue advance would tilt northward along the rim of the Mandate, moving directly and swiftly toward the inner bastions of Formosa, Okinawa, and Japan itself. "Thus," Nimitz said in 1943 as he prepared to knife deeply into the Mandate, "we get on with the war."[1]

Naval planners had admired Eniwetok, from 1907 speculations of a secret rendezvous through the cautionary plans of 1921–22 that named it "our intended fleet base."[2] But Through Ticket devotees of the late 1920s demoted it to a convoy station. The cautionaries of 1934 also rejected Eniwetok, the only Marshall Island nearer to Japan than Hawaii, as too far forward for fleet protection and too dangerous a site for B-1. The enemy might deviate from its expected policy of limited atoll defenses and arm it with heavy artillery.[3] Thus the 1935 Orange Plan earmarked it for a "temporary" seaplane base to aid the Wotje-to-Truk movement,[4] so temporary that it might be manned only by aviation personnel who could evacuate by air.

The notion of Eniwetok as a fleet base, if only a transient one, reappeared in studies by the Fleet Base Force, the outfit responsible for building and guarding advanced bases. In the summer of 1935 Captain

Damon E. Cummings of that force was on the faculty of the Army War College and in touch with both Op-12 and Reeves. Current estimates regarded Wotje as a tough nut to crack so that the fleet would have to patrol near Truk for an extended period during the operation. Cummings therefore urged preliminary seizure of Eniwetok as a sanctuary in the forward cruising zone (Map 21.1). He predicted light resistance if Blue pounced "at once." Inside the big lagoon the fleet would replenish in safety under an umbrella of VPs flown out from Hawaii, presumably via new commercial air stations on Midway and Wake. Air corps planes would be uncrated and assembled there to cut Japan's aviation pipeline and by staging through simultaneously occupied fields on Bikini and Rongelap—the latter only two hundred miles from Wotje—would assure sky control over Wotje and the flanking atolls. Although the preliminaries in the northwestern Marshalls would delay the main assault on Wotje, Cummings claimed they would ensure its success and insulate Base One from attack so that it could be ready sooner for the Truk assault.[5]

Cummings's ingenuity was received coolly at Op-12, which was wedded to a rigid sequence of short advances.[6] Besides, the logisticians had little data on islands other than Wotje.[7] But King, who took command of Base Force aviation in 1936, was probably aware of the idea, and it was kept alive by Naval War College teachers who noted Eniwetok's "outstanding capabilities" as a fleet base.[8]

Not until 1939, however, after the army had shriveled its role in the Mandate campaign, did senior admirals reconsider Eniwetok. The impetus came from Rear Admiral King, who was nearing retirement in a "sunset cruise" on the General Board. King's opinions were never taken lightly by the war planners.[9] On 21 September 1939 he declared it "essential" that the Blue attack overleap the outer wall of Japanese islands to a base in the northwestern Marshalls.[10] Op-12 rounded up all the known data on Eniwetok,[11] which confirmed its attractions: a lagoon wide, deep, and clear enough for any armada, two defensible passes, and two midsized islets for airstrips. (Bikini and Rongelap were hydrographically unappealing and were dropped from consideration. Taongi and Bikar, the northern outliers of the group, were useless.[12]) From that moment Eniwetok was designated Base One in U.S. war plans in lieu of Wotje (Map 21.2). Strangely, the decision was not documented in a plan until March 1941, when the fleet confirmed the target, citing the rationales of bypassings and striking nearer to Truk.[13] The fleet war plans officer intended to write an "Eniwetok Plan" later

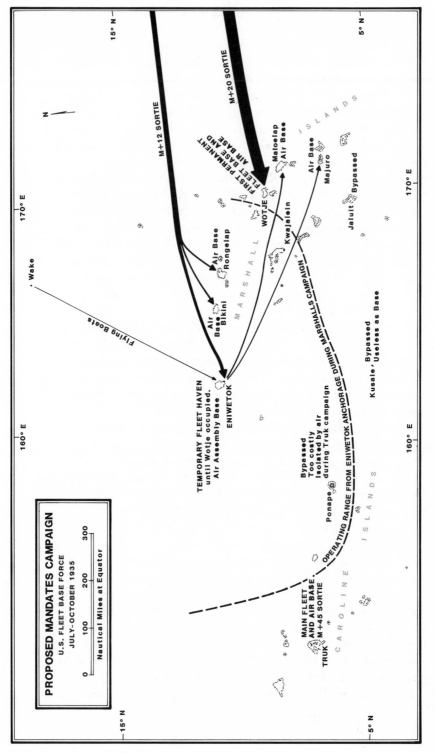

PROPOSED MANDATES CAMPAIGN

U.S. FLEET BASE FORCE
JULY-OCTOBER 1935

Nautical Miles at Equator

0   100   200   300

MAP 21.1

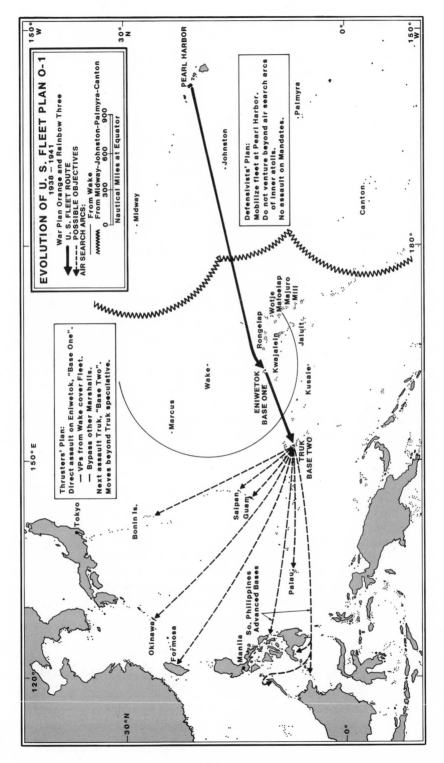

EVOLUTION OF U. S. FLEET PLAN O-1
1938 – 1941
War Plan Orange and Rainbow Three

→ U. S. FLEET ROUTE
- - - - - POSSIBLE OBJECTIVES
AIR SEARCH ARCS:
From Wake
wwwww From Midway-Johnston-Palmyra-Canton

0   300   600   900
Nautical Miles at Equator

Defensivists' Plan:
Mobilize fleet at Pearl Harbor.
Do not venture beyond air search arcs
of inner atolls.
No assault on Mandates.

Thrusters' Plan:
Direct assault on Eniwetok, "Base One".
— VPs from Wake cover Fleet.
— Bypass other Marshalls.
— Next assault Truk, "Base Two".
— Moves beyond Truk speculative.

150°W

30°N

PEARL HARBOR

· Midway

· Johnston

· Palmyra

· Canton

180°

150°W

0°

Rongelap

· Wotje
Maloelap
Majuro
Mili

Wake ·

Kwajalein

· Jaluit

· Marcus

ENIWETOK
BASE ONE

· Kusaie

TRUK
BASE TWO

150°E

Tokyo

Bonin Is.

Saipan ·
Guam ·

Palau ·

Okinawa ·

Formosa ·

Manila ·
So. Philippines
Advanced Bases

120°E

30°N

0°

MAP 21.2

in 1941 but apparently never did, so no landing plan for the island was prepared between the marine study of 1921 and the first wartime essay of December 1942.[14]

King admonished the planners that success at Eniwetok would depend on speed and especially the immediate availability of an air base to support the assault.[15] He had in mind Wake Island, where the navy had just decided to develop a base after four years of dithering. Because the final peacetime plans lacked details about the Eniwetok campaign, the Wake Island project must serve as a proxy in understanding how U.S. strategy shifted to the northerly track that became the dominant maritime attack path of World War II.

Wake Island lay in no-man's land, 1,100 miles west of Midway and 530 miles north of Eniwetok. Alone among U.S. possessions it was a place from which Blue could deploy offensive air power over Japanese territory (because Guam and the Philippines were considered lost and other U.S. atolls were out of range; Midway and Johnston would stage planes to Wake). But Wake's enticing location was counterbalanced by its physical defects. It was a true desert island, never inhabited by Micronesian wanderers. Its four square miles of flat, sandy land, although ample by central Pacific standards, rose barely above sea level; the "safe" fifteen-foot elevation of one of its three islets had not been noticed by the seven U.S. military parties that waded ashore to scan the island before 1920. There was evidence that typhoons had often swamped the atoll. A geographer had snickered that Wake was "here to-day and away to-morrow . . . occasionally disappearing beneath the water. . . . It seems to be a coral reef which the insects have not finished. . . . What the United States government wants with this island is difficult to say."[16]

Certainly the navy had no use for an island with "nothing in the way of natural advantages."[17] The two-and-a-half-square-mile lagoon was comparable in extent to Apra but was shallow and encased by a granite-hard reef that blocked entry to all but the tiniest skiffs. It could never be upgraded to a fleet anchorage. At most, by extraordinary effort and expense, a channel and small basin might be excavated for extending submarine and destroyer operations in the war zone.

Wake could have sunk beneath the water for all that war planners of the 1920s cared. During the Washington Conference, Japan suggested placing the nonfortification frontier at 150° east longitude, which would have allowed martial use of Wake, but American indifference let it slip to the treaty's demilitarized zone.[18] Seaplanes that surveyed the other Blue atolls never got to Wake, and the navy ignored a clever suggestion to snap photos from a balloon tethered above a passing vessel.[19] Two enterprising naval skippers did heave to and land (one earning a reprimand),[20] and a minesweeper delivered a scientific expedition ashore for a few days in 1923. The impromptu naval explorers reported the lagoon "an excellent place" for flying boats, which needed only six-foot depths. The naive intelligence officer accompanying the scientists thought the reef a splendid defensive shield for planes; unfortunately, it was also a barrier to tenders they depended on.[21] In any case, the sad performance of VPs and the fetish for the Through Ticket foreclosed strategic interest in the island. At the end of the decade the navy disavowed any jurisdiction over Wake, and government maps omitted legends of U.S. ownership because it was not "of sufficient importance for specific mention."[22]

Wake was rediscovered by the planners of the Royal Road campaign. OpNav deduced from an inspection in 1933 that three VProns (thirty-six planes) could operate from Wake—no small number when the fleet had only seven VProns—if tenders could only get inside.[23] In 1935 a commercial venture dramatized the possibility. Pan American Airways decided to inaugurate Flying Clipper service to Asia by way of the central Pacific. (A survey by Charles Lindbergh had eliminated a shorter Alaskan route.) Passenger seaplanes could follow the all-Blue cable line from California to Manila, with overnight stops on Oahu, Midway, and Guam and another at Wake. (The twenty-four-hundred-mile-range Clippers could have skipped either Midway or Wake by reducing payloads, but profits would have suffered.) Juan Trippe, Pan Air's president and a former naval flyer with ties to the service, obtained a mail contract and appealed for other government assistance.[24] King, as chief of BuAer, jumped at the chance for some air activity in the central Pacific. He had learned while playing the Blue-Orange game at the War College that air bases on Midway and Wake could aid the Blue offensive.[25] He urged President Roosevelt to place Wake under naval control. The navy shipped a seaplane out to map it, leased the best ground to Pan Air, and urged Congress to fund clearance of coral snags from the lagoon "for obvious reasons."[26] The airline sent a crew of young men to build seadromes on "the new frontier of the air"; they captivated the public's imagination (and received many an unsolicited proposal of marriage). Mail flights commenced in November 1935. A year later Pan Air began hauling passengers in luxurious four-engined Martin Clippers. Until the war, one or two round-trips per month brought the famous, the powerful, and those who could afford the $1,845 intercontinental fare to spend a night in the airline's little hotel.[27]

The navy wanted to use the Pan Air stations to exercise flying boats, but the massed flights of naval doctrine would have been impossible at Wake. (No warplane landed there until a VPron flew to Manila in late 1939.) Gasoline had to be manhandled over the reef in steel drums. In the absence of machine shops or tenders, breakdowns would soon have terminated the flying. Op-12 realized that VPs could not perform offensively as bombers at forward islands until proper bases were set up.[28]

At the end of 1935 Pye, as director of Op-12, recommended that air bases be built on U.S. atolls and incorporated into Plan Orange. The navy and its friends in Congress had to conspire to obtain funding for "civil works" because of the voters' isolationist mood. The charade began with surveys in 1936 by the Army Corps of Engineers, the normal routine for domestic harbor work. Although Pan Air needed only a small entry for drainage and delivery of goods, Op-12 expected the work to be "confidentially guided to meet naval requirements."[29]

At Midway the sham worked brilliantly; development of a defensive air station commenced in 1938. At Wake, however, nobody knew what to design for what purpose. Proposals came and went with fluctuating perceptions of need, cost, and politics. Some officers thought that VPs with strong underbodies and beaching wheels could self-establish camps for patrolling in the opening days of war.[30] The WPD wanted channel digging, a slow and expensive process, to be done gradually.[31] Air enthusiasts wanted an optimized outpost, like Midway, for operation of three VProns for surveillance and attack over an indefinite period, supported by tankers and depot ships (AVDs) of ten thousand tons and ultimately by onshore machine shops, hangars, and buried fuel dumps. A deep channel, however, would have leaked sand with disastrous consequences to the island. Others, chafing for quick action, demanded a simple perch improvised without special funding, the only project CNO Leahy would bless. In 1938 the Hepburn Board recommended a shore base, which its opponents shrank to a simple gas station watched by caretakers. BuDocks thought a few men could dynamite coral pinnacles in the lagoon and a passage for motor lighters and set up a crude ramp and fuel cache so that a couple of VProns could scout until mechanical failures beached them after four weeks—long enough to cover an Eniwetok landing. Orange submarines would have prevented the dragging of nine thousand drums of aviation gasoline (avgas) ashore for fresh squadrons.[32]

The frustrations over how to make Wake Island profitable accentuated the problems of seaplane tender operations, still regarded by the General Board in 1939 as the worst constraint in readying the navy for war.[33] For years King had lobbied for craft able to steam swiftly and operate in shallow lagoons, but the bureaucracy had spurned his appeals. He had suggested converting destroyers, tugboats, or even yachts.[34] He had toyed with lifting VPs for repair by broaching submarines beneath them (unworkable except in calm harbors). The navy looked into barge-mounted catapults and considered submarine tankers to fuel planes at sea or even in unwatched lagoons of the Mandates.[35] The General Board studied a special class of vessel bearing small seaplanes for inshore work,[36] hardly the solution to a strategic aviation problem.

In 1939 a compromise design for Wake was arrived at. A channel would be dug to admit thousand-ton tenders converted from light warships (AVPs and AVDs). They would follow their flocks from Hawaii when war began, hopefully arriving in time to sustain them after shore tanks were depleted.[37] The navy began adapting a few destroyers, faster but no more commodious than the 1918-vintage Bird class minesweepers.[38] Op-12's "Maintenance Plans" presumed that men and equipment would rush out when mobilization began and within sixty days establish a self-sustaining base on Wake.[39] It was a fatuous idea. Gear could not be landed over the surf-swept reef with Japanese raiders in the offing, nor could dredges complete the job under attack.[40]

In December 1938 the Hepburn Board had named Wake as third in importance among Pacific islands after Oahu and Midway,[41] yet a coherent rationale for developing it was lacking until late the following year when naval planners adopted the Wake-Eniwetok attack formula. (Wake was strictly a naval bailiwick; the army had "no particular interest" in it.[42]) Publicly the navy said it needed island bases for "vital" defensive patrols at the outbreak of war.[43] But for defense of what? The district commandant of Hawaii had dismissed Wake fifteen years earlier as "not deserving of much consideration" as a sentinel of Oahu.[44] An Orange fleet headed for Pearl Harbor could easily avoid the search arcs of its planes. More to the point for an offensive-minded service, naval planners had been grumbling since 1935 that the lack of an aerial scouting post was the "most serious obstacle" to initiation of a central Pacific attack. The fleet needed "unsinkable carriers" for air cover and light craft bases.[45] It needed an aircraft assembly station and a strip for bombers en route "to Operating Forces in advanced areas," that is, to Base One during and after its occupation.[46]

Wake Island's potential role in war plans was retarded by its apparent indefensibility. Japan was expected to recognize it as a threat and covet it as a place from which to spot Blue forays toward the Marshalls, the Marianas, and the home islands. Op-12 expected Orange promptly to raid and occupy it but had no clue as to how to hold or reclaim it.[47] Preliminary studies had suggested that planes and tenders would have to depart each dawn and evacuate permanently if attacked.[48] Hardly more promising was a scheme of the fleet aviation staff in which PBYs would alight on M+2 crammed with marines to hold the island with hand weapons until the fleet appeared.[49] In 1939 a marine staff expert went out to study defenses against "attacks not of a minor character." To fend off armored ships, he reported, Wake would need big-caliber guns dug in before the war, not midsized pieces dispatched from California on M+12.[50] Even more serious was the danger of Orange air attacks launched from carriers, the Marshalls, or Marcus Island. The naval antiaircraft guns used by marines, which could train only on directly approaching planes, were useless to shield several square miles by crossfire. They could bring a bomber under fire for twelve seconds to no effect except psychological. Since naval opinion was not ready to concede the need of a fighter plane defense, the study glumly advised dispersing VPs passively about the lagoon. It concluded that the enemy would carry the island because the fleet could not stand by it.[51] Improvement of Wake would thus ultimately benefit Orange.[52]

Before the summer of 1939 the dimly understood purpose of Wake invited opponents to savage the project. The State Department professed horror at the navy's jurisdiction. Roosevelt vetoed fleet maneuvers near it lest Japan feel provoked.[53] America Firsters and antiwar activists damned it as beyond America's legitimate venue of defense.[54] Worse, Leahy behaved like the enemy within. He vetoed the loan of an army dredge. He shared Ingersoll's disdain of Wake as merely an air transit point for reinforcing Guam; when Congress ruled out a proposed base on Guam (Chapter 22), he deemed the atoll worthless even though BuAer and fleet admirals valued it for other uses. Lawmakers, skeptical of other justifications such as using it as a training post or an advanced guard for the popular Midway base, refused the money.[55] Congressman Carl Vinson, chairman of the House Naval Affairs Committee and the navy's best friend on the Hill, managed in April 1939 to stave off death amendments and salvage a mini-base proposal, although it was to be starved of cash until 1940.[56]

Ghormley, the head of Op-12 since mid-1938, decided to join the proponents of a Wake-Eniwetok strategy. Stung by the setback in Congress, he confronted the obstinate Leahy. He declared in WPL-35 that "Wake is beyond doubt the most important [U.S. island] strategically from the view of both Blue and Orange. Its central location makes it of inestimable *offensive* and defensive value to Blue; especially as a patrol plane base from which the Marshalls and Eastern Carolines can be subjected to observation and *attack*" (emphasis added).[57] When Leahy left Naval Operations on 1 August 1939, his successor was greeted by a chorus of supplicants for Wake: Captain Marc A. Mitscher of BuAer, the Shore Station Development Board, Commander in Chief Bloch, who said it was essential to fleet operations, and the master builder Ben Moreell (who probably orchestrated the clamor) fuming that bungling had made the navy a joke. Stark gave in. Wake soared on the navy's master project list from priority number 730 (far behind the officers' club on Oahu) to number 8.[58] The base on Wake was assured—if time didn't run out. The once-despised island rose figuratively from the brine to become the gun barrel of Pacific offensive plans.

Wild schemes abounded to get started before Congress acted[59]— Wake was already two years behind Midway. On 26 June 1940 war-frightened legislators finally voted generous funding in connection with a ten thousand-plane rearmament program.[60] A survey team spent the summer on Wake producing a cursory design.[61] OpNav ordered a ship-sized entry, grander than any previously imagined, for completion in May 1942, and naval engineers designed big air and submarine stations.[62] But at the end of 1940 not a shovel of sand had been turned. The development of Wake had slipped three years behind that of Midway.

Ironically, as naval opinion embraced the more vigorous model of the central Pacific attack, it soured on one of its underpinnings, the VPB striking force. By 1939 big seaplanes were grossly outclassed by wheeled aircraft. Kalbfus, back in the fleet as commander of the Battle Force, urged confining them to patrolling. Sending the sluggish craft toward the Orange fleet in daylight would result in their slaughter unless they were shepherded by carrier fighters, which, of course, would negate their premium of range.[63] The commander of the VProns considered solo bombing runs "questionable except as a last resort." Massed formations might fare better, he conceded, but only "desperate circumstances" would justify torpedo attacks.[64] Even King had backed off and was talking of a *defensive* striking force to cover the Midway-Aleutians gap[65] (through which Japanese carriers were later to sail to Pearl Harbor).

In February 1940 Captain Crenshaw silenced the debate. Op-12 had lost faith in the PBYs as bombers, massed or otherwise, after learning the sad experiences of the Royal Air Force with the planes.[66] The navy relegated its flying boats to reconnaissance, auxiliary duties, and small-scale night raids. During the Pacific war they flew daylight attack missions only as rare acts of desperation. Nevertheless, two decades of hoping and planning for a seagoing heavy bomber force had been instrumental in drawing the navy to a strategy of advance through wide-open seas, a strategy that was robust enough to outlive an obsolete weapon.

Although the need for VPs as "eyes of the fleet" still justified ocean bases, the long-range punch for a Wake-Eniwetok-Truk campaign would have to come from the Army Air Corps. B-17 Flying Fortresses, which were operational from 1938 on and outclassed flying boats in speed, altitude, defense, and even range, were thought by their admirers to be capable of hitting ship and shore targets with pinpoint accuracy. Astonishingly, however, most generals and admirals resisted incorporating them into the offensive plan until late 1941. In 1939 and 1940 the Army Hawaiian Department first suggested building bomber fields on five Pacific atolls for "joint offensive action against a hostile fleet," but its omission of Wake bespoke a strategically defensive mindset. Major General Henry H. Arnold, head of the air corps, wished to encourage aggressive thinking, yet the Army War Plans Division insisted on confining bombers to a massed defense of Hawaii, fretting that the need to defend outlying atoll fields would result in scattering or diversion to reconnaissance. Army war planners made it clear that they had no interest in the Orange fleet unless it approached Oahu.[67]

The navy did not object. Rear Admiral Turner, director of the WPD and a fierce critic of the army, early in 1941 felt that heavy bombers were not needed in Hawaii either. (He probably wished to avoid the assignment of VPs to scouting for them[68] and, one suspects, to keep the central Pacific a preserve for naval strategic forces.) In May Lieutenant General Walter C. Short, commander of the Hawaiian Department, advised that B-17s could operate from atolls, including Wake, by day and night if the navy provided airstrips with underground tanks and magazines and guaranteed protection.[69] Again the navy was not interested. The idea lay fallow until the autumn of 1941, when thirty-five B-17s flew to the Philippines by way of Midway and a primitive airstrip on Wake that was lengthened for them, then over the Mandate at night to Rabaul, Australia, and Manila.[70]

In the last years before the war, fleet intelligence got wind that the Japanese were urgently making preparations in the Mandates. Although direct espionage was impossible (the mythical exploits of the famous aviatrix Amelia Earhart notwithstanding[71]), arcane sources indicated that the Japanese had developed eight anchorages and a dozen airfields stocked with 262 planes. By 1941 seventy steamers were said to be engaged in carrying construction materials to the islands.[72]

Rear Admiral Patrick Bellinger of Patrol Wing Two (the combined command of fleet VPs in the Pacific) worried that U.S. aircraft carriers would be mauled in the thicket of Orange bases. A better alternative, he proposed in October 1940, would be to reduce the Mandates through continuous pounding by tough, long-legged aircraft. Bellinger recommended that until the navy could acquire heavy bombers air corps groups of sixty planes each be allocated, two to Hawaii and a third to Midway, ready to "proceed immediately to Wake to start offensive operations." Wake would be transformed into a major army base defended by army interceptors, radar, and flak.[73]

Most of the fleet admirals applauded Bellinger's idea as "sound as a rock." John S. McCain, another air officer, thought land bombers were proper naval tools; Vice-Admiral William F. Halsey, the top carrier commander, "heartily agreed." The fleet war planners, however, were aghast at an air corps usurpation of a naval mission. B-17s from Wake, they argued, could reach only "outer outer" objectives. They were not accurate enough to hit ships or other small targets. Without fighter protection many would perish and, since the carriers would have to enter the Mandate to provide escorts, their dive bombers could also knock out the enemy by "sheer force of numbers." Furthermore, construction of a "miniature Ford Island" (like the air station at Pearl Harbor) would be a nightmarish task on a besieged atoll such as Wake. If Blue had to build replicas of Ford Island for bombers to reduce every outpost on the way to Truk, they warned, the war would be very long.[74]

By late 1941 events were moving too fast for naval chauvinism to resist. On 19 November the Joint Board amended Rainbow Five, the only operative U.S. war plan since its promulgation in May. In that plan's sole prewar revision, tiny Wake was the subject of five amendments. Most significant for the offensive strategy, the army was directed to "support the Navy in the capture and establishment of control over the Caroline and Marshall Islands by air operations within tactical operating radius of Army and Navy air bases equipped for effective

246 • WAR PLAN ORANGE

operations by Army Air Forces." Wake alone fit the description; in the
Asiatic theater the air force was to hit maritime targets defensively in
lieu of naval action. Four years after the army had virtually written off
the central Pacific drive, its strategic air power was ordered to join with
naval might in executing the Orange Plan strategy. When Stark informed the president, Wake as the centroid of the joint Pacific offensive
became national policy.[75]

By then the fleet welcomed air force support as long as it did not
encroach on its spearhead role.[76] The army agreed to immediate preparation of Midway and Wake for "temporary offensive operations" of
Flying Fortresses.[77] Bloch, who was responsible for Hawaii's defenses
and until then had opposed any improvement of Wake, recommended
"an airport of first magnitude."[78] The loading of ground equipment
began in Hawaii on 1 December 1941. General Short had hoped to
send a dozen B-17s on that date[79] and soon to accumulate a full group,
but transfers to the Philippines had drained his squadrons. On 4 December he promised to send them "when and if required and if any such
are then available."[80] Not one heavy bomber reached the atolls before
the war began.

Historians have speculated that if Japan had not struck as early as
December 1941 the buildup of MacArthur's Philippines air force to
more than three hundred heavy bombers by the spring of 1942 (Chapter 6) might have changed the course of the war. It is just as interesting
that the facilities on Wake would have been completed in the same
period so that, secured by a powerful air force and an undamaged fleet,
the United States might have started an ocean offensive much earlier in
the war.

The promise of Wake Island had motivated naval thrusters (and by
late 1941 army sympathizers) to preserve the central Pacific attack plan
even though the kick-off date had to be pushed back to M+180
(Chapter 24). During the last two years of peace, however, it became
obvious that the British Commonwealth would be an ally in a Pacific
war and that a different offensive route could be available via its
territories south of the equator. A few American cautionaries tried to
promote a campaign in southern waters as a less risky alternative to one
in the northern Mandate.

The South Pacific had often been suggested as an avenue of advance
in early Orange Plans but had always been rejected (except in the Quick
Movement of 1932 in which stealth overrode all other considerations).
Strategists of the Through Ticket in the 1920s had assigned the region
to supply convoys until the Mandate could be cleared, but even this

minor role evaporated after adoption of the Royal Road in 1934. Interest revived briefly in late 1939 and early 1940, the period of the Rainbow Two concept of a fleet deployment to Singapore or Java (Chapter 22), when incursions into the Mandate from the south were seen as useful to shorten the communications line.[81] In the spring of 1940 the drafters of Rainbow Three toyed with Blue advances from the vicinity of Rabaul to establish a fleet base in the Palaus or at TawiTawi, a Philippine port near Borneo, but concluded that the United States would first have to reduce the Mandate in a difficult campaign as in Plan Orange.[82] After the middle of that year Cooke found all such ideas embarrassing and jettisoned them.[83]

Yet Roosevelt was intrigued with British Empire islands of the South Pacific such as the Gilberts, Fijis, and Solomons, where bases might be established under the Lend-Lease arrangement begun in the Atlantic. Stark dissuaded him from making overtures to Churchill because he felt that operations from the south, whether to scout, raid Orange traffic, or invade the Mandate, demanded strict secrecy lest Japan "smell a rat" and grab the islands first.[84] Turner insisted that the overobligated fleet should not "operate continuously a large part of [its] force very far to the Southward." In 1941 he made certain that Rainbow Five forbade major naval operations in the South Pacific west of 180°, where most of the foreign groups lay; only minor Blue missions such as escorting and hunting for raiders could proceed as far as the coast of Australia to free the small navies of Australia and New Zealand to fight for Malaysia.[85]

In May 1941 a neocautionary lobby favoring a South Pacific campaign germinated in Op-12. It sought to counter the determination of Admiral Husband E. Kimmel, the combative new commander in chief at Pearl Harbor, to operate the fleet in the dangerous Wake-Eniwetok region. Captain Charles J. "Carl" Moore, head of the division's Plans Section, probed gently at first, suggesting U.S. air bases in the Gilbert Islands as a ploy that might draw Kimmel toward safer waters. The Gilberts, a sprawl of atolls south of the Marshalls but lacking that group's excellent lagoons, had not gone unnoticed. The army had been eyeing them as air links to Australia.[86] Bellinger, fretful about the "inherent vulnerability" of Wake, enthused that VPs shuttled between Tarawa in the Gilberts and Wake could safely overfly the entire Marshall group within a fifteen-hundred-mile ellipse because they could land at Wake after dark and depart by sunrise. When the planes were forced to abandon Wake, flights between Tarawa and Johnston could still observe most of the Marshalls. But Moore understood that patrols from the Gilberts could not observe the most dangerous sector of Japanese naval approach to the fleet operating zone, even from Makin, an island closer than Tarawa to the Marshalls.[87] Besides, Kimmel was resisting the nudge to the south by declining to explore the British islands.[88] The Navy Department looked into a Lend-Lease deal for the Gilberts, but nothing was accomplished before the war.[89]

Moore shifted to a more vigorous southern strategy by proposing a fleet base at Rabaul. (A check of the Solomon Islands had turned up no suitable alternative in that group.[90]) Rabaul was a magnificent sheltered body of water on New Britain, an Australian Mandated island seven hundred miles south of Truk (about the same as the distance from Eniwetok to Truk). In studies of Rainbow Two the JPC had imagined it as a den for a Blue killer force to neutralize the Carolines and protect supply lines, and drafts of Rainbow Three had envisioned it as a base for advancing toward Borneo.[91] Australia, fearful that the United States would neglect its needs, appealed for American strength at Rabaul.[92] Moore got the bureaus working on logistical studies of the harbor.[93] He induced the pliable Stark to tell the army that Rabaul's attractions were leading the navy to contemplate two routes into the Mandate. Moore hoped that a southern base would draw the fleet via friendly islands toward the strategically important region between the Philippines and Borneo and, above all, deflect Kimmel away from the central Pacific.[94]

The cautionary trial balloon from OpNav fell flat in Pearl Harbor. Kimmel, though tactfully conceding that Rabaul might prove "exceedingly useful" later in the war, refused in mid-1941 to send any Blue units.[95] Unwilling to override the commander in chief, Stark offered Canberra sympathy but no help.[96] Rabaul's defenses were so pathetic—a battalion, two guns, and a few planes—that an Australian inspection team recommended evacuation. In October 1941 the navy unbent slightly to offer a bit of material assistance: harbor patrol boats and sonobuoys, later shore and antiaircraft guns, radar, and mines to be sowed by U.S. ships. Nevertheless, the ordnance accumulation fell behind and the shipment was rescheduled for February 1942.[97] By then, Rabaul had fallen. Eventually the Japanese developed it into a great South Pacific base.

In the last months of peace the Army Air Forces created another inducement for a South Pacific strategy. The vulnerability of Wake so troubled Brigadier General Carl Spaatz, chief of air staff, that he demanded a more secure route for ferrying bombers to the Philippines. In October 1941 the army began erecting a chain of airports on U.S.

and Allied South Pacific islands with such speed that flights began in January 1942.[98] To Kimmel, the implication was intolerable. On 2 December 1941 he complained bitterly to Stark that Blue outposts were breeding like rabbits all over the ocean. There were navy bases on the Aleutians, Samoa, and four atolls; air force strips on Christmas, Canton, Fiji, and New Caledonia; and still more bases mooted in the "far flung" Gilberts, New Hebrides, Solomons, and Bismarcks. Each might require the fleet's protection, draining its offensive power. The admiral pleaded for curtailment of the buildup except on islands that would foster "success in the Western Pacific." "A Fleet in being behind a series of defensive positions in the Central and South Pacific," he grumbled, "cannot contribute very much toward victory."[99]

The commander in chief wanted no distraction from his resolve to project the fleet offensively into the central Pacific and to prepare Wake for a vital role in that mission (Chapter 25).[100] His commitment to the aggressive legacy of War Plan Orange remained steadfast even as Japanese aircraft carriers bore down on Pearl Harbor.

The Great Western Arsenal, Dead at Last

The evolution of Pacific strategy from 1938 through 1941 reflected other struggles in addition to those of loyalists of the central Pacific offensive against the undertows of army reticence, home defense, and dangers from Europe. Their Orange Plan formula was also challenged by unreformed thrusters intent on reviving discredited strategies—the Through Ticket and especially that most ancient of canards, a prepared Gibraltar in the western Pacific.

A fleet base on Guam had dominated U.S. strategic thought from 1910 until the treaty freeze of 1922. The idea lay dormant thereafter until 1935 when, as the treaty was about to lapse, King told Roosevelt of the island's utility for military aviation,[1] and the General Board noted its value for submarine and cruiser operations as well. The board pointed out that any base erected under the shadow of Saipan would need "unusual powers of resistance" and might rekindle an arms race. It advised the president to do nothing.[2] But the irrepressible Savvy Cooke, the fleet war plans officer, took up a personal crusade to resurrect the dream of Mahan, Dewey, and Coontz. In late 1937, while the army was flinching from the Mandate campaign, he visited Op-12, then, wearing civilian clothes and with Sherman in tow, boarded a Clipper to Guam.[3]

Cooke's report, an enthusiastic call for a fleet base, reverberated with the cosmic conceptions that were his hallmark. A base on Guam, he claimed, would cow Japan even if the United States were engaged in the Atlantic. If Japan unwisely began a war, a fleet concentration there would assure Blue dominance of the western Pacific and forestall an invasion of the Philippines. A swift voyage could be made to Guam, either directly or after pausing at one of the Carolines (Truk or an atoll such as the Halls or Ulithi) because stores prepositioned on Guam would ease the shipping bottleneck, a major defect of the Orange Plan. The army, he was sure, would join the campaign and even cease its clamor for a huge defensive air corps (a competitor for military funds) because the fleet would never be subject to major losses. At the very least, the base would assure easy clearance of the Mandate, which Cooke described as a fruit dangling from Japan with its stem ripe for snapping at Guam.[4] Bloch concurred and urged recasting the Orange Plan's objective to "the Guam-Truk Area."[5]

The ardor of the CinCUS and his planner was premature. Leahy recognized the value of some sort of base but thought it was a bad time to raise the subject because public feeling was averse to overseas involvements.[6] The proposal could be tested, and the president may have suggested the way. In May 1938 Congress passed the Naval Expansion Act authorizing construction of new ships and a buildup to three thousand planes. Because shore facilities were inadequate, especially for air and light forces, it appointed a team of five officers under Rear Admiral Arthur Hepburn, the previous CinCUS, to recommend new bases and improvements to old ones. In December (without bothering to consult the army[7]) the Hepburn Board prescribed an ambitious program of twenty-seven stations for planes and small warships in the United States and on Pacific islands. Of "far-reaching importance" was its recommendation that a $200 million "Main Base" be built on Guam, with docking and repair capabilities for "at least the major part" of the fleet and with defenses strong enough for a prolonged stand.[8]

In 1939 military programs had to be cloaked under the shroud of "defense." To acknowledge that America plotted offensive war was unthinkable. Cooke fibbed when he said at congressional hearings that the Guam project wold be of "negligible" aggressive value. It was intended for deterrence and to guarantee the safety of U.S. territory, even as distant as California. The board, however, had injudiciously

252 • WAR PLAN ORANGE

TABLE 22.1 *Guam Base Proposals, 1937–1939*

Scope	War purpose	Defenses	Proponents	Cost ($ million)
Main fleet base	Primarily offensive	Fully defended, resist indefinitely, 15,000 troops	Fleet, especially Cooke Some WPD officers	$200+
Air and submarine base	Primarily defensive, some aid to offense	Fairly strong, resist for six months, 6,500 troops	CNO Leahy Dir WPD Ingersoll Hepburn Board Chief BuDocks Moreell	$80
Minimal VP base, tenders, one or two VProns	Scouting, air transit	None	President Roosevelt Congressional Naval Committees Asst SecNav Edison Leahy (later) Moreell (later)	$5
No development	Demolition only	Minor police garrison	Isolationist groups Majority of Congress	Nil

listed among the purposes of the base "the prosecution of naval operations in the western Pacific."[9]

Leahy and Roosevelt dared not solicit money for a project that had offensive overtones. The new Guam lobby began to backpedal, as its predecessor of 1910–22 had done, from a fleet base to an outpost for lesser forces (Table 22.1). The Hepburn Board reduced its formal recommendation to an $80 million station for submarines and planes; it could not save the Philippines but would render an invasion of the group "precarious," impede other Orange aggressions, and later assist fleet operations in the Far East.[10] Ghormley viewed the smaller base as enhancing a Mandates drive by drawing Orange forces to attempt to reduce it, especially if it could resist until M+180, the revised date under consideration for the Truk campaign. The board judged that a defense of "moderate strength" (estimated by the planners at 6,500 to 15,000 men) could survive against "anything short of a major effort" comparable to a Japanese invasion of the Philippines, while brawny air defenses would repel Orange bombers with "heavy and unrequited losses." Even if Japan controlled the surface waters, submarine and air reinforcements could get through (although nobody explained how supplies would be delivered).[11]

In the climate of 1939, however, even an air-submarine base was beyond political tolerance. The president backed away. The Hepburn Board's multibase program was scaled back by 80 percent, although nine eastern Pacific projects survived.[12]

The final option for an installation on Guam was a seaplane scouting base, touted by the fleet as an insurance policy for an opening campaign in the Mandate.[13] Moreell adapted Pan Air studies of coral removal into blueprints for a typhoon-safe harbor for forty-eight VPs to be fed in via Wake and later from the Marshalls.[14] Ingersoll thought it might be financed as a commercial project, but FDR and Leahy supported only a "very minor" program, $5 million for a breakwater and dredging of a roost for a VPron or two whose planes might survive for a few weeks to screen the Eniwetok campaign.[15]

To isolationists and peace advocates *any* development of Guam was suspect. The National Peace Conference and the Keep America Out of War Congress espied a plot to fortify the island and provoke war.[16] Representative Hamilton Fish called Guam "a dagger at the throat of Japan."[17] The State Department also worried about irritating Tokyo.[18] The most telling arguments, however, addressed the island's vulnerability. Former Congresswoman Jeannette Rankin claimed that many naval officers who dared not speak out viewed any base on Guam as a hostage rather than a deterrent. General Hugh Johnson called the island a salient, "something like a nose or thumb stuck into the enemy's mouth where he can bite it off."[19] The reborn Guam lobby, like its ancestor, squirmed under the political ax. Representative Vinson denied that the navy had ulterior motives.[20] Leahy swore that Guam ranked as "the most strategically valuable point in the Pacific" after Hawaii; without it the navy would be "decidedly handicapped" in defending national interests.[21] BuAer officers told incredulous congressmen that flying boats were capable only of reconnaissance and might be needed to detect threats from Australia or Singapore![22]

The opposition won. The House of Representatives struck Guam from the naval appropriations bill. Leahy halfheartedly laid the case before the Senate, trying to explain the difference between a naval base and a seaplane harbor. He swore to pristine motives (among them support for "defensive" movements beyond the 180th meridian).[23] Roosevelt kept mum. Some felt he was testing public opinion about a real base or Japan's reaction, which was predictably negative.[24] In any event, the cause was hopeless. In May 1939 the chairman of the Senate Committee on Naval Affairs talked with the president. Guam was chopped.[25]

The planners forgot about Guam, but a few naval die-hards did not. The General Board sulked about the "great need" for an outpost.[26] As late as November 1940 Moreell suggested that it was not too late to consider a first-class fortified base.[27] But it was too late, as events would prove—and just as well because a fleet base on Guam would have been an albatross, probably America's Singapore. Nevertheless, the quixotic attempt had been educational. The novice fleet planners learned the pitfalls of Washington politics and tailored future ideas accordingly. Wake Island displaced Guam as the air station they sought to aid the offensive, in a locale the fleet could hope to support. Above all, a modern generation of naval leaders who studied Guam's potential rediscovered the strategic value of the Marianas, knowledge they carried forward into World War II.

The Guam story had a morose conclusion. Under Moreell's prodding the Shore Station Development Board overstepped its authority to conjure up an amateurish scheme for an air surveillance line from Hawaii to the Philippines. In February 1941 a free-spending Congress authorized a VP harbor on Guam. Stark was opposed but shuddered at another confrontation. When he was overruled, he refused to send a defense battalion to an island his planners considered lost.[28] But when contractors reported that they could install an airstrip by autumn, the oft-vacillating CNO wondered if Guam might prove useful after all. The staff resisted; U.S. war plans had long ago consigned Guam to Defense Category F specifying demolition of facilities as the sole reaction to a Japanese attack. Kimmel said the island was beyond the bounds of fleet support. Stark reversed again in November 1941 and vetoed the airfield. Three weeks later the Rising Sun flew over Guam. The civilian workmen, having accomplished nothing of value, were carried off into captivity along with the token marine garrison.[29]

Older than the quest for a Mahanian Gibraltar at Guam was the yearning for a great dockyard in the Philippines, squelched by Theodore Roosevelt in 1908 but simmering still in the hearts of a few naval thrusters. The ember flickered momentarily in 1935 when a question arose of keeping a U.S. base in the Philippines after the islands achieved independence in 1945. Embick was appalled at the idea of retaining "a military-naval liability" that would lure the United States to bleed for European colonial interests. The Navy Section of the JPC countered in shopworn clichés with appeals for a base that would enhance American prestige and commerce and white supremacy. When Roosevelt sided with the army, Pye lamely explained that the navy had meant to have a local station, not a fleet base, and shelved the matter.[30] In 1938 Leahy ruled out Philippine bases except for local needs.[31]

Nevertheless, late in 1940 President Manuel Quezon offered the United States permanent sovereignty over a harbor of any island of its choice (except Luzon) and triggered a surrealistic debate among naval officers about the site—not the reality—of a fleet base. Old favorites popped out of the files. Malampaya Sound and Polillo had their admirers. The General Board liked Jolo, in the extreme southwest. Stark brought everyone to heel with a caustic reminder that all would prove worthless when Orange surrounded the Philippines.[32] But Moreell again convinced the Shore Station Board that he could help by upgrading Cavite, in Manila Bay, into a main outlying base. Op-12 protested that the place could neither be held nor supported. Turner relented slightly for a modest seaplane facility but forbade airfields for carrier planes that would never be sent. Congress funded some shops for the Asiatic Fleet anyway. The job was half finished when Japanese bombers leveled Cavite on 10 December 1941.[33] The Asiatic Fleet surface vessels had already fled.

With or without a western base the Through Ticket still roused the blood of a few aging thrusters, especially former war planners holding commands at Manila. Rear Admiral George Julian Meyers, commandant of the Sixteenth Naval District, clamored in 1938 for an invincible arsenal in the Philippines to receive the fleet surging forward "unencumbered by a train, free to give battle, with rapidity of movement and capable of continuing its offensive attitude after its arrival in these waters."[34] His fellow strongheart Asiatic Fleet CinC Harry Yarnell had warned the navy that after slogging through the Mandate for six months it would find the Japanese entrenched throughout the Philippines and no base available. Far better and worth any risk, he vowed, would be a brave sprint to the islands with an astounding three hundred thousand troops. Like Leonard Wood, he counted on Yankee ingenuity to improvise the means.[35] In September 1939 the two fossil thrusters called on Op-12 to press the case for saving the archipelago. Crenshaw retorted that "this independence stuff" had switched off the navy's interest. Let the army tend to the Philippines, he said, and dismissed them because the division was busy with urgent war news.[36]

The prospect of an Allied coalition revolutionized the calculus of involvement in the Far East. The European dependencies in Malaysia—Hong Kong, North Borneo, Sarawak, Brunei, Malaya, French Indochina, and the Netherlands East Indies (NEI)—were more opulent prizes than the Philippines, rich in oil and resources and worthy of major Western exertions to preserve. Their civilized infrastructure could maintain naval forces in ports more safely removed from Japanese aggression than those of the Philippines, especially at the mighty fortified dockyard of Singapore. From such bases, supplied from either the Atlantic or Pacific, America and its friends might thwart Japan's designs of conquest in the region. The arc of islands stretching from Sumatra to the coast of Australia that formed the boundary between the Pacific and Indian oceans, known as the Malay Barrier, could become a rampart at which Japan's expansion would be halted and eventually rolled back. (After it fell in World War II it formed a barrier in reverse, preventing Allied forces from penetrating the Japanese Empire from the southwest.)

Rainbows Two and Three, the Pacific strategies summoned forth by Joint Board directives in the spring of 1939, were plans to commit Blue power to defense of the barrier. For Rainbow Two the board proposed a mission of protecting U.S. "vital interests" in the Orient, alone or in cooperation with allies, "by securing control in the Western Pacific, as rapidly as possible."[37] The joint planners began working on it in August 1939, when the European democracies still seemed secure. (They could not consult with future allies because the sharing of secret war plans was not yet politically feasible.) The JPC found the board's directives to be nebulous guides. What would provoke the United States to fight? Would it intervene if Japan engulfed Southeast Asia during a European war but respected American territory? The Army Section under Colonels F. S. Clark and Joseph T. McNarney felt that America would *have* to fight for Malaysia for political and trade reasons but primarily to deny Japan resources and bases that it would turn against U.S. interests. The Navy Section under Cooke agreed that loss of the Indies would so endanger the Philippines as to constitute a casus belli. The committee therefore decided to project a war against Japan involving the United States in binding alliances from the outset with Britain, France, and Holland (but not China) on behalf of "the interests of the White race."[38]

At first the planners trifled with easy fixes such as fleet visits to Malaysian harbors and reinforcement of Luzon that would awe Japan into passivity (a faint echo of the 1932 Quick Movement). Alternatively, a wartime naval surge under air cover from Wake and Guam might relieve Blue forces gallantly resisting at Manila Bay (as in plans of the Teddy Roosevelt and Harding eras). From Luzon the avengers would cut off and demolish Orange forces advancing against the barrier and chase the remnants into the East China Sea, making for a "vastly easier war." And if the Blue sortie were delayed, why worry? The Allies, unhampered by "time-space factors" of the wide Pacific, would advance smartly from the south to save the Philippines.[39]

The skylarking came to an end with the outbreak of World War II on 3 September 1939. The planners turned from giddy notions of saving Manila to sober contemplation of war in Malaysia. The colonels, still optimistic, predicted that Allied forces in the theater—215,000 troops (most of them natives), 381 aircraft, and some light flotillas—could blunt the Orange juggernaut at an outpost line just south of the Philippines. But Cooke, reticent for once, expected that before Blue could intervene, Japan would overrun Indochina and the Borneo oil fields, isolate the Philippines, and stand poised to achieve its paramount goal of neutralizing Singapore by seizing undefended Dutch islands that surrounded the great base. By sheer tenacity, however, and with three Royal Navy battleships to fend off Orange heavy units, the Allies would preserve a few sanctuaries at the barrier. Cooke believed their resistance would induce the United States to dispatch its navy immediately. (A delay might stretch the recovery of Malaysia over "several months.") The fleet, journeying south of the Mandate and possibly south of New Guinea, would fuel at Rabaul or Darwin and steam full tilt to a stoutly resisting port of the barrier (Map 22.1). Cooke devoutly hoped it would fetch up at Singapore because the Dutch ports of Java were none too promising; Surabaya's dockyard, though well guarded, was so shallow that capital ships would have to anchor at a bay a hundred miles away, Batavia was small and ill-defended, and other anchorages were virtually undeveloped.[40]

After securing a base, the Blue posse would venture northward toward "places of contact" at Japanese forward bases and halt the enemy advance by naval actions. Aided by reinvigorated Allies, Cooke figured on retaking the lost outposts from a dispersed and "decidedly vulnerable" foe that would hold its stations anemically, like minor atolls of the Mandate, each with two thousand men and a couple of guns. Army planners, conversely, foresaw grueling combats between large ground elements. They proposed to send a pioneer echelon with the fleet to guard its base and three divisions (forty-five thousand men) on 20 M (previously designated M+20) for the counterattack, followed by a buildup to one hundred thousand in the theater within ninety days and a flow of one hundred thousand a month thereafter. (It was the sailing pattern of the 1929 Orange Plan but with troop numbers doubled.) Recaptured ports would be fixed up for air and naval

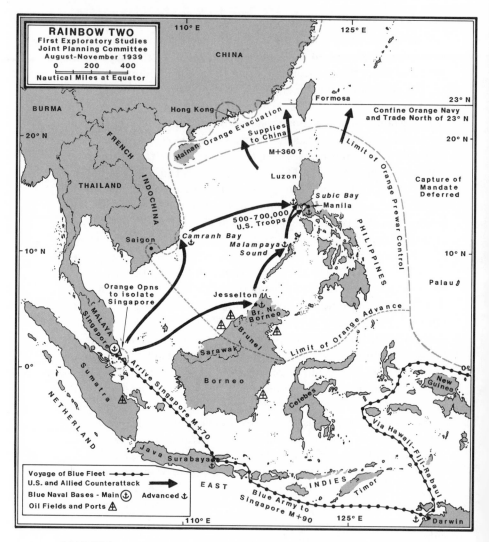

RAINBOW TWO
First Exploratory Studies
Joint Planning Committee
August-November 1939

0   200   400
Nautical Miles at Equator

MAP 22.1

use. One or more would be adapted as advanced fleet bases, probably
Jesselton or Brunei Bay on the north coast of Borneo, where Blue sea
power would assure control, rather than Camranh Bay in Indochina,
which might fall prey to a Japanese army marching overland from
China.[41]

With sublime confidence in American naval eminence, Cooke assumed the Orange navy would sequester its battle line north of For-

mosa to guard against an Allied breakthrough. It would confine itself to attrition tactics and raids on bases by carriers, cruisers, and landing parties, but to no avail. "In short order," Cooke predicted, the avenging armies and navies would stride along both margins of the South China Sea and converge on Malampaya Sound and there ready a great assault to reclaim Manila, an undertaking the Allies would be honor-bound to assist.[42]

In his usual thorough way, Cooke also examined a more gloomy drama of Allied resistance so limp that Japan would subjugate the NEI and encircle or reduce Singapore before Blue could supervene.[43] If the United States chose to prosecute a Rainbow Two campaign anyway, it would find "progress slow, the cost of the war multiplied, and the issue problematical. . . . The principal advantage of Allied participation will have been lost and the problem becomes essentially that of an Orange war."[44]

By November 1939 the drafts of Rainbow Two were complete but not approved. Over the winter confidence eroded. There were rumors of Italy or the USSR joining the Nazis, or of Japan striking in several directions from its position on Hainan Island off the southern Chinese coast. It could certainly occupy the Philippines and Indochina and dominate the South China and Celebes seas before America could do anything. Singapore looked less and less inviting. Murphy, the fleet war plans officer, warned that his boss "wouldn't like" Rainbow Two,[45] a gross understatement—Richardson must have been horrified. In March 1940, when Hill brought to Washington a review of the CinCUS's thinking,[46] OpNav was ready for a shove toward conservatism. Richardson warned that if the fleet went gallivanting about the China Sea, Japan would not hesitate to ravage the eastern Pacific, including the atoll bases, Hawaiian sea lanes, and even the U.S. West Coast. Since the fleet would have to detach units to defend these places, a Malaysian expedition could not be "much, if any," superior to the Orange navy.[47]

In April the JPC came up with a less strident draft of Rainbow Two (Map 22.2).[48] The fleet's mission was softened to a limited campaign to halt Japan's drive and deny it resources by wresting command of the sea near the petroleum ports of Borneo. Coalition armies would counterattack far more cautiously, creeping forward in short movements until the oil fields were recaptured. The U.S. Army would shift emphasis from ground to air support. Troop levies could be limited mainly to base defense outfits, while the air corps would fly 102 heavy bombers directly to the battlefront and ship 420 lighter planes to arrive by 80M. Air officers began studying transit fields in the South Pacific, Australia,

RAINBOW TWO
Second Exploratory Studies
Navy War Plans Division
April-May 1940

0   200   400
Nautical Miles at Equator

CHINA

110° E

125° E

Air attacks on
Orange bases in China,
supplied from India

Part of
Blue Fleet in
E. Pac. defends
communications,
keeps most of
Orange Navy
in home waters

BURMA

Formosa

20° N

Hong Kong

20° N

Hainan

FRENCH INDO-CHINA

Luzon

Economic pressure causes
Orange withdrawal from
European Colonies.
If not, Allies retake
Phil. Is., clear S.
China Sea.

THAILAND

Blue capture
of Mandate
deferred

Manila

PHILIPPINES

10° N

Saigon

Camranh
Bay

SOUTH
CHINA
SEA

10° N

Palau

Allied Interdiction of
oil shipments

Jesselton

Limit of Orange Prewar Control

MALAYA

Blockade

Br. N.
Borneo

Blockade

Limit of Orange Advance

Singapore

SOUTH

Relief effort if
Singapore held
(unlikely)

Brunei

Sarawak

Sumatra

0°

Borneo

Celebes

Slow arduous advances

New
Guinea

0°

NETHERLAND

Java Surabaya

Voyage of
Major Part of Blue Fleet
U.S. and Allied Counterattacks
Blue Naval Bases - Main   Advanced
Oil Fields and Ports

EAST

Blue Army
arrives via
Atlantic

INDIES

Timor

Darwin

110° E

125° E

MAP 22.2

and China, and OpNav sent a "most anxious" request to the fleet for details.[49]

Rainbow Two's revival of a Through Ticket cruise to a doomed port in the Orient was out of touch with reality. The truth was driven home by the German blitzkrieg of May 1940 that overran Holland and France and threatened Britain's survival, nullifying fantasies of all-out Allied efforts in the Pacific. The plight of the orphaned colonies in Asia undermined the core assumption of a dependable Allied resistance pending Blue's arrival. During the summer the planners, deluged with emergency projects for defending the Atlantic and South America, shelved the plan.[50] In October Richardson urged the department to scrap it altogether.[51] Turner and Stark heartily agreed. Rainbow Two thereby expired, never having evolved beyond the drafting stage. The Joint Board never acted on it, and no army or navy supporting plans were outlined.

The last plan to direct the main U.S. war effort against Japan, Rainbow Three, was first explored in April 1940, when the Joint Board elevated its priority as it became evident that the Allies could not spare much for the Pacific. The plan assumed that the friendly powers would be able to shield the Atlantic and enable the United States to dedicate itself to common interests in the western Pacific. But unlike Rainbow Two, the country would get little help in that distant theater. The JPC's outlines presumed that in response to a Japanese onslaught against Malaysia the United States would first secure the eastern Pacific, then extend its control westward "as rapidly as circumstances permit" with the help of whatever aid the Allies could render. But the dispatch of maximum power directly to Asia would be "inadvisable or unnecessary" for both military and public opinion reasons.[52]

Rainbow Three was a daunting strategic conception, neither a brazen thrust like Rainbow Two nor a prudent crawl like Plan Orange. It was a hybrid with the worst features of both. The navy, perhaps for that reason, left the drafting to the Army War Plans Division, an odd venue for a maritime plan. For lack of a better idea, Colonel McNarney hypothesized an opening scene like that in Rainbow Two: the Philippines and northern Indies lost, Orange closing on Singapore, heavy casualties to both sides yet, miraculously, the "weak" Allies holding the Malay Barrier. The Blue objective would still be to deny Orange the oil of Borneo, although without the "great advantage" of a direct rescue expedition. Instead, the fleet and a full army corps would concentrate gradually at Hawaii. In considering a movement "well to the westward"—although not as far as Singapore or Java—McNarney found himself ensnarled in old thruster-versus-cautionary trade-offs of speed, route, and destination. Sketchy intermediate objectives, barely mentioned, included Rabaul, the Celebes, and the Palaus (Chapter 21).[53] He had not progressed far when the Allied collapse in Europe pushed the plan into limbo.

In the fall of 1940 the JPC took a brief second look at Rainbow Three and proposed to shrivel it to a frail script of hemisphere defense and prowlings against trade rather akin to Rainbow Four with token support of the British and Dutch in Malaysia.[54] This feeblest of versions evaporated in a few weeks.

In mid-October, when Richardson came to Washington to meet the president, he and Murphy, his war plans officer, put their heads together with Op-12 to invent a stopgap model of Rainbow Three. They concocted a weak mixture of Plan Orange and Rainbow Two concepts that linked a naval feint in the central Pacific with dispatch to the Malay Barrier of a strong task force known as the Asiatic Reenforcement.[55] It was a bad compromise that violated the maxims of concentration and powerful strokes by scattering forces about the Pacific for illusive goals. Stark went along despite an abhorrence of a Rainbow Three war because the navy had to be ready, as he told Marshall, to help the Allies if ordered by "higher authority."[56] In December 1940 Turner melded it with those elements of Stark's famous "Plan Dog" memo (Chapter 23) dealing with the Pacific into Navy Rainbow Three, WPL-44.[57] There was not and never would be a Joint Rainbow Three. Turner's plan was a transitional case to be superseded by Rainbow Five as soon as possible.[58]

WPL-44 presumed that denial of oil and of trade with lands beyond the barrier would have a "profound effect" on Japan's capacity to fight, a curious assumption since Japan had significant fuel stores and all ports outside its sphere of sea control were under Allied ownership or influence. Stark believed that the Asiatic Reenforcement would ensure "effective and continued" closure of the barrier.[59] The plan assumed that the Allies and local U.S. units could hold Singapore and Java without major relief for ninety days—a prescient guess.[60] Its unstated hypothesis was that a big injection of British naval power into the region would extend the period of resistance considerably, to mesh with a delayed Blue drive into the Mandate (Chapter 25).

A great deal was thus expected of the Asiatic Reenforcement. It was to consist of the carrier *Yorktown* bearing a marine aircraft group for a guerrilla defense of the Indies, accompanied by four heavy cruisers, a VPron with tenders, minecraft, and a small train. It would hasten from Hawaii on 5M to join Admiral Thomas C. Hart, commander in chief of the Asiatic Fleet (CinCAF). Stark, in a typical dither, sent confusing signals. Hart was to meet secretly with local Allied commanders to coordinate operations but not to promise specific help. The Asiatic Reenforcement was not a firm commitment, but he could "depend on" its timely arrival.[61] Hart wanted to base it at Manila. In that case, Turner said, safe passage might require a detour *south of Australia—*

the only time in thirty-five years that a planner suggested such a round-about route. When Hart bemoaned the obvious problems of timing and logistics, he was told to work out a deal with Admiral Kimmel, the newly appointed commander in chief of the Pacific Fleet (CinCPac). (In February 1941 the U.S. Fleet was subdivided into Atlantic and Pacific fleets. The latter, the larger of the two, is hereafter meant in references to "the fleet.") The two CinCs agreed on a path north of Australia and a turnover to Hart's control at Darwin. The flying boats would hop-scotch independently across the South Pacific by way of tenders at friendly lagoons, overtaking the Asiatic Reenforcement in time to scout the narrow Torres Strait between Australia and New Guinea. The warships would not reach Darwin until 24M, slowed by two old seaplane tenders, which Hart did not want. (Kimmel did not care but resented diversion of the nimble small tenders he would need for central Pacific operations.)

Hart wished to steer the Asiatic Reenforcement from Darwin to Singapore. OpNav insisted that he find a base in the NEI and defend the eastern end of the Malay Barrier, a safer zone in spite of the CNO's worry that Orange might roll up the Indies from east to west. The *Yorktown* was to operate in open waters south of the barrier; the marine planes, guided by flying boats from advanced coves and aided by the Anzac navies, would seal the straits north of Java. Nobody imagined it would challenge the Orange fleet.[62]

As Kimmel dutifully rounded up units for "distant service,"[63] he was vexed about his aircraft carriers. The Pacific Fleet's three flying decks were the "main requisite" for his primary mission, a foray into the Mandate, where Orange flattops might lurk and where "too many carriers [was] an impossibility." But OpNav had rejected various pleas to send the marine air group before the war, or aboard an aircraft ferry, or hopping to Australia "from carrier to carrier." The CinCPac sourly decided he would have to lend the *Lexington,* loaded with naval squadrons geared for fleet action, and powerful escorts, to ride shotgun as far as Torres Strait. Thus only one carrier would remain for early fighting in mid-Pacific.[64] Stark, ambivalent as ever, stressed the urgency of the Asiatic Reenforcement yet agreed to its "temporary retention" if needed for central Pacific tasks.[65]

The Asiatic Reenforcement expired two months after its conception. At a White House meeting on 16 January 1941 Roosevelt vetoed any meaningful buildup of the Asiatic Fleet. Stark, dumbfounded, thought it "not impossible" that the idea would pop up again and armed Secretary of the Navy Frank Knox with talking papers.[66] But it never did. Hart never drew an operational plan. Australia was told to forget about transit bases. Strangely, nobody informed Kimmel so his planners worked fruitlessly on the moribund cruise for another two months.[67]

Throughout 1941 romantic imaginations still fancied demonstrations of naval force in the Orient. Yarnell urged a cruiser outing to Manila to frighten Japan and secure the bay until Stark, loyal to FDR's decision, warned that an augmentation of the Asiatic Fleet would provoke hostilities that would result in its destruction.[68] Secretary of State Cordell Hull was also keen to show the flag, and the president could not resist messing with schemes for cruises to Manila or Allied ports. Stark had to convince him that yachting parties would neither deter nor retard Japan. To split the Pacific Fleet, he explained, would be a "grave strategic error" that would allow Orange to defeat its parts in detail.[69] When Roosevelt mused of carriers delivering warplanes to the Soviets in Siberia, Kimmel advised him that the entire Pacific Fleet would have to escort them through the Japanese straits, a provocation sure to foment war. If war were desired, he pleaded, allow him to begin it with offensive blows.[70] No more was heard of the matter.

Early in 1941 the U.S. Navy was offered the chance to fulfill its ancient craving for a great fortified base in the Orient. In September 1940 a Royal Navy commission had recommended that His Majesty's government urge America to deter Japanese aggression and "safeguard our joint interests" by positioning its fleet deeper in the Pacific, "say at Singapore." The United States, it thought, would be delighted.[71]

Singapore was the stuff of dreams: an anchorage capacious enough for the largest navy afloat; four square miles of shore facilities with docks and cranes to refit great ships; abundant stores of food and munitions; an excellent commercial seaport next door; and proximity to the oil wells and refineries of Sumatra. It was ringed with artillery, minefields, and aerodromes. To the north lay a jungle impenetrable, it was thought, to overland attack.[72] The British were about to offer all this on a silver platter.

When Roosevelt aligned himself at the end of 1940 with the Rainbow Five thesis of alliance with the British Commonwealth (Chapter 23), he also agreed to secret staff talks with British and Canadian planners on global strategy and among Allied Far Eastern commanders on local plans.[73] Ghormley, as special naval observer in London, passed the word.[74] An American-British conference of planning officers known as ABC-1 convened in Washington on 29 January 1941. The British readily agreed to the Rainbow Five theme of primacy of the

European war. Regarding the Pacific, they alleged that their effort the world over depended on the resources and manpower of Australia, New Zealand, and India and that Singapore was essential to the security of those lands. If Singapore fell, Japan would penetrate the Indian Ocean and isolate the eastern reaches of the British Empire. India would revolt. China would quit the war. Russia would join the Axis. Without Singapore, the "card of re-entry" to the Orient, the Allies would never beat Japan. Its loss, they asserted, would constitute "a disaster of the first magnitude, second only to the loss of the British Isles," and result in "the disintegration of the British Commonwealth."

The British, alas, could not hold Singapore with the scanty land and air forces they could spare. The Admiralty had long hoped to send a fleet in the hour of need, but because of losses and obligations in other theaters it could release only a battle cruiser and a carrier. With Nelsonian pluck, however, these two would deny Orange the freedom of the South China Sea, repel it from the Indies, nip at its naval flanks, and keep open the supply lines to Singapore. The Royal Navy had no fear of Japanese aviation—it operated from Alexandria and other places within range of hostile airfields and surely Japanese airmen were inferior to the Italians. Singapore could endure for a while, but the "only real solution" for its long-term survival lay in a fleet of capital ships. Only the United States could provide one.

The American government had just canceled the Asiatic Reenforcement, the last whisper of a naval rush to the Far East. It was intent on campaigning in the central Pacific. Its war planners regarded Singapore as expendable because the British imperial sea lanes could be maintained without it.[75] It was indefensible because it could be easily surrounded and rendered untenable. Although the Britishers did not quantify their plea, Turner and Embick surmised that they "would like the United States to send their whole fleet" and a large army, too,[76] which was out of the question. Nor would the United States split the Pacific Fleet and send part of it westward in the face of superior Orange power; the advanced segment could never be extracted to the Atlantic in case of a need and would no doubt be destroyed. The remainder would be so weak that "the naval threat against Japan would be removed for years to come."[77]

Desperate for a quarter loaf, the English begged for a carrier task force to slash at Orange convoys closing on Singapore and compel its capital ships to battle. The Americans stared flintily. Last-ditch supplications to enfeeble Japan by petroleum embargoes or raids on its home islands fared no better.[78] In the end, the United States offered a token of direct support. The Asiatic Fleet would help defend the Malay Barrier within a combined theater command set up by the local chieftains. (Unification of the entire Pacific under U.S. leadership was not feasible because of extreme distances, the Americans said, and, one surmises, because they feared entrapment in a rescue expedition.) Under no circumstances would Blue heavy units steam to the Far East. They would, however, lend important help indirectly. The Atlantic Fleet would cross to Gibraltar at the outbreak of war to relieve British ships for the barrier defense, and the Pacific Fleet would raid the Mandates to distract Japan from the onslaught.[79]

The British bowed with ill grace. They insisted that the record declare the Far East crucial to victory, the U.S. position in error, and the correct strategy forsaken because of "nonmilitary" factors.[80] The ABC-1 report of 27 March 1941 merely acknowledged the case for Singapore alongside the American refusal to go there. The barrier resistance was to be commanded by a Briton. The planners stated that land and air forces would somehow "hold" Malaya and Java and "defend" the rest of the Indies and the Philippines. Local sea and air units would lash back in tactical stabs. The British Empire pledged troops, planes, and "ultimately" a mighty armada. The United States pledged nothing.[81]

Churchill's lieutenants behaved self-destructively at ABC-1. They exhibited a "vague attitude of condescension" that the naive Yankees would see it their way.[82] They obtained their leader's heartfelt desire, a U.S. pledge to beat Germany first, yet contrary to that intent they sought to gamble America's strongest military asset on a mission of extreme peril. The fall of Singapore a year later did not in fact collapse the Commonwealth war effort. Had its fleet gone there and suffered annihilation, however, the United States might have turned its back on Europe to prosecute the war against Japan with all its power.

The country did reaffirm its commitment at ABC-1 to an aggressive policy in the central Pacific. The importance of naval action there grew in prominence later in 1941, when the British decided they could, after all, send a sizable fleet to Singapore. In the last few months of peace American naval planners were obliged to invent an unusual variant of the prompt ocean attack inherited from Plan Orange to honor that commitment, just as that venerable strategy seemed about to be abandoned.

The American Way of Planning:
On the Eve of War

The American planning system in the last year of peace evolved further toward the processes that would govern wartime strategy making. Army-navy disputes over home security versus a counterattack in the Pacific yielded to universal expectation of a global war, with the European theater standing highest in priority. The convergence of views brought the services, or at least officers in Washington contemplating grand strategy, into World War II in a cooperative frame of mind.

In September 1941 the Joint Board was bound more tightly into the military structure by orders to send advice via the service chiefs rather than directly to Roosevelt. The senior air leaders, Arnold and Towers, joined the board, and it met more frequently. The JPC "moved upstairs" to become a committee of two, chief war planners Turner and Brigadier General Leonard Gerow, who coordinated the joint plans. To write the plans, they formed a Joint Strategic Committee (JSC) of at least three officers from each War Plans Division and various subcommittees. The JSC, although nominally lower in the hierarchy, was an improvement because its members were able to concentrate on war planning free of the paperwork inundating the plans divisions as they expanded to three or four dozen officers apiece.[1]

Within the navy, the CNO and his chief planner sought to steer the service away from its traditional obsession with Japan. Rearmament was accelerating, but few heavy warships had yet come on line. England's perilous situation so haunted Stark that in the spring of 1941 OpNav transferred a large part of the Blue fleet from Hawaii to the Atlantic Coast to guard against a British collapse and surrender of the Royal Navy. All thoughts of a Rainbow Two or Three campaign in Southeast Asia were set aside. The Pacific Fleet, reduced to not much more than half the power of the former United States Fleet, was distinctly weaker than the Imperial Navy. Revised war plans abridged its offensive role and tethered it to the eastern half of the ocean, where it could speedily rejoin the Atlantic Fleet. Hitler's invasion of the Soviet Union in June 1941 had no discernible effect on the maritime dispositions. (The most obvious implication for the military balance of the Pacific—the release of Japanese troops guarding the Manchuria-Soviet border—meant little to naval minds.) Nevertheless, a hard-core thrusting faction coalesced in Hawaii during 1941. Under the leadership of an attack-minded CinC, the fleet planning staff navigated among conflicting orders and invented a combative reaction that cleaved to the spirit of the suspended Orange Plan.

Officers at naval headquarters contrived the turn away from offensive aspirations in the Pacific. Harold Stark's innate caution had been bolstered throughout 1940 by Richardson's fulminations against all offensive plans. When the CNO weighed the world situation near the end of the year, he concluded that U.S. and Allied interests in the Pacific would have to wait until Hitler was defeated. Stark set about to pry the navy away from its fixation about Japan and redirect national concerns to Europe. To engineer this extreme reorientation of policy he needed a forceful and like-minded planning officer.

Stark got his man on 19 October 1940 when he dumped the torpid Crenshaw and hired Captain (soon Rear Admiral) Richmond Kelly Turner as the nineteenth director of war plans. Turner, a gunnery expert with a "career flirtation" in aviation—he had gone to flight school in midlife and served on a carrier and as a BuAer planner—had gone back to the line because air billets seemed like dead ends in the 1930s. In 1936–38, as head of the War College's Strategic Section, he gained a reputation as a deep thinker and student of war.[2] Stark and Ingersoll believed that Turner was "the right man";[3] he held the navy's top planning post until he left for a Pacific command in the middle of 1942.

The director's overpowering manner inspired both hate and venera-
tion. Officers who ran afoul of "Terrible Turner" knew him as a
vile-tempered, ambitious martinet whose dark brows beetled intimi-
datingly. Postwar memoirs are strewn with sobriquets like "abrasive,"
"tricky," "pigheaded," "s.o.b." Some said he was a heavy drinker;
others denied it. To his admirers, including the CNO, Turner was
"intelligent . . . a man who got things done . . . the Navy's Patton."
"Every time I think of Kelly Turner," Stark said later, "I warm a little
about the heart." Since the director often spoke for the navy at high-
level meetings, some thought Stark was "absolutely under his thumb"
and that Turner was the real chief of naval operations.[4]

Despite his aggressive personality, Turner viewed the Pacific
through cautionary eyes. He supported Stark's advocacy of a
Germany-first policy and a strong Atlantic Fleet. He restricted the
planning of amphibious attacks in the Pacific, ironically since he went
on to fame and four stars as the victor of a dozen island invasions, the
"alligator" of Japanese lore.[5] Only once before in the history of Pacific
war planning, under Standley and Bryant in the early 1930s, had a
CNO and his chief planner worked together so effectively to drive the
service toward facing the strategic realities of a difficult war.

"Things began to hum" at Op-12. Turner jettisoned the existing
war plans as obsolete and took personal charge of writing new ones
during the next six months. Viscerally mistrustful of the army, he
bullied the Joint Board and its committees, rejecting all solutions but
his own. He removed all thrusters from planning, firing Cooke and
shunting Hill and Sherman into base and logistical studies. Despite
some brawls with the ever-cautionary Carl Moore, he kept Moore on
hand to grapple with fleet thrusters (unsuccessfully, it turned out).[6]
Turner also gathered the Office of Naval Intelligence under his wing, a
violation of the rule of separating information and decision making,[7]
and forbade the division's Negro messengers from handling secret
documents.[8]

Throughout 1940 Stark had despaired of America's being drawn
into a global war. In the autumn he resolved to persuade the president
to recast the nation's priorities. Parleying with his staff by day and
working alone through the nights, he wrote a personal think piece "to
clear his mind."[9] On 12 November 1940, a week after Roosevelt was
reelected to a third term, the CNO issued the result of his labor, one of
the most significant policy documents of the era. In the style of naval
planners, he examined and demolished strategic alternatives he found
unpalatable, which he labeled strategies A through C, respectively, for

hemisphere defense, all-out war against Japan, and equal effort in both oceans. They would all prove indecisive, he felt, by failing to apply full power against the strongest enemy, Germany. If Britain succumbed, the United States could not win anywhere. If Britain survived, even with armaments from America its feeble strategy of blockade, bombing, and peripheral jabs would never beat Hitler. Only Plan D, a U.S.-led land offensive in Europe, would bring him down. Regarding Japan, the United States and Allied Powers would have to accept loss of the western Pacific stoically and wage a limited defensive war until they could turn their full weight against Japan.[10]

Stark's paper, known as the Plan Dog memorandum ("Dog" meaning "D" in naval letter code), was the true parent of Plan Rainbow Five. General Marshall found its reasoning "entirely favorable" because the Nazi threat had invalidated other strategies.[11] The Joint Board also approved. The two service chiefs, knowing Roosevelt's cagey style, looked for a tacit rather than an open presidential endorsement. FDR was "probably delighted." He gave the nod to Plan Dog's strategic premise and assented to secret talks with the British to cast it into a combined plan for use when the nations became combat allies.[12]

Turner and his staff worked diligently to create new war plans. In December 1940 they completed WPL-44 (Navy Rainbow Three) as a stopgap strategy for the Pacific because Plan Orange was about to be repealed. Their version bore no resemblance to the 1939 Joint Board directive for a strong push against Japan. It was, rather, a prototype of Rainbow Five, which adopted the Germany-first and Pacific defensive decisions, slightly modified by deputizing the Asiatic Reenforcement posse. Secretary Knox okayed WPL-44,[13] but it ran into trouble with army planners because it was not founded on a joint plan. Gerow damned it as "black indeed" because the country had means enough for one early operation against Japan, but the plan's scattershot deployments meant that "we stand to lose everywhere and win nowhere." Turner arrogantly retorted that he would not alter the naval campaigns one iota.[14] Stark and Marshall smoothed their underlings' ruffled feathers by putting them to work writing Rainbow Five together. The senior planners, mollified, also pooled their talents in a paper for the president on global strategy that urged accelerated rearmament and avoiding provocations of Japan such as overt alliances, economic sanctions, or sending arms to China.[15]

On 17 December 1940, thirty-four years after the inception of Navy War Plan Orange, Stark ordered its disestablishment. It was stricken officially from the register of national plans in July 1941, although the districts, bureaus, and fleets were urged to continue to tap it as a reservoir of information. The Orange Plan, said Stark, had been "drawn up to guide the prosecution of a war under circumstances which do not now exist."[16] The venerable color title disappeared, but its much-studied conceptions remained available for strategists who would steer the nation through the war.

The convening of the ABC-1 Conference at the end of January 1941 induced the army and navy to close ranks against the well-rehearsed British. Old disputes were forgotten as Ghormley and Embick co-chaired the American delegation and Turner and McNarney presented its positions.[17] (Cooke, the navy's preeminent thruster, was excused because his views on a Pacific offensive were "in such violent opposition" to Turner's.[18]) The future Allies embraced the Germany-first doctrine but disagreed sharply about the Pacific, especially the importance of Singapore (Chapter 22). The Americans held all the cards and virtually dictated the strategy of war in that ocean. In the conference and in subsequent dealings with a British liaison committee established in Washington during the rest of 1941, the United States ordained the nature of combined planning against Japan in time of war: the process would be nominally binational, but the Americans would utterly dominate it.

The translation of the ABC-1 report of 27 March 1941 into a plan for global coalition war was anticlimactic. The JPC smoothly converted the conference decisions into Joint Plan Rainbow Five, which projected an M-Day of 1 September 1941. Op-12 simultaneously presented WPL-46, a naval supporting plan that added little new to the Pacific strategy of its predecessor under Rainbow Three except to cancel the Asiatic Reenforcement and stress the army's duty to support maritime operations with air power. Stimson and Knox endorsed Joint Rainbow Five and sent it to Roosevelt on 2 June 1941.[19] The president said he would approve it if war broke out and returned it, ostensibly because Churchill had not yet endorsed the ABC-1 conclusions.[20] But FDR's support was clear enough to Stark, who inactivated the navy's four other Rainbow plans. Rainbow Five alone fit the world situation.[21]

Army strategic planning against Japan in 1941, for example, the decision to commit heavy bombers to a central Pacific offensive (Chapter 21), was largely an offshoot of the joint planning effort. Local staffs overseas continued to update defense programs, notably in the Philippines, where in the summer of 1941 Douglas MacArthur took charge of what was virtually a theater command. Although the army sent reinforcements as the year wore on, its plans for the Philippines and the eastern Pacific strong points remained tactically defensive and of limited strategic importance once the idea that Luzon could be a base for bombing Japan was ruled out (Chapter 6). Nevertheless, the experience gained there was significant for the future war planning system because when MacArthur and his staff were removed to Australia in 1942 they took on the mantle of theater planners, a function in which they became nearly autonomous during the war in parallel with the stature of the Pacific Fleet's staff.

After promulgating Navy Rainbow Five in the spring of 1941, OpNav lost interest in Pacific strategy. Stark preferred to leave campaign planning to commanders afloat. He had told the CinCPac to prepare WPUSF-44, an operating Plan O-1 for Rainbow Three,[22] then a few weeks later switched to a demand for WPPac-46, a Rainbow Five accessory. He ordered the Asiatic Fleet to draw up a Plan O-2 for fighting in the Netherlands East Indies under a British theater commander.[23] Turner busied himself with the "undeclared naval war" against German U-boats and with contingent studies of occupations of the Azores, Iceland, and European islands of the Caribbean.[24] He believed he had restrained the Pacific Fleet behind a geographical fence where it could not get into trouble.

Thus the initiative for planning offensive campaigns against Japan passed to the Pacific Fleet during the last half year of peace. The strategists in Hawaii acted fairly independent of Op-12 because they had a back-door channel through Kimmel's personal correspondence with the CNO. Stark's replies, in spite of his innate wariness, were peppered with cries for bold action (Chapter 25). He probably intended them as ritualistic exhortations, but he was no longer addressing the arch-defensivist J. O. Richardson. That sullen admiral had been relieved because, he later claimed, he had "hurt the President's feelings" by telling him that the navy's leaders mistrusted his administration for provoking Japan diplomatically and economically before the United States was ready for war.[25]

On 1 February 1941 Husband E. Kimmel raised his flag in Pearl Harbor. The fifty-nine-year-old admiral from Kentucky was a proud and humorless man yet with reserves of charm and courtesy. He had climbed an impressive career ladder in battleships and ashore in budgeting and administration. Still, he was astonished when he was rocketed from command of the cruiser squadrons over the heads of forty-six senior admirals. Kimmel had spent a few days as FDR's aide long ago, but, contrary to later allegations, his promotion was not a result of favoritism. Stark and Richardson simply thought he was the best-qualified man. So did Rear Admiral Chester W. Nimitz, who as head of the Bureau of Navigation had a strong voice in personnel assignments. Kimmel's coterie of admirers was wide and included future heroes Halsey and Raymond Spruance. Pratt had called him "a humdinger."[26] According to navy gossip, Roosevelt wanted "the two toughest sons-of-bitches" to run the new fleets. When Stark proposed Kimmel and Ernest King, FDR said to assign one to each ocean. Since King was already commanding units in the Atlantic and Kimmel in the Pacific, convenience was apparently a key factor in the decision.[27] One may wonder what the course of events would have been on 7 December 1941 and throughout World War II had the admirals been posted the other way round.

Because much of the blame for the debacle at Pearl Harbor was placed on Kimmel, his character has been assessed over the decades since by many observers, from colleagues, to witnesses at investigations of the disaster, to memoirists and historians. Two traits stand out. The admiral was obsessive about detail and appearances, a workaholic with a bent for efficiency and routine that "reached almost frightening proportions." He was also a warrior "full of fight" who relished the prospect of hurling his fleet full tilt at Orange and realized "the great value of speed" in doing so. Some historians have commented that he lacked the flair of a great commander because he did not intuitively grasp the broad implications of his situation. Although he had studied and taught at Newport and took to poring over war plans aboard his flagship at night, his strategic thinking was mundane, "unfired by the spark of creative imagination."[28] To translate his zeal for aggressive action into a systematic plan, Kimmel needed an inventive war plans officer who was also a certified thruster.

He chose Captain Charles Horatio McMorris, known in the navy as "Soc" for his Socrates-like wisdom. McMorris was shrewd and tough, a self-styled "born sonofabitch," in appearance "the ugliest man in the Navy," yet a delightful side of his personality helped him sell ideas. He was an experienced surface sailor, but his planning background consisted only of the course at Newport and a year as operations officer of the Scouting Force. (His shore jobs had mostly involved personnel, teaching English and history, and editing the *Naval Institute Proceedings*.) Nevertheless, the CinCPac had the "highest confidence" in this "very able, outspoken officer." When the possibility of a substitution arose, he protested to Nimitz, "I sincerely believe that McMorris is the one officer of the Navy best fitted for the preparation of War Plans for the Pacific Fleet."[29]

A thruster without peer in 1941, McMorris translated the admiral's instinctive ferocity into vivid plans of maneuver. Some commanders griped that he went too far, that he "let his imagination and enthusiasm carry him out to sea." Yet he survived the catastrophe of 7 December with his reputation intact in spite of his blind conviction that Pearl Harbor was secure.[30] During the war his stature grew as "a fighting man of the first water." In 1943 Nimitz reclaimed McMorris as a top-level fleet strategist. For the rest of the war he continuously advocated thrusting campaigns.[31]

By 1941 the Fleet War Plans Section was no longer a one-man show. McMorris took as his aide and scrivener of plans Commander Lynde D. McCormick, an athletic and intelligent graduate of the War College (and subsequently its president) with submarine, surface, and staff experience. He was later tapped by the Joint Chiefs of Staff to serve as their senior logistical planner, which suggests that in 1941 he worked on fleet supply and force allocations, not operations.[32] McMorris retained Richardson's protégé Murphy, Lieutenant Francis R. Duborg (a young Rhodes Scholar and teacher of languages with little planning experience), and Lieutenant Colonel Omar T. Pfeiffer, USMC.[33] The section left the cramped quarters afloat for more efficient offices ashore; the admiral and the rest of the fleet staff soon followed.[34] Hovering in the background was the unsinkable Savvy Cooke, who, having taken refuge from Terrible Turner as skipper of Kimmel's flagship, the *Pennsylvania,* stood ready to whisper thrusting solutions in his ear.[35]

The CincPac and his chief planner met every day without fail.[36] By March 1941 McMorris had drafted WPUSF-44,[37] which drew many comments from Washington and Manila but lapsed upon the demise of Rainbow Three. In May he switched to WPPac-46, Plan O-1 under Rainbow Five, the final U.S. peacetime plan against Japan. Kimmel considered it realistic and free of wishful thinking. He submitted it to Washington on 25 July, describing it (perhaps to stifle critics) as a guidebook to be adjusted when war came.[38] But in the admiral's mind it was gospel. In any case, it satisfied Turner and Stark. On 9 September 1941 the CNO approved WPPac-46 without comment.[39] It remained essentially unchanged until the war began.

Kimmel's task force commanders were supposed to write subsidiary plans, but they had no planning staffs and were busy with training and other chores. To encourage them McMorris set up a chart maneuver of WPPac-46 in August 1941. Admirals Pye, Halsey, Bellinger, and Wilson Brown acted out their wartime assignments against Japan, whimsically named "Sallow" and played by Kimmel's staff, while the CinCPac umpired. Because of their absences at sea the game stretched over four months, and it was only partway along when the war erupted. It was apparently not a good motivator since no task force subsidiary plan has come to light.[40]

A historical parallel deserves comment. Of the eighteen interwar commanders in chief only two are known to have submitted war plans for Pacific operations that were accepted by the Navy Department: Coontz in 1925 and Kimmel in 1941. Their superiors, CNOs Eberle and Stark, believed in wide powers of decentralized campaign planning for the fleet. Both CinCs presented thrusting programs when cautionary headquarters planners were backing away from boldness. Coontz, who had infinite leeway under the permissive system of his day, brewed the most rampaging of all Through Ticket onslaughts. Kimmel's freedom was severely constrained, but he, too, stretched his bonds to unexpected limits in creating an audacious opening gambit.

The American way of planning on the eve of war embodied many long-term continuities. Strategy, as always, was the province of uniformed officers who received virtually no guidance from Congress, the State Department, civil agencies, or even the service secretaries. The president was, of course, consulted in those crisis days on large matters of mobilization, alliances, and theater priorities, but he rarely influenced campaign designs. Amity between the armed services, an often elusive condition, had been assured in 1940 when the navy yielded its passion for an immediate amphibious drive against Japan to the needs of a European war the generals would dominate. The army, satisfied, lapsed into its traditional junior role in Blue-Orange strategy making. In the navy, the CNO and the War Plans Division turned their attention to global affairs and the Atlantic in particular. They relinquished campaign planning to the Pacific Fleet, taking care first to hobble it by halving its power, banning an immediate amphibious attack, and restricting its reach to the nearest fringes of the Japanese Empire. Nevertheless, keepers of the thrusting flame in Pearl Harbor revolted. They fashioned a new mission of strategic aggressiveness, the final offshoot of War Plan Orange before the fighting began.

Instant Fury Delayed

The ascendancy of the Rainbow Five principles at the end of 1940 came close to expunging the amphibious drive from American war plans. The strategists who framed the Eurocentric policy expected to shrivel the mission of the Pacific Fleet to guarding the eastern ocean and making hit-and-run jabs at Japan's outer perimeter. A Phase II offensive would be delayed for many months and possibly several years if held in abeyance until Germany was beaten. In the most extreme case, the United States might never launch a counterattack. The issues bearing on when—and if—a drive would be mounted ranged from simple operational constraints such as the reduced size of the Pacific Fleet and the time needed to prepare assault forces, to more cosmic matters of grand strategy such as conserving the navy for an Atlantic emergency and even the relevance of an offensive strategy to the stated war aims.

The augmented Atlantic Fleet of 1941 was powerful enough to conduct the missions Rainbow Five assigned it, including relief of Royal Navy units to go to Singapore. Rainbow Three had already endowed Admiral King with two of the navy's five carriers, three battleships, and many lesser craft.[1] The United States and Great Britain agreed that maintaining more than half the Blue navy in the Pacific would have a chilling effect on Japanese adventurism[2] so Kimmel retained most of the capital ships, modern light warships and naval planes, and a train adequate for supporting Blue advanced bases.[3] Under Rainbow Five additional ships were allocated to the Atlantic; at Turner's urging, they were transferred during the spring of 1941 (Table 24.1).[4] Army ground and air units guarding the eastern Pacific were also scaled back to bolster the Atlantic.[5]

The departures cost Kimmel one-fourth of his fleet—more than the Pearl Harbor attack![6] He reorganized the remainder from "type commands" into ten task forces (TFs) of varying potency, from powerful battle squadrons to homogeneous submarine and air patrol commands to minor local defense units. The CinCPac remained bitter to the end about being left inferior to the Orange navy in all types except battleships. "I must insist," he wrote typically in November 1941, "that more consideration be given to [our] needs." "The butter," Stark apologized, was "spread extremely thin" around the world.[7] No ships were returned to the Pacific until after the shock of Pearl Harbor.

The two-ocean deployment violated Mahanian orthodoxy of concentration, but OpNav strategists reasoned that partition was acceptable if the Pacific Fleet stayed intact and within reassembly range of the decisive Atlantic theater, literally within a twenty-one-day cruise of Panama.[8] It must not, Stark said, venture far to the west, where it could be mauled by Japan, because it might have to disengage in response to an actual or potential collapse of the British Isles, or suffer any defeat that would arouse a public outcry to beat Japan first. The new policy, set forth in his Plan Dog memo of November 1940, negated all previous offensive strategies, including the Orange Plan's rapid seizure of the Mandates (Table 24.2).[9]

At the nadir of faith late in 1940, the navy almost canceled the central Pacific offensive. Defensivists decried even the contemplation of plans involving an assault on Truk. Stark told the president that the island was so heavily armed that an attack would result in severe casualties.[10] Richardson believed that the entire navy could not penetrate to Truk because it would be "barely superior" to the Japanese navy at the outset of a war and would soon degenerate from attrition.[11] Captain Moore, who had studied Truk at the War College, considered landings on its steep islands far inside the reef a "murderous prospect."[12] Furthermore, speed was now out of the question. Holcomb had reported that he could not assemble enough marines by 75M and

TABLE 24.1   *Principal U.S. Naval Forces, Disposition, 1940–1941*

	Pacific Fleet (U.S. Fleet before 1 Feb 1941)			Asiatic Fleet	Atlantic Fleet +NW Europe detachment	
	Dec 1940[a] Plan Orange[a]	Dec 1940 Rainbow 3[b]	July 1941 Rainbow 5[c]	July 1941 Rainbow 5	Dec 1940 Rainbow 3	July 1941 Rainbow 5
Aircraft carriers	3	2	3		2	3
Battleships	12	12	9		3	6
Heavy cruisers	8	4	8	1	5	5
Light cruisers	9	9	8	1	4	8
Destroyers, modern	67	67	41		15	51
Destroyers, old	4	4	4	13	30	30
Submarines, modern	32	32	27	11		7
Submarines, old	6	6	6	6	56	56
Minecraft	9	5	13		11	9
Patrol craft				8		19
Train and other	64	59	59	12	21	59
Patrol planes	84	72	107	24	18	120
Patrol plane tenders	8	6	12	4	3	11
Fleet Marine Force:						
Divisions			1			1
Brigades	3	3				
Defense battalions	4	4	3			1
Smaller units				1		1
Air groups	1		1			1

Sources: WPL-44, Dec 1940, App II. WPL-46, May 1941, App II.

Note: Does not include Southeast Pacific, District, and Miscellaneous forces.

[a] Before detachment of Asiatic Reenforcement.

[b] After detachment of Asiatic Reenforcement.

[c] After transfers to Atlantic and cancellation of Asiatic Reenforcement.

TABLE 24.2 *Timetables for Base One[a] and Base Two,[b] 1935–1941*

	War Plan, Including Related Analyses and Studies		
Concept and goals	Amended Orange Plan 1934–1937	New Orange Plan 1938–1939	Rainbow Three and Five 1940–1941
Strategic concept	Mandates campaign adopted; major joint forces; rapid campaign and base development	Army support reduced after Base One captured; campaign slightly delayed; base development much delayed	Preparations only; decisions delayed until war; campaign and base development greatly delayed (dates below tentative)
Date Base One captured	M+32	M+40 to M+55	Several months— M+180?
Date Base One completed	M+60 to M+75	M+60 to M+90 (Budocks: M+180)	M+180 to M+360?
Date Base Two captured	M+75 to M+85	M+75 joint force M+180 marines alone	Indefinite—M+360?
Date Base Two completed	M+180, approx.	M+360; possibly as late as M+720	"Years"

[a] Base One: Wotje 1934–39, Eniwetok after September 1939.
[b] Base Two: Truk.

would be desperately short of guns and aircraft until 1942.[13] Stark concurred that training seventy-five thousand men for the "strong effort" would take far longer than the Orange Plan had assumed.[14]

But even if the difficulties were eventually resolved, how, asked Sherman, would Blue proceed from Truk to win the war?[15] To Richardson Truk was merely an anchorage bare of facilities and "still hundreds of miles from the enemy country." Stark agreed that it was not "a satisfactory final geographical objective" for projecting war into the China seas, where "real pressure" could be put on Japan, or even a suitable springboard to the Philippines. At best, it could serve as an advanced outpost for better diverting and pummeling Orange forces.[16] Furthermore, dry docks would be a necessity in the Mandate, where bottom fouling would reduce the battle line to fifteen knots.[17] Richardson thought that developing a proper base at Truk would require "the order of years rather than months."[18] Fellow cautionaries in Op-12 suggested that it would take two to five years to construct the sort of Base Two envisioned in the Orange Plan.[19] Meanwhile, the fleet would have to suspend the attack to protect itself and its communications. The result, Sherman frowned, would be "a bad one."[20]

Even if the United States did establish a fleet base at Truk within a reasonable time, the specter of recall to the Atlantic would prohibit further advance.[21] Op-12 reckoned that to survive if the fleet left the Pacific, Truk would have to be fortified with artillery in concrete emplacements and twelve thousand troops and cushioned by half a dozen outlying sea-air stations. In other words, Blue would have to occupy and arm virtually all of the Mandates including the western Carolines. Since the Army Air Corps refused to participate, six hundred naval planes, the cream of fleet and marine aviation, would be frozen in place for defense.[22] Even so, Stark did not think that Truk could be held without continuous support of capital ships; once they were withdrawn, all gains in the mid-Pacific would "undoubtedly" be lost. "We would have then to choose," he cautioned, "between a lengthy evacuation process, and a major loss of men, material and prestige."[23]

The most fervent antioffensivists demanded not merely deferral of the Truk campaign but its cancellation, with reconsideration only in extraordinary circumstances such as a sudden favorable opening or as an act of political desperation.[24] In December 1940 this view came close to prevailing. In WPL-44 Turner adopted a premise of indefinite delay by instructing the fleet to *prepare* to occupy the Mandates as far as Truk but specified no date of execution. Conceivably, said Stark, the attack might never be launched because it would depend on verification beyond doubt that the Atlantic was secure. An appendix containing timetables and logistical data was promised; it was never sent to Kimmel and was probably never written.[25] Thus the fleet's draft Plan O-1 of March 1941 stipulated only mobilization and training for the assault "if"—not when—"developments should warrant."[26]

If Truk were to be indefinitely delayed, why bother to take the Marshalls? In Plan Orange the group had been wanted as the jumping-off point for the Carolines. Messages about ammunition shipments and air and antisubmarine equipment indicate that as late as the summer of 1940 OpNav was still intent on quick occupation of an atoll for Base One.[27] But ominous intelligence about the Marshalls kept trickling in. Before 1940 Japan had considered atolls too vulnerable for military use and had confined its preparation of the Mandates to "civilian" airfields and seaplane ramps on a few of the Carolines and Marianas. Then the Imperial Navy acquired modern long-range bombers and changed its mind. It built an aviation hub on Kwajalein supported by outlying fields on Maloelap and Wotje and a seaplane station on Jaluit. Most disconcerting, naval intelligence believed that an airstrip was "definitely" being readied at Eniwetok. (In fact, Japan did not site a field there until the middle of the war.[28])

Still, the planners had only the "vaguest ideas" about the mysterious atolls. Richardson considered that the taking of Base One would be a "major" operation beyond the ability of the Fleet Marine Force.[29] Op-12 cautionaries warned that capital ships would be sitting ducks for Orange raiders in the Marshalls.[30] Stark, in a rare show of optimism, saw "no difficulty" in seizing places the Orange navy would not defend with main forces, but he derided all atolls as "weak positions" suited only for sheltering seaplanes and submarines to aid attacks on "real islands." Furthermore, Base One would be useless without the fleet nearby to support it and would be lost if the big ships left the Pacific.[31] Richardson, true to form, took the most jaundiced view. Lacking physical data, the United States would not know if it had an island suitable for B-1 until it was captured. Thus matériel and shipping could not be intelligently assembled beforehand. The Orange Plan's assumption that the base could be commissioned between 60M and 90M was "greatly out of proportion." Six to twelve months was a sounder estimate.[32]

If the obsession with the Atlantic of late 1940 had continued unabated, the Blue drive through the Pacific would have receded into the far future, perhaps to be revived after Germany was beaten, if at all. But early in 1941 it became necessary to reassess an amphibious Phase II in the context of a war involving a coalition with allies. At the ABC-1 Conference the United States refused to send a fleet to Singapore but yielded to British pleadings to render aid indirectly by naval operations in the central Pacific. Turner boasted that the Pacific Fleet could take actions so threatening that it "might be considered unlikely" that Japan would send the main body of its fleet against the Malay Barrier. Under "ideal" circumstances Kimmel could force it to emerge and fight for a vital position covering Japanese sea lanes (presumably a reference to Truk). Turner's posturing did not console the British. To appear credible, a strategy of saving the barrier would have to include a definite— and early—landing date.

Turner's innuendo about invading the Carolines early in the war set Embick to fuming about a commitment he considered far too hazardous. The army would not furnish troops, he said, and when the Atlantic offensive began it would terminate other support for the Pacific drive. Turner backed off to suggest a "possible" assault if, for example, an enemy mistake opened the way. After unrecorded discussion the army assented to a few soothing words for the ruffled Ally. Although the final ABC-1 report did not fix a date for attacking Truk, Turner held out a ray of hope by hinting that the fleet might attempt an early seizure of the Marshalls. The group was not vital per se, he noted, but U.S. control or interdiction would imperil or even deny the Carolines, which were vital to Japan. A capture of Base One would be scheduled after all. Therefore, Joint Rainbow Five was to direct the fleet to conduct, not just prepare for, "denial and capture" operations.[33] Navy Supporting Plan WPL-46 specified a "Task b" for execution on M+180 by the Fleet Marine Force and thirty thousand soldiers, defined confusingly as capture of the Marshalls *and* Carolines.[34] Although Op-12 still coaxed the logisticians for base layouts at both Eniwetok and Truk,[35] the M+180 commitment was intended only for the Marshalls because the ground force for Task b would have been too puny to take Truk.

Throughout 1941 OpNav worried that the headstrong admiral in Pearl Harbor might try to reaccelerate the deferred amphibious drive. His tigerish planning officer favored taking the Marshalls "as expeditiously as possible" and moving on to Truk.[36] Stark barraged them with warnings. The Carolines were "held rather strongly," he advised, and backed by powerful defenses in the Palaus that would soon extend to New Guinea.[37] Op-12 confined the vessels of the Naval Transportation Service to the vicinity of Hawaii, barring them from offensive deployment even though scheduled conversions would have been adequate for an attack force (Table 24.3). (The navy's own auxiliaries would be kept busy in wartime supplying Blue atoll bases.[38])

Kimmel's first reaction to the postponement of landings was to manipulate it as a lever to increase his strength. He blustered that the public would compel reinforcement of his fleet when it saw how impotent it was to do anything. Stark bridled. The plan did not imply that naval combat units would be returned for attacking Truk at any known date, only that troops and a train should be made ready within some period of time.[39] About April or May 1941 Kimmel, after brooding that Japan's vital interests lay far beyond the Mandate, bowed to the no-quick-landings policy. He acknowledged that the fleet amphibious force was "wholly unprepared" to attack in the teeth of "the hardest kind of opposition to overcome." Most of its transports and landing craft had gone to the Atlantic. To fashion civilian ships into an assault train might take twelve months. The fleet could not even rehearse the storming of a fortified atoll until it received men and boats, amphibious tractors, and bombardment ammunition.[40]

TABLE 24.3   *Planned Size of Naval Transportation Service, 1938–1940*

Estimated vessels for Naval Transportation Service at outbreak	WPL-14 Orange 1938	WPL-42 Rainbow One mid-1939	WPL-44 Rainbow Three late 1940
Transport	63	71	26
Ammunition	14	12	4
Stores	17	9	9
Cargo	88	20	17
Hospital	10	1	0
Oiler	121	15	0[a]
Other	66	9	0
Total all types	379	137	56

Source: Dir WPD to CNO, Planning for Use of Merchant Marine, 25 Feb 41, A16/QS1, Signed Ltrs, Box 81, WPD Files, OA, NHD.

[a] Eliminated because more naval tankers were available and civilian tanker crews were deemed more reliable.

OpNav sympathetically sped a marine regiment and some equipment to Kimmel during the fall of 1941 but refused to return the agile destroyer-transports that the CinCPac coveted for entering lagoon passes.[41] Nor were homemade nostrums promising. Vice-Admiral Wilson Brown, charged with commanding island invasions, suggested that the fleet build motor lighters and stash them at Wake or the Gilberts for towing to the Marshalls. Perhaps musing over a Mai Tai at Waikiki, Brown also recommended surfboard-riding commandos to dynamite beachhead obstacles. "I think we can skip this," Murphy said.[42]

By late 1941 Kimmel had grown completely averse to amphibious adventures. When Stark persisted in needling him about preparing for Truk,[43] the CinCPac retorted that he had one transport instead of the thirty to forty needed and scarcely any other auxiliaries. The marines were far from ready, even for the Marshalls. In November he declined an opportunity to free up marines to train for landings by rejecting substitute army guards for Blue atolls.[44] A Mandate campaign could not be launched, he reckoned, until his sea and air power was augmented by 50 percent,[45] which was inconceivable for a long time to come. As Kimmel's chief of staff acknowledged after the war, "We could not possibly have taken any of the Marshall Islands. . . . Obviously the capture of Truk was impossible."[46] The Navy Department's haranguing to make ready for an invasion to be launched no earlier than M+180 may have blinded it to signals of an instantaneous combat alternative abrew at fleet headquarters in Pearl Harbor.

What was the Pacific Fleet supposed to do for six months? According to Rainbow Five, it would steam about on mid-ocean sweeps, raids, and feints to confuse Orange and divert some of its forces from the Malay Barrier yet stay free to run for the Atlantic.[47] To assure Kimmel's absolute compliance, OpNav limited the distance to which he might penetrate into the central Pacific. In November 1940 army war planners had urged that offensive naval activities not proceed beyond the 180th meridian, a mindless insult because no enemy targets lay on the near side of the International Dateline. Planners at OpNav who were piecing together the diversionary concept examined a boundary at 160° east longitude to allow cruises to the Marshalls. It was stretched, with army concurrence,[48] to 155° east longitude, permitting large-scale naval operations in the eastern Carolines although not as far as Truk. Within the permitted cruising zone the fleet could neutralize the Marshalls by air raids and submarine patrols and deny them to Japan along with Wake and the Gilberts.[49]

In 1941 U.S. war plans contained a defect of logic that strategists in Washington seemed unwilling to face. A fundamental goal, handed down from the Rainbow Two and Three studies, was to restrict Japan's access to oil. When the oceanic diversionary strategy was first proposed, planners expected that demonstrations in the central Pacific would help the Malay Barrier hold out for three months, long enough for a strong British fleet to arrive after a journey from Europe estimated by the Admiralty at seventy to ninety days.[50] But during the year losses in the Mediterranean and Atlantic diminished the Royal Navy's capacity for a rescue (although the British clung to the hope that a weaker relief effort might do the job).[51] Prolonged resistance at the barrier for the strategic purpose of denying Japan petroleum could therefore be achieved only if the U.S. Pacific Fleet advanced to positions from which it could jeopardize Orange traffic with Malaysia. But the deferral of the Eniwetok assault until M+180 and Truk until at least M+360 meant the almost certain collapse both of the barrier defense and of the coordinated alliance strategy. It is unclear whether the American and British planners misunderstood the mismatched timing of their missions or indulged in self-delusion. In any event, another irony of history had decreed that Japan's domination of Micronesia, abetted by London twenty-five years earlier as an anti-American ploy, would seal the fate of Britain's Oriental empire.

By November 1941, with the Nazis preoccupied in Russia, the Admiralty regained a modicum of self-assurance. It dispatched two capital ships to Singapore, which it expected U.S. Asiatic Fleet destroyers to screen in action. Hart and MacArthur looked forward to discussing combined strategy with Admiral Tom Phillips, RN, when he arrived with the *Repulse* and *Prince of Wales* about 2 December 1941.[52] The U.S. Army was reinforcing the Philippines (Chapter 6) and promising heavy bombers for a Mandate campaign (Chapter 21). Stark exulted that by mid-December Allied strength in the Far East would pose a real hazard to Japan. The British boasted that by February or March 1942 they would muster at Singapore six battleships, a carrier, and many cruisers and airplanes, a force that Stark deemed "impressive" and possibly decisive. Nevertheless, the time had passed to consider reaccelerating central Pacific landings as part of a coherent coalition strategy. It was left to the hawkish crew at Pearl Harbor, who lacked the means and by then the desire for amphibious attack, to invent an aggressive gambit to fulfill the U.S. pledge of ensuring the Allied position in the Orient.

Fleet Battle in the Central Pacific, 1941

Rainbow Five specifically instructed the Pacific Fleet to act "offensively in the manner best calculated to weaken Japanese economic power, and to support the defense of the Malay Barrier."[1] OpNav confidently believed that the fleet's relocation to Hawaii in mid-1940 had persuaded Orange to keep its big ships at home.[2] It expected that demonstrations against Japanese central Pacific atolls would induce the Combined Fleet to hover watchfully at its Inland Sea bases and perhaps tie down "important" detachments in the Carolines.[3] By the end of 1940 the mission of diversion had been enshrined in WPL-44.[4] The fleet was ordered to design "a vigorous offensive" in the Marshalls as its centerpiece.[5]

From the moment Kimmel took command on 1 February 1941 he was bombarded with virile advice. Hart urged him to act combatively to relieve unbearable pressure on the Asiatic front. Savvy Cooke assured him that courageous attacks would undermine enemy psychology. The CinCPac, who was by nature a fighting man and aware that his predecessor had been fired for squeamishness, promised "to damage Japan as situations present themselves or can be created." When he asked his superior if "bold aggressive action" was expected of him, Stark pithily replied, "Concurred in."[6] But the leash binding the fleet to nearby seas was "not conducive to the most vigorous offensive effort." Kimmel asked, "Does it imply that severe losses shall not be risked in accomplishing the tasks assigned?"[7] The CNO, in a rare display of certitude, assured him that "the restrictions . . . do not imply that severe losses shall not be risked . . . provided compensating gains appear probable."[8] "Light and ineffective blows," Kimmel was admonished, would "reduce respect for our power [and] increase enemy morale and reduce our own."[9] When the British wondered if the fleet might loll about "comparatively inactive" in Pearl Harbor imposing "no restraint at all on Japan," Turner retorted that it was drawing properly ferocious plans.[10]

The admiral got the message. Soc McMorris, his war plans officer, set to work on a program to distract Japan.[11] With the verve of the old Orange Plan, the reaction would be swift, vigorous, and offensive.

By the spring of 1941 Kimmel understood that Rainbow Five posed a paradox. His mission was to help save the Malay Barrier, yet his fleet had been scalped for the Atlantic, its amphibious drive postponed, and its radius of action circumscribed. It was unable to harm vital enemy interests; to raid Japan was inconceivable, and harassment of Japanese sea lanes from distant Hawaii would be of little consequence. Blue's carrier force was "woefully deficient," and its powerful battle line would be impotent until advanced bases were gained. The Combined Fleet could afford to play a waiting game until the United States threatened a vital interest or attrition had "broken our backs" during the deferred amphibious drive. Kimmel came to see the diversionary strategy as a dead end: "Quick results may only be hoped for—common sense dictates that it is largely a hope, based upon the idea that Japan will make a fundamental mistake, and that bold action may be able to take advantage of it."[12] Casting about for a better mission, the admiral flailed at discredited schemes. Send a big army to Luzon. Develop Guam. He toyed frivolously with bagging German raiders in the Pacific and had to be restrained from slipping submarines into the Mandate to find their reputed lairs.[13]

Kimmel was not alone in believing that fleabite raids would be ineffective. Hart demanded powerful actions that would prevent capital ships from shredding his command.[14] McMorris pointed out the fallacy of expecting fleet demonstrations to draw off "considerable" Orange strength: if the main body was going to hover near home for contingencies in any event, only smaller warships and air power could be distracted from the barrier.[15] Stark privately admitted to Hart that this was probably true.[16]

McMorris wondered how blows at the Marshalls could prove strategically significant. Warlike developments were suspected on at least four atolls so he postulated strong Orange defenses, each guarded by a shore battalion and submarines with two hundred aircraft dispersed among them and a striking force of cruisers and subs lurking somewhere in the Mandate.[17] Op-12 thought otherwise, citing intelligence estimates of minimal Japanese defenses east of the Carolines.[18] The Marshalls were weakly held, it insisted, and no match for the Pacific Fleet.[19] McMorris therefore reduced his estimate of hostile aircraft to seventy-five[20] and concluded that if the Japanese didn't take the Marshalls seriously, harassing them would do little good. Kimmel agreed that "mere denial" of the Marshalls, Gilberts, and Wake would be an "extremely doubtful" way to distract enemy strength.[21] The fleet would fail in its strategic mission unless it invented a more daring plan.

If the fleet could not threaten vital areas, perhaps it could draw the enemy to fight in its own corner of the ocean. Kimmel's eye fell on the most forward position of his theater, Wake Island. Its importance, he wrote to Stark, was "increasingly evident as one inquires into means by which . . . [to] carry on offensive operations to the westward." If captured by Japan, it would constitute "a serious obstacle" to all Blue activities in the central Pacific. A secure American base there, however, would assure successful raids on the Marshalls and bolster more valiant initiatives if the fleet's operating frontier were later extended. Above all, a fortified U.S. base on Wake would generate an opportunity for sea combat. As Kimmel explained, "If Wake be defended, then for the Japanese to reduce it would require extended operations of their naval force in an area where we might be able to get at them; thus affording us opportunity to get at naval forces with naval forces. We should try, by every possible means, to get the Japanese to expose naval units. In order to do this, we must provide objectives that require such exposure."[22]

The CinCPac never defined the magnitude of the "naval units" he hoped to lure to Wake. After he was relieved on 16 December 1941, he told investigators, "We felt that an expedition to Wake, to attack it, would force the Japanese to expose some of their fleet, which we hoped we would be able to get there and catch. . . . We felt that if we could keep Wake reasonably well defended—it would serve as bait to catch detachments of . . . the Japanese fleet coming down there."[23] McMorris's appraisal of a "detachment" Orange might send can be gleaned from the chart maneuver he set up, which consisted of a carrier with some cruisers and destroyers.[24] When Halsey embarked on a plane-delivery voyage to Wake early in December 1941, McMorris told him that in case of war a weak Japanese "raiding force" approaching the island would afford the single-carrier U.S. task force a profitable encounter.[25] (Later that month, after a scruffy Japanese gunnery and landing force failed to reduce the island, Japan did send a pair of light carriers to pound Wake into submission.)

Wake as naval bait was a novel idea. Under Plan Orange its development had been justified for supporting an immediate capture of Eniwetok, but deferral of the landing on Eniwetok to M+180 rendered Wake's function uncertain (and imposed a burden on the fleet to hold it for at least six months). Rainbow Three of December 1940 restored its importance at the outbreak as a scouting post for Blue raids on the Marshalls. In both plans, flying boats were supposed to rush to the atoll on M Day and rely on a cache of aviation gasoline and Pan Air's shops for two or three weeks. When their tenders arrived, they would face a dubious life expectancy outside the reef because no entry channel had yet been dug. Before Kimmel's show of interest OpNav felt so lethargic about Wake that it offered the navy's only portable air base equipment to the Asiatic Fleet.[26]

When Kimmel and McMorris took over fleet planning early in 1941, they insisted that two VProns would have to fly to Wake at the outbreak to cover the fleet's line of approach to the Marshalls and especially to spy far to the west to detect naval surprises from Truk or Japan.[27] Development of the atoll began in January. A pioneer construction party blasted a thirteen-foot-deep entry for supply barges (Map 25.1). By the summer of 1941 a work force of twelve hundred was pressing ahead smartly with shore facilities, undeterred by four typhoons that year.[28] Sustained flying boat operations became possible when it was discovered that onshore gasoline tanks could be filled through a floating hose from a vessel moored precariously near the surf line.[29] Each month a VPron flew in for practice, once to hunt for a reported submarine.[30] Tenders hovering outside sent bombs into the lagoon in launches. Some officers derided the drills as "stunts" because in wartime a squadron would drain the tanks in a week. (In early December a VPron had to leave after a day or two because of the fuel shortage.[31]) Engineers designed a beach station for self-service of a VPron;[32] the second squadron would have to roost at Midway in the meantime.[33]

Harbor work lagged behind progress ashore. The dredge kept

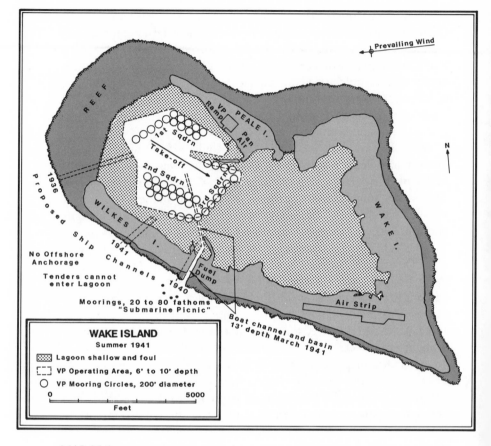

Prevailing Wind

N

REEF

VP Ramp
PEALE I.
Pan Air

1st Sqdrn

Take-off

2nd Sqdrn

3rd Sqdrn

WAKE I.

WILKES I.

Proposed Ship Channels

1936

1941

1940

Fuel Dump

No Offshore Anchorage

Tenders cannot enter Lagoon

Moorings, 20 to 80 fathoms "Submarine Picnic"

Boat channel and basin 13' depth March 1941

Air Strip

WAKE ISLAND
Summer 1941

Lagoon shallow and foul

VP Operating Area, 6' to 10' depth

O VP Mooring Circles, 200' diameter

0   5000

Feet

MAP 25.1

breaking down because the navy insisted on cutting through the widest, toughest part of the reef to align the channel to windward, consenting too late to an easy slice through one of the sandy islets.[34] In late 1941 it still took a week to unload using lighters from a ship—four weeks in bad weather—an "impossible situation" in war.[35] To limit exposure, only one ship at a time was allowed at the island.[36] By 7 December none of the seaplane facilities was ready. At the war's beginning, Wake's capacity for its originally intended strategic task, the launching of long-range aircraft, was extremely limited.

Until Kimmel's appeal for fortification, the war planners had trusted to improvising a defense of Wake. The WPD expected "early raids by enemy air, submarine or surface units, one or all." McMorris glumly hoped the Base Force could jury-rig air and submarine stations and that marines sailing from California on 5M would arrive in time and wrestle artillery ashore.[37] But naval intelligence was reporting that the Japanese Fourth Fleet in the Mandate had landing units ready to pounce. The island needed a quick fix.[38]

Defense of Wake was nominally the responsibility of the Hawaiian Naval Coastal Frontier (formerly known as the Fourteenth Naval District). But Commandant Claud Bloch had virtually no combat elements[39] and protested his hollow responsibility. Orange would destroy a base on Wake with big-caliber shells, he pointed out, because the fleet would be unable to stand by continuously and the five-inch cannon of marine defense outfits were popguns. Massive fixed batteries could not be gotten ashore until the deep channel was finished—in 1943. Until then, vessels lying outside would be meat for "a submarine picnic." Bloch concluded that protecting the island and its communications would become an intolerable burden on the navy.[40] In the War Plans Division he found an ally in Carl Moore (whose father had marched a five-piece band ashore to claim Wake for the United States in 1899).[41] Wishing to deflect the fleet away from the northerly road to Truk (Chapter 21), Moore ridiculed the bait theory, arguing in May 1941 that the fleet's weakened condition ruled out a sea clash on advantageous terms and that shielding Wake would be a "serious handicap" that would impair its other missions. If war erupted soon, the island would be "of no great value in operations against Orange anyhow." Abandon it forthwith, he advised.[42]

But the CinCPac had his own claque of supporters inside Op-12: former fleet planners Hill and Murphy, who believed that the man on the scene best understood the situation. They snorted at Bloch's U-boat picnic as "exaggerated and misleading" and calculated with more zeal than honesty that monthly stores for a garrison could be landed in nine runs of a motor launch (by conveniently omitting ammunition and aviation gas). BuDocks had told them the channel would be opened in February 1942. Meanwhile, a semi-improved base would serve adequately as naval bait.[43]

Kimmel spurned Moore's advice to shift fleet operations to the South Pacific and especially his assertion that for the Japanese navy the Gilbert Islands would be "probably more inviting" as a battle milieu.[44] He was sure the Combined Fleet would never steam in force to such a remote salient. Wake, by contrast, offered a golden opportunity of getting at Orange forces trying to reduce it. Kimmel's frequent pleas for return of departed warships were couched in terms of rendering the

Japanese gambit "a highly hazardous undertaking."[45] (After 7 December he acknowledged another motivation for fortifying Wake: the moral duty to give the men, like the boy with the best shooter in a game of marbles, "some chance for the white alley." He insisted that the casualties the defenders inflicted on Orange before the island fell had justified his decision.[46])

The reactions of Stark and Turner were not recorded. After the war they claimed they had opposed arming Wake. The CNO testified that the island "stuck out" in a region the fleet would be hard-pressed to defend.[47] Turner added that he was sure it lay beyond support range and would fall. He simply did not believe Kimmel would try to fight an "engagement with the Japanese Fleet" to save it.[48] Their actions, however, belied their recollections. In May 1941 Stark ordered fortification to proceed and granted the task a priority higher than base development. Wake, he declared, would become "extremely important to mid-Pacific operations."[49] Having badgered the commander in chief to behave aggressively, he could scarcely deny him a hardy outpost in the arena of first contact.

Kimmel moved swiftly. The Fleet Marine Force was activating island garrisons;[50] by robbing units slated for other atolls he got elements of the First Defense Battalion onto Wake in August 1941. On his own authority he sent more guns and in the autumn the remainder of the 388-strong battalion under Major James P. S. Devereux. The CinCPac was satisfied that the marines would put up a good fight against shelling or invasion.[51] For sea protection, the navy had on the drawing boards an elegant base for six submarines that would require massive dredging and bulkheading. Turner pushed for a simpler station, but time ran out before anything was ready. In October, however, the crisis atmosphere induced Kimmel to send a pair of subs to patrol near the island. In November they painted out identification, darkened ship, and stayed below in daylight.[52]

Antiaircraft defenses were last to arrive. An airfield for carrier-type planes had been authorized in 1940 along with workshops for two squadrons.[53] By late summer of 1941 a coral strip was made operative. In November Kimmel decided to station marine light bombers on Wake for sea defense or possibly a naval battle (they could not have reached and raided the Mandate), but after mulling over Turner's warning to expect "repeated bombing attacks" he opted to send a Marine Fighting Squadron instead. On 4 December the dozen Wildcat fighters of VMF-211 flew in from a carrier. Radars and modern antiaircraft guns were scheduled to follow but never arrived.[54] Meanwhile, the service chiefs decided that army P-40s were better interceptors. (Kimmel and General Short, commander of the Hawaiian Department, took this as a sign that Washington deemed Oahu safe enough to get along without some of its defensive power; in fact, Marshall was concerned about guarding bombers staging through the atolls to the Philippines.) Short also wanted to put soldiers on Wake and Midway. Kimmel convinced him to wait until the bases were finished.[55] To Short's demand for army jurisdiction over the islands Kimmel retorted, "Over my dead body."[56] His bait was in place and he meant to control it. Wake was "by no means impregnable," he reflected, but the Japanese would have to expose "quite a force" to capture it, probably "a substantial portion of their Combined Fleet."[57]

It is virtually certain, however, that Kimmel and McMorris did not believe the Pacific Fleet could accomplish its mission decisively by defending Wake any more than by raiding minor Orange outposts. Only one action would prove decisive beyond doubt: defeating the Combined Fleet. They might be able to bring about a great sea battle under conditions of maximum advantage. The most opportune moment would occur at the outset of the war, when much of Japan's strength would be committed elsewhere. The frontier of the fleet's permitted operating zone lay closer to Pearl Harbor than to Japanese home bases; parts of it were protected by Blue's air bases and beyond reach of the enemy's. To induce the commander in chief of the Combined Fleet, Admiral Isoroku Yamamoto, to engage at a favorable time and place, it will be argued, they were willing to offer an irresistible lure: the American aircraft carriers.

A battle climax had been a constant element of U.S. Pacific strategy since 1906. Planners had always assumed that the great battle would be fought when and where Japan elected, probably late in the war after attrition had equalized capital ship strength and in waters relatively close to Orange main bases. In the 1930s the zone of possible contact was extended to the Marianas and Carolines but never to the Marshalls. Stark believed, as he told Roosevelt, that the Mandate campaign of Plan Orange had been designed to "induce the Japanese to expose their fleet in action against our fleet, and lead to their naval defeat." Even diversionary raids, he claimed, might induce a battle in a favorable place.[58] The CNO stoked Kimmel's appetite by asserting in February 1941 that "a properly vigorous offensive" might give him a shot at "an important section" of the Orange fleet.[59] Turner went further than previous strategists when he told the British the same month that the Japanese main body would fight straightaway for the Marshalls.[60]

Neither OpNav's nor the fleet's war plans of 1941 explicitly projected a full-scale battle. To the contrary, McMorris's Plan O-1 specified that after raiding the Marshalls the fleet would either conduct "further operations of a similar nature" or return to Pearl Harbor. His admonition to "detect and destroy" expeditions against outlying Blue islands was consistent with a skirmish at Wake, and his stricture to avoid fighting at a disadvantage was a normal platitude. The formal plans never mentioned a massive combat.[61] The evidence given here of a battle design is circumstantial, derived from analysis of the extraordinary deployments and timetables of the fleet planners. WPPac-46, submitted in July 1941 and approved by OpNav in September, is a document long known to historians that was published as an exhibit in the Pearl Harbor Hearings conducted by Congress after the war. Its predecessor, McMorris's draft WPUSF-44 of March, was not appended; it has been located only recently and apparently has not been previously researched.[62] Taken together, the fleet plans and the related commentaries demonstrate an almost certain battle orientation of the Pacific Fleet during 1941.

The hundred or so books that have been written about the Pearl Harbor attack[63] have largely overlooked the scheme for a Pacific Jutland. Typically, they note the fleet's assigned task of raiding and sometimes the prospect of a limited fight at Wake, which Kimmel discussed in letters to Stark, but they rarely allude to a greater strategic design. The following assay of the grand intention offers a fresh slant on the conditions preceding the "day of infamy." It begins with a strategic overview and proceeds through deployments of Blue forces, operations in the Marshalls, and prebattle maneuvers, suggesting alternative interpretations of each move. It speculates about Japanese reactions that U.S. planners might have anticipated and on a battle and its outcome. Five maps depict the dispositions, planned for Blue and presumed for Orange. Finally, the attitudes of U.S. naval leaders of 1941 are explored for further clues, and the bearing of the presumptive battle plan on the events of 7 December is discussed. The presentation ends with a gnawing question: why has such an important strategic intention—if indeed it existed—gone unreported for fifty years?

The offensive deployments of the Fleet O-1 Plans commenced with independent sorties of submarines, flying boats, and cruisers, primarily for reconnaissance (Map 25.2). The Rainbow Three version of March 1941 (WPUSF-44) dispatched the fleet submarine force of twenty-eight boats into the Mandate, four to hunt quarry at Truk and Saipan and the rest to observe and report on the Marshalls, then concentrate at Kwajelein (still unsuspected as a major Orange air base) to avoid entanglement with an onrushing Blue task force.[64] McMorris changed his mind after cancellation of the Asiatic Reenforcement allowed for a stronger carrier raiding unit that did not need direct undersea aid and after the decision to fortify Wake promised reliable aerial scouting. By July Task Force Seven had grown to thirty-two, mostly modern, submarines. A few were to stand guard at American atolls. Most would sortie from Oahu on J Day (the Planning Section's eponym for M Day) "or earlier, if so directed." They would top up fuel tanks at Midway and, sweeping on a wide front, advance to the sea gates of the Combined Fleet: Yokohama, Bungo and Kii channels (the outlets from the Inland Sea), and the exits from the Sea of Japan. They were to radio word of *"important* enemy movements" and damage *"important* enemy units" (emphasis added).[65]

The submarine sprint to Japan would have been an excellent pre-battle deployment. If the boats got off to an early start and cruised most of the way on the surface at fourteen or fifteen knots—they were rated at twenty—they would approach stations as early as 8J, in time to observe and injure the Combined Fleet as it debouched in response to the appearance of Blue carriers in the Marshalls. This rate of advance may appear optimistic compared with the first wartime patrol passages of seventeen to twenty days, but in the traumatic days after 7 December the subs were ordered to run on one engine and surface only at night when within five hundred miles of enemy bases. Submerged speeds were as slow as two and a half knots so they made an average of eight knots. (After being criticized for excessive caution, the skippers cut the transit time significantly.[66]) Before the war a swift passage would have seemed plausible to McMorris. He foresaw no aerial snoopers because he believed Orange had few long-range planes, and he expected picket boats only near Japan.[67] If the submarines did not arrive on time, they could still form a scouting line across the Japanese path as they later did in several World War II battles.

There are alternative explanations for the submarine movement. McMorris might simply have expected profitable ship hunting because the run to Japan was to occur even if the rest of his plan were scrubbed and he expected permission for the boats to sink merchantmen on sight (Chapter 26).[68] But if commerce raiding were his intention, it would have been more appropriate to mount a sustained campaign in Japanese waters than to assign the returning boats to soften up the Mandate for eventual invasion with only "occasional" sweeps toward the Marianas and Japan.[69] Furthermore, the orders to report and attack "im-

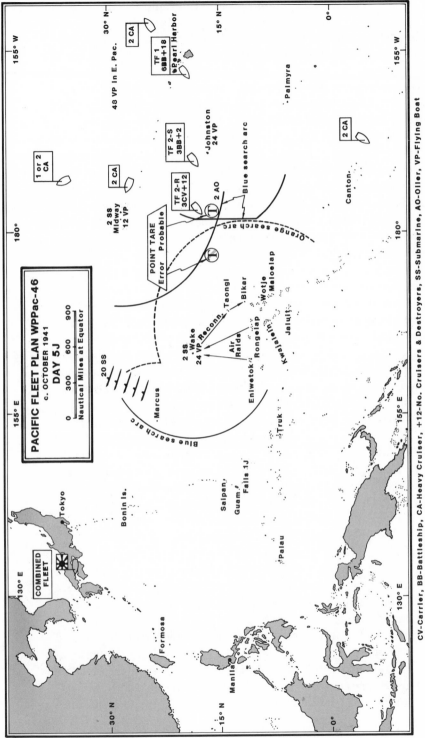

PACIFIC FLEET PLAN WPPac-46
c. OCTOBER 1941
DAY 5J

0   300   600   900
Nautical Miles at Equator

COMBINED FLEET

Tokyo

Bonin Is.

Saipan.
Guam
Falls 1J

Palau

Formosa

Manila

Marcus

20 SS

Blue search arc

Eniwetok

Rongelap
Kwajalein
Jaluit

Truk

2 SS
Midway
12 VP

1 or 2 CA

2 CA

POINT TARE
Error Probable

2 CA

TF 2-R
3CV+12

2 AO

2 SS
Wake
24 VP Reconn.

Air
Raids
24 VP

Taongi
Bikar
Wotje
Maloelap

TF 2-S
3BB+2

·Johnston
24 VP

Orange search arc

Blue search arc

Canton·

TF 1
6BB+18
·Pearl Harbor

2 CA

48 VP in E. Pac.

·Palmyra

30° N

15° N

0°

15° N

0°

30° N

155° E

180°

155° W

130° E

155° E

180°

155° W

130° E

155° W

CV-Carrier, BB-Battleship, CA-Heavy Cruiser, +12-No. Cruisers & Destroyers, SS-Submarine, AO-Oiler, VP-Flying Boat

MAP 25.2

portant" enemy units implied a Japanese naval sortie. Had McMorris not expected such a reaction, the subs could better have served the strategy by prowling in the Mandate and watching for an Orange detachment bound for Wake. Moore, always anxious to trim Kimmel's sails, tried in June 1941 to reinstate the original submarine deployment to the Mandate.[70] McMorris ignored him.

The vitality of the submarine movement was sapped in October 1941 when OpNav detached twelve boats for Manila. Rear Admiral Thomas Withers of TF 7, who was no doubt disgruntled, complained that with allowances for overhauls, training, and sentinel duty only four to seven subs could sail for Japan until new construction made up the difference about March 1942. His supporting plan of 12 November cannot be found,[71] but his calculation was unduly pessimistic and the surge to Japan remained embedded in Plan O-1.

The United States enjoyed an edge in long-range aerial scouting. McMorris allocated five of the fleet's nine VProns—the "maximum practicable" number—to fly to the atolls for "the earliest possible information of advancing enemy forces" (Map 25.2).[72] The improvement and arming of Wake promised their availability for a sea battle in the vicinity. By late 1941 two VProns, possibly three, could operate from the lagoon with a semblance of security. From their scheduled arrival on 5J to the limit of their mechanical endurance they were assigned to search westward for Orange warships closing for a surprise attack on Blue forces "operating toward the Marshalls." Midway's patrol arcs were laid out to the southwest for the same purpose.[73] (A proposal by Cooke for deep penetration flights refueled by submarines was not acted on.[74])

The seaplane dispositions do not necessarily demand a battle rationale. Naval practice stipulated VP coverage of fleet operations beyond 175° west (approximately the longitude of Midway). Flying boats from the Blue atolls could observe wide swaths of ocean and would have done so even if the Marshalls raid had been canceled.[75] Yet the particulars of their deployment mesh exceptionally well with a battle scenario. Patrol Wing Two rounded up every fuel drum it could find in Hawaii to support flights at Wake for three or four weeks,[76] a duration well beyond the Marshalls raid but correlating with a potential date of engagement. McMorris knew that the fleet's doctrine of evacuating planes to avoid heavy losses would have to be discarded at Wake.[77] In his chart game a vicious carrier-cruiser raid cost the island half its facilities and heavy casualties, although some VPs escaped the carnage and later returned.[78] He did not intend to expend the big planes over the fortified Marshalls; his plan directed them to peek only at Taongi and Bikar, minor islands thought to be unarmed that the Blue carriers would pass close aboard.[79] Nor were the VP search arcs directed toward a raiding detachment that might have issued from the Marshalls toward Wake. The plan's undoctrinaire exposure of irreplaceable assets is best explained as a hunt for momentous quarry.

The third scouting element, the heavy cruisers of TF 3, was mostly assigned to sweep the eastern Pacific clear of raiders. But two of the long-range ships were detailed to set out immediately—possibly two days before the war by virtue of warnings—and race in the direction of the Ryukyus (Map 25.2). Their stated mission was to catch enemy convoys. Their eight floatplanes could also have formed a scouting line hundreds of miles wide to watch for Yamamoto if he were steaming across the Philippine Sea.[80]

As the scouting dragnet slipped into place, Task Force Two under Vice-Admiral William F. Halsey was to penetrate the Marshall Islands (Map 25.3). In the Rainbow Three version only one aircraft carrier would have been available because the other two would be headed for the Malay Barrier.[81] Cooke was aghast at risking such a weak carrier force in a densely defended web.[82] But cancellation of the Asiatic Reenforcement early in 1941 freed all the carriers, the *Lexington*, *Saratoga*, and *Enterprise*, for the Marshalls. (The *Yorktown* had gone to the Atlantic.[83])

In McMorris's unusual conception TF 2 was to sail in and out of the Marshalls on two separate excursions a week apart. The instantly ready vessels would sortie from Pearl Harbor on 1J and make twenty knots to Point Tare, a spot of ocean within the scouting envelope of Blue atolls, to rendezvous with an oiler dispatched two days earlier thanks to war warnings. (Otherwise the carriers would refuel the destroyers.) The task force would then gallop westward through waters inspected by Wake's VPs. From 6J to 9J it would reconnoiter the Marshalls, from northwest to southeast, in search of Orange sea- and aircraft and shore installations. The plan was strangely ambivalent about strikes. Halsey was authorized to attack by air and gunshot if Orange defenses were "comparatively weak," the reverse of what one might expect.[84] McMorris fine-tuned the schedule periodically to reflect changing ship locations. For example, on 6 December 1941 the two operative carriers (the *Saratoga* was on the West Coast) were delivering marine squadrons to the atolls so if war broke out in the next twenty-four hours the *Lexington* was to fuel at sea near Midway and the *Enterprise* in Pearl Harbor and proceed to the Marshalls independently.[85]

On completing the reconnaissance Halsey would link up with the rest of the fleet at Point Tare as the battleships joined from Hawaii and the heavy cruisers reappeared from sweeps around the eastern Pacific (Map 25.4). For two days all vessels would refuel from oilers and shuffle into reconstituted Task Forces One and Two, while the admirals studied photographs and chose targets. Then the carriers, cocooned by three dozen fast gunships, would hasten back to the northern Marshalls to blast any ships and planes they could find, with shore facilities as secondary targets. Marine teams would go ashore temporarily to "demolish installations and eliminate enemy personnel," but no ship was to expend more than 25 percent of its shells or bombs against fixed targets (Map 25.5).[86]

The double cruise through the Marshalls was a bizarre stratagem. Even in 1941, striking a week after a reconnaissance in force had alerted the foe would have been unorthodox. The first cruise would have wasted the element of surprise by failing to wound the enemy at once. The second would have courted disaster because the Japanese would have had time to pour in air reinforcements. Carrier raids of World War II, both U.S. and Japanese, were stealthy approaches announced by full-deckload strikes. In its chart maneuver Blue suffered 20 percent damage to planes and carriers from Orange air attacks on the first day and TF 2 had to fight its way out. (Halsey characteristically spurned passivity in the game and bashed whatever he found.[87])

Stark understandably criticized the dual maneuver. Prodded by Moore, he urged Kimmel to combine the two forays or at least shorten the interval between them.[88] The CinCPac replied that "exploratory measures [had to] precede large-scale efforts." He was willing to accept "grave risks" to the carriers to obtain priceless information.[89] McMorris conceded only that TF 2 might launch "supplementary" air strikes during the reconnaissance in highly favorable and risk-free circumstances.[90]

The fleet strategists were reacting to a lack of information about the Mandates that was keenly felt by all. An incident of late 1941 illustrates the lengths to which the United States was willing to go to obtain knowledge. General Marshall, worried about bombers passing through Wake, suggested an aerial reconnaissance of the Mandate.[91] Since slow naval VPs might be shot down and provoke a crisis, air force bombers were assigned to a scouting mission at high speed and altitude

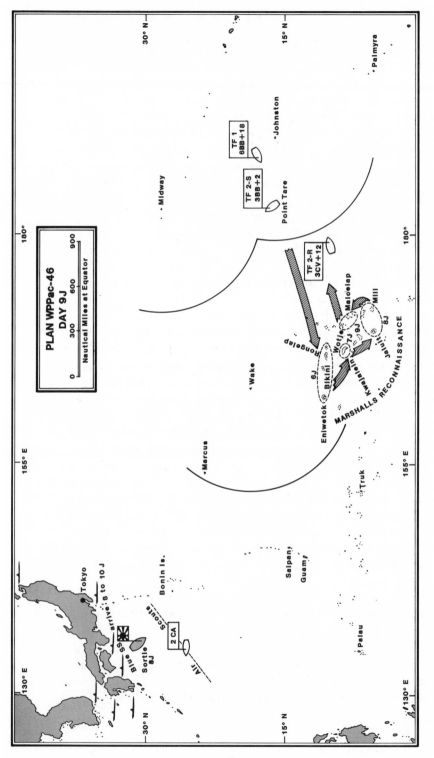

PLAN WPPac-46
DAY 9 J

Nautical Miles at Equator

0   300   600   900

MAP 25.3

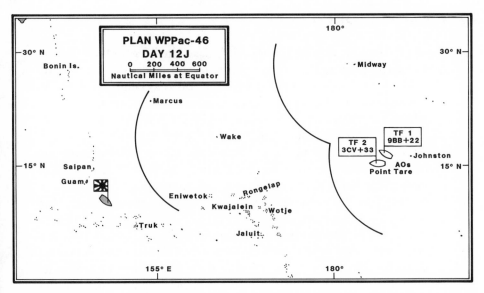

MAP 25.4

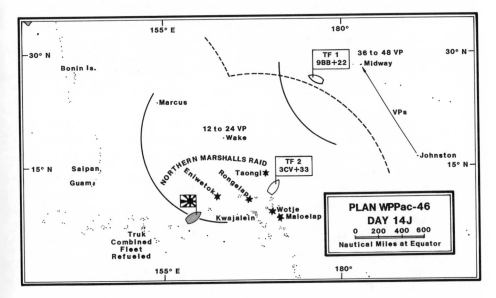

MAP 25.5

while ostensibly in transit to Manila.[92] Fleet Intelligence Officer Edwin T. Layton proposed an inspection of eleven islands; the Joint Board reduced it to single passes of B-24s over Truk and Jaluit.[93] But equipment problems delayed the planes' arrival in Hawaii to 5 December 1941, and the spy flights were aborted by the Japanese attack.[94] The fleet got no firsthand intelligence before the war began.

Still, it is difficult to accept Kimmel's weighing of the risk-reward trade-off. To expose three carriers solely for news of Orange's outermost bases would have been a grossly disproportionate gamble, even factoring in the possibility of spotting a Wake-bound detachment (which would more than likely have hit and run before the reconnaissance). Yet McMorris refused to revise the dual-pass pattern. His logic best fits the context of a prebattle maneuver. The first cruise, it may be supposed, was to signal a forthcoming raid and tantalize Yamamoto to sail to the central Pacific. The second voyage would neutralize the northern Marshalls and destroy air reinforcements sucked in by the previous visit, thereby improving the odds and assuring Wake's operability at the moment of battle.

The supreme riddle of the 1941 fleet plans concerns deployment of the battle line. The United States and its Allies were outnumbered in the Pacific in every class of war vessel save the biggest gunships. Kimmel had nine battleships. Japan had six battleships and four battle cruisers, but some of them might be needed to oppose two British capital ships coming to Singapore and others, the fleet plan supposed, for operations in the Mindanao-Celebes area.[95] Orange dreadnoughts were faster and their crews better adapted to night fighting. Blue's had longer steaming range and thicker armor. In sixteen-inch guns (the most potent batteries afloat until Japan's eighteen-inch leviathans were commissioned during the war) Kimmel held a three-to-two advantage. It was possible for the Pacific Fleet to achieve momentary superiority for a climactic gun battle, the legendary grail of the Orange Plan.

Husband Kimmel was a "black shoe" artillery officer. He had served aboard at least seven battlewagons and as chief of staff of the big-gun force. He had instructed in shot and shell and had supervised production at the Naval Gun Factory.[96] Although a battleship orientation was not uncommon in the navy of 1941, Kimmel's case was extreme; King and Halsey, for example, were skilled carrier commanders and Nimitz had trained as a submariner. Of all his deprivations the CinCPac most keenly felt the removal of three battleships to the Atlantic.[97] He begged fruitlessly for the *North Carolina* and *Washington*, fast, heavily gunned new dreadnoughts.[98] In a meeting of

9 June 1941 the president casually suggested detaching three more battleships, leaving three to defend Hawaii and three for raiding. "That's crazy!" Kimmel exploded. Roosevelt backed down.[99]

To cast his beloved battleships in a decisive role would have suited the admiral's proclivities. His Plan O-1 sent them forth from Pearl Harbor in two waves. The *Pennsylvania, Nevada,* and *Arizona* were to sortie immediately as a "Support Force" and arrive at Point Tare while the carriers reconnoitered the Marshalls. They would hover outside enemy air range as a force for Halsey to retire on. Their contingent tasks—fending off night torpedo attacks by destroyers and cruisers that might pursue Halsey or shepherding wounded vessels home— seem unworthy of their power. Hanging about a fixed point for six days with only a pair of destroyers, the slow battleships would have made prime submarine targets.[100] There was probably another reason for their presence. Kimmel was "very reluctant" to remain ashore when the shooting began.[101] Perhaps he wanted to be on the bridge of his flagship while the great armada assembled. "The Fleet will be kept informed of the location of the Commander-in-Chief," the plan said laconically.[102]

The six other battlewagons, reorganized as Task Force One under Vice-Admiral William S. Pye, were to put to sea on 5J with a strong escort. After a feint southward to throw off snoopers they would reach Point Tare on 11J for a magnificent rendezvous (Map 25.4). Milling about in the middle of the Pacific Ocean, with Kimmel himself proba- bly in tactical command, would be all sixty-seven of the fleet's oceango- ing men-of-war drinking from fresh oilers. TF 1 would absorb the Support Force to form a monolithic battle line of nine dreadnoughts.[103] To simplify their concentration, McMorris's later updates merged all the battleships in Pearl Harbor under a unified command.[104]

When the conferences and refuelings ended, Halsey would hightail it back to pummel the Marshalls. There would be no further business at Point Tare (a place oddly mislocated in the plans).[105] The battleships would steam toward a position north of the Marshalls to furnish during the raid "such support . . . as developments require" (Map 25.5).[106] In later testimony Kimmel and McCormick (McMorris's aide) amplified the mission of TF 1. It was to "cover" Halsey's raid and be there for him to retire on[107] (even though his normal line of retreat would have been eastward toward Hawaii rather than northward). Nobody envisioned the ponderous battleships raiding Japanese out- posts. They might have lumbered up to an Orange detachment sacking Wake (which would likely have hit and run by that date) or dealt with harriers of wounded Blue carriers, but in either instance the entire U.S. battle line would have been a sledgehammer against a flea. To the contrary, its presence would have been counterproductive to the raiding strategy. Halsey was obliged to "furnish security as practicable" to TF 1,[108] an unwelcome chore to a carrier admiral who despised the slow leviathans.[109]

Kimmel unquestionably intended to launch every ship of his command on "offensive operations." McMorris considered the fleet "virtually mobilized," buttoned up, and ready to sortie as an entirety within one to four days.[110] Pye remembered that the chart game rehearsed the full plan including the battleship sortie.[111] Halsey was "quite certain that [Kimmel] would not have split his Fleet and let it be taken in detail by sending a portion out."[112] Was it a matter of pride for the CinCPac to send—or take—his proud dreadnoughts to sea for the big show, if only to stand by? No, it will be argued. He intended to engage Yamamoto. The stakeout of the battle line makes no sense except as a disposition for that event.

Task Force One, nine battleships screened by eighteen light cruisers and destroyers, would have reached its waiting position in two or three days while Halsey ravaged the Marshalls.[113] No duration of the raid was set. One day might have been adequate to knock out the four suspected northern bases nearest to both Wake and the battleship loitering zone. (The Pacific Fleet was able to hit six atolls of the Marshalls and Gilberts on 1 February 1942.) Or a second day might have been dedicated to follow-up strikes on weak targets.[114] The raid could not have lasted long because Halsey was enjoined to conserve 75 percent of his ordnance. Afterward he was to join TF 1 and pass under command of the senior black-shoe admiral present, probably Kimmel, and if not, Pye.[115]

The scene of the rendezvous was to be the "area to the northward of the Marshalls." In a plausible context this encompassed half a million square miles of sea. The fleet would logically have sought a place under friendly air cover and far from prying eyes in the sky. (Moore, who worried that the wild men of Hawaii might seek battle near Japan, advised Turner in June 1941, "If a Fleet engagement is sought it should be undertaken in an area where support can be had from our VPs."[116] It was the last known acknowledgment of a battle scenario by an officer in Washington.)

McMorris noted that the battleships might shelter under Wake's air umbrella,[117] but after two weeks of war the island's VProns would have suffered grievously from breakdowns and combat. Midway, however, was assumed to be immune from serious danger. Bellinger intended to shift his headquarters there for control of all fleet VP operations.[118] By ferrying replacements from Hawaii, and from Johnston after Point Tare was vacated, forty-eight flying boats could have massed at Midway for patrols to the southwest[119] (a force similar to the long-range air scouts of thirty-two Catalinas and thirteen B-17s on the island during the battle of June 1942).[120]

This reconstruction suggests a fleet concentration somewhere along the 1,028-mile Wake-Midway line, although not adjacent to either because Kimmel had a phobia about danger from submarines within 200 miles of the atolls.[121] An assemblage close to Wake would also risk detection by Orange scouts from the northern Marshalls if their bases had not been fully suppressed or from Marcus Island. A position nearer to Midway would offer a safer prospect (Map 25.5). Japanese carriers could close by 432 miles on a winter's night and launch a dawn search to a distance of 300 miles.[122] With the dense reconnaissance pattern at Midway, such a force would surely be spotted at a distance. The fresh flying boats there might also lend a hand in combat. The fleet plans retained a shred of the 1930s striking force idea by recommending VP attacks on targets beyond range of other weapons when their importance justified loss of the planes.[123] The Orange battle line could not close so rapidly, but no U.S. admiral would have wished to blunder into it in the dark because Blue ships had few radars, and exercises had shown them ill prepared to match the Japanese with rapid, sustained night fire.[124]

The hypothesized waiting position would eerily have resembled the fleet's ambush site at Point Luck before the Battle of Midway: northeast of a "bait" island (Wake) on the flank of an unsuspecting Japanese armada, under the wing of the best U.S. advanced base, and beyond the eyes of shore-based aerial prowlers. Wherever its precise locale, the entire Pacific Fleet would be concentrated and ready about 15J or 16J, the battleships' magazines full and those of the carriers and cruisers nearly so.[125] Kimmel believed it could keep the sea for four to six weeks, the endurance of maximum VP strength in the central Pacific.[126] He would have ample time and information to maneuver for engagement should Yamamoto be heading his way.

One may speculate on what Japanese reaction the fleet planners anticipated (remembering always that they did not seriously expect the war to commence with a blow at Pearl Harbor). Yamamoto, at anchor in the Inland Sea when the war erupted in the Far East, would be aware from spies and U-boats that Blue task forces had sortied from Oahu.[127]

He would learn on 6J that Halsey was scanning the Marshalls, presumably preparatory to a raid. He would grasp the opportunity for a fight (Map 25.3). (During the February 1942 U.S. raid on the Marshalls, Japan's First Carrier Air Fleet of four flattops, two battleships, and a powerful screen raced out of Truk to try to catch the Blue carriers.[128]) How quickly could Yamamoto react? The Pacific Fleet, regarded as virtually mobilized, was expected to set sail on the second through sixth days of the war. U.S. planners might have assumed an equally rapid Orange sortie after getting word of the Marshalls reconnaissance on 6J, say anchors aweigh on 8J. Kimmel would probably learn of it from the submarine cordon, the cruisers in the Philippine Sea, or perhaps from arcane sources such as code breaking. "Information of the enemy will be disseminated prior to and on the execution of the Plan, by means of intelligence reports," McMorris promised.[129]

Where would Yamamoto head? A northerly end run to cut off Halsey in the Marshalls would have been too dicey because of Midway's search net and the drag of relying on slow oilers while the prey slipped away. He would also have wished to avoid Wake's patrol circle as long as possible. His soundest course might have been to put in at Truk for fuel and then approach the Marshalls from the west-southwest (Maps 25.4 and 25.5). Assuming a movement at fifteen knots—the customary assumption for the Blue battle line—the Combined Fleet, goaded on by TF 2's reappearance to scorch the northern Marshalls on 14J, would be spotted in the vicinity of Eniwetok by Wake's air scouts about 15J to 17J. The Orange carriers might sprint ahead to bash Wake or hunt for Halsey, but Kimmel would probably have expected Yamamoto to keep them close to his battle line, as he would have done. The two fleets, a thousand miles apart, would close rapidly near Wake Island (Map 25.6).

What might have been the outcome of a battle in 1941? The Orange navy outnumbered the Pacific Fleet in carriers by ten to three. Their five hundred planes constituted a two-to-one edge[130] (perhaps more if Halsey had suffered losses). To readers knowing the superiority of carriers over battleships in World War II the Blue situation might appear suicidal, but in 1941 this was far from clear. American naval planes were "ineffective for modern air operations," according to the General Board that summer,[131] and Japan's aerial capabilities were unknown. Kimmel's appreciation of air power was rather primitive. He prized long-range scouting but tended to view carriers as auxiliaries. They could be detached for raids, but their place in a fleet engagement was with the battle line. (A "very controversial" matter, he acknowl-

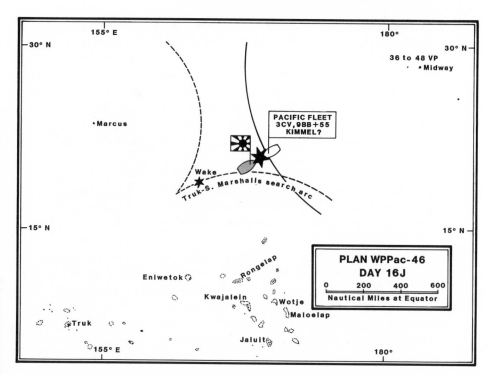

MAP 25.6

edged.) His administrative reorganization had dispersed the flying decks among three task forces while keeping the battleships well concentrated.[132] The CinCPac did not understand and sometimes irritated his aviators. "Flyboys," he called them. The senior air expert of his forty-officer staff held the modest rank of commander.[133] McMorris, too, was somewhat contemptuous of airmen to judge by his relationships on Nimitz's wartime staff.[134]

The situation of the Pacific Fleet's battle line might have been good. It would be assembled in toto, whereas some Orange dreadnoughts would be occupied in Southeast Asia. Blue submarines might have exacted a toll on the main body as it emerged. The United States would enjoy the exclusive benefit of long-range air scouting. By November 1941 plans were afoot to place army heavy bombers on the atolls; more could have flown from the mainland to Hawaii and Midway in time for action. Kimmel might well have had the advantage of surprise. Years later he mused that a clash would have been "a nice mix-up" and not at all one-sided in favor of Japan.[135] In the best of all outcomes he might have achieved the fabled maneuver of interposing his fleet between the enemy and its base. It is tempting to think again of the Battle of Midway when the benefits of the sole air base, an ambush strategy, poor enemy dispositions, and of course intelligence, offset terrible odds against America. (Some elements of McMorris's plan resembled Yamamoto's agenda for that battle, however, with scattered task forces weaving about the ocean and the battle line poised to the rear for a coup de grace after air preliminaries.)

Some may hold that Plan O-1 could never have been implemented because of material deficiencies of the Pacific Fleet. In post-disaster hindsight, Kimmel claimed his dreadnoughts' top speed was seventeen knots, not twenty-one,[136] and Turner scoffed that they were suited only for sinking a slow Orange landing convoy if one had appeared at Hawaii.[137] Normal overhauls might have reduced the number of ships available for action by one-fifth.[138] Keeping the entire fleet at sea was problematical; it had four oilers equipped for servicing warships under way but needed twenty-five for extended operations.[139]

A supposition that the fleet would not have executed the plan, however, denies certain facts. On 9 September 1941 the chief of naval operations approved Plan WPPac-46 without significant comment.[140] McMorris's update on the morning of 6 December implied that if war had broken out the next day where expected—in the Orient, not at Pearl Harbor—the plan would have been activated with some adjustments for current ship locations.[141] Many witnesses later testified that the fleet was ready to spring forth as an entirety. Its chief of staff remembered that preparations for the movement were "a major preoccupation" of the commander in chief. McMorris recalled his boss fretting about the risks yet confident that he controlled a mighty armada and determined to strike. The hawkish strategist also "knew the power in our Fleet and expected it to be effective." McCormick thought Kimmel would have plunged ahead with every ship. The CinC-Pac himself believed to the end that it was his duty to act aggressively. Halsey was "anxious to go." Even the cautious Pye accepted the propriety of the plan.[142]

The dedication of fleet officers to an offensive sortie at full strength does not prove that a program for naval battle existed. It was never enshrined in the joint or OpNav plans, which instructed the fleet to divert the Imperial Navy, not engage it. McMorris, despite the implication of his deployments, did not explicitly inject a combat into his plan. If a battle plan existed, why has it never come to light? The players are long dead, and the world may never know. At this late date, two speculations are plausible.

First, perhaps the battle scenario was held secret by Kimmel and McMorris, who deliberately kept it from fleet colleagues and the cautionaries in Washington. Both officers were known to hold their cards close to the chest at times. Kimmel, for example, never told Bellinger about his well-documented idea of blindsiding an Orange detachment at Wake,[143] nor did McMorris regularly inform his aides of intelligence briefings or his chats with Kimmel. Pye knew he was supposed to get the battleships ready "for the conduct of a major action" but, since he did not say how soon he expected it, the extent of the second-ranking admiral's knowledge is uncertain.[144] No other senior fleet officer is known to have expressed an opinion about whether Orange heavy forces would turn up. A common conviction held that they would not venture "out of the Western Pacific,"[145] which, taken literally, would have meant only no intrusion past Midway.

The second speculation is that after the Pearl Harbor disaster it was antithetical to everyone's self-interest to admit to a "harebrained" scheme that was never articulated in a plan or other written communication and that bordered on insubordination unless it had been blessed by a nod and a wink from headquarters. To acknowledge its existence once the frailty of battleships was demonstrated at Hawaii and Malaya would have cast the naval leadership as greater fools than they appeared already. By the time the higher-ups of OpNav and the War Plans Division were called to the witness stand it was late in the war or after it was over and they had towering reputations to preserve. This does not suggest a conspiracy of silence or a cover-up, simply that they might have preferred to forget a vague, personal, unrecorded, and, in hindsight, bizarre concept. Besides, the interrogators never asked them about it. In adversarial proceedings it is best for witnesses to reaffirm authenticated policies and not volunteer gossip.

Kimmel faced a dilemma during the investigations of the Pearl Harbor attack. He had been fired from his command nine days after the raid. In February 1942 he told Stark he would keep his "mouth shut . . . as long as humanly possible,"[146] but he turned bitter in the belief that he had been made the scapegoat of defeat. In later testimony and memoirs he reproached his superiors for failing to give him adequate warning of the attack. It would hardly have been wise to disclose any sensationally thrusting intention he may have harbored. To the contrary, the admiral played down the planned concentration of the fleet at sea. He told the congressional joint committee investigating the attack that the battleships had been better off in the supposedly well-defended harbor, where most were salvaged, than on the "dangerous course" of cruising without carrier cover[147]—the very course his plan dictated.

McMorris, by then a war hero, remained faithful to the rationality of the battleship deployment. "It was intended to have the entire available strength in easy supporting distance of the reconnoitering forces," he said, although adding equivocally that "it was not expected that the main part of the Japanese Fleet would be encountered."[148] His true feelings shone through, however, when he rose to the bait of a hypothetical question. What would he have advised had he known that Admiral Chuichi Nagumo's flattops were bearing down on Pearl Harbor? The Blue battleships, he replied, "certainly" should not have been at their moorings but massed to the westward for contact. Given Nagumo's six-to-two carrier dominance that day, the dreadnoughts would have "suffered quite severely," he admitted, but the U.S. hope lay in bringing the foe to bay with gunfire no matter how awkward and improbable the chances.[149]

Between 1941 and 1946 eight government committees conducted investigations that filled forty published volumes. Nearly all high commanders and planners of 1941 testified under oath. The inquiries, along with countless interviews and reminiscences, spawned a cottage industry of publications about the attack. How the United States was caught off guard on a Sunday morning, the use and misuse of code-breaking "Magic," and the blunders that magnified the Japanese success have become part of American folklore. Revisionist writers have touted theories of conspiracy, suppressed information, venality, and fraud in high places up to and including the White House. Historians have expended barrels of ink debating whether Kimmel and Short understood the import of the famous "war warning" of 27 November 1941, a message from Washington that said hostilities were imminent but did not name Pearl Harbor as a target. It contained the fateful words, "Execute an appropriate defensive deployment preparatory to carrying out the tasks of WPL-46."[150]

The tasks of the fleet in that plan were primarily offensive. On the witness stand Stark waffled by saying the message meant Kimmel should have prepared both for defense and for a decision to raid the Marshalls. Turner disagreed, insisting that it voided even preparation of an offensive move. The fleet, he claimed, should have gone to sea only to defend Hawaii and other vital bases.[151] Other OpNav officers downplayed the fleet's offensive capabilities. Ingersoll said the prevalent opinion considered it ready only for "primarily defensive" tasks regardless of the plan's "diversionary trips."[152] Captain R. O. Glover of Op-12 said that the division regarded Kimmel's mission as defense of his base and felt the fleet was incapable of "total movement [for an] outright offensive."[153] Kelly Turner, a bona fide war hero when he was interrogated, pinned all blame for the defeat on the Hawaiian commanders and assumed none himself. But to his credit, he reaffirmed the fleet's obligatory mission: "So far as Admiral Kimmel was concerned," he attested, "his part in the plan was not defensive." Conditions would have confined him initially to naval and air actions, Turner explained, but "it would be a grave error for anyone to get the idea that the war in the Central Pacific was to be purely defensive. Far from it."[154]

The two foremost thrusters of the fleet differed in their post-mortems. Kimmel, languishing in disgrace and furious at having been denied inside information, decided after years of soul-searching that he had correctly tried to honor both of Stark's interpretations. Some last-minute steps were defensive, he argued, such as reconnoitering by the carriers near the atolls and holding the battleships in port. A key question concerned the inactivity of the forty-nine flying boats sitting on Oahu the morning of 7 December. Kimmel argued that because he had been ordered several times to get set to slam the Marshalls, he needed the planes in tip-top condition for operations at primitive U.S. atoll bases, not worn out by patrols around Oahu. In hindsight he grimly acknowledged that if he had known what was coming he would have sent them out to scout, shelved the attack, and gone to a defensive crouch.[155]

McMorris, his reputation unsullied, was unrepentant. He recalled that the prevailing attitude held that the fleet *was* defensively deployed and hence no further change was necessary. He took the war warning to mean that national leaders worried that "in our enthusiasm to strike as promptly as possible we might advance forces to a position that would be regarded as threatening," to the Gilberts, for example, or near the Marshalls, "and thus destroy any remote chance of retaining peace." This interpretation seemed so evident that neither he nor the commander in chief sought clarification of the message. The fleet's assignment, McMorris said, was to hover in or near Pearl Harbor ready to lunge forward immediately. Hypnotized by the glory of offensive action, the heir of the thrusting tradition of naval planning scarcely thought about base protection.[156] Captain W. W. Smith, Kimmel's chief of staff, confirmed that the security of Pearl Harbor was not weighed seriously because of the navy's absolute enchantment with the offensive.[157] Thirty-five years of Orange war planning had indoctrinated the U.S. Navy to a mission of instantaneous attack. It was too late to change.

The cautionaries of the military headquarters had diluted the swift revenge of War Plan Orange to trivial demonstrations. The thrusters in Hawaii were tightly circumscribed and left with only one weapon of dominance. Never ordered to seek a gunnery Trafalgar, neither were they told to avoid one. Four decades after the event, the publication of interviews with many who were present by Gordon W. Prange, a scholar who devoted a lifetime of study to the Pearl Harbor episode, offered confirmations that "Kimmel proposed to sail forth to engage Yamamoto and waste no time about it."[158] The commandant of the Pearl Harbor air station understood that the "grandiose concept" visualized two navies maneuvering "so as to force each other out in battle array where they could settle the question of supremacy."[159] The author of the congressional report that condemned the commander in chief but who admired him as a man summed it up: "The admiral," he said, "appeared consumed with the idea . . . of becoming himself 'the American Nelson.'"[160]

Total or Limited War?

The story has reached the eve of the Pacific war anticipated by American strategists for thirty-five years. Before assessing the value of their legacy, a thorny question remains: what was the nature of the war they expected the United States to pursue after advancing halfway across the Pacific?

The clearly stated objective of War Plan Orange, from inception in 1906 through the early 1930s, was the complete subjugation of Japan. As described in varying detail in its many versions, that goal was to be achieved by an economic siege after maritime campaigns had resulted in acquisition of island bases close to Japan and destroyed its navy. After 1934, however, detailed offensive planning was truncated two thousand miles short of Japan—at Truk in the case of Plan Orange and Rainbow Five and somewhere in Southeast Asia in the aborted Rainbows Two and Three—and the time to reach those positions was stretched out. The capture of Truk slid from the second month of war in 1935 to the twelfth month—or even later—in the 1941 plans. Development of a fleet base would probably delay continuation of the advance for another year or more. Therefore, the duration of the entire war, having expanded from six or twelve months in pre-1914 conceptions to two years in the 1920s, was estimated by pessimistic observers of the 1930s at three, four, or even more years. Some strategists began to play with scenarios of a softer war for limited objectives, especially after 1937. The clear vows of unlimited retribution that had echoed through older plans dissipated.

Hovering always in the minds of both thrusters and cautionaries were perceptions of America's willingness to wage a long, expensive conflict and, most fundamentally, what it would seek to achieve. Not until January 1943 did the United States adopt the basic war aim of unconditional surrender of the Axis powers, a close derivative of the Orange Plan assumption in the case of Japan. The question explored here is whether, in the absence of outright statements in the final years of peace, U.S. policy makers remained dedicated, consciously or otherwise, to the total vengeance of the old Orange Plan or turned instead toward an assumption of limited war.

World War II was conducted by the United States largely in accordance with Rainbow Five, the global plan that was promulgated in May 1941 and remained in effect until its recision in March 1946, several months after the war ended.[1] At the time of its adoption, or within a few weeks after, all previous plans were deactivated, including Orange and Rainbows One through Four. The governing plan stated unequivocally that the United States would devote its energies primarily to Europe, "the decisive theater," to defeat Germany, "the predominant enemy." It stipulated a sequence of holding the Mediterranean and knocking out Italy, a sustained air assault against Germany, and eventually a land offensive on the Continent. The bulk of America's air strength would be deployed to Europe. Most of its ground forces would go to that theater commencing with a ten-division expedition on 180M and perhaps building, in accordance with the AWPD's "Victory Program" of the summer of 1941, to an astounding four hundred divisions within two years. The preeminent task of the navy under Rainbow Five was to protect transatlantic shipping.

In contrast, the U.S. mission in the Pacific was to be strategically defensive. Local forces in the Far East would have to fend for themselves without naval reinforcement. The Pacific Fleet would shield the eastern Pacific and the atoll bases, create diversions in a narrow central band of the ocean, harass Orange trade, and prepare to assault the Mandate as far as Truk. A maximum of one army division would be available for an operation west of the strategic triangle—in the Marshalls—by 180M. Air force support would be limited and might cease altogether when the European offensive began.[2] In other words, Rainbow Five sketched out a limited war in the Pacific for at least two years in the tentative hope that relatively cheap actions could exploit Japan's economic vulnerability. (The chance of a decisive moment early in the war, implicit in Fleet Plan O-1, was not addressed in higher-level plans.) The course of the struggle after Hitler's defeat was left unstated.

The possibility of less than total war against Japan had been considered by earlier strategists from time to time. For example, the reorganized Joint Board of 1919 took as its first question Captain Harry Yarnell's inquiry as to whether national interests (which he defined as trade and the Philippines) would be better served by decisive defeat of Japan or by a limited war and, if the former, at what cost.[3] He got no answer. Planners of the 1920s turned to two-year scenarios of all-out war, but in the early 1930s defensivists saw that such a policy would entail far more time and expense than predicted. They split as to the alternative solutions. A few naval analysts recommended building a vast new fleet and then taking the offensive. General Embick argued that the outcome would not be worth the cost and recommended a permanent defensive stance (Chapter 15). Naval planners dodged the issue by halting campaign planning at Truk after 1934 and even logistical studies of islands beyond it after 1938.

The issue of a limited war arose seriously in high councils during disputes between the services over global priorities from November 1937 to February 1938, after Japan invaded China (Chapters 19 and 20). Embick and his army planning staff urged a temperate strategy of "military and economic pressure" for "the limited objective of isolating Orange." Colonel Krueger argued that a goal of crushing the enemy "so utterly that he will accept any terms" suited neither the U.S. public will nor the stakes involved in the Pacific, especially when a limited sea campaign of isolation promised satisfactory results. The navy acknowledged that the foe might yield to "sufficient pressure," which it defined in traditional terms of "offensive operations" and "interruption of Orange vital sea communications." Its objective, to defeat Japan in "an economic war of exhaustion," therefore differed only slightly from previous statements.[4] The Joint Board waffled, endorsing a more gradual naval offensive to impose "increasing military and economic pressure" without defining whether the payoff was to be unlimited victory or limited containment.[5] In early 1939 the joint planners, concerned with the growing threat to home security from the European Axis, speculated that Japan might settle rationally if punished just enough to render further fighting "unprofitable and useless." It seemed doubtful, they remarked, that it could be "completely overcome . . . in an unlimited war" without an ironclad blockade that would require a large American army in China.[6]

In the summer of 1939 the Rainbow Two exploratory studies suggested how the United States might prevail in a limited Pacific war. Savvy Cooke, at heart an advocate of furious vengeance, harbored doubts that the American public would support the shedding of blood for the primary purpose of salvaging foreign colonies. Such a motivation would not warrant the "economic and military crushing" of Orange. If the Allies could prevent Japan from conquering an empire, it would have to trade to live. Thus, he reasoned, the recovery of U.S. and European colonies and closure of trade routes south of Formosa might so constrict Japan's economic life as to compel a settlement.[7]

By March 1940, however, the darkening European scene had dimmed the always faint prospect of combined operations to eject Orange from the South China Sea. The Rainbow Two formula was diminished to cutting off oil movements from Borneo to Japan and gradually recapturing the oil fields. The planners hoped wistfully that a fuel squeeze and a show of military firmness would induce Japan to quit, relinquish its spoils, and yield equal rights in China—a euphemism for withdrawal from that suffering country. But if Japan fought on, the picture would be bleak. Merely to eject it from all bases captured from the Allies would demand exertions of "major proportions." To advance beyond the Hong Kong–Luzon line would magnify the struggle into a war with gruesome casualties.[8] The Rainbow Three drafts of the same era expressed similar hopes that denial of resources, piecemeal defeats, and financial woes would induce Japan's economic collapse.[9]

Although these Rainbow Two and Three studies never matured into approved war plans, the seeds of doubt they sowed sprouted into disenchantment about programs for total victory whatever the cost. Richardson, the most ardent naval defensivist, implored Stark to impress upon "the boss" the enormous burden and small benefit of an unlimited war.[10] The CNO, who was groping throughout 1940 for a Pacific stance consistent with the Germany-first doctrine, was receptive. His Plan Dog memo of November 1940 asserted that imposing starvation and the "complete destruction" of Japanese military power as stipulated in the old Orange Plan would consume "the full military, naval, and economic energy of the American people" for years to come. Japan's powers of aggression had to be curtailed, of course, but shriveling it to a third-rate nation was not in America's interest. He urged on

Roosevelt "a more limited objective."[11] The army, eager to confirm the policies that had eluded it three years earlier, agreed that the United States should pursue "only a limited war" in the Pacific.[12] Thus Rainbow Three of December 1940 restricted offensive goals to gaining positions for applying "vitally important" economic pressure against Japan.[13] Even this vague formulation was omitted from Rainbow Five a few months later.

How to wage a cheap but effective war across the wide Pacific for several years was a conundrum. The Joint Orange Plans of 1935 and 1938 deleted campaigns west of Truk. The lengthening estimates of the time needed to prepare bases and, by late 1940, Stark's warning that an advance from Truk to the Philippines would require a maximum national exertion, insinuated that these operations would have to await Germany's surrender.[14] For all the bravura talk to the British in 1941, there is little evidence that U.S. leaders thought the Malay Barrier could be held for longer than a few months.

One attractive possibility was to seek decisive naval results in the Philippine Sea, the waters between Truk, the Philippines, and Japan. Since 1932 the idea had fascinated officers who had soured on an unlimited war (Chapter 18). Turner told the British military emissaries early in 1941 that the navy was considering deep probes beyond the fleet's operating frontier of 155° east to interrupt Orange communications with the Mandate.[15] Cooke, then in Op-12, told the CincPac that Rainbow Five was elastic enough to sanction such strikes.[16] Kimmel and McMorris, taken with the idea, proposed "sweeps in force" to raid the Marianas and Bonins, blows that Stark agreed might prove "very profitable" in distracting the Japanese until Kimmel tried too hard in May 1941: "Consideration is being given to making the initial major offensive operation a sweep far to the westward of Midway instead of a raid on the Marshalls," he reported, apparently thinking of striking the Bonins.[17] The CincPac was probably angling to stop the stripping of his carriers, but he pushed the wrong button. OpNav forbade heavy-duty operations west of the Marshalls, allowing only minor flexibility for detachments to probe beyond that group. Fleet Plan O-1 of July retained a residual supposition of full-power sweeps toward the Philippine Sea at some vague date after the Marshalls operations.[18]

In 1941 "general operations" near Japan itself or in the East China Sea were beyond the navy's ambition. The British urged such forays, which Turner rejected.[19] Kimmel, in a late bid for reinforcements, asked in November 1941 for permission to cruise "on occasions to

Japanese home waters." Stark vehemently declined, pointing out that such excursions were not contemplated in Rainbow Five. They might be feasible, however, "under certain auspicious conditions," including a huge augmentation of the Pacific Fleet and absolute security of Singapore,[20] conditions that were patently impossible at any foreseeable date. Kimmel shrugged and said afterward that he never had the means to try.[21]

The possibility of a proxy war through an ally on the Asian continent never gained a following among American planners. Primitive musings that China or Russia, motivated by revenge, would join the United States for the kill were filed away.[22] Cooperation with the Soviet Union seems rarely to have been mentioned.[23] As for China, a nation at war with Japan from 1937 on, the authors of Rainbow Two noted that an Allied advance from Malaysia would open its ports to a flow of arms.[24] In the Rainbow Three drafts of 1940 they asserted that Chinese aid would be essential if Japan did not quit after being rolled back from its island conquests.[25] But an entanglement with China was not an eventuality the Joint Board welcomed, and it did not survive in Rainbow Five. The opening of a major front in China, a strategy the United States tried to pursue during World War II, received little consideration by the military before the American entry into the war. For example, on 5 November 1941 Marshall and Stark dissuaded the president from military gestures to discourage Japan from severing the Burma Road, China's only link to the outside world. To send forces to China, they warned, the services would have to denude the Atlantic and thereby imperil Britain and the Germany-first strategy of Rainbow Five.[26]

Aspirations of sharing a combined Pacific offensive with the Royal Navy fared no better. In 1932 the WPD had suggested that Orange might be defeated by purely naval action if England joined in because empire bases would ease logistical problems and an Allied fleet (even with just the British China and Mediterranean squadrons) would heavily outgun Japan.[27] (This from a staff that had just completed Plan Red to fight Britain!) By late 1939, however, the drafters of Rainbow Three figured that the British would not assist any attack north of the Philippines and perhaps not even one north of Borneo. Army planners who contemplated an "expanded concept" in which a Western alliance would crush Japan with massive power relinquished the thought when the "life and death struggle" in Europe became clear in 1940.[28] By 1941 the planners had written off Britain's offensive power in the Pacific and deeply mistrusted its defensive capability there.

While naval advocates of limited war scenarios tempered the Orange Plan's unbridled offensivism, most still clung to other familiar assumptions of Pacific strategy. Long-term passivity was an unacceptable alternative except to extremists such as Embick, who was content to huddle behind America's sea moats, or Richardson, who called for responses of blockade and raids from afar with perhaps a counterattack in the distant future, if ever.[29] Leahy, however, spoke for the mainstream of naval thought when he told the Senate Naval Affairs Committee in 1939: "The only way that war, once begun, can be brought to a successful conclusion is by making the enemy want to stop fighting. . . . Prompt and effective injury to an enemy at a distance from our shores is the only correct strategy to be employed."[30] Hovering over naval planners were the wraiths of Admiral George Dewey, who believed that "the object of war is to defeat the enemy, [and] that object is best attained when defeat is complete," and Alfred Thayer Mahan, who had long ago instructed the nation that "war once declared must be waged offensively, aggressively. The enemy must not be fended off, but smitten down."[31]

In spite of ponderings of limited war strategies and a dearth of ringing declarations of unlimited goals during the last years of peace, the record shows a bias among naval strategists to pursue the classical objectives of Plan Orange when the opportunity arose. Even at lowest ebb between 1937 and 1941, planners adhered to two of the plan's fundamental theses, that Japan could be defeated by the economic havoc of blockade and bombardment and that a Pacific fight would be a long one.

Submarines were the best weapons for long-distance disruption of Japanese shipping. But the United States was a signatory to the London Naval Conference of 1930 that outlawed unrestricted sinkings. The national mood, recalling the evils of 1917–18, regarded such behavior as abhorrent to "civilized" norms. The Orange Plan had supposed that America would comply with the rules—interception, fair warning, and removal of crews—that would "render a shark a sitting duck." For two decades U.S. submariners had protested the restraints. Their colleagues, who held a Mahanian distaste for *guerre de course*, pointed out that submarines were technically incapable of transpacific patrols. Not until the late 1930s did fast, long-range submersibles enter service. Although designed to operate as adjuncts to the battle fleet, they were also well suited to blockade duty.

In 1941 the navy reviewed the rules afresh, cheered on by the British, who had abandoned all scruples in the face of German U-boat depredations. Rainbow Five adopted a half-measure proposed by the

Naval War College authorizing fleet commanders to declare trade excluded from designated "strategic areas" in the Far East and near Japan. Specific instructions, OpNav added with a figurative wink, would be "issued later." The General Board objected bitterly to the implications of a "sink on sight" policy even though the commanders in chief were piously instructed to comply with international law.[32] As late as October the navy decreed that unrestricted torpedoings would be forbidden—unless justified by events after the outbreak.[33] The only known declaration to the contrary from a high commander was a message of 27 November 1941 from Stark notifying the Asiatic Fleet that it would receive orders to wage "unrestricted sub and aerial warfare" south of a line from Shanghai to Guam.[34] This granted it a free hunting license around Allied territories and Orange bases directly threatening them although with a hint of extension to Japanese waters. From Hawaii Soc McMorris, unburdened by diplomatic niceties, expected Orange merchantmen to be armed or under naval control and therefore legitimate prey everywhere. His plan's dispatch of fleet submarines to Japan in connection with a putative battle plan (Chapter 25) included an alert to the boats to stand by for orders to inflict "maximum damage" on shipping.[35] His surmise was correct. Six hours after the attack on Pearl Harbor, the Navy Department radioed, "Execute unrestricted air and submarine warfare against Japan."[36] The deadly blockade commenced on the first day of war.

Air bombardment of Japan, the other element of siege, had hardly been mentioned in plans since the studies of 1928. In a limited war Japan would sit safely beyond reach of American shore-based bombers. In 1938 Bloch had daydreamed of raids on Japan for psychological effect carried out by flying boats of unspecified type from an unspecified base somewhere in the "Eastern Pacific,"[37] presumably Midway or the Aleutians. Scarcely more realistic were the urgings of Asiatic theater commanders in the spring of 1941 that B-17s from Luzon should bomb southern Japan, which was vetoed by the U.S. high command (Chapter 6), or Op-12 suggestions that air power based in China and maintained via India could strike at Japan.[38]

Carrier raids were the only means left to punish the enemy homeland during a limited war. As early as 1920 Captain Thomas Craven, director of naval aviation, had imagined shipborne planes as "the most direct means by which military pressure could . . . carry the destructive influence of war home to Japan,"[39] but planners of the 1920s had envisioned only surgical strikes on naval bases. A more potent concept was broached in February 1941. OpNav alerted Kimmel to think about carrier attacks on Japan's flammable cities, "ostensibly on military objectives," to divert forces and sap morale. Like it or not, Stark added, the navy might be ordered to do it.[40] The notion may have been planted via the White House from London since British envoys were urging the United States to "a live and active threat" against Japan's industries and cities to help Singapore. Even occasional raids, they claimed, would arouse an outcry and draw off the Combined Fleet more surely than thrashing about in the Mandate. McMorris, ever the hawk, put "the Japanese homeland" on his list of fleet targets. But the idea upset the cautionaries at the WPD. Carriers, they believed, would be "ineffectual" for sustained attacks and best manipulated as potential threats. Turner thought that petty blows would actually soothe enemy trepidations and free the Combined Fleet from home ports.[41] Privately, however, he set about to procure firebombs for "certain naval aircraft task groups [that] may be called upon to employ incendiaries in numbers far in excess of the current allowances." By August 1941 the Bureau of Ordnance had worked out the requirements and set a delivery date of July 1942.[42] On the eve of war, "uncivilized" U-boats and firebombers were being viewed as probable instruments for inflicting the economic devastation of Plan Orange within a Rainbow Five strategy of restricted war goals.

A crucial tenet of the traditional Orange Plan, that a war against Japan would be a long one, unquestionably remained intact in Rainbow Five because the defeat of Germany would absorb U.S. power for several years while the difficulties of campaigning in the Pacific would grow worse as Japan looted its conquests and dug in. There was also the issue of building a vastly superior fleet contemplated by a few naval analysts of the 1920s and 1930s to overcome distance and attrition. In 1939 the JPC calculated the capital ship strength that Blue would have to deploy to assure parity for battle after detaching units for base defense, escort, invasions, raids, and blockade. An advantage of four to three was reckoned as ample in the Marshalls, where a sea battle was unlikely and big ships could act in support of landings. A five-to-three margin of battleships and carriers (the old treaty ratio) would be needed in the central Mandate. A six-to-three edge would be essential when approaching the Philippines to compensate for stretched-out communications and intensified attrition from the air.[43] It would take years to build such a navy. Many analysts believed that just getting the fleet into position by capturing and developing advanced bases would take a long time. Roosevelt, it was reported, "doubted" that the Marshalls or Carolines could be seized until the second or third year.[44]

Stark believed that the industrial and civil engineering works of Base Two would take two to five years to construct.[45] Richardson, scornful of those who imagined the fleet could "sail away, kick Orange and be back at home in a year or so," predicted a Pacific conflict lasting five to ten years.[46] On the brink of war, American leaders had no illusions that a struggle against Japan, even one for limited objectives, would be brief.

Notwithstanding the deliberate vagueness of Rainbow Five, the aggressive compulsions of War Plan Orange lived on in the search for means to implement a siege and attain ultimate victory in a long war. Informal processes of memory and conviction carried these war aims and other hallowed precepts of the ancient strategy through the years of doubt, preserved for instinctive application when the shooting began. For all that some strategists rustled about for softer solutions, or simply deferred thinking about how to finish the war, the logic of the old plan was compelling. It was never far from the minds of those who formulated strategy when the war came.

The American Way of Planning: The Planners at War

When war came, the United States relied on peacetime experience as the foundation of its planning system. There were modifications and additions, of course, but strategy making for the Pacific followed recognizable patterns of earlier days. Table 27.1 contrasts the multilayered planning system of World War II with the simpler prewar setup.[1]

Franklin D. Roosevelt and Prime Minister Winston Churchill carved the world into three strategic sectors. The Allies shared responsibility in all, but the United States was paramount in the Pacific and Britain in the Middle East and Indian Ocean. In the Atlantic-European theater they joined in a unified command. The direction of planning for all theaters was entrusted to a senior military committee, the Combined Chiefs of Staff (CCS). In the Pacific, however, the CCS was more symbolic than real. Britain's junior voice was heard infrequently, usually to protest diversions of strength from the Atlantic. After a year or two it faded to a whisper, and the United States ran the Pacific war almost unhindered as it had long expected to do.

The president, as head of state and commander in chief of the armed

TABLE 27.1 U.S. Prewar and Wartime Command and Planning Agencies for Pacific War

Prewar Orange Plan Era	World War II
No alliances.	Combined Chiefs of Staff (CCS). U.S. and British service chiefs. Reported to President and Prime Minister. Allied grand strategy.
	Combined Staff Planners (CSP). Permanent planning staff of CCS.
Joint Board (JB), 1903–41. Consultative Army-Navy Board. Appointed individuals, 1903–18, service chiefs and Directors of War Plans Divisions ex officio, 1919–41. Reported to Secretaries of War and Navy, 1903–39, to President, 1939–Aug 41, to service chiefs, Sep 1941. National war plans. Minor in WWII. Joint Planning Committee (JPC), 1919–41, Joint Strategic Committee, 1941. Chiefs and selected staff members of Army and Navy WPDs. Joint war plans for Joint Board. Army and Navy Sections of JPC.	Joint Chiefs of Staff (JCS). Three U.S. service chiefs plus personal Chief of Staff of President. Reported to President. National grand strategy, inter-Allied and interservice matters.
	Joint Staff Planners (JPS). Chief planners and chief air planners of Army and Navy as part-time duty. Senior war plans arm of JCS.
	Joint U.S. Strategic Committee (JUSSC), 1942, renamed Joint War Plans Committee (JWPC), 1943–45. Planning advisers from all services. Working staff of JPS for war plans.
	Other JCS committees on logistics, transportation, intelligence, etc. Input to war plans, supporting plans.
	Joint Strategic Survey Committee (JSSC). "Retired elders," advice to JCS on strategy.
Army Chief of Staff, 1903–41.	Army Chief of Staff.
Army War Plans Division (AWPD), 1903–41. War plans, mainly mobilization and logistical.	Operations Division (OPD), ex AWPD.
	Strategy and Plans (S&P) Group of OPD. Strategic plans, later review and liaison.
	Theater (Operations) Group of OPD. Theater liaison, planning of details.

No Army theater commands.	Supreme Commander Southwest Pacific. Theater planning staff.
General Board (GB), 1903–41. By appointment. Advisory "elders." Reported to Secretary of the Navy. Naval war plans, 1900–1923 except 1910–11. Second Committee of GB. Naval war plans, 1901–19.	Not significant.
Chief of Naval Operations (CNO), 1915–41.	Chief of Naval Operations (CNO) and CinC U.S. Fleet (Cominch).
War Plans Division (WPD, Op-12), 1919–41. Naval war plans. Op-12A Policy and Projects Section, Op-12B, Plans Section, 1928–41.	Assistant Chief of Staff for Plans, F-1. Cominch Plans Division, F-12. Broad naval war plans. Ex Op-12B. Logistics Plans Division. Ex Op-12A. Futures Plans Section, F-126, 1942–43.
Commander in Chief U.S. Fleet (CinCUS), 1919–40, Commander in Chief Pacific Fleet (CinCPac), 1941. War Plans Officer, 1935–40, War Plans Section, 1941. Fleet war plans.	Commander in Chief Pacific Fleet (CinCPac) and CinC Pacific Ocean Areas. Fleet staff and war planners. Pacific Fleet operating plans. Subsidiary commands and planning staffs, e.g., Third Fleet, Fifth Fleet, amphibious commands.
Naval War College (NWC). Orange planning studies, 1906–9, naval war plans, 1910–11. Army War College. Orange planning studies.	Not significant.

forces, held supreme responsibility for direction of the American war effort. Continuing his practices of 1939 onward, he focused on large matters of mobilization, dealings with Allies, articulation of war aims, and theater priorities. He rarely intervened in campaign strategy in the Pacific. Exceptions such as the Doolittle raid on Tokyo or MacArthur's liberation of Manila were usually politically motivated. Roosevelt tended to be reactive rather than creative. He did not personally direct military strategy in the style of Churchill, Hitler, or Stalin. As in prewar days, it was left mainly to the admirals and generals.

Congress and civil officials, including the secretaries of the army and navy, continued to play negligible roles in operational planning. This suited the uniformed commanders, who rarely concerned themselves with nonmilitary objectives. The navy, especially, agreed with the founding authors of Plan Orange of three decades earlier that it understood national policy and could independently decide its own best course.

Most wartime planning agencies evolved from the existing establishment. New entities arose and old ones mutated, but the pluralistic American way of planning persisted. Whatever the formal structures, exhortations of outspoken officers could still override them.

Interservice cooperation in Washington was fairly good during the Pacific war—far better than that of the quarrelsome Japanese army and navy. High commanders did not often dispute geopolitics or grand strategy. Their wranglings usually concerned the designs of campaigns.

The Joint Chiefs of Staff (JCS), a descendant of the Joint Board, emerged as the principal agency to prosecute the war under the president. The old board shriveled to insignificance. Of the four JCS members, the two service chieftains, General Marshall and Admiral King, had the strongest say. Arnold of the Army Air Forces usually sided with Marshall. Admiral Leahy, the president's personal chief of staff, acted as impartial chairman. King's devotion to the "navy's war" and the army's preoccupation with Europe meant that his was the foremost will on Pacific matters. He encouraged an early counteroffensive and masterminded the maritime grand strategy.

The planning staff of the Joint Chiefs, known as the Joint Strategic Committee (JSC) and later as the Joint War Plans Committee (JWPC), paralleled the prewar Joint Planning Committee. Like its predecessor, it was staffed by competent professionals who worked together effectively on interservice matters.

There was no exact equivalent of the independent naval staffs of

1906–14 that had identified the great strategic principles—what a later age would call think tanks. The closest analog was the Joint Strategic Survey Committee (JSSC), a council of three retired officers with links to the past who rendered advice on high strategy with "unusual wisdom and objectivity."[2] Admiral Russell Willson, an aide to Clarence Williams when the latter wrote the first plan for the central Pacific, and General Embick, a thinker on strategy since early in the century whose opinion Marshall valued[3] and who recanted his defensivism, favored the Orange Plan solution and assisted mightily in persuading doubters.

The army centralized its war planning in a new Operations Division (OPD), a descendant of the Army War Plans Division. Like its predecessor, it focused on mobilization. In a service that had little experience in wide-angle campaign planning the responsibility for operational programs soon gravitated to theater commanders far from the capital.

As expected, no unified command was established in the Pacific. But the arrangement chosen was nothing like the one expected before the war. In the 1920s the army had rejected a unified theater leadership under a naval officer (and perhaps under a general late in the war, which would have occurred if an invasion of Japan had been mounted in 1945). The prewar idea of co-management by equals, with the service having "paramount interest" at the moment supposedly dominating choices, was untenable. It gave way to a solution that sprang from circumstances early in the war. Marshall, anxious to help the soldiers trapped on Luzon by the Japanese onslaught, summoned Brigadier General Dwight D. Eisenhower to the Army War Plans Division. MacArthur's former aide recommended only token efforts to help the Philippine garrison and consignment of available forces to Australia as a base for long-term resurgence. In March 1942 MacArthur was extracted from Corregidor by presidential order and awarded responsibility for holding Australia and islands to its north. The general clamored to launch a counterblow through his sector, but the navy refused to serve under army direction and the army would not subordinate him to an admiral. In a face-saving compromise the Joint Chiefs carved the Pacific into separate jurisdictions under MacArthur and Nimitz (Map 28.1), a split that continued until nearly the end of the war. Within each theater interservice relations were relatively harmonious. Outside the boundaries that was not always the case.

In the army's Southwest Pacific theater the magisterial general and his intensely loyal staff took over planning. MacArthur was offensive-

328 • WAR PLAN ORANGE

minded although cautionary in his style of campaigning. Marshall and the OPD nearly always backed his plans despite their necessary favoring of the Atlantic front with larger reinforcements.

Naval planning, like the peacetime experience, was complex, overlapping, and frequently reshuffled. After Pearl Harbor King took over the dormant title of commander in chief of the United States Fleet—rebaptized Cominch in lieu of the embarrassing "Sink-Us"—which endowed him with hands-on control of fleet strategy. Stark, having been tarnished by Pearl Harbor, was sent to Europe in March 1942, and King took on the mantle of chief of naval operations. But administration bored the admiral; he left the running of OpNav to others. Vice-CNO Frederick J. Horne, prolific writer of Orange Plans of the 1920s, took charge of the material side of the navy's war, assisted by a Logistics Plans Group descended from Op-12A, the former Policy and Projects half of Op-12.

King relished the job of supercommander of the fleets and spent 90 percent of his time on it.[4] He recruited Kelly Turner as assistant chief of staff for plans (F-1). Turner converted Op-12B, the Plans Section of the WPD, into the Cominch Plans Division (F-12). Within a few months, however, King preempted Savvy Cooke as his F-1 to plan the transition to Phase II of the war. Later Rear Admirals Bernhard H. Bieri and Donald B. Duncan filled the headquarters planning job, but King always relied on Cooke, despite the latter's frail health, as his "chief strategical advisor"[5] holding successive titles of deputy chief and chief of staff. The team of King (a man willing to take "very considerable calculated risks"[6]) and Cooke, thrusters both and loyal to the traditions of the Orange Plan, shaped the Pacific war to fit its mold.

After Pearl Harbor Admiral Chester W. Nimitz was appointed commander in chief of the Pacific Fleet and of the Pacific Ocean Areas, a naval theater encompassing that part of the ocean not reserved to MacArthur or to a short-lived Allied command of the Malay Barrier. Nimitz decided to retain Kimmel's staff, including McMorris and McCormick as war planners. During 1942 most of the prewar naval strategists of Hawaii and Washington drifted off to ship and operational commands, leaving the JCS and its staff to plan campaigns in the Southwest Pacific. Many of them were recalled to Oahu after the middle of 1943 for the central Pacific push. Nimitz, impressed with Sherman's "erudition and genius" and his aviation credentials, selected him as top fleet planner. "Ask Forrest" became the byword at Pearl Harbor. Soc McMorris headed the fleet's joint planning activities and mastered operational details. Carl Moore came out from the JWPC as

A long-range scouting plane was essential to planning a cautionary drive through the central Pacific. These later Catalina VPs were little changed from those first ordered by the navy in 1933. (U.S. Naval Institute)

The U.S. Fleet at anchor at Lahaina Roads, Hawaii, before the war. The anchorage was to have been the assembly point for the Blue offensive because Pearl Harbor could not accommodate heavy warships. (NH 77331, Naval Historical Center)

Vision of the great Blue offensive: U.S. battleships, 1938. (Watercolor by Arthur Beaumont, NH 89577, Naval Historical Center)

Part of U.S. Pacific Fleet, Majuro, 1944. An advanced naval Base One at a lagoon of the Marshall Islands was the first goal of the War Plan Orange offensive. (80-G-253060, National Archives)

Japanese base on Truk under attack by U.S. aircraft in 1944. Truk was
scheduled to become Base Two in War Plan Orange but was bypassed,
and the magnificent facilities designed for it were installed on other
islands of comparable strategic location. (80-G-227427, National
Archives)

The Blue offensive timetable depended on getting floating drydocks to
the western Pacific. Cautionaries believed their lack would prolong the
war. Not until World War II were docks like these (at Manus)
constructed. (80-G-380416, National Archives)

Wake Island, inadequate as a naval base, was nevertheless the focus of American attack plans in 1941. Seven VPs anchored in the lagoon and a Pan Am Clipper at the dock demonstrate its value for flying boats. (80-G-451194, National Archives)

Navy Department, Washington, D.C., in 1942. Most versions of War Plan Orange were crafted in this building. (80-G-33183, National Archives)

Admiral Harold R. Stark, chief of naval operations, August 1939 to March 1942. The author of the beat-Germany-first policy was ambivalent about offensive war plans for the Pacific. (80-G-42569, National Archives)

"Terrible Turner," Stark's director of war plans, shown during the war. After completing the global design of Plan Rainbow Five he left detailed campaign planning to the Pacific Fleet. (80-G-309855, National Archives)

Commander-in-Chief J. O. Richardson, an arch-defensivist who despised Plan Orange. In 1940 he succeeded in slowing the offensive timetable but was sacked by President Roosevelt. Vice Admiral William S. Pye [right] was a three-time director of the War Plans Division in earlier years. (NH 77336, Naval Historical Center)

"Savvy" Cooke, the most thrusting naval war planner in the last years of peace, kept the spirit of the Pacific offensive alive in a multi-threat world. (80-G-302333, National Archives)

Admiral Husband E. Kimmel, commander-in-chief of the Pacific Fleet in 1941, was the scapegoat for the debacle at Pearl Harbor. Kimmel had hoped to induce a gunnery engagement against the Japanese battle line at the outset of war. (NH 48588, Naval Historical Center)

"Soc" (for Socrates) McMorris, Kimmel's war planner in 1941; who worked out a fighting plan to ambush the Imperial Japanese Navy. (NH 89414, Naval Historical Center)

Forrest P. Sherman, a
brilliant young aviator
who became Nimitz's top
planner during the war
and chief of naval opera-
tions afterward. He influenced prewar plans
significantly despite his
modest rank of com-
mander. (80-G- 16543,
National Archives)

Commander Chester W. Nimitz
[right] in 1923 with a director of
the War Plans Division. Nimitz
studied at the Naval War College
under Clarence Williams, the most
farsighted of all Orange Plan
authors, a graphic illustration of
the continuity of U.S. strategy over
half a century. (NH 58313, Naval
Historical Center)

Cover of the 1922 Orange Plan
signed by the chief of naval
operations and the secretary of the
navy.

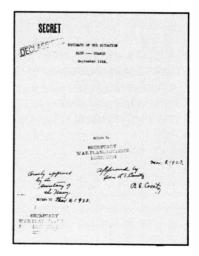

chief of staff to Admiral Raymond Spruance. Turner and Hill took charge of the amphibious business, a specialty in which sophisticated planning know-how was crucial. As the central Pacific offensive began to roll, Nimitz and Company assumed control of campaign planning, and the thrusting psychology inherited from prewar fleet planners overcame the cautionary policy necessitated by early defeats.

Other former strategists found niches in staff work. Lynde McCormick became head logistical planner for the Joint Chiefs of Staff. Education called some, including Kalbfus and Pye to the War College, Murphy to the Naval Postgraduate School, and Magruder to a training slot. Standley, the only chief planner to rise to CNO until Sherman did the trick in 1951, served as ambassador to the Soviet Union. Few planners got operating plums other than the amphibians. The prime exceptions were two former WPD directors who had moved to higher posts in OpNav before the war: Ingersoll commanding the Atlantic Fleet and Ghormley briefly in charge in the Southwest Pacific. The seagoing supremos of the Pacific, Halsey and Spruance, had never served in Op-12, although Spruance had taught strategy at Newport. The great task forces they took to sea became the property of airmen with little war planning background. Only a few other fighting leaders had done a hitch in the WPD, including Admirals Hart of the Asiatic Fleet, Wilson Brown, Robert A. Theobald, A. S. Carpender, and submariner Robert H. English, and Generals Thomas Holcomb and Holland Smith of the Marine Corps.

The personal traits of the navy's ablest strategists were the same as those on the General Board's checklist of 1900. All were line officers with long experience at sea, men of high intelligence who had an aptitude for the work. The vital attribute of good judgment remained as mysterious as ever—it could reflect "unremitting study" or "imagination, even dreams"—but both styles were useful and even coexisted in the most competent individuals. The naval planners made no blunders of decisive consequence during the war.

The stereotyping of gallant old warriors as thrusters and modern managers as cautionaries no longer held true after the war began. Both aggressiveness and prudence seemed to correlate better with lifelong attitudes. Preachers of firm action such as King, MacArthur, Halsey, Cooke, and McMorris remained true to form. So did cautionaries such as Turner, Sherman, and Moore. Early in Phase II, from about mid-1942 to mid-1943, the cautionary view emphasizing small gains with economy of force and low risk necessarily dominated campaign plans. But as U.S. military power waxed, cautionaries joined the thrusting faction, goaded on by the old fear of public intolerance for an excessively long war. The swing from gradualism to boldness reversed a four-decade trend of naval planning.

Wartime planning papers were drawn in the format prescribed in 1910. An Estimate of the Situation with four elements (mission, enemy circumstances, own circumstances, and courses of action) set the stage for a final element, the decision. Logistical plans evolved as works of intricate detail. One may ask whether the authors consulted the prewar plans. They did not do so literally, as cookbooks. The most detailed of 1941 plans, WPPac-46, was checked out of OpNav's safe three times in 1942 and then gathered dust until the postwar investigations.[7] Old plans were not mentioned in wartime strategy papers and rarely in later memoirs. Nevertheless, first drafts of campaign plans such as those for seizing the Mandate in 1944 echoed exact concepts and sometimes exact phrases of the Orange Plans.[8] It was not necessary to study the old plans again. Hundreds of officers already had done so. Wartime plans were "an almost unbroken continuation of prewar planning."[9] The decision makers of World War II carried the Orange strategy "genetically encoded" in their memories.

The American way of planning for war in the Pacific continued as it had always been: pluralistic, diffuse as to responsibility, competitive, and untidy—but it worked.

Plan Orange at War: The Ocean Strategy Implemented

T he remaining chapters will compare the U.S. Pacific strategy of World War II with the Orange Plan to determine to what extent the plan was implemented. It is assumed that the reader is familiar with the main episodes of the war; hence source notes to well-known events and strategic decisions are omitted.

War Plan Orange has been defined in this work as synonymous with strategies broadly accepted by the American leadership before the war, whether called Orange or Rainbow and whether found in official plans or informal writings and opinions of responsible officials. This treatment comports with the free-form American way of designing war plans. Those older versions of the plan that were repudiated before the war—the "failed strategies"—have been excluded from the definition. Those that were not explicitly superseded have been included even if not recently updated, for example, the siege of Japan set forth in the plans of the 1920s, a subject not restudied until 1943–45.

The Orange Plan as understood at the outbreak of hostilities posited a sudden strike by Japan to eject the United States from the western Pacific so it could protect the flank of its conquests of China and

Southeast Asia. Japan would then settle into a long war of attrition to retain sea mastery and eventually negotiate to retain most of its profits. The authors of Plan Orange judged this policy to be a fatal miscalculation because the United States would choose to fight long and hard to defeat Japan unconditionally. The nation would amass forces of enormous power, launch a transpacific counterattack to gain advanced bases and control of the sea by battle, and reduce Japan by blockade and air bombardment. The overarching themes were that sea (and air) power would neutralize a formidable ground army and that victory would flow from destruction of the enemy's economy. These geopolitical and grand strategic principles that had endured for three and a half decades remained valid, as Chapter 1 has shown, in spite of the concurrent war in Europe and its effects on mobilizations, alliances, and the extent of the Pacific combat zone.

Historians have been unkind to War Plan Orange. Although no comprehensive study has heretofore been compiled, several scholars have criticized it harshly, and most others have accepted their views.[1] The plan has been condemned as "little more than [an] abstract exercise" and "a literary artifact" irrelevant to a world war.[2] Certain defects have been claimed, unfairly, to have nullified it. The United States *was* too weak before the war to execute it, but it does not follow that offensive planning should therefore have ceased.[3] The services *did* have self-serving motives—the navy needed a dramatic mission and the plan certainly helped it win budget battles—but to dismiss it as a bureaucratic ploy, "a building plan [not] a sailing plan," is myopic. The untidy American planning system and the navy's stubborn offensiveness have been labeled faults[4] rather than strengths that kept the strategy alive and relevant.

A common misconception that the plan was designed to save the Philippines has brought about a slew of criticisms: that U.S. deficiencies (including lack of a western base) made it "an exercise in frustration"; that a slow central Pacific offensive rendered it "even more unrealistic than before"; that prewar atoll bases were intended (and failed) to save Manila;[5] and that MacArthur's inability to repel the Japanese on the Luzon beaches "spelled the doom for War Plan Orange." Other reproofs have been patently wrong. Underfunding did not mean failure of the strategy, nor was it more costly than conceivable alternatives.[6] The offensive agenda was not a trick to lure Britain into an alliance.[7] To assert that Plan Orange did not provide details of operations or establish a long-range program for the defeat of Japan is absurd. And the claim that "a total war strategy was simply not compatible with naval warfare"[8] is a complete error.

Praise of the Orange Plan has been guarded. A few rare plaudits appear in an unpublished paper by the Office of the Chief of Military History acknowledging that "it succeeded quite well, if less than perfectly," as a tool of national policy, in the limited sense of helping leaders "distinguish quickly and clearly between hopes and possibilities" once they calibrated it to real-war conditions.[9]

The poor reputation of the plan is the result of lapses in research. Many of the planning papers remained classified "secret" until the 1960s or 1970s. The army historians apparently looked only at joint and army documents, not at the voluminous naval records. The official navy operational histories of Samuel Eliot Morison and most private works also missed the prewar naval story. Some scholars drew negative conclusions from examining the failed strategies. There has also been an unfortunate tendency to focus on certain details of the plan which were wrong or simply quaint rather than on principles that stood the test of time.

The Prussian strategist Count Helmuth von Moltke the elder once said, "No plan survives contact with the enemy."[10] On 7 December 1941, while the smoke still roiled across Pearl Harbor, the United States activated Plans Rainbow Five and Navy WPL-46 but annulled their attack missions in the Pacific. Their scrappy progeny, Fleet Plan WPPac-46, was canceled. The maimed Pacific Fleet would not sortie immediately to divert Orange by raid or battle. The Atlantic Fleet, its recent increments hastening back to the Pacific, would not relieve the Royal Navy for Singapore. Arms for Rabaul were canceled. The navy hunkered down in the strategic triangle to defend the eastern Pacific and to maintain contact with outposts in those waters and along the line to Australia. The sole shred of offensive response that survived the first awful day was the directive to execute unrestricted air and submarine warfare against Japan.

In the Atlantic Rainbow Five's premises remained intact. The United States reaffirmed its commitment to beat Germany first. As the war unfolded, however, the corollary of holding Japan with minimal force for several years was discarded. American dedication to the Pacific was substantial, exceeding that in the Atlantic in naval effort throughout and rivaling it in ground forces until 1944. U.S. policy was thus a "near paradox of an unwavering commitment to a Europe-first strategy and an almost equal expenditure of effort in the Pacific."[11]

Rainbow Five neither identified the long-range objective of fighting Japan nor fixed a complete strategy or timetable. When the United States cured those omissions during the second year of war, the design it chose was a clone of Plan Orange.

Prewar strategists had foreseen a war of three phases shaped by geography. Japan's offensive of Phase I, which lasted for six months, has been compared to their expectations in Chapters 5 and 6. In summary, the violation of the eastern Pacific on the opening day did not vitiate its function as an American sanctuary and springboard for future offensives. When Japan tried to penetrate the region a second time, it reaped defeat at Midway. In the western Pacific the Philippine garrison failed in an ill-advised strategic defense, fell back on the Plan Orange citadels of Bataan and Corregidor, and, with no hope of relief, succumbed. Similar Japanese amphibious blitzkriegs secured Malaysia and its resources. As in Plan Orange, the U.S. response was to deploy sea raiders to interdict the resource traffic. Phase I ended with the naval victory at Midway in June 1942, a battle noted in Chapter 25 as resembling somewhat the expectations of the fleet planners of 1941.

The most analyzed aspect of Plan Orange over its long life was the Blue offensive of Phase II. It was to begin at Japan's outer defense line on M + 180 and end when an expanded fleet and an expeditionary army were established at bases in the Philippines and on intermediate islands. American leaders never doubted that they would counterattack when conditions allowed. The key strategic choice, as in prewar plans, was the route of advance. A maritime drive by Blue forces from the Indian Ocean, rejected at the dawn of Orange planning, remained unthinkable even though other campaigns from that quarter, such as recovery of Burma to aid the Chinese, had their adherents. Approaches to the Japanese Empire from the west were no more viable in 1944 than in 1907. The Chinese were incompetent, the British disdainful of them and averse to a strong offensive, and the United States unwilling to expend much strength in that theater. The high road to Japan still ran through the Pacific.

Wartime strategists reviewed all the transocean routes again. A northern advance via the Aleutians, scorned since Mahan's sophomoric plea of 1911, was reexamined out of frustration with slow progress elsewhere. The evils listed in the Orange Plan—weather, topography, logistics, remoteness from vital objectives—were still daunting so schemes for seizing the Kuriles as bomber fields or invading the home island of Hokkaido were blackballed. Soviet contributions such as lending Siberian airfields or opening a land front in Manchuria were mooted as dazzling prospects, but Stalin had no intention of enlisting against Japan until Hitler was finished. The north remained a strategic backwater.

After the Japanese drive had been halted in the spring of 1942, the situation favored an initial counterstroke in the Southwest Pacific. Since the beginning of the war the navy's second-priority assignment (after holding the U.S.-Hawaii-Midway line) had been to maintain sea and air links with Australia by erecting a chain of island bases and patrolling and raiding along the line. The mission had culminated in the May 1942 Battle of the Coral Sea, which thwarted Japanese penetration toward Australia and guaranteed that the communications line would be held.

The islands of the Southwest Pacific were large and mostly unfortified. MacArthur and his staff concocted a two-pronged advance through New Guinea and the Solomon Islands to retake Rabaul, where the Japanese were developing a base dominating the region. Army planes and Australian troops were available for New Guinea. The navy and marines could blunt Japan's creep through the Solomons by operating from stations improvised on islands to the south and from rear bases in Australia and New Zealand. Conversely, the preferred target of Plan Orange, the Marshall Islands, lay two thousand miles from any U.S. base and beyond the grasp of a weakened fleet lacking sophisticated means of assaulting hardened targets. Guadalcanal was nowhere near Eniwetok, but the old plan was almost correct in one particular: the marines initiated Phase II on 7 August 1942, just two months later than the postulated kickoff date.

Admiral King called the Southwest Pacific attrition campaign of 1942–43 the offensive-defensive phase of the war; the true offensive began, he said, in late 1943, when Allied bases were no longer threatened and the United States could attack when and where it chose.[12] Over the years of peacetime planning the expected locale of Japanese efforts to sap U.S. strength and morale had migrated outward, from the Ryukyus to the Philippines and eventually to the Mandate. In fact, Japan chose to wage attrition battles throughout the war, but it did so most effectively on the approaches to Rabaul, in jungle grapplings, combats aloft by day and in narrow straits by night, and in ten sea battles. It confounded old presumptions that it would resist lightly in fringe regions of no great importance and conserve its sting for the inner defense zone.

If wrong as to location and time, the prewar analysts were partially correct as to the scale of enemy efforts. A 1939 estimate that Orange would commit sixty warships and its entire naval air arm to attrition in distant seas was borne out. But Japan did not rigorously hoard its big ships. It willingly exposed carriers and battleships on several occasions. But the outcome of the campaign validated the prediction that Blue would prevail. Warship casualties in the Southwest Pacific were about equal, but the United States was able to restock and Japan was not. Japanese air forces were savaged; factories made good the losses, but ace pilots were irreplaceable and their successors were later slaughtered in the North Pacific. Japanese transports, not American, slid beneath the waves with their battalions aboard. When it was over, the grim tally of the South Pacific attrition campaign had not altered the grand design of Plan Orange. By the end of 1943 the United States was ready to mount a drive toward vital objectives.

A southern offensive had been a necessity in 1942, as even King acknowledged. But after one year of campaigning, the United States had advanced less than two hundred miles in the Solomons and New Guinea. At that rate it might take fifteen years to reach Tokyo! A sense of urgency to speed up the war began to envelop Washington. The choices for acceleration boiled down to two: bypass the citadel of Rabaul and break out of the "Bismarcks Barrier" toward the Philippines, or launch the ocean blitzkrieg of War Plan Orange.

The mid-Pacific had been the navy's favored avenue of attack since 1907, even before Japan acquired Micronesia. The region had been embraced by planners of various schools for divergent motives: by the Guam lobby to further its pet project, by Through Ticket zealots in quest of speed, and by cautionaries eyeing a "natural line of advance" that was secure and flexible. After 1933 the Royal Road to Truk formed virtually the whole of the formal Orange Plan. Even gun-shy cautionaries of 1939–41 had blessed a slowed-down Mandate drive and Blue outlying bases to support it. King had been fascinated by the central Pacific route at the War College games in 1933. Later in the 1930s he had promoted it as VP commander, advocate of atoll bases, and sponsor of a bold movement along the northern rim of the Mandate. In 1942 he proposed to begin Phase II at a place closer than Guadalcanal to the Mandate, in the Ellice, Santa Cruz, or Gilbert groups, but Nimitz and Halsey resisted the idea as unfocused and leading nowhere.

In mid-1943, as carriers and shock divisions were reaching the Pacific in quantity, King and Cooke urged the opening of the ocean front. This time they persuaded the fleet strategists because the wide sea was best suited to the new task forces and a place where the imperial main body would more surely fight. The drive could be launched from great bases on the West Coast and Hawaii. It could progress rapidly through useful islands spaced at wide intervals and put American forces in position to bomb Japan and lunge at a variety of Far Eastern objectives. And to the liking of the independent-minded navy, no Allies need be involved and the army only in a supporting role.

In 1944 Americans crossed the Pacific via both the central and southern routes. Discussion of the latter campaign is deferred to Chapter 30, which deals with wartime strategies not contemplated in Plan Orange. The remainder of this chapter addresses the central Pacific offensive. As analogies with Plan Orange are drawn, an intriguing phenomenon will emerge. At first, the United States enacted campaigns resembling its most recent prewar conceptions. As it plunged farther to the west, it followed strategies of the 1930s, then those prescribed in the 1920s, and finally, as it neared Japan, the primordial plans of the Dewey-Mahan era. It was not a perfect regression but close enough to remark that, like a film run backward, U.S. strategy rolled backward in time (Table 28.1 and Map 28.1).

The congruence of Orange and wartime plans may be conveniently assessed by viewing the ocean drive as three successive movements. The opening strokes in eastern Micronesia conformed roughly with the prewar sequence. The Gilbert Islands furnished a preliminary position in lieu of Wake, followed by the advance into the western Marshalls that procured Base One and bypassed other Japanese fortresses. The next stage, however, diverged significantly from the old itinerary. Truk was neutralized and Base Two was erected instead at Manus, a fine harbor obtained in an unexpected coup by MacArthur's men. In a momentous strategic decision the navy then shifted the axis of advance to the Marianas, a group often considered by planners before the war but not one of their definite goals. The final movement of Phase II, through the western Mandate to the southern Philippines, returned to a closer approximation of the old strategy.

Only a few of the islands the Americans seized in the central Pacific were those specifically designated in Plan Orange (although the old choices were carefully scrutinized). Except for the decision to go to the Marianas instead of Truk, however, the changes were rather nominal because the chosen targets served the plan's strategic aims as well as or better than the original selections.

The opening U.S. attacks of November 1943 to February 1944 delivered the prewar goals of a low-cost penetration of Japan's outer

TABLE 28.1 *Sequence of Plans for Phase II Offensive, 1906–1941: Selected Campaigns, in Approximate Chronological Order of Appearance in Orange Plans*

☐ = closest approximation to World War II strategy

Campaigns in order of execution in World War II	← Oldest Concept		Latest Concept →	
Mandate campaign concept	Ignore Mandate (Through Ticket)	Use for brief replenishment, possibly surreptitiously	Occupy for communications after fleet in Philippines	Occupy step by step, develop fleet bases
Pre-Marshalls outpost	None (Pre–air age)	Johnston (air staging)	Wake	Gilberts
Marshalls campaign	Occupy whole group from east to west	Take eastern atoll, neutralize rest	Take western atoll, neutralize rest	
Eastern Carolines campaign	No value	Take high islands en route to Truk	Bypass high islands	
Central Carolines campaign	Occupy atolls near Truk	Occupy Truk[a] as Base Two after Marshalls	Prewar fleet base at Rabaul instead	
Marianas campaign	Prewar fleet base on Guam or else bypass and take after Philippines	Occupy as long-range air base, induce naval battle, decisive politically	Develop Guam as prewar scouting base	
Western Carolines campaign	Bypass	Occupy Palaus and/or atolls	Bypass, occupy Palaus after Philippines if necessary	
Southern Philippines campaign	Ignore or pause briefly for replenishment of fleet	Major western base	Temporary western base, roll-up to Manila	Advance from East Indies (Rainbow 2)
Largest fleet battle	Near Philippines, midwar	Near Japan, late war	Philippine Sea area, midwar	Central Pacific, early war

[a] Base Two at Manus in lieu of Truk.

barrier and a site for Base One. The sequence of steps—approach to the Marshalls, the Marshalls campaign, and bypassing of the eastern Carolines—conformed to Orange Plan precepts.

It was natural that Wake Island, the focal point of offensive plans between 1939 and 1941, should be eyed as the first stepping-stone, yet the atoll was destined to disappoint the hopes invested in it. Kimmel's dream of catching an Orange naval detachment there came closest to reality. A week after Pearl Harbor he sent his carriers out to cover a reinforcement of the beleaguered marines, but a combination of bad luck, bad weather, and cold feet in Washington induced Pye (temporarily in charge pending Nimitz's arrival) to sound the recall as they closed unknowingly on two Japanese carriers. The island fell. For a fleet battle in the central Pacific, Midway provided the lure six months later. Other sea battles might have occurred near Wake on two other occasions when the fleet raided in the vicinity and powerful enemy task forces sortied in vain to catch it. It happened in February 1942 and again in October 1943 when Admiral Mineichi Koga with six battleships escorted by carriers rushed to Eniwetok and nearly to Wake.

In prewar plans Wake's air power was supposed to provide cover for landings on Eniwetok. Wartime planners, in search of a preliminary base before tackling the Marshalls, replayed the 1941 comparison of Wake (for bold penetration and possible fleet encounter) against the Gilberts (a prudent step from a safe quarter). At a strategy meeting in January 1943 King pressed for his old favorite, the Midway-Wake-Eniwetok axis, for a speedier advance and to "whipsaw" the Japanese in the South Pacific, but his staff preferred the safer path. Cooke steered the joint planners toward a compromise of reaching Eniwetok by short hops through the Marshalls, which eliminated a difficult operation to recapture Wake without the help of land-based aircraft. (Only Nimitz's air deputy John Towers thought carriers could handle the job alone.) Besides, Wake was no sea base because the Japanese had not completed the channel, and it was not worth much for post-Marshalls operations. The decision was made to leave it alone to starve for the rest of the war.

The Gilberts, the pet islands of the 1941 cautionaries, were nominated. In November 1943 Tarawa and Makin were occupied. A hundred B-24s from the Ellice Islands carried out warm-up raids of the kind once imagined as spewing from Blue atolls. The Gilberts served adequately for air support of the Marshalls campaign but otherwise yielded few benefits except a high-cost lesson in amphibious tactics at Tarawa. The Orange fleet, its carrier squadrons having recently been shot down defending Rabaul, did not appear.[13]

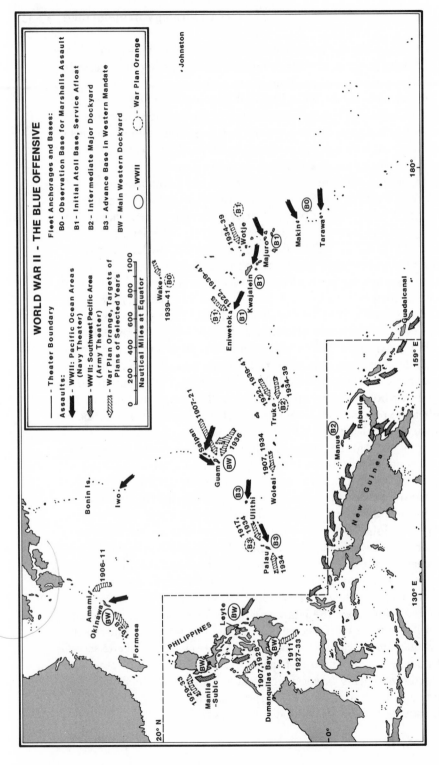

WORLD WAR II - THE BLUE OFFENSIVE

Fleet Anchorages and Bases:
BO - Observation Base for Marshalls Assault
B1 - Initial Atoll Base, Service Afloat
B2 - Intermediate Major Dockyard
B3 - Advance Base in Western Mandate
BW - Main Western Dockyard

○ - WWII   ⊂⊃ - War Plan Orange

--- - Theater Boundary

Assaults:
▼ - WWII: Pacific Ocean Areas (Navy Theater)
◁ - WWII: Southwest Pacific Area (Army Theater)
◿ - War Plan Orange, Targets of Plans of Selected Years

0 200 400 600 800 1000
Nautical Miles at Equator

Johnston

Bonin Is.
Iwo
Amami
Okinawa 1906-11
(BW) 1898
Formosa

PHILIPPINES
Leyte (BW)
Manila -Subic (BW) 1928-33
Dumanquilas Bay (BW) 1911 1927-33
1907, 1925

Palau (B3) 1917, 1934
Z 1934

Ulithi (B3) 1934

Woleai 1907, 1934

Guam (BW) 1936
Saipan 1907-21

Truk (B2) 1934-39
1922, 1938-41

Wake 1939-41 (BO)

Eniwetok (B1) 1922, 1939-41
Kwajalein (B1)
Majuro (B1)
Wotje (B1) 1934-39

Makin (BO)
Tarawa (B1)

New Guinea
Manus (B2)
Rabaul
Guadalcanal

20° N
0°
130° E
159° E
180°

MAP 28.1

Planning for the Marshalls was another case of déjà vu. In the 1930s strategists had debated whether to begin at an eastern atoll and roll up all Orange bases seriatim or to thrust deeply to a western island and bypass the rest. Sea and air cover had posed dilemmas for both schools. In 1943 Nimitz and his staff opted at first for the cautionary concept of a decade earlier, proposing landings on Jaluit and Mili, the islands nearest to American bases, and slogging on through five other atolls. Cooke fretted at bogging down in the sticky web. He rallied his JWPC confreres to a bolder overleap, to Wotje, Maloelap, and Kwajalein simultaneously, to secure the eastern and central Marshalls at a stroke. But a triple landing would have absorbed all U.S. forces in the Pacific. Spruance and other fleet cautionaries uncharacteristically suggested lunging directly to Eniwetok even though it lay beyond air reach of Tarawa. The issue was put to Nimitz. Worried about an enemy buildup in the group, he opted for a compromise proposed by Sherman: a thrust to the single, deep target of Kwajalein.[14]

The big atoll was assaulted on 31 January 1944 and secured in a few days. The operation borrowed much from the plans of the 1930s. It was mounted half from Hawaii and half from the West Coast. Simultaneous occupation of lightly held Majuro assured the fleet of a safe anchorage. Landing tactics hewed to the prewar scenarios. Bypassed islands were subdued by air barrage for the rest of the war. As the Orange planners had predicted, the Combined Fleet did not come out to save its atoll bases.

The next move was a clean reversion to the prewar itinerary. An impromptu decision was made to take Eniwetok immediately rather than wait until May 1944. The island had been recognized as extraordinarily useful in at least eight studies by imaginative planners, from Williams in 1907 to McMorris in 1941. As planned before the war, the fleet ranged forward to batter and neutralize Truk. Occupation of Eniwetok cut Japan's air pipeline to orphaned outposts and brought Truk and the Marianas within flying range. The atoll was adapted as a supply depot through which millions of tons of war goods passed. In tandem with Majuro, it neatly provided an excellent Base One lagoon, the place, for example, from which Halsey sortied to scourge the Philippines in the autumn of 1944. The Eniwetok operation proved beyond doubt the efficiency of the Mandate route. It marked "the beginning of a new phase of the Pacific war," the approach to an inner Japanese defense line.[15]

Regarding the eastern Carolines old wisdom triumphed again. Marine studies of 1937 had convinced the naval planners to outflank them, yet in 1943 neocautionaries demanded that Kusaie and the Australian island of Nauru be seized before the Marshalls, and Ponape be taken as a prelude to Truk. Fortunately for American fighting men, the high islands were bypassed for reasons stated in Plan Orange: poor physical and locational value, dispersion of effort, and avoidance of casualties.

The middle stage of the Mandate drive diverged markedly from prewar thinking. The United States bypassed Truk, the sine qua non of the Orange Plan. Truk had been coveted as Fleet Base Two in the 1922 version and in every model from 1934 on. In Rainbow Five it was still the grail of the central Pacific, to be occupied six months after clearing the Marshalls. In the spring of 1943 the Joint Chiefs reconfirmed both the objective and the timetable. Nimitz, who was keen to fly his flag at Japan's main ocean base, scheduled the operation for August 1944, to be preceded by taking the Mortlocks, near Truk, for air support (another detail cribbed from the old plan).[16]

But marine analysts of the 1930s had warned of bloody losses on mountainous islands deep inside Truk's reef. Current reviews again looked daunting, and Carl Moore once more objected to the "murderous prospect" as he had in the 1930s. In fact, Truk was not so formidable as believed. Its air power was a pale shadow of prewar forecasts, its big guns had been uprooted for Rabaul, and the Imperial Navy had fled. The garrison of 7,500 (reinforced to 12,356 after the first raid) scattered on several islands was closer in strength to Kwajalein's 8,000 than to the 27,663 predicted on Truk in the Orange Plan or the 31,000 later encountered on Saipan and an octave below the 97,000 dug in at the bristling redoubt of Rabaul.[17] Nevertheless, strategists of all stripes realized simultaneously that bypassing Truk could foster sweeps to more treasured goals. Moore had in mind his 1940 notion of a slant to the Celebes Sea. MacArthur wanted the fleet to skip ahead to the Palaus and join him in the Philippines, an idea Nimitz liked. King and Sherman were impatient to get to the Marianas.

Truk had been a magnet when it seemed the only island of a Blue-Orange ocean theater suitable for a fleet base. In early 1944, however, army forces occupied Manus in the Australian-mandated Admiralty Islands. Manus lay adjacent to "one of the largest and best" harbors of the Pacific, twenty square miles of deep waters that planners early in the century had wistfully noted could accommodate a huge fleet. The United States developed it into "a major naval and air base, capable of service, supply and repair to forces afloat, air forces, and other Allied units in the forward area," at a cost exceeding the cumulative investment in all previous advanced bases. Outfitted with three enormous floating dry docks, Manus was functionally equivalent to the industrial arsenal long scheduled for Truk.[18] The fleet had its Base Two seventeen hundred miles from the Philippines. The sequence of Plan Orange was intact. The Joint Chiefs voted to bypass Truk.

The most important command decision of the Mandate drive was to take the Marianas. The American assault of June 1944 yielded four profound results. First, the Japanese carriers came out, lost their squadrons in the "Great Marianas Turkey Shoot," and never again threatened U.S. forces. Second, Guam was transformed into a naval depot and headquarters of the Pacific Fleet, one of a triad of great western bases for Phase III. Third, Saipan, Tinian, and Guam were carpeted with aerodromes for massive raids on Japan that began six to nine months sooner than scheduled and terminated the China strategy that until then had gripped U.S. planners. Finally, the government of General Hideki Tojo fell when Saipan fell. "Never before had a modern Japanese leader gathered to himself so much power," it was said of Tojo,[19] warlord of Japan since 1941. Moderates in Tokyo began seeking a way out of the war. The unthinkable became thinkable.

The Marianas campaign is one of the most difficult to reconcile with Plan Orange. The group had often been studied before the war, with mixed conclusions. Its naval benefits were understood in a general way. A fleet base at Guam, an obsession of the thrusting faction, had been killed by government animosity in 1922 and again during a revival attempt in 1939. The political naiveté of sponsors of an "American Gibraltar" and its probable fate as an "American Singapore" have been noted. Although the idea of developing Guam as a major base was a bad one, it rested on a sound appreciation of the island's "commanding strategic position." Many planners felt that bases in the Marianas, lying equidistant from the large islands of the Japanese Empire from Honshu to Mindanao, could dominate the western Pacific. As early as 1907–9 Oliver and Williams had predicted that possession of the group would have a "decisive influence" on the outcome. U.S. control, they observed, would isolate Japan's outposts, constrain its freedom, yield communications and interdiction advantages, and perhaps bring the Orange fleet to action.

King had been fascinated by the Marianas even while the Royal Road planners downplayed them in the 1930s. In June 1942 he pinpointed them as future targets, although he foresaw their value only as providing naval and flank protection. MacArthur, however, derided the idea as a nonsupportive diversion from his theater, and fleet cautionaries saw neither good harbors nor vital objectives beyond. (Nimitz had not been impressed by his planning assignment during the War College's "Battle of the Marianas" game in 1923.) Despite King's fancy for the group as "the key to the situation,"[20] naval reasons alone would probably not have pointed the U.S. sword at the Marianas in 1944.

The other attractions had shallower roots in prewar strategy. Colonel Walter Krueger had best appreciated the potential of the Marianas for long-range air power. His Strategic Plan Orange of 1936 envisioned planes from Saipan and Guam controlling the Philippine Sea and suppressing the rest of Japan's island barrier for a Blue breakthrough to the Far East. Strategic bombing was a mainstay of the Orange Plan, but no plane of Krueger's day could reach from the Marianas to Japan. The home islands would have to be raided from the Ryukyus. But Krueger did foresee the political ramifications of piercing Japan's "Main Line of Resistance." The Orange Fleet would be compelled to fight "to avoid collapse at home." The expected Blue naval victory would be tantamount to winning the war.

In midwar King's yen for the Marianas got a big assist from the Army Air Forces. Nobody had given much thought to Pacific airfields for the new B-29 Superfortresses that could drop five to ten tons of bombs on targets fifteen hundred miles away. The first squadrons were ready in the spring of 1944, but no suitable islands were expected to be in hand for at least a year and the planes were sent to China. They began to swat at Japan, but it was soon apparent that defense of their bases and resupply by air over "the Hump" of the Himalayas were formidable obstacles. Airfields in the Marianas, within range of Japan and easily defended and supplied, would dramatically accelerate the siege.

In summary, the decision to attack the Marianas was generally in tune with Plan Orange concepts. Their geographical importance and the forcing of Japan to naval combat had been correctly perceived, but the strategic air and political effects were only murkily glimpsed. A succinct appraisal is that the occupation, though not definitively predicted before the war, fit neatly with the grand strategy of Plan Orange. The Marianas campaign yielded a naval victory, bases for advancing to the Far East, and despair in Tokyo, all hoped-for benefits of the central Pacific offensive, and the new airfields comported with the principle (if not the location) of strategic bombing from Pacific islands and thus eradicated other notions of bombing from China or Siberia.

The last stage of the ocean offensive during the final four months of 1944 carried the war to the southern Philippines, the customary terminus of Phase II. The navy's route lay through the western Carolines. Early planners had known the Palaus were adaptable as a fleet base but deemed them irrelevant because so many good harbors lay just beyond in the Philippines. The group had been omitted from the Royal Road itinerary (unless it became necessary to deny them to raiders after the fleet reached the Philippines). Nimitz's planners, however, proposed to capture as many as four of the large western Carolines. The CinCPac canceled a plan to attack Yap and other islands, but the assault on Peleliu resulted in a brutal battle to gain an air base and harbor of no great importance. The Orange planners had admired atolls of the western Carolines such as Woleai and Ulithi for anchorage and aviation use. In 1944 Ulithi was taken easily and developed as a splendid depot that served the fleet for the rest of the war. The old assessment of the western Carolines had been the more perceptive one.

Plan Orange had always defined the end of Phase II as the date when the fleet was established in the Philippines in superior strength and ready to continue operating offensively. Ever since the Naval War College's recommendation of 1907, the goal had usually been a bay in the southern islands, not Manila Bay. The choice was confirmed in 1911, 1914, and, except for Coontz's foolhardy sprint of 1923–25, in the Through Ticket Plans of the 1920s. In the air age the chosen locale receded from islands relatively near Manila to those most distant. In 1926–28 the planners dismissed "for all time" a direct assault on Luzon and opted for Dumanquilas Bay on Mindanao. Early ideas of a primitive waiting post for the train gave way to the great Western Base project. The realization that Blue would have to fight its way ashore encouraged studies of carrier strikes and landing tactics.

In World War II the consensus goal of nearly all commanders and planners was the southern Philippines, where the twin Pacific offensives converged naturally. Naval strategists dwelled on severing Japan from its oil, enticing its fleet to final defeat, and establishing a base for the next advance (which, until mid-1944, was aimed at China). The army had additional motivations: the islands were its *only* feasible target, and MacArthur felt passionately about his pledge to return.

U.S. strategists still expected to reenter the Philippines at Mindanao, the island selected by the old planners, but in the autumn of 1944 carrier raids disclosed a softness in local defenses. The expedition was ratcheted forward to Leyte Gulf, a fine harbor that had been overlooked in the prewar plans and not even surveyed until 1938. The gulf fully satisfied the Orange Plan's criteria for a Western Base: a big anchorage buffered from sea and air raids, with a large hinterland and easy communications to the south and east. (Interestingly, the train amassed for the operation approximated the seven hundred vessels slated for the Western Base movement of the 1920s.) The Leyte-Samar area was developed as another of the troika of harbors, along with Guam and eventually Okinawa, that became the functional equivalents of the Western Base.

At the end of 1944 the war had reached a point matching the end of Phase II of the Orange Plan. Overwhelming fleet strength and a large army were poised in the southern Philippines and on intermediate islands of the Pacific, including harbors equivalent to Bases One and Two. The sea blockade had cut all Japanese trade except with Northeast Asia. The Imperial Fleet, although imagined in some older plans as a continuing threat, finally had been destroyed in the sea Battle of Leyte Gulf.

The United States was ready to embark on Phase III to compel Japan to unconditional surrender. It was during that phase that Plan Orange faced its most serious challenges. Before turning to the war's finale, however, the viability of the old plan in meeting technological changes and other surprises will be evaluated.

Plan Orange at War: Innovation and Surprise

S trategists are not clairvoyants. A war plan nurtured over thirty-five years could not apprehend all the kaleidoscopic shifts in nations' behavior or the revolutions in military technology that characterized World War II. Innovation and surprise tested the plan's validity throughout the war. Certain changes had been anticipated by the planners, in outline if not in detail, and did not materially alter its relevance. Most of the unexpected developments were easily co-opted within the plan's framework, a tribute to its flexibility and broad aims. Only a few surprises compelled wartime leaders to depart from it. None compromised its most fundamental principles.

The technology of war changed radically in the first four decades of the century. The internal combustion engine made possible the airplane and submarine, the landing and fast patrol vessel, and the tank, truck, and bulldozer. The switch from coal to oil gave warships oceanic range and tenure. Ordnance became more deadly and more accurate. Technologies of communication—radio and eventually radar and electronic warfare—transformed command and control. Modern historians view such innovations as packages that were bonded into new integrated fighting systems such as carrier task forces, U-boat wolf packs, and assault landing expeditions.

Before the war the Orange Plan incorporated several new weapons and techniques that were virtually unprecedented in warfare. Three examples will be stressed here: air power, amphibious operations, and seagoing logistics.

War Plan Orange was very air-minded. Its authors understood the value of the "overwhelming" aerial mass that American industry could provide. The 1928 forecast of eighteen thousand warplanes a year was a perceptive glimpse of the numbers actually deployed to the Pacific. Japan's effort to destroy American air power by campaigns of attrition was bound to fail because of its much lower productive capacity.

The aircraft carrier is an enduring symbol of the Pacific war. Experts may debate whether the United States or Japan led in carrier capability at the outset (although both were superior to other naval powers). Japanese aircraft and ships were good but vulnerable. The ample squadrons of American carriers were more flexible, but their planes were mediocre. Both sides understood concentration and surprise. In the late 1920s U.S. planners had assigned a variety of roles to the fast carriers joining the fleet, including spearheading landings in the Philippines, long-range patrolling, and neutralization of Orange bases in the Mandate. They expected that carriers, screened by fast gunships and informed by shore-based air scouts, would strike deeply into enemy waters. They recoiled from the risk of immobilizing them to cover bases or beachheads. During World War II the durability of U.S. flattops against land-based planes was a pleasant surprise that assured their effectiveness even in the face of kamikaze attacks.

Planners were hazy about the role of the flying deck in sea battles, although possibilities were studied and even rehearsed at sea. Their scenarios said nothing of the carrier-versus-carrier donnybrooks in which surface units rarely spotted each other such as occurred on five occasions during 1942–44. (Interestingly, each battle began with a task force of one side deployed forward to support a fight for an island, a prime mission of carriers in 1930s plans.) Most strategic planners had inaptly viewed carriers as auxiliaries to the battle line, imagining them hovering near the battleships for scouting, artillery spotting, and sky brawls before the decisive gunnery exchange.[1] Even though it astonished naval traditionalists, the new style of combat did not undermine American strategy. In most ways the elevation of the carrier to capital ship enhanced the pertinence of Plan Orange. The prowess of Japan's carriers amplified its Phase I victories, and the mass and quality of U.S.

carrier aviation were crucial in Phase II and for closing the noose in Phase III. Flight decks made possible the amphibious offensive of Plan Orange in the central Pacific; they were ancillary in the South Pacific approach and absent from mainland campaigns.

Concerning long-range air power at sea, the planners' vision was farsighted as to doctrine but immature as to technology. Naval aviation had been hampered by bureaucratic constraints. The Pratt-MacArthur Agreement of 1931 had reserved multiengined landplanes to the Army Air Corps, which showed little interest in combat over the sea. The navy had to bet on clumsy flying boats that were outmoded by the time war came. It is easy in hindsight to criticize the VPB striking force as archaic, but the superiority of the landplane was not conclusively proved until the eve of war in the Pacific.

The planners realized the urgency of a mature scouting system for ocean operations. During World War II information was gathered in abundance by long-range planes flown by army, navy, and marine crews, by improved carrier and submarine scouting, and by the electronic arts of eavesdropping and code breaking. Reconnaissance proved crucial to the outcome of every naval battle (including Pearl Harbor, for its absence). After the initial defeats American forces at sea or ashore were rarely taken by surprise. Modern means of intelligence freed the navy to roam at will and to erect bases in wide seas, whereas before the air age fleets were expected to secure themselves behind narrow straits. Information technology made the Orange Plan work better.

The efficacy of devastating the Japanese economy by air was fully understood in the 1920s. By 1928 a full-fledged bombing campaign had been enshrined as coequal with the blockade in bringing about a capitulation. The Army Air Corps embraced the role. Although city-burning protagonists such as Billy Mitchell did not divert the air planners from recommending precision bombing of industry and transportation, all understood the horrible effect that incendiary bombs might have on Japan's flimsy metropolises.

The action radii of early bombers of a few hundred miles (and only a thousand miles by 1941) reinforced the traditional decision to advance to the Ryukyus and other small islands near Japan. In 1944 the advent of the B-29s shifted U.S. attention to the Marianas (although conventional bombers redeploying from Europe were expected to operate from Okinawa by late 1945). Nevertheless, the underlying premise of Plan Orange remained valid. It was indeed feasible to operate a huge air force from small islands. Conversely, the old plans had shrugged off the utility of air bases on the Asian continent, and rightly so, because the Soviets refused to provide any and bombing from Chinese fields was a short-lived fiasco.

An aerial weapon the planners missed was the escort carrier. The "XCVs" envisioned in the late 1920s, auxiliary fleet carriers converted from liners, never appeared. The small, cheap CVEs that were launched in abundance during World War II took over the auxiliary tasks of covering invasions, hunting U-boats, and ferrying planes. By excusing fleet carriers from immobile stakeouts at beachheads they alleviated a worrisome aspect of the amphibious campaign strategy.

The air war of 1941–45 was marked by many technical advances. (The most dramatic, the atomic bomb, will be dealt with in the final chapter.) Some merely extended prewar trends toward machines that could fly higher, faster, farther, and with more ordnance. Others were marvels of invention. Radar became essential at sea and aloft; Nimitz considered it as revolutionary as the steam engine.[2] Aerial photography and minelaying matured, as did precision antiaircraft fire using proximity fuses. Control and vectoring techniques won air battles. Such miracles were not predicted by the Orange Plan (whose authors refrained from technological speculation), but the inventions that made aviation more deadly enhanced their air-minded strategy.

The planners deserve high marks for anticipating the conditions of amphibious warfare in World War II. Early notions of seizing empty ports had given way to plans to assault fortified islands. The infantry and field weapons of wartime landing units were about the same as expected. The planners did not predict the gaggle of innovative landing craft such as amphibious tractors and beachable tank-hauling vessels, although they were aware of a need for specialized barges for heavy equipment. The hoped-for endurance of soldiers in tropical campaigning was boosted by wartime advances in medicine and sanitation. These and other innovations that guaranteed no U.S. landing would ever be repelled (a setback that would undermine public support) helped assure the success of Plan Orange.

The planners' best insights into amphibious war concerned doctrine. The tactics of storming an atoll worked out by Ellis in 1921 identified the patterns that became familiar in wartime: bombardment, minesweeping, combat loading, debarking of successive troop waves at dawn, seizure of weak flank positions, and winning an island primarily on the beaches. Battles for mountainous islands were correctly analyzed by other marines in the mid-1930s. The need for air bases to support landings was well understood. During the war U.S. forces established airfields within range before seizing most of the central and Southwest Pacific objectives. (Some landings, as at Hollandia and Okinawa, initially relied on carrier air.) The dispute during the 1930s about the duty of fleet carriers in invasions flared up again at the time of the Gilberts operation. Should they hover near the beaches or prowl ahead to destroy enemy threats? Kelly Turner, as amphibious chieftain, argued the old marine case for close support. Air officers Sherman and Towers championed the forward doctrine of the prewar WPD and usually prevailed. The controversy subsided when "jeep" carriers arrived in quantity. Nevertheless, the mission of fleet carriers during invasions proved a thorny issue at Saipan and Leyte, where Spruance and Halsey chose opposite courses of screening a landing and chasing Japanese flattops, and finally at Okinawa, where kamikazes extracted a high price for immobility.

By 1937 the planners had rejected the notion of clearing all enemy islands along the ocean highway in favor of bypassing the nonessential or the too stoutly defended. The conviction had to be relearned during the war. Early offensives in the Southwest Pacific slogged through each Japanese fortress in succession, a slow and costly method. Central Pacific campaign plans at first presumed the same technique. But early in 1944 the United States returned to the Orange Plan thesis, plunging deeply into the Mandate and skipping past half a dozen Japanese strongholds. Rabaul and Truk, Japan's two great outlying bases, were outflanked and left in the wake of the fleet. The bypassing of citadels on such a grand scale was almost unprecedented in the history of warfare.

Americans excelled at maritime logistics. The hundreds of Liberty ships that were launched to haul men and goods were protected, as prescribed in Plan Orange, by convoying, ports of refuge, and anti-raider patrols. (Japan failed effectively to do the same, to its regret.) The United States, alone among naval powers, mastered the art of carrying bases with the fleet. Logisticians had been compelled by vetoes of overseas dockyards and the dilemma of Pacific distances to invent giant colliers in 1908–14 and the Western Base project in the 1920s. They designed modular advanced base units for assembly by special construction battalions (Seabees). Halsey called the bulldozer one of the three decisive weapons of the war. The floating service depot was perfected. The war lasted long enough for delivery of the huge floating dry docks that had worried two generations of planners, although new damage-control techniques and antifouling paints rendered them somewhat less critical. A U.S. Navy unaccompanied by mobile bases could probably not have defeated the Japanese at sea once they adopted a defensive posture. In contrast, the Royal Navy was helpless to return after the loss of Singapore until the Americans provided logistical support in 1945.

Prewar perceptions of two familiar naval weapons, the submarine and the battleship, were faulty. Conventional U.S. submarine duties of ambushing warships near their bases or in advance of sea battles were foreseen and were executed effectively, but unrestricted submarine and air attacks against merchant ships had been banned out of respect for "civilized" rules (although many officers expected the rules to change). The adoption of a sink-on-sight policy on 7 December 1941 greatly strengthened the blockade program of Plan Orange (although defective torpedoes hobbled results for almost two years). Of the 8 million tons of Japanese merchant shipping sunk, submarines accounted for 60 percent, aircraft 30 percent, mining (mostly airborne) 5 percent, and surface gunfire only 1 percent. Said the U.S. Strategic Bombing Survey, "The war against shipping was perhaps the most decisive single factor in the collapse of the Japanese economy and the logistic support of Japanese military and naval power."[3] The old concept of blockade by surface vessels could not have been made effective until late in the war. The decision for undersea predation magnified the success of one of the Orange Plan's most basic prescriptions.

The submarine restriction had also influenced prewar offensive itineraries. The shortcomings of destroyers and auxiliary cruisers for blockade work had goaded the planners to favor lunges for blockade stations at Guam, Truk, or in the Philippines as soon as possible. But in World War II there were no neutral cargoes to intercept en route to Japan, and a swift movement to western Pacific bases was not feasible. Modern submarines took up the slack by raiding from Hawaii and Australia, their productivity improving as advanced bases were captured. The planners had also reckoned that final severing of Japan from Northeast Asia would require naval stations in the Ryukyus. But modern weapons of bombing as well as blockade allowed the siege to be conducted from more distant islands. (Okinawa was grabbed anyway, more for use of tactical aircraft and for staging troops in case of an invasion of Japan than for blockade.) In summary, Plan Orange had wrongly identified the weapons, rules, and bases of the blockade. Yet it had established the undeniable gospel that Japan and its outposts would be exceedingly vulnerable to an un-Mahanian *guerre de course*. Once again, innovation and change added to the success of an immutable grand strategy.

American reverence of the battleship as the arbiter of victory was clearly wrong. Both sides commissioned huge dreadnoughts before and during the war, but the battle lines never met en masse. As their vulnerability to air power became painfully apparent, the United States realized they did not need to be hoarded for battle and reassigned them to unaccustomed roles: old ones to shore bombardment (a duty the Orange Plan had endorsed in mid-Pacific waters) and new ones as antiair shields for the carriers (feasible because of speed and electronics). In their new jobs the battleships fit comfortably into the grand strategy except for the climactic battle scenario, which will be discussed shortly.

The naval war was decided more by the sheer weight of U.S. naval force than by a specific weapon. The planners had predicted an abundance of submarines and light warships arriving at the battlefront after a year or so. But because they proposd to win within the limit of public tolerance—assumed at two years in the 1920s—and because battleships and carriers took three years to build, they expected to make do with the capital ships in being. Only a few Cassandras prophesied a doubled or quadrupled fleet of great ships. In fact, during the war U.S. shipyards added 50 percent more battleships and 75 percent more heavy cruisers to the prewar fleet and a stunning 400 percent more fast carriers, all of improved design. The growth was more the result of unforeseen political and social factors, like the head start of the 1940 building program and public sufferance of a long war, although speedier construction techniques also contributed.[4] Without doubt the building of a "second fleet" enhanced the Orange Plan formulation of naval superiority as the guarantor of success.

A review of technology and surprise would be incomplete without further remarks on intelligence. The United States was reading Japanese diplomatic codes at the time of the Washington Conference in 1921 and military codes as well by 1941. But the planners could not design strategy on such windfalls. They rarely mentioned arcane sources and felt rather condescending about them: "We got most of our Intelligence from the newspapers or something else," one had snickered.[5] The Office of Naval Intelligence, lacking prestige and suffering rapid turnover of leadership, played a minor role in prewar planning.[6] During the war both belligerents were skilled at radio analysis, but neither got much help from spies above tactical levels such as coast watchers. The Americans gained an incredible edge through code breaking, however. Unexpected intelligence certainly improved the U.S. ability to win at sea, notably in the "Miracle at Midway," where the navy violated a doctrinal taboo and engaged a superior enemy fleet.

Intelligence also had its failures, as at Pearl Harbor and Savo Island (Guadalcanal). The most impressive and continuous application was in the blockade. Half the merchant sinkings by U.S. submarines resulted from intercepting Japanese communications.[7] Once more, an innovation enhanced a basic strategic concept of Plan Orange.

Enemy behavior provided some surprises, although on a grand strategic level Japan conformed to most expectations, such as fighting without regional allies, striking suddenly for early gains, and relying on attrition and demoralization for a favorable peace settlement. The war opened with the surprise raid on Pearl Harbor. U.S. planners had occasionally reflected on the possibility but judged it unlikely because the fleet was not stationed at Hawaii until 1940 and the base was expected to function mainly as a transit point for ships en route to western Pacific anchorages. During the war Pearl Harbor assumed the more vital function of permanent outlying fleet base in a secure area (as it was except on 7 December 1941) and, after massive improvement, as springboard for the central Pacific drive. The loss of some old battleships in the raid was of little consequence for the broader strategy. What really mattered was arousal of the American spirit to the goal of coercing Japan to unconditional surrender. The planners had not believed Orange would act so foolishly because Hawaii, unlike the Philippines, was regarded by Americans as an integral part of their country. As the General Board observed in 1914, an attack would "arouse a greater spirit of resentment . . . and result in a more determined prosecution of the war."[8] The attack on Pearl Harbor, a tactical surprise, assured fulfillment of the ruthless goals of Plan Orange.

Another veering from the script was Japan's predilection to seek naval battles frequently and far from home. Orange Plans had universally predicted a single decisive engagement, a Mahanian concept borrowed from land warfare. The confident, superior U.S. Navy had welcomed the prospect, but because Japan would determine the time and place, the planners had rarely agreed on details. During the first twenty years their thoughts had ranged from a battle near the Philippines within a few weeks of the outbreak to one near Japan after two years of attrition. Air age planners later speculated on battles in open waters more congenial to fleet aviation, in the Philippine Sea or by 1941 at the center of the Pacific.

In World War II there were a dozen major naval engagements. Several have a claim to decisiveness—Midway, Philippine Sea, Leyte Gulf, the series around Guadalcanal as a whole, and Pearl Harbor for its moral effect. The Imperial Navy did not wait until attrition had inflicted maximum pain. It fought early and late, at the sea frontier and in the inner defense zone. There was no cataclysmic shoot-out of a score of dreadnoughts. Carrier-versus-carrier battles were as common as gunnery frays. The Battle of Leyte Gulf, the largest of the war, was not its climactic moment. It was an anticlimax, the outcome preordained (despite mutual tactical errors) because the U.S. Navy had grown beyond the 25 or 50 percent superiority of the treaty years to several times the enemy's strength, just as shrewd analysts of the 1930s had said would happen in a long war. The rare encounters of battleship detachments at Guadalcanal and Leyte were not decisive turning points. There was no need for Blue to cosset its dreadnoughts for another Jutland. After the depletion of Japanese carriers at Midway, Pye suggested a possible slugfest, but even that battlewagon devotee conceded they should be consigned to auxiliary duties for the rest of the war. Thus at Saipan Vice-Admiral Willis Lee declined the option of a night battleship duel in favor of protecting the carriers, and at Okinawa Spruance chose to nail the gargantuan *Yamato* from the air rather than send his six dreadnoughts for some sport.

The Orange Plan, fallacious in every detail of large naval encounters, was nevertheless correct in strategic principle. It stipulated destruction of the Imperial Navy as a prerequisite of victory. Japan, it decreed, could not adopt a battle-shunning, "fleet-in-being" policy to tie down opposing strength as Germany had done in World War I. It could not turn the Combined Fleet after Phase I to missions like raiding bases or shipping. It had to fight somewhere, sometime, in some manner. It did. It lost—as predicted.

Japan had some technological and tactical surprises up its sleeve. Among the best known were its excellent Zero fighter plane, the "long lance" torpedo, and a carrier doctrine of audacious strikes. The innovations enhanced its successes of Phase I but did not retard the United States more than temporarily when it fielded better and more abundant weaponry during the ensuing phases. Prewar planners had expected enemy sea, air, and ground forces to exhibit a high level of competence. America had to adjust some of its tactics to cope but not its grand strategy.

A final surprise was the Japanese predilection for fanatical, even suicidal, combat. (One notes wryly that tables of matériel in Orange landing plans included barbed wire for prisoner compounds.) Its troops fought to the last man. Bypassed garrisons never surrendered. During the final ten months Japan mounted kamikaze attacks, primarily by air—"the first guided missiles." Conduct of Japanese warriors in earlier battles had convinced prewar strategists that they would fight near suicidally in such special instances as night torpedo boat attacks, but the kamikazes, as Nimitz observed, were a complete surprise.[9]

The impact of suicidal Japanese behavior on U.S. strategy was mixed. At the campaign level it encouraged the United States to adopt the bypassing policy of Plan Orange. On the level of grand strategy it fostered a potentially serious deviation. The prewar planners had expected the Japanese people to endure great hardships yet believed that a rational government would yield when it recognized its cause as hopeless. The suicide methods, by exacting grim casualties and making the Japanese seem bestial rather than heroic, intensified American racial animosity and stiffened the will to fight.[10] Near the end many U.S. leaders became convinced that Japan could endure years of siege and that unlimited victory could be achieved only by invading the home islands, an anathema to the old planners. If last-ditch behavior had induced such an invasion, the most sacred principle of the classical strategy would have been abandoned at the final moment. Fortunately for American and Allied fighting men, the siege delivered the timely unconditional surrender predicted by War Plan Orange.

Plan Orange at War:
The Better Strategy

A litmus test of the relevance of Plan Orange is to evaluate it against other Pacific strategies the United States formulated during World War II. Four significant deviations from the plan were devised in the war years. Two were executed at the behest of MacArthur—the South Pacific offensive of Phase II and the recapture of Luzon in Phase III. Although neither campaign had been prescribed in the Orange Plan, neither was so drastic a departure as to negate its basic principles. The other two variances were scheduled for Phase III but were never executed. They were proposals to land in China and open a continental ground-air front, which proved infeasible and superfluous, and a final proposal to invade the Japanese home islands, for which planning was under way when Japan surrendered in August 1945. Had either landing been carried out, it would be difficult to sustain the argument that Plan Orange provided the war-winning strategy. In the end, none of the four variances was as satisfactory as the traditional prewar solutions.

The first of the departures was the South Pacific offensive (the amphibious jumps of 1944 from Papua to Leyte, not the 1942–43 actions that have been likened to the attrition scenarios of Plan Orange). Peacetime planners had occasionally considered movements south of the equator but spurned them because of the drawbacks of long supply lines and a dearth of U.S. or Japanese islands for bases. (A rare exception was the 1932 Quick Movement to Mindanao by a southerly route.) Rainbows Two and Three of 1939–40 had the fleet advancing to Malaysia by way of Allied harbors of the South Pacific, and in 1941 the possibility of a fleet base at Rabaul was studied, but until the war began there was no acceptable script for threatening Japan from its southeastern flank.

The South Pacific offensive was a product of the persuasiveness of Douglas MacArthur. (Imagine the course of events, it has been asked, if he had been ordered to Hawaii instead of Australia or left on Corregidor.) The general touted the advantages of his theater with help from naval allies, including Nimitz for a while. The Southwest Pacific was an attractive milieu in 1944 for the swelling numbers of troops, planes, and naval light units that could stage from Australia and advanced bases already set up in the area. A breakthrough of the Bismarcks Barrier would yield an excellent harbor (at Rabaul, later switched to Manus), after which the advance could proceed by short hops to the Philippines. Casualties would be minimized by "hitting 'em where they ain't." Carrier support would assure that occasional giant strides could be made. The campaign would expose the Japanese southern empire to bombing and open the way either to China or to a large island for operations against Japan itself.

Predictably, the services disparaged each other's choice of route. The navy warned that an attack from the south would cross the area where the Japanese were massing most heavily. It would be strategically inflexible because it could debouch only in the southern Philippines. Even MacArthur admitted that his intermediate targets were mere stepping-stones. The general's supporters lashed back against the central Pacific alternative. Movements spaced at long intervals, they argued, would be less disconcerting than frequent short jumps. Truk would prove too costly. Strategic bombing from the Marianas would be nothing but a "stunt." MacArthur said that carriers would be sunk in the Mandate by land-based planes—as at Midway, he added egregiously. Die-hards of both camps conceded only that diversionary actions in the other theater could marginally assist their favored campaign.

Since the United States attacked along both routes in World War II, the question germane to Plan Orange is whether the central Pacific route it fostered was paramount, secondary, or equal in importance.

Opinions of commanders during and after the war and of historians were swayed by factors of army or navy allegiance, political versus military goals, preferred style of warfare, and loyalty to personalities. The best impartial evidence is found in pronouncements of authorities who shared responsibility for both theaters. The president did not take sides so this means the interservice and combined military planning agencies. The Joint War Plans Committee at first suggested that the two fronts should be nearly equal in value. The seniors of the Joint Strategic Survey Committee, however, demanded "unequivocal" primacy of the central Pacific, noting the confusion in Europe that had resulted from failure to define the main Allied effort. They prevailed upon the Joint Chiefs. The Washington planners then made an "unequivocal decision" for the Mandate as the region of principal exertion and relegated the parallel attacks along its Aleutian and southern flanks to supporting status. At the "Quadrant" Conference in August 1943 the JCS confirmed to the British that the Mandate drive would constitute the main Pacific push and that all other operations would be subsidiary.[1]

By the end of 1943 both attacks had been firmly launched. An Overall Plan for the Defeat of Japan presented at the Cairo meeting of Roosevelt, Churchill, and Generalissimo Chiang Kai-shek confirmed the policy of dual offensives with mutual support and occasional interchanges of forces. It made clear, however, that priority of sequence and resources would favor the central Pacific because of its promise of "a more rapid advance toward Japan and her vital lines of communications; the earlier acquisition of strategic air bases closer to the Japanese homeland; and, of greatest importance, [its] more likely precipitat[ion of] a decisive engagement with the Japanese Fleet."[2] Mac-Arthur's advance was approved only as far as the western tip of New Guinea. Although the general's complaints caused Marshall to fret about dissipation of mass, both offensives rolled along in high gear. Operations meshed so well in practice that a hard test of primacy never proved necessary. By mid-1944 the strategic debate shifted to the course of action after the two offensives merged in the southern Philippines later in the year.

Events demonstrated that the central Pacific attack was indeed paramount. It brought naval power and mobility to bear most effectively. It drew the Orange carriers and their squadrons to destruction. Its intermediate objectives, especially the Marianas, were strategically unique (whereas the naval and air bases of the South Pacific could have been duplicated in the Mandate). The route led to a splendid array of Far Eastern objectives and accelerated the war by a more direct plunge toward Japan. In grand strategic terms the central Pacific offensive was primary and decisive, comparable to the Allied invasion of France. The South Pacific attack was secondary and supportive, like the campaign in the Mediterranean. This judgment does not belittle MacArthur's cause. The twin advances were indeed mutually supportive. They relieved pressure on each other and confused the enemy. Perhaps, though, a single, massed offensive might have been even more successful. The historian of the Joint Chiefs judiciously opined that the dual attacks and divided command complicated U.S. problems and "undoubtedly reduced the efficiency with which the war was fought."[3] The indulgence was tolerable for a war machine of unsurpassed might.

Even had the greater (or sole) effort been made in the South Pacific, the war script would have diverged only temporarily from Plan Orange. The United States would still have followed its broad prescriptions of crossing the Pacific by a sequence of amphibious landings, bypassing enemy strongholds and erecting mobile bases, to arrive in the Philippines in overwhelming strength for Phase III. The route would have changed but not the grand strategy.

An obsession to invade China transfixed American planners during World War II. If carried out, it would have nullified Plan Orange in a fundamental way. Prewar strategists had always rejected entanglement on the mainland. Speculations of the 1920s about a march through China had been filed away. The services had agreed that it would be both contrary to public opinion and logistically infeasible, and "might well result in disastrous defeat." Even in 1939, when China and Japan were already fighting, the JPC could not interest the Joint Board in incorporating China into a Rainbow Two campaign that would parallel its coast.

Wartime plans, however, were abrim with schemes for China. Roosevelt believed it was potentially a great power and that its millions could be shaped into effective legions. In the spring of 1943 the joint planners submitted a tentative Strategic Plan for the Defeat of Japan that hinged on a China campaign. Since progress in the South Pacific was discouragingly slow, they urged that air power introduced into China through the back door from India could disrupt Japanese shipping traffic much sooner than other blockade methods. Most important, they believed the bombing of Japan would have to be mounted from China. Pressures on the British for actions to open the way by clearing Burma or forcing the straits to Singapore and beyond produced interminable wranglings but few results. A seaport—preferably Hong Kong—would have to be seized by American forces after the

Philippines. By August 1943 the China plan had been adopted as the primary American strategy, its glittering benefits enlarged to include a base for invasion of Japan should that prove necessary. In other words, whether Japan were to be crushed by siege or invasion, China was the place from which to launch the blow.

In the first half of 1944 the hopes for China soured. An army mission under General Joseph "Vinegar Joe" Stilwell failed miserably to prepare Chiang's armies or induce them to fight in Burma. Meanwhile, as the first squadrons of B-29s were being readied, the Pacific timetable implied that the Marianas would not be won until the end of the year and that the laggardly pace in the South Pacific would rule out access to a Chinese port until 1946. The air force therefore sent the Superfortresses to inland China, supplying them by air from India. But full deployment of all the B-29s scheduled for production would ultimately have required the services of seven thousand conventional heavy bombers converted to flying tankers, more than were hurled against Germany. Air planners flailed at lame expedients like knocking out the coke ovens of Manchuria, the railway yards of Bangkok, or the dry docks of Singapore. In a plan appropriately named Twilight, the B-29s were supposed to ferry their own fuel from India to Chinese staging fields, a mad scheme in which only 14 percent of sorties would have dropped bombs.

By June 1944, as Nimitz's ocean sweep gained momentum, the Japanese began a land offensive to overrun the Chinese airfields. The planners threw in the towel. In September the last studies of occupying a Chinese port were shelved. By common consent, China was removed from the itinerary. The B-29s went to the Marianas. As the historian of the Joint Chiefs observed, "It is difficult indeed to discover any essential military contribution [of the China effort]. Certainly its contributions did not balance the effort expended."[4] The Orange Plan's dictum to shun China had been rich in wisdom.

The final gasp of a mainland strategy wheezed to the surface in the last months of the war, when fleet admirals and planners recommended taking harbors in North China and Korea to complete the encirclement of Japan. The old plans had rejected such notions. The Joint Chiefs did the same in 1945, scotching them as needless diversions. Had the United States needed additional bases, there were plenty of useful islands between Okinawa and the Straits of Tsushima that Plan Orange had identified.

As an aside, a mainland strategy might have profoundly affected the postwar order in Asia. But U.S. strategists both before and during the war focused single-mindedly on the defeat of Japan, which the Orange Plan promised to deliver by offshore campaigns, the most expeditious method. The old planners had sometimes pondered the long-term consequences to Japan of limited versus total war but gave no thought to the effects of U.S. strategy on China's postwar fate.

As the China option slipped away in 1944, a controversy heated up over where to go after Leyte, which was secured by the end of the year. Planners agreed that a large island closer to Japan would be essential for bombing and perhaps staging an invasion. The choices were Luzon and Formosa. Debates arose that resembled those of long ago.

Early naval strategists had considered the bypassing of Luzon as "entirely practicable" except in the impetuously thrusting plans of 1914 and 1923–25. Army planners had been schizophrenic, yearning to rescue Corregidor but conceding the task as impossible except when hypnotized by imperious Filipinists like Leonard Wood and MacArthur. They estimated in the late 1920s that three hundred thousand motorized troops would be needed to reclaim Luzon. Spurning a Joint Board injunction to retake Manila, they had declined to write a plan. Neither service had shown any taste for the mountainous island of Formosa, which had no good harbors and would absorb an equally large army (although it might prove useful as an enclave for airports). Naval planners joined in warning that defeat of an assault on either island could lose the war. The customary itinerary of Plan Orange was a vault from the southern Philippines to smaller islands that could be dominated by Blue sea power and lesser ground expeditions, Polillo perhaps, but most likely the Ryukyus.

In the fall of 1943 the joint planners decided that seizure of Formosa was "the most promising way of finishing the war comparatively soon." King and the JSSC advisers viewed it as the way to sever Japan from its southern resources. Fleet aviation, they believed, would be strong enough to cover the landings. Needless to say, Formosa lay in the navy's theater. But MacArthur, backed by Marshall, urged a descent on Luzon. The island had excellent natural features that he believed could be won more cheaply under land-based air cover. Its liberation would also fulfill his pledge to free the Philippine people. Needless to say, Luzon lay in the army's theater.

The Joint Chiefs punted. Concerned with speeding up the war by skipping nonessential places, they told Nimitz and MacArthur to study the choices again. The issue festered until their famous meeting with the president in Hawaii in July 1944. FDR decided in MacArthur's favor, primarily on political grounds of recouping American honor and prestige. King put up a spirited fight to send the fleet against Formosa, yielding only when Leahy estimated that five hundred thousand troops would be needed (three times Cooke's estimate and about the number assumed for a landing in Japan), and when Nimitz and Sherman, aghast at big ground battles, suggested thrusting consolation prizes: after Luzon they proposed that the fleet should pounce on smaller islands close to Japan—Iwo Jima and Okinawa.

The reasoning of the Orange Plan to bypass Formosa had been sound. The United States neutralized the big island by sea and air power and marooned its garrison. With the conviction growing that it would be necessary to invade Japan, it seemed logical "to make an England out of Luzon."[5] MacArthur proceeded to the attack. He realized his political goal, but the island did not come cheaply. The city of Manila and one hundred thousand Filipinos were destroyed in the process. Although the campaign completed the oil blockade and chewed up more Japanese air power, Luzon never became a naval or air post of prime importance, nor was it required for invading Japan.[6] The Orange Plan's direct leap from the southern Philippines to the Ryukyus attracted no serious wartime sponsorship but might have been the more economical procedure.

The final amphibious campaigns on the approaches to Japan conformed closely to prewar thought, including expectations of fanatical resistance. The invasion of the Ryukyus, although abbreviated to Okinawa and adjacent islets, was planned initially as a broad-front seizure of several islands as in Plan Orange (Chapter 14). The range of modern sea and aircraft, however, made the old plan's call for moving onward to islands virtually in sight of Japan unnecessary. Iwo Jima was taken to help Marianas-based bombers, a need not foreseen before the war. (Iwo had not interested naval planners because it had no harbor.) The nearby Bonin Islands had a decent anchorage, but wartime strategists agreed with their forebears that they were strategically unimportant and not worth the price of overcoming heavy fortifications.

The greatest challenge to War Plan Orange arose at the very end of the struggle and on the brink of its full vindication when American leaders proposed to invade Japan. To understand this stunning reversal of policy, one must review U.S. war goals and the perceptions of time and cost to achieve them.

The goal established by American military planners from 1907 onward was the "complete" defeat of Japan, couched in terms such as "enforcing submission" and "imposing our will." After twenty years of repetition, the theme became muted, although planners apparently never wavered in their innermost minds (Chapter 26). Rainbow Five had temporized by decreeing that until Germany was defeated, the United States would merely act in the manner "best calculated to weaken Japanese economic power."[7] Thus the nation fought during the first year with no clearly articulated aim in the Pacific.

On 24 January 1943, at a famous press conference during the Casablanca summit meeting, Roosevelt offhandedly announced the most far-reaching command decision of World War II: a demand for unconditional surrender of the Axis powers. Unconditional surrender was a term unfamiliar to Orange planners (although it was first uttered by General U. S. Grant during a battle and linked by legend with his initials). But their expressions conveyed a similar meaning. Faith in absolute victory befitted the confident eras of swelling naval power during the last years of both the Theodore and Franklin Roosevelt administrations. The wartime public mood, a compound of moral outrage and growing assurance, embraced the draconian objective. The Combined Staff Planners of the Allies were puzzled by the imprecise meaning and felt the term would be alien to a people whose warriors never surrendered. They proposed instead "the destruction of Japanese capacity to resist" by all means necessary. But the president's formulation stood. As clarified later, Japan was to be occupied, disarmed, and stripped of all overseas territories and its leaders unseated and prosecuted. Only at the end of the war was Emperor Hirohito's retention of a symbolic throne conceded.

For thirty-five years the bedrock ideologies of Plan Orange had been victory by neutralization of land power from the sea and by destruction of the enemy's economy. The siege philosophy had been written into the first draft plan of 1906 and reiterated endlessly. The corollary was to avoid invasion of Japan, an operation deemed unnecessary, logistically impossible, and self-destructive because of the bloodshed and public revulsion it would cause. The planners had reckoned that given several years America could mobilize enough troops and munitions to invade, but before World War II its merchant marine could have sustained only a million men in the Far East and could not have lifted enough in one movement to gain a lodgment against a concentrated foe or have kept them supplied. Blue's heavy motorized equipment would bog down in Japan's rice paddies and mountains. Invasion, they concluded, was "a physical impossibility" with "almost no prospect of success." (Nevertheless, the *threat* of invasion by massing troops on nearby islands was noted as a useful bluff to tie down enemy resources and hasten termination of the war.)

The authors of Plan Orange believed that blockade and bombardment would succeed if maintained unremittingly. But no one knew how long a trial the enemy might endure. They hoped Japan would sue for peace after loss of its navy and commercial isolation even though history suggested that blockades worked slowly. The past offered few clues on the effect of bombing; demonstrations in Spain and China in the 1930s had been inconclusive, although by 1941 British and German experience suggested a toughness of disciplined populations and modern economies.

Plan Orange had projected a "long and exhausting" struggle, defined after the World War as two years' duration, including a year of siege. Cautionaries had warned that it might take two years just to establish a central Pacific naval base. Pessimists who argued the need to build a "second fleet" estimated a three- to four-year struggle. By 1940 Stark was bemoaning a siege of "several years" and Richardson a five- to ten-year war. Every planner had worried that national patience would be "severely tried" by a long war, which thrusters sought to obviate by bold strokes and cautionaries by avoidance of disheartening early defeats. None had foreseen that a crusade against evil dictatorships would energize the American public for a war that lasted three years and eight months.

The penultimate U.S. command decision of World War II was to authorize *planning and preparing* to invade the home islands. Outpourings of arms and transport far exceeding the most extravagant prewar vision rendered invasion in late 1945 a viable option after preliminary siege operations and redeployment of forces from Europe. Suicide tactics were fostering gloomy prognoses that Japan as an organized society would never yield unconditionally to a siege. Only an invasion would allow the fixing of a war termination date.

By mid-1943 the tide had turned in Europe and optimism was budding that the Soviets and Western Allies would do in Hitler in 1944. But the glacial advance on Rabaul begat estimates of a Pacific struggle stretching dismally for years ahead. In May the Trident Conference of Allied strategists could spout only platitudes of beating Japan in the shortest possible time. The Combined Staff Planners in August 1943 laid out a schedule of clearing the Japanese southern empire during 1946 and conducting a siege and/or invasion of Japan in 1947 but did not estimate a surrender date. Signs of weariness began to appear in the United States.

Into the breach stepped Savvy Cooke to urge—for planning purposes—the defeat of Japan within one year after Germany.[8] U.S.

leaders eagerly grasped at his schedule, as did Churchill, despite the inferred diversion of effort from Europe. The goal of victory in 1945 quickly became etched in stone—but not the method. The Combined Staff Planners reported in October 1943 that an invasion could be scheduled within the deadline date but left it an "if necessary" choice. Then in June 1944 the U.S. Joint Staff Planners concluded that a siege strategy would entail "unacceptable delay" in concluding the war. Only "invasion of the industrial heart of Japan" on Honshu could guarantee unconditional surrender by the requisite date. They proposed to mount it at the end of 1945, after intensified blockade and bombing and the occupation of the home island of Kyushu. The Joint Chiefs blessed the strategy—for planning purposes.

The defining moment arrived in April 1945, on the eve of Germany's collapse. The joint planners reported that a siege could probably deliver only a negotiated peace, an outcome that most leaders had come to equate with losing the war. Only invasion could ensure unconditional surrender within a year. They described the assault as economical in casualties while claiming spuriously that a siege would require placing almost as many divisions in China and would stretch the war into late 1946 despite the USSR's promise to attack the Japanese in Manchuria three months hence. Again the JCS, for planning purposes, endorsed the invasion. Following a month of hassles about which admiral or general would command it, on 25 May 1945 the Joint Chiefs issued a directive for a landing at Kagoshima Bay, Kyushu, on 1 November 1945. (A follow-up directive for a March 1946 assault on Honshu was never issued.)

Predictably, each military service favored a closure strategy suited to its abilities. The army, with MacArthur anointed supreme commander of the invasion, regarded landings as inevitable. He and Marshall told President Harry Truman, who had succeeded to the White House upon Roosevelt's death on 12 April, that invasion was the only way to impose on Japan a feeling of "utter helplessness."[9] Kyushu would be a cheap exercise, they said, costing thirty-one thousand American casualties in thirty days, the same number as on Luzon and only half as many as on Okinawa.[10] (After the war, the Army Operations Division reported a sober calculation of thirty thousand per day.[11]) Truman agreed to get on with the planning.

Meanwhile, the siege was progressing smartly. Japan's conventional naval and air power had been destroyed. Its imports had been reduced by 90 percent. Its few surviving vessels were confined to the home islands and Korea.[12] Blue submarines had run out of prey, even in the

Sea of Japan, where Nimitz was considering deploying carriers. U.S. battleships were shelling exposed ports. Starvation lay in the offing. The "robust" aerial campaign by swarms of bombers envisioned in Plan Orange was well under way. Studies of 1943 had reckoned that 784 B-29s could "reduce the Japanese war effort to impotency" in six months.[13] But high-altitude precision attacks on industry failed to put many bombs on target in 1944, and U.S. plane losses ran high. Planners had long understood that the dispersed workshops, pinched transportation lines, and wood-and-paper cities of Japan would be ideal targets for area firebombing. U.S. doctrine forbade it until the discouraging results of precision bombing were assessed. Then the real fury of devastation began. In March 1945 General Curtis LeMay sent the Twenty-First Bomber Command in at night loaded with napalm incendiaries. The heart of Tokyo was burned out and eighty-three thousand Japanese died. Similar raids on other cities followed. By the summer of 1945 flights of up to six hundred planes had gutted the hearts of the largest cities and were methodically incinerating smaller towns as well. In a few months there would be no targets left.

Still, nobody could offer an estimate of the cost of persevering in the siege. Unofficial postwar guesses ranged from casualties in the "low thousands," reflecting minor air and naval losses near Japan in the final days,[14] to seven thousand Allied casualties per week if superfluous battles to clear the southern empire continued, to an extremely heavy toll should Japan let fly against the besiegers the thousands of kamikaze planes it was hoarding.[15]

Whether the United States officially abandoned the Orange Plan strategy is open to question. No one can know for sure if an invasion of Japan would have been attempted, although its success has rarely been doubted. The rush of events in August 1945—the atomic bombs, the Soviet attack, the frantic peace feelers from Tokyo—changed everything. Speculations about the choice of siege versus invasion have necessarily addressed a hypothetical situation that excludes those extraordinary events.

Official postwar assessments echoed the biases of 1945. The U.S. Strategic Bombing Survey opined that Japan would have been so badly incapacitated by the siege that it would have yielded by the end of the year and in all probability by 1 November.[16] Army Air Forces leaders loyally supported Marshall and MacArthur in justifying invasion as the only way to beat the enemy without destroying him.[17] An army historian claimed that unconditional surrender would not have ensued without the means, plans, and *intent* to invade.[18] But most admirals asserted that they had felt the invasion would not have been tried. Nimitz doubted it would be needed. Spruance called it "a terribly bloody, unnecessary proposition." Leahy thought the siege would succeed "in due course" and preened that "the Army did not appear to be able to understand that the Navy with some Army air assistance, already had defeated Japan." King explained his passivity toward invasion in front of the president as an obligatory show of unanimity among the Joint Chiefs but said he expected to have a chance to change his mind.[19] There was also semantic obfuscation as to whether the Kyushu operation would constitute a "real" invasion or merely the winning of a final siege base. Nevertheless, the navy's acquiescence in plans to convert the maritime war to a land war reverberates as a faltering of conviction in the classic strategy that had served it so well.

This review is not intended to second-guess the decision makers but to evaluate the status of War Plan Orange in August 1945. Apparently none of them referred to the cumulative findings of three and a half decades of planning at that time or in recollections and later studies. Granting that old plans may have seemed antediluvian by then, it would still have been informative to exhume and review the historic annals. Roosevelt must have been familiar with the siege doctrine since his Navy Department days of 1913–20, yet he raised no objection to preliminary planning for an invasion. Truman probably had no knowledge of Plan Orange even though nearly all its principles and many details had just been executed with superlative success. Military chieftains with memories of prewar studies and games could have contemplated the situation from a longer baseline of perspective. If so, their judgment might have been tempered by the reasoning of cooler days, before the thirst for revenge and the massing of great legions, that a siege must inexorably yield total victory. In the end, however, events took charge and vindicated Plan Orange.

There were no equivalents of the atomic bombings in Orange or wartime plans. The weapon was unknown to most strategists and unproven until three weeks before it was dropped on Hiroshima and Nagasaki. The decision to use it was made by Truman based on recommendations of his military and civilian advisers. The bombings were acclaimed by American and Allied peoples. Every fighting man in or headed for the Pacific breathed a prayer of thanks. Japan surrendered within the week.

After the war reinterpretations set in. Stimson and Churchill claimed that the bombs had obviated a million or more Allied invasion casualties. Truman's memoirs claimed that half a million American deaths had been avoided. All implied even more horrendous Japanese losses.[20] The invasion toll has become the standard justification of the atomic bombings, even though it is questionable that after 292,000 American deaths in all theaters of World War II, any president would have accepted carnage on that scale as the only option for ending the war. The casualty rationale has been the easiest for the decision makers to cleave to and best for America's moral posture in the world. Other interpretations, tinged with emotional attitudes of a later age toward nuclear weapons, have since appeared. They have included speculations about alternative possibilities of warning or negotiation; of hidden agendas of awing the Soviets, or ending the war before they could demand a role in occupying Japan, or avoiding a communist revolution in that ruined land if the war continued; of justifying the huge expense of the bomb program; of immorality and racism; and simply of *having* the bomb as its own imperative.

In the summer of 1945 the United States had two deliverable atomic bombs. The leadership from Truman down viewed them as weapons of devastation, instruments of siege notwithstanding musings of tactical use on beachheads. The Orange Plan had covenanted absolute victory by siege, but it could not preclude an excruciatingly long process that would exhaust American will. The bombs were perfect weapons to bring a swift conclusion. If the civil and military captains had not wavered by calling for an invasion, the bombs would be remembered for what they were, the ultimate implements of the nation's longest-standing war policy. It had been defined thirty-five years earlier as "the eventual impoverishment and exhaustion of Orange by such acts of repression as the circumstances of the war may make necessary or desirable."[21] At the culminating moment of the strategy's execution, the bombs cured its last defect, the possibility of an unbearably protracted war. The start of the nuclear age marked the finale of War Plan Orange.

Appendixes

UNITED STATES LEADERS AND PLANNERS INVOLVED IN WAR PLAN ORANGE, 1906 TO MID-1919

	1906	1907	1908	1909	1910	1911	1912	1913	1914	1915	1916	1917	1918	1919
President of the United States														
Theodore Roosevelt	••••	••••	••••	•										
William Howard Taft				•••	••••	••••	••••	•						
Woodrow Wilson								•••	••••	••••	••••	••••	••••	••
Secretary of the Navy														
Charles J. Bonaparte	••••													
Victor H. Metcalf		••••	••••											
Truman H. Newberry			•	•										
George von L. Meyer				•••	••••	••••	•••	•						
Josephus Daniels								•••	••••	••••	••••	••••	••••	••
Assistant Secretary of the Navy (partial listing)														
Franklin D. Roosevelt								•••	••••	••••	••••	••••	••••	••
Senior Member of the Joint Army-Navy Board														
Adm George Dewey	••••	••••	••••	•••	•••	•••	•••	•••	•••	•••	•••	•		
Chief of Staff of the Army														
MajGen J. Franklin Bell	••••	••••	••••	••••	••									
MajGen Leonard Wood					••	•••	•••	•••	••					
MajGen William Wotherspoon									••					
MajGen Hugh L. Scott									•	••••	••••	••••	••	
Gen Peyton C. March													••	••
General Board of the Navy (president[a] and certain other members)														
Adm George Dewey	••••	••••	••••	••••	••••	••••	•••	•••	•••	•••	•••			
Cp/RAdm R. Wainwright	••	••		??	••••	••••	•?							
Cp Raymond P. Rodgers	••••	••••	••••	••••	••••	•••								
Cp Nathan Sargent	••••	••												
Cp/RAdm Sidney Staunton			??••	•?	•?	??	•??	??••		•?				
Cp Bradley A. Fiske	••				??	•••?		??••	••••					

Cp William L. Rodgers

Cp William R. Shoemaker

Cp Harry S. Knapp

Cp James O. Oliver

RAdm Charles J. Badger

RAdm William S. Benson

Staff duty with General Board (partial listing)

LCd Frank K. Hill

Lt/LtC Clarence S. Williams

Cd Victor Blue

Cd Lusius A. Bostwick

Naval War College (president[a] and certain other staff members)

Cp/RAdm John P. Merrell

Cd/Cp James O. Oliver

RAdm Raymond P. Rodgers

RAdm Alfred T. Mahan (consulting)

Cd/Cp Frank K. Hill

Cd William V. Pratt

Cp William L. Rodgers

RAdm Austin Knight

Cp/RAdm William S. Sims

Chief of Naval Operations

Adm William S. Benson

Notes

?—indicates date of assignment uncertain.   [a]The president is indicated by underlining.   [b]NWC had three acting presidents 1917–1919.

UNITED STATES LEADERS AND PLANNERS INVOLVED IN WAR PLAN ORANGE, 1917 TO 1928

	1917	1918	1919	1920	1921	1922	1923	1924	1925	1926	1927	1928
President of the United States												
Woodrow Wilson	•••	••••	••••	••••	•							
Warren G. Harding					•••	••••	••					
Calvin Coolidge							••	••••	••••	••••	••••	••••
Secretary of the Navy												
Josephus Daniels	•••	••••	••••	••••	•							
Edwin Denby					•••	••••	••••	• ••				
Curtis D. Wilbur								••	••••	••••	••••	•••
Assistant Secretary of the Navy (partial listing)												
Franklin D. Roosevelt	•••	••••	••••	••								
Theodore Roosevelt, Jr.					•							
Senior Member of the Joint Army-Navy Board[a]					•	••••	••••	••••	••••	•••	••••	•••
Chief of Staff of the Army[a]												
MajGen Hugh L. Scott	•••	••										
Gen Peyton C. March		•••	••••	•••	••							
Gen John J. Pershing					••	•••	•••	•• ••				
MajGen John L. Hines								••		•		
Gen Charles P. Summerall										•		
General Board of the Navy (through 1923, when ceased war planning; president[b] and certain other members)												
Adm George Dewey	•											
RAdm Charles J. Badger	••••	••••	••••	••••	•							
Cp William R. Shoemaker	••••	••••	••									
Cp James O. Oliver	••											
RAdm William L. Rodgers					•••	••• •••	••• •••					
Cp Frank H. Schofield					••	•••	•• ••					
Chief of Naval Operations[a]												
Adm William S. Benson	••••	••••	•••									
Adm Robert E. Coontz			•	•••	•	•••	••					
Adm Edward W. Eberle							••	••••	••••	••••	••••	
Adm Charles F. Hughes											• •	••••

President of Naval War College (through 1927)
Cp/RAdm William S. Sims ●c
RAdm Clarence S. Williams
RAdm William V. Pratt

War Plans Division d (director b *and certain other members*)
Cp Harry E. Yarnell
RAdm James H. Oliver
Cp Thomas C. Hart
Cd/Cp William S. Pye
Cp Lusius A. Bostwick
RAdm Clarence S. Williams
Cp Sinclair Gannon
RAdm William R. Shoemaker
Cp William H. Standley
Cp R. M. Griswold
RAdm Frank H. Schofield
Cp Frederick J. Horne
Cd/Cp Merlyn G. Cook

Commander-in-Chief, United States Fleet
Adm Henry T. Mayo
Adm Hugh Rodman e
Adm Edward W. Eberle e
Adm Hilary P. Jones
Adm Robert E. Coontz
Adm Samuel S. Robison
Adm Charles F. Hughes
Adm Henry A. Wiley

Fleet War Plans Officer
Cp S. Gannon, Asst Chief of Staff f

Notes
?—indicates date of assignment uncertain.   a The Senior Member of Joint Board from July 1919 was the more senior of the Chief of Staff or the Chief of Naval Operations. Name is underlined.   b The president or director is indicated by underlining.   c NWC had three acting presidents 1917–1919.   d Planning Division July 1919 to January 1922.   e C-in-C Pacific Fleet; U.S. Fleet was disestablished July 1919 to December 1922.   f De facto war plans officer.

UNITED STATES LEADERS AND PLANNERS INVOLVED IN WAR PLAN ORANGE, 1926 TO 1935

	1926	1927	1928	1929	1930	1931	1932	1933	1934	1935
President of the United States										
Calvin Coolidge	••••	••••	••••	•						
Herbert Hoover				•••	••••	••••	••••	•		
Franklin D. Roosevelt								•••	••••	•••
Secretary of the Navy										
Curtis D. Wilbur	••••	••••	••••	•						
Charles F. Adams				•••	••••	••••	••••	•		
Claude A. Swanson								•••	••••	•••
Senior Member of the Joint Army-Navy Board [a]										
Chief of Staff of the Army [a]										
MajGen John L. Hines	•••									
Gen Charles P. Summerall	•	••••	••••	••••	•••ǀ					
Gen Douglas MacArthur					•ǀ	•••ǀ	•••ǀ	••	•••ǀ	•••ǀ
Chief of Naval Operations [a]										
Adm Edward W. Eberle	••••	••••ǀ								
Adm Charles F. Hughes		•ǀ	••••ǀ	•••ǀ	••ǀ					
Adm William V. Pratt					••	••••	••••	••ǀ		
Adm William H. Standley								••	•••ǀ	•••ǀ
War Plans Division (*director* [b] *and certain other members*)										
Cp William H. Standley	•ǀ									
Cp/RAdm William S. Pye	••••	•								
Cp R. M. Griswold	?•••	••••	•••							
RAdm Frank H. Schofield	••ǀ	••••ǀ	••••ǀ	•ǀ						

Cp Frederick J. Horne
Cd/Cp Merlyn G. Cook
RAdm Montgomery M. Taylor
RAdm Edward C. Kalbfus
Cp R. F. Dillen
Cp George J. Meyers
Cp/RAdm Samuel W. Bryant
Col Thomas Holcomb, USMC
Cp Royal E. Ingersoll

Commander-in-Chief, United States Fleet

Adm Samuel S. Robison
Adm Charles F. Hughes
Adm Henry A. Wiley
Adm William V. Pratt
Adm John V. Chase
Adm Frank H. Schofield
Adm Richard H. Leigh
Adm David F. Sellers
Adm Joseph M. Reeves

Fleet War Plans Officer

Cd Cary W. Magruder

Notes

?—indicates date of assignment uncertain.   ᵃSenior Member of Joint Board was the more senior of the Chief of Staff or the Chief of Naval Operations.   ᵇThe director is indicated by underlining.   Name is underlined.

UNITED STATES LEADERS AND PLANNERS INVOLVED IN WAR PLAN ORANGE, 1933 TO 1941

	1933	1934	1935	1936	1937	1938	1939	1940	1941
President of the United States									
Franklin D. Roosevelt	••	••••	••••	••••	••••	••••	••••	••••	••••
Secretary of the Navy									
Claude A. Swanson	••	••••	••••	••••	••••	••••	••		
Charles Edison								••	
Frank Knox								••	••••
Assistant or Under Secretary of the Navy									
Henry L. Roosevelt	••••	••••	••••						
Charles Edison				•					
James V. Forrestal					••••	••••	••••	••••	••••
Senior Member of the Joint Army-Navy Board[a]									
Chief of Staff of the Army[a]									
Gen Douglas MacArthur	••••	••••	••						
Gen Malin Craig			•	••••	••••	••••	••		
Gen George C. Marshall							••	••••	••••
Chief of Naval Operations[a]									
Adm William V. Pratt	••								
Adm William H. Standley	••	••••	••••	••••					
Adm William D. Leahy					••••	••••	••		
Adm Harold R. Stark							••	••••	••••
War Plans Division *(director*[b] *and certain other members)*									
Cp/RAdm Samuel W. Bryant	••••	••							
Cp R. F. Dillen	••••	••••							
Cp George J. Meyers	••••	••••	••						
Col Thomas Holcomb, USMC	••••	••••							
RAdm William S. Pye			••	••					

Cp Royal E. Ingersoll
LtC Vincent R. Murphy
Cp Robert L. Ghormley
Cp Russell S. Crenshaw
Cp Charles M. Cooke
Cp Charles J. Moore
Cp Harry W. Hill
Cd Forrest P. Sherman
Cp Oscar Smith
Cp/RAdm Richmond K. Turner

Commander-in-Chief, United States Fleet

Adm Richard H. Leigh
Adm David F. Sellers
Adm Joseph M. Reeves
Adm Arthur J. Hepburn
Adm Claud C. Bloch
Adm James O. Richardson
Adm Husband E. Kimmel[c]

Fleet War Plans Officer[b] and aides

Cd Cary W. Magruder
Cd Charles M. Cooke
Cp Harry W. Hill
Cd Forrest P. Sherman (aviation)
Cd Vincent R. Murphy
Cp Charles H. McMorris
Cd Lynde W. McCormick
Lt Francis R. Duborg

Notes

? —indicates date of assignment uncertain.   [a]Senior Member of Joint Board was the more senior of the Chief of Staff or the Chief of
Naval Operations. Name is underlined.   [b]Indicated by underlining.   [c]C-in-C Pacific Fleet (established February 1941)

Abbreviations

AA	Antiaircraft
AAC	Army Air Corps
AAF	Army Air Forces
ABC-1	U.S.-British Conference of military staffs, early 1941
A/C	Aircraft
ACOS	Assistant Chief of Staff
Actg	Acting
Adm	Admiral
Admin	Administrative
Adv	Advance, Advanced
AG	Adjutant General
AGO	Adjutant General's Office
A&N	Army and Navy
App	Appendix
Asst	Assistant
Astc	Asiatic
Atl	Atlantic
Avn	Aviation
AWC	Army War College
AWPD	Army War Plans Division
B-1, B-2, B-3	Base One, Base Two, Base Three

BasFor	Base Force
BatFor	Battle Force
Bd	Board
Biog	Biographical
Blue	United States; or designating U.S. forces, strategy, and so on
Br Gen	Brigadier General
Brit	British
Bu	Bureau
BuAer	Bureau of Aeronautics, Navy Department
BuC&R	Bureau of Construction and Repair, Navy Department
BuDocks	Bureau of Yards and Docks, Navy Department
BuEquipt	Bureau of Equipment, Navy Department
BuNav	Bureau of Navigation, Navy Department
BuOrd	Bureau of Ordnance, Navy Department
B-W	Base Western
Cdg	Commanding
Cdr	Commander
Cdt	Commandant
Centr Div	Central Division of the Office of Naval Operations
CG	Commanding General
Chrmn	Chairman
CinC	Commander in Chief
CinCAF	Commander in Chief, Asiatic Fleet
CinCPAC	Commander in Chief, Pacific Fleet
CinCPOA	Commander in Chief, Pacific Ocean Areas (in WWII)
CinCUS	Commander in Chief, United States Fleet (pre-WWII)
CinCUSJAF	Commander in Chief, United States Joint Asiatic Force
CNO	Chief of Naval Operations
CO	Commanding Officer
Color Plans	U.S. plans for war with various countries code-named by color, e.g., Orange, Red, Black
ComAirBasFor	Commander Aircraft, Base Force
ComAirBatFor	Commander Aircraft, Battle Force
ComAirScoFor	Commander Aircraft, Scouting Force
ComBasFor	Commander Base Force
ComBatFor	Commander Battle Force
Cominch	Commander in Chief, United States Fleet (WWII)
Comm	Committee
ComMinBatFor	Commander Mine Craft, Battle Force
ComScoFor	Commander Scouting Force
ComSubFor	Commander Submarine Force
Conf	Confidential
Corresp	Correspondence
COS	Chief of Staff
Cpt	Captain

Def	Defense, Defenses
Dept	Department
Dev	Development
Dir	Director
Div	Division
Encl	Enclosure
Est	Estimate
FAW	Fleet Air Wing
FE	Far East
Flt	Fleet. Any of the following U.S. Navy organizations:
	The aggregate of large warships of the navy up to 1919, sometimes known as the Battle Fleet
	The combined Atlantic and Pacific fleets, mid-1919 through 1922
	The United States Fleet, first half of 1919 and from 8 December 1922 to 31 January 1941
	The Pacific Fleet from 1 February 1941 through the end of World War II
	At any time the bulk of U.S. naval forces regardless of formal organization
	"Fleet" includes aircraft, auxiliaries, and attached units such as the Fleet Marine Force
	Smaller American fleets, like the Asiatic Fleet, Atlantic Fleet, and Scouting Fleet, are referred to by name
FMF	Fleet Marine Force
F-1	Assistant Chief of Staff for Plans, Office of Cominch (in WWII)
F-12	Cominch Plans Division (in WWII)
GB	General Board of the Navy
Gen	General
Gov-Genl	Governor-General (of the Philippines)
GS	General Staff (of Army)
G-2	G-2 Division (Intelligence) of Army General Staff
Haw, Hawn	Hawaii, Hawaiian
Hbr	Harbor
HQ	Headquarters
I, Is	Island, Islands
JB	Joint Army and Navy Board, known as Joint Board
JCS	Joint Chiefs of Staff (of WWII)
JPC	Joint Planning Committee of Joint Board
JPS	Joint Staff Planners (of WWII)
JSSC	Joint Strategic Survey Committee (of WWII)
Jt	Joint
Jt A&N	Joint Army and Navy
JUSSC	Joint U.S. Strategic Survey Committee (of WWII)
JWPC	Joint War Plans Committee (of WWII)
LC	Library of Congress
Lectr	Lecture

Lt	Lieutenant
Lt Cdr	Lieutenant-Commander
Ltr, Ltrs	Letter, Letters
Maj Gen Cdt	Major-General Commandant, U.S. Marine Corps
Mil	Military
Mmbr	Member
NA	National Archives, Washington, D.C., and annex at Suitland, Maryland, when indicated
Nav	Naval
NAS	Naval Air Station
ND	Naval District
n.d.	No date
NHC	Naval History Collection, Naval War College, Newport, Rhode Island
NHD	Naval History Division (now Naval Historical Center), Washington Navy Yard, Washington, D.C.
NWC	Naval War College, Newport, Rhode Island
OA, NHD	Operational Archives, Naval History Division (now Naval Historical Center)
O-1	Plan of United States Fleet or Pacific Fleet
O-3	Plan of Asiatic Fleet (until 1926, of United States Fleet)
ONI	Office of Naval Intelligence
Op, Opg	Operating
OPD	Operations Division (Army, WWII)
Opns	Operations
OpNav	Office of the Chief of Naval Operations
Op-12	Same as War Plans Division; also its director
Op-12A	Policy and Projects Section of WPD; also its head
Op-12B	Plans Section of WPD; also its head
Orange	Japan, Japanese. In context, War Plan Orange or the strategy of the plan
Pac	Pacific
PatWing	Patrol Wing
PHH	Pearl Harbor Hearings of U.S. Congress, Joint Committee on the Investigation of the Pearl Harbor Attack, 79th Congress, 1946, including exhibits and reprinted records of prior hearings by other agencies
Phils	Philippine Islands
PIs	Philippine Islands
Portf	Portfolio
Prob	Probably
Prepn	Preparation
Pres	President
Rainbow Plans	U.S. war plans Rainbow One through Five, 1939–46
RAdm	Rear Admiral
Reconn	Reconnaissance

Red	Great Britain, British
Rept	Report
RG	Record Group
Rte	Route
ScoFor	Scouting Force
2d Committee	Second Committee of the General Board of the Navy
SecNav	Secretary of the Navy
SecWar	Secretary of War
SecState	Secretary of State
Secy	Secretary
Ser	Serial
Sitn	Situation
Spenavo	Special Naval Observer, London
Sqn	Squadron
Sr	Senior
Sta	Station
Subj	Subject
Supt	Superintendent
TF	Task Force
USAF	United States Asiatic Force
USJAF	United States Joint Asiatic Force
USMC	United States Marine Corps
USN	United States Navy
VAdm	Vice-Admiral
VP	Patrol seaplane, flying boat
VPB	Patrol bomber (flying boat)
w	With
Wash Conf	Washington Conference of 1921–22
WP	War Plan
WPD	War Plans Division, Office of the Chief of Naval Operations
WPL + number	War Plan of Office of the Chief of Naval Operations
WPO	War Plan Orange
WPPac + number	War Plan of Pacific Fleet
WPUSF + number	War Plan of United States Fleet
WWI	World War I
WWII	World War II

Notes

Chapter 1 Plan Orange and the Global War

1. At least twenty-three colors were assigned, including Black (Germany), Gold (France), Purple (Russia), Green (Mexico), Red (Great Britain, with Crimson, Scarlet, Ruby, and so on for the British Dominions), and White (Domestic Emergency). JB Minutes, 29 Oct 04, Box 2; Vlahos, *Blue Sword*, App I. The origins of the colors are unknown; perhaps the British Empire's red tinting on maps or Japan's rising sun ensign were suggestive.
2. Secy of JB to COS, Jt A&N Basic WP—Rainbow 5 and Report of US-Brit Staff Conversations ABC-1, 9 Jun 41, JB Rainbow 5 File.
3. Distribution lists are attached to some archival copies of Orange Plans.
4. Lehman, *Command of the Seas*, 217, used in reference to procurement policy. Byron, lecture, NWC, 15 Jun 89.
5. See Chapter 27 for instances of wartime use of prewar plans.
6. Williams had been the navy's third director of war plans. Patekewich, "Book of NWC Admirals." Hoyt, *How They Won*, 43.
7. Geopolitics refers broadly to national conduct and expectations. Fundamental policy, meaning ends and goals set by highest civilian authorities, was not generally relevant to Plan Orange. See Lowenthal, *Leadership and Indecision*, 1:4–5.
8. Matloff, *Strategic Planning, 1943–1944*, App E.

Chapter 2 The American Way of Planning: The Independent Staffs

1. Admiral James D. Watkins, "The Maritime Strategy," *U.S. Naval Institute Proceedings,* supplement, January 1986, 15–17.
2. GB to Pres NWC, Plan of a war portf, 6 Jun 12, #425, Box 123, GB Subj File.
3. Special Comm, NWC Staff to Pres NWC, Educational Work of War College as Related to War Plans, 19 Oct 11; Pres NWC to GB, Plan of a war portf, 23 Mar 12; GB to Pres NWC, same title, 6 Jun 12, #425, Box 123, GB Subj File.
4. Horne, lecture, ca. mid-1922.
5. SecState to SecWar & SecNav, 17 Jan 22, in Davis, *History of Joint Chiefs,* 1:18–19.
6. Cpt H. Yarnell to Col J. W. Gulick, Natl Policy & War Plans, 28 Oct 19, JB Ser Misc 18, in Morton, "War Plan ORANGE," 225. Cpt William D. Puleston to SecNav via Cdt AWC, 9 Sep 30, in Davis, *History of Joint Chiefs,* 1:20–21.
7. Lowenthal, *Leadership and Indecision,* 1:62–66, 159, 262–64. Davis, *History of Joint Chiefs,* 1:34.
8. 2nd Comm to GB, Memo on Prepn of Genl War Plans, read by Cpt Howard to GB 23 Nov 09; Acting SecNav (Winthrop) to GB, 1 Oct 10, #425, Box 122, GB Subj File.
9. SecNav, Annual Repts, various years, passim.
10. Coletta, "Josephus Daniels," 564–72.
11. Rep. Carl Vinson, Nav Avn Facilities, 21 Feb 39, Hepburn Rept Notebooks.
12. Brune, *Origins of Security Policy,* 59.
13. Braisted, *Navy in Pacific, 1897–1909,* 123. Morton, "War Plan ORANGE," 222. Davis, *History of Joint Chiefs,* 1:7, 11. Lowenthal, *Leadership and Indecision,* 1:60, 106–8.
14. JB to SecNav & SecWar, 18 Jun 07, #325, JB Records. Ainsworth to Wood, 6 Jul 07, RG 94, AGO File No. 1260092, in Braisted, *Navy in Pacific, 1897–1909,* 204–5.
15. JB Proceedings, 8 May 13, #301, roll 1. Braisted, *Navy in Pacific, 1897–1909,* 124–29, 132–40; Lowenthal, *Leadership and Indecision,* 60.
16. Costello, "Planning for War," 11–12, 17. Vlahos, "NWC and Origins," 23–41.
17. SecNav to Dewey, 30 Mar 00, #401, GB Subj File.
18. Leech, *Days of McKinley,* chap. 18.
19. Spector, *Professors of War,* chap. 8. Costello, "Planning for War," 23, 34.
20. Crowl, "Mahan."
21. Albion, *Makers of Policy,* 82. Costello, "Planning for War," 29–34. Spector, *Admiral of New Empire,* 123, 127.
22. Wheeler, *Pratt,* 70–71.
23. Hattendorf et al., *Sailors and Scholars,* 70–72; Reynolds, *Admirals,* 280.
24. Albion, *Makers of Policy,* 82. SecNav to CinCs US Nav Forces, 15 Dec 00; CinC US Nav Forces on Astc Statn to SecNav, 28 Feb 01; CinC US Nav Force Pac Station to SecNav, 25 Mar 01, #401.2, Box 3, GB Subj File.
25. Crenshaw, lecture, NWC, 10 May 40.
26. Horne, lecture, USMC School, 27 Apr 28. Pye, lecture, NWC, 7 Jan 26.
27. James Harrison Oliver, Flag Officer Biog Files. Dorwart, *Office of Naval Intelligence,* 96–105.

28. NWC, Problem of 1907, Tentative Plan of Campaign & Strategic Game, 12 Jul 07, 17–18, 118–19, 156–58; Cdr James H. Oliver, Concerning Problem of the Year (1907), pt. III, NWC Problems & Solutions.
29. Clarence Stewart Williams, Flag Officer Biog Files.
30. 2d Comm to GB, Memo on Prepn of Genl War Plans, read 23 Nov 09, #425, Box 122, GB Subj File.

Chapter 3   The Geopolitics of the Pacific War

1. Roosevelt to Theodore Roosevelt, Jr., 10 Feb 04, in Morison, *Letters of Theodore Roosevelt*, 4:724.
2. Stephan, *Hawaii under Rising Sun*, chap. 1.
3. Spector, *Professors of War*, 197.
4. NWC 1911 Plan, 4. GB 1914 Plan, Strategic Section, 8.
5. James K. Eyre, Jr., "Japanese Imperialism and the Aguinaldo Insurrection," *U.S. Naval Institute Proceedings*, no. 558 (Aug 1949):901–7.
6. NWC Rept of Conference of 1907, pt. 1, 26, 101. NWC 1911 Plan, 4. GB 1914 Plan, 8.
7. Esthus, *Roosevelt and Japan*, chaps. 8–10, passim.
8. GB 1906 Plan.
9. William Loeb, Jr., to SecNav, 27 Oct 06; GB to Asst SecNav, 29 Oct 06, #425.2, Box 141, GB Subj File.
10. Ainsworth to Wood, 6 Jul 07, RG 94, AGO File #1260092, in Braisted, *Navy in Pacific, 1897–1909*, 204–5.
11. Esthus, *Roosevelt and Japan*, passim.
12. NWC Rept of Conference of 1907, pt. 1, 26, 101.
13. NWC 1911 Plan, Sec. II, 5.
14. Braisted, *Navy in Pacific, 1909–1922*, 124–29. GB Proceedings, 5:84–85; Corresp between GB and SecNav, 29 Apr–13 May 13, #425, Box 123, GB Subj File. JB Proceedings, 8 May 13, #301, roll 1.
15. Mahan to SecNav George von L. Meyer, 24 Sep 10, #404, GB Records, in Challener, *Admirals, Generals*, 17.
16. Leech, *Days of McKinley*, 481, 514–17. Esthus, *Roosevelt and Japan*, 5–8. Challener, *Admirals, Generals*, 18, 180–81, 203–4, 218.
17. GB to RAdm Frederick Rodgers, 16 Feb 01; Rodgers to SecNav, 13 May 01, #92, #425.2, Box 140, GB Subj File.
18. GB Proceedings, 29 May 02. NWC, "Solution of the Problem of 1902," RG 12, NHC, NWC, 14–19, in Vlahos, "NWC and Origins," 26. 2d Comm of GB, n.d. (approved by GB 29 Jul 03), #425, Box 122; Pres NWC to GB, 1 Sep 03, #425.2, Box 141, and 18 Jan 04, #425, Box 122, GB Subj File.
19. Taylor to JB, 10 Jun 04, #325, JB Records.
20. Br Gen Tasker Bliss to JB, 10 Jun 04, #303, JB Records.
21. JB to SecNav, 24 Jun 04, #425, Box 122, GB Subj File.
22. GB to CinC Astc Flt, 26 Apr 06; GB to Pres NWC, 2 Oct 06, #425.2, Box 141, GB Subj File.
23. GB to RAdm Frederick Rodgers, 16 Feb 01; Rodgers to Sec Nav, 13 May 01; GB to CinC US Nav Force on Astc Station, #165, 18 Oct 01; GB to CinC Astc Flt, 17 Sep 03, #425.2, all in Boxes 140–42, GB Subj File.

24. Dewey, *Autobiography,* 175–78.
25. Taylor to JB, 10 Jun 04, #325, JB Records.
26. NWC 1911 Plan, 1–10.
27. Special Comm, NWC Staff, to Pres NWC, Method of Preparing Strategic Plans, 18 Oct 11, #425, Box 123, GB Subj File.
28. GB 1914 Plan, 3, 8–10.
29. CinCAF (F. B. Upham) to CNO, Shall US retain Phil Is; or . . . a Naval Base . . . ? 2 Jan 35, File EG62, Box 255, SecNav & CNO Secret Corresp.
30. SecWar to JB, WPD 532-9, 7 Mar 24, cited in JB to SecNav, Relations w Phil Is & Mil & Nav Bases in Case Independence Granted, 14 Mar 24, #305, Ser 227; JB to SecWar, Mil Value of the Phil Is to US, 23 Oct 31; Asst COS G-2 to COS, International aspects of Phil independence, 6 May 30, #305, Ser 499; JPC to JB, 2 Feb 34, #305, Ser 227, JB Records.
31. CNO to CinCAF, 7 Feb 41, CNO-CinCUS-CinCAF WPL-44 corresp, Jan–Feb 1941.
32. GB 1914 Plan, 3–4. RAdm A. T. Mahan to Cdr J. Oliver, 22 Feb and 4 Mar 11, Mahan-Oliver Corresp 1911.
33. NWC Rept of Conference of 1907, pt. 1, 14–16. GB 1914 Plan, 11.
34. The forty-day assumption appears in Plan O-3, ca. Jan 1925, 7.
35. Lt Cdr W. D. MacDougall, Study of Special Situation, 5 Apr 07, JNOpP, RG 8, NHC, NWC, in Vlahos, "NWC and Origins," 32.
36. NWC Conference of 1906, pt. 2, 26.
37. GB 1914 Plan, foreword, 10, 14–15, 50, App A.
38. These observations appeared frequently in Orange Plans of the 1920s, most fully in JPC Est, Jan 1928.
39. WPD Est 1922, 12–13.
40. GB 1906 Plan, 1–3.
41. NWC 1911 Plan, 2(a):1.
42. Cdr James H. Oliver, NWC, Concerning Problem of the Year (1907), Jun 1907, pt. 3, NWC Problems & Solutions.
43. WPD Est 1922, 3.
44. JPC Est, Jan 1928, 41.
45. Dewey to Pres NWC, 19 Jun 12, GB Records, in Spector, *Professors of War,* 110. GB 1914 Plan, 73.
46. GB 1914 Plan, 13.
47. Mahan, 22 Feb & 4 Mar 11, Mahan-Oliver Corresp 1911.
48. Oliver, 1907 Problem, 8.
49. Dir WPD to GB, Questions concerning Limitation of Armament, 19 Oct 21, #425, GB Subj File.
50. Mahan, 22 Feb & 4 Mar 11, Mahan-Oliver Corresp 1911.
51. GB 1914 Plan, 36–38, 125–26.
52. For example, Army Est, Aug 1927.
53. Actg Dir WPD to CNO, Strategic Survey of Pacific, 3 May 23; CNO to SecNav, same title, 10 May 23, 198–26, roll 80, SecNav & CNO Secret & Conf Corresp.
54. JPC Est, Jan 1928, 38.
55. JPC to JB, Jt A&N Basic War Plan—Orange, 12 Mar 24, JPC Plan 1924.
56. Cpt R. A. Koch, NWC, Blue-Orange Study, 31 Mar 33, w Apps 1 to 3; Head of

Research Dept NWC to COS NWC, Position of US in Far East, 3 Apr 33, UNOpP, Box 49, RG 8, NHC, NWC.

Chapter 4 Grand Strategy

1. Schofield, lecture, 23 Mar 28.
2. For a modern citation of the 10 percent rule see Friedman, *U.S. Maritime Strategy*, 72, n. 10.
3. Hughes, *Fleet Tactics*, 35–37.
4. WPD Est 1922, 8.
5. SecNav to Pres NWC, 16 Nov 10, Box 122, GB Subj File.
6. Richardson, *On the Treadmill*, 266.
7. Cdr James H. Oliver, NWC, Concerning Problem of the Year (1907), Jun 1907, pt. III, NWC Problems & Solutions.
8. Crowl, "Mahan," 444–77.
9. Robert Debs Heinl, Jr., *Dictionary of Military and Naval Quotations* (Annapolis: Naval Institute Press, 1966), 122.
10. Mahan, 22 Feb & 4 Mar 11, Mahan-Oliver Corresp 1911.

Chapter 5 The Eastern Pacific Bastion

1. Cpt Charles M. Cooke to Dir WPD, Atlantic War Plans, 7 Oct 38; Cooke to Dir WPD, 7 May 39, Al6-3 Warfare Misc, Box 90, WPD Files. JB, Jt A&N Basic WPs, Rainbow Nos. 1, 2, 3, and 4, 12 May 39, #325, Ser 642, Box 1942, JB, Plans & Opns Div.
2. Vlahos, "NWC and Origins," 24.
3. Bd of Officers, Plans of Campaign against Spain & Japan, 1897, 4–5.
4. John M. Ellicott, Sea Power of Japan, Apr 00, File JN; Strategic Features of Phil Is, Hawaii & Guam, 14 Jun 00, File XSTP, RG 8, NHC, NWC, in Vlahos, "NWC and Origins," 25–26.
5. JB to SecNav & SecWar, 18 Jun 07, #325, JB Records.
6. NWC Conference of 1906, 15–16.
7. NWC 1911 Plan, 2(b), 6–7.
8. GB 1910 Plan, 5–6.
9. AWPD to COS, draft memo, Revision of Jt A&N Basic WP–Orange, Jan 1935; COS to JB, same title, 18 Jan 35, File 234, Box 70, AWPD Color Plans.
10. GB 1914 Plan, 39–44.
11. AWC Repts, 13–14 Apr 1925. JPC Est, Jan 1928, 26, 42–44.
12. Bywater, *Great Pacific War.*
13. AWPD Plan 1936, 28.
14. GB 1917 Strategic Problem.
15. AWC Repts, 13–14 Apr 1925.
16. JPC Plan 1924.
17. AWPD Plan 1936, 22–23, 28. WPL-35, CNO, June 1939, vol. 1, pt. 1. JPC, Exploratory Studies, 21 Apr 39, Sec III, 23.
18. Cdg Gen 4th Army to ACOS AWPD, Def of Alaska under Army Strategical Plan–Orange, 17 Nov 38, #2720-107, AWPD Files. JPC, Exploratory Studies, 21 Apr 1939, Sec III, 11–13.

19. Watson, *COS: Prewar Plans*, 454–57. Personal Ltr, Marshall to the Pres, 22 Nov 39, ibid. Matloff and Snell, *War Dept.: Strategic Planning, 1941–42*, endpaper table.
20. GB 1914 Plan, 13, 29–31, 62.
21. Dir WPD to CNO, Nav Air Sta, Seattle, 18 Jun 38, NA13, Signed Ltrs, Box 78, WPD Files. Maj A. Frank Kibler, Memo for file w Secret Ltr HQ 4th Army, May 1939, #2720-135, RG 165, NA.
22. Chief BuAer to SecNav, Best Location for Air Bases in PIs, Guam & Alaska, 24 Jan 35; GB to SecNav, Policy regarding nav bases in Pac, 22 Apr 35, #404, Ser 1683-1, GB Files.
23. Lt Cdr Frederick H. Hewes to Chief BuDocks, Rept of Special Investigations & Surveys in Alaskan Waters, 17 Jul 37, H1-3, SecNav & CNO Secret & Conf Corresp.
24. Hepburn Rept.
25. Swanborough and Bowers, *US Navy Aircraft*, 80.
26. WPL-13 revision Mar 1939.
27. WPL-35, CNO, June 1939, vol. 1, pt. 1, Sec IV.
28. Lt Col R. W. Crawford to Gen Gerow, 3 Feb 41, WPD 4297-2 in Watson, *COS: Prewar Plans*, 456.
29. Charles Wilkes, USN, *Narrative of the United States Exploring Expedition during the Years 1838, 1839, 1840, 1841, 1842* (Philadelphia, 1845), vol. 5, chap. 7.
30. Morgan, "Strategic Factors in Hawaiian Annexation," 13–15.
31. U.S. Congress, House, Comm on Nav Affairs, *Establishment of a Naval Base at Pearl Harbor in the Hawaiian Islands*, 1908, cited in PHH, Hearings, pt. 6, 2768–70.
32. GB to SecNav, 18 Jun 07, #405; GB to SecNav, 6th Endorsement, 23 Jul 07, #404, vol. 5, GB Ltrs.
33. Roosevelt to SecWar, 11 Feb 08, #305, JB Records.
34. JB to Pres, 5 Mar 08, #303, ibid.
35. Braisted, *Navy in Pacific, 1909–1922*, 40.
36. Bd of Officers, Plans against Spain & Japan, 1897, 4–5.
37. NWC Conference of 1906.
38. NWC 1911 Plan, 2(b):10.
39. JB to SecNav and SecWar, 18 Jun 07, #325, JB Records.
40. Cdr C. S. Williams, Extract from paper, Nov 09, UNOpP 1910, Box 48, RG 8, NHC, NWC. NWC, Problem of 1907, 17–18, 118–19, 156–58.
41. NWC 1911 Plan, 2(b):4–6, 19, 2(c):16–22.
42. Mahan-Oliver Corresp 1911.
43. GB, Honolulu & Pearl Hbr, 24 Nov 08, Ref #5-E, War Portf No. 3, Box 6, GB War Portfs.
44. Mahan-Oliver Corresp 1911.
45. JB to SecNav, 27 Nov 11; JB, Pac Coast Defs, Insular Possessions, 14 May 13, #303, JB Records.
46. GB 1914 Plan, 11–13, 25–26, 33–44, 62, 117–25.
47. JB, Strategy of the Pacific, 1919; JB to CNO, Mission US Forces, Oahu, 22 Dec 19, Ser 87, #325, JB Records.

48. JPC to JB, Jt A&N Basic War Plan–Orange, 12 Mar 24; JB to JPC, Proposed Jt A&N Basic War Plan–Orange, 7 Jun 24, #325, Ser 228, JB Records.
49. JPC Plan Oct 1926. JPC Plan Nov 1926. JPC Army Section Revision, May 1927. JPC Est, Jan 1928, 29, 42–44, 46–47. JB Points, Feb 1928. JPC Navy Section Revision, Mar 1928. JPC Revision, Apr 1928. JPC Navy Section Revision, Apr 1928. JPC Army Section, Jul 1928. CNO Plan, Mar 1929, 1:16, 27–29, 34, 4:App II.
50. AWPD, Study of Time Factors Affecting Major Attacks on Hawn Is, 27 Dec 35, File A16/ND14, SecNav & CNO Secret Corresp.
51. JPC to JB, 3 Dec 36; JB to SecNav, Changes in Jt Basic WP, Orange, 9 Dec 36, #325, Ser 594, JB Records.
52. Draft WPUSF-44, 24 Mar 41, 6–7, Annexes A, B. WPPac-46, 25 Jul 41, Annex I, 4–5. C. M. Cooke, Memo for the CinC, 7 Apr 41, Cooke Papers.
53. Memo Re Initial Stages of Japanese War, 4 Feb 07, JNOpP, RG 8, NHC, NWC, 4–5, in Vlahos, "NWC and Origins," 32.
54. NWC Rept of Conference of 1907, 26–27; GB 1914 Plan, 125–26.
55. AWPD, Study of Time Factors Affecting Major Attacks on Hawn Is, 27 Dec 35, File A16/ND14, SecNav & CNO Secret Corresp.
56. JPC Army Section, Jul 1928.
57. Hepburn Rept, passim.
58. Bryan, *American Polynesia,* 157–60.
59. CinCPac War Diary, 10 Dec 41, in Hoyt, *How They Won,* 9.
60. Message, ComInCh to CinCPac, 301740 Dec 41, cited in Hayes, *Joint Chiefs,* 56.
61. NWC Conference of 1906, 5–6, 16.
62. GB 1914 Plan, 26–28.
63. ONI, Quick, accurate, economical survey of possible bases for a/c & surface craft in Pac, 7 Feb 20, PD 196-3, SecNav & CNO Conf Corresp. CO Nav Air Sta Pearl Hbr to CNO, Rept of Results of Avn Reconn of Is to Westward including Midway, 12 Nov 20, Box 10, ONI, NHC, NWC.
64. District Intelligence Officer to Dir Nav Intelligence, Mil Aspects of Leeward Is of Hawaii, Johnston & Wake Is, 8 Oct 23, Box 10, ONI, NHC, NWC.
65. Cdt 14th ND to CNO, Midway I–Radio traffic sta, Recommendations for establishment, 2 Aug 23, 196-3, SecNav & CNO Conf Corresp.
66. CO Nav Air Sta Pearl Hbr to Cdt 14th ND, Rept of Annual Inspection of Naval Reservation of Midway & Reconn of Coral Is between Midway & Pearl Hbr, 16 May 24, 111-61, SecNav & CNO Conf Corresp.
67. Cook to Standley, Inspection of Nav Reservation Midway & Reconn of Coral Is between Midway & Pearl Hbr, 19 Aug 24, 111-61, SecNav & CNO Conf Corresp.
68. Local Jt A&N Planning Comm to Cdt 14th ND and CG Hawn Dept, Jt A-N Action, Def of Oahu, 13 Nov 24, Ser 350, JB Records. JPC, Army Section, Jul 1928.
69. CinCUS to CNO, Midway I, 31 Mar 34, N1-9, SecNav & CNO Secret & Conf Corresp. *New York Times,* 10 May 35, 1:8. "US Naval Administrative Histories of WWII," no. 28(d), Deputy CNO (Air), 6:1404.

70. Dir WPD to CNO, Dev of Midway & Wake Is for naval use, 12 Dec 35, File NB/ND14, SecNav & CNO Secret Corresp.
71. Actg Chief of Engineers to SecWar, Prelim examination of . . . Midway I, 30 Jun 36; Actg SecWar to SecNav, 26 Mar 38, H1-18/EG60 (360109), SecNav Genl Records. CNO to CinCUS, Dev of Midway, Wake & Guam, 18 Mar 38, Box 21, Records of Base Maintenance Div, Shore Sta Dev Bd, RG 38, NA.
72. CNO, Statement to House Comm, n.d. (prob Jan 1939), Hepburn Rept Notebooks.
73. Hepburn Rept.
74. CinCUS to CNO, 28 Feb 38, File NB/ND14 1936–39, Box 259, SecNav & CNO Secret Corresp. WPL-35, CNO, Jun 1939, vol 1.
75. CNO to CinCUS, Def of is in Pac west of Honolulu belonging to US, 10 Jun 37; CNO to Maj Gen Cdt USMC, same title, 15 Sep 37, File A16/QH (Pacific), SecNav & CNO Secret Corresp.
76. Records for 1939 on defense of Midway are voluminous. See correspondence among CNO, BuAer, WPD, CinCUS, and subsidiary fleet commanders, Commandant USMC, and others in Files A16/JJ to A16/KK, Box 22, File A16-3, Box 57, Files NB/ND14 and A16-1/EG12-1, Box 236, SecNav & CNO Conf Corresp. File A16-3/FF, Box 91, File Defs of Midway Folder 1, Box 147G, WPD Files. A lengthy report is in Col Harry K. Pickett, USMC, The Defenses of Midway, n.d., ca. Aug 1939, File same name, Box 147G, WPD Files; also WPL-35, CNO, Jun 1939, vol. 1.
77. There are also many records on the development of Midway in 1940–41. Correspondence involving the WPD appears on 29 May, 13 Jul, and 22 Jul 40 in Signed Ltrs, Boxes 79–80, WPD Files. Several histories of the Battle of Midway also cover the story, as does Woodbury, *Builders for Battle,* chaps. 7, 10, and 11.
78. Pac Sta War Portf #3, Is & Anchorages in N Pac Belonging to US, 20 Nov 12, Folder #141, GB Records. GB to SecNav, Examination of Is of Caroline & Marshall Groups, 10 May 13, #409, GB Subj Files.
79. GB, 2d Endorsement, #414-3, 24 Jan 18, GB Subj File.
80. CO Nav Air Sta Pearl Hbr to Cdt 14th ND, Nav Reconn of Johnson [sic] I, 11 Sep 23, Box 10, ONI, NHC, NWC. Cdt 14th ND to CNO, same title, 14 Sep 23, 196-3, Sec Nav & CNO Secret & Conf Corresp. WPD, Study of Certain Pac Is, 6 Aug 27.
81. VP Sqns 1-B & 1-F to Cdr A/C Sqns, Rept of Reconn of Johnston I . . . , 6 May 33, Box 10, ONI, NHC, NWC. Tentative Plan O-1, 26 Aug 33.
82. Col Harry K. Pickett USMC, Def of Johnston I, 30 Oct 39, WPD Files.
83. ComAirBatFor to CinCUS, Flt Organization—proposed change in . . . , 3 May 38, File A16-3/A21 Warfare Air Services, Box 91, WPD Files.
84. Draft WPUSF-44, 24 Mar 41, Opns Plan O-1, 1-7, 10, Annex E.
85. WPPac-46, 25 Jul 41, 25, 43. The earlier draft of WPUSF-44 with the stronger speculation was not among the exhibits turned over to postwar investigators of the disaster.
86. Bd of Officers, Plans against Spain & Japan, 1897, 4–5.
87. NWC 1911 Plan, 2(b):5–6, 2(c):16–19, 21–22.
88. JPC Navy Section Revision, Mar 1928.

Chapter 6   The Western Pacific Capitulation

1. NWC Conference of 1906, 15, 31–33. NWC Rept of Conference of 1907, 14–19, 24–25.
2. HQ Phil Dept, Proceedings of Jt A&N Bd, 23 Jun 16; JB to SecNav, Rept of a Jt Bd on cooperation of A&N in Phils, 2d endorsement, 10 Nov 17; JB to Pres, SecWar, & SecNav, Phil Is, mission of forces, 14 Nov 16, #303, Ser 49, JB Records.
3. GB 1910 Plan, 2–3, 8–9. NWC 1911 Plan, 8–11, 52–54.
4. JB to Pres, SecWar, & SecNav, 14 Nov 16.
5. GB 1917 Strategic Problem.
6. Cdt 16th ND to CinCAF, Strategic sitn in Pac, 9 Mar 34, A16-3(1)(100), Box Cominch-CNO, CinCUS Op Plans 1932–39.
7. JB, Strategy of the Pacific, 1919.
8. Belote and Belote, *Corregidor*, 10–14. JB to Pres, SecWar, & SecNav, 14 Nov 16.
9. AWPD to Deputy COS, Mission, Strength & Composition of Phil Garrisons, 20 Oct 22; SecWar to Gov-Genl, 4 Nov 22, File #532, Box 22, AWPD Records.
10. SecNav to Dewey, 30 Mar 00, #401, GB Records.
11. Oliver, 1907 Problem.
12. GB, 1906 Plan, 9, 12.
13. 2d Comm to GB, Memo on Prepn of Genl War Plans, read 23 Nov 09, #425, Box 122, GB Subj File. Cdr C. S. Williams, Extract from paper, Nov 09, UNOpP 1910, Box 48, RG 8, NHC, NWC.
14. SecNav to SecWar, Objectives . . . by mil forces . . . in Phils . . . in case of war, 1 Jul 15, #303, JB Records.
15. CinC Astc Flt to Office of Nav Opns, n.d., ca. Apr 1916, Cable 18129, #303, Ser 49, JB Records.
16. JB, Strategy of the Pacific, 1919.
17. Dir WPD to CNO, Bearing of "Treaty for Limitation of Naval Armaments" upon def of our overseas possessions, 29 Apr & 1 Jun 22, 226-103:24/1; CNO to Pratt, same title, 12 May 22; Pratt to CNO, 13 May 22, 226-103:24/1, roll 112; Dir WPD to CNO, Jt A&N Bd—Its origin and work, 10 May 22, 233-16, roll 116, SecNav & CNO Secret & Conf Corresp.
18. GS to ACOS, AWPD, Action Taken by War Dept [re] defs in Phil Is to conform with . . . Four-Power Treaty, 25 Feb 22; Actg SecWar to SecState, 27 Feb 22; ACOS AWPD to AG, Policies & plans re def of Phil Is, 18 Jul 22, #565, Box 24, AWPD Records.
19. JB-JPC Plans, May–Jul 1923. Actg Dir WPD to CNO, Strategic Survey of Pacific, 3 May 23; CNO to SecNav, same title, 10 May 23, 198-26, roll 80, SecNav & CNO Secret & Conf Corresp.
20. Gov-Genl to SecWar, 5 Feb 23, #305, Ser 209, JB Records.
21. CinCAF & Cdg Gen Phil Dept, Combined A&N War Plans (Orange), 2 Jan 25, File same name, Box 64, WPD Files.
22. Edwin Alexander Anderson, Flag Officer Biog Files. Anderson and Wood had both won Medals of Honor during punitive expeditions in Mexico, against Geronimo's tribe and Vera Cruz respectively.

23. Astc Flt War Plan, 1922. Cdt 16th ND, War Portf, Register #2, forwarded 26 Mar 23, 198-37, roll 90, SecNav & CNO Secret & Conf Corresp.
24. AWC Repts, 13–14 Apr 25. Maj W. G. Kilner, Air Corps, Executive, Memo for SecWar, 1 Jan 27, File 232, Box 69, AWPD Color Plans. JB Points, Feb 1928. JPC Navy Sect Revision, Mar 1928. JPC Navy Section Revision, Apr 1928. JB Plan, Jun 1928. CNO Plan, Mar 1929, vol. 1, 15, I:61, 64, 68–73, 78–80, II:130, vol. 3, Apps I:22; II:129–30.
25. JPC Army Members to JB, Revision of Defensive Sea Area Plans, Manila Bay & Subic Bay, 30 Jul 28, File 353, JB Records.
26. CinCAF & Cdg Gen Phil Dept, Jt Ltr to CNO & COS, Inadequacy present mil & naval forces Phil Area to carry out Assigned Mission . . . , Disposition of Available Forces, and . . . Future Policy, 1 Mar 34, A16-3(9)/ND16, Box 243, SecNav Secret Corresp.
27. Phil Dept Plan Orange 1934.
28. Maj Gen Cdg Phil Dept to CinCAF, Army Phil Def Plans, 28 Jan 33, File CinCUS prior 3 Sep 39, CinCUS Op Plans 1932–39, vol. 1.
29. ACOS Phil Dept, 1st Phase Orange Plan, G-4 app, 6 Apr 36, File 173, Box 64, AWPD Color Plans.
30. Phil Dept Plan Orange 1934.
31. CNO to CinCAF, Plan O-2 Orange, US Astc Flt Operating Plan–Orange, 3 Nov 32, A16-3/FF6; CinCAF to CNO, WPs Orange–basic change in, 31 Jan 33, A16-3(CF 192); CNO to CinCAF, same title, 18 Mar 33, A16/ND16; CinCAF to CNO, same title, 16 Jun 33, A16-3 (CF586), CinCUS Op Plans 1932–39.
32. CNO to JB, 21 Nov 35, JB Records. Dir WPD to CNO, Marivales Ammunition Depot–Status, 15 & 30 Apr 36; Actg SecNav to SecWar, 2 May 36, A16-3(11)ND16, Box 245, SecNav & CNO Secret Corresp. JPC to JB, 15 May 36, JB Records. CNO, Change #2 to WPL-15, 3 Sep 36. CNO, Navy Plan Orange, vol. 1, Mar 1939.
33. CNO to JB, Inadequacy present mil & nav forces Phil Area to carry out Assigned Missions, 28 Apr 34, A16/ND16, CinCUS Op Plans 1932–39. JB #324, Ser 533, cited in Change #3 to WPL-13, 26 Feb 35.
34. JPC to JB, 15 May 36. JB, 19 May 36, #325, Ser 570, JB Records. Actg ACOS AWPD to AG, Revision of Jt A&N Basic WP–Orange, 28 May 36, File 2720-71, AWPD Files.
35. NWC Rept of Conference of 1907, 17–19, 27.
36. GB 1910 Plan, 8–9, 11. NWC 1911 Plan, 8–9.
37. CinCAF & Cdg Gen Phil Dept, Combined A&N War Plans (Orange), 2 Jan 25.
38. Phil Dept Plan Orange 1934, G-2 App.
39. Asst COS AWPD, Memo for Gen Moseley, Extracts from G-2 Est of Possible Orange Air Opns in Phil Is, 12 Oct 32, File 2720-7, AWPD Records.
40. Pres NWC to CNO, Material and Equipment for Nav Adv Base Force, 18 Dec 33, File A16-3(3) to (5)/SS, Box 237, SecNav Secret Corresp.
41. Meyers, WPs–Orange change, 27 Feb 34.
42. Lt Col A. L. Sneed, 1st Phase Orange Plan, Phil Dept Air Officer, 1 Nov 35, File 183, Box 65, AWPD Color Plans.
43. Lt jg Fitzhugh Lee, 2d to CinCAF, AAC Exercises in . . . Mindinao [sic], 21 Feb 35, File A16-3/(5)1935, Box 60, SecNav & CNO Conf Corresp.

44. CinCAF to Cdt 16th ND, Mil Reconn Surveys of Phils: plans for completion, 14 Jan 38, File A16-3/A6-8 to /FF3-5, Box 237, SecNav & CNO Secret Corresp.
45. CNO to Adm Greenslade, 11 Sep 39, Scholarly Microfilms, roll 5. WPD to Stark, 9 Dec 39, File A16-3/EF37, Box 237, SecNav & CNO Secret Corresp.
46. Crenshaw to CNO, Sending of Patrol Plane Sqn of 12 Planes to Phils for neutrality duty, 28 Aug 39, A4-3/VP, Signed Ltrs, Box 78; Cooke to CNO, Guidance for the CinCAF in event of growing tension in W Pac, 30 Jan 40, Box 79, WPD Files.
47. CNO to CinCAF, Instructions concerning Prepn of Astc Flt for War under WP Rainbow 3, 12 Dec 40, File A16(R-3)(1940), Box 241, CNO Secret Corresp. WPL-44, Dec 1940. CNO-CinCUS-CinCAF WPL-44 corresp, Jan–Feb 1941.
48. Cpt W. R. Purnell, Certain Strategical Considerations . . . [re] Orange War–Rainbow No. 3, 13 May 41; CinCAF to CNO, 13 May 41, File A16(R-3)(1941), Box 241, CNO Secret Corresp.
49. CNO to CinCAF, Opn Plan No. 1–US Astc Flt (incl Change #1), 9 Jul 41, A16/FF6, Signed Ltrs, Box 82, WPD Files.
50. CNO to CinCAF, Proposed assignment of shore-based VSB sqns to Astc flt, 17 Oct 41, A4-3/VZ; CNO to CinCAF, Reenforcement of Brit Naval Forces in Far East Area, 7 Nov 41, A16-1/EF3-13, Signed Ltrs, Box 82, WPD Files.
51. Purnell, Certain Strategical Considerations, 13 May 41.
52. Morton, *Fall of the Philippines,* 8–13, 19–22, 61–63. Watson, *COS: Prewar Plans,* chap. 13.
53. American-Dutch-Brit Conversations, Apr 1941, PHH, *Exhibits,* pt. 15, 1562, 1565, 1576. Layton with Pineau and Costello, *"And I Was There,"* 531 (map).
54. Watson, *COS: Prewar Plans,* 397.
55. Lt Cdr Robert W. Morse to Turner, Staging Landplane Bombers to Far East, 25 Aug 41, VB, Signed Ltrs, Box 82, WPD Files. Williams, "Deployment of the AAF," 178–79, 182. AAF Historical Office, *South Pacific Route,* 26, 29, 32–33, 54. Morton, *Fall of Philippines,* 14–19, 31–45, 64–71.
56. Blair, *Silent Victory,* 1:60.
57. CNO to CinCAF, 7 Nov 41. CNO to Spenavo, 6 Nov 41, Section Pac-Far E Jt Staff Corresp.
58. Morton, *Fall of Philippines,* 61–64.
59. US Secy for Collaboration to Jt Secys Brit Jt Staff Mission, US-Brit Commonwealth cooperation in Far East Area, 11 Nov 41, Section Aid to China; Spenavo to CNO, 26 Oct 41; CNO to Spenavo, 6 Nov 41; First Sea Lord to Stark, 5 Nov 41, Section Pac-Far East Jt Staff Corresp.
60. CNO to CinCAF, 17 Oct & 7 Nov 41.
61. Morton, *Strategy and Command,* 151.

Chapter 7 The Great Western Base

1. Bradford, "Coaling Stations." Costello, "Planning for War," 45, 176–78.
2. GB to RAdm Frederick Rodgers, 16 Feb 01, #425.2, Box 140; 2d Comm of GB, n.d. (approved by GB 29 Jul 03), #425, Box 122, GB Subj File.
3. Dewey to SecNav, 29 Aug 98, 15 Jun 03, in Costello, "Planning for War," 202, 206.

4. Dewey to Roosevelt, 4 Aug 04, GB Letterpress, in Spector, *Admiral of New Empire,* 167.

5. Dewey to SecNav, 26 Sep 01; Long to Roosevelt, 9 Nov 01, #405, GB Records, in Costello, "Planning for War," 206.

6. Dewey to Pres NWC, 8 Dec 02; Pres NWC to GB, 13 Jan 03, #425.2, Box 140, GB Subj File.

7. Pres NWC to GB, 10 Oct 03, #425.2, Box 141, GB Subj File.

8. Pres, Message to Congress, 7 Dec 03, in Costello, "Planning for War," 206. Roosevelt to Dewey, 5 Aug 04, in Spector, *Admiral of New Empire,* 167.

9. Moody to Root, 22 Nov 02, SecNav Conf Ltrs Sent, RG 45, NA, in Braisted, *Navy in Pacific, 1897–1909,* 122.

10. Wood to Roosevelt, 1 Jun 04; Folger to SecNav, 1 Jun 04, #404-1, GB Records, in Costello, "Planning for War," 208–9.

11. Dewey to Roosevelt, 4 Aug 04; Roosevelt to Dewey, 5 Aug 04, Dewey Papers, in Spector, *Admiral of New Empire,* 167.

12. U.S. Congress, Senate, *Coast Defense of the United States and the Insular Possessions,* 59th Cong., 1st sess., Senate Doc. No. 248 (Washington, 1906), 26, in Costello, "Planning for War," 207.

13. Costello, "Planning for War," 211.

14. GB 1906 Plan, 1–3, 15, 46. NWC Rept of Conference of 1907, 14–18, 20, 24, 27, 31–32.

15. GB to SecNav, 18 Jun 07, #405, Ltrs, GB Records, 5:85.

16. Jt Comm to Pres AWC, Consideration of Special Sitn, 18 Feb 07; Cdr H. S. Knapp, War between US & Japan, Possibility of Gr Brit Becoming Japan's Ally, 19 Jan 07, in Vlahos, "NWC and Origins," 31–32.

17. JB to SecNav & SecWar, 18 Jun 07, #325, JB Records.

18. Lt Col W. W. Wotherspoon to C/S, Rept of Meeting at Oyster Bay, 29 Jun 07, AG 1260092, in Morton, "Military Preparations."

19. GB to SecNav, 26 Sep 07, #408, 26 Sep 07, #405, Ltrs, GB Records, vol. 5.

20. Lt Cols F. V. Abbott & S. D. Embick to Gen Wood, 27 Nov 07, AG 1260092; Maj Gen Leonard Wood to AG, 23 Dec 07, AG 1260092, in Morton, "Military Preparations."

21. JB Minutes, 31 May 10.

22. Morton, "Military Preparations." JB, Proceedings, 6 Nov 07, Box 301-3, JB Records.

23. Roosevelt to SecWar, 11 Feb 08, #305, JB Records.

24. GB to SecNav, 31 Jan 08, in Braisted, *Navy in Pacific, 1897–1909,* 219.

25. Cdr L. S. Van Duzer, Extracts from endorsement of ltr by Lt Cdr Ralph Earle, n.d. (ca. early 1910), UNOpP 1910, Box 48, RG 8, NHC, NWC.

26. Braisted, *Navy in Pacific, 1909–1922,* 70.

27. Wood to Roosevelt, 1 Jun 04; RAdm Wm Folger to SecNav, 1 Jun 04, #404-1, GB Records, in Costello, "Planning for War," 208–9. Abbott & Embick to Wood, 27 Nov 07, Wood to AG, 23 Dec 07.

28. GB to SecNav, 31 Jan 08. Actg Gov-Genl, 8 Sep 09, with JB Proceedings, 19 Oct 09, #301-3; GB, Rept of base in Phils, 21 Jun 09, cited in JB, Rept of JB in Matter of Establishment of Naval Sta in PIs, 8 Nov 09; Capt S. A. Staunton, Memo, 9 Oct 09, #305, JB Records. COS to SecWar, 2 Dec 09, with JB

Proceedings, 10 Dec 09. GB to SecNav, 8 Jan 10, #425, Box 122, GB Subj File. JB Proceedings, 31 May 10.
29. GB 1917 Strategic Problem.
30. Pres NWC to GB, 24 Feb 10, #425, Box 122, GB Subj File.
31. GB, Rept of base in Phils, 21 Jun 09. Staunton, Memo, 9 Oct 09.
32. GB to SecNav, proposed ltr, 10 Aug 20, #404, Ser 1000, XSTP, NHC, NWC. CNO to SecNav, 12 Aug 20, SecNav Genl Records, in Braisted, *Navy in Pacific, 1909–1922,* 483–84. Belknap, lecture, NWC, 5 Nov 21.
33. Lt Cdr C. S. Williams, Proposed Routes between US & Phils, Nov 07, approved by GB Nov 07, Ref 7-C, War Portf No. 3, Box 7, GB War Portfs.
34. SecNav to CO USS *Charleston,* 10 May 98, Naval War Bd, 1898, Records. Davis, "Taking of Guam."
35. Pomeroy, *Pacific Outpost,* 24–25, 32. GB to SecNav, 3 Oct 07, #405, 5:131; GB Endorsement, Naval Sta Guam . . . new coal shed, 18 Jun 09, #414-1, 6:97, GB Ltrs.
36. Braisted, *Navy in Pacific, 1909–1922,* 72–73. Pomeroy, *Pacific Outpost,* 24–25, 32; Committee, Cdr T. M. Potts, Plan for def of Guam, 29 Sept 05, #425.2, Box 141, GB Records. GB to SecNav, 3 Oct 07, #405, 5:131, GB Ltrs. Pres NWC to GB, 12 Oct 09; SecNav to CinC Astc Fleet, Addition to fortifications at Guam, 25 May 11, #425.2, Box 141, GB Subj File.
37. Mahan to Pres NWC, 28 Jul 10, 196-7, Roll 70, SecNav & CNO Secret & Conf Corresp.
38. Mahan-Oliver Corresp 1911. Mahan to Pres NWC, 17 Mar 11, Binder 1911 #17, UNOpP, Box 48, RG 8, NHC, NWC. Mahan to SecNav, 21 Apr 11, in Seager, *Mahan,* 485.
39. Pres NWC to GB, Forwarding . . . strategic plan of campaign of Blue against Orange, 14 Mar 11, roll 1, Scholarly Microfilms. Pres NWC to GB, Recommending appointment of Bd . . . on def and equipment of Guam as naval base, 14 Mar 11, #425.2, Box 141, GB Subj File.
40. Fiske favored a base on Polillo, an island off the east coast of Luzon with a good anchorage in the vicinity of worthwhile objectives—"our Gibraltar" he called it, mimicking Mahan (Fiske to GB, Permanent Base in the East, 25 Mar 11, #408, Box 32, GB Subj File).
41. Braisted, *Navy in Pacific, 1909–1922,* 74.
42. Dewey to SecNav, 4 Dec 12, #403, GB Subj File, in Costello, "Planning for War," 223.
43. GB 1914 Plan, 19–24, 52–56, 61.
44. GB 1917 Strategic Problem.
45. Rodgers urged an investigation (Pres NWC to GB, Recommending appointment of Bd . . . on def and equipment of Guam as naval base, 14 Mar 11, #425.2, Box 141, GB Subj File). Braisted, *Navy in Pacific, 1909–1922,* 74.
46. JB, Proceedings, 8 May 13; SecWar to SecNav, 27 May 13; SecNav to SecWar, 7 Jan 14, JB Proceedings.
47. GB 1917 Strategic Problem.
48. BuOrd to Maj Gen Cdt USMC, 2d Endorsement, Temporary def of Guam, 16 Sep 15; Office of Chief of Engineers to COS, 4th endorsement, 3 Feb 16, #322, JB Records. JB, Proceedings, 17 Aug 16.

49. Douglas, "Coontz," 23–35, including (p. 25) an undated clipping and printed address about Coontz's successor.
50. James H. Oliver, Flag Officer Biog Files. Dorwart, *Office of Naval Intelligence*, 96–105.
51. Braisted, *Navy in Pacific, 1909–1922*, 470. Morton, "War Plan ORANGE," 25.
52. Adm McKean, Statement for conference, 21 Oct 19, SecNav & CNO Secret & Conf Corresp. Oliver to CNO, 22 Oct 19, in Braisted, *Navy in Pacific, 1909–1922*, 473. JB, Strategy of Pacific, 1919. JB to SecWar & SecNav, Dev & Def of Guam, 18 Dec 19, Ser 28, #322, JB Records.
53. JB, Strategy of Pacific, 1919. Pye, lecture, AWC, 21 Oct 24.
54. CNO to War Portf Distribution List, Extent & Dev of Pac bases . . . for Campaign in the Pac, 9 Aug 20, 190-6:1, roll 67; Bd for Dev of Navy Yard Plans on Limited Dev of . . . Guam, 28 Sep 21, EG 54, Box 255, SecNav & CNO Secret Corresp. The board included Captains Arthur J. Hepburn and Edward C. Kalbfus.
55. Pye, lecture, 10 Oct 1924.
56. CNO to Maj Gen Cdt USMC, Function of Marine Corps in War Plans, 28 Jan 20; Maj Gen Cdt to CNO, same title, 16 Feb & 26 Mar 20, Def of Guam, 22 Apr 20; Dir Plans Div to CNO, Def of Guam, 29 Apr 20; GB to SecNav, Def of Guam, 2d endorsement, 2 Jul 20, 198-7, roll 78, SecNav & CNO Secret & Conf Corresp.
57. CNO to SecNav, 15 Jul 20, 190-6:1, Ser 90, JB #304, SecNav & CNO Secret & Conf Corresp, in Braisted, *Navy in Pacific, 1909–1922*, 482. CNO to War Portf Distribution List, 9 Aug 20. Bd for Dev of Navy Yard Plans, 28 Sep 21.
58. GB Pre-Conference Papers, 1921.
59. Dir WPD to GB, Questions concerning Limitation of Armament, 19 Oct 21, #425, GB Subj File.
60. Office of COS to JB, 29 Dec 19; CNO to JB, 7 Jan 21, 196-7, Ser 28-e, #325; JB to SecWar, Action upon recommendations of Bd, 7 Mar 22, #322, JB Records. Pye, lecture, 21 Oct 24.
61. Wheeler, "Denby," 584. Dingman, *Power in the Pacific*, 226. Buckley, *US and Conference*, 47, 92.
62. Buckley, *US and Conference*, passim. Roosevelt diary, 29 Jan 22, in Braisted, *Navy in Pacific, 1909–1922*, 646.

Chapter 8 The American Way of Planning: Thrusters and Cautionaries

1. NWC Conference of 1906. GB 1906 Plan. Lack of ratification is in 2d Comm to GB, Prepn of Genl War Plans, read to Bd 23 Nov 09, #425, Box 122, GB Subj File. Oliver, 1907 Problem.
2. Janowitz, "Professional Soldier," 17.
3. Pye, lecture, NWC, 7 Jan 26. Schofield, lecture, USMC, 23 Mar 28. JPC Est, Jan 1928, 36–38.
4. Hattendorf, Simpson, and Wadleigh, *Sailors and Scholars*, 64. Reynolds, *Admirals*, 368–70.
5. 2d Comm to GB, 23 Nov 09.
6. GB 1910 Plan. Pres NWC to GB, Solution and Discussion of Problem 12, 14 Nov 10, Box 122, #425, GB Subj File.

7. Actg SecNav to GB, 1 Oct 10; SecNav to Pres NWC, 16 Nov 10, Box 122, #425, GB Subj File.
8. Secy GB to Pres NWC, Forwarding binders for War Plans, 23 Dec 10, ibid.
9. Special Comm, NWC Staff to Pres NWC, Educational Work of War College as Related to War Plans, 19 Oct 11, #425, Box 123, ibid.
10. Fiske to GB, Permanent Base in the East, 25 Mar 11, #408, Box 32, ibid.; Pres NWC to GB, Prepn of Strategic Plans or War Portfs by NWC, 19 Oct 11; GB to Rodgers, 22 Mar 11; SecNav to GB, Prepn of War Portfs, 26 Oct 11, #425, Box 123, ibid.
11. Patekewich, "Book of NWC Admirals." The six were Oliver, Williams, Schofield, Pye, Taylor, and Bryant.
12. GB 1914 Plan, Strategic Section.
13. Coletta, *Fiske,* passim. Hattendorf, Simpson, and Wadleigh, *Sailors and Scholars,* 83.
14. Reynolds, *Admirals,* 9–10.
15. GB, 1917 Strategic Problem.
16. Pye, lecture, AWC, 4 Feb 36.
17. Love, ed., *Chiefs of Naval Operations,* xiv–xvii.
18. Crawley, "Checklist of Strategic Plans," 2. Wheeler, *Pratt,* chap. 4.
19. RAdm A. M. Knight, Evolution of War Plans, 30 Mar 15; GB to SecNav, Prepn of War Plans by GB, 28 Jan 15, #425, Box 123, GB Subj File.
20. Coletta, "Josephus Daniels," 564–72.
21. Trask, "Benson," 3–6, 10–15. Wheeler, *Pratt,* 114, 119. Albion, *Makers of Policy,* 90. Crawley, "Checklist of Strategic Plans," 2.
22. Crawley, "Checklist of Strategic Plans," 2–3. Albion, *Makers of Policy,* 90–92. Pye, lecture at Naval Post Graduate School, 6 Nov 26. *Navy Directory,* various years.
23. Douglas, "Coontz," 23–35.
24. Crawley, "Checklist of Strategic Plans," 3.
25. Davis, *History of Joint Chiefs,* 14–29. Horne, lecture, ca. mid-1922. Pye, lecture, AWC, 21 Oct 24.
26. JB, Strategy of the Pacific, 1919.
27. Pye, lecture, AWC, 21 Oct 24.
28. Davis, *History of Joint Chiefs,* 38. ,

Chapter 9 The Through Ticket

1. GB 1906 Plan, 1–3, 46.
2. William Loeb, Jr., to SecNav, 27 Oct 06; GB to Asst SecNav, 29 Oct 06, #425.2, Box 141, GB Subj File.
3. JB to SecNav & SecWar, 18 Jun 07, #325, JB Records.
4. Sargent to GB, 15 Jun 07, in Vlahos, "NWC and Origins," 35. Capt S. A. Staunton, Memo, 9 Oct 09, #305, JB Records.
5. GB to Pres NWC, 6 Jun 07, #425.2, Box 141, GB Subj File. GB 1914 Plan, 50.
6. NWC 1911 Plan, 2(c):16.
7. GB 1914 Plan, 11.
8. GB to SecNav, Strategic Sitn, Orange War Plan, & readiness for war, 14 Mar 14, #425, Box 123, GB Records. Wrongly filed under 1913.

9. GB 1914 Plan, 2–3, 65, 73–74. BuC&R to SecNav, Prepn for war, 20 Jun 11; BuOrd to GB, same title, 16 Jul 12, #425, File Prepn for War, Bureaus, Box 123, GB Subj File.
10. GB 1906 Plan, 40, 43. GB 1910 Plan, 19–24. GB 1913 Admin Plan, 12–13. GB 1914 Plan, 65.
11. Staunton, Memo, 9 Oct 09. GB 1910 Plan, 35–36. GB 1914 Plan, App B.
12. GB 1910 Plan, 15–17, 33–36. GB 1906 Plan, 16–18. GB 1917 Strategic Problem.
13. GB 1914 Plan, Transfer of Blue Nav Forces, 66–67, App C, Blue Trans-Pac Rtes, 133–39.
14. Sargent to GB, 15 Jun 07. NWC 1911 Plan, 2(c):16–17. GB 1914 Plan, 17.
15. GB 1910 Plan, 3, 14.
16. Hart, *Great White Fleet*, passim. Carter, *Incredible Great White Fleet*, passim. Braisted, *Navy in Pacific, 1897–1909*, 223–39. Reckner, *Roosevelt's Great White Fleet*, passim.
17. GB 1910 Plan, 15–16, 38–39. NWC 1911 Plan, 2(c):16–19, 3:1–5.
18. NWC Rept of Conference of 1907, pt. 1, 65. NWC 1911 Plan, Proposed Rte around S. America, 2. GB 1910 Plan, 38–39. Braisted, *Navy in Pacific, 1909–1922*, 37–38. Hart, *Great White Fleet*, 198–99. Alden, *American Steel Navy*, 224. GB 1914 Plan, 45. GB 1906 Plan, 16–18, 33–38, 48.
19. Alden, *American Steel Navy*, 224, 229.
20. NWC Rept of Conference of 1907, pt. 1, 65, 74–75, 87. Miller, Coaling articles, 1899–1914, passim. GB to Navy Dept, 3d Endorsement, Conversion of Colliers, 20 Dec 1911, #420-2, GB Ltrs, 7:345.
21. GB to Navy Dept, 3d Endorsement, Conversion of Colliers Vestal & Prometheus into Supply & Repair Ships, 20 Dec 11, #420-2, vol. 8, GB Ltrs. BuOrd to GB, 16 Jul 12. NWC Conference of 1906, pt. 2:42–48. NWC Rept of Conference of 1907, pt. 1, 14–16. GB 1910 Plan, 19–21. GB 1913 Admin Plan, 12–13. Maj Gen Cdt USMC to GB, Prepns for War, 9 Aug 12, #425, Box 123, GB Subj File.
22. William Rawle Shoemaker, Flag Officer Biog Files.
23. GB 1914 Plan, introduction, para. 2.
24. GB 1913 Admin Plan, Steps Which Should Be Taken, 12–13. GB to SecNav, 14 Mar 14. GB 1917 Strategic Problem.
25. NWC Rept of Conference of 1907, 1–4.
26. NWC 1911 Plan, 2(c):24–26. Mahan-Oliver Corresp 1911.
27. WPD Est 1922, 22–24.
28. GB 1910 Plan, charts (apparently by Pratt). NWC 1911 Plan, 2(c):25–26. GB 1914 Plan, 28–30.
29. NWC 1911 Plan, 2(c):25.
30. NWC Rept of Conference of 1907, 34.
31. Oliver, 1907 Problem. Knapp, Memo, 31 Jan 07, in Vlahos, "NWC and Origins," 31.
32. NWC Conference of 1906, pt. 2, 4–6, 9, 15–19. Oliver, 1907 Problem. GB 1910 Plan, 2–4, 8–9, 11. NWC 1911 Plan, 2(b):2–4, 8–11.
33. Mahan-Oliver Corresp 1911.
34. GB 1914 Plan, 13, 29–31, 62.
35. GB 1906 Plan, 16–18. GB 1910 Plan, 25–30.

36. NWC Conference of 1906, pt. 3, 34. NWC Rept of Conference of 1907, pt. 1, 65, 74–75, 87. GB to Navy Dept, 20 Dec 11.
37. Miller, Coaling articles, 1899–1914. GB 1913 Admin Plan, 12–13.
38. NWC 1911 Plan, 2(d), passim. Shoemaker, lecture, 23 & 25 Aug 14, 67–69.
39. Miller, Coaling articles, 1899–1914.
40. Aid for Opns to ONI, 22 Nov 12; GB to SecNav, Examination of Is, Caroline & Marshall Groups, 20 Nov 12; T. S. Rodgers to Aid for Opns, 25 Nov 12; CinC Pac Flt to SecNav, 4 Dec 12, same title; GB to SecNav, same title, 10 May 13, #409, GB Subj File.
41. C. S. Williams, Proposed Rtes between US and Phils, approved by GB Nov 1907, Ref 7-C, War Portf #3, box 7, GB War Portfs. ONI, charts, Rtes & Distances U.S.-Japan, Dec 1910, for Register #672, part of Memo re Plans of Campaign—Orange, Box 48, RG 8, NHC, NWC. GB 1914 Plan, 77, Transfer of Blue Naval Forces, 132.
42. Shoemaker, lecture, 23 & 25 Aug 14, 67–69.
43. Williams, Proposed rtes, 1907. GB 1914 Plan, App C. WPD, Study of Certain Pac Is, 6 Aug 27. Jose, *Australian Navy,* 21. Shoemaker, lecture, 23 & 25 Aug 14, 67–69.
44. Staunton, Memo, 9 Oct 09. Rept of JB in Matter of Establishment of Naval Sta in PIs, 8 Nov 09, #305, JB Records.
45. GB 1906 Plan, 1–3. NWC Rept of Conference of 1907, pt. 1, 18, 27.
46. NWC 1911 Plan, 2(c):40–41.
47. GB 1910 Plan, 8.
48. GB 1914 Plan, 68–69. NWC 1911 Plan, 2(c):31–36, 40–41. NWC Rept of Conference of 1907, 17–18, 118–19, 156–58. GB to NWC, Request of War College for repts [on] military (naval) features . . . of Phils . . . and . . . accurate reconn, 22 Dec 10, #425, Box 122, GB Subj File.
49. GB 1914 Plan, 1.
50. GB 1917 Strategic Problem.
51. CNO to SecNav, 15 Jul 20, 190-6:1, Ser 90, JB #304, SecNav & CNO Secret & Conf Corresp, in Braisted, *Navy in Pacific, 1909–1922,* 482.
52. Beigel, "Battle Fleet's Home Port," 54–63.
53. Sub-Bd for Dev of Navy Yd Plans to Planning Div, Present available berthing space at Pearl Hbr—Pac War Plan, 26 Jan 20, roll 78, SecNav & CNO Secret & Conf Corresp.
54. JB, Strategy of the Pacific, 1919.

Chapter 10 The Cautionary Strategy

1. Oliver, 1907 Problem.
2. 2d Comm to GB, Prepn of Genl War Plans, read to Bd 23 Nov 09, #425, Box 122, GB Subj File. Cdr C. S. Williams, Extract from paper, Nov 09, UNOpP 1910, Box 48, RG 8, NHC, NWC.
3. GB 1914 Plan, 13, 71.
4. Bywater, *Great Pacific War,* chap. 12.
5. Re Midway: US Legation Tokio to SecState, 20 Mar 01, #537; Actg SecState to SecNav, 27 Aug 02, SecNav Genl Records. Lyle S. Shelmidine, "The Early History of Midway Islands," *American Neptune,* July 1948, 179–95. Re

Wake: Corresp among Master USAT *Buford,* Hydrographer, BuEquipt, SecState, SecNav, Legation of Japan, various dates Aug 1902, File 9642, SecNav Genl Records. *New York Tribune,* 11 Aug 02, 1:3, 28 Aug 02, 2:4. *New York Herald,* 2 Nov 02, 5th Sec. RAdm Robley D. Evans, USN, *An Admiral's Log* (New York: D. Appleton and Co., 1911). Re other Leeward atolls: Bryan, *American Polynesia,* 187.

6. Gerard Ward, ed., *American Activities in the Central Pacific, 1790–1870* (Ridgewood, N.J.: Gregg Press, 1967), 1870 entries. U.S. Congress, Senate, Nav Affairs Comm, Rept No. 194, 40th Cong., 3d sess., 1869. George H. Read, Pay Inspector, USN (Ret.), *The Last Cruise of the Saginaw* (Boston: Houghton Mifflin, 1912).

7. Pres of US, Executive Order, 20 Jan 03, in Shelmidine, "Early History of Midway," 192.

8. NWC 1911 Plan, 4, 9. Pac Sta War Portf #3, Isls & Anchorages in N Pac Belonging to US, 20 Nov 12, Folder #141, GB Records. CinC Pac Flt, Examination of . . . Caroline & Marshall groups, 4 Dec 12, War Portf #3, 20 Nov 12, GB War Portfs. GB to SecNav, same title, 10 May 13, #409, GB Subj File. GB 1914 Plan, 13–14, 27–28, 45, 71, 147.

9. WPD, Study of Certain Pac Is, 6 Aug 27.

10. GB, 2d Endorsement, #414-3, 24 Jan 18, GB Subj File.

11. Charles Wilkes, USN, *Narrative of the United States Exploring Expedition during the Years 1838, 1839, 1840, 1841, 1842* (Philadelphia, 1845), vol. 5, chap. 7, entry Dec 20, 1841.

12. Dierdorff, "Pioneer Party—Wake Island," 501.

13. SecNav to Chief BuEquipt, 2 Feb 99, 153877, File DT Misc Telegraph & Cable, RG 45, NA. "Old Glory on Wake Island," *U.S. Naval Institute Proceedings,* no. 388 (Jun 1935), 807. Harry W. Flint, "Wake Island," *Pacific Commercial Advertiser* (Honolulu), 22 Feb 99.

14. F. V. Greene to Adj Genl, US Expeditionary Forces, 5 Jul 98, 114945 AGO, Bureau of Insular Affairs, RG 350, NA.

15. Evans, *Admiral's Log,* 293–96. Evans, Rept #3-D, 7 Jan 04, in Pac Sta War Portf #3, 20 Nov 12, GB War Portfs.

16. NWC 1911 Plan, 2(b):9.

17. GB 1914 Plan, 27.

18. Ibid., 22.

19. NWC 1911 Plan, 2(b):8, 2(c):26–30. GB 1914 Plan, 13, 21–23, 50.

20. NWC 1911 Plan, 2(b):8, 2(d):43, 2(c):13–15.

21. GB 1910 Plan, 3, 9.

22. GB 1914 Plan, 56.

23. Williams, Extract from paper, Nov 09. GB to Pres NWC, 18 Oct 10, #425, Box 122, GB Subj File. GB 1910 Plan, passim.

24. NWC 1911 Plan, 2(c):26–30, 2(d):51–52. Mahan-Oliver Corresp 1911.

25. GB 1914 Plan, 23–24, 55–56, 70–74, 77.

26. GB 1917 Strategic Problem.

27. JB, Strategy of the Pacific, 1919.

28. Dir WPD to GB, Questions concerning Limitation of Armament, 19 Oct 21, #425, GB Subj File.

29. WPD Est 1922, 8, 16, 24–27.

30. For the colonial era see Pomeroy, *Pacific Outpost*, 3–5. Peattie, *Nan'yō*, passim. Richard G. Brown, "The German Acquisition of the Caroline Islands, 1898–99"; Stewart G. Firth, "German Firms in the Pacific Islands, 1857–1914," both in John A. Moses and Paul M. Kennedy, eds., *Germany in the Pacific and Far East, 1870–1914* (St. Lucia, Queensland: University of Queensland Press, 1977), passim.

31. Bryan, *American Polynesia*, 12–13; Bryan, comp., *Guide to Place Names*. Judy Tudor, ed., *Pacific Islands Year Book and Who's Who*, 10th ed. (Sydney: Pacific Publications, 1968).

32. Long to Dewey, 16 May 98; Dewey to Long, 19 May 98, Annual Rept of SecNav, 1898 (Washington, 1899).

33. SecNav to T. M. Irvin, #130, 17 June 98, #608, 21 Sept 98, roll 364, microfilm ser M-625, Navy Area Files, 1775–1910, RG 45, NA. SecWar to Maj Gen Wesley Merritt, 26 Jun 98, Box 593, AGO 79350, Orders to Merritt, etc., RG 107, NA.

34. Leech, *Days of McKinley*, 328–30; Morgan, *Making Peace with Spain*, 143–44.

35. Bradford, "Coaling Stations."

36. Corresp among officials of Pacific Cable Co. and State Dept, 11 Jul–18 Oct 98, File DT, Misc Telegraph & Cable 1898, RG 45, NA.

37. Hay to Day, 1 Nov 98, Diplomatic Archives Branch, Civil Archives Div, SecState, RG 59, NA. Brown, "Caroline Islands," 144–48.

38. Actg Ambassador Berlin to SecState, 29 Dec 98, #681; Ambassador A. D. White to Hay, 11 & 12 Jan 99; Bradford to SecState, 27 Jan 99, Diplomatic, RG 84, NA.

39. Kennedy, *Samoan Tangle*, 234, 250.

40. Bradford to Long, 14 Feb 99, File DT, Misc Telegraph & Cable 1898, RG 45, NA.

41. Pratt, *Expansionists of 1898;* Peattie, *Nan'yō*, chap. 1.

42. For von Spee's campaign and the occupation of Micronesia see Jose, *Australian Navy*, 22–29, 31–33, 47–52, 54, 58, 63, 104–6, 121–22, 129–31, 136, chaps. 3 and 5, passim; Edwin P. Hoyt, *Kreuzerkrieg* (Cleveland: World Publishing Company, 1968), 59–60, 84, chaps. 12–20, passim; Clinard, "Japan's Influence on American Naval Power," 118–21; "Operations, Japanese Navy in the Indian and Pacific Oceans during War, 1914–18," typescript translated from French source, n.d., JNOpM 1915–23, NHC, NWC; Peattie, *Nan'yō*, chap. 2.

43. Jose, *Australian Navy*, 135–36. Blakeslee, "Japan's New Possessions," 186–87. Dept of State, *Papers Relating to the Foreign Relations of the United States, 1914*, supplement, 184, in Fifield, "Disposal of Carolines, Marshalls and Marianas," 475. Sprout and Sprout, *Toward a New Order of Sea Power*, 89. Braisted, *Navy in Pacific, 1909–1922*, 333, 444.

44. GB 1917 Strategic Problem Pacific.

45. Shoemaker, lecture, 23 & 25 Aug 14.

46. Mahan to Roosevelt, 18 Aug 14; Ellen Lyle Mahan to Roosevelt, 9 Jan 15, Asst SecNav Collection, Box 137, Roosevelt Library, Hyde Park, N.Y. Seager, *Mahan*, 601–2.

47. Daniels, *End of Innocence*, 242.

48. GB 1917 Strategic Problem. GB, 2d Endorsement, 24 Jan 18. GB 1914 Plan, 42–43, Transfer of Blue Naval Forces, Dec 1916, 77. Draft ltr by 1st Secy w note, 10 Apr 17, Niblack to SecNav, 18 Oct 17, #414-3, GB Subj File, in Braisted, *Navy in Pacific, 1909–1922*, 442. GB to CNO, 2 Dec 18, #438, Ser 879, GB Subj File.

49. Planning Comm to CNO, n.d., prob fall 1918, #438, GB Subj File.

50. Fifield, "Disposal of Carolines, Marshalls and Marianas," 473.

51. Sprout and Sprout, *Toward a New Order of Sea Power*, 92. Blakeslee, "Japan's New Possessions," 189.

52. George Louis Beer, *African Questions at the Paris Peace Conference* (New York, 1923), 454–55, in Fifield, "Disposal of Carolines, Marshalls and Marianas," 474.

53. Planning Comm, prob fall 1918. GB, 2 Dec 18. Memo by Hornbeck, 20 Jan 19, Paris Peace Conference Records, 7, RG 256, NA, in Braisted, *Navy in Pacific, 1909–1922*, 448.

54. Trask, "Benson," 3–6.

55. Braisted, *Navy in Pacific, 1909–1922*, 427–28n.

56. Frank H. Schofield, Flag Officer Biog Files.

57. Braisted, *Navy in Pacific, 1909–1922*, 446–53. Fifield, "Disposal of Carolines, Marshalls and Marianas," 474–78.

58. Roskill, *Naval Policy between the Wars*, 1:89. *New York Times*, 31 Jan 20, p. 3, in Sprout and Sprout, *Toward a New Order of Sea Power*, 94.

59. Braisted, *Navy in Pacific, 1909–1922*, 446.

60. Ibid., 530.

61. Rodman to SecNav, Mandate awarded Japan over No Pac Is, 14 Apr 21, 102-41, SecNav & CNO Secret & Conf Corresp.

62. Bostwick, handwritten note prob to CNO, n.d., ca. early 1921, ibid.

63. SecNav to SecState, 20 Oct 21, GB Pre-Conference Papers, 1921.

64. GB 1914 Plan, Transfer of Blue Naval Forces, Dec 1916, 77. GB, 2d Endorsement, 24 Jan 18.

65. Rodman to SecNav, 14 Apr 21.

66. Pye to CNO, 23 Apr 21, 102-41, SecNav & CNO Secret & Conf Corresp.

67. Dir WPD to ONI, 21 Dec 21, 178-6:1, roll 64, SecNav & CNO Secret & Conf Corresp.

68. GB Pre-Conference Papers, 1921.

69. SecNav to SecState, n.d., prob 23 Apr 21, 102-41, SecNav & CNO Secret & Conf Corresp.

70. Buckley, *US and Conference*, 142–43.

71. *Navy Directory*, 1921 issues. Clarence Stewart Williams, Flag Officer Biog Files. Article, *Portland Oregonian*, 15 May 27, ibid. Sr Mmbr of Comm to Pres NWC, Co-operation between Army and Navy, 29 May 16, 112-1, roll 26, SecNav & CNO Secret & Conf Corresp.

72. NWC, 10 Aug 21. Dir WPD to Pres NWC, Est of Blue-Orange Sitn submitted by NWC, 4 Oct 21, 112-33, roll 26, SecNav & CNO Secret & Conf Corresp. The two were Sinclair Gannon, who joined the division when school was out, and William H. Standley.

73. Sims to SecNav, Gen recommendations concerning War College, 15 Jan 19, 112-19, SecNav & CNO Secret & Conf Corresp.

74. Pres NWC to GB, Matters Connected with Pac, 13 Aug 20, File XSTP, Box 105, RG 8, NHC, NWC.
75. Dir WPD to GB, 19 Oct 21.
76. T. Roosevelt, Jr., to GB, 13 Jun 22, #425, GB Subj File.
77. WPD Est 1922.
78. Actg Dir WPD to CNO, Jt Blue-Orange Est, 21 Dec 22, 112-33:1, roll 26, SecNav & CNO Secret & Conf Corresp.
79. WPD Est 1922, cover page.
80. Rowcliff to Williams, Shipping Requirements for Orange Plan, 11 Aug 22, File 178-6:2, Roll 8, SecNav & CNO Secret & Conf Corresp. Baker, lecture, NWC, 22 Sep 22. Bd for Dev, 31 Oct 22.
81. Ellis, Adv Base Opns, Jul 1921. Logan Feland, Div Opns & Training HQ USMC to Maj Gen Cdt, 23 Jul 21, AO-41, Marine Corps Historical Center, Washington, D.C.
82. NWC, 10 Aug 21. WPD Est 1922, 14–16, 21a, 24–27b.
83. Pye to CNO, 23 Apr 21.
84. WPD Est 1922, 24.
85. Williams, Proposed Rtes between U.S. and Phils, approved by GB Nov 1907, Ref 7-C, War Portf #3, Box 7, GB War Portfs. ONI, Map, Rtes & Distances US-Japan, Dec 1910, UNOpP 1910, Box 48, RG 8, NHC, NWC. NWC 1911 Plan, Tables of is by Cdr W. V. Pratt. GB 1914 Plan, Transfer of Blue Nav Forces, 66–67, App C, Blue Trans-Pac Rtes, 129–39, map following 147.
86. Shoemaker, lecture, 23 & 25 Aug 14, introduction. GB 1914 Plan, 22, 131.
87. Dir WPD to GB, 19 Oct 21. WPD Est 1922, 3–5a, 10–11. Bd for Dev, 31 Oct 22. Peter N. Davies, "Japanese Merchant Shipping and the Bridge over the River Kwai," in Clark G. Reynolds, ed., *Global Crossroads and the American Seas* (Missoula, Mont.: Pictorial Histories Publishing Co., 1988), 214.
88. Williams, Proposed Rtes, 1907.
89. Ellis, Adv Base Opns, Jul 1921, 32, 37; NWC, 10 Aug 21. Dir WPD to GB, 19 Oct 21. WPD Est 1922, 16, 24–27. Bd for Dev, 31 Oct 22.
90. GB 1914 Plan, 27.
91. Horton, "Midway Islands," 1156–57.
92. Ellis, Adv Base Opns, July 1921, 1, 14–15, 18–33, 37–38, 45–80. Dir WPD to GB, 19 Oct 21. Bd for Dev, 31 Oct 22.
93. "Operations, Japanese Navy . . . 1914–18."
94. Williams, Proposed Rtes, 1907.
95. Rodman to SecNav, 14 Apr 21.
96. WPD Est 1922, 24–27. Baker, lecture, NWC, 22 Sep 22. NWC, 10 Aug 21. Ellis, Adv Base Opns, Jul 1921, 14–17. Dir WPD to GB, 19 Oct 21. Bd for Dev, 31 Oct 22.
97. NWC, 10 Aug 21.
98. Baker, lecture, NWC, 22 Sep 22.
99. WPD Est 1922, 14, 25. Dir WPD to GB, 19 Oct 21.
100. Bd for Dev, 31 Oct 22.
101. WPD Est 1922, 25.
102. Dir WPD to GB, 19 Oct 21.
103. Williams Biog file.

Chapter 11 The Thrusters' Resurgence

1. Lane, *Armed Progressive*, 250–63 and passim. Francis Russell, *The Shadow of Blooming Grove: Warren G. Harding and His Times* (New York: McGraw-Hill, 1968), 267, 325–30, 351–57, 385, 442.
2. AWPD to Deputy COS, Mission, Strength & Composition of Phil Garrisons, 20 Oct 22; SecWar to Gov-Genl, 4 Nov 22, #532, AWPD Records.
3. Morton, *Strategy and Command*, 24. Gov-Genl to SecWar, 16 Jan 23, quoted in SecWar to SecNav, 16 Jan 23; Office CNO to CinC Astc Flt, Receipt of Secret Ltr, 10 Jan 23, 198-37, roll 90, SecNav & CNO Secret & Conf Corresp.
4. Gov-Genl to SecWar, 5 Feb 23, #305, Ser 209, JB Records.
5. Andrew Sinclair, *The Available Man: The Life behind the Masks of Warren Gamaliel Harding* (New York: Macmillan, 1965), 67–68. Lane, *Armed Progressive*, 252–53.
6. Gov-Genl to SecWar, 5 Feb 23. The staff of the Ohio Historical Society, which holds the Warren G. Harding Papers, could find no evidence of a written directive.
7. Douglas, "Coontz," 23.
8. Actg Dir WPD to CNO, Jt Blue-Orange Est, 21 Dec 22, 112-33:1, roll 26, SecNav & CNO Secret & Conf Corresp.
9. *Navy Directory*, 1921–23. Sinclair Gannon, Flag Officer Biog Files.
10. Judge Advocate Genl of Navy, Memo of Adm Latimer, 13 Feb 23, 198-1:2; CNO, Circular Letter, Basic War Plans, War Portf, vol. 1, 22 Mar 23, 198-1, roll 71, SecNav & CNO Secret & Conf Corresp. WPD Est 1922, changes interleaved with text, dated July 1923 but probably begun earlier.
11. GB Strategic Survey, Apr 1923. Coontz to SecNav, Strategic Survey of Pac, 10 May 23, 198-26, roll 80, SecNav & CNO Secret & Conf Corresp.
12. Actg Dir WPD to CNO, Jt Blue-Orange Est, 21 Dec 22, 112-33:1, roll 26, SecNav & CNO Secret & Conf Corresp.
13. AWPD to ACOS G-2, War Plan Orange, 6 Mar 23, File Orange 1039-1, AWPD Records. JB-JPC Plans, May–Jul 1923.
14. Actg Dir WPD to CNO, Modifications of Navy Orange Estimate, 9 Jun 23, File Orange Studies, Box 64, WPD Files.
15. SecWar to Gov-Genl, 24 Jul 23, #532, Box 22, AWPD Records.
16. JPC Plan 1924. JB Plan 1924. Morton, *Strategy and Command*, 30.
17. AWPD Plan 1925.
18. WPD to circulation list, Tentative Basic Strategic Plan Orange, 1 Nov 23, cited in Rept of Comm #5, AWC, G-4, 27 Feb 24, UNOpP, Box 49, RG 8, NHC, NWC. CNO to Basic War Plans Distribution List, War Plans, 29 Dec 23, w encl, Discussion of War Plans . . . & Cooperation & Coordination necessary, 198-1:2/1, roll 71, SecNav & CNO Secret & Conf Corresp.
19. GB Strategic Survey, Apr 1923. JB-JPC Plans, May–Jul 1923.
20. JB to SecNav, Recommendations by Gov-Genl of Phils Concerning Measures of Def, 7 Jul 23, #305, Ser 209, JB Records. Gov-Genl to SecWar, 5 Feb 23.
21. JB-JPC Plans, May–Jul 1923.
22. Actg Dir WPD to CNO, Strategic Survey of Pac, 3 May 23, 198-26, roll 80, SecNav & CNO Secret & Conf Corresp.

23. GB Strategic Survey, Apr 1923.
24. Gov-Genl to SecWar, 5 Feb 23.
25. JB to SecWar, Def of Phils, 7 Jul 23, JB-JPC Plans, May–Jul 1923.
26. Actg Dir WPD to CNO, 9 Jun 23.
27. CinCUS to CNO, Flt Operating Plan—Information Relating to, 23 Oct 24, 198-13, roll 79, SecNav & CNO Secret & Conf Corresp.
28. *Navy Directory*, 1924–25.
29. Plan O-3, ca. Jan 1925.
30. Gov-Genl to SecWar, 5 Feb 23.
31. Actg Dir WPD to CNO, 9 Jun 23.
32. AWPD Plan 1925.
33. GB Strategic Survey, Apr 1923.
34. Plan O-3, ca. Jan 1925, 14–23.
35. Actg Dir WPD to CNO, 9 Jun 23.
36. WPD to circulation list, 1 Nov 23. Plan O-3, ca. Jan 1925, 6–7.
37. Plan O-3, ca. Jan 1925, 48–54. CinCUS to CNO, 23 Oct 24. (Prob) Capt F. H. Schofield, GB, to Standley, Notes on Orange Plan, 14 Dec 23, 198-1:2, roll 71, SecNav & CNO Secret & Conf Corresp.
38. JB to SecWar, Def of Phils, 7 Jul 23.
39. Ibid.
40. Plan O-3, ca. Jan 1925, 35–36, 52, 59. CinCUS to CNO, 23 Oct 24.
41. Plan O-3, ca. Jan 1925, 55–59. CNO to Distribution List for Basic Readiness Plan, App F—Mobile Base Project, 20 Dec 23, 198-1, roll 71, SecNav & CNO Secret & Conf Corresp.
42. Moore, "Eagle and the Roo."
43. Plan O-3, ca. Jan 1925, 55–59.
44. Actg Dir WPD to CNO, 9 Jun 23.
45. Plan O-3, ca. Jan 1925, 55–60. WPD to CNO, 9 Feb 27; CNO, Fueling at Sea, 28 Mar 27, BuC&R Gen Corresp, File S55-(9), vol. 1, Box 4157, RG 19, NA. Communication from Thomas Wildenburg, New City, N.Y., 4 Mar 1990.
46. Plan O-3, ca. Jan 1925, 42–52, 55–60.
47. JB-JPC Plans, May–Jul 1923.

Chapter 12   The American Way of Planning: The Professionals

1. JPC Est, Jan 1928, 63–64.
2. JB Plan 1924. JPC Plans Oct & Nov 1926. JPC Plan, Apr 1928.
3. JPC Army Section Revision, May 1927.
4. JPC and JB Plans, 1924. JPC Plan Nov 1926.
5. JPC Plan Nov 1926. Army Est, Aug 1927. Deputy COS to Schofield, Coordination of Opns, Orange Plan, 5 Jun 28, JB #325, Ser 280, AWPD Records. JB Plan, Jun 1928. CNO Plan, Mar 1929, 1:19–20, 26.
6. The home reserve is cited in most planning documents of October 1926 to March 1929.
7. Braisted, "On the American Red and Red-Orange Plans." Holt, "Joint Plan Red." CNO, Plan Red (WPL 22), Feb 1931, approved by SecNav 15 Feb 31, roll 4, Scholarly Microfilms.

8. Pye, lecture, Naval Post Graduate School, 6 Nov 26.
9. William Rawle Shoemaker, Flag Officer Biog Files. Turk, "Eberle." *Navy Directory,* 1923, 1924.
10. CNO to Basic War Plans Distribution List, War Plans, 29 Dec 23, w encl, Discussion of War Plans . . . & Cooperation & Coordination necessary, 198-1:2/1, roll 71, SecNav & CNO Secret & Conf Corresp.
11. William Harrison Standley, Flag Officer Biog Files. Walter, "Standley." RAdm Kemp Tolley, USN (Ret.), "Admiral-Ambassador Standley," *Shipmate* 40 (Sep 1977):27–28.
12. Frank H. Schofield, Flag Officer Biog File. Wheeler, *Pratt,* 70–71, 106, 351 illus., 424–25. SecNav, Genl Index to Genl Corresp, Schofield entries, Microfilm Ser M 1052, RG 80, NA. Patekewich, "Book of NWC Admirals." Authors File, NWC, Schofield entries. Braisted, "Hughes."
13. *Navy Directory,* 1926–29. Lectures at USMC School: Horne 27 Apr 28, Dillen 26 Apr 29, Cook 27 Feb 31.
14. William Satterlee Pye, Flag Officer Biog File. Pye, address to University Club, Larchmont, N.Y., 20 May 37, ibid. Patekewich, "Book of NWC Admirals." Authors File, NWC, Pye entries.
15. Frederick Joseph Horne, Flag Officer Biog Files. Naval Historical Foundation, *Manuscript Collection,* iv. Horne Papers, Box 3, passim. Authors File, NWC, Horne entries. Albion, *Makers of Policy,* 392, 485, 533–36.
16. See bibliography for plans and revisions of 1927–29.
17. Schofield, lectures, AWC 22 Sep 23, USMC School 23 Mar 28. JPC Est, Jan 1928, 36–38, 54–55.
18. Merlyn Grail Cook, Flag Officer Biog Files. *Navy Directory,* 1928–31.
19. Montgomery Meigs Taylor, Flag Officer Biog Files. Cdr J. H. Slypher, Supt Naval Records & Library, biog ltr re Taylor, 1924, ibid. Frank H. Rentfrow, article re *Olympia,* source & date unknown, ibid. Patekewich, "Book of NWC Admirals." Authors File, NWC, Taylor entries.
20. Slypher, biog ltr re Taylor, 1924. Braisted, "Hughes," 53, 65. Symonds, "Pratt," 71–86. Wheeler, *Pratt,* 324, 349, 361. CNO to Chiefs All Bureaus, Representatives for WPs in Navy Dept Bu & Offices, 8 Jan 30, EG 55 to EY, Box 255, SecNav Secret Files. *Navy Directory.*
21. Edward Clifford Kalbfus, Flag Officer Biog Files. Hope R. Miller, article on Kalbfus, *Washington Post,* 11 Nov 42, ibid.
22. George Julian Meyers, Flag Officer Biog Files. Authors File, NWC, Meyers entries.
23. CNO Plan, Mar 1929, 1:30, 3:212, 219–20.
24. *Navy Directory,* 1929–32.
25. JPC and JB Plans, 1924.

Chapter 13   A Marginally Saner Policy

1. (Prob) Schofield, GB, to Standley, Notes on Orange Plan, 14 Dec 23, 198-1:2, roll 71, SecNav & CNO Secret & Conf Corresp. Schofield, lectures, AWC 22 Sep 23, USMC 23 May 28. JPC Est, Jan 1928, 36–38.
2. GB 1906 Plan, 1–3.
3. GB 1914 Plan, 24, 68–69.

4. GB Strategic Survey, Apr 1923.
5. JPC Plan, Nov 1926. JPC Army Section Revision, May 1927. JPC Est, Jan 1928, 57–58.
6. JPC Est, Jan 1928, 36–38, 54–60. Schofield, lecture, USMC, 23 Mar 28.
7. NWC, 10 Aug 21.
8. WPD to circulation list, Tentative Basic Strategic Plan Orange, 1 Nov 23, cited in Rept of Comm #5, AWC, G-4, 27 Feb 24, UNOpP, Box 49, RG 8, NHC, NWC. CNO to Distribution List for Basic Readiness Plan, App F—Mobile Base Project, 20 Dec 23, 198-1, roll 71; Dir WPD to CNO, Def of the Phils, 17 Jan 24, 200-17, roll 91, SecNav & CNO Secret & Conf Corresp.
9. Schofield, Notes on Orange Plan, 14 Dec 23. Schofield, lecture, AWC, 22 Sep 23. Actg Dir WPD to CNO, Modifications of Navy Orange Estimate, 9 Jun 23, File Orange Studies, Box 64, WPD Files. GB Strategic Survey, Apr 1923.
10. JPC Plan 1924. AWPD Plan 1925. JB Plan 1924.
11. Army Est, Aug 1927. JPC Est, Jan 1928, 22–27, 78–80. Cdr Lt Cruiser Div 3 to CinCAF, Advanced Nav Base in S Phil Is, 29 Feb 28, w repts by COs of USS Cincinnati & Richmond & Capt H. K. Cage, 27 Feb and 3 Mar 28; Col R. M. Cutts USMC to Dir WPD, Malampaya Sound—Tactical Study, 7 May 27, File same name—Problem 2, Box 56, WPD Files. JPC Est, Jan 1929.
12. JPC Est, Jan 1928, 57–58. JPC Navy Section Revision, Mar 1928. JPC Revision, Apr 1928.
13. Schofield, lecture, USMC, 23 Mar 28.
14. JPC Est, Jan 1928, 65–67. JB Plan, Jun 1928. CNO Plan, Mar 1929, 1:21–25.
15. JPC Navy Section Revision, Mar 1928. JPC Revision, Apr 1928.
16. Maj P. H. Worcester to Horne, Blue Orange Est, Air Plans, 30 Jul 27, File 232, Box 69, AWPD Color Plans.
17. Chief BuAer to CNO, New Basic Plan Orange, 28 Aug 28, File Orange Basic Plan—Comment, Box 64, WPD Files. WPD, Est of Sitn, Blue-Orange, 8 Jul 27, File 232, Box 69, AWPD Color Plans.
18. JB Points, Feb 1928.
19. Originator not stated, Problem No. 1, Tactical Study—Orange War, n.d., ca. late 1927; Horne to Capt Bingham, 4 Nov 27; Office of Nav Opns, Study of Adv Base, 1 Feb 28, File Dumanquilas Bay—Tactical Studies File 1, Box 42; Sherman comment from NWC, Sr Course 1927, Operations Problem II, File Malampaya Sound—Tactical Study—Problem 2, Box 56, WPD Files. Schofield, lecture, USMC, 23 Mar 28.
20. JPC Navy Section Revision, Mar 1928. JPC Revision, Apr 1928.
21. Shoemaker, handwritten note on Navy Est, n.d., prob Jul–Aug 23, File Orange Studies, Box 64, WPD Files.
22. Chief BuOrd to CNO, Lahaina Roads Def Project: Mine Barrages, Submarine Nets, Torpedo Nets, 18 Apr 27, UNM, Box 42, RG 8, NHC, NWC.
23. JPC Est, Jan 1928, 49. CNO Plan, Mar 1929, 1:16.
24. Shoemaker, note on Navy Est, prob Jul–Aug 23.
25. CNO, Basic Readiness Plan, 20 Dec 23. WPD, Def of Phils, 17 Jan 24.
26. JPC to JB, Jt A&N Basic War Plan—Orange, 12 Mar 24; JB to JPC, Proposed Jt A&N Basic War Plan—Orange, 7 Jun 24, #325, Ser 228, JB Records.
27. Pye, lecture, NWC, 7 Jan 26. JPC Revision, Oct 1926.
28. JPC Plan, Nov 1926. WPD Est, May 1927. JPC Est, Jan 1928, 36–38, 44–45,

54–55. JB Points, Feb 1928. JPC Navy Section Revisions, Mar & Apr 1928. JPC Plan, Apr 1928. JB Plan, Jun 1928. CNO Plan, Mar 1929, vol. 1, pt. 2, 132, pt. 3, app II, pt. 4, app III. WPL-16, change #3, Jul 1933.
29. Army Est, Aug 1927. JPC Est, Jan 1928, 15–18.
30. Worcester to Horne, 30 Jul 27. Horne, Memo for Maj Jenkins, 28 Jul 27, File 232, Box 69, AWPD Color Plans. JPC Est, Jan 1928, 15–17, 44–45.
31. JPC Est, Jan 1928, 65–67. JB Plan, Jun 1928. CNO Plan, Mar 1929, 1:21–25. WPD, Study of Certain Pac Is, 6 Aug 27.
32. AAC Plans, 1929–31, esp Table I, 1931.
33. WPL-16, change #3, Jul 1933.
34. Friedman, *US Aircraft Carriers*, chap. 6.
35. JB Comment, Oct 1926. JPC Plan, Nov 1926.
36. JPC Plan and Revision, Oct 1926. JB Comment, Oct 1926. JPC Plan, Nov 1926. JPC Army Section Revision, May 1927. Army Est, Aug 1927. JPC Est, Jan 1928, 46–48, 80. JB Points, Feb 1928. JPC Navy Section Revision, Mar 1928. JPC Revision, Apr 1928. JPC Plan, Apr 1928. CNO Plan, Mar 1929, 1:25, 45, 99–100, 2:126.
37. WPD, Def of Phils, 17 Jan 24. Baker, lecture, NWC, 12 Oct 23.
38. AWC Repts, 13–14 Apr 25.
39. CNO, Basic Readiness Plan, 20 Dec 23.
40. JPC Navy Section Revision, Mar 1928. JPC Revision, Apr 1928. JPC Plan, Apr 1928. JB Plan, Jun 1928. CNO Plan, Mar 1929, vol. 1, pt. 1, 24–25, pt. 2, 121–22, 126, 139, 189, vol. 3, app II, vol. 4, app III.
41. JB Points, Feb 1928. JPC Navy Section Revision, Mar 1928. CNO Plan, Mar 1929, vol. 1, pt. 2, 141.
42. Baker, lecture, NWC, 12 Oct 23.
43. JPC Est, Jan 1928, 33–34. CNO Plan, Mar 1929, vol. 1, pt. 2, 132.
44. NWC 1911 Plan, 2(c):28–29, 2(d):52–58.
45. CNO, Basic Readiness Plan, 20 Dec 23. JPC Est, Jan 1928, 64. JPC Plan, Apr 1928. CNO Plan, Mar 1929, vol. 1, pt. 2, 131, 136–38.
46. Dir WPD to GB, Questions concerning Limitation of Armament, 19 Oct 21, #425, GB Subj File.
47. CNO, Basic Readiness Plan, 20 Dec 23.
48. Shoemaker, note on Navy Est, Jul–Aug 23. WPD, Def of Phils, 17 Jan 24.
49. Schofield, Notes on Orange Plan, 14 Dec 23.
50. JPC Est, Jan 1928, 64.
51. BuDocks, *Building Navy's Bases*, 2:232, 299.
52. Flt Adm Ernest J. King, "U.S. Navy at War, Final Official Report" (1 Mar to 1 Oct 45) (Washington: reprint by *The United States News*, 1946), 24.

Chapter 14 The Siege of Japan

1. GB Strategic Survey, Apr 1923.
2. Dir WPD to GB, Questions concerning Limitation of Armament, 19 Oct 21, #425, GB Subj File. WPD Est 1922, 14, 16, 25–27b.
3. Many versions of the plan contained summaries similar to that described here, for example, JB, Strategy of Pacific, 1919; WPD Est 1922, 2–5; JPC Est, Jan 1928; JB Plan, Jun 1928.

4. JB, Strategy of Pacific, 1919. WPD Est 1922, 16, 25.
5. JPC Est, Jan 1928, 62. CNO Plan, Mar 1929, 1:17.
6. WPD, Quick Movement, 1932.
7. Day, lecture, NWC, 16 Feb 23. JPC Est, Jan 1928, 31–32, 44, 62–63, 68–73. JPC Navy Section Revision, Apr 1928. CNO Plan, Mar 1929, 1:19.
8. GB 1906 Plan, 46. NWC Rept of Conference of 1907, pt. 1, 20.
9. GB 1914 Plan, 69. JPC Plan 1924. JB Plan 1924. Memorandum re NWC Conference of 1906, 14 Feb 07, in Vlahos, "NWC and Origins," 32. NWC, Problem of 1907, 119.
10. GB Strategic Survey, Apr 1923.
11. NWC 1911 Plan, 2(c):40–41.
12. JB Points, Feb 1928. JPC Navy Section Revision, Mar 1928. CNO Plan, Mar 1929, vol. 1, pt. 2, 131, 136–38, 4:app VII, 1, 3.
13. AWC Repts, 13–14 Apr 25. JB Est, Jan 1928, 78–80.
14. Army Est, Aug 1927. JPC Navy Section Revision, Mar 1928. JPC Est, Jan 1928, 56–57, 68–73, 78–80.
15. CNO Plan, Mar 1929, 4:app VII.
16. JPC Navy Section Revision, Apr 1928. JB Plan, Jun 1928.
17. CNO Plan, Mar 1929, vol. 1, pt. 2, 136–37, 4:app VII, 2–4. Change #3 to WPL-13, 26 Feb 35, 132. Change #4 to WPL-16, 31 Jan 34, app VII, secs 1, 2, 6.
18. Army Est, Aug 1927. JPC Est, 1928, 26–27, 56–57, 67–76, 81.
19. Corresp among GB and CinC Astc Flt, various dates 1901–3, #425.2, Boxes 140 and 141, GB Subj File. GB 1906 Plan. JPC Est, Jan 1928, 26.
20. Mahan-Oliver Corresp 1911.
21. NWC 1911 Plan, 2(c):36–40, 52–58.
22. NWC Conference of 1906, pt. 2, 3–4. GB 1906 Plan, 1–3.
23. Army Est, Aug 1927. JPC Est, Jan 1928, 26–27, 67–73. NWC, 10 Aug 21.
24. Mahan-Oliver Corresp 1911. WPD Est 1922, 14–16.
25. NWC 1911 Plan, 2(c):53–55. NWC Conference of 1906, pt. 2, 42–48.
26. AWPD to ACOS G-2, War Plan Orange, 6 Mar 23, File Orange 1039-1, AWPD Files.
27. NWC, 10 Aug 21. WPD Est 1922, 14–16.
28. Army Est, Aug 1927. WPC Est, Jan 1928, 26–27, 56–57, 67–73.
29. NWC, 10 Aug 21.
30. JPC Plan, Apr 1928. CNO Plan, Mar 1929, 4:app III.
31. JPC Est, Jan 1928, 56–57.
32. Bd for Dev of Navy Yd Plans to Chief BuDocks, Adv Bases in a Pac Campaign, Material and Facilities, 31 Oct 22, 198-13, roll 79; CNO to Distribution List for Basic Readiness Plan, App F—Mobile Base Project, 20 Dec 23, 198-1, roll 71, SecNav & CNO Secret & Conf Corresp.
33. Hayes, *Joint Chiefs,* 658. Cate and Craven, "Army Air Arm between Two World Wars, 61–62.
34. GB 1910 Plan, 6–7, 40–45.
35. NWC 1911 Plan, 2(a):1. GB 1914 Plan, 68–69. JPC Est, Jan 1928, 64–65.
36. NWC 1911 Plan, 2(a):1, 2(c):55.
37. GB 1914 Plan, foreword, 15, 50. CNO Plan, Mar 1929, 1:16.
38. Cdr L. S. Van Duzer, Extracts from endorsement of ltr by Lt Cdr Ralph Earle,

414 • Notes to Pages 160–65

n.d., ca. early 1910, UNOpP 1910, Box 48, RG 8, NHC, NWC. GB 1910 Plan, 6–7, 40–45.

39. Vlahos, "War Gaming." Fleet Problems, 1923–41, passim.
40. WPD to GB, 19 Oct 21.
41. NWC 1911 Plan, 2(c):26–27. Plan O-3, ca. Jan 25, 42–52, 59–60. NWC 1911 Plan, 2(c):27.
42. Ellis, Adv Base Opns, Jul 1921, 37. WPD, Marshall Is Plan, ca. 1927.
43. GB 1906 Plan, 1–3. NWC Rept Conference of 1907, pt. 1, 14–16, 20–21. GB 1914 Plan, 72.
44. GB 1910 Plan, 40–45.
45. NWC 1911 Plan, 2(c):27. JPC Est, Jan 1928, 57–58.
46. WPD, Landing Opns, Oct 1927. JPC Est, Jan 1928, 42–44, 64–65.
47. NWC 1911 Plan, 2(a):1, 2(c):36–40, 52–58.
48. NWC Conference of 1906, 3–6, 11–14. GB 1910 Plan, 44–45.
49. Mahan-Oliver Corresp 1911.
50. WPD Est, May 1927. WPD Landing Opns, Oct 1927. JPC Est, Jan 1928, 33–34, 38, 64–65.
51. NWC Rept of Conference of 1907, pt. 1, 21.
52. NWC Conference of 1906, pt. 1, 6.
53. WPD Est 1922, 3–4. Schofield, lecture, USMC, 23 Mar 28.
54. NWC Conference of 1906, pt. 1, 6, pt. 2, 2–4, 8.
55. WPD Est 1922, 3–4.
56. GB 1906 Plan, 1–3.
57. NWC Conference of 1906, pt. 2, 5–6, 11–14, 17–20.
58. WPD Est 1922, 2–5, 14–16.
59. GB Strategic Survey, Apr 1923.
60. JPC Navy Section Revision, Apr 1928. JPC Est, Jan 1928, Tables pp. 80–82.
61. JPC Est, Jan 1928, 63–64.
62. JB Plan, Jun 1928.
63. JPC Est, Jan 1928, 38.
64. NWC Conference of 1906, pt. 2, 5–6.
65. Mahan-Oliver Corresp 1911.
66. NWC 1911 Plan, 2(c):39–40. GB 1914 Plan, 24.
67. JPC Est, Jan 1928, 32–33.
68. Ibid.
69. JPC Est, Jan 1928, 15–17. JB Plan, Jun 1928.
70. Army Est, Aug 1927.
71. Sherry, *Rise of American Air Power*, 31, 58–59.
72. CNO Plan, Mar 1929, 1:17–18.
73. Col James H. Reeves, AC/S G-2, Sitn Monograph Orange, 1 Jan 27, File 166, Box 63, AWPD Color Plans.
74. Sherry, *Rise of American Air Power*, 90.
75. JB-JPC Plans, May–Jul 1923. JPC Plan 1924.
76. AWPD to ACOS G-2, 6 Mar 23.
77. Maj P. H. Worcester, GS, Memo for Capt Rowan w Comments on Est of Sitn Blue-Orange, 30 Jun 27, File 232, Box 69, AWPD Color Plans.
78. Asst COS G-2 to Asst COS AWPD, Info assisting in dev of Orange Plan, 28 Feb 28, JB #325, Ser 280, AWPD Records.

79. WPD Est, May 1927. Army Est, Aug 1927. JPC Est, Jan 1928, 55–56. JPC Navy Section Revision, Mar 1928. JPC Revision, Apr 1928.
80. WPD Est 1922, 2–5.
81. Worcester, Memo, 30 Jun 27.
82. AWC Repts, 13–14 Apr 25.
83. Army Est, Aug 1927.
84. JB Points, Feb 1928.
85. ACOS, G-2, GS, to ACOS WPD, 28 Feb 1928.
86. AWC Repts, 13–14 Apr 25.
87. Morgan, "Planning the Defeat of Japan," 183–91.
88. GB Strategic Survey, Apr 1923. Actg Dir WPD to CNO, Strategic Survey of Pac, 3 May 23, 198-26, roll 80, SecNav & CNO Secret & Conf Corresp.

Chapter 15 Quest for a Strategy

1. Pres NWC to CNO, Basic WPs (vol. 2)—Basic Orange Plan, 10 Dec 23, 198-1:2, roll 71, SecNav & CNO Secret & Conf Corresp.
2. JB Comment, Oct 1926. Army Est, Aug 1927. JB Plan, Jun 1928. CNO Plan, Mar 1929, 1:19.
3. Vlahos, *Blue Sword*, 144.
4. Cpt R. A. Koch, NWC, Blue-Orange Study, 31 Mar 33, w apps 1 to 3; Head of Research Dept NWC to COS NWC, Position of US in Far East, 3 Apr 33, UNOpP, Box 49, RG 8, NHC, NWC.
5. Army Est, Aug 1927.
6. Embick, Memo for Cdg Gen Phil Dept, 19 Apr 33, WPD 3251-15, in Schaffer, "Embick."
7. Koch, 31 Mar 33. Head of Research Dept NWC, 3 Apr 33.
8. Maj P. H. Worcester, GS, Memo for Capt Rowan w Comments on Est of Sitn Blue-Orange, 30 Jun 27, File 232, Box 69, AWPD Color Plans. JPC Est, Jan 1928, 48–52, 54–55. JB to JPC, Jt A&N Basic WP—Orange, 26 Jan 28, JB #325, Entry 184, Ser 280, AWPD Records. JPC Est, Jan 1929, para 57. D. Staton (?) to Koch, 31 May 33, UNOpP, Box 49, RG 8, NHC, NWC.
9. WPD, Quick Movement, 1932. Pencil notation indicates ca. Oct 1932, but CNO to CinCUS, 13 Jul 33, File A16-3/FF1, Box 237, SecNav Secret Files, states that the study was prepared in OpNav and hand delivered to CinCUS in April 1932. Thus Meyers probably had main responsibility for its preparation.
10. JPC Navy Section Revision, Apr 1928. CNO Plan, Mar 1929, 1:12–14.
11. RAdm Taussig COS US Flt to Bryant, 23 Jan 33; Bryant to Taussig, 1 Feb 33, in CNO to CinCUS, 13 Jul 33, A16-3/FF1, Box 237, SecNav Secret Files. CinCUS to Cdrs of subsidiary forces, Prepn Plan No. 1, Orange, 21 Jan 33, A4-3, CinCUS Op Plans 1932–39.
12. David Foote Sellers, Flag Officer Biog Files. Wheeler, *Pratt,* 362–67. Roskill, *Naval Policy between the Wars,* 2:284.
13. Tentative Plan O-1, 26 Aug 33. Memoranda (total eleven) from CinCUS to CNO or among CinCUS and subsidiary fleet commanders, re War Plans, Battle Force Mobilization Plan, or Organization of Train for Orange War, 22 Sep 33 to 28 Apr 34; CNO to CinCUS, Composition of Train for Western Adv of US Flt, 21 Jun 34, vol. 2; ComBatFor to Flt Cdrs, Mobilization Plan—Orange—

Aircraft, 21 Mar 34, File BatFor prior 3 Sep 1939, Box BasFor & BatFor Commands, all in CinCUS Op Plans 1932–39.

14. Tentative Plan O-1, 26 Aug 33.

15. WPD (prob Meyers) to Cdg Gen FMF, 20 Nov 33, cited in Dir WPD to Cdg Gen FMF, Wotje Attack Plan, 12 Oct 34, File Wotje Attack Plan, Box 77, WPD Files.

16. CinCUS to CNO, Operating Plan O-1 Orange, 31 Mar 34, A16-3; CNO to CinCUS, 16 Mar 34, CinCUS Op Plans 1932–39.

17. A recent detailed discussion of Japanese secrecy is in Peattie, *Nan'yō,* chap 8.

18. Pomeroy, *Pacific Outpost,* 106.

19. Nomura interview, Jun 1982.

20. Wilds, "How Japan Fortified Mandated Islands." Peattie, *Nan'yō,* 236.

21. Hines, lecture, NWC, 1 Nov 21.

22. 1927 Asst Naval Attaché, Tokyo, rept, File Marshall Is, PL, Pacific—Logistics—Mandated Is, RG 8, NHC, NWC. SecNav to SecState, 2 Feb 33, EF 37, Box 173, SecNav & CNO Secret & Conf Corresp. FMF, Attack of Ponape, 5 Oct 35.

23. Asst COS G-2, Sitn Monograph Orange, 1 Jan 27, File 166, Box 63, AWPD Color Plans. JPC Est, Jan 1928, 66–67.

24. Corresp between Dir ONI, CNO, and WPD re cruises of scout cruisers: 9 Oct 22, 162-78:3, roll 46; 31 May, 12 & 13 Jun 23, 162-30, roll 55; Corresp between SecNav and State Dept, 26 Jun, 8 & 18 Oct 23, 162-78:3, roll 46, SecNav & CNO Secret & Conf Corresp.

25. Dir ONI to CNO, Information lacking regarding certain . . . Caroline & Marshall Is, 6 & 15 Oct 24, 232-43, roll 115, SecNav & CNO Secret & Conf Corresp. Rept by USS *Milwaukee,* 1923, File Marshall Is, PL Pac Logistics, Mandated Is, RG 8, NHC, NWC.

26. ONI, Intelligence Rept, Truk, Caroline Is, 30 Sep 23, File PL Caroline Is, RG 8, NHC, NWC.

27. ONI to CNO, 6 & 15 Oct 24. Dir WPD to CNO, Proposed itinerary 38th & 39th Destroyer Divs, 22 Oct 24, 232-43, roll 115, SecNav & CNO Secret & Conf Corresp.

28. Montross, "Mystery of Pete Ellis." Ballendorf, lecture, Naval History Symposium, 20 Oct 1989.

29. Peattie, *Nan'yō,* 239–40.

30. Intelligence Section FMF, Monographs of Japanese Mandate Is, 2 Aug 34 and later, File Mandate Islands, same subtitle, Box 57, WPD Files.

31. Hydrographer to ComAirBasFor, Information on Pac Is, 2 Dec 33, A7-3/FF5-4; Chief BuAer to Hydrographer, Conf Aviation Chart Program of Principal Japanese Is, 19 Jan 34, EF37, Box 173, SecNav Conf Corresp.

32. Corresp between ComAirBasFor, CinCUS, and CNO, Proposed Operating Plan 1935—Flight to Phils, 25 Jul, 8 & 14 Aug 34, A16-3(5)/A21 1934–37, Box 62, SecNav Conf Corresp.

33. WPD, Quick Movement, 1932.

34. Hughes, "Strategy-Tactics Relationship."

35. For their history and development see Knott, *American Flying Boat;* Jablonski, *Sea Wings.* For data on aircraft types see Swanborough and Bowers, *US Navy Aircraft;* Chief BuAer to Asst SecNav, Charts of Characteristics . . . of US

Navy Airplanes, 29 Sep 33, Aer-D-19-CRP H1-3, SecNav & CNO Secret and Conf Corresp. For activity in the Pacific, see Horvat, *Above the Pacific*. For chronology of events, see NAVAIR, *US Naval Aviation*.

36. JB, Rept, 11 Sep 23, RG 255, NA.
37. Cdr Air Sqns rept, CinCUS annual repts, 1925.
38. NAVAIR, *US Naval Aviation*, 37.
39. Cate and Craven, "Army Air Arm between Two World Wars," 61–62.
40. ComAirScoFor to CNO, Patrol Seaplanes—Requirements of, 13 Apr 31, VP/A4-3; Chief BuAer to CNO, same title, 7 May 31, VP/FF11-1, CNO Secret & Conf Files.
41. CinCUS annual repts, 1932, 1933 w rept of Cdr Scouting Force, 1934.
42. CO USS *Wright* to ComAirBasFor, Experiments Suggested by CinC, 25 Jan 34, AVI/A16-3, ONI Files, Box 15, NHC, NWC. CNO to CO USS *Astoria*, 30 Apr 34, H1-3, Box 246, SecNav & CNO Secret & Conf Corresp.
43. CinCUS annual repts, passim.
44. Cdr Scouting Flt, rept, CinCUS annual repts, 1928.
45. CinCUS & Subsidiary Cdrs, CinCUS annual repts, 1932. Dir Ship Movements Div to WPD, Assignment of VP Sqns, 14 Aug 35, VP to VT, Box 264, SecNav & CNO Secret & Conf Corresp.
46. CinCUS, ComBatFor & ComBasFor repts, CinCUS annual repts, 1933.
47. GB to CNO, 6 Sep 34, File VP, Box 212, SecNav & CNO Secret & Conf Corresp.
48. Smith, *Airships Akron and Macon*, xii, xxi–xxii, and passim.
49. Tentative Plan O-1, 26 Aug 33. WPL-16, change #3, 17 Jul 33.
50. Memos among CinCUS, CNO, and subsidiary fleet commanders re War Plans, Mobilization Plan or Organization of Train, various dates 17 Feb to 21 Jun 34.
51. Catalina was suggested by the manufacturer, Consolidated Aircraft Corporation, and adopted first by the British in 1941.
52. Swanborough and Bowers, *US Navy Aircraft*, 84.
53. ComAirBasFor, conference, 15 Nov 34, A to A2-1, Box 1, ComAirBasFor Genl Corresp, RG 313, NA. ComAirBasFor rept, CinCUS annual rept, 1935.
54. CNO to CinCUS, Design of Patrol planes, n.d., prob Jan 1935; ComAirBasFor to CinCUS, Characteristics of VP Planes, 9 Jun 35, File VP, SecNav & CNO Secret & Conf Corresp.
55. "US Naval Administrative Histories of WWII," 47a, BuAer, 6:1752.
56. CinCUS annual repts 1937, 1938.
57. CNO to CinCUS, Design of Patrol Planes, prob Jan 1935. CNO to CinCUS and Pres NWC, Characteristics of VP planes, 1 Apr 35; Pres NWC to CNO, same title, 15 Jul 35, UANP, ONI Box 15, NHC, NWC. Dir WPD to CNO, Reconciling Statements on VP Planes & Employment, 4 Apr 35, VP to VT, Box 264, SecNav & CNO Secret & Conf Corresp.
58. CinCUS to CNO, Characteristics of VP Planes, 28 Jun 35, File VP, SecNav & CNO Secret & Conf Corresp.
59. King and Whitehill, *Fleet Admiral King*.
60. Chief BuAer to CNO, Comment on proposed . . . Secret Ltr . . . "Design of Patrol Planes," 25 Feb 35; Chief BuAer to CNO, Comment on Dir WPD Secret Memo . . . Patrol Plane Program, 22 Mar 35, File VP, SecNav & CNO Secret

& Conf Corresp. (Prob) BuAer, n.d., possibly 6 Mar 34, Aer-P1-EMN-A1-3(1) A21-1 QB/EN15, GB Records.
61. Dir WPD to CNO, Characteristics of VP Planes, 23 Jul 35, File VP, SecNav & CNO Secret & Conf Corresp.
62. ComAirBasFor rept, in CinCUS annual rept 1937.
63. CinCUS annual repts, 1937, 1938.
64. CinCUS annual rept 1939.
65. Swanborough and Bowers, *US Navy Aircraft*, 80.

Chapter 16 The American Way of Planning: Cooperation and Campaign Plans

1. Samuel Wood Bryant, Flag Officer Biog Files. *Navy Directory*. Patekewich, "Book of NWC Admirals."
2. Dir WPD, Operation Plan No. 1, 28 Jul 32, UNO, Box 44, RG 8, NHC, NWC.
3. For example, WPL-13, Change #1, Jul 32, pt. 1, chap. 1, p. 43, chap. 4, p. 86; pt. 2, chap. 1, p. 112; pt. 3, chap. 6, p. 233.
4. Ibid., pt. 3, chap. 2, p. 219.
5. RAdm Taussig COS US Flt to Bryant, 23 Jan 33; Bryant to Taussig, 1 Feb 33, cited in CNO to CinCUS, 13 Jul 33, A16-3/FF1, Box 237, SecNav Secret Files.
6. CNO to CinCUS, 13 Jul 33, A16-3/FF1, Box 237, SecNav Secret Files.
7. Wheeler, *Pratt*, 274–75, 422–25. Reynolds, *Fast Carriers*, xi, 17. Melhorn, *Two-Block Fox*, 112–14. Braisted, "Hughes," 52, 60. Walter, "Standley," 94. Harry W. Hill, oral history, 162, 169. William T. Tarrant, oral history, 43.
8. CNO to CinCUS, 3 Nov 33, Box 147-D, WPD Files. WPD, Some Plans & Studies Required . . . Plan O-1, Orange, 2 Dec 33, CinCUS Op Plans 1932–39.
9. CinCUS to CNO, US Flt's O-1 (Color) Plans—Prepn of, 8 Dec 33; CNO to CinCUS, same title, 17 Jan 34, A16/FF1, CinCUS Op Plans 1932–39.
10. CinCUS to CNO, Operating Plan O-1 Orange, 31 Mar 34, A16-3, ibid.
11. Cary Walthall Magruder, Flag Officer Biog Files. *Navy Directory*.
12. CNO to Basic War Plans Distribution List, War Plans, 29 Dec 23, w encl, Discussion of War Plans . . . & Cooperation & Coordination necessary, 198-1:2/1, roll 71, SecNav & CNO Secret & Conf Corresp.
13. George Julian Meyers, Flag Officer Biog Files. *Navy Directory*.
14. WPD to Asst COS AWPD, Plan O-1 Orange of CinC US Jt Astc Force—Expeditionary Forces required in 1st movement, 29 Jan 35, File 365, Box 70, AWPD Color Plans.
15. Memos among JB, JPC, COS, WPD, and AWPD, Jan to Apr 1935, Files 234 & 365, Box 70, AWPD Color Plans. See Chapter 17 for details.
16. Asst COS AWPD to COS, Revision of Jt A&N Basic WP—Orange, 8 Apr 35, File 365, Box 70, AWPD Color Plans.
17. JB to SecWar & SecNav, Revision of Jt A&N Basic WP—Orange, 8 May 35, #325, Ser 546, JB Records.
18. Morton, *Strategy and Command*, 37, indicates that MacArthur was interested in conforming the Orange Plan with revised army mobilization schedules and field organization and did not understand the change in the basic concept.

19. CNO to Distribution List for Navy Basic Plan—Orange, Change #4 to WPL-13, 1 Jul 35, w encl, roll 2, Scholarly Microfilms.
20. Lt Col J. P. Smith, GS to Maj Spalding, Capture of certain Orange possessions, n.d., early 1935; Embick to Dir WPD, Orange Plan, Army opns M+12 Group, 15 Jun 35, File 234, Box 70, AWPD Color Plans. Cpt D. E. Cummings to Maj Spalding, GS & Lt Col Cauldwell, USMC, Planning for attacks under O-1 Plan, 30 Jul 35, File BasFor & BasFor Projects, Box 39, Op Plan Files. Cdr P. L. Carroll to Dir WPD, Meeting of O-1 Group, 15 Jul 36, A16-3/FF, Box 91; CNO to CinCUS, 23 Sep 36, File Wotje, Attack of—Army Est, Box 77, WPD Files.

Chapter 17   Royal Road: The Ocean Campaign

1. JPC Est, Jan 1928, 24–27, 33–34, 56, 77.
2. WPD, Quick Movement, 1932.
3. Tentative Plan O-1, 26 Aug 33. CinCUS to CNO, Operating Plan O-1 Orange, 31 Mar 34, A16-3; CNO to CinCUS, 16 Mar 34, CinCUS Op Plans 1932–39.
4. WPD Memo, Some Plans & Studies Required . . . Plan O-1, Orange, 2 Dec 33, CinCUS Op Plans 1932–39.
5. WPD, Royal Road, Jul 1934, v, 4, 8–9, 12, 64, 69.
6. Ibid., v, 4, 51–52, 55–59.
7. JB to SecWar & SecNav, Revision of Jt A&N Basic WP—Orange, w encl, 8 May 35, #325, Ser 546, JB Records.
8. WPD, Royal Road, Jul 1934, 67, 70, 73–74. CNO to CinCUS, Operating Plan O-1—Orange, 10 Dec 34, Op-12-CTB A15(0), Box 147-D, WPD Files.
9. WPD, Royal Road, Jul 1934, v, 18–20, 67–74, 78–80, 84–89.
10. Change #2 to WPL-15, 3 Sep 36.
11. Change #4 to WPL-15, Apr 1938.
12. WPD, Royal Road, Jul 1934, 35. CNO to JB, 26 Nov 35; CinCUS to CNO, 20 Jun 35, A16/ND14, Box 229, SecNav & CNO Conf Corresp. JB, 15 Jul 36, #353, Box 16, JB Records.
13. CinCUS to CNO, Employment of Blue Submarines—Orange War, 20 Jan 36, A16-3, File Misc Studies, Box 73, WPD Files. Same title, Dec 1935, cited in Cdr Submarine Sqn 5 to CinCAF, Study of Initial Submarine Opns, 5 Jan 38, A16-3/(22) to A17-26, Box 245, SecNav & CNO Conf Corresp.
14. Change #4 to WPL-15, Apr 1938.
15. WPD, Royal Road, Jul 1934, 25A, 28, 43–44, 48, 58, 60, 75, 85.
16. Tentative Plan O-1, 26 Aug 33.
17. Cdg Gen FMF, Submission of "F-2 Study of Mandates," w attachment, 28 Mar 35, File Mandates—an F-2 Study of, Box 58, WPD Files. WPL-35, CNO, Jun 1939, vol. 1.
18. Asst COS G-2, Sitn Monograph Orange, 1 Jan 27, File 166, Box 63, AWPD Color Plans. WPD, Landing Opns, Oct 1927.
19. Chief BuDocks to CNO, Possibilities of developing facilities for . . . land-planes . . . in Marshall Is, 1 Aug 35, N1-9, SecNav & CNO Secret Corresp.
20. WPD, Marshall Is Plan, ca. 1927. JPC Est, Jan 1928, 77. Army Est, Aug 1927.
21. WPD, Royal Road, Jul 1934, 55, 77.

22. Dir WPD to Asst COS AWPD, Plan O-1 Orange of CinC US Jt Astc Force— Expeditionary forces required in 1st movement, 29 Jan 35, File 234, Box 70, AWPD Color Plans.
23. WPD, Study of Certain Pac Is, 6 Aug 27. WPD, Royal Road, Jul 1934, 78–79. CNO to BuDocks, Possibilities of developing facilities for . . . landplanes . . . in Marshall Is, 11 Feb 35; Chief BuDocks to CNO, same title, 1 Aug 35, File N1-9, SecNav & CNO Secret Corresp.
24. Ellis, Adv Base Opns, Jul 1921, 31. Col James H. Reeves, AC/S G-2, Sitn Monograph Orange, 1 Jan 27, File 166, Box 63, AWPD Color Plans. WPD, Study of Certain Pac Is, 6 Aug 27. WPD, Marshall Is Plan, ca. 1927. JPC Est, Jan 1928, 77.
25. AWPD, Wotje Attack, 31 Jul 36. Change #5 to WPL-16, 10 Jul 37, app 7, chap. 7.
26. BuDocks to CNO, 1 Aug 35. Bryan, comp., *Guide to Place Names.*
27. CNO to CinCUS, 10 Dec 34.
28. WPD, Some Plans & Studies Required . . . Plan O-1, 2 Dec 33. WPD, Royal Road, Jul 1934, v, 79, 82–83. JB, Revision of Jt A&N Basic WP—Orange, 8 May 35.
29. Ellis, Adv Base Opns, Jul 1921, 18, 29–32. WPD, Study of Certain Pac Is, 6 Aug 27. WPD, Landing Opns, Oct 1927.
30. BuDocks to CNO, 1 Aug 35. WPD, Royal Road, Jul 1934, 78, 81–83. WPD, Study of Certain Pac Is, 6 Aug 27. WPD, Landing Opns, Oct 1927.
31. WPD, Royal Road, Jul 1934, 19–20. WPD, Study of Certain Pac Is, 6 Aug 27.
32. AWPD Plan 1936, 8, 25–27.
33. WPD, Study of Certain Pac Is, 6 Aug 27.
34. WPD, Plan O-1 of CinC—Expeditionary forces 1st movement, 29 Jan 35.
35. WPD, Marshall Is Plan, ca. 1927. D. C. McDougal, Est of Sitn . . . for Seizing & Def of Eniwetock [sic], 26 Oct 27, File Orange Studies, Folder #2, Box 64, WPD Files. FMF, "F-2 Study of Mandates," 28 Mar 35.
36. FMF, Wotje Attack, 9 Aug 34. FMF, Maloelap Attack, 22 Oct 34.
37. USMC, Wotje Attack, 25 May 36.
38. JPC Est, Jan 1928, 77.
39. AWPD Plan 1936, 8–9, 22–26, 29.
40. AWPD, Wotje Attack, 31 Jul 36.
41. Col Sherman Miles AWPD to Dir WPD, Est of Sitn, Attack of Wotje, 27 Aug 36, File 2720-73, AWPD files. CNO to CinCUS, 23 Sep 36, File Wotje, Attack of—Army Est, Box 77, WPD Files.
42. FMF, "F-2 Study of Mandates," 28 Mar 35.
43. USMC, Truk Attack, 28 Apr 37. FMF, "F-2 Study of Mandates," 28 Mar 35. WPL-35, CNO, Jun 1939, vol. 1.
44. Change #2 to WPL-15, 3 Sep 36.
45. WPD, Plan O-1 of CinC—Expeditionary forces 1st movement, 29 Jan 35.
46. USMC, Wotje Attack, 25 May 36. Change #2 to WPL-15, 3 Sep 36. Change #4 to WPL-15, Apr 1938.
47. Asst COS AWPD to COS, Revision of Jt A&N Basic WP—Orange, 8 Apr 35, File 365, Box 70, AWPD Color Plans. USMC, Truk Attack, 28 Apr 37.
48. Operation Roadmaker, in CinCPac (by McMorris, COS), Granite, 13 Jan 44, Ser 0004, File Granite, Box 138, WPD Files, 17.

49. USMC, Truk Attack, 28 Apr 37.
50. RAdm Charles J. Moore, oral history, 897–902.
51. WPD, Landing Opns, Oct 1927. Col T. C. Holcomb USMC to Dir WPD, Denial of base to enemy in Marshall-Carolines, 31 Mar 33, WPD Files.
52. Cpt D. E. Cummings, Problems of Cdr Blue Astc Force, 6 Aug 35; Establishment of B-1, 30 Jul 35; Def of B-1 Area, gen requirements, 3 Aug 35, Base Force Plans, Jul–Oct 1935.
53. WPD, Plan O-1 of CinC—Expeditionary forces 1st movement, 29 Jan 35. WPL-13 revision Mar 1939, vol. 1.
54. Holcomb, Denial of base to enemy, 31 Mar 33. WPD, Royal Road, Jul 1934, 80.
55. WPD to Cdg Gen FMF, 20 Nov 33.
56. FMF, Rongelap Attack, 26 Jul 35. USMC, Wotje Attack, 25 May 36.
57. WPD, Plan O-1 of CinC—Expeditionary forces 1st movement, 29 Jan 35.
58. Cpt D. E. Cummings, Rapidity of Adv of Flt under O-1 Plan, Attack Force point of view, 30 Jul 1935, Base Force Plans, Jul–Oct 1935.
59. USMC, Truk Attack, 28 Apr 37.
60. Chart, Possible Opns, n.d., early 1935, File 234, Box 70, AWPD Color Plans.
61. FMF, Maloelap Attack, 22 Oct 34. Cdg Gen FMF to Dir WPD, Wotje Attack Plan, 7 Jan 35, File Wotje Attack Plan, Box 77, WPD Files.
62. Dir WPD To Cdg Gen FMF, Wotje Attack Plan, 12 Oct 34, File Wotje Attack Plan, Box 77, WPD Files, including citation of WPD (prob Meyers) to FMF, 20 Nov 33.
63. Cdg Gen FMF, Wotje Attack Plan, 7 Jan 35.
64. FMF, Wotje Attack, 9 Aug 34. FMF, Maloelap Attack, 22 Oct 34.
65. FMF, Wotje Def Plan, 27 Mar 34.
66. USMC, Wotje Attack, 25 May 36. USMC, Truk Attack, 28 Apr 37.
67. FMF, Majuro Attack, 18 Jan 35.
68. WPD, Some Plans and Studies Required, Plan O-1, 2 Dec 33. FMF, Rongelap Attack, 26 Jul 35.
69. Sherrod, *History of Marine Aviation,* 30.
70. GB, Small Patrol Plane Tenders, 6 Apr 36, GB Hearings, GB Records.
71. Maj I. Spalding GS to Col Smith AWPD, Avn in new Orange Plan, 2 Mar 35; Spalding to Col Krueger, Army avn cooperation w Navy in Orange Plan, 6 Mar 35, File 365, Box 70, AWPD Color Plans. FMF, Rongelap Attack, 26 Jul 35.
72. Cdg Gen FMF, Wotje Attack Plan, 7 Jan 35. USMC, Wotje Attack, 25 May 36. AWPD Plan 1936, 8, 26, 29.
73. Spalding, 2 & 6 Mar 35. Cdg Gen FMF to WPD, 7 Jan 35. Cpt D. E. Cummings, Plans for ejecting Orange from Marshalls & E Carolines, 3 Oct 35, Base Force Plans Jul–Oct 1935.
74. USMC, Wotje Attack, 25 May 36. FMF, Rongelap Attack, 26 Jul 35.
75. FMF, Wotje Attack, 12 Oct 34.
76. BuDocks to CNO, 1 Aug 35. Change #2 to WPL-15, 3 Sep 36. Change #6 to WPL-13, 26 Mar 37. Change #5 to WPL-16, 10 Jul 37. Change #6 to WPL-16, 23 Apr 38. WPL-13 Revision Mar 1939, vol. 1.
77. FMF, "F-2 Study of Mandates," 28 Mar 35. BuDocks to CNO, 1 Aug 35. USMC, Truk Attack, 28 Apr 37.
78. WPD to Cdg Gen FMF, 20 Nov 33.

79. WPD, Plan O-1 of CinC—Expeditionary forces 1st movement, 29 Jan 35. Chart, Possible Opns, early 1935. JB, Revision of Jt A&N Basic WP—Orange, 8 May 35.
80. BuDocks to CNO, 1 Aug 35.
81. Cummings, Plans for ejecting Orange, 3 Oct 35. AWPD Plan 1936, 8, 25–27.
82. FMF, Attack of Ponape, 5 Oct 35.
83. Ibid.
84. Cummings, Plans for ejecting Orange, 3 Oct 35.
85. Cpt D. E. Cummings, Problems of Cdr Blue Astc Force, 6 Aug 35; Establishment of B-1, 30 Jul 35; Def of B-1 Area, gen requirements, 3 Aug 35, Base Force Plans, Jul–Oct 1935. USMC, Truk Attack, 28 Apr 37.
86. USMC, Truk Attack, 28 Apr 37.
87. Ibid.

Chapter 18 Royal Road: The Path Divides

1. CNO to CinCUS, Operating Plan O-1—Orange, 10 Dec 34, Op-12-CTB A15(0), Box 147-D, WPD Files.
2. CNO to Basic War Plans Distribution List, War Plans, 29 Dec 23, w encl, Discussion of War Plans . . . & Cooperation & Coordination necessary, 198-1:2/1, roll 71, SecNav & CNO Secret & Conf Corresp.
3. WPL-13, Change #1, Jul 1932, pt. 3, chap. 2, p. 219. WPD, Quick Movement, 1932.
4. CNO, Operating Plan O-1 Orange, 10 Dec 34.
5. Plan O-3, ca. Jan 1925. Tentative Plan O-1, 26 Aug 33.
6. WPD, Royal Road, Jul 1934, v, 11, 71–73, 86–89.
7. WPD, Some Plans & Studies Required . . . Plan O-1, Orange, 2 Dec 33, CinCUS Op Plans 1932–39.
8. WPD, Royal Road, Jul 1934, 86–89.
9. WPD, Study of Certain Pac Is, 6 Aug 27.
10. Change #3 to WPL-13, 26 Feb 35, 56, 132, App 2.
11. Change #6 to WPL-13, 26 Mar 37. Richardson, *On the Treadmill,* 267.
12. Change #5 to WPL-13, 15 Sep 36.
13. Change #5 to WPL-16, 10 Jul 37.
14. Asst COS AWPD to COS, Revision of Jt A&N Basic WP—Orange, 8 Apr 35, File 365, Box 70, AWPD Color Plans.
15. JB to SecWar & SecNav, Revision of Jt A&N Basic WP—Orange, 8 May 35, #325, Ser 546, JB Records.
16. WPD, Quick Movement, 1932.
17. Change #1, WPL-13, Jul 1932, 3: app 2, and pt. 2, chap. 6, pp. 169–74. CNO to Distribution List for Navy Basic Plan—Orange, re ibid., 21 Jul 32, roll 2, Scholarly Microfilms.
18. USMC, Truk Attack, 28 Apr 37.
19. Asst COS AWPD to Dir WPD, 22 Apr 35, File 234, Box 70, AWPD Color Plans.
20. AWPD Plan 1936, 8–9, 22–26, 29.
21. Ibid., 8–9, 24–27.
22. JPC Est, Jan 1928, 81.

23. Corresp of 1928–32 among SecNav, CNO, CinCAF, Governor of Guam, Commandant of Guam, and USMC staff officers concerning defense of Guam, A16-3/FF3 to /VV, Box 58; EG 54, Boxes 178 & 255, SecNav Secret Files, RG 80, NA. The story of Samoa was similar. Despite musings of a southern convoy station, it had only "slight possibility" of wartime value. The puny defenses were removed in 1931. See CNO to SecNav, Naval Sta Samoa, policy, 9 Jun 31; CNO to Dir Naval Communications, Return of Basic War Plans by Gov of Samoa, 26 Jun 31, EG 53, Box 255, SecNav Secret Files.

24. Pomeroy, *Pacific Outpost,* 120.

25. WPD, Royal Road, Jul 1934, 20. Cpt D. E. Cummings, Rapidity of Adv of Flt under O-1 Plan, Attack Force point of view, 30 Jul 1935, Base Force Plans, Jul–Oct 1935.

26. Cpt D. E. Cummings to Maj Spalding and Lt Col Cauldwell, Planning for attacks under the O-1 Plan, 30 Jul 35, Base Force Plans, Jul–Oct 1935.

27. AWPD Plan 1936, 25–27.

28. USMC, Saipan and Uracas Attack, 1937.

29. Cdg Gen FMF, Submission of "F-2 Study of Mandates," w attachment, 28 Mar 35, File Mandates—an F-2 Study of, Box 58, WPD Records. WPL-35, CNO, Jun 1939, vol. 1. USMC, Saipan and Uracas Attack, 1937.

30. AWPD Plan 1936, 8–9, 24–27.

31. Cate and Craven, "Army Air Arm between Two World Wars," 65–66.

32. Carl Berger, *B-29: The Superfortress* (New York: Ballantine Books, 1970), chap. 2.

33. JB, Revision of Jt A&N Basic WP—Orange, 8 May 35.

34. FMF, "F-2 Study of Mandates," 28 Mar 35.

35. Dir Flt Maintenance Div to CNO, Class A and B Floating Dry Docks, Brief History of evolution & present status of ARD-3, 23 Sep 36; CNO, Floating Drydocks, File Drydocks, Floating, Box 42, WPD Files.

36. Change #5 to WPL-13, 15 Sep 36. Dir WPD to CNO, Naval Base Battalions, 12 Aug 36; CNO to Chief BuNav, same title, 29 Sep 36, A16/EN4, File Naval Base Battalion, Box 39, WPD Files.

37. Change #5 to WPL-16, 10 Jul 37.

38. Change #6 to WPL-16, 23 Apr 38.

39. WPL-13 Revision Mar 1939, vol. 1.

40. Ibid.

41. Cpt D. E. Cummings, Establishment of B-1, 30 Jul 35; Problems of Cdr Blue Astc Force, 6 Aug 35, Base Force Plans, Jul–Oct 1935. Change #5 to WPL-16, 10 Jul 37.

42. Change #6 to WPL-16, 23 Apr 38.

43. WPL-13 revision Mar 1939, vol. 1.

44. Flt Maintenance Div, Floating Dry Docks, 23 Sep 36.

45. WPL-13 revision Mar 1939, vol. 1. Change #5 to WPL-13, 15 Sep 36.

Chapter 19 The American Way of Planning: The Defensivists' Revolt

1. Haight, "FDR's 'Big Stick.' " Roskill, *Naval Policy between the Wars,* 2:367. Ingersoll, oral history, 68.

2. ACOS AWPD, Statement w App A, 2 Dec 35, JPC Dev File, #305, Ser 573, JB Records, in Schaffer, "Embick."
3. Pye to CNO, Phil Sitn, 22 Apr 36, EG 62, Box 255, SecNav & CNO Secret Corresp. CNO to Cpt Bastedo, 12 Jan 37, A16-3, Warfare Misc, Box 90, WPD Files.
4. Schaffer, "Embick."
5. ACOS AWPD, Statement, 2 Dec 35.
6. Asst SecWar to Pres, Jt A&N Basic WP—Orange, ca. late 1937. It is the only Orange Plan document in the president's files of the FDR Library at Hyde Park, N.Y., according to William R. Braisted, private communication to author, 16 Aug 1983.
7. Davis, *History of Joint Chiefs*, 30–31.
8. AWPD, Memo, Some Thoughts on Jt Basic WP Orange, 22 Nov 37, File 225, Box 68, AWPD Color Plans. COS to CNO, Two drafts of proposed Jt Basic WP—Orange submitted by JPC, 7 Dec 37, 2720-1045, AWPD Files.
9. Dir WPD to CNO, 11 Jul 39, Signed Ltrs, Box 78, WPD Files. Morton, *Strategy and Command*, 72n. Davis, *History of Joint Chiefs*, 40–41. Lowenthal, *Leadership and Indecision*, 1:159.
10. WPD, Diary of Activities, 2 Oct 39, File WPD Diary, WPD Files.
11. Major, "Leahy," 101–7, 111–14. Albion, *Makers of Naval Policy*, 171, 383–84. Moore, oral history, 772. Simpson, "Stark," 119–36. Ingersoll, oral history, 82. Patekewich, "Book of NWC Admirals."
12. Royal Eason Ingersoll, Flag Officer Biog Files. Ingersoll, oral history, 33, 48, 53, 59.
13. Robert Lee Ghormley, Flag Officer Biog Files. Moore, oral history, 1351. Major, "Leahy," 113–14. Buell, *Master of Sea Power*, 198.
14. WPL-13 revision, Mar 1939.
15. Russell Snydor Crenshaw, Flag Officer Biog Files. *Navy Directory*. Hill, oral history, 186. Moore, oral history, 590, 634. Dir WPD to CNO, "Are We Ready?" 7 Aug 39, File A16-3 Warfare Misc, Box 90, WPD Files. WPL-35, CNO, June 1939. CNO to Distribution list of WPL-38, 8 Oct 40, A16-3(17) to (22)EF13, Box 253, SecNav & CNO Secret Files. Cpt John L. McCrea, Testimony, PHH, *Hart Inquiry*, pt. 26, 291–94.
16. Arthur J. Hepburn, Flag Officer Biog Files. Waldo Drake, "Admiral Hepburn Takes Over Fleet," *United States Navy Magazine*, 20 Jun 36, and articles from *Washington Times-Herald*, 25 Feb 42, and *Washington Evening Star*, 25 Feb 42, in ibid. Walter, "Standley," 96–97.
17. Cpt C. M. Cooke, Jr., to Dir WPD, Atlantic War Plans, 7 Oct 38, File A16-3 Warfare Misc, Box 90, WPD Files. Cpt Harry W. Hill to Cooke, 4 Feb 39; Cooke to Hill, 22 Jun 39, Cooke Papers.
18. Hill, oral history, 170.
19. Cooke to Bloch, 11 Nov 37; Cooke to Hill, 2 May 38; Hill to Cooke, 14 Oct 38, Cooke Papers. CNO to CinCUS, CinC's Operating Plan O-1, Orange—WPUSF-44 & 45, 22 May 39, Signed Ltrs, Box 78, WPD Files.
20. Richardson, *On the Treadmill*, 109–10, 255, 272–76, 294, and passim. Hill, oral history, 5, 176, 183–85, 256, 461. Cdr Forrest P. Sherman to Dir WPD, CinCUS's Operating Plan O-1, 30 Apr 40, A16-3/FF, Box 91, WPD Files. CNO Conference, 1 May 40.

21. Richardson, *On the Treadmill,* 461, 279, chap. 14. CinCUS to CNO, War Plans—Status & readiness in view current international sitn, 22 Oct 40, File A16/FF1, Box 233, SecNav & CNO Secret Corresp. CinCUS to CNO, 26 Jan 40, PHH, *Hearings,* pt. 14, 924–35.
22. Cary Walthall Magruder, Flag Officer Biog Files.
23. Samuel Wood Bryant, Flag Officer Biog Files.
24. Richardson, *On the Treadmill,* 116–17, 132–33.
25. Major, "Leahy," 112. Cooke to Hepburn, 28 Jan 36; Hepburn to Cooke, 31 Jan 36, Cooke Papers. Commendation from Charles Maynard Cooke, Jr., Flag Officer Biog Files.
26. Reynolds, *Admirals,* 306–7. Hill, oral history, 164.
27. Vincent Raphael Murphy, Flag Officer Biog Files. Richardson, *On the Treadmill,* 174, 399. Cooke to Richardson, 13 Dec 39, Cooke Papers.
28. Cooke to Richardson, 10 Aug 37 & 15 May 38, Cooke Papers.
29. CNO to CinCUS, 31 Oct 39, A16/FF1, Box 224, SecNav & CNO Secret Corresp.
30. CNO, Change in Navy Membership JPC, 2 Aug 39; WPD to CNO, Opns Slate for 1940, 15 Aug 39, Signed Ltrs, Box 78, WPD Files.

Chapter 20   Defensivism versus Plan Orange

1. AWPD, Memo, Some Thoughts on Jt Basic WP Orange, 22 Nov 37, File 225, Box 68, AWPD Color Plans.
2. Office of COS to Asst SecWar, Mil Priority Policy to Guide Industrial Planning, 25 Oct 37; COS to CNO, Jt A&N Basic WP—Orange, 3 Nov 37, File 225, Box 68, AWPD Color Plans. Asst SecWar to Pres, Jt A&N Basic WP—Orange, n.d., prob. late 1937, PSF 105, Franklin D. Roosevelt Papers, FDR Library, Hyde Park, N.Y.
3. COS to CNO, Two drafts of proposed Jt Basic WP—Orange submitted by JPC, 7 Dec 37, 2720-1045, AWPD Files.
4. AWPD, Some Thoughts on Jt Basic WP Orange, 22 Nov 37.
5. Deputy COS to Asst COS AWPD, Draft of directive to Planning Comm re new Orange Plan, 5 Nov 37, File 225, Box 68, AWPD Color Plans.
6. Office of COS, Mil Priority, 25 Oct 37.
7. Brig Gen W. Krueger AWPD to COS, Jt A&N Basic WP—Orange, 29 Oct 37; AWPD to COS, Draft of Directive to JPC re New Jt A&N Basic WP—Orange, 9 Nov 37; JB to JPC, Jt A&N Basic WP—Orange, 10 Nov 37, Ser 617; JPC to JB, same title, 27 Dec 37, Ser 618, #325, File 365, Box 68, AWPD Color Plans. COS, Two drafts of proposed Jt Basic WP—Orange, 7 Dec 37.
8. Deputy COS, Draft of directive to Planning Comm, 5 Nov 37.
9. Author unknown, Memo for Gen Krueger, New Orange Plan, 24 Nov 37, File 225, Box 68, AWPD Color Plans. JPC, Jt A&N Basic WP—Orange, 27 Dec 37.
10. Memo for Krueger, New Orange Plan, 24 Nov 37. COS, Two drafts, 7 Dec 37. AWPD, Some Thoughts, 22 Nov 37. COS, Jt A&N Basic WP—Orange, 3 Nov 37.
11. JB Plan, 21 Feb 38.
12. JB to JPC, Study of Jt Action in Event of Violation of Monroe Doctrine by

Fascist Powers, 12 Nov 38, #325, Ser 634, JB Records. Morton, *Strategy and Command,* 68–69.

13. JPC, Exploratory Studies, 21 Apr 39, pt. 5, 1–7.
14. Dir WPD to CNO, Opns & forces . . . for campaign against Germany, Italy & Japan, acting in concert against U.S., 12 Jan 39; Cooke to Dir WPD, Study of Jt Action in event of violation of Monroe Doctrine & simultaneous attempt to adv Japanese influence in PIs, 13 Feb 39, A16-3, Signed Ltrs, Box 78, WPD Files.
15. Dir WPD to WP Officer of Staff of CinCUS, Studies prepared by Navy Members of JPC, 15 Feb 39, A16/EN, ibid.
16. Dir WPD to CNO, Division of available vessels, Atl-Pac, 12 Apr 39, ibid.
17. JPC, Exploratory Studies, 21 Apr 39, pt. 2, 2, pt. 4.
18. Ibid., pt. 2, 2–4, pt. 3, 1–5, 24, pt. 4, passim, pt. 5, 1–7.
19. Asst COS to COS, Subj JB 325 (634), 2 May 39, #4175, AWPD Records.
20. Ibid.
21. Cooke to Dir WPD, Atlantic War Plans, 7 Oct 38; Cooke to Dir WPD, 7 May 39, File A16-3 Warfare Misc, Box 90, WPD Files.
22. Cooke to Cpt Harry W. Hill, 22 Jun 39, Cooke Papers.
23. JPC to JB, draft directive, Jt A&N Basic WPs, Rainbow Nos. 1, 2, 3, and 4, 6 May 39; JB to JPC, same title, 12 May 39, #325, Ser 642, Box 1942, Plans & Opns Div, JB Records. Actg Secs War & Navy to Pres, 14 Aug 39, A16(A&N), File A16-3 Warfare Misc, Box 90, WPD Files. Rainbow 1, 9 Aug 39. Morton, *Strategy and Command,* 70–71.
24. Dir WPD to CNO, 11 Jul 39, Signed Ltrs, Box 78, WPD Files. Morton, *Strategy and Command,* 72n.
25. Rainbow 1, 9 Aug 39. Morton, *Strategy and Command,* 72.
26. CNO to Cdts Atlantic Nav Districts, Navy Basic WP—Rainbow 1, 16 Feb 40, A16(R-1), File A16-3 Warfare Misc, Box 90, WPD Files.
27. WPD, Diary of Activities, 2 Oct 39, File WPD Diary, WPD Files.
28. JB Plan, 21 Feb 38. WPD, Opns & forces . . . for campaign, 12 Jan 39. Cooke, Study of Jt Action, 13 Feb 39.
29. CNO Conference, 1 May 40. Moore, oral history, 632–35.
30. WPD, Opns & forces, 12 Jan 39. WPL-35, CNO, Jun 1939, vol. 1.
31. JB Plan, 21 Feb 38.
32. CNO to CinCUS, Army Forces for Employment w US Flt, 25 Jul 39; CinCUS to CNO, same title, 29 Aug 39, A16-3(9) to (9)/A6, Box 239, SecNav & CNO Secret Files. Capt J. B. Earle WPD to Col F. S. Clark AWPD, same title, 9 Sep 39, File A16-3/FF Warfare US Flt, Box 91, WPD Files.
33. Cooke to Dir WPD, 7 May 39.
34. JB, Jt A&N Basic WPs, Rainbows 1 to 4, 12 May 39.
35. JB Plan, 21 Feb 38. CNO, Army Forces, 25 Jul 39. CinCUS, Army Forces, 29 Aug 39. Earle to AWPD, 9 Sep 39. Maj Gen Cdt to CNO, Ability of Marine Corps to carry out its part of Navy Basic WPO, 30 Apr 40, A16/KK, Box 235, SecNav & CNO Secret Corresp.
36. Cpt Harry W. Hill to Dir WPD, 27 Apr 40, A16-3/FF, Warfare US Flt, Box 91, WPD Files. WPD, Plan O-1, 30 Apr 40.
37. WPD, Plan O-1, 30 Apr 40.
38. CNO Conference, 1 May 40. Hill, oral history, 190–92.

39. WPL-42, 12 Jul 40, 12, 14–19, 23–24, Apps 2, 7. Richardson, *On the Tread-mill,* 283–86.
40. Acting CNO to Cdts of NDs, Jt A&N WPs, 4 Nov 40, Signed Ltrs, Box 80, WPD Files.
41. Sr A&N Members JPC to COS & CNO, Views on questions propounded by pres on war sitn, 26 Jun 40; Cpt Jules James, Asst Dir ONI, Memo, World Sitn, 15 Jun 40, File A16-3 Warfare Misc, Box 90, WPD Files.
42. Dir WPD to CNO, Conference—Jun 17, 1940, Signed Ltrs, Box 79, WPD Files.
43. ComAirScoFor to CNO, Study of Patrol Plane Requirements to Patrol sea approaches of continental US & principal outlying possessions, 20 Jun 40, w endorsements, ComScoFor, A16-3, Entry 89, Box 78, CinCUS Conf Gen Corresp, RG 313, NA.
44. Naval History Div, Checklist of Plans. Navy Rainbow 4, ca. Aug 40. CNO to CinCUS, Jt A&N Basic WP—Rainbow 4, 11 Jun 40; CNO to Chief BuNav, Maj Gen Cdt USMC & Judge Atty Gen, same title, 9 Sep 40, File A16-3, Warfare Misc, Box 90; Dir WPD to Div Dirs, Navy Plan for Execution of Missions in Jt Task No. I of Jt . . . Rainbow 4, 6 Sep 40, A16(A&N), Signed Ltrs, WPD Files. Morton, *Strategy and Command,* 70–75. Richardson, *On the Treadmill,* 300.
45. Moore, oral history, 641–43. Dyer, *Amphibians,* 1:163. Acting CNO to Cdts all NDs, Jt A&N WPs, 4 Nov 40, 16(A&N), File A16-3 Warfare Misc, Box 90; Dir WPD to Dir Flt Maintenance Div, WPL Project under WPL-42, 21 Jan 41, Signed Ltrs, Box 80, WPD Files.

Chapter 21   Tilting the Offensive Northward

1. CinCPac Ser 00151 to CominCh, 30 Aug 43, cited in Lt Col Robert D. Heinl and Lt Col John A. Crown, Historical Branch G-3 Div HQ USMC, *The Marshalls: Accelerating the Tempo* (Washington: U.S. Government Printing Office, 1954), 7.
2. Ellis, Adv Base Opns, Jul 1921, 32.
3. CNO to CinCUS, Operating Plan O-1—Orange, 10 Dec 34, Op-12-CTB A15(0), Box 147-D; Cdg Gen FMF, Submission of "F-2 Study of Mandates," w attachment, 28 Mar 35, File Mandates—an F-2 Study of, Box 58, WPD files.
4. WPD to Asst COS AWPD, Plan O-1 Orange of CinC US Jt Astc Force—Expeditionary Forces required in 1st movement, 29 Jan 35, File 365, Box 70, AWPD Color Plans.
5. Cummings to Maj Spalding GS, & Lt Col Cauldwell USMC, Planning for attacks under O-1 Plan, 30 Jul 35; Cummings, Plans for ejecting Orange, 3 Oct 35, Base Force Plans, Jul–Oct 1935.
6. WPD, Plan O-1 of CinC, 29 Jan 35. Chart, Possible Opns, n.d., early 1935, File 234, Box 70, AWPD Color Plans.
7. ComMinBatFor to CinCUS, 22 Jul 39, Encl H, Base One, A16-1/EG12-1, Box 236, SecNav & CNO Secret Corresp.
8. Pence, lecture, 10 Jul 36.
9. For example, his influence on the VP striking force debates of the 1930s,

Chapter 15; and the WPD's endorsement of his proposal to enlarge the base at Midway: Dir WPD to CNO, Dredging Midway I, 3 Oct 39, N22, Signed Ltrs, Box 79, WPD Files.

10. RAdm Ernest J. King, Advanced Base West of Hawaii—Measures to Expedite Use, 21 Sep 39, File NB—Nav Bases, Box 96, WPD Files.

11. Lt D. E. Smith, WPD to Adm King, Rongelap, Bikini, and Eniwetok Atolls—Available information & studies, 12 Dec 39, File QG Pacific, Box 97, WPD Files.

12. WPD, Study of Certain Pac Is, 6 Aug 27. WPD, Plan O-1 of CinC, 29 Jan 35. FMF, Rongelap Attack, 26 Jul 35. Chief BuDocks to CNO, Possibilities of developing facilities for . . . landplanes . . . in Marshall Is, 1 Aug 35, File N1-9, SecNav & CNO Secret Corresp. Dir WPD to CNO, vol. 2, Landing Opns Blue Orange, 5 Oct 40, A16-3/FF, Signed Ltrs, Box 80, WPD Files. WPL-36, 8 Oct 40, 111–12.

13. Draft WPUSF-44, 24 Mar 41, passim.

14. WPPac-46, 25 Jul 41, 52f. Ellis, Adv Base Opns, July 1921. Future Plans Section, OpNav, Capture of Wake, Eniwetok, and Chichi Jima, Dec 1942, Box 153, WPD Files.

15. King, Adv Base West of Hawaii, 21 Sep 39.

16. Hubert Howe Bancroft, *The New Pacific* (New York: Bancroft Co., 1900), 709.

17. Dir WPD to CNO, Dev of Midway & Wake Is for naval use, 12 Dec 35, File NB/ND14, SecNav & CNO Secret Corresp.

18. Dingman, *Power in the Pacific,* 204–12. Buckley, *US and Conference,* 100.

19. CO Nav Air Sta Pearl Hbr to CNO, Rept of Results of Avn Reconn of Is to Westward including Midway, 12 Nov 20, Box 10, ONI, NHC, NWC.

20. Cdt Twelfth ND to CNO USS *Newport News,* Rept of Landing on Wake I, 6 Nov 20, w CO's Rept, 8 Oct 20, N-5-a 13732 ONI, CNO Records, RG 38, NA. Picking, "Wake Island," 2075–77.

21. District Intelligence Officer to Dir Nav Intelligence, Mil Aspects of Leeward Is of Hawaii, Johnston & Wake Is, 8 Oct 23, Box 10, ONI, NHC, NWC.

22. Holbrook, "U.S. Defense and Trans-Pacific Air Routes," 35.

23. WPD, Study of Certain Pac Is, 6 Aug 27. Dir WPD to Dir Nav Intelligence, Wake I—Information concerning, 2 Nov 33; CNO to CO USS *Nitro,* Wake I—Accurate Information of, 13 Nov 34; Lt jg Johnson, A/C BasFor to CNO, Wake I—Preliminary Information, 10 Jan 35, H1-3, SecNav & CNO Secret & Conf Corresp.

24. Holbrook, "U.S. Defense and Trans-Pacific Air Routes," 52–56, 60–62.

25. King and Whitehill, *Fleet Admiral King,* 239 and passim.

26. Chief BuAer to Asst SecNav, 6 May 35, A21-5, H1-3, SecNav & CNO Secret & Conf Corresp. CNO, Wake I, 30 Oct 34. Logbook, USS *Nitro,* 8 Mar 35, RG 80, NA. Holbrook, "U.S. Defense and Trans-Pacific Air Routes," 76–84, 95. SecNav to Chrmn, House Comm on Merchant Marine & Fisheries, 20 Apr 35; Dir Ship Movements Div to Dir Central Div, H.R. 6767—Comments on, 1 Apr 35, A18(350326), File QG Wake I, Box 3891, SecNav Gen Records.

27. Josephson, *Empire of the Air,* 111–12. Holbrook, "U.S. Defense and Trans-

Pacific Air Routes," 114. Dorothy Kaucher, *Wings over Wake* (San Francisco: Joseph Howell, 1947), 64, 102.
28. WPD, Dev of Midway & Wake, 12 Dec 35.
29. Ibid. Chief of Engineers to CNO, 17 Jul 36, File MI-18/EG(360109), Box 835, SecNav General Corresp. U.S. Congress, House, Doc. No. 84, Ltr from SecWar, Wake I, w Rept of Bd of Engineers for Rivers & Hbrs, 29 Jun 36, 75th Cong., 1st sess.
30. CNO to CinCUS, Design of Patrol Planes, n.d., prob Jan 1935; ComAirBasFor to CinCUS, Characteristics of VP Planes, 9 Jun 35, File VP, SecNav & CNO Secret & Conf Corresp.
31. WPD, Dev of Midway & Wake, 12 Dec 35.
32. Congress, Rept of Bd of Engineers, 29 Jun 36. Hepburn Rept. Chief BuAer to Chief BuDocks, Analysis of Hepburn Bd Rept Developments, 10 Jan 39, Hepburn Notebooks. CNO to CinCUS, Dev of Midway, Wake & Guam, 18 Mar 38, Box 21, Shore Sta Dev Bd. Dir Nav Districts Div to Dir WPD, same title, 14 Mar 38; Dir WPD to CNO, Supply of nav aviation gasoline to Wake, 18 Mar 39; Dir Ship Movements Div to CNO, same title, 1 Apr 39, File NB/ND14, Box 259, SecNav & CNO Secret Corresp.
33. Acting Chrmn GB to CNO, 11 Sep 39, File A16-1, Box 236, SecNav & CNO Secret Corresp.
34. Corresp among BuAer, CNO, and WPD re WPL-10, 18 May to 5 Jun 33, A16/EN11, SecNav & CNO Secret & Conf Corresp. ComScoFor annual rept, 1932. CinCUS to CNO, 27 Jul 35, File VP to VT, Box 264, SecNav & CNO Secret & Conf Corresp.
35. Corresp among CNO, CinCUS, ComSubFor, ComAirBasFor, BuConstruction, BuEngineering, Use of Submarines for Servicing Patrol Planes, Apr to Jul 1937, A16-3, Box 105, ComAirScoFor Records. Cdr R. P. Molten to Dir WPD, Patrol Planes, "assisted take-off," 4 Aug 38; Dir WPD to CNO, Catapult Barge, for "assisted take-off" for Patrol Planes, 5 Aug 38, S83-2, Signed Ltrs, Box 78, WPD Files. The Mandate idea appears in Cdr PatWing 2 to CinCUS, Tarawa, Gilbert Is—Suggestions, 27 Dec 40, File A8-2/EF13-50, Box 228, CNO Secret Corresp.
36. GB Hearings re Seaplane Tenders & Seaplane Carriers, 29 Dec 39 & 26 Jan 40, GB Records.
37. Dir WPD to Dir Nav Districts Div, Dev of . . . Midway—Opns of similar project at Wake, 20 Jan 39, A21-5/N22, Signed Ltrs, Box 78, WPD Files. Chief BuDocks to CNO, same title, 30 Jan 39; Chief BuDocks to Cdt 14th ND, Avn facilities for Wake I, 9 Feb 39; Actg SecNav to SecWar, 20 Feb 39; Chief BuDocks to CNO, Wake I—Dev of, 25 Aug 39, NA39/A1-1, BuDocks Conf Corresp.
38. CinCUS annual repts, 1938, 1939.
39. WPL-13 revision, Mar 1939. WPL-35, CNO, June 1939, vol. 1.
40. Actg Chrmn GB to SecNav, "Are We Ready?" 31 Aug 39; to CNO, 11 Sep 39, File A16-1, Box 236, SecNav & CNO Secret Corresp.
41. Hepburn Rept.
42. Congress, Rept of Bd of Engineers, 29 Jun 36.
43. Hepburn Rept.

44. Cdt 14th ND to CNO, Nav Reconn of Johnson [sic] I, 14 Sep 23, 196-3, SecNav & CNO Secret & Conf Corresp.
45. WPD, Dev of Midway & Wake, 12 Dec 35. CinCUS atoll Plan, 28 Feb 38.
46. WPL-13 revision Mar 1939, vol. 1. WPL-35, CNO, June 1939, vol. 1. USMC, Defs of Wake, 11 Aug 39.
47. WPL-35, CNO, June 1939, vol. 1.
48. ComAirScoFor to CinCUS, AA Def for Adv Bases for Patrol Plane Opns, 27 Jul 39, File A16-3, Box 57, SecNav & CNO Conf Corresp.
49. ComMinBatFor to CinCUS, 22 Jul 39, Encl G, Wake.
50. CNO to Chief BuOrd, Early Requirements of Ordnance Material for National Emergency, 23 Feb 38, A16(0)/EN, File A16-3 Warfare Misc, Box 90, WPD Files.
51. USMC, Defs of Wake, 11 Aug 39.
52. WPL-35, CNO, June 1939, vol. 1.
53. Holbrook, "U.S. Defense and Trans-Pacific Air Routes," 76–84, 95. CNO to CinCUS, Flt Problem XVI, 9 Oct 34, A16-3(5-XVI), Folder 1, SecNav & CNO Conf Corresp. Pomeroy, *Pacific Outpost*, 122–23.
54. Hepburn Hearings, House, early 1939, passim.
55. Actg SecNav to SecWar, 8 Feb 38; SecWar to SecNav, 17 Feb 38, File H1-18/EG60 (36109-1), Box 246, SecNav & CNO Conf Corresp. Cpt James S. Woods to Dir WPD, Our position in Pac, 1 Feb 38, File A16-3/EG54 Guam, Box 91, WPD Files. CNO, Statement to House Comm, prob Jan 1939, Hepburn Rept Notebooks. CNO, Dev of Midway, Wake & Guam, 18 Mar 38. Dir Nav Districts Div, same title, 14 Mar 38. CinCUS, Dev of Midway, Wake, & Guam, 28 Feb 38. CNO, Statement to House Comm, prob Jan 1939. Chief BuAer Statement (draft), n.d., prob Jan 1939, Hepburn Rept Notebooks.
56. Chief BuDocks to Shore Establishments Div, Air Base Dev at Wake I, 1 Aug 39, Box 21, Records of Base Maintenance Div, Shore Sta Dev Bd.
57. WPL-35, CNO, Jun 1939, vol. 1.
58. Chief BuDocks, Air Base Dev at Wake I, 1 Aug 39. Actg Chief BuAer to Chief BuDocks, same title, 7 Aug 39; Sr Mmbr Shore Sta Dev Bd to SecNav, Master Priority List, 1939—change in—Wake I dev, 10 Aug 39, File EN11/A1-1, BuDocks Conf Corresp. CinCUS to CNO, Wake I—Dev of, 16 Aug 39, File NA39/A1-1 Box 185, SecNav & CNO Conf Corresp. Master Priority List, 25 May 39, Hepburn Notebooks.
59. Chief BuDocks, Wake I—Dev of, 25 Aug 39. Dir WPD to Dir Nav Districts Div, Rivers & Harbors improvements—War Dept, 15 Sep 39, N22, Signed Ltrs, Box 79, WPD Files.
60. "Naval Administrative Histories of WWII," no. 58, BuAer, vol. 11.
61. Woodbury, *Builders for Battle*, 243–44.
62. ComMinBatFor to CinCUS w endorsements, Wake I Channel, 10 Oct 40, File H1-18/EG60/A1(400214), SecNav & CNO Secret & Conf Corresp. BuDocks, Charts of Wake I Seadrome & Submarine Base, Dec 1940, Envelopes 40 & 49, File EG 61, Entry 109, Box 4875, US Flt Records, 1940–41.
63. ComBatFor, Jt Carrier & Patrol Plane Opns, 11 Mar 39, A16-3, Box 89, CinCUS Conf Genl Corresp.
64. ComAirScoFor to Cdr Patwings, Effective Use of Patrol Planes, 5 Sep 39,

A16-3(3), Box 118; ComAirScoFor to Exercise Fleet Cdr, Minor Jt Army-Navy Exercise, 23 Jan 40, A16-3, Box 107, ComAirScoFor Records.

65. ComAirBatFor to CinCUS, Flt Organization—proposed change in composition of BatFor & ScoFor, 3 May 38, A3-1/00, File A16-3/A21 Warfare Air Services, Box 91, WPD Files.

66. GB, Proceedings, 19 Feb 40, GB Records.

67. Cdg Gen Hawn Dept to AG, Hemisphere Def, 5 Oct 39; AWPD to COS, 2 Jan 40, File Christmas & Midway Is, AG 580; Cdr 18th Wing to Cdg Gen Hawn Dept, 18 Sep 40 w 1st Endorsement, Cdg Gen Hawn Dept to AG, 19 Oct 40, AAC Bulk 381, Plans, Hawn Dept, cited in AAF Historical Office, "South Pacific Route," 7–12, 15–16.

68. Dir WPD to CNO, Opinion of War Plans concerning employment of modern Army . . . bombers, 21 Feb 41, Signed Ltrs, Box 81, WPD Files.

69. Cdg Gen Hawn Dept to AG, 10 May 41, 5th endorsement to Cdr Air Corps 12 Dec 40, AAC 600, Misc, East Indies, in AAF Historical Office, "South Pacific Route," 21–22.

70. Lt Cdr Robert W. Morse to Turner, Staging Landplane Bombers to Far East, 25 Aug 41, VB, Signed Ltrs, Box 82, WPD Files. Williams, "Deployment of the AAF," 178–79, 182. AAF Historical Office, "South Pacific Route," 26, 29, 32–33, 54.

71. Earhart's plane was lost without a trace on a round-the-world flight in July 1937 while en route from New Guinea to Hawaii via Howland Island. Public clamor led to dispatch of the *Lexington* to conduct a search. Persistent rumors have been stirred by a movie and several books that claim she was on a mission to scout the Mandate (or feign a disappearance or even crash purposely so that naval planes could reconnoiter) and that she may have been shot down, captured, and executed by the Japanese. See, for example, Foley, "Looking for Earhart." There is no evidence that the United States received any reconnaissance information from her. The *Lexington*'s log shows that no planes flew nearer than three hundred miles from a Marshall Island: Rept on Earhart Search, 1937, File UANOp, Box 15, RG 8, NHC, NWC.

72. Pac Flt, Intelligence Bulletin #45-41, 27 Nov 41, PHH, *Exhibits,* pt. 17, pp. 13–14.

73. Cdr PatWing 2 to CinCPac, Types of Combatant A/C for a Pac Campaign, 22 Oct 41, PW2/A16-3/0026, File A16, CinCPac WPs file late 1941.

74. Ibid. Author unknown, summarized comments on Bellinger paper; V. R. Murphy, handwritten note to McMorris, L. McCormick to McMorris, n.d., prob late Oct 1941; McMorris to Davis, n.d., prob Dec 1941, CinCPac WPs file late 1941.

75. JPC to JB, Proposed changes in Jt A&N Basic WP—Rainbow 5, 7 Nov 41; JB, Extract of Minutes of Meeting of 19 Nov 41, #325, Ser 642-5 (Revision), Box 1942, Plans & Opns Div, Numerical File, JB Records.

76. CinCPac to CNO, Defs, Outlying Bases, 2 Dec 41, Ser 0114W, EG61/(16), File A16, Box 4846, Entry 109, CinCUS Secret Corresp.

77. CinCPac message to CNO, 28 Nov 41, 280627, PHH, *Exhibits,* pt. 17, 2480.

78. Cdt 14th ND to Greenslade Bd, Annual Rept on Program for Wake I, 28 Nov 41, NNO 730051, Entry 275, Box 40, RG 38, NA.

79. CinCPac to CNO, 28 Nov 41.

80. CinCPac to CNO, Defs, Outlying Bases, 4 Dec 41, Ser 0113W, NB/ EG61(16), File A16, Box 4846, Entry 109, CinCUS Secret Corresp. Cdg Gen Hawn Dept to AG, 3 Dec 41, Radiogram no. 1018, in AAF Historical Office, "South Pacific Route," 58–59.

81. AWPD, Jt Basic WP Rainbow 2, Outline, Additional Est & Assumptions on which to base provisions of Jt . . . Rainbow 2, Sept 1939, Tab 2; WPD, Jt A&N Basic Plan—Rainbow 2, Navy Draft, 22 Sep 39, Tab 3; WPD, Supplement 1, same title, 22 Mar 40, Tab 8, JB Rainbow 2 Dev File.

82. AWPD, 1st Army draft, Annex "A" to Jt A&N Basic WP Rainbow 3, A Study of Sitn Presented by Directive of JB for Prepn of . . . Jt Rainbow 3, 29 Apr 40, #325, Ser 642, Box 1942, JB Rainbow 2 Dev File.

83. Moore, oral history, 639–40.

84. CNO to Pres, Memorandum, 11 Feb 41, PHH, *Exhibits,* pt. 16, 2149–51. CNO to CinCUS, Tarawa, Makin, Gilbert Is, 10 Mar 41, File QG Pacific, Box 97, WPD Files. Naval Aide to Pres, Memorandum for the Pres, 3 Mar 41, PHH, *Exhibits,* pt. 20, 4304.

85. Meeting 3, 3 Feb, Meeting 11, 26 Feb, US & Brit Navy Sections Meeting, 6 Mar 41, ABC-1 Conference, Jan–Mar 1941. WPL-46, 26 May 41, app 1.

86. CinCUS to CNO, Christmas & Makin Is—Preliminary Reconn of, 31 Oct 40; Dir WPD to Dir Ship Movements Div, 1st endorsement to CinCUS Ltr 31 Oct, 6 Nov 40, File H1-18/EF13-13, Box 255, CNO Secret Corresp.

87. Cdr PatWing 2 to CinCUS, Tarawa, Gilbert Is—Suggestions, 27 Dec 40, File A8-2/EF13-50, Box 228, CNO Secret Corresp. Moore to Dir WPD, Wake I—Policy . . . construction on & protection of, 24 May 41, File QG Pacific, Box 97, WPD Files. Moore, oral history, 647–48.

88. CinCPac to CNO, Proposed Visit of Task Group 19 to certain Brit Ports, 25 Jul 41, File A16/EF12-50/(16), Box 223, CNO Secret Corresp.

89. CNO to SecNav, Possible Methods of Repayment by Lend-Lease Debtors, 19 Aug 41, L11-7, Signed Ltrs, Box 82, WPD Files.

90. Moore, Wake I, 24 May 41. CNO to COS, 22 May 41, File A16-3(9) to A16-3(11)/ND5, Box 249, SecNav & CNO Secret & Conf Corresp.

91. AWPD, Jt Rainbow 2, Sep 1939. AWPD, 1st Army draft, Annex "A" to Jt A&N Basic WP Rainbow 3, A Study of Sitn Presented by Directive of JB for Prepn of . . . Jt Rainbow 3, 29 Apr 40, #325, Ser 642, JB Rainbow 2 Dev File 1939–40.

92. Jt Secys Brit Jt Staff Mission to US Secy for Collaboration, Rabaul . . . defs of, increase in, 12 Aug 41, A16-1/EF13, Sects Pac-Far East Jt Staff Corresp & Aid to China, Brit Jt Staff Mission 1941.

93. Dir WPD to Dir Nav Districts Div, Adv Bases, prob requirements of, 1 Jul 41, NB, Signed Ltrs, Box 82, WPD Files.

94. Moore, Wake I, 24 May 41. CNO to COS, 22 May 41.

95. CinCUS to CNO, Rabaul, 31 May 41, File A8-2/EF13-47, Box 228, CNO Secret Corresp.

96. CNO to Distribution List of WPL-46, Interpretation of Cooperation between US & Brit Commonwealth in Pac, 5 Sep 41, A-16(R-5), roll 5, Scholarly Microfilms.

97. Jt Secys Brit Jt Staff Mission to US Secy for Collaboration, Rabaul . . . def of, increase in, 25 Sep 41; US Secy for Collaboration to Brit Jt Staff Mission, same

title, 29 Aug 41, A16-1/EF13, Sects Pac-Far East Jt Staff Corresp & Aid to China; RAdm V. H. Danckwerts to Turner, 25 Sep 41, Brit Jt Staff Mission 1941. CNO to various bureaus, Rabaul . . . defs of—increase in, BaseF (Pac), 25 Oct 41, A16-1/EF13-47, Signed Ltrs, Box 82, WPD Files. Cdt 14th ND to CinCUS, Rabaul . . . Defs of, 27 Nov 41, A1-1/EF13-50, File A16, Box 4846, Entry 109, CinCUS Secret Corresp.

98. Morse, Staging Landplane Bombers to Far East, 25 Aug 41. Williams, "Deployment of the AAF," 178–79, 182. AAF Historical Office, "South Pacific Route," 26, 29, 32–33, 54.

99. CinCPac, Defs, Outlying Bases, 2 Dec 41.

100. Kimmel, testimony, PHH, *Roberts Commission,* pt. 22, 397–98, 453–55.

Chapter 22   The Great Western Arsenal, Dead at Last

1. Chief BuAer to SecNav, Best Location Air Bases Phil Is, Guam & Alaska, 24 Jan 35, GB Files.

2. GB to SecNav, Policy re naval bases in Pac, 22 Apr 35, #404, Ser 1683-1, GB Subj File.

3. Cdr C. M. Cooke to Adm C. C. Bloch, 11 Nov 1937, Cooke Papers. On Guam they noted a site that became Pacific Fleet Headquarters in 1945 (George E. Jones, "Brain Center of the Pacific War," *New York Times Magazine,* 8 Apr 45, 39).

4. Cpt James S. Woods to Dir WPD, Our position in Pac, 1 Feb 38, File A16-3/EG54 Guam, Box 91; Dir WPD to CNO, Detailed Statement for Nav Affairs Comm, 13 Jan 39, Signed Ltrs, Box 78, WPD Files.

5. CinCUS atoll Plan, 28 Feb 38.

6. CNO to CinCUS, Dev of Midway, Wake and Guam, 18 Mar 38, Box 21, Records of Base Maintenance Div, Shore Sta Dev Bd.

7. Adm A. J. Hepburn, Testimony, Hepburn Hearings, House.

8. Dir WPD to Dir Centr Div, Naval Air Bases, 31 May 38, Box 50, WPD Files. Hepburn Rept, 27–28 and passim. Woods, Our position in Pac, 1 Feb 38.

9. Cooke, Statement to House Comm, n.d. prob Feb 1939; author unknown (prob WPD), n.d., ca. Mar 1939, Base at Guam, handwritten end note, Hepburn Rept Notebooks. Hepburn Rept, 26–28.

10. Dir WPD, Detailed Statement for Nav Affairs Comm, 13 Jan 39. Hepburn Rept, 26–28.

11. Dir WPD to Chief BuDocks, Hepburn Bd Rept, 30 Dec 38, Signed Ltrs, Box 78, WPD Files. Dir WPD, Detailed Statement for Nav Affairs Comm, 13 Jan 39.

12. Major, "Leahy," 111–12. Source unknown (prob BuAer), Recapitulation [of Costs], 17 Jan 39, Hepburn Rept Notebooks.

13. CinCUS atoll Plan, 28 Feb 38.

14. Memos all titled Apra Hbr, Guam, Improvements: Chief BuAer to CNO, 15 Mar 37; Chief BuDocks to CNO, 12 Jan 38, File NB to NB/NC, Box 185; Cdt Nav Sta Guam to Chief BuDocks, 19 Oct 37 and to Chief BuAer, 11 Feb 38, File EG 54 to 56, Box 179, SecNav & CNO Conf Corresp. Woods, Our position in Pac, 1 Feb 38.

15. Dir WPD to Dir Nav Districts Div, Apra Hbr . . . Temporary flt avn facilities, 24 Feb 38, File EG 54 to 56, Box 179, SecNav & CNO Conf Corresp. Chief

BuAer to Chief BuDocks, Proposed Expansion Nav Aeronautical Shore Facilities, 23 Jan 39; (prob) BuAer, Recapitulation, 17 Jan 39, Hepburn Rept Notebooks.

16. Hepburn Hearings, House, passim.
17. Pomeroy, *Pacific Outpost*, 128.
18. Major, "Leahy," 112.
19. Hepburn Hearings, House.
20. Rep. Carl Vinson, Nav Avn Facilities, 21 Feb 39, Hepburn Rept Notebooks.
21. CNO, Statement to House Comm, n.d. prob Jan 1939, Hepburn Rept Notebooks.
22. RAdm A. B. Cook, Testimony, Hepburn Hearings, House.
23. CNO, Statement to Senate Comm, n.d. prob Mar 1939, Hepburn Rept Notebooks.
24. Pomeroy, *Pacific Outpost*, 132.
25. Hearings on S 830, Comm on Nav Affairs, U.S. Congress, Senate, 76th Cong., 1st sess. Major, "Leahy," 112. Pomeroy, *Pacific Outpost*, 133.
26. GB to SecNav, "Are We Ready?" 31 Aug 39, roll 5, Scholarly Microfilms.
27. Chief BuDocks to CNO, 28 Oct 40, File A16-3/FF, Warfare US Flt, Box 91, WPD Files. CNO to Greenslade Bd, Suggestions [re] . . . Policy & Strategic Factors of . . . Location & Dev of Naval Bases, 29 Nov 40, Greenslade Board files, RG 45, NA.
28. Chief BuDocks to CNO, 28 Oct 40, File A16-3/FF, Warfare US Flt, Box 91, WPD Files. CNO to RAdm John W. Greenslade, Sr Mmbr Bd to Survey & Rept on Adequacy & Future Dev of Nav Shore Establishment, Suggestions as to Certain Policy & Strategic Factors of Problem of Location & Dev of Nav Bases, 29 Nov 40, Greenslade Bd files, RG 45, NA. CNO to Cdt Nav Sta Guam, Def of Guam, 3 Feb 41, A16-1/EG54; Dir WPD to Dir Centr Div, Questions . . . from Senator Walsh to Sec Knox, 25 Feb 41, A18; Dir WPD to CNO, Comment on Greenslade Bd Rept, 25 Mar 41, Signed Ltrs, Box 81, WPD Files. BuDocks, *Building Navy's Bases in WWII*, 1:34, 2:344.
29. Dir WPD to CNO, Landplane Runway—Guam, 2 Aug 41, EG54; Dir WPD to Dir Nav Districts Div, Guam—present status, 15 Oct 41, A16-1/EG54; CNO to Cdt Nav Sta Guam, same title, 4 Nov 41, A16-1/EG54; CNO to Dir Nav Districts Div, Air field dev for landplanes, 14 Nov 41, N1-9/NS8, Signed Ltrs, Box 82, WPD files. CNO to CinCPac, 14 Nov 41, PHH, *Exhibits*, pt. 16, 2221.
30. ACOS AWPD, Statement w App A, 2 Dec 35; Roosevelt to SecNav, 9 Dec 35; Navy Members JPC, Memo, 14 Jan 36, same to JB, 6 Feb 36, JPC Dev File, #305, Ser 573, JB Records, all cited in Schaffer, "Embick," 89–95. Pye to CNO, Phil Sitn, 22 Apr 36, File EG 62, Box 255, SecNav & CNO Secret Corresp.
31. CNO to Cdt 16th ND, Manila Bay Area Nav Base, 4 May 38, NB/ND16, Signed Ltrs, Box 78, WPD Files.
32. Op-12A to Cpt C. M. Cooke, 25 Sep 40, EA-EZ Conf; CNO to CinCAF, Nav Base in PIs, 2 Oct 40, NB; Dir WPD to CNO, 3 Dec 40, A16-3/ND16, Signed Ltrs, Box 80, WPD Files.
33. BuDocks to CNO, 28 Oct 40. CNO to Greenslade Bd, Suggestions . . . Nav Bases, 29 Nov 40. WPD, Comment on Greenslade Bd Rept, 25 Mar 41.

BuDocks, *Building Navy's Bases in WWII*, 2:392. Woodbury, *Builders for Battle*, 327.

34. George Julian Meyers, Flag Officer Biog Files. *Navy Directory.* Cdt 16th ND to High Commissioner to Phils, 3 Oct 38, A16-3/ND16, Signed Ltrs, Box 78, WPD Files.
35. Cdt 14th ND to Dir WPD, 7 Aug 35, w unsigned attachment Memo on Pac Campaign, n.d., File A16-3/A6-8 to /FF3-5, Box 237, SecNav & CNO Secret Corresp.
36. Cpt R. S. Crenshaw to ComBasFor, 22 Sep 39, ND16, Signed Ltrs, Box 79, WPD Files.
37. JPC to JB, draft directive, Jt A&N Basic WPs, Rainbow Nos. 1, 2, 3, and 4, 6 May 39, #325, Ser 642, Box 1942, Plans & Opns Div, JB Records.
38. WPD, Est to Provide for Special Sitn Set Up in . . . Rainbow 2, 5 Aug 39, Tab 1; AWPD, Jt Basic WP Rainbow 2, Outline, Additional Est & Assumptions on which to base provisions of Jt . . . Rainbow 2, Sep 1939, Tab 2; WPD, Supplement 1, same title, 22 Mar 40, Tab 8, JB Rainbow 2 Dev File 1939–40.
39. AWPD, Jt Rainbow 2, Sep 1939; WPD Est . . . Special Sitn, 5 Aug 39.
40. AWPD, Jt Rainbow 2, Sep 1939. WPD Est . . . Special Sitn, 5 Aug 39. (Prob) WPD, basic rte for movement of Flt to NEI, Jul 1940, File Netherland East Indies, Box 63, WPD Files.
41. AWPD, Jt Basic WP Rainbow 2, Outline, Additional Est & Assumptions on which to base provisions of Jt A&N Basic Plan—Rainbow 2, 1st draft, Aug 1939, Tab 3, Rainbow 2, Sep 1939. (Prob) AWPD, Est of Land Force Requirements in S China Sea Area, n.d., prob late 1939, File S China Sea Area Bases, pt. 1, Box 71, WPD Files.
42. AWPD, Rainbow 2 Outline, 1st draft, Aug 1939. AWPD, Est of Land Force Requirements, late 1939.
43. WPD Est . . . Special Sitn, 5 Aug 39.
44. AWPD, Jt Rainbow 2, Sep 1939.
45. Cdr Vincent R. Murphy to Cooke, 29 Mar 40, Cooke Papers.
46. Richardson, *On the Treadmill*, 286–88.
47. WPD, Supplement 1, Jt Rainbow 2, 22 Mar 40.
48. JPC to JB, Jt A&N Basic WPs—Rainbow, 9 Apr 40, Tab 9; JB to JPC, 15 Apr 40, Rainbow 2, 1939–40.
49. WPD, Supplement 1, Jt Rainbow 2, 22 Mar 40. WPD, drafts of Jt A&N Basic WP—Rainbow 2, 11, 18 & 25 Apr, 1 May 40, Tab 10; AWPD, 5th Army drafts of Jt A&N Basic WP—Rainbow 2, 11 May 40, Tab 11; AWPD, 6th draft, same title, 20 May 40, Tab 12, Rainbow 2, 1939–40. CNO to CinCUS, Jt A&N Basic WP—Rainbow 2, 24 May 40, A16(A&N), Signed Ltrs, Box 79, WPD Files. Richardson, *On the Treadmill*, 286–88.
50. Moore, oral history, 615–26, 632.
51. Richardson, *On the Treadmill*, 286–88.
52. Morton, *Strategy and Command*, 71. JPC to JB, Jt A&N Basic WPs—Rainbow, 9 Apr 40.
53. AWPD, 1st Army draft, Annex "A" to Jt A&N Basic WP Rainbow 3, A Study of Sitn Presented by Directive of JB for Prepn of . . . Jt Rainbow 3, 15 Apr 40 w updates through late May, Tab 13, Rainbow 3, early 1940.

54. JPC, Problem of Production of Munitions [re] Ability of US to Cope with Def Problems, 27 Sept 40, File A16-1 (Aug–Dec 1940), Box 241, CNO Secret Corresp.
55. Richardson, testimony, PHH, *Hearings*, pt. 1, 319. CinCUS to CinCAF, International Sitn—Reenforcement of Astc Flt, 16 Oct 40, PHH, *Exhibits*, pt. 14, 1007–11.
56. CNO, Memo for Marshall, Jt Basic WPs, Rainbow 3 & 5, 29 Nov 40; Actg COS to COS, same title, 2 Dec 40, Rainbow 3.
57. Dyer, *Amphibians*, 1:163–65.
58. Turner, testimony, PHH, *Hearings*, pt. 26, 268.
59. CNO, Plan Dog, 12 Nov 40.
60. CNO to CinCAF, 12 Nov 40, PHH, *Exhibits*, pt. 16, 2449.
61. Ibid. WPL-44, Dec 1940. CNO to CinCAF, Instructions Concerning Prepn of Astc Flt for War under WP Rainbow 3, 12 Dec 40, File A16(R-3)(1940), Box 241, CNO Secret Corresp. CNO-CinCUS-CinCAF WPL-44 Corresp, Jan–Feb 1941.
62. CNO to CinCAF, 12 Nov 40. WPL-44, Dec 1940. CNO to CinCAF, Instructions. . . Rainbow 3, 12 Dec 40. CinCUS to CinCAF, 26 Dec 40, File WPL-46, Box 147J, WPD Files. CinCAF to CNO & CinCUS, 18 Jan 41, CNO-CinCUS-CinCAF WPL-44 corresp, Jan–Feb 1941. CinCUS to Cdrs Subsidiary Flt Commands, Opns Plans O-1, Rainbow 3, 24 Mar 41, Annex C; CinCPac to CNO, WPL 44—Passage of Astc Flt Reenforcement—Reconn of Ellice & Santa Cruz Is, 2 May 41; CinCUS to CNO, WPL 44—Passage of Astc Flt Reenforcement, prepn for, 7 Mar 41, File A16(R-3)(1941); CNO to CinCPac, same title, 17 Mar 41, File A16-1, Box 241, SecNav & CNO Secret Corresp.
63. CinCPac to ComBasFor, Prepn for Detachment for Distant Service, 28 Feb 41, A16/0335, File A16; CinCPac to CNO, Logistic requirements, US Astc Flt, Rainbow 3 War, 7 Mar 41, A16-3/(S-16), CinCUS Secret Corresp.
64. CinCUS to CinCAF, 26 Dec 40. CinCUS to CNO, WPL-44, 28 Jan 41, CNO-CinCUS-CinCAF WPL-44 corresp, Jan–Feb 1941. CinCUS, WPL-44—Passage, 7 Mar 41. CinCUS, Plans O-1, 24 Mar 41, Annex C.
65. WPL-44, Dec 1940. CNO to CinCUS, 10 Feb 41, CNO-CinCUS-CinCAF WPL-44 corresp, Jan–Feb 1941.
66. CNO to SecNav, Far Eastern Sitn, 21 Jan 41, A16-3/EF37, Signed Ltrs, Box 80, WPD Files. Morgan, "Planning the Defeat of Japan," 51.
67. CNO to CinCPac, WPL-44, Passage of Astc Flt Reenforcement—prepn for, 10 Apr 41, File A16(R-3)(1941), Box 241, CNO Secret Corresp.
68. CNO, Far Eastern Sitn, 21 Jan 41.
69. CNO to CinCUS, 10 Feb 41. CNO to Pres, Memorandum, 11 Feb 41; CNO to CinCPac, 25 Feb 41, PHH, *Exhibits*, pt. 16, 2149–51.
70. Kimmel, testimony, PHH, *Roberts Commission*, pt. 23, 944.
71. To First Sea Lord, Rept of Comm on Nav Cooperation w USN in event USA entering the war, 11 Sep 40, Corrigendum 20 Sep 40, Section Adm Bailey's Comm, roll 5, Scholarly Microfilms. In June 1939 the British ambassador had met with Leahy and Ghormley to explore sending the U.S. fleet to Singapore; they refused to discuss it in detail. Lowenthal, *Leadership and Indecision*, 1:132.
72. Puleston, *Armed Forces of the Pacific*, 124–26.

73. Simpson, "Admiral Stark," 142, 152.
74. CNO, Memo for Marshall, Jt Basic WPs, Rainbow 3 & 5, 29 Nov 40; Actg COS to COS, same title, 2 Dec 40, JB Rainbow 3 Dev File 1940.
75. Note by UK Delegation, 31 Jan; Plenary Meeting, 31 Jan; Meeting 3, 3 Feb; UK Delegation, Results of Brit Staff Conversations w the Dutch, 4 Feb; Meeting 6, 10 Feb; UK Delegation, The Far East, Appreciation, 11 Feb; Meeting 7, 14 Feb; Meeting 11, 26 Feb; UK Delegation, Reply to Note by Navy Section of US Staff Comm, 15 Mar, all in ABC-1 Conference, Jan–Mar 1941.
76. UK Far East Appreciation, 11 Feb; US Navy & Army Sections . . . , Jt Meeting, Minutes, 13 Feb, ABC-1 Conference, Jan–Mar 1941.
77. Meetings 3, 6, 11, of 3, 10, 26 Feb; UK Reply to Navy Section, 15 Mar, ABC-1 Conference, Jan–Mar 1941.
78. UK Far East Appreciation, 11 Feb, US Navy & Army Sections Meeting, 13 Feb; Meeting 6, 10 Feb; Meeting 11, 26 Feb, ABC-1 Conference, Jan–Mar 1941. CNO to CinC's Pac, Atl & Astc Flts, Observations on present international sitn, 3 Apr 41, Ser 038612, File Planning, Misc, Box 67, WPD Files.
79. Plenary Meeting, 31 Jan; Meetings 3, 4, 11, of 3, 5, 26 Feb; UK Reply to Navy Section, 15 Mar 41, ABC-1 Conference, Jan–Mar 1941.
80. Meeting 11, 26 Feb 41, ABC-1 Conference, Jan–Mar 1941.
81. ABC-1, Rept, 27 Mar 41, 3–4, Annex III, 7–9.
82. Lowenthal, *Leadership and Indecision*, 1:465.

Chapter 23   The American Way of Planning: The Planners at War

1. Davis, *History of Joint Chiefs*, 43, 46–49, 55, 58–59. Lowenthal, *Leadership and Indecision*, 1:512–14. *Navy Directory.*
2. Richmond Kelly Turner, Flag Officer Biog Files. Reynolds, *Admirals*, 362–63. Hill, oral history, 177.
3. Dyer, *Amphibians*, 1:154.
4. Ibid., 150–51, 188, and passim. Layton with Pineau and Costello, *"And I Was There,"* 21, 96, 99–100. Prange with Goldstein and Dillon, *Pearl Harbor: The Verdict*, 331–32. Moore, oral history, 644, 655–56. Hoyt, *How They Won*, 137.
5. Dyer, *Amphibians*, 1:159–60. Reynolds, *Admirals*, 362–63.
6. Hill, oral history, 185–86. Moore, oral history, 641–44. Dyer, *Amphibians*, 1:163.
7. Layton with Pineau and Costello, *"And I Was There,"* passim.
8. Turner, Memo for WPD, 29 Oct 40, Signed Ltrs, Box 80, WPD Files.
9. L. P. McDowell, Memo for WPD, 30 Oct 40, Signed Ltrs, Box 80, WPD Files. Simpson, "Admiral Stark," 142.
10. CNO, Plan Dog, 12 Nov 40.
11. AWPD Tentative Draft COS to Stark, Navy Basic WP—Rainbow 3, 29 Nov 40, JB Rainbow 3 Dev File 1940.
12. Simpson, "Admiral Stark," 142, 152.
13. WPD to Dir, Nav Communications Div, WPL-44, 9 Jan 41, A-16(R-3), Signed Ltrs, Box 80, WPD Files.
14. AWPD, COS to Stark Tentative Draft, Navy Basic WP—Rainbow 3, n.d., late Nov 1940; WPD, same title, 27 Nov 40, File 3, JB Rainbow 3 Dev File 1940.

Asst COS to COS, same title, 29 Nov 40, File 4175-15, AWPD Files. Dyer, *Amphibians*, 1:164.

15. Turner & Col Joseph T. McNarney, Study of Immediate Problems concerning involvement in War, 21 Dec 40, JB 325, Ser 670, in Dyer, *Amphibians*, 1:157–60.
16. CNO to CinCUS, War Plans—Status & Readiness in view current International Sitn, 17 Dec 40, File A16-3/FF Warfare US Flt, Box 91, WPD Files. Chrmn GB to SecNav, "Are We Ready III," 14 Jun 41, GB #325, Ser 144, roll 5, Scholarly Microfilms.
17. CNO to RAdm R. L. Ghormley, Appointment of Nav Comm to Conduct Staff Conversations w British, 24 Jan 41, A16-1/EF13, Ser 09212; US Navy & Army Sections of US-British Conference, Jt Meeting, Minutes, 31 Jan 41, Section US UK Staff Conversation Minutes (all Ser BUS(J)41 + 2 digits), ABC-1 Conference, Jan–Mar 1941.
18. Cooke to Cpt V. R. Murphy, 12 Feb 42, Cooke Papers.
19. CNO to WPD & Distribution, Prepn of Nav Establishment for war under Navy Basic WP Rainbow 5, 1 Apr 41, File A16(R-5) (Jan–Jul 1941), Box 241, CNO Secret Corresp. WPL-46, 26 May 41, including App I. SecWar & SecNav to the Pres, 2 Jun 41, JB Rainbow 5 File 1941.
20. Secy of JB to COS, Jt A&N Basic WP—Rainbow 5 & Rept of US-Brit Staff Conversations ABC-1, 9 Jun 41, JB Rainbow 5 File 1941.
21. CNO, Priority in Prepn of Plans, 11 Jun 41, Scholarly Microfilms. Chrmn GB to SecNav, "Are We Ready III," 14 Jun 41.
22. CNO to CinCUS, War Plans—Status & Readiness, 17 Dec 40. CNO to Distribution, Order of priority in prepn of wps, 18 Jan 41, A16/EN, Signed Ltrs, Box 80, WPD Files. CinCPac to Subordinate Commands, CinC's Operating Plan O-1, Orange—Quarterly Repts assignment of forces, 7 Feb 41, File A16/EN28 to /FF12, Box 233, CNO Secret Corresp.
23. CNO to CinC's Pac, Atl & Astc Flts, Observations on present international sitn, 3 Apr 41, Ser 038612, File Planning, Misc, Box 67, WPD Files. WPL-46, 26 May 41, including App I.
24. Dyer, *Amphibians*, 1:chap. 5.
25. Richardson, *On the Treadmill*, 424, 435.
26. Prange, *At Dawn We Slept*, 44, 49–52. Prange with Goldstein and Dillon, *Pearl Harbor: the Verdict*, 103–4. Reynolds, *Admirals*, 175–76. Richardson, *On the Treadmill*, 8–9.
27. RAdm Robert E. Milling, USN (Ret.), ltr to Simpson, 5 Sep 1978, in Simpson, "Admiral Stark," 134. Kimmel also was awarded the title of CinCUS. He would have outranked King if the fleets had been reunited in one ocean.
28. Prange, *At Dawn We Slept*, 49–52, 139. Prange with Goldstein and Dillon, *Pearl Harbor: The Verdict*, 466–71, 477. Kimmel, *Story*, 59–62. Reynolds, *Admirals*, 175–76.
29. Charles Horatio McMorris, Flag Officer Biog Files. Prange, *At Dawn We Slept*, 68–69, 703. Hoyt, *How They Won*, 322–23, 55. Reynolds, *Admirals*, 213–14. Ltr, Kimmel to Nimitz, 8 May 41, cited in Hoyt, *How They Won*, 55.
30. Prange, *At Dawn We Slept*, 68–69, 401.
31. Layton with Pineau and Costello, *"And I Was There,"* 330–34, 345–46. Dyer, *Amphibians*, 2:742. Hoyt, *How They Won*, 233, 237.

32. Lynde D. McCormick, Flag Officer Biog Files. McCormick, testimony, PHH, *Hart Inquiry*, pt. 26, 74–75.
33. Francis R. Duborg, Flag Officer Biog Files. CinCUS, US Flt Memo 4USM-41, 25 Jun 41, File A2-11/FF1(1) 1941, RG 313, NA (Suitland, Md.).
34. Prange, *At Dawn We Slept*, 135.
35. Charles Maynard Cooke, Jr., Flag Officer Biog Files.
36. Prange, *At Dawn We Slept*, 703.
37. Draft WPUSF-44, 24 Mar 41.
38. WPPac-46, 25 Jul 41, 5–7, 13.
39. CNO to CinCPac, US Pac Flt Operating Plan, Rainbow 5 (Navy Plan O-1, Rainbow 5), WPPac46, review & acceptance of, 9 Sep 41, File QG Pac, Box 97, WPD Files.
40. CinCPac (per McMorris) to Cdrs of TFs, Flt Chart Maneuver #1-41, moves of 26 Aug, 27 Sep, 21 & 29 Oct, 26 Nov 41, A16-3/(16), CinCPac WPs file late 1941. Archival records indicate that TF 7, the submarine force, submitted a plan which is missing from the file.

Chapter 24 Instant Fury Delayed

1. WPL-44, Dec 1940, CinCUS to CNO, WPL-44, 28 Jan 41, CNO-CinCUS-CinCAF WPL-44 corresp, Jan–Feb 1941.
2. AWPD Tentative Draft COS to Stark, Navy Basic WP—Rainbow 3, 29 Nov 40, JB Rainbow 3 Dev File 1940.
3. WPL-44, Dec 1940, App II.
4. Dir WPD to CNO, Transfer of certain units of Pac Flt to Atl Flt—recommendation for, 2 Apr 41, Signed Ltrs, Box 81, WPD Files.
5. WPL-44, Dec 1940. CinCUS to CNO, WPL-44, 28 Jan 41.
6. Prange, *At Dawn We Slept*, 133.
7. CinCPac to CNO, 15 Nov 41; CNO to CinCPac, 25 Nov 41, PHH, *Hearings*, pt. 5, 2103–5.
8. AWPD Tentative Draft COS to Stark—Rainbow 3, 29 Nov 40. WPPac-46, 25 Jul 41, 5–7, 13.
9. CNO, Plan Dog, 12 Nov 40.
10. Ibid.
11. CinCUS to CNO, War Plans—Status & readiness in view current international sitn, 22 Oct 40, File A16/FF1, Box 233, SecNav & CNO Secret Corresp.
12. Moore, oral history, 632–35.
13. Maj Gen Cdt to CNO, Ability of Marine Corps to carry out its part of Navy Basic WPO, 30 Apr 40, A16/KK, Box 235, SecNav & CNO Secret Corresp.
14. CNO, Plan Dog, 12 Nov 40.
15. WPD, Plan O-1, 30 Apr 40.
16. CinCUS to CNO, 26 Jan 40, PHH, *Hearings*, pt. 14, 924–35. CNO, Plan Dog, 12 Nov 40. CNO to CinCPac, Adv Flt Base in Caroline Is, 9 Apr 41, A16(R-3)(1941), Box 241, CNO Secret Corresp.
17. CNO to Cpt Crenshaw, 2 May 40, A16-3/FF, Warfare US Flt, Box 91, WPD Files.
18. CinCUS, WPs—Status & readiness, 22 Oct 40.
19. CNO, Plan Dog, 12 Nov 40. CNO, Adv Flt Base in Carolines, 9 Apr 41.

20. WPD, Plan O-1, 30 Apr 40.
21. Ibid.
22. CNO, Adv Flt Base in Carolines, 9 Apr 41.
23. CNO, Plan Dog, 12 Nov 40.
24. CNO, Adv Flt Base in Carolines, 9 Apr 41.
25. WPL-44, Dec 1940. CinCUS to CNO, WPL-44, 28 Jan 41. CNO to CinCUS, 10 Feb 41, CNO-CinCUS-CinCAF WPL-44 corresp, Jan–Feb 1941.
26. Draft WPUSF-44, 24 Mar 41.
27. Actg CNO to Chief BuOrd, Mobilization Requirements 15M Concentration, 22 Jun 40, A16(0)/EN, Signed Ltrs, Box 79, WPD Files. CNO to 5 Bureaus, Assembly of Equipment for Adv Bases, 15 Aug 40, A16/JH; CNO to Bureaus & Districts, same title, 12 Oct 40, File A16/JN, Box 118, ComAirSco-For Records.
28. WPL-36, 8 Oct 40, 110–12, 125, 170–75. Wilds, "How Japan Fortified Mandated Islands." CNO to ComBatFor, Publication re "Physical Characteristics of Mandate Is," 4 Apr 40, A7-3(1); Dir WPD to Dir Nav Intelligence Div, Studies in connection w Landing Opns in Blue-Orange War, 30 Aug 40, A16-3/FF; CNO to Distribution List of WPL-36, Basic Studies for Landing Opns in Blue-Orange War, 8 Oct 40, A16-3/FF, Signed Ltrs, Boxes 79–80, WPD Files.
29. CinCUS, WPs—Status & readiness, 22 Oct 40.
30. WPD, Plan O-1, 30 Apr 40.
31. CNO, Plan Dog, 12 Nov 40.
32. CinCUS, WPs—Status & readiness, 22 Oct 40.
33. Meeting 11, 26 Feb, US Navy & Army Sections, Jt Meeting Minutes, 19 Feb, Section United States–Brit Staff Conference, ABC-1 Conference, Jan–Mar 41. Actg COS to COS, Jt Basic WPs, Rainbow 3 & 5, 2 Dec 40, JB Rainbow 3 Dev File 1940. ABC-1, Rept, 27 Mar 41, Annex III, p. 5.
34. WPL-46, 26 May 41.
35. Dir WPD to Dir Naval Districts Div, Adv Bases, prob requirements of, 1 Jul 41, NB, Signed Ltrs, Box 82, WPD Files.
36. McMorris, testimony, PHH, *Hart Inquiry*, pt. 26, 245–48. WPPac-46, 25 Jul 41, 26–27.
37. CNO to CinCPac, Opn Plans O-1, Rainbow 3, 13 May 41, A16-3/FF Warfare US Flt, Box 91, WPD Files.
38. WPL-46, 26 May 41.
39. CinCUS to CNO, WPL-44, 28 Jan 41. CNO to CinCUS, 10 Feb 41.
40. CinCPac to CNO, Survey of Conditions in Pac Flt, 26 May 41, A16/FF12, Box 233, CNO Secret Corresp. ComScoFor to CNO, Urgent & Immediate Requirements in Pac to Provide Nucleus for a Landing Force, 17 Jun 41, A16-3/(0046); CinCPac to CNO, same title, 1st endorsement, 27 Jun 41, A16/; CinCPac to CNO, Balanced Marine Landing Force Unit, 11 Jul 41, A16/KA(16), File A16, CinCUS Secret Corresp.
41. CNO to CinCPac, Transfer of a Reinforced Regiment of Marines to Hawaii, 25 Jul 41, A16-1/KK, Signed Ltrs, Box 82, WPD Files.
42. Cdr TF 3 to CinCPac, US Open Landing Lighter, Self-Propelled—Immediate Construction of at Pearl Hbr, 25 Sep 41, File A16; Cdr TF 3 to Cdt 14th ND,

Assistance of Personnel of 14th ND in Preparing for Landing Opns in Pac Area, 11 Dec 41, A16-3/A16-3/(00), File A16, CinCUS Secret Corresp.

43. CNO, Adv Flt Base in Carolines, 9 Apr 41.
44. CNO to CinCPac, 26 Nov 41, 270038, PHH, *Exhibits,* pt. 17, 2479. CinCPac to CNO, Defs, Outlying Bases, 2 Dec 41, Ser 0114W, EG61/(16), File A16, CinCUS Secret Corresp.
45. CinCPac to CNO, 6 Nov & 2 Dec 41, Ser #8, PHH, *Exhibits,* pt. 16, 2251–53.
46. Adm W. W. Smith, testimony, PHH, *Hart Inquiry,* pt. 26, 66–68.
47. WPL-44, Dec 1940. CinCUS to CNO, WPL-44, 28 Jan 41.
48. AWPD, COS to Stark Tentative Draft, Navy Basic WP—Rainbow 3, n.d., late Nov 1940; Memo for Marshall, Jt Basic WPs, Rainbow 3 & 5, 29 Nov 40; Actg COS to COS, same title, 2 Dec 40, File 3, JB Dev File Rainbow 3.
49. WPL-44, Dec 1940. CinCUS, WPL-44, 28 Jan 41. Draft WPUSF-44, 24 Mar 41.
50. Roskill, *Naval Policy between the Wars,* 2:437, 476. Some British estimates ran as high as 180 days; see Christopher Thorne, *The Limits of Foreign Policy* (New York: G. P. Putnam's Sons, 1973), 71.
51. Secy Brit Mil Mission, Possible Re-Distribution of US Nav Forces, 8 May 41, Section Pacific–Far East Jt Staff Corresp.
52. Brit Mil Mission in Washington, Note by Jt Secys, Movements of Units of US Pac Flt, 11 Jun 41; Brit Jt Staff Mission to Secy for Collaboration, US-Brit Commonwealth Co-operation in Far East Area, 26 Nov 41, Section Pac-Far East Jt Staff Corresp. Spenavo to CNO, 26 Oct 41; Admiralty to B.A.D. for CNO, n.d., early Nov 1941; CNO to Spenavo, 6 Nov 41; US Secy for Collaboration to Jt Secys Brit Jt Staff Mission, US-Brit Commonwealth Cooperation in Far East Area, 11 Nov 41, Section Aid to China.

Chapter 25   Fleet Battle in the Central Pacific, 1941

1. ABC-1, Rept, 27 Mar 41.
2. WPL-44, Dec 1940. CNO to CinCUS, 10 Feb 41, CNO-CinCUS-CinCAF WPL-44 corresp, Jan–Feb 1941.
3. WPPac-46, 25 Jul 41, 23–24.
4. Plan Dog, 12 Nov 40. WPL-44, Dec 1940.
5. Draft WPUSF-44, 24 Mar 41, 7, Opns Plan O-1, 4, Annex F.
6. CinCAF to CinCUS, 18 Jan 41; CinCUS to CNO, WPL-44, 28 Jan 41, CNO-CinCUS-CinCAF WPL-44 corresp, Jan–Feb 1941. CNO to CinCUS, 10 Feb 41. Cooke, Memo for CinC, 7 Apr 41, Cooke Papers. CinCUS to CNO, CNO's Plan Dog, 25 Jan 41, PHH, *Roberts Commission,* pt. 22, 329–31.
7. CinCUS to CNO, WPL-44, 28 Jan 41.
8. CNO to CinCUS, 10 Feb 41.
9. CNO to CinCPac, Opn Plans O-1, Rainbow 3, 13 May 41, A16-3/FF Warfare US Flt, Box 91, WPD Files.
10. Plenary Meeting, 31 Jan, Meeting 3, 3 Feb; Meeting 4, 5 Feb; Meeting 11, 26 Feb 41, ABC-1 Conf Jan–Mar 41.
11. Draft WPUSF-44, 24 Mar 41, passim.

12. CinCPac to CNO, Survey of Conditions in Pac Flt, 26 May 41, A16/FF12, Box 233, CNO Secret Corresp.
13. CinCPac to CNO, Initial Deployment Pac Flt under Plan Dog, 14 May 41, File CinCPAC Plan Dog Comments; Moore to Dir WPD, CinCPAC Plan Dog Comments, 3 Jun 41, File A16-3/FF Warfare US Flt, Box 91, WPD Files.
14. CinCAF to CNO, 18 Jan 41.
15. Draft WPUSF-44, 24 Mar 41, 7, Opns Plan O-1, 4, Annex F. CNO to CinCAF, 7 Feb 41, CNO-CinCUS-CinCAF WPL-44 corresp, Jan–Feb 1941.
16. CNO to CinCUS, 10 Feb 41.
17. Draft WPUSF-44, 24 Mar 41, 7, Opns Plan O-1, 4, Annex F.
18. WPL-44, Dec 1940. CNO to CinCUS, 10 Feb 41.
19. CNO to CinCPac, Opn Plans O-1, Rainbow 3, 13 May 41.
20. Pac Flt Chart Maneuver, Autumn 41.
21. CinCUS, WPL-44, 28 Jan 41.
22. CinCPac to CNO, Wake I—Policy . . . construction on & protection of, 18 Apr 41, File CinCPAC Plan Dog Comments, Box 91, WPD Files.
23. Kimmel, testimony, PHH, *Roberts Commission*, pt. 22, 397–98, 453–55, and *Hearings*, pt. 6, 2572.
24. Pac Flt Chart Maneuver, Autumn 1941, move of 26 Aug 41.
25. McMorris, testimony, PHH, *Navy Court of Inquiry*, 567–72.
26. WPL-44, Dec 1940, App 2. Draft WPUSF-44, 24 Mar 41, Annexes E, F. CNO to CinCAF, Instructions Concerning Prepn of Astc Flt for War under WP Rainbow 3, 12 Dec 40, File A16(R-3)(1940), Box 241, CNO Secret Corresp.
27. Draft WPUSF-44, 24 Mar 41, Opns Plan O-1, 4-7, Annexes E, F.
28. Dierdorff, "Pioneer Party," 503. ComMinBatFor to CinCUS w endorsements, Wake I Channel, 10 Oct 40, File H1-18/EG60/A1(400214), SecNav & CNO Secret & Conf Corresp. Cdt 14th ND to CNO, Policies . . . Midway & Wake Is, 2 Apr 41, EG61/ND14, File EG61, Box 4849, Entry 109, RG 313, NA (Suitland, Md.). Woodbury, *Builders for Battle*, 257–64.
29. Dir WPD to Dir Ship Movements Div, Gasoline storage—Guam, Midway, Wake—Pan Am Airways proposal, 12 Jan 40; Dir WPD to Dir Central Div, same title, 13 Mar 40, JJ7-6, Signed Ltrs, Box 79, WPD Files.
30. Marine Detachment Wake to Cdr 14th ND, 25 Nov 41, Ser 11-766, PHH, *Hewitt Inquiry*, pt. 37, 793.
31. Cdr Patrol Sqn 25 to Cdr Patwing 2, Rept on Adv Base exercises May 19–28, 1941, n.d.; C.O. USS *Thornton* to Cdr Patwing 2, Hbr Facilities at Outlying Bases, 3 Sep 41, File A16-3(3) Adv Bases, Box 118, ComAirScoFor Records. Patwing 2 Opn Orders #S1-41 26 Aug, #21-41 10 Oct 41, FAW2 Op Plans 1941. CinCPac to ComAirBatFor & Cdr Patwing 2, Nav Air Sta Wake & . . . Midway—Basing of A/C at, 10 Nov 41, Ser 01825, Box CinCPac Jul–Dec 1941, CNO Plans Files. CinCPac to CNO, Defs, Outlying Bases, 4 Dec 41, Ser 0113W, NB/EG61(16), File A16, Box 4846, Entry 109, CinCUS Secret Corresp.
32. Bellinger, testimony, PHH, *Hearings*, pt. 8, 3459.
33. Cdt 14ND to Chief BuNav, Nav Air Sta, Wake I . . . personnel, 22 Aug 41, File EG12-1/ND14/(0823), Box 4849, Entry 109, RG 313, NA (Suitland, Md.). Cdr TF 9 to TF 9, Tentative Organization & Standard Plans, 15 Nov 41, File FAW2 Op Plans. CinCPac, NAS Wake & Midway, 10 Nov 41.

34. Woodbury, *Builders for Battle*, 257–64.
35. ComBasFor, Movement Order 3-41, 23 Jul 41, Ser 0789, CNO Plans Files. CinCPac to CNO, Defs, Outlying Bases, 2 Dec 41, Ser 0114W, EG61/(16), File A16, Box 4846, Entry 109, CinCUS Secret Corresp.
36. Bellinger, testimony, PHH, *Hearings*, pt. 8, 3459.
37. Draft WPUSF-44, 24 Mar 41, Opns Plan O-1, 7-8, Annexes E, F.
38. CNO to Cdt 14th ND, Policies . . . Midway & Wake Is, 2 May 41, EG60, File EG, Box 4849, Entry 109, RG 313, NA (Suitland, Md.). CinCPac, Wake I—Policy, 18 Apr 41.
39. WPPac-46, 25 Jul 41, 10, 32.
40. Cdt 14th ND, Policies . . . Midway & Wake Is, 2 Apr 41. Cdt 14th ND to CNO, Local Def Measures of Urgency, 7 May 41, A16-1(WP)(4)/ND14; Cdt 14th ND to CinCPac, Study of Defs & Installations of Outlying Pac Bases, 17 Oct 41, S-A16-1/A1-1/EG/ND14, File A16, Box 4846, Entry 109, CinCUS Secret Corresp.
41. Moore, oral history, 23.
42. Moore to Dir WPD, Wake I—Policy . . . construction on & protection of, 24 May 41, File QG Pac, Box 97, WPD Files. Moore, oral history, 647–48.
43. V. R. Murphy to McMorris, Questions & Answers on Wake, 19 Apr 41, File EG61, Box 4849, Entry 109, RG 313, NA (Suitland, Md.). Hill to Dir WPD, Wake I, 28 May 41, File QG Pac, Box 97, WPD Files.
44. Moore, Wake I, 24 May 41.
45. CinCPac to CNO, 12 Sep 41, PHH, *Exhibits*, pt. 16, 2248. CinCPac to CNO, 15 Nov 41, PHH, *Hearings*, pt. 5, 2103–4.
46. Kimmel, testimony, PHH, *Roberts Commission*, pt. 22, 397–98, 453–55.
47. Stark, testimony, PHH, *Hearings*, pt. 5, 2156.
48. Turner, testimony, ibid., pt. 26, 270, 278. Moore, oral history, 646–48.
49. CNO to Cdt 14th ND, Policies . . . Midway & Wake Is, 2 May 41.
50. Dir WPD to CNO, Organization of Additional Marine Def Battalions, 2 Dec 40; CNO to Maj Gen Cdt, same title, 10 Jan 41, KE/A16-1, Signed Ltrs, Box 80, WPD Files.
51. CinCPac, Wake I—Policy, 18 Apr 41. Hill, Wake I, 28 May 41. Heinl, *Defense of Wake*, 4, 8. CinCPac to CNO, Defs at Wake, 26 Aug 41, A16/EG60/(86), File A16, Box 4499, Entry 106, RG 313, NA (Suitland, Md.). CNO to CinPac et al., Employment of Marine Def Battalions in Pac Area, 12 Aug 41, KE/A16-1, Signed Ltrs, Box 82, WPD Files.
52. Dir WPD to Dir Nav Districts Div, Wake I Channel & Turning Basin, 6 Sep 41, Signed Ltrs, Box 82, WPD Files. Cdt 14th ND to Greenslade Bd, Annual Rept on Program for Wake I, 28 Nov 41; Wake I Base Blueprint, 27 Nov 41, NNO 730051, Entry 275, Box 40, RG 38, NA. CinCPac to ComSubScoFor, 17 Oct 41, 170354, PHH, *Exhibits*, pt. 17, 2478. CinCPac Opn Order #36-41, 17 Oct 41, Ser 01681, Box CinCPac Jul–Dec 1941; Submarines, ScoFor, Opn Order 28-41, 17 Nov 41; various Opns Orders Jul–Dec 1941, Box Scouting Force, Sqn 40T, CNO Plans Files.
53. Cdr Forrest Sherman to Pres NWC, Def of outlying air bases, 13 Jul 40, A16-3/KK; CNO to All Bureaus & Offices, Avn Shore Facilities to support 10,000 plane program, 22 Jul 40, A21-1; CNO to All Bureaus & Offices, Avn

shore facilities to support 15,000 plane program, 18 Mar 41, A21-1, Signed Ltrs, Boxes 79–81, WPD Files.

54. WPD, Wake I Channel, 6 Sep 41. CinCPac, Defs, Outlying Bases, 4 Dec 41.
55. Cdg Gen Hawn Dept to AG, 3 Dec 41, Radiogram 1018, in AAF Historical Office, "South Pacific Route," 58–59. CinCPac to CNO, Defs, Outlying Bases, 2 Dec 41. CNO to CinCPac, 26 Nov 41, 270038; CinCPac to CNO, 28 Nov 41, 280627, PHH, *Exhibits,* pt. 17, 2479–80.
56. PHH, *Hewitt Report,* summary, pt. 16, 2287.
57. CinCPac to CNO, 12 Sep & 15 Nov 41.
58. CNO, Plan Dog, 12 Nov 40.
59. CNO to CinCUS, 10 Feb 41.
60. Meeting 11, 26 Feb 41, ABC-1 Conference, Jan–Mar 1941.
61. WPPac-46, 25 Jul 41, Annex II, 3, 9.
62. Draft WPUSF-44, 24 Mar 41. I discovered this document in an apparently untouched box of records in the National Archives annex in Suitland, Maryland. In several respects it is more detailed than the subsequent WPPac-46 of July 1941.
63. In 1989 there were 163 book entries under Pearl Harbor in the Library of Congress catalog, including some duplicate and foreign entries.
64. Draft WPUSF-44, 24 Mar 41, Annex D.
65. WPPac-46, 25 Jul 41, 12–13, 27, 45–47, Annex I, 7–9, Annex II, 8.
66. Morison, *History of U.S. Naval Operations in WWII,* vol. 4, *Coral Sea, Midway and Submarine Actions, May 1942–August 1942,* 190–91. Blair, *Silent Victory,* 1:84–90, 97.
67. WPPac-46, 25 Jul 41, 45.
68. Kimmel, testimony, PHH, *Hearings,* pt. 6, 2530.
69. WPPac-46, 25 Jul 41, 45–48.
70. Moore, CinCPac Plan Dog Comments, 3 Jun 41.
71. ComSubScoFor to CinCPac, Submarines Available for War Service, 22 Oct 41, FF12-10/A16; Subordinate Supporting Plan to O-1, 12 Nov 41, File A16, Box 4846, Entry 109, CinCUS Secret Corresp, file index only.
72. WPPac-46, 25 Jul 41, 44, Annex II, 7. Draft WPUSF-44, 24 Mar 41, Opns Plan O-1, 7.
73. WPPac-46, 25 Jul 41, Annex II, 8.
74. Cooke, Memo for CinC, 7 Apr 41.
75. Draft WPUSF-44, 24 Mar 41, Annex E, 5. Kimmel, testimony, PHH, *Hearings,* pt. 6, 2530.
76. Cdr TF 9, Tentative Organization & Plans, 15 Nov 41. Patwing Two Opn Order, 10 Oct 41.
77. Draft WPUSF-44, 24 Mar 41, Opns Plan O-1, Annex E, 5–6.
78. Pac Flt Chart Maneuver, Autumn 41.
79. WPPac-46, 25 Jul 41, Annex II, 3–5, 7–8.
80. WPPac-46, 25 Jul 41, Annex I, 4, 6. Pac Flt Chart Maneuver, Autumn 41. On 6 December McMorris suspended the patrol temporarily because the cruiser force was scattered about on exercises that day (CinCPac, Steps to be taken in case of American-Japanese war within next 24 hrs, 6 Dec 41; Kimmel, testimony, PHH, *Hearings,* pt. 6, 2529–37).
81. Draft WPUSF-44, 24 Mar 41, Annex F.

82. Cooke, Memo for CinC, 7 Apr 41.
83. WPPac-46, 25 Jul 41, 12, Annex II, passim.
84. Draft WPUSF-44, 24 Mar 41, Annex F. WPPac-46, 25 Jul 41, Annex II, 1–5.
85. CinCPac, Steps to be taken, 6 Dec 41. Kimmel, testimony, PHH, *Hearings*, pt. 6, 2529–32. Murphy, testimony, PHH, *Hart Inquiry*, pt. 26, 204–5.
86. Draft WPUSF-44, 24 Mar 41, 7–8, Annex G, 2–4. WPPac-46, 25 Jul 41, Annex II, 1–9.
87. Pac Flt Chart Maneuver, Autumn 41.
88. CNO to CinCPac, Opn Plans O-1, Rainbow 3, 13 May 41.
89. CinCPac to CNO, WPL 44, 28 Mar 41, Serial 019W, File CinCPac Tentative Opns in Case of War, Box 91, WPD Files.
90. WPPac-46, 25 Jul 41, Annex II, 4.
91. Summary of testimony, PHH, *Hearings*, pt. 36, 420.
92. Cpt Edwin T. Layton, testimony, PHH, *Hewitt Inquiry*, pt. 36, 158–60. Summary of Hewitt Inquiry, PHH, *Exhibits*, pt. 16, 2339–40.
93. Layton to CinCPac, Projected Reconn Flight over Mandates Is, 28 Nov 41, PHH, Exhibit 28, *Hewitt Inquiry*, pt. 37, 801–2. Maj Gen E. S. Adams to Cdg Gen, 26 Nov 41, PHH, *Hearings*, pt. 14, 1328. JB, Minutes of Meeting, 26 Nov 41, PHH, *Exhibits*, pt. 18, 1642.
94. Summary of Hewitt Inquiry, PHH, *Exhibits*, pt. 16, 2339–40.
95. WPPac-46, 25 Jul 41, 23.
96. Husband E. Kimmel, Flag Officer Biog Files. Reynolds, *Admirals*, 175–76. Prange, *At Dawn We Slept*, 49–52.
97. Kimmel, testimony, PHH, *Hearings*, pt. 6, 2566.
98. CinCPac to CNO, 12 Sep 41. Prange, *At Dawn We Slept*, 139–40, 292, 337.
99. Kimmel, Interview with the Pres, 9 Jun 41 (Op-12-D-2), in Prange, *At Dawn We Slept*, 139–40.
100. Draft WPUSF-44, 24 Mar 41, Annex F. WPPac-46, 25 Jul 41, 11, Annex II, 3–9. Pac Flt Chart Maneuver, Autumn 41.
101. McMorris, testimony, PHH, *Hart Inquiry*, pt. 26, 250.
102. WPPac-46, 25 Jul 41, 59.
103. Draft WPUSF-44, 24 Mar 41, Annexes F, G. WPPac-46, 25 Jul 41, 11, Annex II, 3–9.
104. CinCPac, Steps to be taken, 6 Dec 41.
105. The stated location of Point Tare at 16° N, 177° E made no sense. It lay beyond air range of Midway and Johnston. Though barely within Wake's search arc, the fleet would have gotten little protection from that island's battered squadrons until replacements were sent. (Prewar plans assumed that the Catalinas had an 800-mile radius, although after 7 December 600 to 700 miles proved more realistic. See Bellinger, testimony, PHH, *Navy Court of Inquiry*, pt. 34, 505–6.) The designated Point Tare lay only 585 miles from the presumed hornet's nest at Wotje. Since McMorris expected three or four long-range Japanese squadrons in the Mandate and bombing runs against Wake from bases 530 miles away, he would have anticipated surveillance over that short distance and probably attack. It is conceivable that he wished the fleet to be seen at the rendezvous to entice Yamamoto forward, a reckless idea because Orange submarines would have converged after a sighting. The most likely explanation is a typographical error. A correction to longitude 177°

west would have put the rendezvous a comfortable 450 miles west of Johnston (instead of 360 miles beyond that island's air reach) and within cover of Midway as well. McMorris specifically limited flights of Johnston's two VProns to 178° west, sixty miles beyond the "corrected" Point Tare, presumably to circle the fleet for hours and avoid chance encounters with Orange air patrols farther west. The corrected point, 950 miles from hostile bases, would have been thought in 1941 to lie beyond reach of all but four-engined landplanes, of which Japan had none. Finally, the oilers, even with a head start, could not have reached the uncorrected site in time for Halsey's first refueling. See Draft WPUSF-44, 24 Mar 41, Plan O-1, 6; WPPac-46, 25 Jul 41, 45, Annex II, 7–8. The corrected location is used in the narrative and maps.

106. WPPac-46, 25 Jul 41, Annex I, 2–3.
107. Kimmel, testimony, PHH, *Hearings,* pt. 6, 2529. McCormick, testimony, PHH, *Hart Inquiry,* pt. 26, 74–75.
108. WPPac-46, 25 Jul 41, Annex II, 3.
109. Prange, *At Dawn We Slept,* 401. Kimmel, *Story,* 72–73.
110. WPUSF-44, 24 Mar 41, Plan O-1, 10. WPPac-46, 25 Jul 41, 8.
111. Pye, testimony, PHH, *Hearings,* pt. 26, 157.
112. Halsey, testimony, PHH, *Hart Inquiry,* pt. 26, 323.
113. Draft WPUSF-44, 24 Mar 41, Annex G, 4.
114. WPPac-46, 25 Jul 41, Annex II, 6.
115. Ibid., Annex I, 2–3.
116. Moore, CinCPac Plan Dog Comments, 3 Jun 41.
117. WPPac-46, 25 Jul 41, Annex II, 2.
118. Bellinger, testimony, PHH, *Navy Court of Inquiry,* pt. 34, 498.
119. WPPac-46, 25 Jul 41, Annex II, 7.
120. Morison, *History of U.S. Naval Operations in WWII,* 4:92–93.
121. Lt Gen Walter C. Short, testimony, PHH, *Roberts Commission,* pt. 23, 988.
122. Bellinger, testimony, *Hart Inquiry,* pt. 26, 124–25, and *Navy Court of Inquiry,* pt. 34, 505–6.
123. Draft WPUSF-44, 24 Mar 41, Opns Plan O-1, Annex E, 5–6. WPPac-46, 25 Jul 41, 43–44.
124. Richardson, *On the Treadmill,* 249–50.
125. WPPac-46, 25 Jul 41, Annex II, 5–6.
126. Kimmel, testimony, PHH, *Hearings,* pt. 6, 2531.
127. Draft WPUSF-44, 24 Mar 41, Opns Plan O-1, 3, Annex F, 6–7.
128. J. Rohwer and G. Hummelchen, *Chronology of the War at Sea, 1939–1945,* trans. Derek Masters, 2 vols. (New York: Arco Publishing, 1972), 1:183–84.
129. WPPac-46, 25 Jul 41, 19.
130. Anthony J. Watts and Brian G. Gordon, *The Imperial Japanese Navy* (London: Macdonald, 1971), 167–209.
131. GB #425, Ser 144, 14 Jun 41, cited in "US Naval Administrative Histories of WWII," no. 52, BuAer, 5:28.
132. Kimmel, testimony, PHH, *Roberts Commission,* pt. 22, 429.
133. Prange with Goldstein and Dillon, *Pearl Harbor: The Verdict,* 471, 507. CinCUS, US Flt Memorandum 4USM-41, 25 Jun 41, File A2-11/FF1(1) 1941, RG 313, NA (Suitland, Md.).
134. Hoyt, *How They Won,* 322–23.

135. Kimmel, testimony, PHH, *Hearings*, pt. 6, 2565.

136. Ibid., 2536.

137. Turner, testimony, PHH, *Hearings*, pt. 4, 1951.

138. WPPac-46, 25 Jul 41, 17.

139. Prange with Goldstein and Dillon, *Pearl Harbor: The Verdict*, 475.

140. CNO to CinCPac, US Pac Flt Operating Plan, Rainbow 5 (Navy Plan O-1, Rainbow 5) WPPac-46, review & acceptance of, 9 Sep 41, File QG Pac, Box 97, WPD Files.

141. CinCPac, Steps to be taken, 6 Dec 41; Kimmel, testimony, PHH, *Hearings*, pt. 6, 2529–37.

142. W. Smith, testimony, PHH, *Hart Inquiry*, pt. 26, 66–68. McCormick, ibid., 75. Pye, ibid., 157–60, 168–69. McMorris, ibid., 245–48, and *Hewitt Inquiry*, pt. 36, 177. Kimmel, testimony, PHH, *Hearings*, pt. 6, 2543.

143. Bellinger, testimony, PHH, *Navy Court of Inquiry*, pt. 34, 567.

144. Pye, testimony, PHH, *Army Pearl Harbor Board*, pt. 27, 537.

145. Murphy, testimony, PHH, *Hart Inquiry*, pt. 26, 205. McCormick, ibid., 76.

146. Kimmel, *Story*, 182.

147. CinCPac, Seps to be taken, 6 Dec 41. Kimmel, testimony, PHH, *Hearings*, pt. 6, 2536. Kimmel, *Story*, 72–73.

148. McMorris, testimony, PHH, *Hart Inquiry*, pt. 26, 245–48.

149. McMorris, testimony, PHH, *Navy Court of Inquiry*, pt. 34, 573, *Hart Inquiry*, pt. 26, 260, *Army Pearl Harbor Board*, pt. 28, 1500, 1506–7.

150. Prange, *At Dawn We Slept*, 406.

151. Stark, testimony, PHH, *Hearings*, pt. 5, 2152–55, 2376–77. Turner, ibid., pt. 26, 282.

152. Ingersoll, testimony, PHH, *Hart Inquiry*, pt. 26, 461.

153. Glover, ibid., 180–83.

154. Turner, ibid., 265.

155. Kimmel, testimony, PHH, *Hearings*, pt. 6, 2529–37, 2543.

156. McMorris, testimony, PHH, *Hart Inquiry*, pt. 26, 229, 259, *Hewitt Inquiry*, pt. 36, 191.

157. W. Smith, testimony, PHH, *Hart Inquiry*, pt. 26, 66–68.

158. Prange, *At Dawn We Slept*, 139.

159. Interview with RAdm James Shoemaker, Ford I. CO, 31 Jan 1963, in Prange with Goldstein and Dillon, *Pearl Harbor: The Verdict*, 475.

160. Interview with Edward P. Morgan, 26 Oct 1976, ibid., 475.

Chapter 26 Total or Limited War?

1. The Joint Staff Planners observed in 1946 that termination of the war and obsolescence of assumptions had rendered Rainbow Five obsolete (Jt Staff Planners, JCS, to various officers, Cancellation of Jt A&N Basic WP Rainbow No. 5, 25 Mar 46, reel 11, Microfilm Series M1421, JB Records).

2. Rainbow 5, May 1941, passim. Mead, "United States Peacetime Planning," 301–6. In contemporary calculations a division was taken as fifteen thousand combat troops plus support elements of fifteen thousand for a total "slice" of thirty thousand, the number slated for the Pacific counterattack.

3. Yarnell to Col J. W. Gulick, National Policy & War Plans, 28 Oct 19, JB Ser Misc 18, in Morton, "War Plan ORANGE," 225.

4. AWPD, Memo, Some Thoughts on Jt Basic WP Orange, 22 Nov 37, File 225; JPC to JB, Jt A&N Basic WP—Orange, 27 Dec 37, Ser 618, File 365; AWPD, Redraft of . . . Opns in Western Pac, 1 Feb 38; Author unknown, Memo for Gen Krueger, New Orange Plan, 24 Nov 37, File 225, Box 68, JB # 325, AWPD Color Plans.

5. JB Plan, 21 Feb 38.

6. JPC, Exploratory Studies, 21 Apr 39, pt. 3, 8–9, 11, 16–22.

7. AWPD, Rainbow 2 Outline, 1st draft, Aug 1939, Rainbow 2 1939–40.

8. WPD, Supplement 1, Jt Basic WP Rainbow 2, Outline, Additional Est & Assumptions on which to base provisions of Jt . . . Rainbow 2, 22 Mar 40, Tab 8, JB Rainbow 2 Dev File 1939–40.

9. AWPD, 1st Army draft, Annex "A" to Jt A&N Basic WP Rainbow 3, A Study of Sitn Presented by Directive of JB for Prepn of . . . Jt Rainbow 3, 15 Apr 40 w updates through late May, Tab 13, Rainbow 3, early 1940.

10. Richardson, *On the Treadmill*, 279.

11. CNO, Plan Dog, 12 Nov 40.

12. Turner & Col Joseph T. McNarney, Study of Immediate Problems concerning involvement in War, 21 Dec 40, JB #325, Ser 670, in Dyer, *Amphibians*, 1:157–60.

13. WPL-44, Dec 1940. CinCUS to CNO, WPL-44, 28 Jan 41, CNO-CinCUS-CinCAF WPL-44 corresp, Jan–Feb 1941.

14. Plan Dog, 12 Nov 40.

15. Meeting 11, 26 Feb 41, ABC-1 Conference, Jan–Mar 1941.

16. Cooke, Memo for CinC, 7 Apr 41, Cooke Papers.

17. Draft WPUSF-44, 24 Mar 41, 8. CinCPac to CNO, Wake I—Policy . . . construction on & protection of, 18 Apr 41, File CinCPac Plan Dog Comments, Box 91, WPD Files. CNO to CinCUS, 10 Feb 41, CNO-CinCUS-CinCAF WPL-44 corresp, Jan–Feb 1941. CinCPac to CNO, Initial Deployment of Pac Flt under Plan Dog, 14 May 41, File CinCPac Plan Dog Comments, A16-3/FF Warfare US Flt, Box 91, WPD Files. ComBatFor, Mining Plan—Approaches to Chichi Jima, 5 May 41 (file slip only), File A16, Box 4499, Entry 106, CinCUS Secret Corresp.

18. Draft WPUSF-44, 24 Mar 41, 8. WPPac-46, 25 Jul 41, 46.

19. Meeting 11, 26 Feb 41, ABC-1 Conference, Jan–Mar 1941.

20. CinCPac to CNO, 15 Nov 41; CNO to CinCPac, 25 Nov 41, PHH, *Hearings*, pt. 5, 2103–5.

21. Kimmel, testimony, PHH, *Hearings*, pt. 6, 2565.

22. NWC 1911 Plan, 2(c):39–40. AWPD to ACOS G-2, War Plan Orange, 6 Mar 23, File Orange 1039-1, AWPD Records.

23. A reference by a War College strategist appears in D. Staton (?) to Koch, 31 May 33, UNOpP, Box 49, RG 8, NHC, NWC.

24. AWPD, Rainbow 2 Outline, 1st draft, Aug 1939.

25. AWPD, 1st Army draft, Annex "A" to Jt A&N Basic WP Rainbow 3, 15 Apr 40 w updates.

26. COS and CNO, Memorandum for the Pres, Est Concerning Far East Sitn, 5 Nov 41, File Planning Misc, Box 67, WPD Files.

27. WPD, Quick Movement, 1932.
28. AWPD, Jt Basic WP Rainbow 2, Outline, Additional Est & Assumptions on which to base provisions of Jt . . . Rainbow 2, Sep 1939, Tab 2, Rainbow 2 1939–40.
29. AWPD, Memo, Some Thoughts on Jt Basic WP Orange, 22 Nov 37. CinCUS to CNO, War Plans—Status & readiness in view current international sitn, 22 Oct 40, File A16/FF1, Box 233, SecNav & CNO Secret Corresp.
30. Cited in PHH, *Hearings*, pt. 1, 294.
31. Dewey to Pres NWC, 19 Jun 12, GB Records, in Spector, *Professors of War*, 110. Mahan, "Preparedness for Naval War," *Harpers* 94 (1897), in Brune, *Origins of Security Policy*, 4.
32. Talbott, "Weapons Development," 53–71.
33. US Secy for Collaboration to Jt Secys, Brit Staff Mission, Action by Submarines against merchant ships, A16-1/EF13, 20 Oct 41, Section Aid to China.
34. CNO to CinCAF, #271422, 27 Nov 41, Flt dispatches, in Talbott, "Weapons Development," 55.
35. WPPac-46, 25 Jul 41, Opns Plan O-1, 44, 46, 72.
36. Blair, *Silent Victory*, 84.
37. CinCUS to CNO, Information for cdr of a raiding force operating against Japanese territory from a base in Eastern Pac, 28 Sep 38, A8(01354), File EF37 Japan, Box 4438, CinCUS Records, RG 313, NA (Suitland, Md.).
38. WPD, Supplement 1, Rainbow 2, 22 Mar 40.
39. Brune, *Origins of Security Policy*, 44.
40. CNO to CinCPac, 25 Feb 41, PHH, *Exhibits*, pt. 16, 2149.
41. Meeting 3, 3 Feb; Meeting 11, 26 Feb; UK Far East Appreciation 11 Feb; UK Reply to Navy Section, 15 Mar 41, ABC-1 Conference, Jan–Mar 1941. ABC-1, Rept, 27 Mar 41. Draft WPUSF-44, 24 Mar 41, 8.
42. Dir WPD to Dir Flt Maintenance Div, Incendiary Bombs, 10 May 41, F41-C; same 2 Aug 41, F41-6, Signed Ltrs, Boxes 81 & 82, WPD Files.
43. JPC, Exploratory Studies, 21 Apr 39, pt. 3, 1–5, 7–8.
44. Adm H. E. Kimmel, Memorandum of Conversation with the Pres, 9 Jun 41, File A3-2, CNO Corresp 1940–41, cited in Heinrichs, "Role of US Navy," 223.
45. CNO to CinCPac, Adv Flt Base in Caroline Is, 9 Apr 41, A16(R-3)(1941), Box 241, CNO Secret Corresp.
46. Richardson, *On the Treadmill*, 278. CinCUS to CNO, 26 Jan 40, PHH, *Hearings*, pt. 14, 924–25.

Chapter 27   The American Way of Planning: The Planners at War

1. Many works are available on World War II strategic planning in the Pacific. Among the most useful are the following, all of which cite original source documents:
   Joint and combined plans and general: Hayes, *Joint Chiefs*. Morgan, "Planning the Defeat of Japan." United States Strategic Bombing Survey, various divisions, many reports on campaigns of the Pacific War (Washington: U.S. Government Printing Office, various dates, mostly late 1940s).
   Army plans: Office of the Chief of Military History, Department of the Army,

United States Army in World War II (Washington: U.S. Government Printing Office, various dates), especially Morton, Strategy and Command; Cline, War Department, Washington Command Post; Matloff and Snell, War Department: Strategic Planning, 1941–1942; Matloff, War Department: Strategic Planning, 1943–1944; Leighton and Coakley, War Department: Global Logistics and Strategy, 1940–1943; and all volumes of The War in the Pacific, much about campaign plans.

Navy plans: Morison, History of U.S. Naval Operations in WWII, 15 vols., of which 9 deal with the Pacific, all with planning information on specific campaigns. Crawley, "Checklist of Strategic Plans," guide to naval operational plans. Hoyt, How They Won, informal but much information on Pacific Fleet planning. Moore, oral history, 7 vols., recollections of a war planner with excellent recall.

Army Air Force plans: Craven and Cate, eds., Army Air Forces in WWII, 7 vols., with details of air planning.

Marine Corps plans: Various authors, Historical Branch, G-3 Division, U.S. Marine Corps, Operational Narratives of the Marine Corps in World War II, also known as Marine Corps Monographs (Washington: U.S. Government Printing Office, various dates), 14 vols., with details of planning of Marine Corps campaigns.

In addition, most of the vast outpouring of general histories, campaign and battle accounts, biographies, and autobiographies contain useful information on World War II planning.

2. Morgan, "Planning the Defeat of Japan," 75.
3. Lowenthal, Leadership and Indecision, 1:532.
4. Albion, Makers of Policy, 392.
5. Cooke to Actg Chief Mil History, 14 Aug 59, in Morgan, "Planning the Defeat of Japan," 78.
6. Hoyt, How They Won, 214.
7. WPPac-46, 25 Jul 41, checkout card, Plans Files copy, OA, NHD.
8. A good example is CinCPac (by McMorris, COS), Granite, 13 Jan 44, Ser 0004, Pac-1-op, Folder Granite, Box 138, WPD Files. The proposed invasion of Truk (Operation Roadmaker) was to begin at Tol Island and proceed stepwise to other islands as in the 1937 Marine Plan.
9. Morgan, "Planning the Defeat of Japan," 71.

Chapter 28   Plan Orange at War: The Ocean Strategy Implemented

1. The sources most often cited are studies by historians of the U.S. Army Office of the Chief of Military History, circa 1960, especially Morton, "War Plan OR-ANGE" and Strategy and Command, chap. 1. Less well known but more focused on the plan's role in the war is an unpublished study by Morton's assistant, Lt Col Henry G. Morgan, Jr., "Planning the Defeat of Japan." A voracious army descendant is Martin, "War Plan Orange." A naval writer critical of the plan and with a viewpoint to push is Doyle, "The U.S. Navy and War Plan Orange." General criticisms are found in Heinrichs, "Role of the United States Navy." Examples of criticisms limited to certain years are Morton, "Military and Naval Preparations for the Defense of the Philippines," and Vlahos, "Naval

War College." A rare balanced presentation is Crowl, "Pacific War" (audio-taped lecture).

2. Morton, "War Plan ORANGE," 222. Doyle, "US Navy and War Plan Orange," 49–50.

3. Martin, "War Plan Orange," 33–34.

4. Heinrichs, "Role of the United States Navy," 201–6. Doyle, "US Navy and War Plan Orange," 50–51.

5. Morton, "War Plan ORANGE," 221, 232, 241, 249. Doyle, "US Navy and War Plan Orange," 58. Morgan, "Planning the Defeat of Japan," 55.

6. Martin, "War Plan Orange," 33–34.

7. Doyle, "US Navy and War Plan Orange," 50–51.

8. Morgan, "Planning the Defeat of Japan," 63, 183–85.

9. Ibid., 70–71, 174.

10. Allen, *War Games*, 139.

11. Morgan, "Planning the Defeat of Japan," 177.

12. Admiral Ernest J. King, "Our Navy at War: Report Covering Combat Operations up to March 1, 1944," reprint, *United States News*, 27 Mar 1944, 25.

13. Hayes, *Joint Chiefs*, 289, 415–17, 421–24. Philip A. Crowl and Edmund G. Love, Office of the Chief of Military History, *Seizure of the Gilberts and Marshalls* (Washington: U.S. Government Printing Office, 1955), 54, 69, 167. Morison, *History of U.S. Naval Operations in WWII*, vol. 7, *Aleutians, Gilberts and Marshalls*, 201–8. Hoyt, *How They Won*, 310.

14. Hayes, *Joint Chiefs*, 416, 424. Hoyt, *How They Won*, 315.

15. Hoyt, *How They Won*, 328, 414.

16. Hayes, *Joint Chiefs*, 289, 372–73, 428, 545–47. Moore, oral history, 908.

17. The United States Strategic Bombing Survey, Naval Analysis Div, *The Reduction of Truk* (Washington: U.S. Government Printing Office, 1946), passim; United States Strategic Bombing Survey, Naval Analysis Div, *The Allied Campaign against Rabaul* (Washington: U.S. Government Printing Office, 1947).

18. The navy spent $132 million on Manus. The most expensive previous advanced naval bases were at Espiritu Santo, $36 million; Noumea, $24 million; Eniwetok, $23 million; and Milne Bay, $11 million (BuDocks, *Building the Navy's Bases*, 2:iii, 124, 234, 295, 299–301).

19. John Toland, *The Rising Sun* (New York: Random House, 1970), 523.

20. Hayes, *Joint Chiefs*, 280.

Chapter 29   Plan Orange at War: Innovation and Surprise

1. For analyses of carrier-versus-carrier warfare before World War II see Hughes, *Fleet Tactics*. The dominance of carriers could not be taken for granted, especially at night and in bad weather, or until the range and lifting power of carrier aircraft improved in the late 1930s.

2. Hoyt, *How They Won*, 288.

3. U.S. Strategic Bombing Survey, *The War against Japanese Transportation, 1941–1945* (Washington: U.S. Government Printing Office, 1947), 6, 47, fig. 44.

4. Construction of battleships and heavy cruisers was shortened by only 10 to 20

percent, although fleet carriers were built in less than half the prewar time (Vlahos and Pace, "War Experience and Force Requirements," 30–31).
5. Moore, oral history, 64.
6. Heinrichs, "Role of US Navy," 200.
7. VAdm C. A. Lockwood to CNO, Communications Intelligence against the Japanese in WWII, 17 Jun 47, cited in Ronald H. Spector, ed., *Listening to the Enemy: Key Documents on the Role of Communications Intelligence in the War with Japan* (Wilmington, Del.: Scholarly Resources, 1988), 135.
8. GB 1914 Plan, 36.
9. Cited in Naval War College Foundation, Newport, R.I., "Foundation Briefs," #15, Apr 1990, 4.
10. In a Gallup public opinion poll of 1 June 1945 Americans favored by a margin of nine to one continuing the war rather than accepting a hypothetical peace offer with no occupation of Japan (Leon V. Sigal, *Fighting to a Finish: The Politics of War Termination in the United States and Japan, 1945* [Ithaca: Cornell University Press, 1988], 95).

Chapter 30   Plan Orange at War: The Better Strategy

1. Morgan, "Planning the Defeat of Japan," 88–89, 127–28, 180. Hayes, *Joint Chiefs*, chap. 19.
2. Morgan, "Planning the Defeat of Japan," 124–25.
3. Hayes, *Joint Chiefs*, 728.
4. Ibid., 459–60, 470, 492–98, 728–29.
5. Morgan, "Planning the Defeat of Japan," 120–21, 142–43.
6. By the end of the war the investment in naval bases on Luzon was $48 million. Naval expenditures on the three principal western bases was $379 million at Guam-Saipan-Tinian, $216 million at Leyte-Samar, and $114 million at Okinawa (BuDocks, *Building the Navy's Bases*, 2:iii.)
7. Rainbow 5, May 1941, App. 1.
8. Hayes, *Joint Chiefs*, 461–62.
9. Ibid., 707.
10. Rufus E. Miles, Jr., "Hiroshima: The Strange Myth of Half a Million American Lives Saved," *International Security* 10 (Fall 1985): 121–40.
11. David A. Rosenberg, commentary at joint session of American Historical Association and American Committee on the History of the Second World War, New York, December 1985 (hereafter AHA-ACHSWW Dec 1985).
12. United States Strategic Bombing Survey, *The War against Japanese Transportation, 1941–1945* (Washington: U.S. Government Printing Office, 1947), 3–4.
13. Hayes, *Joint Chiefs*, 493.
14. Miles, "Hiroshima."
15. Paul Fussell, *Thank God for the Atom Bomb and Other Essays* (New York: Summit Books, 1988), 13–37.
16. United States Strategic Bombing Survey, Summary Report (Pacific War), 26, cited in Morgan, "Planning the Defeat of Japan," 188–89.
17. Herbert Feis, *The Atomic Bomb and the End of World War II* (Princeton: Princeton University Press, 1966), 9.

18. Morgan, "Planning the Defeat of Japan," 183–91.
19. E. B. Potter, *Nimitz* (Annapolis: Naval Institute Press, 1976), 381. Thomas B. Buell, *The Quiet Warrior: A Biography of Admiral Raymond A. Spruance* (Boston: Little, Brown, 1974), 367. Barton J. Bernstein, commentary, AHA-ACHSWW Dec 1985. Admiral William D. Leahy, *I Was There* (New York: Whittlesey House, 1950), 259. King and Whitehill, *Fleet Admiral King*, 605n.
20. Miles, "Hiroshima."
21. NWC 1911 Plan, 2(a):1.

Bibliography

RECORD COLLECTIONS

Note: Initial phrase is used in notes to identify collections.

Authors File, NWC: Card File, Authors of Papers, 1910–38, RG 8, NHC, NWC.

AWPD Color Plans: Army, Adjutant General's Office, Administrative Services Division, Operations Branch, Special Projects—War Plans, "Color," 1920–48, RG 407, NA.

AWPD Records: Army War Plans Division Records, 1903–41, RG 165, NA.

Brit Jt Staff Mission 1941: Joint Secretaries of British Joint Staff Mission to United States, 1941, roll 6, Scholarly Microfilms. Sections include Pacific–Far East and Aid to China.

BuDocks Conf Corresp: Bureau of Yards and Docks, Confidential Correspondence, RG 71, NA.

CinCPac annual rept: Commander in Chief Pacific Fleet, Annual Report, fiscal year 1941, microfilm series M971, RG 313, NA.

CinCPac WPs file late 1941: Commander in Chief United States Fleet, Secret, re War Plans, Box 4846, Entry 109, RG 313, NA (Suitland, Md.).

CinCUS annual repts: Commander in Chief United States Fleet, Annual Reports of United States Fleet, fiscal years 1920–41, microfilm series M971, RG 313, NA. Most include reports of subsidiary commands including

Commanders, Battle Force, Scouting Force, Submarine Force, Base Force, and Aircraft Base Force.

CinCUS Conf Gen Corresp: Commander in Chief United States Fleet, Confidential General Correspondence, RG 313, NA.

CinCUS Op Plans 1932–39: Commander in Chief United States Fleet, Operating Plans File, 1932–39, OA, NHD.

CinCUS Secret Corresp: Commander in Chief United States Fleet, Secret Correspondence, 1940–41, RG 313, NA (Suitland, Md.).

CNO Plans File: Chief of Naval Operations, Plans Files, OA, NHD.

Columbia Oral History: Naval History Project, Oral History Research Office, Columbia University, New York, mostly 1960s.

ComAirScoFor Records: Commander Aircraft, Scouting Force, Records, RG 313, NA.

Cooke Papers: Admiral Charles M. Cooke, Jr., Collected Papers, Hoover Institution Archives, Stanford, Calif.

FAW2 Op Plans 1941: File Fleet Air Wing Two—Operations Plan Material, Box Fleet Air Wings 2 and 4 including predecessor Patwing 2, Fleet Op Plan Files, OA, NHD.

Flag Officer Biog Files: Flag Officer Biographical Files, OA, NHD.

Fleet Op Plan Files 1941: United States (later Pacific) Fleet Operating Plans Files, 1941, OA, NHD.

Fleet Problems, 1923–41: Fleet Problems, U.S. Navy, 1923–41, Problems I to XXII, Microfilm Series M-964, RG 38, 80, and 313, NA.

GB Hearings: General Board of the Navy, Hearings, RG 80, NA.

GB Ltrs: General Board of the Navy, Letters, RG 80, NA.

GB Proceedings: General Board of the Navy, Proceedings, 1900–1947, RG 80, NA.

GB Subj File: General Board of the Navy, Subject File, 1900–1947, RG 80, NA.

GB War Portfs: General Board of the Navy, War Portfolios, 1900–ca. 1912, RG 80, NA.

Hepburn Hearings, House: Hearings on HR 2880, Naval Affairs Committee, U.S. Congress, House, 75th Cong., 1st sess., 1939.

Hepburn Rept Notebooks: Hepburn Report Notebooks, early 1939, QB(119)/A9-10 (390101), SecNav General Correspondence, RG 80, NA.

Horne Papers: Vice-Admiral Frederick J. Horne, Collected Papers, Manuscript Division, Library of Congress.

JB, Minutes: Joint Board, Minutes of Meetings, 1903–41, RG 225, NA.

JB, Plans & Opns Div: Joint Board, Plans and Operations Division, many reports in War Department, General and Special Staffs, RG 165, NA.

JB Proceedings: Joint Board Proceedings, 1903–47, Microfilm Series M1421, RG 225, NA.

JB Rainbow 2 Dev File, 1939–40: Development File Joint Basic War Plan Rainbow Two, Ser 642-2, Box 1942, Plans and Operations Division, Joint Board Numerical File, RG 165, NA.

JB Rainbow 3 Dev File 1940: Development File, Joint Army and Navy Basic

War Plan Rainbow No. 3, #325, Ser 642, Box 1942, Plans and Operations Division, Joint Board Numerical File, RG 165, NA.

JB Rainbow 5 File 1941: File, Joint Army and Navy Basic War Plan Rainbow No. 5, #325, Ser 642-5 (Revision), Box 1942, Plans and Operations Division, Joint Board Numerical File, RG 165, NA.

JB Records: Joint Army and Navy Board, Records (filed by Serial Number), 1903–41, RG 225, NA.

Naval War Board, 1898, Records, RG 80, NA.

Navy Directory: U.S. Navy, Bureau of Navigation, *Navy Directory: Officers of the United States Navy and Marine Corps* (Washington: U.S. Government Printing Office, 1908–42). Copies in Navy Department Library, Naval Historical Center, Washington, and Nimitz Library, U.S. Naval Academy, Annapolis.

NHC, NWC: Naval Historical Collection, Naval War College, Newport, R.I.

NWC Problems & Solutions: Naval War College Problems and Solutions, RG 12, NHC, NWC.

PHH: Pearl Harbor Hearings, U.S. Congress, Joint Committee on the Investigation of the Pearl Harbor Attack, *Hearings.* 79th Cong. (Washington: U.S. Government Printing Office, 1946):

Hearings (Joint Congressional Committee), 15 Nov 45 to 15 Jul 46

Exhibits (of Joint Committee, except other hearings listed below)

Proceedings of Hart Inquiry (navy), 22 Feb to 15 Jun 44.

Proceedings of Roberts Commission (civilian and military), 22 Dec 41 to 23 Jan 42.

Proceedings of Army Pearl Harbor Board, 20 Jul to 20 Oct 44.

Proceedings of Navy Court of Inquiry, 24 Jul to 19 Oct 44.

Proceedings of Hewitt Investigation (navy), 15 May to 11 Jul 45.

Proceedings of Clausen Investigation (army), 23 Nov 44 to 12 Sep 45.

Proceedings of Clarke Investigation (army), 14–16 Sep and 13 Jul to 14 Aug 45

Roosevelt, Franklin Delano, Papers, Franklin D. Roosevelt Library, Hyde Park, N.Y.

Scholarly Microfilms: "Strategic Planning in the U.S. Navy, Its Evolution and Execution, 1891–1945." Wilmington, Del.: Scholarly Resources, 1977, rolls 1 to 9.

SecNav Annual Rept: Secretary of the Navy, Annual Report. Washington: U.S. Government Printing Office, various years 1898 to 1941.

SecNav Gen Records: Secretary of the Navy, General Records, RG 80, NA.

SecNav & CNO Secret & Conf Corresp: Secretary of the Navy and Chief of Naval Operations, Secret and Confidential Correspondence, 1919–41, RG 80, NA (also in Microfilm Series M1140, RG 80, NA). In some years secret papers filed separately from confidential.

Section Aid to China: U.S. Secretary for Collaboration and British Joint Staff Mission, Section Aid to China, Correspondence, 1941, Scholarly Microfilms, roll 6.

Section Pac-Far East Jt Staff Corresp: U.S. Secretary for Collaboration and

British Joint Staff Mission, Section Pacific–Far East, Correspondence, 1941, Scholarly Microfilms, roll 6.

Shore Station Dev Bd: Records of Base Maintenance Division, Shore Station Development Board, RG 38, NA.

US Flt Records, 1940–41: Records of Commander in Chief United States Fleet and subsidiary commanders, 1940 and January 1941, RG 313, NA (Suitland, Md.).

WPD Files: Navy War Plans Division Files, in Records of the Strategic Plans Division, Office of the CNO, OA, NHD.

WAR PLANS, ESTIMATES OF THE SITUATION, AND SIMILAR DOCUMENTS (IN CHRONOLOGICAL ORDER)

Bd of Officers to SecNav, Plans of Campaign against Spain & Japan, 30 Jun 97, War Portfolios, GB Records.

GB War Portfs: General Board, War Portfolios, 1897–1914, GB Records, RG 80, NA.

NWC Conference of 1906: Naval War College, Conference of 1906, Solution of Problem, Problems and Solutions, NWC Problems & Solutions.

GB 1906 Plan: General Board, In Case of Strained Relations with Japan, Sep 06, #78, File UNOpT(T) Orange-Blue Situation, RG 8, NHC, NWC.

NWC, Problem of 1907: Tentative Plan of Campaign and Strategic Game . . . , NWC Problem of 1907, 12 Jul 07, NWC Problems & Solutions.

Oliver, 1907 Problem: Cdr James H. Oliver, NWC, Concerning Problem of the Year (1907), Jun 1907, NWC Problems & Solutions.

NWC: Rept of Conference of 1907: Naval War College, Report of Conference of 1907, Orange Strategic Exercise, summer 1907, NWC Problems & Solutions.

GB 1910 Plan: Second Committee of General Board to Executive Committee, General Plan of Campaign for War against Japan, n.d., ca. Nov 1910, UNOpP 1910, Box 48, RG 8, NHC, NWC.

NWC 1911 Plan: Naval War College, Strategic Plan of Campaign against Orange, 15 Mar 11, Scholarly Microfilms, roll 1.

Mahan-Oliver Corresp 1911: Correspondence between RAdm A. T. Mahan and Cdr James Oliver re NWC 1911 Plan, Feb and Mar 1911, UNOpP, Box 48, RG 8, NHC, NWC.

GB 1913 Admin Plan: Second Committee, General Board, Orange Plan Administrative Section, 29 May 13, revised May 1915, Scholarly Microfilms, roll 1.

GB 1914 Plan: General Board, Second Committee, Strategic Section, Orange War Plan, 25 Feb 14, Scholarly Microfilms, roll 1.

GB 1917 Strategic Problem: General Board to Secretary of the Navy, Strategic Problem, Pacific, 15 Jan 17, 196-1, Box 192, SecNav & CNO Secret & Conf Corresp.

JB, Strategy of the Pacific, 1919: Joint Board to Secretary of War, Strategy of the Pacific, 18 Dec 19, Ser 28-d, #325, JB Records.

Ellis, Maj Earl H., USMC, Advance Base Operations in Micronesia, n.d., ca. Jul 1921, Marine Corps Historical Center, Washington Navy Yard.

NWC, 10 Aug 21: President Naval War College to Chief of Naval Operations, 10 Aug 21 with enclosure Class of 1921, Strategic Problem VII (Strat 35, Mod 7), Solution by NWC Staff, Blue and Orange Estimates of the Situation, 7 Jul 21, 112-33, roll 26, SecNav & CNO Secret & Conf Corresp.

GB Pre-Conference Papers, 1921: General Board to Secretary of the Navy, Limitation of Armaments, Part IV: Fortifications of Oahu, Guam, and the Philippines, 20 Oct 21, Ser 1088-g; Ex-German Islands in the Pacific, 22 Oct 21, Ser 1088-L; Limitation of Armaments, Part IV: Ex-German Islands, 27 Oct 21, Ser 1088-p, #438, GB Subj Files.

WPD Est 1922: War Plans Division, Estimate of the Situation BLUE-ORANGE, 1 Sep 22, Orange Studies, Box 64, WPD Files.

Bd for Dev 31 Oct 22: Board for Development of Navy Yard Plans to Chief, Bureau of Yard and Docks, Advanced Bases in a Pacific Campaign, Material and Facilities . . . , 31 Oct 22, 198-13, roll 79, SecNav & CNO Secret & Conf Corresp.

Astc Flt War Plan, 1922: Commander in Chief Asiatic Fleet to Chief of Naval Operations, War Plans, 29 Nov 22, 198-37, roll 90, SecNav & CNO Secret & Conf Corresp.

GB Strategic Survey, Apr 1923: From Senior Member Present (W. L. Rodgers), General Board, to Secretary of the Navy, Strategic Survey of the Pacific, 26 Apr 23, #425, Serial No. 1136, 198-26, roll 80, SecNav & CNO Secret & Conf Corresp.

JB-JPC Plans, May–Jul 1923: Joint Planning Committee to Joint Board, Synopsis of Joint Army & Navy Estimate of Orange Situation, 25 May 23; Joint Board to Chief of Naval Operations, same title, 7 Jul 23, Ser 207; Joint Board to Secretary of War, Defense of the Philippines, 7 Jul 23, Ser 208; Joint Board to Secretary of the Navy, Recommendations by Governor-General of the Philippines Concerning Measures of Defense, 7 Jul 23, Ser 209, #305, JB Records.

JPC Plan 1924: Joint Planning Committee to Joint Board, Joint Army and Navy Basic War Plan—Orange, 12 Mar 24; Joint Board to Joint Planning Committee, Proposed Joint Army & Navy Basic War Plan—Orange, 7 Jun 24, #325, Ser 228, JB Records.

Jt Bd Plan 1924: Joint Board to Secretary of War, Joint Army and Navy Basic War Plan—Orange, 15 Aug 24, #325, Ser 228, JB Records.

AWPD Plan 1925: Brig Gen Le Roy Eltinger, Army War Plan Orange, Strategical Plan, 29 Jan 25, File 230, Box 69, AWPD Color Plans.

Plan O-3, ca. Jan 25: United States Fleet Contributory War Operating Plans O-3, ca. Jan 25, 198-13, roll 79, SecNav & CNO Secret Corresp.

AWC Repts, 13–14 Apr 25: Army War College, Committee Reports on War Plan Orange, 13–14 Apr 25, File Army War College War Plans Studies, Box 37, WPD Files.

JPC Plan Oct 1926: Joint Planning Committee, Joint Army and Navy Basic War Plan—Orange, 6 Oct 26, File 2720-119, AWPD Files.

JPC Revision, Oct 1926: Joint Planning Committee to Joint Board, Revision of Joint Army and Navy Basic War Plan—Orange, 11 Oct 26, JB #325, Ser 280, Entry 184, Box 1931, AWPD Records.

JB Comment, Oct 1926: Joint Board to Joint Planning Committee, Army, Revision of Joint Army and Navy Basic War Plan—Orange, 23 Oct 26, Ser 280, Box 1931, AWPD Records.

JPC Plan Nov 1926: (prob.) Joint Planning Committee, Joint Army and Navy Basic War Plan—Orange, 23 Nov 26, File 2720-119, AWPD Files.

JPC Army Section Revision, May 1927: Army Section Joint Planning Committee to Capt Rowan, Revision of Joint Army and Navy War Plan Orange, 27 May 27, Entry 184, File 280, JB Plans & Opns Div.

WPD, Study of Certain Pac Is, 6 Aug 27: War Plans Division, Study of Certain Pacific Islands from the Standpoint of Facilities for Sea and Air Craft Fueling Bases, 6 Aug 27, Box 64, WPD Files.

WPD Est, May 1927: (prob) War Plans Division, Estimate of the Situation Blue-Orange, 4 May 27, File 232, Box 69, AWPD Color Plans.

Army Est, Aug 1927: Maj J. L. Jenkins, General Staff, Comments on Blue-Orange Estimate dated Aug 9, 1927, n.d., File 232, Box 69, AWPD Color Plans.

WPD, Marshall Is Plan, ca. 1927: D. C. McDougal, Estimate of the Situation . . . to Seize Two Bases in the Marshall Islands . . . , n.d., ca. late 1927/early 1928, File Orange Studies, Folder 2, Box 64, WPD Files.

WPD, Landing Opns, Oct 1927: Captain R. M. Griswold to Director War Plans Division, WPD, Studies of Landing Operations, Orange, 3 Oct 1927, File Orange Studies, Folder 2, Box 64, WPD Files.

JPC Est, Jan 1928: Joint Planning Committee to Joint Board, Joint Estimate of the Situation—Blue Orange, and Joint Army and Navy War Plan Orange, 9 Jan 28, Entry 194, File 280, AWPD Records.

JB Points, Feb 1928: Joint Board, Points . . . for discussion at Joint Board Meeting . . . [re JPC] . . . development of War Plan Orange, 9 Feb 28, Entry 184, Ser 280, AWPD Files.

JPC Navy Section Revision, Mar 1928: (prob) Horne, Entry 184, Ser 280, AWPD Files.

JPC Navy Section Revision, Apr 1928: Capt F. J. Horne, Joint Army and Navy Basic War Plan—Orange, 17 Apr 28, AWPD #2720-119, Ser 280, RG 165, AWPD Files.

JPC Revision, Apr 1928: Joint Planning Committee to Joint Board, Revision of Joint Army and Navy Basic War Plan Orange, 24 Apr 28, #325, Ser 280, JB Records.

JPC Plan, Apr 1928: Joint Planning Committee, Joint Army and Navy Basic War Plan—Orange, 24 Apr 28, #325, Ser 280, JB Records.

JB Plan, Jun 1928: Joint Board, Joint Army and Navy Basic War Plan Orange, 14 Jun 28, #325, Ser 280, JB Records.

JPC Army Section, Jul 1928: Army Section Joint Planning Committee to Joint Board, 5 Jul 28, Ser 292-B, #349, 1928–33, JB Records.

JPC Est, Jan 1929: Joint Planning Committee, Blue-Orange Joint Estimate of the Situation, 11 Jan 29, #325, Ser 280, JB Records, RG 225, NA. This estimate accompanied the revised Orange Plan sent to the service secretaries for approval in January 1929 but is virtually a verbatim copy of the JPC Est, Jan 1928.

CNO Plan, Mar 1929: Chief of Naval Operations, Navy Basic War Plan—Orange, 1 Mar 29, Scholarly Microfilms, rolls 2 & 3.

AAC Plans, 1929–31: Army Air Corps, Special Mobilization Plan—Orange, 30 Nov 29, File 143; War Department, same title, Arms and Services Plan, Army Air Corps Annex, Registered #35, WD Series, AC-SPOE-A, 4 Mar 31, File 142, Box 60, AWPD Color Plans.

WPD, Quick Movement, 1932: War Plans Division, Battle Problem—Quick Movement, Special Study Blue vs. Orange, ca. Apr 1932, Box 39, WPD Files.

WPL-13, Change #1, 15 Jul 32: (prob) War Plans Division, Change #1, WPL-13, Navy Basic Plan—Orange, 15 Jul 32, Scholarly Microfilms, roll 2.

Tentative Plan O-1, 26 Aug 33: Commander in Chief U.S. Fleet to Chief of Naval Operations, War Plans—Orange, 26 Aug 33, A7-3 2282, File CinCUS prior 3 Sep 1939, vol. 1, CinCUS Op Plans 1932–39.

WPL-16, change #3, Jul 1933: Chief of Naval Operations to Distribution List for WPL-16, change #3, 17 Jul 33, Scholarly Microfilms, roll 3.

Change #4 to WPL-16, 31 Jan 34: Chief of Naval Operations to Distribution List for WPL-16, Change #4, 31 Jan 34, Scholarly Microfilms, roll 3.

Meyers, WPs—Orange change, 27 Feb 34: Capt G. J. Meyers to Director War Plans Division, War Plans Orange—basic change, 27 Feb 34, File CinCUS prior 3 Sep 39, CinCUS Op Plans 1932–39, vol. 1.

FMF, Wotje Defense Plan, 27 Mar 34: Headquarters Fleet Marine Force, Operations Plan #2-34, 1st Advanced Base Defense Force, Reenforced, Wotje Atoll, 27 Mar 34, File Wotje Defense Plan, Box 77, WPD Files.

WPD, Royal Road, Jul 1934: Cdr C. W. Magruder, War Plans Division, Plan O-1 Orange, "The Royal Road" (US Jt Astc Force Operating Plan—Orange, CinCUS—1 Jul 1934), 21 Jul 34, File Royal Road, Box 64, WPD Files.

Phil Dept Plan Orange 1934: Philippine Department First Phase Plan Orange, 1934, Document HPD WPO-1-G2, 1 Aug 34, G-2 App, File 365, Box 65; G-3 Estimate of the Situation, File 171, Box 64, AWPD Color Plans.

FMF, Wotje Attack, 9 Aug 34: Headquarters Fleet Marine Force, Operations Plan #1-34, 2d Marine Brigade, Reenforced, Wotje Atoll, 9 Aug 34, File Wotje Attack Plan, Box 77, WPD Files.

FMF, Maloelap Attack, 22 Oct 34: Headquarters Fleet Marine Force, Operations Plan #3-34, 2d Marines, Reenforced, Maloelap Atoll, 22 Oct 34, File Maloelap Attack Plan, Box 56, WPD Files.

FMF, Majuro Attack, 18 Jan 35: Headquarters Fleet Marine Force, Operations Plan #4-34, 1st Marines, Reenforced, Majuro, 18 Jan 35, File Majuro Attack Plan, Box 56, WPD Files.

Change #3 to WPL-13, 26 Feb 35: Chief of Naval Operations to Distribution

List for Navy Basic Plan—Orange, Change #3 to WPL-13, 26 Feb 35, w enclosure dated Nov 1934, Scholarly Microfilms, roll 2.

FMF, Rongelap Attack, 26 Jul 35: Headquarters Fleet Marine Force, Rongelap Attack Plan, Operations Plan #5-35, 26 Jul 35, Box 69, WPD Files.

FMF, Attack of Ponape, 5 Oct 35: War Plans Section, Headquarters Fleet Marine Force, Attack of Ponape, Estimate of the Situation, 5 Oct 35, File Ponape Attack, Box 69, WPD Records.

Base Force Plans, Jul–Oct 1935: Captain D. E. Cummings, U.S. Fleet Base Force, 8 memoranda re Pacific island bases, July to October 1935, File BasFor & BasFor Projects, Box 39, Op Plan Files, OA, NHD.

AWPD Plan 1936: Colonel W. Krueger, Acting Assistant Chief of Staff, Army War Plans Division, to the Adjutant General, Revision of Joint Army and Navy Basic War Plan—Orange, 28 May 36, File 2720-71, AWPD Records.

USMC, Wotje Attack, 25 May 36: War Plans Section U.S. Marine Corps, Study of Wotje Attack 1-36, 25 May 36, File same title, Box 77, WPD Files.

AWPD, Wotje Attack, 31 Jul 36: Army War Plans Division, Estimate of Situation for Attack of Wotje (from Viewpoint of Landing Force Commander), 31 Jul 36, File Wotje, Attack of—Army Est, Box 77, WPD Files.

Change #2 to WPL-15, 3 Sep 36: Chief of Naval Operations to Distribution List of WPL-15, Change #2 to WPL-15, 3 Sep 36, w enclosure dated July 1936, Scholarly Microfilms, roll 2.

Change #5 to WPL-13, 15 Sep 36: Chief of Naval Operations to Distribution List of WPL-13, Change #5 to WPL-13, 15 Sep 36, w enclosure, Scholarly Microfilms, roll 2.

Change #6 to WPL-13, 26 Mar 37: Chief of Naval Operations to Distribution List of WPL-13, Change #6 to WPL-13, 26 Mar 37, Scholarly Microfilms, roll 2.

USMC, Truk Attack, 28 Apr 37: War Plans Section, U.S. Marine Corps, Truk Attack #1-37, 28 Apr 37, File Truk Attack, Box 75, WPD Files.

Change #5 to WPL-16, 10 Jul 37: Chief of Naval Operations to Distribution List of WPL-16, Change #5 to WPL-16, 10 Jul 37, Scholarly Microfilms, roll 3.

USMC, Saipan and Uracas Attack, 1937: Author unknown, prob. U.S. Marine Corps, Estimate of Marine Corps Forces Required for Attack of Saipan and Uracas, n.d. (prob 1937), File Saipan & Uracas, Attack of, Box 69, WPD Files.

JB Plan, 21 Feb 38: Joint Board to Secretary of War, Joint Army and Navy Basic War Plan—Orange (1938), 21 Feb 38, #325, Ser 618, File 223, Box 68, AWPD Color Plans.

CinCUS atoll Plan, 28 Feb 38: Commander in Chief U.S. Fleet to Chief of Naval Operations, 28 Feb 38, File NB/ND14, Box 259, SecNav & CNO Secret Corresp.

Change #4 to WPL-15, Apr 1938: Chief of Naval Operations to Distribution List for Navy Basic Plan—Orange, Change #4 to WPL-15, Apr 1938, Scholarly Microfilms, roll 2.

Change #6 to WPL-16, 23 Apr 38: Chief of Naval Operations to Distribution List for Navy Basic Plan—Orange, Change #6 to WPL-16, 23 Apr 38, Scholarly Microfilms, roll 3.

Hepburn Rept: Board, Rear Admiral Arthur J. Hepburn, Senior Member, Report on Need of Additional Naval Bases, 23 Dec 38, U.S. Congress, House Doc #65, 76th Cong, 1st sess.

WPL-13 revision Mar 1939: Chief of Naval Operations, Navy Basic War Plan Orange, WPL-13, vol. 1, 8 Mar 39, Box 147C, WPD Files.

JPC, Exploratory Studies, 21 Apr 39: Joint Planning Committee to Joint Board, Exploratory Studies in Accordance with JB 325 (Ser 634), 21 Apr 39, JB Records.

WPL-35, CNO, June 1939: Chief of Naval Operations, Landing Operations Blue-Orange, vol. 1, Jun 1939, Box 147E, WPD Files.

Rainbow 1, 9 Aug 39: Joint Board, Joint Army and Navy Basic War Plan—Rainbow No. I, 9 Aug 39, in Chief of Naval Operations, WPL-42, Navy Basic War Plan—Rainbow 1, 12 Jul 40, App I, Scholarly Microfilms, roll 5.

USMC, Defs of Wake, 11 Aug 39: Col Harry K. Pickett USMC, The Defenses of Wake, 11 Aug 39, WPD Files.

Rainbow 2, 1939–40: Army War Plans Division, War Plans Division and Joint Planning Committee, drafts of Plan Rainbow Two, August 1939 to March 1940, JB Rainbow 2 Dev File, 1939–40.

Rainbow 3, early 1940: Army War Plans Division and War Plans Division, drafts of Plan Rainbow Three, Mar–Apr 1940, #325, Ser 642, JB Rainbow 2 Dev File, 1939–40.

WPD, Plan O-1, 30 Apr 40: Commander Forrest P. Sherman to Director War Plans Division, CinCUS's Operating Plan O-1, 30 Apr 40, A16-3/FF, Box 91, WPD Files.

CNO Conference, 1 May 40: Digest of Conference Held 1 May 40 in Office of CNO, 2 May 40, A16-3/FF, Box 91, WPD Files.

WPL-42, 12 Jul 40: Chief of Naval Operations, WPL-42, Navy Basic War Plan—Rainbow One, 12 Jul 40, App I, Scholarly Microfilms, roll 5.

Navy Rainbow 4, ca. Aug 40: Navy Basic Plan Rainbow Four, Annex I, Navy Plan for Execution of Missions in Joint Task No. I of Joint . . . Rainbow Four, n.d., ca. Aug 40, Scholarly Microfilms, roll 5.

WPL-36, 8 Oct 40: Chief of Naval Operations, WPL-36, Basic Studies for Landing Operations in a Blue-Orange War, vol. 2, pt. 1, 8 Oct 40, CNO Plans File.

Rainbow 3, late 1940: Army War Plans Division and War Plans Division drafts and correspondence of Plan Rainbow Three, Nov–Dec 1940, #325, Ser 642, JB Rainbow 3 Dev File, 1940.

CNO, Plan Dog, 12 Nov 40: Chief of Naval Operations, Memo for the Secretary, 12 Nov 40, File 4175-15, AWPD Files, RG 165, NA.

WPL-44, Dec 1940: Chief of Naval Operations, Rainbow Plan No. III (WPL-44), Dec 1940, Scholarly Microfilms, roll 5. Originals in File WPL-46 ltrs, Box 147J, WPD Files. Interleaved with CNO-CinCUS-CinCAF WPL-44 corresp, Jan–Feb 1941 (see below).

CNO-CinCUS-CinCAF WPL-44 corresp, Jan–Feb 1941: Chief of Naval Operations, Commander in Chief U.S. Fleet and Commander in Chief Asiatic Fleet, correspondence re WPL-44, Jan–Feb 1941, interleaved with WPL-44, Scholarly Microfilms, roll 5. Originals in File WPL-46 letters, Box 147J, WPD Files, OA, NHD. Most of the correspondence also appears in PHH, *Exhibits.*

ABC-1 Conference, Jan–Mar 1941: United States–British Staff Conferences, Washington, 24 Jan to 27 Mar 41, Scholarly Microfilms, roll 6.

Draft WPUSF-44, 24 Mar 41: Commander in Chief U.S. Fleet to Commanders of Subsidiary Fleet Commands, Operations Plans O-1, Rainbow 3, 24 Mar 41, File A16(R-3) (1941), Box 241, CNO Secret Corresp, RG 80, NA (Suitland, Md.).

ABC-1, Rept, 27 Mar 41: United States–British Staff Conversations, ABC-1, Report, 27 Mar 41, Scholarly Microfilms, roll 6.

Rainbow 5, May 1941: Joint Army and Navy Basic War Plan—RAINBOW No. 5, May 1941, in WPL-46, 26 May 41, Appendix I.

WPL-46, 26 May 41: Chief of Naval Operations, Navy Basic War Plan Rainbow Five (WPL-46), 26 May 1941, Scholarly Microfilms, roll 5.

WPPac-46, 25 Jul 41: Commander in Chief Pacific Fleet to Chief of Naval Operations, U.S. Pacific Fleet Operating Plan—Rainbow 5 (Navy Plan O-1, Rainbow 5, WPPac-46), 25 Jul 1941, Box 147F, WPD Files. Also in PHH, *Exhibits,* pt. 17, 2570–2600.

Pac Flt Chart Maneuver, Autumn 41: Commander in Chief Pacific Fleet (per McMorris) to Commanders of Task Forces, Fleet Chart Maneuver #1-41, moves of 26 Aug, 27 Sep, 21 and 29 Oct, 26 Nov 41, A16-3/(16), CinCPac WPs file late 1941.

BOOKS

Albion, Robert Greenhalgh. *Makers of Naval Policy, 1798–1947.* Annapolis: Naval Institute Press, 1980.

Alden, Commander John D., USN (Ret.). *The American Steel Navy . . . 1883 to 1909.* Annapolis: Naval Institute Press, 1972.

Allen, Thomas B. *War Games.* Annapolis: Naval Institute Press, 1987.

Bartlett, Colonel Merritt L., USMC (Ret.), ed. *Assault from the Sea: Essays on the History of Amphibious Warfare.* Annapolis: Naval Institute Press, 1983.

Belote, James H., and William M. Belote. *Corregidor: The Saga of a Fortress.* New York: Harper & Row, 1967.

Blair, Clay, Jr. *Silent Victory: The U.S. Submarine War against Japan.* 2 vols. Philadelphia: J. B. Lippincott, 1975.

Borg, Dorothy, and Shumpei Okamoto, eds. *Pearl Harbor as History: Japanese-American Relations, 1931–1941.* New York: Columbia University Press, 1973.

Bradford, James C. *The Reincarnation of John Paul Jones: The Navy Discovers Its Professional Roots*. Washington: Naval Historical Foundation, 1986.
Braisted, William Reynolds. *The United States Navy in the Pacific, 1897–1909*. 1958. Reprint. New York: Greenwood Press, 1969.
———. *The United States Navy in the Pacific, 1909–1922*. Austin: University of Texas Press, 1971.
Brune, Lester H. *The Origins of American National Security Policy: Sea Power, Air Power and Foreign Policy, 1900–1941*. Manhattan, Kan.: MA/AH Publishing, 1981.
Bryan, E. H., Jr. *American Polynesia and the Hawaiian Chain*. Honolulu: Tongg, 1942.
———, comp. *Guide to Place Names in the Trust Territory of the Pacific Islands*. Honolulu: Pacific Scientific Information Center, 1971.
Buckley, Thomas H. *The United States and the Washington Conference, 1921–1922*. Knoxville: University of Tennessee Press, 1970.
Buell, Thomas B. *Master of Sea Power: A Biography of Fleet Admiral Ernest J. King*. Boston: Little, Brown, 1980.
Bureau of Aeronautics. *United States Naval Aviation, 1898–1956*. Washington: Department of the Navy, n.d.
Bureau of Yards and Docks. *Building the Navy's Bases in World War II*. 2 vols. Washington: U.S. Government Printing Office, 1947.
Bywater, Hector C. *The Great Pacific War*. 1925. Reprint. Boston: Houghton Mifflin, 1942.
———. *Sea-Power in the Pacific: A Study of the American-Japanese Naval Problem*. Boston: Houghton Mifflin, 1921.
Carter, Samuel, III. *The Incredible Great White Fleet*. New York: Crowell-Collier Press, 1971.
Challener, Richard D. *Admirals, Generals, and American Foreign Policy, 1898–1914*. Princeton: Princeton University Press, 1973.
Cline, Ray S. *The War Department, Washington Command Post: The Operations Division*. Washington: Office of the Chief of Military History, Department of the Army, 1951.
Coletta, Paolo E. *Admiral Bradley A. Fiske and the American Navy*. Lawrence, Kan.: Regents Press of Kansas, 1979.
———, ed. *American Secretaries of the Navy*. 2 vols. Annapolis: Naval Institute Press, 1980.
Craven, Wesley Frank, and James Lea Cate, eds. *The Army Air Forces in World War II*. 7 vols. Vol. 1: *Plans and Early Operations*. Chicago: University of Chicago Press, 1948.
Daniels, Jonathan. *The End of Innocence*. Philadelphia: J. B. Lippincott, 1954.
Davis, Vernon E. *The History of the Joint Chiefs of Staff in World War II, Organizational Development*. Vol. 1: *Origin of the Joint and Combined Chiefs of Staff*. Washington: Historical Division, Joint Secretariat, Joint Chiefs of Staff, 1972.
Dewey, George. *Autobiography of George Dewey, Admiral of the Navy*. New York, 1913.

Dingman, Roger. *Power in the Pacific: The Origins of Naval Arms Limitation, 1914–1922.* Chicago: University of Chicago Press, 1976.

Dorwart, Jeffery M. *The Office of Naval Intelligence: The Birth of America's First Intelligence Agency, 1865–1918.* Annapolis: Naval Institute Press, 1979.

Dyer, George C., Vice-Admiral, USN (Ret.). *The Amphibians Came to Conquer: The Story of Admiral Richmond Kelly Turner.* 2 vols. Washington: U.S. Government Printing Office, 1969.

Esthus, Raymond A. *Theodore Roosevelt and Japan.* Seattle: University of Washington Press, 1966.

Friedman, Norman. *U.S. Aircraft Carriers: An Illustrated Design History.* Annapolis: Naval Institute Press, 1983.

———. *The U.S. Maritime Strategy.* Annapolis: Naval Institute Press, 1988.

Hart, Robert A. *The Great White Fleet.* Boston: Little, Brown, 1965.

Hattendorf, John B., B. Mitchell Simpson III, and John R. Wadleigh. *Sailors and Scholars: The Centennial History of the U.S. Naval War College.* Newport, R.I.: Naval War College Press, 1984.

Hayes, Grace Person. *The History of the Joint Chiefs of Staff in World War II: The War against Japan.* 1953. Reprint. Annapolis: Naval Institute Press, 1982.

Heinl, Lt. Col. R. D., Jr., USMC. *The Defense of Wake.* Washington: U.S. Government Printing Office, 1947.

Horvat, William J. *Above the Pacific.* Fallbrook, Calif.: Aero Publishers, 1966.

Hoyt, Edwin P. *How They Won the War in the Pacific: Nimitz and His Admirals.* New York: Weybright and Talley, 1970.

Hughes, Captain Wayne P., Jr., USN (Ret.). *Fleet Tactics: Theory and Practice.* Annapolis: Naval Institute Press, 1986.

Isely, Jeter A., and Philip A. Crowl. *The U.S. Marines and Amphibious War: Its Theory, and Its Practice in the Pacific.* Princeton: Princeton University Press, 1951.

Jablonski, Edward. *Sea Wings: The Romance of the Flying Boats.* Garden City, N.Y.: Doubleday, 1972.

Jose, Arthur W. *The Royal Australian Navy, 1914–1918.* 11th ed. Vol. 9: *Official History of Australia in the War of 1914–18.* Sydney: Angus and Robertson, 1943.

Josephson, Matthew. *Empire of the Air: Juan Trippe and the Struggle for World Airways.* New York: Harcourt, Brace, 1944.

Kennedy, Paul M. *The Samoan Tangle: A Study in Anglo-German-American Relations, 1878–1900.* New York: Barnes and Noble, 1974.

Kimmel, Husband E. *Admiral Kimmel's Story.* Chicago: Henry Regnery, 1955.

King, Fleet Admiral Ernest J., and Walter Muir Whitehill. *Fleet Admiral King: A Naval Record.* New York: Norton, 1952.

Knott, Captain Richard C., USN. *The American Flying Boat: An Illustrated History.* Annapolis: Naval Institute Press, 1979.

Lane, Jack C. *Armed Progressive: General Leonard Wood.* San Rafael, Calif.: Presidio Press, 1978.

Layton, Rear Admiral Edwin T., USN (Ret.), with Captain Roger Pineau, USNR (Ret.), and John Costello. *"And I Was There": Pearl Harbor and Midway—Breaking the Secrets.* New York: Morrow, 1985.

Leech, Margaret. *In the Days of McKinley.* New York: Harper Brothers, 1959.

Lehman, John F., Jr. *Command of the Seas.* New York: Charles Scribner's Sons, 1988.

Leighton, Richard M., and Robert W. Coakley. *The War Department: Global Logistics and Strategy, 1940–1943.* Washington: Office of the Chief of Military History, Department of the Army, 1955.

Livezey, William E. *Mahan on Sea Power.* Norman, Okla.: University of Oklahoma Press, 1947.

Love, Robert William, Jr., ed. *The Chiefs of Naval Operations.* Annapolis: Naval Institute Press, 1980.

Lowenthal, Mark M. *Leadership and Indecision: American War Planning and Policy Process, 1937–1942.* 2 vols. New York: Garland, 1988.

Matloff, Maurice. *The War Department: Strategic Planning for Coalition Warfare, 1943–1944.* Washington: Office of the Chief of Military History, Department of the Army, 1970.

Matloff, Maurice, and Edwin M. Snell. *The War Department: Strategic Planning for Coalition Warfare, 1941–42.* Washington: Office of the Chief of Military History, Department of the Army, 1953.

Melhorn, Charles M. *Two-Block Fox: The Rise of the Aircraft Carrier, 1911–1929.* Annapolis: Naval Institute Press, 1974.

Morgan, H. Wayne, ed. *Making Peace with Spain: The Diary of Whitelaw Reid, September–December 1898.* Austin: University of Texas Press, 1965.

Morison, Elting E., ed. *The Letters of Theodore Roosevelt.* 8 vols. Cambridge, Mass.: Harvard University Press, 1951–54.

Morison, Samuel Eliot. *History of United States Naval Operations in World War II.* 15 vols. (of which 9 deal with Pacific war). Boston: Little, Brown, 1950–60.

Morton, Louis. *The Fall of the Philippines.* Washington: Office of the Chief of Military History, Department of the Army, 1953.

———. *Strategy and Command: The First Two Years.* Washington: Office of the Chief of Military History, Department of the Army, 1962.

NAVAIR (Naval Air Systems Command). *United States Naval Aviation, 1910–1970.* NAVAIR 00-80P-1. Washington: U.S. Government Printing Office, 1970.

Naval Historical Foundation. *Manuscript Collection: A Catalog.* Washington: Library of Congress, 1974.

O'Gara, Gordon Carpenter. *Theodore Roosevelt and the Rise of the Modern Navy.* Princeton: Princeton University Press, 1943.

Paret, Peter, ed. *Makers of Modern Strategy.* Princeton: Princeton University Press, 1986.

Peattie, Mark R. *Nan'yō: The Rise and Fall of the Japanese in Micronesia, 1885–1945.* Pacific Island Monograph Series, No. 4. Honolulu: University of Hawaii Press, 1988.

Pomeroy, Earl S. *Pacific Outpost: American Strategy in Guam and Micronesia.* 1951. Reprint. New York: Russell and Russell, 1970.

Prange, Gordon W. *At Dawn We Slept: The Untold Story of Pearl Harbor.* New York: McGraw-Hill, 1981.

Prange, Gordon W., with Donald M. Goldstein and Katherine V. Dillon. *Pearl Harbor: The Verdict of History.* New York: McGraw-Hill, 1986.

Pratt, Julius W. *Expansionists of 1898: The Acquisition of Hawaii and the Spanish Islands.* 1936. Reprint. Chicago: Quadrangle Books, 1964.

Puleston, Captain W. D., USN. *The Armed Forces of the Pacific: A Comparison of the Military and Naval Power of the United States and Japan.* New Haven: Yale University Press, 1941.

Reckner, James R. *Teddy Roosevelt's Great White Fleet.* Annapolis: Naval Institute Press, 1988.

Reynolds, Clark G. *Famous American Admirals.* New York: Van Nostrand Reinhold, 1978.

———. *The Fast Carriers: The Forging of an Air Navy.* New York: McGraw-Hill, 1968.

Richardson, James O. *On the Treadmill to Pearl Harbor: The Memoirs of Admiral James O. Richardson, USN (Retired),* as told to Vice-Admiral George C. Dyer. Washington: Naval History Division, Department of the Navy, 1973.

Roskill, Stephen. *Naval Policy between the Wars.* Vol. 1: *The Period of Anglo-American Antagonism, 1919–1929.* New York: Walker and Company, 1968. Vol. 2: *The Period of Reluctant Rearmament, 1930–1939.* Annapolis: Naval Institute Press, 1976.

Seager, Robert, II. *Alfred Thayer Mahan: The Man and His Letters.* Annapolis: Naval Institute Press, 1977.

Sherrod, Robert. *History of Marine Corps Aviation in World War II.* Washington: Combat Forces Press, 1952.

Sherry, Michael S. *The Rise of American Air Power: The Creation of Armageddon.* New Haven: Yale University Press, 1987.

Smith, Richard K. *The Airships Akron and Macon: Flying Aircraft Carriers of the United States Navy.* Annapolis: Naval Institute Press, 1965.

Spector, Ronald H. *Admiral of the New Empire: The Life and Career of George Dewey.* Baton Rouge: Louisiana State University Press, 1974.

———. *Eagle against the Sun: The American War with Japan.* New York: Free Press of Macmillan, 1985.

———. *Professors of War: The Naval War College and the Development of the Naval Profession.* Newport, R.I.: Naval War College Press, 1977.

Sprout, Harold, and Margaret Sprout. *The Rise of American Naval Power.* Princeton: Princeton University Press, 1939.

———. *Toward a New Order of Sea Power: American Naval Policy and the World Scene, 1918–1922.* 2d ed. Princeton: Princeton University Press, 1943.

Stephan, John J., *Hawaii under the Rising Sun: Japan's Plans for Conquest after Pearl Harbor.* Honolulu: University of Hawaii Press, 1984.

Swanborough, Gordon, and Peter M. Bowers. *United States Navy Aircraft since 1911.* Annapolis: Naval Institute Press, 1976.

Tuleja, Thaddeus V. *Statesmen and Admirals: Quest for a Far Eastern Naval Policy.* New York: Norton, 1963.

Vlahos, Michael. *The Blue Sword: The Naval War College and the American Mission, 1919–1941.* Newport, R.I.: Naval War College Press, 1980.

Watson, Mark Skinner. *Chief of Staff: Prewar Plans and Preparations.* Washington: Office of the Chief of Military History, Department of the Army, 1950.

Weigley, Russell F. *The American Way of War: A History of United States Military Strategy and Policy.* New York: Macmillan, 1973.

Wheeler, Gerald E. *Admiral William Veazie Pratt, U.S. Navy: A Sailor's Life.* Washington: Naval History Division, Department of the Navy, 1974.

————. *Prelude to Pearl Harbor: The United States Navy and the Far East, 1921–1931.* Columbia: University of Missouri Press, 1963.

Woodbury, David O. *Builders for Battle: How the Pacific Naval Air Bases Were Constructed.* New York: Dutton, 1946.

ARTICLES AND ESSAYS

Beigel, Harvey M. "The Battle Fleet's Home Port, 1919–1940." *U.S. Naval Institute Proceedings, History Supplement 1985,* pp. 54–63.

Blakeslee, George H. "Japan's New Island Possessions in the Pacific: History and Present Status." *Journal of International Relations* 12, no. 2 (1921): 173–91.

Bradford, Royal Bird. "Coaling Stations for the Navy." *Forum,* February 1899, pp. 732–47.

Braisted, William R. "Charles Frederick Hughes, 14 November 1927–17 September 1930." In Robert William Love, Jr., ed., *The Chiefs of Naval Operations,* pp. 49–68. Annapolis: Naval Institute Press, 1980.

————. "On the American Red and Red-Orange Plans, 1919–39." In Gerald Jordan, ed., *Naval Warfare in the Twentieth Century, 1900–1945,* pp. 167–85. London: Croom Helm, 1977.

Cate, James Lea, and Wesley Frank Craven. "The Army Air Arm between Two World Wars, 1919–39." In Wesley Frank Craven and James Lea Cate, eds., *The Army Air Forces in World War II,* vol. 1: *Plans and Early Operations,* pp. 17–71. Chicago: University of Chicago Press, 1948.

Clinard, Outten Jones. "Japan's Influence on American Naval Power, 1897–1917." *University of California Publications in History,* vol. 36. Berkeley: University of California Press, 1947.

Coletta, Paolo E. "Josephus Daniels, 5 March 1913–5 March 1921." In Coletta, ed., *American Secretaries of the Navy,* 2:525–81. Annapolis: Naval Institute Press, 1980.

Crowl, Philip A. "Alfred Thayer Mahan: The Naval Historian." In Peter Paret, ed., *Makers of Modern Strategy,* pp. 444–77. Princeton: Princeton University Press, 1986.

Davis, Oscar King. "The Taking of Guam." *Harpers Weekly* 42, no. 2174 (1898):829–30.

Dierdorff, Captain Ross A., USN. "Pioneer Party—Wake Island." *U.S. Naval Institute Proceedings*, no. 482 (April 1943).

Douglas, Lawrence H. "Robert Edward Coontz, 1 November 1919–21 July 1923." In Robert William Love, Jr., ed., *The Chiefs of Naval Operations*, pp. 23–35. Annapolis: Naval Institute Press, 1980.

Doyle, Michael K. "The U.S. Navy and War Plan Orange, 1933–1940: Making Necessity a Virtue." *Naval War College Review*, May–June 1980, pp. 49–63.

————. "The United States Navy—Strategy and Far Eastern Foreign Policy, 1931–1941." *Naval War College Review* (Winter 1977): 52–60.

Fifield, Russell H. "Disposal of the Carolines, Marshalls and Marianas at the Paris Peace Conference." *American Historical Review* 51 (April 1946): 472–79.

Foley, Rear Admiral Francis D. (Ret.). "Looking for Earhart." *Air and Space*, February–March 1988, pp. 28–30.

Haight, John McVickar, Jr. "FDR's 'Big Stick.' " *U.S. Naval Institute Proceedings*, no. 809 (July 1980).

Heinrichs, Waldo H., Jr. "The Role of the United States Navy." In Dorothy Borg and Shumpei Okamoto, eds., *Pearl Harbor as History: Japanese-American Relations, 1931–1941*. New York: Columbia University Press, 1973.

Holt, Thaddeus. "Joint Plan Red." *MHQ: The Quarterly Journal of Military History* (August 1988): 48–55.

Horton, 2d Lieutenant Jeter R. "The Midway Islands." *World Today*, November 1907, pp. 1151–57.

Hughes, Wayne P., Jr. "The Strategy-Tactics Relationship." In Colin S. Gray and Roger W. Barnett, eds., *Seapower and Strategy*. Annapolis: Naval Institute Press, 1989.

Janowitz, Morris. "The Professional Soldier." In James C. Bradford, *Reincarnation of John Paul Jones: The Navy Discovers Its Professional Roots*. Washington, D.C.: Naval Historical Foundation, 1986.

Lautenschlager, Karl. "Technology and the Evolution of Naval Warfare." *International Security* 8 (Fall 1983).

Lowenthal, Mark M. "The Stark Memorandum and the American National Security Process, 1940." In Robert William Love, ed., *Changing Interpretations and New Sources of Naval History: Papers from the Third United States Naval Academy History Symposium*, pp. 352–61. New York: Garland, 1980.

Major, John. "William Daniel Leahy, 2 Jan 1937–1 Aug 1939." In Robert William Love, Jr., ed., *The Chiefs of Naval Operations*, pp. 101–17. Annapolis: Naval Institute Press, 1980.

Martin, Major John R., USA. "War Plan Orange and the Maritime Strategy." *Military Review* 69 (May 1989): 24–35.

Maurer, John H. "Fuel and the Battle Fleet: Coal, Oil and American Naval

Strategy, 1898–1925." *Naval War College Review* 34 (November–December 1981): 60–77.

McDonald, J. Kenneth. "The Rainbow Plans and the War against Japan." In National Maritime Museum, *The Second World War in the Pacific: Plans and Reality*, pp. 20–30. Maritime Monographs and Reports No. 9. Greenwich, Eng., 1974.

Miller, Edward S. "War Plan Orange, 1897–1941: The Blue Thrust through the Pacific." In William B. Cogar, general ed., *Naval History: The Seventh Symposium of the U.S. Naval Academy*, pp. 239–48. Wilmington, Del.: Scholarly Resources, 1988.

Miller, Spencer. Coaling articles, 1899–1914. Four articles in *Society of Naval Architects and Marine Engineers Transactions* (annual), New York: "Coaling Vessels at Sea" (1899), pp. 1–17; "Coaling Warships at Sea—Recent Developments" (1904), pp. 177–200; "Coaling Warships from Colliers in Harbor" (1910), pp. 125–41 and plates 33–41; "Refueling Warships at Sea" (1914), pp. 157–84.

Montross, Lynn. "The Mystery of Pete Ellis." *Marine Corps Gazette*, July 1954, pp. 30–33.

Moore, John Hammond. "The Eagle and the Roo: American Fleets in Australian Waters." *U.S. Naval Institute Proceedings*, no. 825 (November 1971): 43–51.

Morton, Louis. "The Development of Political-Military Consultation in the United States." *Political Science Quarterly* 70 (June 1955): 161–80.

———. "Interservice Co-operations and Political-Military Collaboration." In Harry L. Coles, ed., *Total War and Cold War: Problems in Civilian Control of the Military*, pp. 131–60. Columbus: Ohio State University Press.

———. "Military and Naval Preparations for the Defense of the Philippines during the War Scare of 1907." *Military Affairs*, Summer 1949, pp. 95–104.

———. "Origins of Pacific Strategy." *Marine Corps Gazette*, August 1957, pp. 36–43.

———. "War Plan ORANGE: Evolution of a Strategy." *World Politics* 11 (January 1959): 221–50.

Picking, Commander Sherwood. "Wake Island." *U.S. Naval Institute Proceedings*, no. 238 (December 1922): 2075–79.

Schaffer, Ronald. "General Stanley D. Embick: Military Dissenter." *Military Affairs*, October 1973, pp. 89–95.

Simpson, B. Mitchell III. "Harold Raynsford Stark, 1 August 1939–26 March 1942." In Robert William Love, Jr., ed., *The Chiefs of Naval Operations*, pp. 119–35. Annapolis: Naval Institute Press, 1980.

Symonds, Craig L. "William Veazie Pratt." In Robert William Love, Jr., ed., *The Chiefs of Naval Operations*, 69–88. Annapolis: Naval Institute Press, 1980.

Talbott, J. E. "Weapons Development, War Planning and Policy: The U.S. Navy and the Submarine, 1917–1941." *Naval War College Review* 37 (May–June 1984): 53–71.

Trask, David F. "William Shepherd Benson, 11 May 1915–25 September 1919." In Robert William Love, Jr., ed., *The Chiefs of Naval Operations*, pp. 3–20. Annapolis. Naval Institute Press, 1980.

Turk, Richard W. "Edward Walter Eberle, 21 July 1923–14 November 1927." In Robert William Love, Jr., ed., *The Chiefs of Naval Operations*, pp. 37–46. Annapolis: Naval Institute Press, 1980.

Vlahos, Michael. "The Naval War College and the Origins of War-Planning against Japan." *Naval War College Review*, July–August 1980, pp. 23–41.

————. "War Gaming, an Enforcer of Strategic Realism." *Naval War College Review* 39 (March–April 1986).

Vlahos, Michael, and Dale K. Pace. "War Experience and Force Requirements." *Naval War College Review* 41 (Autumn 1988).

Votaw, Homer C. "Midway—The North Pacific's Tiny Pet." *U.S. Naval Institute Proceedings*, no. 453 (November 1940): 52–55.

Walter, John C. "William Harrison Standley, 1 July 1933–1 January 1937." In Robert William Love, Jr., ed., *The Chiefs of Naval Operations*, pp. 89–99. Annapolis: Naval Institute Press, 1980.

Weigley, Russell F. "The Role of the War Department and the Army." In Dorothy Borg and Shumpei Okamoto, eds., *Pearl Harbor as History: Japanese-American Relations, 1931–1941*. New York: Columbia University Press, 1973.

Wheeler, Gerald E. "Edwin Denby, 6 March 1921–10 March 1924." In Paolo E. Coletta, ed., *American Secretaries of the Navy*, 2:583–603. Annapolis: Naval Institute Press, 1980.

Wilds, Thomas. "How Japan Fortified the Mandated Islands." *U.S. Naval Institute Proceedings*, no. 626 (April 1955): 401–7.

Williams, E. Cathleen. "Deployment of the AAF on the Eve of Hostilities." In Wesley Frank Craven and James Lea Cate, eds., *The Army Air Forces in World War II*, vol. 1: *Plans and Early Operations*, pp. 151–93. Chicago: University of Chicago Press, 1948.

DISSERTATIONS AND OTHER UNPUBLISHED MATERIALS

Army Air Force Historical Office. "Development of the South Pacific Air Route." AAF Historical Studies No. 45. Reference Collection 1074. Washington: AAF Historical Office, 1946.

Costello, Commander Daniel Joseph. "Planning for War: A History of the General Board of the Navy, 1900–1914." Ph.D. dissertation, Fletcher School of Law and Diplomacy, 1968.

Crawley, Martha. "Introduction to Checklist, Records of Strategic Plans Division, Office of the CNO, and Predecessor Organizations, 1912–1947." Washington: Operational Archives, Naval History Division, January 1978.

Holbrook, Francis Xavier. "United States National Defense and Trans-Pacific Commercial Air Routes, 1933–1941." Ph.D. dissertation, Fordham University, 1970.

Infusino, Frank J., Jr. "The United States Marine Corps and War Planning (1900–1941)." M.A. thesis, California State University, San Diego, 1973.

Mead, Dana George. "United States Peacetime Strategic Planning, 1920–1941: The Color Plans to the Victory Program." Ph.D. dissertation, Massachusetts Institute of Technology, 1967.

Morgan, Lieutenant Colonel Henry G., Jr. "Planning the Defeat of Japan: A Study of Total War Strategy." Washington: Office of the Chief of Military History, 1961. Manuscript. Copy in Navy Department Library, Washington.

Morgan, William Michael. "Strategic Factors in Hawaiian Annexation." Ph.D. dissertation, Claremont Graduate School, 1980.

Naval History Division. "Checklist, Basic, Joint, Combined & Navy War Plans & Related Documents, 1896–1941." 20 Jun 1966. Operating Archives, Naval History Division.

Patekewich, V. "Book of Naval War College Admirals." Newport, R. I.: Development Programs Office, Naval War College Library, n.d.

Simpson, B. Mitchell, III. "Admiral Harold R. Stark, A Biography." Manuscript. Newport, R.I., 1986. Stark Papers, Navy Department Library, Naval Historical Center, Washington.

"United States Naval Administrative Histories of World War II." ca. 300 unpublished volumes. Washington and elsewhere, 1945–57. Written by various U.S. Navy bureaus, fleets, and agencies. Typescripts and microfiches in Naval History Division, Washington, D.C.

Vlahos, Michael. "War Gaming at Newport, 1919–1941: Prototype for Today's Global Games?" Manuscript. Naval War College, ca. Oct 1985.

LECTURES

Baker, Cdr C. S. (SC), "Logistics—Its Natural Aspect." At NWC, 22 Sep 22. Box 1, WPD Files.

———. "Logistics—Its National Aspect." At NWC, 12 Oct 23. Box 1, WPD Files.

Ballendorf, Dirk Anthony. "Earl Hancock Ellis: A Marine's Multiple Muff-Ups in Mufti in Micronesia." Ninth Naval History Symposium, U.S. Naval Academy, 20 Oct 1989.

Belknap, Cpt R. R. "The Blue-Orange Situation." At Fleet War College Sessions, NWC, 5 Nov 21. Box 1, WPD Files.

Byron, Cpt John, USN, National Defense University. "Framework for Naval Strategy." Informal staff lecture at NWC, 15 Jun 1989.

Cook, Cpt M. G. "Office of Naval Operations." At USMC School, 27 Feb 31. Box 2, WPD Files.

Crenshaw, Cpt R. S. "War Plans." At NWC, 10 May 40. Box 3, WPD Files.

Crowl, Philip. "The Pacific War." At NWC, 3 Oct 1988. NWC audiotape collection.

Day, Cpt George C. "Submarines." At NWC, 16 Feb 23. Box 3, WPD Files.

Dillen, Cpt R. F. "The Office of Naval Operations and the WPD." At USMC School, 26 Apr 29. Box 4, WPD Files.

Hines, Cpt A. W. "The Blue-Orange Situation, Orange." At Fleet War Sessions, NWC, 1 Nov 21. Box 6, WPD Files.

Horne, Frederick J. (probably). "Cooperation between the Army and Navy." N.d. (ca. mid-1922). Speeches, Box 2, Horne Papers.

Horne, Cpt F. J. "The Office of Naval Operations and the War Plans Division." At USMC School, Quantico, 27 Apr 28. Box 7, WPD Files.

Pence, Cpt H. L. "Strategic Areas—Hawaiian Islands." Department of Intelligence, NWC, 10 Jul 36. NHC, NWC.

Pye, Cpt William S. "War Plans from the Navy Point of View." At AWC, 21 Oct 24. Box 10, WPD Files.

———. Untitled. At NWC, 7 Jan 26. Box 10, WPD Files.

———. "War Plans." At Naval Postgraduate School, 6 Nov 26. Box 10, WPD Files.

Pye, Adm William S. "The Office of Naval Operations." At AWC, 4 Feb 36. Box 10, WPD Files.

Schofield, Cpt Frank H. "Some Effects of the Washington Conference on American Naval Strategy." At AWC, 22 Sep 23. Box 11, WPD Files.

Schofield, RAdm Frank H. "Naval Strategy of the Pacific." At USMC Field Officers School, Quantico, 23 Mar 28. Box 11, WPD Files.

Shoemaker, Cpt William R. "Strategy of the Pacific: Exposition of Orange War Plan." At NWC Conference, 23 & 25 Aug 14. Scholarly Microfilms, roll 1.

Vlahos, Michael. "U.S. Naval Strategy in the Interwar Era: The Search for a Mission." Seventh Naval History Symposium, Annapolis, 27 Sep 1985.

SELECTED INTERVIEWS BY AUTHOR

Barber, Lt Cdr Charles F. Greenwich, Conn., 14 Nov 1985. Navy War Plans Division, 1941; flag secretary to Admiral Raymond Spruance, 1943–45.

Kimmel, Cpt Thomas, USN (Ret.) Annapolis, 18 Aug 1988. Son of Admiral Husband E. Kimmel.

McCrea, Adm John L., USN (Ret.). Needham, Mass., 17 Nov 1988. Navy War Plans Division, late 1940; aide to Admiral H. R. Stark, 1941.

Morgan, Lt Col Henry G., USA (Ret.). Arlington, Va., 4 Sep. 1990. Formerly office of Chief of Military History.

Morton, Louis, Chairman, Department of History, Dartmouth College, Hanover, N.H. Apr and May 1974 (by correspondence).

Mott, Adm William. Charlottesville, Va., 10 Oct 1988. Liaison with White House, WWII.

Nomura, Minoru. Tokyo, Jun 1982. Professor, Military History Department, National Defense Institute, Tokyo.

ORAL HISTORIES

Hill, Harry W. Reminiscences, 1966–67. Columbia Oral History.
Ingersoll, Adm Royal E. Reminiscences, 1964. Columbia Oral History.
Moore, RAdm Charles J., Ret. Reminiscences, 1964. Columbia Oral History.
Tarrant, William Theodore. Reminiscences, 1964. Columbia Oral History.

Index

Hill, Harry, 221; as Fleet War Plans
Officer, 221, 259, 379; in War Plans
Division, 217 (fig.), 221, 229–30,
269, 291, 379; in WWII, 222, 329
Himalayas, 344
Hirohito, Emperor, 364
Hiroshima, 368
Hitler, 326
Hokkaido, in WWII, 334
Holcomb, Thomas, 181, 183, 229, 277,
377–78; in WWII, 329
Hollandia, in WWII, 351
Home reserve of troops, 134
Hong Kong, 255, 316, 360
Honshu, invasion of, in WWII, 366
Hoover, Herbert, 10, 132, 167, 376
Hornbeck, Stanley K., 112
Horne, Frederick J.: 136, 153, 167, 216,
217 (fig.), 375–76; in WWII, 136, 328
Hospital ships (see also Fleet train), 128
(table), 147, 283 (table)
House, Edward M., 112
Hughes, Charles Evans, 11, 114
Hughes, Charles F., 132, 374–77
Hull, Cordell, 11, 264

Iceland, 272
Immigration. See Japanese immigration
to U. S.
Immigration act, 22
Incendiary raids on Japan, 321, 349, 367
India, 265, 320; in WWII, 361
Indian Ocean, 88–89, 265; blockade
operations, 58; in WWII, 334
Indochina, 255, 257–58, 258 (map),
259, 260 (map)
Industry. See Japan, mobilization,
production and stockpiling; United
States, industry and mobilization
Ingersoll, Royal E.: as Director of War
Plans Division, 216, 217 (fig.), 242,
252 (table), 377–79; in early 1930s,
138; mission to U. K., 213; in Office
of CNO, 268, 310–11; in WWII, 218,
329
Inland Sea, 162–63, 286, 295, 305
Inner atolls (see also Johnston Island;
Midway; Palmyra), 49, 51, 229–30
Intelligence (see also Office of Naval
Intelligence): army, 164–66, 173;
naval, 306, 309; planners' attitudes

toward, 353; in WWII, 308, 349,
353–54, 358
International law of neutral rights,
88–90, 95
Invasion tactics. See Amphibious tactics
Isolationism. See United States, public
opinion, isolationism
Italy, 259, 265; in WWII, 314
Iwo Jima (see also Volcano Islands),
101, 130, 209; in WWII, 340 (map),
363

J Day, 295
Jaluit (see also Marshall Islands), 107
(table), 194 (table); Japanese base on,
280; U. S. attack, 1920s, 117, 1930s,
192 (map), 198 (map), 199, 201,
1940-41, 300 (map), in WWII, 341; as
U. S. base, pre-WWI, 97, 1930s,
191–93; U. S. reconnaissance, 302
Japan. See also Bombing of Japan;
Economic war against Japan; Siege of
Japan
—bombardment of (by sea), 163–64; in
WWII, 367
—financial weakness, 6, 47, 316
—invasion of, 30, 364; 1920s, 159,
165–66; in WWII, 159, 166, 327,
352, 356, 357, 361, 363, 365–67,
369; value of threat, 364, 366–68
—national character and behavior, 25,
160, 167, 195; in WWII, 354, 356,
365
—logistical problems, 46–47, 163–64,
190, 195; in WWII, 366–67
—mobilization, production and
stockpiling, 6, 27–28, 164, 169, 262;
in WWII, 336
—political vulnerability, 209, 316, 344
—strategy of and planning by, xx;
pre-WWI, 93–94; 1920s, 130, 161,
188 (map), 207 (map); in WWII, 326,
334–36, 354
—surrender of, in WWII, 357, 367–68
Japan, Sea of, 163, 295, 367
Japanese-Americans, removal from West
Coast, 1942, 41
Japanese immigration to U. S., 21, 22
Java, 261–63, 266; as fleet destination,
247, 258 (map), 260 (map); as U. S.
base, 60, 257

About the Author

Edward S. Miller is a retired executive with a life-long interest in business plans and war plans. For twenty years he combed through once-secret archives, discovering the excellence of U.S. strategic thought before World War II.

Mr. Miller is a Phi Beta Kappa graduate of Syracuse University and of the Harvard Advanced Management Program. In his thirty-five-year career he was chief planner of America's largest mining company, where he was involved in joint ventures with Japan, and top financial officer of the government's Synthetic Fuels Corporation. He has lectured to audiences at the Pentagon, the Naval War College, military conferences, and in Japan. He resides in Stamford, Connecticut, with his wife and a few small boats.